Handbook of Counseling and Psychotherapy With Lesbian, Gay, and Bisexual Clients

Handbook of Counseling *and* Psychotherapy *With* Lesbian, Gay, *and* Bisexual Clients

Ruperto M. Perez
Kurt A. DeBord
Kathleen J. Bieschke

AMERICAN PSYCHOLOGICAL ASSOCIATION • WASHINGTON, DC

First Printing, October 1999
Second Printing, February 2001
Published by
American Psychological Association
750 First Street, NE
Washington, DC 20002

Copies may be ordered from
APA Order Department
P.O. Box 92984
Washington, DC 20090-2984

In the U.K., Europe, Africa, and the Middle East, copies may be ordered from
American Psychological Association
3 Henrietta Street
Covent Garden, London
WC2E 8LU England

Typeset in Goudy by EPS Group Inc., Easton, MD

Printer: Automated Graphic Systems, Inc., White Plains, MD
Cover Designer: Berg Design, Albany, NY
Technical/Production Editor: Rachael J. Stryker

Library of Congress Cataloging-in-Publication Data
Handbook of counseling and psychotherapy with lesbian, gay, and bisexual clients /
edited by Ruperto M. Perez, Kurt A. DeBord & Kathleen J. Bieschke.
    p.   cm.
  Includes bibliographical references and index.
  ISBN 1-55798-610-X (alk. paper)
  1. Counseling. 2. Psychotherapy. 3. Lesbians—Counseling of.
4. Gays—Counseling of. 5. Bisexuals—Counseling of. I. Perez, Ruperto M.
II. DeBord, Kurt A. III. Bieschke, Kathleen J.
  BF637.C6 H3125 1999
  158'.3'0866—dc21
                            99-32399
                              CIP

British Library Cataloguing-in-Publication Data
A CIP record is available from the British Library.

Printed in the United States of America

CONTENTS

CONTRIBUTORS

Mary Z. Anderson, Western Michigan University
Augustine Barón, Counseling and Mental Health Center, University of Texas at Austin, and Walden University
Kathleen J. Bieschke, The Pennsylvania State University
Ellen M. Broido, Portland State University
David W. Cramer, Independent Practice, Austin, TX
James M. Croteau, Western Michigan University
Anthony R. D'Augelli, The Pennsylvania State University
Mary Gage Davidson, Counseling Center, Emory University
Kurt A. DeBord, Lincoln University
Teresa M. Distefano, Western Michigan University
Sari H. Dworkin, California State University–Fresno
Ruth E. Fassinger, University of Maryland
Angela D. Ferguson, Counseling Center, University of Florida
Mary A. Fukuyama, Counseling Center, University of Florida
Jennifer L. Grzegorek, The Pennsylvania State University
William F. Hanjorgiris, Private Practice, New York, NY
Marcia J. Hartwig, University of Southern Mississippi
Scott L. Hershberger, California State University–Long Beach
Seth C. Kalichman, Center for AIDS Intervention Research, Milwaukee, WI
Sheila Kampa-Kokesch, Western Michigan University
Michael R. Kauth, Veterans Affairs Medical Center, New Orleans, LA
Suzanne H. Lease, The University of Memphis
Connie R. Matthews, The Pennsylvania State University
Mary McClanahan, The Pennsylvania State University
Susan L. Morrow, University of Utah
Shelly M. Ossana, Center for Family and Individual Counseling, Columbia, MO
Jeeseon Park, The Pennsylvania State University

Ruperto M. Perez, Counseling and Testing Center, The University of Georgia

Julia C. Phillips, Counseling, Testing and Career Center, University of Akron

Amy L. Reynolds, Counseling Center, Buffalo State College

Esther D. Rothblum, University of Vermont

Barry A. Schreier, Counseling and Psychological Services, Purdue University

Erinn Tozer, The Pennsylvania State University

Donald L. Werden, Counseling and Psychological Services, Purdue University

FOREWORD

LAURA S. BROWN

When I began my doctoral studies in psychology in 1973, the notion that psychologists might be interested in serving the needs of lesbian, gay, or bisexual (LGB) clients in an affirmative manner was unknown. Less than 30 years ago, there were indeed specialists in working with the sexual minority population, but these specialists had one, invariant view of people who were not heterosexual. Theirs was a pathological paradigm, in which the absence of heterosexual desire and behavior was equated with the presence of a variety of severe psychopathologies. The concept of a "normal" lesbian or a healthy gay man was considered oxymoronic. Although homosexuality had recently been removed from the official diagnostic manuals, its status as a form of pathology was still strong in the treatment literature.

When I wrote a master's thesis in 1974 in which I conducted an empirical study comparing the mental health and self-esteem of lesbians with a matched group of heterosexual women, I encountered the pathologizing paradigm in my literature review. Were I, as an emerging psychologist, to have been guided by the erstwhile scholarship available by the time I received my degree in 1977, I would have been unable to provide affirmative, nonbiased treatment to the lesbian and gay clients with whom I began to work. The clients and patients portrayed in that scholarly material were never ordinary people with ordinary problems who happened to be lesbian or gay (and also depressed or anxious or having troubles at work). They were described and defined in terms of their sexuality, with the sole treatment goal of changing them into heterosexuals.

I had few places to turn to in the scholarly literature to guide me elsewhere. As scientist–practitioners trained to refer to empirical research and scholarship, I and every other psychologist of that time experienced a lack of such information. There were no studies of the nonpathologizing treatment of bisexual women and men, and there was little research, aside from my own and that of a few other newly minted lesbian and gay psychologists, to give me a conceptual framework for understanding the normal functioning of lesbians and gay men. Like other practitioners of lesbian and gay affirmative psychotherapy in the 1970s and 1980s, I was helping to create a map of the territory for this work, using the rhetoric of the lesbian and gay civil rights movement, my own experiences in a lesbian community, and a commitment to social justice as my guides to developing treatment.

The publication of the *Handbook of Counseling and Psychotherapy With Lesbian, Gay, and Bisexual Clients* marks a clear end to the era of discovery for the affirmative treatment of sexual minority clients. The book reflects a field that has grown to maturity and is solidly based in empirical findings that support a commitment to social justice. This is a landmark work, reflecting the enormous growth of theory and scholarship in the treatment of lesbian, gay, and bisexual clients in the past 3 decades. It also speaks to the precision and specificity with which we may now approach working with sexual minority clients. Because sexual minority clients vary greatly in their age, social class, ethnicity and culture, and other factors, and because they enter therapy for reasons both completely related to and entirely disconnected from the fact of their sexual orientation, the level of conceptual sophistication required to provide effective and competent, as well as LGB-affirmative, therapy can be quite high. As the authors in this book make clear, the development of that sophistication and skill no longer requires self-invention and discovery.

The timing of the publication of this book also mirrors developments within psychology itself in the dealings with sexual minority clients and their needs. In 1997, the Council of Representatives, the governing body of the American Psychological Association (APA), passed a resolution titled Appropriate Therapeutic Responses to Sexual Orientation. The resolution reaffirmed APA's commitment, first made in 1975, to a nonpathologizing construct of homosexuality and called on psychotherapists to define and give clients adequate informed consent when clients approached therapists with questions about sexual orientation. Implicit in this call for informed consent is that psychologists should be knowledgeable about such topics as the presumed etiologies of homosexuality and the extremely high failure rates and negative emotional consequences attendant on attempts to change sexual orientation from homosexual to heterosexual.

Previous studies of APA membership had found that most psychologists did not have this kind of information. A survey of psychotherapist members of APA, conducted in the early 1990s under the joint auspices of the APA Committee on Gay, Lesbian, and Bisexual Concerns and the APA Board of Professional Affairs, found that although most respondents were likely to see at least one client whom they knew to be gay, lesbian, or bisexual, most respondents also had little or no information about ho-

mosexuality. This study, in which critical incidents of superior and problematic practice with sexual minority clients were collected, also uncovered
the persistence of the pathologizing model of homosexuality among practicing psychologists. Similar studies of graduate and internship training programs in clinical and counseling psychology conducted at the beginning of
the 1990s found equivalent gaps in the knowledge being provided to the
next cohort of psychologists. Because information about affirmative, nonpathologizing treatment of sexual minority clients was not easily accessible,
only psychologists with a strong commitment to working with this population became educated. The average psychologist was at risk for working
less than competently with her or his modal one LGB client. All of this
information rested in the context of high use of psychotherapy by lesbians,
gay men, and bisexual women and men, groups who value what therapy
can offer and use it regularly throughout the life span for assistance in
coping with both developmental challenges and psychological distress.

This book's publication by APA fills in those lacunae and makes it
easy for psychologists and other mental health professionals to become fully
and richly informed about the culture and concerns of LGB people. The
therapist, or trainer of therapists, who reads this volume will come away
with a depth of knowledge about the normal lives of LGB people and a
necessary database for working with troubled LGB clients. Readers will also
become familiar with the diversity and complexity of LGB communities,
regarding ethnicity, class background, spirituality, and a host of other factors. Most important, LGB clients and their families will have an improved
chance of receiving the most effective, bias-free, and scholarship-informed
treatment possible.

ACKNOWLEDGMENTS

This book started with a phone call. In a flurry of brainstorming and speculation, the idea for this book was born. From that point in 1996 until now, the three of us have worked as a team of editors to structure, organize, and mold this book. Our goal was to stay true to the scientist–practitioner model while unifying and reviewing the scholarly work relevant to therapy with lesbian, gay, or bisexual clients.

The *Handbook of Counseling and Psychotherapy With Lesbian, Gay, and Bisexual Clients* is truly reflective of a multitude of sincere and careful efforts. Collaboration was the key and essential ingredient to getting this handbook off the ground. The process of collaborating to generate and produce the numerous facets of this project has been stimulating, challenging, fascinating, and truly educational. As editors, we regularly found ourselves sharing and trading the drivers' and passengers' seats as the book gained a momentum that sometimes seemed to be all its own. As people joined us on this journey, we intentionally endeavored to share those seats while steadily drawing attention to the course that we had set.

A number of people have contributed greatly to this collaborative process. We are proud to be associated with such a collection of outstanding professionals. We gratefully express our thanks and appreciation to the fine staff at APA Books, especially to Mary Lynn Skutley, Ed Meidenbauer, Rachael Stryker, and particularly to Ted Baroody, who devoted much of his time and energy shepherding us through the initial stages of the book's development. We are deeply indebted to their genuine interest, creative talent, and unfailing encouragement.

We are also grateful for the opportunity to work with a group of talented, creative, insightful, and sensitive authors. Each of them dedicated themselves to this project and contributed much of their energy, knowledge, and expertise. Our thanks also go to Laura S. Brown for so graciously writing the foreword for this book. We value her generosity and the power and poignancy of her words.

In addition, we extend our appreciation to the individuals who provided valuable assistance in the early stages of developing this volume. We are particularly grateful to Martha L. White from The University of Georgia for her helpful feedback in developing the initial outline for this book. We are also grateful to Amy Eberz, Jennifer Grzegorek, Brad Hieger, Mary McClanahan, Jeeseon Park, Jennifer Sager, and Erinn Tozer from The Pennsylvania State University and to Melissa Bartsch at the University of Tennessee for helping us to review the early drafts of the various chapters. Their reviews provided us with valuable feedback, and their comments were enormously helpful to us in our evaluation and review of the final manuscript.

On a personal note, we would each like to take this opportunity to acknowledge the love and support given to us unselfishly by our friends, colleagues, and families. In particular, we express our sincerest appreciation to our friends and colleagues at The University of Georgia, Lincoln University, and The Pennsylvania State University. Their generous support has been invaluable to each of us throughout this project. We also owe our heartfelt thanks to Daryl Gregory, Wayne Mayfield, and Bella M. Perez for their unending love and steadfast encouragement.

Finally, this book is dedicated to all our friends, colleagues, students, and clients who have challenged us to recognize and appreciate the diversity and complexities of lesbian, gay, and bisexual identities. Their courage, insightfulness, warmth, and wisdom have profoundly affected and inspired our own professional and personal growth.

Handbook of Counseling and Psychotherapy With Lesbian, Gay, and Bisexual Clients

INTRODUCTION

THE CHALLENGE OF AWARENESS, KNOWLEDGE, AND ACTION

RUPERTO M. PEREZ, KURT A. DeBORD, AND KATHLEEN J. BIESCHKE

Since 1975, when the American Psychological Association (APA) supported the removal of homosexuality from the official list of mental disorders, APA has encouraged mental health professionals to provide affirmative and appropriate services to lesbians and gay men (Garnets, Hancock, Cochran, Goodchilds, & Peplau, 1991). APA recently reaffirmed this position in 1997 when it resolved that it "supports the dissemination of accurate information about sexual orientation, and mental health, and appropriate interventions in order to counteract bias that is based in ignorance or unfounded beliefs about sexual orientation" (APA, 1997, p. 2). Despite these formal resolutions, psychologists' attitudes and beliefs about what constitutes effective practice with lesbian and gay clients vary considerably (Garnets et al., 1991; Yarhouse, 1998).

Clients who identify themselves as lesbian or gay use therapy at a high rate (Bradford, Ryan, & Rothblum, 1994; Liddle, 1996; Morgan, 1992). In a recent study, 99% of the psychologists sampled reported seeing at least one lesbian or gay client over the course of their career (Garnets et al., 1991). Psychologists and other mental health professionals, however, still lack knowledge or expertise in the area of lesbian, gay, and bisexual (LGB) psychology (Garnets et al., 1991; Phillips, chapter 14, this volume; Phillips & Fischer, 1998). In addition, the attitudes of clinicians toward LGB clients are often heterosexist and sometimes homophobic (Bieschke, McClanahan, Tozer, Grzegorek, & Park, chapter 13, this volume; Garnets et al., 1991).

We believe that if psychologists are to be effective when working with LGB clients, a professional understanding of the nature of LGB issues and individuals is essential. Specifically, therapists must be knowledgeable about the social history and culture from which past and current issues are born; the current trends in ethical psychological service delivery; and the significant areas that influence theory, research, and practice. This is particularly true for psychologists who have little or no knowledge of LGB culture. Psychologists and other mental health service providers must also obtain knowledge of the issues pertinent to their clients' culture and worldview. Thus, they must be keenly aware of personal biases and assumptions that can hinder effective therapy or research (APA, 1990; Garnets et al., 1991; Lopez, 1989; Morrow, chapter 6, this volume; Murray & Abramson, 1983).

A number of noteworthy books address LGB counseling and therapy (Dworkin & Gutierrez, 1992), theory and research (D'Augelli & Patterson, 1996), and LGB issues in specific settings (Evans & Wall, 1991). On the basis of our familiarity with these publications as well as our clinical work and research, we recognized the need for a book that integrated these areas in a meaningful way. We also believed that this book should stay true to the scientist–practitioner model while unifying and reviewing the burgeoning scholarly work relevant to therapy with LGB clients. The *Textbook of Homosexuality and Mental Health* (Cabaj & Stein, 1996) was the first book to successfully accomplish such an integration.

The purpose of the present volume is to successfully execute this integration while highlighting the developmental perspectives and sociocultural contexts we consider crucial for understanding LGB populations. It is one of the few texts to date that meaningfully integrates LGB theory, practice, and research into an authoritative text. Both researchers and practitioners who are interested in the lives of LGB clients should find this text useful.

There are three major sections to this handbook. Each section begins with an introduction that serves as an overview and guide to each of these major areas. The first section, "Social and Theoretical Perspectives," describes the social and historical contexts from which past and current therapeutic issues with LGB clients evolved. To understand how the socially constructed labels of *lesbian, gay,* and *bisexual* achieved their current status, it is imperative to consider how the dynamics of power and oppression have operated in LGB populations. In addition, existing theory pertaining to counseling LGB clients is presented and reviewed. The next section, "Counseling and Therapy," examines and discusses the competent, informed, and ethical practice of psychotherapy with LGB clients by distilling and unifying the critical conclusions of case studies, theoretical work, and empirical investigations. This section considers individual and group counseling as well as the counseling of adolescents, couples, and older LGB individuals. Finally, the last section, "Relevant Issues for Therapy, Theory, and Research," addresses therapy with LGB clients in a multifaceted, holistic fashion. Again, psychologists committed to conducting ethical and sensitive research and practice with LGB clients will benefit from reading such considerate evaluations of the diverse disciplines that influence LGB lives.

The organizational structure that we adopted was intended to allow any practitioner or researcher to use the book as a comprehensive text. For example, if a practitioner unexpectedly finds her- or himself in need of information about how to work with an LGB couple, a single chapter in this book may serve as an excellent starting point. Or, if a researcher in vocational psychology finds him- or herself contemplating the role that sexual orientation might play in career decision making, a chapter here can provide important groundwork for beginning investigative research in this area. Although the chapters stand alone as valuable contributions to the overall field, we must admit our bias and recommend reading the entire volume. The organizational structure we have chosen leads the reader in a logical sequence from contextual variables to the heart of therapy and then on to the related bodies of scholarly work that are critical to understanding LGB clients.

In developing this book, our aim was to provide a developmental perspective to guide work with LGB clients as well as a perspective from which to develop informative, meaningful research. However, we realize that there is much more to working with LGB clients than we could possibly cover in a single edition. Although we have attempted to be as inclusive and integrative as possible regarding the many facets of LGB research and counseling, we recognize that we have not focused on some dimensions as well as we have others.

For instance, we have encouraged our authors to be inclusive of issues facing bisexual individuals in counseling. The research on bisexual persons is very much in its early stages, and although there are some current resources that examine aspects of bisexuality (e.g., Firestein, 1996; Weinberg, Williams, & Pryor, 1994), much more work needs to be done. In addition, there are no discussions of transgender issues in this edition of the book because of the lack of empirical research in this area.

Authors were also asked to integrate a discussion of racial and ethnic diversity into each chapter. Again, there has been much written in the area of race and ethnicity (e.g., Ponterotto, Casas, Suzuki, & Alexander, 1995), but little is known about the impact that race and ethnicity have on developmental theory and counseling with LGB clients. More research is needed with more racially and ethnically diverse LGB populations to gain increased insight into the unique needs of ethnically and racially diverse LGB clients.

One of the challenges in developing this handbook was making decisions regarding terminology. The terminology used in the LGB psychological literature has grown in diversity as much as the field has grown itself. In addition, because LGB theory and research have developed rapidly, the common usage of terms has become obscured. We therefore asked the chapter authors of this book to attend to and articulate definitional issues that uniquely concerned their subdisciplines. To diminish obscurity, we committed ourselves and our authors to the common usage of a few basic terms. We realize that potential readers of this book may have a wide range of experience and knowledge about working with LGB clients in therapy or working with LGB topics in research. For those readers who find it helpful to have definitions of some of the frequently used terms in this book, we have provided those definitions.

The use of some terms, such as *homosexual* and *sexual orientation*, has evolved in such a way that many psychologists no longer prefer them. The term *homosexual* was used historically as the psychologically appropriate and sensitive term to identify individuals who were primarily sexually aroused by others of the same sex. APA (1991) noted that this is rarely the appropriate term to use because of the psychopathological connotations the term acquired during the period when the *Diagnostic and Statistical Manual of Mental Disorders* listed homosexuality as a psychological disorder. We believe that the terms *homosexual* and *sexual orientation* emphasize the importance of sexuality and ignore the relevance of other aspects of people who identify themselves as LGB. Given this context, we have encouraged authors to use the more inclusive acronym LGB (lesbian, gay, bisexual). Additionally, we have adopted and affirmed the perspective that identifying oneself as lesbian, gay, or bisexual involves one's sense of self in ways that are emotional, intellectual, political, sexual, social, spiritual, and vocational. This multifaceted perspective on LGB identity clearly asserts that there is more to identifying oneself as LGB than simply proclaiming that one is sexually aroused by members of the same or both sexes. However, given the operational definitions used by some noteworthy scholarly work reviewed in this book, terms such as *sexual orientation* and *homosexual* were not entirely abandoned in the text.

Several additional comments are relevant to the basic terms used in this book. First, no term has been widely accepted to replace that of the term *sexual orientation*. Although the term *affectional orientation* allows for interpersonal attractions that are not based solely on sex, it does not necessarily include sexual attraction. APA (1994) advocates the use of the term *sexual orientation* for professional work in this area. Using the combination of the terms *sexual orientation* and *affectional orientation* is probably one of the better, yet underutilized approaches to dealing with this conundrum (Bohan, 1996). Using the term *LGB identity* is another. However analyzed, the definitional problems in this area have been conceived in abstraction and are not going to be solved easily, as Broido (chapter 1, this volume) makes clear in her chapter addressing the socially constructed nature of an LGB identity.

On a simpler level, the term *gay* is used specifically in this book to refer to gay men, not lesbian women. Both gay men and lesbian women are assumed to have a sexual and affectional attraction to members of the same sex. Men and women who identify as bisexual usually experience an affectional and a sexual attraction to both men and women. Such attractions can manifest serially or simultaneously (Bohan, 1996). When appropriate, LGB people are referred to collectively in this book, because members of the groups often face similar psychological and social issues. Obviously, it is not always appropriate to refer to all three groups collectively (Croteau et al., 1998). Subsequently, we have been careful to distinguish between these groups when necessary.

The final definitions concern fear, ignorance, and hate. Collectively, we have used the terms *homophobia*, *biphobia*, and *heterosexism* to define behaviors and attitudes that denigrate or disavow important aspects of the LGB self. If these terms are thought of as part of a continuum, the phobias can involve active acts of denigration and hate, whereas heterosexism involves more passive forms of prejudice, such as the disavowal of LGB identity. The behaviors and attitudes associated with all three forms of prejudice can be intentional or unintentional and can be perpetuated by individuals, groups, or systems. Regardless of the intent and source, the social effects of such prejudices are destructive and far-reaching.

In conclusion, this book was written to serve as an agent of prosocial change. We are fully cognizant of the negative and sometimes violent social effects of homophobia, biphobia, and heterosexism on LGB individuals. Information, knowledge, and learning go a long way to disarm the powerful effects of ignorance, prejudice, and oppression. It is our hope that this handbook contributes to prosocial change by counteracting the harmful biases, perceptions, and actions toward LGB persons in our society.

REFERENCES

American Psychological Association. (1994). *Publication manual of the American Psychological Association* (4th ed.). Washington, DC: Author

American Psychological Association. (1997). *Resolution on appropriate therapeutic responses to sexual orientation*. Washington, DC: Author.

American Psychological Association, Committee on Lesbian and Gay Concerns. (1991). Avoiding heterosexual bias in language. *American Psychologist, 46,* 973–974.

American Psychological Association, Office of Ethnic Minority Affairs–Board of Ethnic Minority Affairs Task Force on the Delivery of Services to Ethnic

Minority Populations. (1990). *Guidelines for providers of psychological services to ethnic, linguistic, and culturally diverse populations.* Washington, DC: Author.

Bohan, J. S. (1996). *Psychology and sexual orientation: Coming to terms.* New York: Routledge.

Bradford, J., Ryan, C., & Rothblum, E. D. (1994). National lesbian health care survey: Implications for mental health care. *Journal of Consulting and Clinical Psychology, 62,* 228–242.

Cabaj, R. P., & Stein, T. S. (Eds.). (1996). *Textbook of homosexuality and mental health.* Washington, DC: American Psychiatric Press.

Croteau, J. M., Bieschke, K. J., Phillips, J. C., Lark, J. S., Fischer, A. R., & Eberz, A. B. (1998). Toward a more inclusive and diverse multigenerational community of lesbian-, gay-, and bisexual-affirmative counseling psychologists. *The Counseling Psychologist, 26,* 809–816.

D'Augelli, A., & Patterson, C. (Eds.). (1996). *Lesbian, gay, and bisexual identities over the lifespan.* New York: Oxford.

Dworkin, S. H., & Gutierrez, F. J. (Eds.). (1992). *Counseling gay men and lesbians: Journey to the end of the rainbow.* Alexandria, VA: American Counseling Association.

Evans, N. J., & Wall, V. A. (Eds.). (1991). *Beyond tolerance: Gays, lesbians and bisexuals on campus.* Alexandria, VA: American Association for Counseling and Development.

Firestein, B. A. (Ed.). (1996). *Bisexuality: The psychology and politics of an invisible minority.* Newbury Park, CA: Sage.

Garnets, L., Hancock, K. A., Cochran, S. D., Goodchilds, J., & Peplau, L. A. (1991). Issues in psychotherapy with lesbians and gay men. *American Psychologist, 46,* 964–972.

Liddle, B. J. (1996). Therapist sexual orientation, gender, and counseling practices as they relate to ratings of helpfulness by gay and lesbian clients. *Journal of Counseling Psychology, 43,* 394–401.

Lopez, S. R. (1989). Patient variable biases in clinical judgement: Conceptual overview and methodological considerations. *Psychological Bulletin, 106,* 184–203.

Morgan, K. S. (1992). Caucasian lesbians' use of psychotherapy. *Psychology of Women Quarterly, 16,* 127–130.

Murray, J., & Abramson, P. R. (1983). *Bias in psychotherapy.* New York: Praeger.

Phillips, J. C., & Fischer, A. R. (1998). Graduate students' training experiences with lesbian, gay, and bisexual issues. *The Counseling Psychologist, 26,* 712–734.

Ponterotto, J. G., Casas, J. M., Suzuki, L. A., & Alexander, C. M. (Eds.). (1995). *Handbook of multicultural counseling.* Newbury Park, CA: Sage.

Weinberg, M. S., Williams, C. J., & Pryor, D. W. (1994). *Dual attraction: Understanding bisexuality.* New York: Oxford University Press.

Yarhouse, M. A. (1998). When clients seek treatment for same-sex attraction: Ethical issues in the "right to choose" debate. *Psychotherapy, 35,* 248–259.

I

SOCIAL AND THEORETICAL PERSPECTIVES

The aim of this section is to provide practitioners and scholars interested in counseling and therapy with lesbian, gay, and bisexual (LGB) individuals with a contextual framework within which relevant issues may be understood. Definitional, historical, and theoretical perspectives are presented and discussed. The relevance of these perspectives to counseling and therapy with LGB individuals is highlighted.

In chapter 1, Ellen M. Broido explores the philosophical assumption underlying the question "What does it mean to be or to identify as lesbian, gay, or bisexual?" Both essentialist and social-constructionist perspectives on this question are presented and discussed. Dr. Broido provides thoughtful commentary on how these perspectives influence both theory and practice.

In chapter 2, Amy L. Reynolds and William F. Hanjorgiris present models of lesbian, gay, and bisexual identity development. This presentation includes models that are thought to be common to all LGB individuals as well as models that uniquely describe subgroups of the population (e.g., bisexual individuals). In addition, they discuss the implications of these models for practitioners. In their considered critique, they highlight the need for empirical research that tests the viability of these proposed models.

Esther D. Rothblum, in chapter 3, presents a focused historical view of LGB culture. In particular, she highlights events in LGB history that have influenced the development of LGB communities and language and, indirectly, the mental health of this population. She then focuses on events that are more specific to mental health. If one is to truly understand LGB individuals, an understanding of their cultural history is imperative.

In chapter 4, Mary A. Fukuyama and Angela D. Ferguson provide readers with more detail about LGB culture, particularly as relevant to people of color. The focus of this comprehensive chapter is on the complicated interaction of cultural variables (including ethnicity, race, and gender), sexual orientation, and oppression. These authors focus on how managing multiple social oppressions influences the identity development of these individuals. In addition to presenting culture-specific perspectives, they discuss implications for counseling.

The section ends with chapter 5, by Ruth E. Fassinger, in which she carefully examines the relevance of four widely used psychotherapy frameworks (i.e., humanist, cognitive–behavioral, psychodynamic, and systems–cultural) for working with LGB clients. She eloquently discusses both the strengths and weaknesses of these approaches and concludes by presenting a model of theoretical integration.

All the chapters in this section provide commentary essential to understanding LGB individuals. Clearly the strength of this section is the presentation of divergent theoretical perspectives. These chapters primarily focus on theoretical perspectives; the results of few empirical studies are presented. There is a need for such studies, however, particularly for studies focused on people of color and those who identify as bisexual; few studies have focused exclusively on these populations. Taken as a whole, this section will challenge, deepen, and broaden the reader's conception of the "typical" LGB client.

1

CONSTRUCTING IDENTITY: THE NATURE AND MEANING OF LESBIAN, GAY, AND BISEXUAL IDENTITIES

ELLEN M. BROIDO

Twenty-five hundred years ago, a man and an adolescent boy engaged in a sexual relationship. One hundred years ago, two women lived and functioned socially together over the course of their lives, saw themselves as in a romantic relationship, but did not have a sexual relationship with each other or with others. One hundred years ago, a Native American woman took on many of the roles usually held by men in her culture, including hunting and warfare. She also took another woman as her wife. Currently, a man married to a woman routinely has anonymous sex with other men he meets in public places. Two other men spend their adult lives together in a sexual, romantic, and monogamous relationship. Two women decide to have a child together and raise the child as coparents. After many years of identifying as gay, both publicly and to himself, and having sexual and romantic relationships with other men, a man enters and maintains a monogamous relationship with a woman but still identifies as gay. A woman who feels no particular sexual identity has sexual and romantic relationships with both women and men. A biological male grows up desiring physical and emotional relationships with women. As an adult this person transforms (including sex reassignment therapy and hormone treatments) into a woman and continues to have relationships with women.

What, if anything, do these people have in common? Do they share an identity? A sexual orientation? Should all or some of these people be considered homosexual? Bisexual? Lesbian? Gay? Would they have considered themselves such? Should they be grouped together as a class? Do their sexual and romantic orientations arise from common sources or have common meanings?

These questions have served as focal points for a debate between two philosophical camps trying to understand how people view their own and others' sexual orientation: the essentialists and the social constructionists. This chapter presents readers with an understanding of the current debate about the nature and meaning of sexual orientation. It reviews definitions of terms often used in this debate, traces the historical development of the positions in the debate, and considers directions the debate might take in the future. Finally, it addresses therapeutic implications of the social constructionist position. Addressed here also, but in more detail in the following chapter, is the issue of how people come to adopt lesbian, gay, or bisexual identities. The focus of this chapter is on the philosophical and ontological assumptions underlying the question, What does it mean to be or to identify as lesbian, gay, or bisexual?

The fundamental question underlying these arguments is this: Is there a difference between experiencing same-gendered desire, engaging in same-gendered sexual relationships, experiencing same-gendered romantic relationships, and identifying as lesbian, bisexual, or gay? This question has been explored by people holding a variety of positions on the subject. However, two predominant points of view have been most evident. One camp, the essentialists, has argued that there is a common element that binds together people in different historical eras and cultures who experience sexual desire for others of their own gender. They believe that same-gender desire (which combines the concepts of sexual–physical desire and emotional desire) is a real and stable phenomenon, existing in an objectively knowable reality, although it may take different forms in different eras and cultures. Bisexuality, both as a behavior and as an identity, generally has been ignored by essentialists. Social constructionists, on the other hand, argue that behaviors and social roles are primarily, if not solely, shaped by historical era and social context, so that there is no "essential" or cross-contextual element to any type of identity or behavior. Identities are chosen or "constructed" from the models available within a given society or context (Clausen, 1997; Jagose, 1996). Thus, if a society did not recognize homosexuality and bisexuality as possible identities, people could not see themselves as homosexual or bisexual. Similarly, if heterosexuality (a condition in which other-gendered sexuality is experienced as a core part of a person's identity) were not seen as a possible identity, people would not identify as heterosexual. Indeed, the latter argument was made by Katz (1995) and underscored in the title of his work, *The Invention of Heterosexuality*.

DEFINITIONS AND CONCEPTS

Use of Language

The use of terminology is particularly important, and problematic, in a chapter discussing social constructionist perspectives on identity. In this chapter the terms *lesbian* and *gay* are used to refer to people whose self-identification includes the use of those labels, who self-acknowledge same-gender physical and emotional desires, and who live in contemporary Western society. The term *homosexual* is used to refer to people who engage primarily in same-gender sexual behavior or who experience same-gender emotional desire, however they identify themselves. The terms *bisexual* and *heterosexual* are used as both behavioral and identity descriptors, because there are no words that differentiate these meanings. Although the use of the term *homosexual* is often discouraged because of its connotation of pathology and its focus on the sexual aspect of identity (Committee on Lesbian and Gay Concerns, 1991), a necessary consequence of taking a social constructionist perspective is to refrain from speaking of people in other eras or non-Western cultures using the terms *lesbian* or *gay*; therefore, the term *homosexual* is used to refer to these people. In addition, the term *homosexual* was used by many of the authors, researchers, and theorists whose work is cited in this chapter, and in those parts of the chapter their usage has been retained.

Essentialism

Essentialism is a theory of social science that posits that some aspects of people are fixed, stable, and fundamental to their sense of themselves (Garnets & Kimmel, 1993). As applied to questions of sexual orientation, essentialist positions look for the causes or sources of same-gender desire. They are split, roughly, into those citing genetic causes and those citing environmental causes (although many essentialists see a combination of these influences as important; LeVay, 1996; Money, 1990). However, non-biological, nonenvironmental arguments have been proposed as well. Perhaps the best known of these is the story presented in Plato's *Symposium* (trans. 1987), in which humans were originally dyads: two people physically connected to each other. Some dyads were two men, others two women, and still others a man and a woman. Once the gods split the dyads in two, each half was instinctively drawn to the gender with whom it had originally been paired; hence, some people desire their own gender and others desire the other gender.

Fundamentally, essentialists believe that homosexuality and same-gender desire are the same thing and that homosexuality has existed, with fundamentally the same meaning, across many different cultures and historical eras, regardless of whether people defined themselves as homosexual. Stein (1990c) said the following in his review of the essentialism–social constructionism debate:

> Essentialists think that the categories of sexual orientation (e.g., heterosexual, homosexual and bisexual) are appropriate categories to apply to individuals. According to essentialists, it is legitimate to inquire into the origin of heterosexuality or homosexuality, to ask whether some historical figure was a heterosexual or homosexual, etc. This follows from the essentialist tenet that there are objective, intrinsic, culture-independent facts about what a person's sexual orientation is. (pp. 4–5)

Social Constructionism

Social constructionists (sometimes called *social constructivists*) approach questions of social roles and identities from a different philosophical perspective, believing that social and historical contexts shape and circumscribe the possible ways in which people can understand themselves and others. In the field of counseling, social constructionism is known particularly as the philosophical underpinning of Kelly's (1955) personal construct theory (see also Neimeyer, 1993). Social constructionist ideas have been applied in many different disciplines and to various aspects of identity, race, and gender in particular. Modern feminism has explicitly challenged the notion that women are "essentially" nurturing and men "essentially" aggressive (Brod, 1987; Butler, 1990; Lorber, 1998), and race has been reframed as a social construction based on issues of power and privilege rather than as a biological reality (Omi & Winant, 1998). Social constructionism also challenges the assumption of a particular and universal coherence among biological sex, gender, and sexual orientation. For example, it is often assumed that biological males see themselves and are seen by others as men and desire women as their sexual and affectional partners, whereas biological females see themselves and are seen by others as women and desire men as their sexual and affectional partners. Social constructionism disrupts this assumption, arguing not only that the three concepts (sex, gender, and sexual orientation) do not necessarily configure in this manner but also that the meanings of the categories themselves are culturally determined.

Looking at issues of sexual orientation and identity, social constructionists care little for questions about the causes of homosexuality. Indeed, many of them argue that the search for a cause or causes is nonsensical, because there is no universal, or essential, commonality about same- or other-gendered sexuality. Social constructionists reject the idea that there exists a fundamental, consistent meaning to or organization of sexuality across cultures and historical eras; they believe, therefore, that labels such as *heterosexual*, *bisexual*, and *homosexual* also have no consistent meaning across cultures and historical eras (Kitzinger, 1995), nor are they "the only or inevitable ways of organizing sexuality" (Clausen, 1997, p. 146).

Rather, social constructionists argue that it is the *meaning* of same- and other-gendered sexuality that is worthy of study and challenge, particularly, how societies define and grant power to ways of being sexual and forming loving relationships. Constructionists examine the ways that particular structures affect people's understanding of themselves.

HISTORICAL PERSPECTIVES

Although many of the arguments supporting constructionist perspectives rely on cross-cultural and particularly non-Western examples, these examples usually are drawn from the recent past, and the construction of sexual identity rarely is examined; the focus is more on the behaviors themselves (Greenberg, 1988; Mondimore, 1996). Texts written after the 1970s usually note that the lack of attention to issues of how people made meaning of same-gendered sexuality is due to absence of historical record, whereas in earlier texts this absence seems due to an essentialized perspective on the meaning of sexual orientation. Historical texts that do address how people made meaning of same-gender sexual and emotional desires focus on European history. The presentation of historical conceptions of sexual orientation in this chapter reflects the extant literature on the topic and is therefore primarily focused on European and, beginning in the twentieth century, North American perspectives.

Rise of Essentialism

The concept of heterosexuality, homosexuality, and bisexuality as identities, or social categories, is a distinctly recent phenomenon (Clausen, 1997; De Cecco & Elia, 1993; Foucault, 1976/1978; Jenness, 1992). Certainly there has been same-gender (and other-gendered) sexual behavior for many millennia. There are documented accounts of same-gender sexual behavior from as far back as the Golden Era of Greece. However, the concept of using sexuality as a way of framing a person's identity dates only as far back as the late seventeenth century (DuBay, 1987; Foucault, 1976/1978; McIntosh, 1968/1981; Mondimore, 1996, but see Saslow, 1989, for evidence supporting the presence of this concept as early as the Renaissance).

The concept of sexual orientation (i.e., of sexual behaviors being indicative of a type of person rather than a behavior distinct from identity) became evident in changes in the British and German penal codes of the nineteenth century (Foucault, 1976/1978; Mondimore, 1996). Although words to describe various aspects of same-gender sexual behavior date at least to the Classical Greek era, the first documented use of the word *homosexuality* was in 1869; the word occurred in a pamphlet arguing for the repeal of sodomy laws, written to a German judge by an early advocate for people who experienced same-gender desire as a core part of themselves (Mondimore, 1996). Whereas several contemporary authors had used a variety of words to describe people in whom same-gender desire was a stable and fundamental aspect of a person's personality, the use of the term *homosexual,* as in this pamphlet, has continued (Mondimore, 1996, p. 3). Documenting the developments of this era in his seminal work, *The History of Sexuality,* Foucault (1976/1978) wrote the following:

> As defined by the ancient civil or canonical codes, sodomy was a category of forbidden acts; their perpetrator was nothing more than the juridical subject of them. That nineteenth-century homosexual became a personage, a past, a case history, and a childhood, in addition to being a type of life, a life form, and a morphology, with an indiscreet anatomy and a mysterious physiology. Nothing that went into his total composition was unaffected by his sexuality. It was everywhere present in him: at the root of all his actions because it was their insidious and indefinitely active principle. . . . It was consubstantial with him, less as a habitual sin than as a singular nature. . . . Homosexuality appeared as one of the forms of sexuality when it was transposed from the practice of sodomy onto a kind of interior androgyny, a hermaphrodism of the soul. The sodomite had been a temporary aberration; the homosexual was now a species. (p. 43)

Foucault (1976/1978) identified this period as one in which, at least from a judicial perspective, a particular behavior was redefined, or reconstructed, as indicative of a fundamental aspect of a person's identity. By the late 1800s, the concept of sexual orientation as a type of identity arose within the literatures of medicine and psychology, as did calls for the acceptance of homosexuals as people with constitutional sickness, rather than as criminals. Early advocates for acceptance based their arguments on the idea that "sexual orientation was inborn, unchangeable, and therefore 'natural'. . . and homosexuality a valid and natural form of human sexual expression" (Mondimore, 1996, pp. 27–28).

Early published accounts of homosexuality, beginning in the mid-1800s and evident most notably in Krafft-Ebing's *Psychopathia Sexualis* (1894), clearly linked same-gender sexual behavior to constitutional degeneracy and thus explicitly conceived of homosexuality as a fundamental and immutable aspect of a person. Krafft-Ebing's work, which linked homosexual behavior with mental illness, emotional shallowness, and the inability to maintain relationships, became the basis for almost all medical and psychological views on homosexuality for much of the following century (Mondimore, 1996).

Whereas early essentialists focused on men's sexuality, women living in same-gender relationships escaped social notice or disapproval. "Boston marriages" (situations in which two unmarried women lived together, were not otherwise married, and functioned socially as a unit) were not uncommon in the United States and Britain in the later 1800s and early 1900s (see, in particular, Lillian Faderman's texts *Surpassing the Love of Men: Romantic Friendship and Love Between Women From the Renaissance to the Present*, 1981, and *Odd Girls and Twilight Lovers: A History of Lesbian Life in Twentieth Century America*, 1991). The extent to which these relationships were sexual generally is not known, and Faderman (1981) has argued that many, if not most, were *not* sexual. It is known that "these women spent their lives primarily with other women, they gave other women the bulk of their energy and attention, and they formed powerful emotional ties with other women" (Faderman, 1981, p. 190). Because women of this era were not considered to be sexual, Boston marriages were not perceived as lesbian relationships, nor were they thought to threaten the social order. It was only when the cases histories of Krafft-Ebing and Freud, among others of that era, portrayed women as sexual that Boston marriages were reconstructed as lesbian and became socially condemned (Faderman, 1981; Mondimore, 1996).

Challenges to Essentialism

Alfred Kinsey and his research group may have presented the first documented challenge to essentialist views of sexual orientation. Kinsey's research into the sexual behavior of human males (Kinsey, Pomeroy, & Martin, 1948) and females (Kinsey, Pomeroy, Martin, & Gebhard, 1953) has been widely cited, as well as misinterpreted, in the literature on homosexuality. Relevant here is Kinsey and colleagues' distinction between sexual behavior and identity, perhaps the first explicit distinction between the two ideas. As DuBay (1987) noted, Kinsey "was careful to point out that his 'homosexual–heterosexual' scale represented ranges of sexual behavior and experiences, *not* sexual orientation as commonly believed" (p. 3). Kinsey et al. (1953) wrote: "These terms [*homosexual, heterosexual*] are of value only because they describe the source of sexual stimulation, and they should not be taken as descriptions of the individuals who respond to the various stimuli" (pp. 446–447). This was the first challenge to the prevailing essentialized view of sexuality, which had been dominant for the previous century.

The next significant challenge to the medicalized, essentialized conception of homosexuality was presented in the 1968 article, "The Homosexual Role," by Mary McIntosh. McIntosh (1968/1981) argued that homosexuality is not a condition intrinsic to a given person or "a condition characterizing certain persons in the way that birthplace or deformity might characterize them" (p. 31), but rather is a role defined by society, which particular people adopt or are forced to adopt. By identifying homosexuality as a socially constructed role, McIntosh articulated an explicitly social constructionist perspective.

McIntosh (1968/1981) identified two major problems with the conceptualization of homosexuality as a condition. First, a condition implies either total membership or absence of membership in the category. This is denied by the prevalence of bisexual behavior. Second, the conceptualization of homosexuality as a condition implies the existence of a causative agent, either genetic or environmental. McIntosh (1968/1981) addressed the causal question:

> The failure of research to answer the question has not been due to lack of scientific rigor or to any inadequacy of the available evidence; it results rather from the fact that the wrong question has been asked. One might as well try to trace the aetiology of "committee chairmanship" or "Seventh Day Adventism" as of "homosexuality." (p. 31)

McIntosh (1968/1981) noted that conceptualizing homosexuality as an essential characteristic allowed society to clearly demark "deviants" from "normals" in that deviant behavior happened only in "deviant" people but never in "normal" people. Thus, if a person were to cross this threshold, he (McIntosh addressed only male homosexuality) made an irreversible step and became part of a culture that because of its separation from "normal" society was better able to retain those who entered.

McIntosh (1968/1981) argued that society has created the role of "homosexual" as a form of social control. Society has defined the characteristics of this role (primarily for men) not only in terms of sexual behavior but also in terms of social behavior, as being effeminate, relating to all men in a sexual manner, and engaging exclusively in same-gender sexual behavior.

The next major challenge to the essentialized view of homosexuality was put forth by Michel Foucault (1976/1978) in his book *The History of Sexuality: Volume I. Introduction.* In this text he argued that homosexuality as an identity first arose in the judicial and medical establishments of the nineteenth century. Making the argument presented earlier in this chapter, Foucault identified the shift from seeing same-gender sex acts as something in which anyone could engage, as a "temptation" with potentially universal appeal, to assigning an identity and specific characteristics to those who had same-gender sex. Faucault's arguments both challenged the current assumptions about what was "natural" sexuality and argued that society furthermore *created* the categories that people then viewed as natural and unnatural (Jagose, 1996).

Although earlier critiques of essentialized views of same-gender desire focused primarily on men, challenges to essentialist perspectives of lesbian identity arose within the lesbian feminist movement of the 1970s. Some women conceived of any relationship with a man as oppressive and saw relationships with women as a form of social change (Esterberg, 1997). Others believed that only sexism kept women from recognizing their innate potential to love other women and thus that "same-sex desire might follow from an acceptance of 'sisterhood' rather than the other way around" (Clausen, 1997, p. 44). This argument was expanded in Adrienne Rich's (1980) article "Compulsory Heterosexuality and Lesbian Existence," in which she asked her readers to

> consider the possibility that all women—from the infant suckling at her mother's breast, to the grown woman experiencing orgasmic sensations while suckling her own child . . . to two women . . . who share a laboratory, to the woman dying at ninety, touched and handled by women—exist on a lesbian continuum, we can see ourselves as moving in and out of this continuum, whether we identify ourselves as lesbian or not. (pp. 650–651)

Although she did not argue that all women could be lesbians, Kitzinger (1987) explicitly discussed the roles of sexism and patriarchy in shaping what it meant to be a lesbian. Kitzinger (1995) summarized the argument she presented in her 1987 text, *The Social Construction of Lesbianism*, as follows:

> "The lesbian" as a type of being does not exist, but is rather actively constructed in a society which . . . is predicated on male subordination of women through prevailing ideas of "femininity," including the requirement that the "feminine" woman be heterosexual. (p. 139)

The feminist movement of the 1970s, then, explicitly attacked essentialist notions of sexual orientation, arguing that lesbianism spanned the range of ways in which women connected to other women; that sexism shaped what it meant to be heterosexual, bisexual, or lesbian; and that women's understandings of their own sexualities and sexual orientations were shifting, rather than fixed.

The idea of the homosexual as a type of person, defined by the gender of the person she or he was attracted to, existed uncontested in Western culture for only a relatively brief period, from the late eighteenth century to the mid twentieth century. It was preceded, not by an absence of homo-

or bisexual behavior or emotions, but by a conception of sexuality that saw these acts and feelings only in behavioral terms rather than as describing types of people whose fundamental nature dictated their expression of their sexuality. The current view of social constructionists in some ways recalls the earlier perspective and is considered in the next part of this chapter.

CURRENT SOCIAL CONSTRUCTIONIST PERSPECTIVES

From the initial conception of homosexuality as reflective of a fundamental, immutable, and central aspect of a person's identity to the feminist arguments of the 1970s that any woman could be a lesbian (popularized on Alex Dobkin's, 1974, record album *Lavender Jane Loves Women*), the understanding of the nature of same-gender desire has shifted radically over 150 years. Social constructionists argue that conceptualizing sexuality on the basis of the gender of the participants is only one possible way of organizing sexuality (Clausen, 1997; Jagose, 1996). Many non-Western cultures, and some Western cultures at different periods of history, have used different paradigms for organizing sexuality, for example, the social status of one's partner or the age of one's partner (Chan, 1995; Clausen, 1997; Greenberg, 1988). Likewise, sexual identity has been defined in different periods or cultures differently. For example, in many current Latin American cultures same-gender sexual behavior labels a man as homosexual only if he is the passive, or receptive, partner. The active partner is considered heterosexual regardless of the gender of his sexual partner.

Current assumptions about the centrality of sexuality and gender are similarly challenged in a social constructionist perspective. Most current psychological theories hold the assumption that one's sexuality is a core aspect of one's identity (Hart, 1984; Richardson, 1993). However, this is not universally true, nor must it be true. The idea that the gender of one's sexual partner is the logical basis for organizing sexuality most often rests on the premise that procreation is the primary goal of sexual behavior and that procreative sexuality is the model against which all sexuality should be evaluated or compared. Yet people engage in sexual behavior for many reasons, and there is no unquestionable reason to grant greater importance to one reason than another. Moreover, people's choice of partner is not necessarily the same for each of these reasons.

In addition, current critiques of the concept of gender as an essential quality (e.g., Butler, 1990; Lorber, 1998) further call into question the necessary construction of sexuality as dependent on the gender of the participants. Clausen (1997) raised this point:

> To accept the notion that orientation to same or opposite sex is biologically determined is to do more than decide that homosexuality and heterosexuality are real categories. It is also to bow to the concept that gender is real in some sense that transcends differences between gen-

itals or chromosomes. It is to decide that the meanings we attach to gender (or through which we "make" gender) are somehow not meanings at all but fixed attributes. (p. 129)

In addition, Jagose (1996) argued that

psychoanalysis makes culturally available a narrative that complicates the assumption that an identity is the natural property of any individual. Sigmund Freud's theorisation of the unconscious further challenges the notion that subjectivity is stable and coherent. In establishing the formative influence of important mental and psychic processes of which an individual is unaware, the theory of the unconscious has radical implications for the common-sense assumption that the subject is both whole and self knowing. . . . Identity, then, is an effect of identification with and against others: being ongoing, and always incomplete, it is a process rather than a property. (pp. 78–79)

Social constructionism holds that the meanings of identities, and the identities that people choose between, are determined by the choices available in a particular sociohistorical context. For people of color living in contemporary Western culture, this context often forces them to choose between their identities as members of a racial or ethnic group and as people identifying as lesbian, bisexual, or gay (Chan, 1993, 1995; Espin, 1987, 1993; Loiacano, 1993).

People experience and respond to pressures to choose a singular identity in a variety of fashions (Chang Hall, 1993), some identifying more with their race or ethnicity, others with their lesbianism, gayness, or bisexuality, some finding ways to integrate the two. No single model is necessarily the best, and people often identify with whichever of their identities is most salient in a particular context. Research on lesbian Latinas (Espin, 1987) and gay and lesbian Asian Americans (Chan, 1993) has indicated that most respondents preferred an identity that integrated their race or ethnicity and their sexual orientation; however, their sexual orientation was perceived by others as so transgressive that it overshadowed their race or ethnicity, and they were identified primarily by their sexual orientation (Chan, 1995). Chan (1995) also maintained that the adoption of a bisexual identity, even in the presence of only same-gender sexual behavior, is not uncommon among Latinos and Latinas. Chan (1995) also noted that in African Americans and Chinese Americans, "attempts may be made to integrate different behaviors into a sense of self, but the integration of a sexual identity may not exist as it does for members of the dominant culture" (p. 93). To identify as lesbian, bisexual, or gay, one must frame one's identity through contemporary Western concepts.

There is no singular "current perspective" on the notion of lesbian, bisexual, or gay identity. Those exploring biological and environmental determinants of sexual orientation largely do not interact with those exploring the social forces shaping the ways in which people construct their identities (but see De Cecco & Elia, 1993; Stein, 1990b). Although the social constructionist perspective seems to be the dominant viewpoint of those working within the humanities and social sciences, representatives of these disciplines frequently critique the absurdities following from a strict constructionist perspective (e.g., if everything is a social construct, what, if any, basis is there for shared realities or questions?; Stein, 1990a).

AREAS FOR FUTURE RESEARCH AND THEORY DEVELOPMENT

Social constructionist perspectives raise a number of important questions for future research and theory development. Although essentialism and social constructionism remain the dominant paradigms for those exploring sexual orientation on a theoretical level, additional perspectives have begun to arise. Some researchers and theorists who are more focused on the current experiences of lesbians, bisexual people, and gay men in contemporary Western cultures have begun to argue for a middle ground between essentialism and social constructionism (see, in particular, Epstein, 1987, and Rhoads, 1995). Their models recognize that people experience and make meaning of their sexual orientation in a variety of ways, some experiencing it as a central, stable, and fundamental part of who they are and others experiencing more fluid identities. Building on a theory first proposed by Epstein, Rhoads developed a model in which sexual orientation is perceived similarly to ethnicity, having both essential and socially constructed components. Rhoads's model is based on the experiences of gay and bisexual men at a particular university at a particular point in time; therefore, further research into the generalizability and implications of such a model is needed.

Studies of how transgendered people understand and make meaning of their gender have only recently been published (e.g., Feinberg, 1996; Griggs, 1998). How do people whose experience of their gender is outside traditionally understood categories understand sexual orientation? What does it mean for a biological female who becomes a man to desire another man? Once gender is deconstructed, the meaning of sexual orientation becomes suspect (Bornstein, 1995), but little research or theoretical exploration of these questions has yet been attempted.

As discussed earlier in this chapter, the little research that exists on how people create identities and understand sexual orientation has occurred in Western cultures. Although the hegemony of American media has ensured the diffusion of Western perspectives into most cultures, this does not mean that endogenous understandings of identity and the meaning of sexual feelings and behaviors have disappeared. As counseling becomes increasingly cross-cultural, there is a great need to understand the range of ways in which contemporary non-Western cultures and societies understand the meanings given to sexual desires and identities.

An additional issue left largely unquestioned has been how, if gender is no longer to be the organizing principle for understanding sexuality, sexuality might be organized or understood and what implications there are for bisexuality as an identity. In an article in a recent edition of *Out* magazine, Graff (1997) asked the following:

> Do stories like Robin's [a person who does not consider the gender of her lovers] point to a future beyond labels, a world where who you desire does not define who you are? Or are *gay* and *lesbian* and even *straight* more popular because the great unknown of bisexuality is scarier? Would "we" disappear as a community if we stopped policing the meaning of the words *lesbian* and *gay*? .... [Author John D'Emelio, interviewed for the article, responded] "Cultures don't change overnight. We're in the process of making those categories more real than ever; they haven't crested yet." (pp. 193–194)

Challenging the idea that sexual orientation is a necessary part of one's sense of self, DuBay (1987) questioned the necessity of adopting a role or holding an identity as lesbian, bisexual, or gay. Research is needed to explore the experiences, development, and self-perceptions of people who do not hold sexual orientation as a central part of their identity.

Changes in how lesbian, bisexual, and gay people are portrayed in popular culture seem to be affecting how they see themselves (Clausen, 1997). It is important to explore the impact and mechanisms of cultural portrayals of lesbian, bisexual, and gay people on the relevance and development of identity. In addition, as conceptions of sexuality and gender continue to change, it is necessary to develop a better understanding of how these issues shape the idea and practice of identity.

IMPLICATIONS OF SOCIAL CONSTRUCTIONISM

Recognizing that sexual orientation is a socially constructed concept has many implications for counselors in terms of challenging assumptions about the nature of sexual orientation, both in work with clients and in work for social justice. However, there are also limitations to the extent to which a largely theoretical concept like social constructionism fits with the reality that many clients experience. The final portion of the chapter explores both the practical consequences of social constructionism and its limits in counseling and therapy.

Examining Assumptions

Social constructionist perspectives call into question many of the assumptions of contemporary Western culture and, by extension, assumptions present in the field of counseling. These challenges lie most clearly in assumptions about the stability of sexual orientation, the centrality of sexual orientation to people's sense of self, and the link between biological sex, gender, and sexual orientation (Jagose, 1996). Therapists often carry with them the effects of socialization in the dominant culture as well as in the particular cultures in which they were raised and trained. If they were raised or trained in contemporary Western culture, they probably were taught that sexuality is a fundamental part of people's self-concept, that erotic attraction is a relatively stable attribute, and that the gender of people's partners is central to their sense of identity (Richardson, 1993). Social constructionist views, which challenge all of these notions, may be profoundly unsettling for someone trying to understand her or his own, or another's, sexuality and identity, and how the two relate. Counselors should be certain to explore and become aware of their own assumptions about the nature and meaning of sexual identity, how their assumptions might be similar to or different from those of their clients, and how those assumptions affect how they and their clients experience and make meaning of their sexuality.

Many people report that their sexual orientation is a stable part of themselves and central to their identity. Others find their sexual orientation to be a more fluid identity. Some find it central to their sense of themselves, and others do not (Brown, 1995; Golden, 1987; Moses, 1978; Ponse, 1978; Rhoads, 1995). Counselors and therapists must be careful not to impose their own definitions of *straight, lesbian, bisexual,* or *gay* or to presume that sexual orientation is always central to identity, because their understanding of those terms and processes may differ from those of clients. Moreover, the use of only one of these terms may preclude clients' comfort in discussing the potentially fluid nature of sexual orientation.

Applications of Social Constructionism

Social constructionism provides several important new ways of understanding the meaning of sexual orientation. Most significant among these are the ideas that categories such as *homosexual, bisexual,* and *heterosexual* are socially constructed and that, therefore, some people may have experiences that do not fit within the ways society defines these labels. Social constructionism alerts therapists to this reality and calls on them to present other options to clients. This presentation may be particularly affirming for clients who experience their sexual orientation as bisexual, or as fluid, or for whom gender is not a determinant in their emotional and erotic relationships.

Because current Western society assumes sexual orientation to be a fixed and stable characteristic, changes in the gender of a person's object choice may be highly disconcerting to clients. Both heterosexual and gay and lesbian communities have placed a great deal of importance on the idea of sexual orientation being a fixed characteristic and sanction those who state that their experiences differ. Esterberg (1997) noted the profound impact on lesbian and bisexual communities when lesbian and bisexual women experience changes in their identities:

> As the stories of women who have experienced change demonstrate, many lesbians are suspicious of women whose sexuality seems fluid. ... These thoughts may be threatening for those who believed their questions and struggles about sexual identity were settled. That for some women sexual fluidity persists in the face of such obstacles is remarkable. (p. 79)

Thus, while acknowledging the socially constructed nature of the categories *lesbian*, *bisexual*, *gay*, and *straight*, therapists must also be prepared to help clients deal with the consequences of not fitting into socially constructed categories. It is particularly important that counselors recognize the potential for loss of support systems when clients experience shifts in their experience of their sexual orientation. Clients who report their experience of their erotic attraction as changing, or as not central to their identities, are likely to experience rejection by both the straight and the lesbian–bisexual–gay communities and to find even less representation of their experiences in the dominant culture than the little that is available to lesbians, bisexual people, and gay men. Bisexuality, in part because it challenges the assumption of stable and singular sexual desire or identity, is particularly threatening to many people and is seen as politically treasonous and indicative of confusion (Weinberg, Williams, & Pryor, 1994/1998).

There is no consensus on what it means to identify as lesbian, gay, or bisexual, and social constructionist perspectives challenge the necessity of doing so. It has long been an assumption, manifested particularly in the identity development models explored in the next chapter, that identifying oneself as lesbian, bisexual, or gay, both to oneself and to significant others, is a healthy thing (Dankmeijer, 1993; De Cecco & Elia, 1993). Hart (1984) questioned the benefit of limiting clients' options by encouraging them to adopt a static identity.

The social constructionist approach challenges many of the standard identity development models that imply a linear progression to a stable sense of one's sexual orientation (particularly Cass's, 1979, 1984, model). Indeed, as Richardson (1993) noted, "without the existence of a specific category of persons labeled as homosexual there can be no development of a discrete homosexual identity" (p. 120) and hence no basis for generalized models of homosexual identity development. Richardson has highlighted the importance of exploring how clients themselves make meaning of their experiences rather than fitting them into models whose very premises are suspect.

The Realities of Essentialism

Regardless of debates between essentialists and constructionists, many people—gay, straight, and otherwise—do experience their sexual orientation as central to their identity and experience it as a stable phenomenon (Epstein, 1987; Rhoads, 1995; Richardson, 1993). Often people seek counseling because they feel the need to come to terms with their "identity," to know their "true nature." Even if they experience their "true nature" as a member of a stigmatized group, acknowledging this identity "provides both a way to accept themselves and to manage being stigmatized by society" (Richardson, 1993, p. 124).

Social constructionist perspectives, arising out of a philosophical discourse, do not address the reality that whether or not people construct their identities, they are still subject to discrimination, violence, and general social disapproval. Although social constructionists have not made the argument, their position can be used to support conversion therapies because social constructionists reject the idea that homosexuality is a fixed and innate aspect of identity. As Rhoads (1995) noted, "poststructural accounts that avoid identity as a source of difference run the risk of whitewashing difference" (p. 155).

DuBay (1987) presented a fictional account of a student speaking with a therapist about being gay. The therapist told the student that being gay was no different from his identity, or role, as a chemist or tennis player and that he could discard the role just as easily as he could quit playing tennis or being a chemist (pp. 156–157). Clearly this constructionist approach is of little use to those who experience their sexual orientation as central to their sense of themselves. Furthermore, social constructionist perspectives can feed into the idea that same-gender desire is a chosen behavior, a voluntary transgression of social norms, and is therefore deserving of condemnation.

Pointing out both the limits and the promise of social constructionist perspectives, Clausen (1997) wrote the following:

> Gay men and lesbians are real; their sexual desires, like those of heterosexuals, are often quite predictable; and they have common interests and a need, ability and right to organize politically around those interests. At the same time, their personal identities are not necessarily static, any more so than are the identities of heterosexuals. Their communities are historically shaped and will change in the future. (p. 137)

While remaining open to the possibility of change in the nature and meaning of various identities in clients (and themselves), therapists must recognize and validate clients' experiences of reality as well as their need for stability and community. Although there exists a diversity of ways in which those identities are assigned meaning, both by our clients and by the surrounding society,

> we need to consider the process whereby, for each individual, either stability *or change* of sexual identity occurs. We must address ourselves not only to the question of how individuals develop a heterosexual or homosexual identity, but also how they do, or do not, maintain this identity thereafter. (Richardson, 1993, p. 121)

The Role of Therapists

We need to be able to affirm people's sense of themselves—whether they perceive their sexual orientation as an internal and fixed aspect of themselves or as fluid. In addition, as Richardson (1993) has noted, "therapists need to be highly conscious of the important issues that acknowledgment of the possibility of either stability *or* change raises" (p. 124).

The ongoing stigmatization of people who identify as lesbian, bisexual, or gay in many parts of modern society renders less important the philosophical distinction between essentialist and constructionist perspectives on identity. The lesbian, bisexual, and gay communities have found ways to use essentialist perspectives as effective tools in the struggle to acquire equal rights; however, constructionist perspectives can be used as well (see Kitzinger, 1995, p. 154). To adopt a strictly constructionist perspective often is not helpful when working with the day-to-day realities of the lives of lesbian, bisexual, and gay people. More important, instead, is to validate the experience of those who find sexual orientation, of any type, to be a central part of their identity, as well as to validate those for whom it is less immediate to their sense of themselves, and to be open to change in the meanings ascribed to these identities. For counselors, the imperative lies on the side of support of members of oppressed social groups and efforts toward a just society (Albee, 1986). Kitzinger (1995) noted that even she can advocate an essentialist position when politically necessary. Clausen (1997) stated that "rather than debating causes, we need to work to insure that same-sex desire will be treated as a valid, and valuable, form of human expression regardless of how it is explained" (p. 32). For the therapist, this means that traditional models of lesbian and gay identity development may or may not be applicable to clients. The challenge is for therapists to be open to multiple interpretations of identity, to increase their tolerance for ambiguity, and to work for a just and equitable society on both individual and institutional levels.

CONCLUSION

The question before us is not, How will definitions of lesbian, bisexual, and gay identity evolve? That question is too narrow, given the questions in the larger academic cultures concerning the meanings of sexuality, sexual orientation, and gender. These questions will permeate into the general, nonacademic consciousness with time and with more accessible presentations of these ideas. The questions that will evolve from current understandings are more likely to address the presumed centrality of sexuality and gender to self-concept and to explore the relationships between the surrounding culture and identity (see Esterberg, 1997, for one example).

Clausen (1997) challenged "experts" to shift their focus from issues of identity based on sexual orientation to issues of justice and equity:

> For over 100 years, anxious laypeople have turned to the experts hoping to be enlightened as to the "truth" of their sexual natures, or to be reassured that their desires are acceptable. Explanation becomes validation—or proscription, taboo. . . . But the wounds will not be healed by advances in knowledge. We already know enough. Instead, we need to work on enlarging the space for different kinds of people to live well with each other. . . . [Experts] cannot tell us what we desire, what our desires mean, which of them are most real or authentic, if or how to act on them, whether they will change in the future, or how best to move from desires and behaviors to descriptions of our selves [sic]. (pp. 148–149)

The role of counselors and therapists is to help those who experience same-gender desire, and those who identify as lesbian, bisexual, or gay, to understand and accept themselves and to work toward a society in which all people are free to express their desire and to identify as they feel is appropriate.

REFERENCES

Albee, G. W. (1986). Toward a just society: Lessons from observations on the primary prevention of psychopathology. *American Psychologist, 41,* 891–898.

Bornstein, K. (1995). *Gender outlaw: On men, women, and the rest of us.* New York: Vintage Books.

Brod, H. (Ed.). (1987). *The making of masculinities: The new men's studies.* Boston: Allen & Unwin.

Brown, L. S. (1995). Lesbian identities: Concepts and issues. In A. R. D'Augelli & C. J. Patterson (Eds.), *Lesbian, gay, and bisexual identities over the lifespan: Psychological perspectives* (pp. 3–23). New York: Oxford University Press.

Butler, J. (1990). *Gender trouble: Feminism and the subversion of identity.* New York: Routledge.

Cass, V. C. (1979). Homosexual identity formation: A theoretical model. *Journal of Homosexuality, 4,* 219–236.

Cass, V. C. (1984). Homosexual identity formation: Testing a theoretical model. *Journal of Sex Research, 20*(2), 143–167.

Chan, C. S. (1993). Issues of identity development among Asian-American lesbians and gay men. In L. D. Garnets & D. C. Kimmel (Eds.), *Psychological perspectives on lesbian and gay male experiences* (pp. 376–387). New York: Columbia University Press.

Chan, C. S. (1995). Issues of sexual identity in an ethnic minority: The case of Chinese American lesbians, gay men, and bisexual people. In A. R. D'Augelli & C. J. Patterson (Eds.), *Lesbian, gay and bisexual identities over the lifespan: Psychological perspectives* (pp. 87–101). New York: Oxford University Press.

Chang Hall, L. K. (1993). Bitches in solitude: Identity politics and lesbian community. In A. Stein (Ed.), *Sisters, sexperts and queers: Beyond the lesbian nation* (pp. 218–229). New York: Plume.

Clausen, J. (1997). *Beyond gay or straight: Understanding sexual orientation.* Philadelphia: Chelsea House.

Committee on Lesbian and Gay Concerns. (1991). Avoiding heterosexual bias in language. *American Psychologist, 46,* 973–974.

Dankmeijer, P. (1993). The construction of identities as a means of survival: The case of gay and lesbian teachers. *Journal of Homosexuality, 24*(3–4), 95–105.

De Cecco, J. P., & Elia, J. P. (1993). A critique and synthesis of biological essentialism and social constructionist views of sexuality and gender. *Journal of Homosexuality, 24*(3–4), 1–26.

Dobkin, A. (1974). *Lavender Jane loves women* [Record]. New York: Women's Wax Works.

DuBay, W. H. (1987). *Gay identity: The self under ban.* Jefferson, NC: McFarland.

Epstein, S. (1987). Gay politics, ethnic identity: The limits of social constructionism. *Socialist Review, 17*(3/4), 9–54.

Espin, O. M. (1987). Issues of identity in the psychology of Latina lesbians: Explorations and challenges. In Boston Lesbians Psychologies Collective (Eds.), *Lesbian psychologies* (pp. 35–55). Urbana: University of Illinois Press.

Espin, O. M. (1993). Issues of identity in the psychology of Latina lesbians. In L. D. Garnets & D. C. Kimmel (Eds.), *Psychological perspectives on lesbian and gay male experiences* (pp. 348–363). New York: Columbia University Press.

Esterberg, K. G. (1997). *Lesbian and bisexual identities: Constructing communities, constructing selves.* Philadelphia: Temple University Press.

Faderman, L. (1981). *Surpassing the love of men: Romantic friendship and love between women from the Renaissance to the present.* New York: Morrow.

Faderman, L. (1991). *Odd girls and twilight lovers: A history of lesbian life in twentieth century America.* New York: Columbia University Press.

Feinberg, L. (1996). *Transgender warriors: Making history from Joan of Arc to RuPaul.* Boston: Beacon Press.

Foucault, M. (1978). *The history of sexuality: Volume I. Introduction* (R. Hurley, Trans.). New York: Vintage Books. (Original work published 1976)

Garnets, L. D., & Kimmel, D. C. (Eds.). (1993). *Psychological perspectives on lesbian and gay male experiences*. New York: Columbia University Press.

Golden, C. (1987). Diversity and variability in women's sexual identities. In Boston Lesbian Psychologies Collective (Eds.), *Lesbian psychologies: Explorations and challenges* (pp. 19–34). Urbana: University of Illinois Press.

Graff, E. J. (1997, September). Sexual disorientation: So you go both ways. And you call yourself gay? *Out, 48*, 190–194.

Greenberg, D. F. (1988). *The construction of homosexuality*. Chicago: University of Chicago Press.

Griggs, C. (1998). *S/he: Changing sex and changing clothes*. New York: Berg.

Hart, J. (1984). Therapeutic implications of viewing sexual identity in terms of essentialist and constructionist theories. *Journal of Homosexuality, 9*(4), 39–51.

Jagose, A. (1996). *Queer theory: An introduction*. New York: New York University Press.

Jenness, V. (1992). Coming out: Lesbian identities and the categorization problem. In K. Plummer (Ed.), *Modern homosexualities: Fragments of lesbian and gay experience* (pp. 65–74). New York: Routledge.

Katz, J. N. (1995). *The invention of heterosexuality*. New York: Plume.

Kelly, G. A. (1955). *The psychology of personal constructs*. New York: Norton.

Kinsey, A., Pomeroy, W., & Martin, C. (1948). *Sexual behavior in the human male*. Philadelphia: W. B. Saunders.

Kinsey, A., Pomeroy, W., Martin, C., & Gebhard, P. (1953). *Sexual behavior in the human female*. Philadelphia: W. B. Saunders.

Kitzinger, C. (1987). *The social construction of lesbianism*. London: Sage.

Kitzinger, C. (1995). Social constructionism: Implications for lesbian and gay psychology. In A. R. D'Augelli & C. J. Patterson (Eds.), *Lesbian, gay and bisexual identities over the lifespan: Psychological perspectives* (pp. 136–161). New York: Oxford University Press.

Krafft-Ebing, R. von (1894). *Psychopathia sexualis* (C. H. Chaddock, Trans.). Philadelphia: Davis.

LeVay, S. (1996). *Queer science: The use and abuse of research into homosexuality*. Cambridge, MA: MIT Press.

Loiacano, D. K. (1993). Gay identity issues among Black Americans: Racism, homophobia, and the need for validation. In L. D. Garnets & D. C. Kimmel (Eds.), *Psychological perspectives on lesbian and gay male experiences* (pp. 364–375). New York: Columbia University Press.

Lorber, J. (1998). The social construction of gender. In P. S. Rothenberg (Ed.), *Race, class and gender in the United States: An integrated study* (pp. 33–45). New York: St. Martin's Press.

McIntosh, M. (1981). The homosexual role. In K. Plummer (Ed.), *The making of the modern homosexual* (pp. 31–49). Totowa, NJ: Barnes & Noble Books. (Reprinted from *Social Problems, 16*(2), 182–191, 1968)

Mondimore, F. M. (1996). *A natural history of homosexuality*. Baltimore: Johns Hopkins University Press.

Money, J. (1990). Agenda and credenda of the Kinsey scale. In D. P. McWhirter, S. A. Sanders, & J. M. Reinish (Eds.), *Homosexuality/heterosexuality: Concepts of sexual orientation* (pp. 41–60). New York: Oxford University Press.

Moses, A. E. (1978). *Identity management in lesbian women*. New York: Praeger.

Neimeyer, R. A. (1993). An appraisal of constructivist psychotherapies. *Journal of Consulting and Clinical Psychology, 2,* 221–234.

Omi, M., & Winant, H. (1998). Racial formations. In P. S. Rothenberg (Ed.), *Race, class and gender in the United States: An integrated study* (pp. 13–22). New York: St. Martin's Press.

Plato. (1987). *Symposium* (Stanley Rosen, Trans.). New Haven, CT: Yale University Press.

Ponse, B. (1978). *Identities in the lesbian world*. Westport, CT: Greenwood Press.

Rhoads, R. (1995). *Coming out in college: The struggle for a queer identity*. Westport, CT: Bergin & Garvey.

Rich, A. (1980). Compulsory heterosexuality and lesbian existence. *Signs: Journal of Women in Culture and Society, 5,* 631–660.

Richardson, D. (1993). Recent challenges to traditional assumptions about homosexuality: Some implications for practice. In L. D. Garnets & D. C. Kimmel (Eds.), *Psychological perspectives on lesbian and gay male experiences* (pp. 117–129). New York: Columbia University Press.

Saslow, J. M. (1989). Homosexuality in the Renaissance: Behavior, identity and artistic expression. In M. B. Duberman, M. Vicinus, & G. Chauncey, Jr. (Eds.), *Hidden from history: Reclaiming the gay and lesbian past* (pp. 90–105). New York: Meridian.

Stein, E. (1990a). Conclusion: The essentials of constructionism and the construction of essentialism. In E. Stein (Ed.), *Forms of desire: Sexual orientation and the social constructionist controversy* (pp. 325–353). New York: Garland.

Stein, E. (Ed.). (1990b). *Forms of desire: Sexual orientation and the social constructionist controversy*. New York: Garland.

Stein, E. (1990c). Introduction. In E. Stein (Ed.), *Forms of desire: Sexual orientation and the social constructionist controversy* (pp. 3–10). New York: Garland.

Weinberg, M. S., Williams, C. J., & Pryor, D. W. (1998). Becoming and being "bisexual" (L. W. Garmer, Trans.). In E. J. Haeberle & R. Gindorf (Eds.), *Bisexualities: The ideology and practice of sexual contact with both men and women* (pp. 169–181). New York: Continuum. (Original work published 1994)

2

COMING OUT: LESBIAN, GAY, AND BISEXUAL IDENTITY DEVELOPMENT

AMY L. REYNOLDS AND WILLIAM F. HANJORGIRIS

Understanding lesbian, gay, and bisexual (LGB) identity development, or the process by which LGB people come to know and value more fully who they are, is central to developing an effective and meaningful relationship with LGB clients. Having a positive identity requires additional developmental effort unique to LGB individuals (Gonsiorek & Rudolph, 1991). This developmental challenge is the result of society's homophobic and heterosexist attitudes and the reality that many LGB individuals internalize these negative attitudes and assumptions about LGB issues and people. For LGB people, the reality of living in a society where their very existence and value are questioned makes it challenging to recognize, accept, and integrate their LGB identity (Fassinger & Richie, 1997). Such realities lead to internalized homophobia and self-hatred, which may have significant deleterious effects for LGB individuals such as addictions, suicide, and other mental health difficulties.

Despite the prevalence of societal homophobia and heterosexism, it is important to acknowledge that same-sex sexual behavior has been present across cultures throughout recorded history (see Fukuyama & Ferguson, chapter 4, this volume) and that reactions to this reality have always been influenced by the particular social structures in place within each culture (see Broido, chapter 1, this volume). Although some individuals who engaged in same-sex sexual behavior may have been uniquely identified within a specific cultural context, their behavior was often integral to the general structure and functioning of the culture. For example, "two-spirited people" were historically valued in many Native American communities (Tafoya, 1997).

The purpose of this chapter is to explore lesbian, gay, and bisexual identity development and its effect on the psychotherapy process. Researchers have highlighted the importance of studying the coming out process as well as gay and lesbian identity formation models (Buhrke, Ben-Ezra, Hurley, & Ruprecht, 1992; Morin, 1977). The chapter also explores future research issues.

IDENTITY DEVELOPMENT LITERATURE

Since the late 1970s there have been many empirical studies and theoretical writings that focused on the process by which an individual acquired a gay or lesbian identity and examined the developmental tasks necessary to form and maintain a positive gay or lesbian identity. Initial investigations of gay identity formation consisted of descriptive studies that sought to examine the identity developmental process for gay men (Dank, 1971). Exploration of the developmental process and unique issues for lesbians and bisexuals did not occur until later. The typical method used by early researchers studying gay men consisted of asking participants to recall the conditions or events they considered important to their acquisition of a gay identity. Researchers then defined developmental milestones believed necessary to the process of gay identity development (Brady & Busse, 1994; Troiden, 1979). According to de Monteflores and Schultz (1978), many early researchers tended to ignore the process and identified coming out with a single event (i.e., publicly identifying oneself as gay). Subsequent models attempted to extend earlier theory by organizing participants' retrospective accounts of coming out into developmental stages (Cass, 1979; Coleman, 1987; Troiden, 1989; Troiden & Goode, 1980).

The contemporary view of lesbian and gay male identity development, like that of racial and ethnic minority identity, has been that identity formation represents an emergent, continuous life process (Garnets & Kimmel, 1993). Erikson's (1963) formulation of ego identity development provided a basis for this belief by highlighting that identity development is an ongoing, interactive process that is highly influenced by the norms and values of individual families, cultures, and society.

The process through which LGB individuals first recognize their sexual orientation is often referred to as *coming out*. The coming out process consists of a series of complex cognitive, affective, and behavioral changes. An awareness of same-sex sexual feelings; initial same-sex sexual encounters; participation in the gay, lesbian, and bisexual subculture; labeling self as *gay* or *lesbian;* and disclosing a gay or lesbian identity to others all are part of coming out. Forming an LGB identity is a challenging process because it means adopting a nontraditional identity, restructuring one's self-concept, and altering one's relations with others and with society (de Monteflores & Schultz, 1978). Coming out typically occurs on two levels: to oneself and to others. The process can occur quickly or over an extended time, and it is the beginning of the lifelong process of developing an LGB identity.

Research increasingly has investigated the process of acquiring a positive gay, lesbian, or bisexual identity, and a wide range of models of LGB identity development have been proposed (Brady & Busse, 1994; Cass, 1979; Chapman & Brannock, 1987; Fassinger & Miller, 1996; McCarn & Fassinger, 1996; Troiden, 1979). Brown (1995) identified a variety of lesbian identity models: "biological models, traditional psychodynamic models, feminist psychodynamic models, and cognitively mediated 'stage' models" (p. 10). Although these models are all important and influential in understanding LGB individuals, this chapter primarily focuses on developmental stage models because of their importance in assisting members of the counseling profession in helping LGB clients to understand and accept who they are (McCarn & Fassinger, 1996).

According to Fox (1995),

> the emergence of lesbian and gay identity theory represented an important shift in emphasis in developmental theory, away from the concern of etiology and psychopathology characteristic of the illness model toward articulation of the factors involved in the formation of positive gay and lesbian identities. (p. 53)

Gonsiorek (1995) described LGB models as filling a "theoretical and clinical vacuum" (p. 25) that developed with the movement away from the illness model. These models moved the focus from trying to understand why people are lesbian and gay toward comprehending how one develops a positive LGB identity in a homophobic culture. Although understanding the fluidity of sexual behavior, attraction, and identity is vital to working with all clients, it is also important to explore fully the unique developmental issues of lesbians, gay men, and bisexuals as separate groups.

Understanding the unique issues of these groups is important but challenging at times because previous writings and research have not always been consistent (and language is sometimes unclear) about whether these models address a generic LGB experience or one that is unique to one or more of those groups. Clearly, there are unique issues for each group that warrant separate attention; however, there are also core issues that have to do with adopting and managing an LGB identity in a homophobic and heterosexist culture. Just as there are an increasing number of models that look at identity development commonalities across racial groups or oppressed groups, there is value in developing models that address common concerns of LGB individuals. Many of these issues and questions must be addressed as LGB identity development models are developed and tested.

An example of a model that describes a common LG experience is the identity model developed by Cass (1979). Cass's six-stage model of gay identity formation addressed many of the shortcomings of previous gay identity models by explaining how a person changed from a pregay to a gay identity. Cass's model, which was created to explain a common gay *and* lesbian experience, was derived from clinical and empirical data and theoretically grounded within interpersonal congruency theory. Cass's (1979) model was based on two broad assumptions: "(a) that identity is acquired through a developmental process, and (b) that locus for stability of, and change in, behavior lies in the interaction process that occurs between individuals and their environments" (p. 219). Walters and Simoni (1993) summarized Cass's six-stage model to include the following: (a) identity confusion (Who am I?), (b) identity comparison (I am different), (c) identity tolerance (I am probably gay), (d) identity acceptance (I am gay), (e) identity pride (Gay is good; heterosexuals are bad!), and (f) identity synthesis (My gayness is one part of me). This model proposes a common path of development for both gay men and lesbians; however, there has not been research to test the validity of this theory for both populations.

Lesbian Identity Development

Throughout history and across cultures, romantic and intimate relationships between women have been documented. These relationships were not necessarily sexual, and it is not known how these women perceived themselves or their relationships. According to Brown (1995), the affection and intimacy between women were not seen by society as a whole as a largely sexual relationship. In fact, such relationships were able to exist without a lesbian identity being assumed. Lesbian identity is a relatively new construct that did not come into existence until lesbians were identified and accepted as a unique group, different from gay men. Brown (1995) also emphasized that because sexuality (and gender) is viewed differently across cultures, lesbian identity, as a psychological construct, is culture bound.

Because of the influence of feminism, many of the models described here are focused on the effects of society and oppression on the identity development process for lesbians. Most of these lesbian identity models are based on clinical observations, are theoretical in nature, and have not been empirically tested or validated.

Lesbian identity development models differ in a variety of ways. Many models address both the social and psychological construction of identity. The genesis of these models appears to be either clinical experiences or research. Some models are theoretically based, such as the labeling theory underlying Moses' (1978) or Ponse's (1978) social constructionist theory. Finally, some models focus on identity formation (e.g., Ponse, 1978), whereas others (e.g., Moses, 1978) highlight the importance of identity management.

Whereas some identity development models address the common identity issues for lesbians and gay men (e.g., Cass, 1979), a variety of models focus on the unique identity formation process for lesbians. For example, Ponse (1978) offered one of the first frameworks to increase understanding of how some women come to self-identify as lesbian. Through her research, she identified five elements that may create a lesbian identity: a subjective feeling of being different, an understanding that that feeling may be lesbian, accepting a lesbian identity, developing a lesbian network, and participating in a lesbian relationship. Although these elements seem to build on each other, Ponse did not conceptualize them in a stepwise manner. Ponse highlighted how identity may differ from sexual and affectional activity and described four different behavior patterns (lesbian identity with lesbian activity, lesbian identity with bisexual or heterosexual activity or celibacy, bisexual identity with lesbian activity, and heterosexual identity with lesbian activity). According to Ponse, these distinct behaviors challenge the notion of a stable lesbian identity.

Rather than develop an identity development stage model, Ettore (1980) proposed a classification system to understand differences among lesbians in terms of their self-definition and social and political behavior. Faderman (1984) also incorporated the sociopolitical context in her discussion of lesbian identity. Although not strictly a developmental model, her conceptualization highlighted the process that lesbians experience as they attempt to make sense of their lesbian selves. She incorporated the influence of feminism on how lesbians may view themselves.

Sophie (1985/1986) created one of the first developmental models in her lesbian identity development stage theory, which is based on the commonalities among six LGB theories as well as qualitative data from structured interviews with 14 women. She suggested four core stages: first awareness, testing and exploration, identity acceptance, and identity integration. Sophie found some support for her model of identity development in her interviews as well as some contradictory results. She highlighted the variability of the identity development process (in terms of timing and context) especially during later stages, thus challenging the accuracy and value of linear models.

Chapman and Brannock (1987) also developed a model of lesbian identity but with five stages: same-sex orientation, incongruence, self-questioning/exploration, identification, and choice of lifestyle. Through a quantitative study, these authors examined the process of self-labeling that many lesbians experience. According to Chapman and Brannock, some dissonance, particularly from heterosexual surroundings, may be necessary for women to embrace a lesbian identity. The contrast provided by interaction with a heterosexual environment increases self-awareness in lesbians, which begins the process of self-labeling. In another example of a lesbian-focused identity development model, Kitzinger (1987), using Q-sort methodology, identified five types of lesbians on the basis of their differing views of their lesbianism.

Rust (1992) described the process by which lesbian and bisexual women self-identify. She viewed LGB identity as a process of self-definition that grows out of an individual's social context. Rather than providing a developmental model, Rust's research identified the fluidity of sexual orientation and challenged the assumption of linear development found in many LGB identity models. On the basis of similar concerns about current lesbian identity models, McCarn and Fassinger (1996) proposed an alternative model that incorporated important insights from racial–ethnic and gender identity models. They used notions from the racial identity work of Cross (1987), which highlighted a dual identity process encompassing personal identity and reference group orientation. The existence of these two developmental processes may explain why LGB identity models appear to describe later stages less effectively and reliably. According to McCarn and Fassinger, most lesbian and gay models describe individual identity in the first several stages, followed by attention to group identity in the later, sociopolitical stages. In creating their lesbian identity model, McCarn and Fassinger (1996) challenged the notion that "political activism and universal disclosure become signs of an integrated lesbian/gay identity" (p. 519). Instead, their model proposed a dual process that allows lesbians to incorporate the reality of important factors, such as work environment, geographic location, and racial or ethnic group membership, that affect whether disclosure is a reasonable reality. Rather than stating that a political consciousness is needed to be fully developed as a lesbian, McCarn and Fassinger proposed such consciousness to be only part of the process. Their model proposed separate individual sexual identity and group membership identity processes, with four phases: awareness, exploration, deepening/commitment, and internalization/synthesis. Their model, through its complexity and its ability to embrace multiple realities, offers an important advancement in the understanding of LGB identity. This model has been initially validated, and the results indicate that it may be useful for understanding the experiences of diverse lesbians (McCarn, 1991).

Gay Male Identity Development

Various gay identity theories introduced the notion of a developmental process in coming out and offered important information for counseling gay men. Like many developmental theories, gay identity theories initially focused on men and their development; however they often were used to describe the coming out process for all. When lesbian identity models were created, they focused on the aspects unique to lesbian identity. Unfortunately, few gay identity models speak to issues unique to gay men and how such issues affect their identity formation.

Similar to the findings among women, same-sex sexual behavior and relationships between men have been thoroughly documented throughout history, long before notions of gay identity existed. According to Greenberg (1988), "male homosexuality was not stigmatized or repressed so long as it conformed to norms regarding gender and the relative ages and statuses of the partners" (p. 182). However, despite the acceptance of same-sex sexual behavior among men in various cultures in premodern times, modern Western terms cannot be applied to premodern societies (Gonsiorek & Rudolph, 1991).

A wide range of studies examining gay male development, from both linear and nonlinear perspectives, have been published over the years. McDonald (1982) analyzed retrospective information from 199 self-identified gay men and determined that the coming out process occurs in an orderly sequence as described in the stage models of gay identity development. Troiden (1989), however, elaborated on these findings by suggesting that even though a stage-sequential linear progression was assumed in gay male identity development, the data indicate the process to be a repeating spiral pattern. Similarly, Finnegan and McNally (1987) have stated the following:

> Although the models contain stages, they are not distinct entities. Individuals may move back and forth between stages or may, while in one stage, have an experience that ordinarily occurs in a different stage. However, for the sake of clarity, models are presented in a linear and ordered fashion. (p. 78)

Recently, one new model of development has emerged that provides some conceptual clarity to the gay identity construct by separating the identity development process into two parallel, mutually catalytic branches of development: (a) an internal individual sexual identity development process and (b) a contextual group-membership identity development process (Fassinger & Miller, 1996). These authors' inclusive model of homosexual identity formation (HIF), which is an extension of the previously cited work of McCarn and Fassinger (1996), includes the effects of societal homophobia and heterosexism on the development of an individual gay male identity. The model also addresses the many forms of difference and diversity that exist within the gay male community that influence the identity development process (e.g., race, class, age, geographic location, occupation, and community support). Previous models of gay male identity development emphasized public disclosure as an indication of identity progression or achievement. However, as noted by Fassinger and Miller (1996),

> disclosure is so profoundly influenced by environment and external oppression that to use it as an index of identity development . . . ignores the harsh realities that race, religion, socioeconomic status, geographic location, and other sources of demographic diversity often impose on the identity development process. (p. 6)

In addition to disclosure, it is important to address issues such as how gay men deal with same-sex attraction and how their mode of coping relates to their relationship patterns, as well as how gender socialization affects the identity development process. Troiden (1993) has stated, "In keeping with their gender-role training, males are much more likely to gain sexual experiences with a variety of partners before focusing their attentions on one special person" (p. 209). Researchers have found that gay males become sexually active at an earlier age than heterosexual males; however, after an awareness of being gay has developed, disclosure to others may be delayed for more than 4 years (Friedman & Downey, 1994). Lessening the social isolation that may accompany coming out to oneself and others may be an important step in the achievement of a positive identity by gay men.

Identification with the gay community has been found to promote understanding of, coping with, and ultimately accepting of a gay identity and behavior (Martin, 1993; Martin, Dean, Garcia, & Hall, 1989). Conversely, a lack of connection and identification with the larger gay community, which is dependent, in part, on a self-concept as gay, may prevent the individual from internalizing the community expectation for safer sex behavior or using community-based sources of support:

> Gay men look to the gay community for support in the broadest sense: to provide an alternative, non-stigmatizing definition of their status, and to provide role models and a "career path," as well as a range of social and sexual opportunities. (Berger and Mallon, 1993, p. 156)

Berger and Mallon further emphasized that community plays a vital role in the social creation and maintenance of gay identity and behavior.

Bisexual Identity Development

Historically, human sexual activity has included much diversity, yet most individuals have found the notion of a fluid sexual nature hard to accept. Even though research has documented the existence of bisexuality and bisexuals (Klein, 1993), American society continues strenuously to promote heterosexuality as the norm, and individuals who participate in same-sex sexual activities continue to be stigmatized. Although there was a bisexual social movement in the mid-1970s, bisexual individuals did not become nationally organized or create a community until the early 1990s (Udis-Kessler, 1995). The bisexual movement continues to grow, and its members have attempted to gain access to academic circles by the creation of bisexual studies courses and the inclusion of studies of bisexuality in predominantly lesbian and gay conferences and publications (Udis-Kessler, 1995).

Whereas a substantial proportion of women and men have reported participation in some sort of same-sex sexual activity during their lives, only some self-identify as bisexual (Klein, 1993). In other words, same-sex sexual behavior does not always lead to self-labeling as gay, lesbian, or bisexual.

Although much theory has been developed to explain the process through which gay men and lesbians develop a positive gay identity, limited scholarly activity has been dedicated to bisexual identity development (Zinik, 1985). This oversight is surprising when one considers the fact that the Kinsey, Wardell, Martin, and Gebhard (1948) study provided empirical support for the existence of lesbians, gays, and bisexuals. In fact, Kinsey et al. suggested that bisexuality may be more prevalent than homosexuality. Although Kinsey et al. encouraged researchers to think of sexuality in terms of a continuum rather than as a rigid set of dichotomous categories, most research continues to view human sexuality as a dichotomous variable (Blumstein & Schwartz, 1993). Kinsey et al. used a case-study approach to determine, through interviews with 5,300 white males and 5,940 white females, the ways in which sexuality influences how individuals think, feel, and behave. Study findings revealed that more participants identified themselves as bisexual than as exclusively gay. Limited follow-up studies that investigated the same-sex sexual behavior of heterosexually identified men and women (Blumstein & Schwartz, 1993; Humphrey, 1970) provided further evidence of the fluidity of sexual behavior. These investigators discovered that many of the men and women in their studies were heterosexually married and did not consider themselves to be gay, lesbian, or bisexual despite participation in same-sex sexual behavior. Findings such as these led Bell and Weinberg (1978) to state,

> It should be clear by now that we do not do justice to people's sexual orientation when we refer to it by a singular noun. There are homosexualities and there are heterosexualities, each involving a variety of different interrelated dimensions. (p. 329)

Subsequent research on sexual orientation has indicated that the use of a continuum is a valid way to describe the fluid nature of sexual orientation (Klein, Sepekoff, & Wolf, 1985). In Blumstein and Schwartz's (1993) study of sexuality, the findings suggested that sex-object choice and sexual identification could change in many ways and many times over the life cycle.

A major scholarly advance was provided by Klein et al. (1985), who investigated sexual orientation as a multivariable concept that included variables related to the sexual self (attraction, fantasy, and behavior), to the composition of sexual orientation (emotional preference, social preference, and heterosexual or gay lifestyle), and to self-identification. Klein (1993) stated, "The total range of bisexual preference is extremely broad, from almost complete preference for one sex, to enjoying sex with either gender, to almost complete preference for the other sex" (p. 21).

The distinction among the concepts of sexuality, sexual orientation, sexual behavior, and sexual identity may help to explain why same-sex sexual activity does not always lead to a self-definition as gay or bisexual. Sexuality relates to affection, affiliation, and genital behavior. As such, participation in same-sex sexual activity does not always lead to self-labeling. De Cecco and Shively (1984) reported that same-sex sexual behavior was not limited to a small proportion of individuals but seemed to be an integral aspect of human sexuality. Sexual orientation was defined by Bell and Weinberg (1978) as the direction of an individual's sexual preference toward male or female partners. Sexual identity, however, represents a consistent, enduring self-recognition of the meanings that sexual orientation and sexual behavior have had for an individual (Savin-Williams, 1990).

Despite this view of sexual identity and orientation, bisexuality is generally regarded as a behavior without an identity to back it up (du Plessis, 1996). Zinik (1985) defined bisexuality as sexual behavior with both female and male partners, which may be simultaneous, concurrent, or serial behavior. Hansen and Evans (1985) offered three explanations for the lack of a defined bisexual orientation: (a) the belief that bisexuals are promiscuous and nonmonogamous, (b) the idea that individuals cannot simultaneously eroticize men and women, and (c) the fact that LGB definitions are often based on the heterosexual norm. Both Paul (1984) and Cox and Gallois (1996) proposed that the lack of a social identity for bisexuals (until recently) was the reason many bisexuals defined their sexuality by their current partner rather than by their true orientation.

Multiple barriers to the development of a healthy bisexual identity exist that need to be addressed within the bisexual identity development literature. Like lesbians and gay men, bisexual individuals face homophobia and heterosexism when they participate in same-sex behavior or relationships. However, unlike lesbians and gay men, until recently bisexual people did not have an active and visible community where they could feel fully accepted and understood. The heterosexual community viewed them as lesbian and gay, and the lesbian and gay community often perceived them as hiding behind heterosexual privilege and not willing to face their lesbian and gay selves. Some authors described these realities as based in biphobia, or the discomfort and distrust of bisexual attractions, behaviors, and identity (Pope & Reynolds, 1991). This bias and, sometimes, discrimination has been visible not only in the lesbian and gay communities but in the psychology profession in its practice and research.

A content analysis of 144 LGB studies published from 1974 to 1993 revealed that women and bisexuals were underrepresented and that the sexual orientation of participants was often assumed rather than assessed (Chung & Katayama, 1996). Although progress has been made in the assessment of sexual orientation in LGB research studies, and distinct bisexual identity development processes have begun to emerge, much work remains to be done. Fox (1995) highlighted the uniqueness of the bisexual identity formation models that have been developed. Unlike lesbian and gay identity models, the process in bisexual models is not usually viewed as linear with specified outcomes. Instead, the formation of a bisexual identity is seen as more open-ended and complex because of the incorporation of lesbian, gay, and heterosexual attractions, behaviors, and relationships (Fox, 1995). Some authors have researched and identified the process of bisexual identity development and sometimes even proposed stage models (e.g., Fox, 1993; Rust, 1992; Twining, 1983; Weinberg, Williams, & Pryor, 1994). For example, Weinberg et al. (1994) developed a four-stage model on the basis of fieldwork and interviews (initial confusion, finding a label, settling into the identity and self-acceptance, and continued uncertainty).

The development of a bisexual identity is an understudied and misunderstood construct that needs more exploration. The study of bisexuality is way behind the research that examines lesbian and gay identity formation. Unlike lesbian and gay identity models, the development of bisexuality often presumes an absence of closure, partially owing to the fluidity of sexuality (Weinberg et al., 1994). Although the various bisexuality identity models have proposed diverse approaches to the coming out process, all have described the formation process as complex and multifaceted, complicated by a lack of social validation and support from lesbians, gay men, and heterosexuals (Fox, 1995).

CRITICISMS OF LGB IDENTITY MODELS

Although significant criticisms have been directed at the various LGB identity development models, the models continue to influence psychological theory and practice. Stage models of identity development have been especially criticized for their reductionistic and simplistic view of the developmental process and their emphasis on linear growth (Broido, chapter 1, this volume; Eliason, 1996). Increasingly, researchers examining lesbian, gay, and bisexual development have highlighted the fluidity of sexual orientation and the importance of envisioning such growth in nonlinear ways. One of the most consistent criticisms of lesbian and gay models is that they usually do not acknowledge the existence of bisexuality (except as a passing phase) or a bisexual identity (Rust, 1992). Similarly, these traditional models have rarely incorporated the reality of race and culture, thus making their use with LGB people of color questionable if not inappropriate (Brown, 1995; Chan, 1987; McCarn & Fassinger, 1996).

Brown (1995), because of her belief in the centrality of gender, was highly critical of efforts to develop LGB identity models that describe the experiences of both lesbians and gay men. Similarly, Gonsiorek (1995) postulated the importance of considering gender when conceptualizing sexual orientation:

> Lesbians appear to perceive affectional orientation and political perspectives as central to self-definition, while gay men appear to view sexual behavior and sexual fantasy as central. It may even be that the nature of sexual orientation is different for men and women. (p. 26)

Many scholars, including de Monteflores and Schultz (1978), Brown (1995), and Gonsiorek (1995), have emphasized the importance of studying and understanding gender differences in the coming out process as well as the lifelong process of LGB identity development. These gender differences challenge the assumption that there is uniform LGB identity development.

In addition to gender differences within the identity development process, until recently there was little written on the developmental process of coming out and managing an LGB identity for LGB people of color. According to Smith (1997),

> many assumptions about coming out have been developed through research involving predominantly White or White-identified lesbians, gay men, and bisexuals, for whom individualism, independent identity, and separation from family of origin are important parts of growing up. There has been little discussion of cultural differences in the meaning, process, or role of coming out, particularly but not exclusively for people who are not White and middle class. (p. 281)

This inattention to the issues, developmental concerns, and interpersonal and social realities of LGB people of color makes it difficult to apply their experiences to current models. In the past 10 years, however, there has been increased attention to these issues and concerns (cf. Chan, 1987; Greene, 1994, 1997). Smith highlighted the importance of addressing cultural factors in the therapy process, especially when discussing coming out issues. Attention to the complexity and multidimensionality of the identity development process for all LGB individuals is necessary to develop and deliver effective and ethical clinical services (Reynolds & Pope, 1991; Smith, 1997).

Eliason (1996) highlighted some additional challenges created for LGB identity models because of poststructuralism and its emphasis on deconstruction and difference. See Broido (chapter 1, this volume) for further exploration of the constructive aspects of identity development. The theory of social constructionism challenges traditional notions of LGB identity as essential or natural and instead describes it as socially constructed. Kitzinger (1987) highlighted this perspective by stating, "In sum, the assumption that humans have no basic, fundamental sexual nature that is transhistorical and transcultural, and to which labels such as 'heterosexual,' 'homosexual,' and 'bisexual' can unproblematically be applied, is a key feature of social constructionist theory" (p. 141).

A newer criticism of LGB identity models has been postulated by Fassinger and Miller (1996) and by McCarn and Fassinger (1996). Their view is that the personal sexual identity process is inappropriately commingled with the group identification process in most LGB identity models. They emphasize the importance of separating the individual process that focuses on sexual awareness from the group process that focuses on group membership and affiliation. The implication of the mixture of these two models is that individuals cannot be fully integrated in their LGB identity unless they are completely open about their sexual orientation and same-sex relationships. According to McCarn and Fassinger (1996), "models of racial/ethnic minority identity development do not place the burden of political awakening on the individual and imply negative judgement of members who have not reached advanced stages in quite the same way that the lesbian/gay models do" (p. 520). In fact, the reality of lesbians and gays as members of an invisible minority group emphasizes the importance of redefining their view of lesbians and gays as a group. Such self-awareness and self-acceptance must be incorporated into LGB models.

A final critique of the LGB identity development literature has focused on the limited research on the proposed models (McCarn & Fassinger, 1996). Over the past 20 years, many models have been proposed, but few have been researched (e.g., Ettore, 1980; Rust, 1992; Troiden, 1993). Until data are collected that examine the validity of these models, it is difficult to determine their accuracy and therapeutic value.

AREAS FOR FUTURE RESEARCH AND THEORY DEVELOPMENT

Major conceptual and theoretical advances have been made in the understanding of LGB identity development since the publication of Hooker's (1957) pioneering research and the declassification of homosexuality as a psychiatric disorder. Extant models of LGB identity development suggest that individuals may progress through a linear or cyclical developmental process beginning with a period of self-awareness of same-sex attraction or "differentness." This development then involves a period of intrapsychic and interpersonal experimentation and adaptation (e.g., self-labeling and resolving of internalized homophobia) and may terminate with public self-disclosure (global or situational), integration of sexual orientation into an overall self-concept, and some degree of identification with the larger LGB community. Although they are useful for understanding the developmental process of identity development in some LGB individuals, current models do not reflect the diverse multiracial, multiethnic, and transgendered individuals who identify as, or who are labeled, lesbian, gay, or bisexual.

With few exceptions, most research on LGB identity development has been conducted with samples of White middle-class, middle-aged gay men (and sometimes lesbians; Kitzinger, 1987; McDonald, 1982; Sophie, 1985/1986; Troiden, 1993). As such, problems with generalizability have become a focus of concern, and several avenues of future research have been noted. First, questions remain as to how to define and measure the construct of sexual orientation. It has been pointed out that prior research has failed to distinguish between same-sex sexual behavior among gays, lesbians, heterosexuals, and bisexuals and the concepts of gender identity, sexual orientation, sex role orientation, and sexual behavior (Iasenza, 1989). Second, the effects of different individual and cultural worldviews on the meaning and definition of same-sex sexual behavior have yet to be articulated. Chan (1989) suggested that cultural values may affect the "meaning" provided to same-sex sexual behavior and desire. Third, Loiacano (1989) highlighted the importance of investigating how racism, dual identities, and reference group salience affect LGB identity development among people of color. Fourth, the effects of other variables, such as ethnicity, ability or disability, religion, internalized homophobia, social background, socioeconomic status, social isolation, support networks, self-labeling, age of coming out, transgender issues, drug and alcohol use or abuse, and AIDS, on the identity development process have yet to be explored. Last, bisexual identity has received relatively little empirical attention to date (Fox, 1995; Klein, 1993). Although the current theories of LGB identity development provide insight into the developmental process of some LGB individuals, much work remains to be done before a clear understanding of identity development among such a diverse community can be achieved. The work of Klein (1993) and others on the multivariable nature of sexuality and identity development offers insight into the complex nature of sexuality and sexual orientation. Exploration and understanding of this complexity are necessary to develop models that address the needs, experiences, emotions, and realities of lesbians, gays, and bisexuals.

Buhrke et al. (1992) made two additional recommendations that are vital to the future of LGB research in the counseling profession. First, they stated that more research is needed to further the understanding of LGB people and issues. Second, they pointed out that historically a heterosexual paradigm has been used to conceptualize LGB issues and research. Heterosexism in the counseling literature must be addressed, specifically the overall paradigm used to conceptualize and implement the research, which has led to such practices as comparing lesbian and gay relationships to heterosexual relationships. Brown (1989) encouraged the psychology profession to create a lesbian–gay paradigm in which lesbians and gay men and their experiences can serve as models to allow better understanding of identity development, relationships, and other important psychological variables.

IMPLICATIONS FOR COUNSELING AND PSYCHOTHERAPY

Research has documented that lesbians and gay men are involved in therapy in greater numbers than heterosexuals (Bell & Weinberg, 1978); therefore, it is especially important that therapy be delivered in LGB-affirmative ways. Garnets and Kimmel (1993) stressed that despite gains in the acceptance of LGB people by the psychological community, bias, discrimination, and inappropriate or inadequate therapy with LGB clients still exist. One of the areas of concern highlighted by Garnets and Kimmel was identity. Having an adequate appreciation and knowledge of coming out issues and life span identity development issues for LGB clients is central to providing appropriate and affirmative psychotherapy.

Because much has been written about therapy issues for LGB individuals elsewhere, in this section we focus on LGB identity-related concerns. Four significant themes to consider when addressing these issues in a therapeutic context are (a) coming out and early awareness of LGB feelings and identity, (b) identity management, (c) internalized homophobia and its effect on the identity formation process, and (d) societal homophobia and heterosexism.

To handle these issues, self-assessment and self-awareness on the part of the therapist are vital. Without an understanding of one's biases and internal barriers, it may be difficult to serve this group effectively. Without knowledge of the unique issues, concerns, and cultural dynamics of LGB communities and individuals, therapists will most likely be unable to meet their clients' needs. Without requisite skills, therapists may have difficulty reaching out to their LGB clients.

First, in terms of assisting clients in the coming out process, therapists need to understand developmental models. The most challenging aspect of working with LGB clients is their invisibility. Many individuals are so uncomfortable, even with their therapist, that they hesitate to share their same-sex attractions and issues. Unless a therapist can be truly LGB-affirmative and antiheterosexist (e.g., not use other-gender pronouns when discussing relationships), hesitant clients may never disclose what they are questioning. Therapists also need to serve a source of support, because clients often do not come out to others in their support system. Therapists often act as a bridge between their clients and the services that allow LGB clients to find a community in which they can immerse and normalize their feelings and desires. Because other sources of support often are unavailable, it is crucial that therapists be sensitive to the vulnerability of their LGB clients (Rust, 1992). In general, therapists need to apply LGB developmental theories with caution. On the basis of the criticisms described earlier, therapists need to evaluate whether a given theory fits the client rather than try to make the client fit the model.

Second, therapists must assist clients in the process of identity management. Therapists must help clients examine how their LGB identity intersects with and affects other aspects of their life such as career, relationship with family of origin, religion or faith, and coming out to others. Identity management requires that LGB individuals redefine what it means to be LGB. According to Browning, Reynolds, and Dworkin (1991), increased contact with the LGB community is one way for LGB individuals to redefine their identity in a positive direction. Identity management issues and concerns are lifelong and multidirectional. For example, coming out to others affects how LGB individuals perceive themselves, and one's self-perception affects how and whether one comes out to others. Therapists must be aware of these lifelong issues and be comfortable with the dynamic, ever-changing process of identity development and management.

A third important area for therapists to address in therapy is internalized homophobia and its impact on the identity development process. All individuals regardless of their sexual orientation learn the same anti-LGB messages and heterosexist assumptions. Therapists need to understand what internalized homophobia is, how it operates, and how it affects other aspects of identity, self-esteem, and relationships. In addition, therapists need to develop strategies for helping clients counteract these negative assumptions and messages. Because of the strength and tenacity of homophobia, therapists need to go beyond creating a "null environment" (Freeman, 1979) in which LGB behavior and relationships are seen as a neutral, albeit appropriate, option. Instead, to challenge the strength of homophobic beliefs, therapists must feel comfortable to go beyond by providing affirmative therapy in which they encourage clients to explore and embrace LGB feelings within themselves.

Finally, another vital issue for therapists to consider in their work with LGB clients is the powerful effect of societal homophobia and heterosexism on their clients' behavior and identity. When clients experience bias and discrimination, therapists must be willing to act as their advocate to ensure it does not happen again. This may require that therapists be willing to leave the comfort of their office to engage with the surrounding community and, when necessary, take on a more activist role in an effort to create societal change. For many therapists, this role is unfamiliar, and there are few role models and not much literature to teach professionals how to act in this manner. Ongoing supervision and consultation with appropriate community members may be necessary for therapists to feel strong enough to take such risks.

CONCLUSION

Working with LGB clients is an effective and ethical means of challenging the status quo of psychology. No longer is it possible to do business as usual now that it has become clear that the core assumptions of psychology and its theories are laden with heterosexism and homophobia. Therapists must address bias, discrimination, and invisibility on multiple fronts such as education and training and institutional change. LGB advocates within psychology might benefit from exploring the efforts of multicultural psychologists who have made some inroads during the past 10 years infusing multiculturalism into the theory and curriculum of psychology. New and more effective strategies should be developed for creating individual change through education and creating institutional change through organizational work. As Brown (1997) stated,

> preventing heterosexist and antisexual minority bias in psychotherapy should be a simple matter of ethical, effective practice. This goal will be accomplished when the equation of the two is taken for granted by all mental health professionals and by those who educate and train them (p. 57)

REFERENCES

Bell, A. P., & Weinberg, M. S. (1978). Homosexualities: A study of diversity among men and women. New York: Simon & Schuster.

Berger, M. B., & Mallon, D. (1993). Social support networks of gay men. Journal of Sociology and Social Welfare, 20, 155–174.

Blumstein, P. W., & Schwartz, P. (1993). Bisexuality: Some social psychological issues. In L. D. Garnets & D. C. Kimmel (Eds.), Psychological perspectives on lesbian and gay male experiences (pp. 168–184). New York: Columbia University Press.

Brady, S., & Busse, W. J. (1994). The gay identity questionnaire: A brief measure of homosexual identity formation. Journal of Homosexuality, 26(4), 1–22.

Brown, L. S. (1989). New voices, new visions: Toward a lesbian/gay paradigm for psychology. *Psychology of Women Quarterly, 13,* 445–458.

Brown, L. S. (1995). Lesbian identities: Concepts and issues. In A. R. D'Augelli & C. J. Patterson (Eds.), *Lesbian, gay, and bisexual identities over the lifespan: Psychological perspectives* (pp. 3–23). New York: Oxford University Press.

Brown, L. S. (1997). Preventing heterosexism and bias in psychotherapy and counseling. In E. R. Rothblum & L. A. Bond (Eds.), *Preventing heterosexism and homophobia* (pp. 36–58). Thousand Oaks, CA: Sage.

Browning, C., Reynolds, A. L., & Dworkin, S. H. (1991). Affirmative psychotherapy for lesbian women. *The Counseling Psychologist, 19,* 177–196.

Buhrke, R. A., Ben-Ezra, L. A., Hurley, M. E., & Ruprecht, L. J. (1992). Content analysis and methodological critique of articles concerning lesbian and gay male issues in counseling journals. *Journal of Counseling Psychology, 39,* 91–99.

Cass, V. C. (1979). Homosexual identity formation: A theoretical model. *Journal of Homosexuality, 4*(3), 219–235.

Chan, C. (1987). Asian lesbians: Psychological issues in the coming out process. *Asian American Psychological Journal, 12,* 16–18.

Chan, C. S. (1989). Issues of identity development among Asian-American lesbians and gay men. *Journal of Counseling and Development, 68,* 16–20.

Chapman, B. E., & Brannock, J. C. (1987). A proposed model of lesbian identity development: An empirical investigation. *Journal of Homosexuality, 14*(3/4), 69–80.

Chung, Y. B., & Katayama, M. (1996). Assessment of sexual orientation in lesbian/gay/bisexual studies. *Journal of Homosexuality, 30*(4), 49–62.

Coleman, E. (1987). Assessment of sexual orientation. *Journal of Homosexuality, 14*(1/2), 9–24.

Cox, S., & Gallois, C. (1996). Gay and lesbian identity development: A social identity perspective. *Journal of Homosexuality, 30*(4), 1–30.

Cross, W. E. (1987). A two-factor theory of Black identity: Implications for the study of racial identity development in minority children. In J. S. Phinney & M. J. Rotheram (Eds.), *Children's ethnic socialization* (pp. 117–133). Beverly Hills, CA: Sage.

Dank, B. M. (1971). Coming out in the gay world. *Psychiatry, 34,* 180–197.

De Cecco, J. P. (1981). Definition and meaning of sexual orientation. *Journal of Homosexuality, 6*(4), 51–67.

De Cecco, J. P., & Shively, M. G. (1984). From sexual identity to sexual relationships: A contextual shift. *Journal of Homosexuality, 9*(2/3), 1–26.

de Monteflores, C., & Schultz, S. J. (1978). Coming out: Similarities and differences for lesbians and gay men. *Journal of Social Issues, 34*(3), 59–71.

du Plessis, M. (1996). Blatantly bisexual; or unthinking queer theory. In D. E. Hall & M. Pramaggiore (Eds.), *Representing bisexualities: Subjects and cultures of fluid desire* (pp. 19–54). New York: New York University Press.

Eliason, M. J. (1996). Identity formation for lesbian, bisexual and gay persons: Beyond a minoritizing view. *Journal of Homosexuality, 30,* 31–58.

Erikson, E. (1963). *Childhood and society.* New York: Norton.

Ettore, E.M. (1980). *Lesbians, women, and society.* London: Routledge & Kegan Paul.

Faderman, L. (1984). The "new gay" lesbians. *Journal of Homosexuality, 10*(3/4), 85–95.

Fassinger, R. E., & Miller, B. A. (1996). Validation of an inclusive model of homosexual identity formation on a sample of gay men. *Journal of Homosexuality, 32*(2), 53–78.

Fassinger, R. E., & Richie, B. S. (1997). Sex matters: Gender and sexual orientation in training for multicultural counseling competency. In D. B. Pope-Davis & H. L. K. Coleman (Eds.), *Multicultural counseling competencies: Assessment, education, training, and supervision* (pp. 83–110). Thousand Oaks, CA: Sage.

Finnegan, D. J., & McNally, E. B. (1987). *Dual identities: Counseling chemically dependent gay men and lesbians.* Center City, MN: Hazelden.

Fox, R. C. (1993). *Coming out bisexual: Identity, behavior, and sexual orientation self-disclosure.* Unpublished doctoral dissertation, California Institute of Integral Studies, San Francisco.

Fox, R. C. (1995). Bisexual identities. In A. R. D'Augelli & C. J. Patterson (Eds.), *Lesbian, gay, and bisexual identities over the lifespan: Psychological perspectives* (pp. 48–86). New York: Oxford University Press.

Freeman, J. (1979). How to discriminate against women without really trying. In J. Freeman (Ed.), *Women: A feminist perspective* (2nd ed., pp. 194–208). Palo Alto, CA: Mayfield.

Friedman, R. C., & Downey, J. I. (1994). Homosexuality. *New England Journal of Medicine, 331,* 923–930.

Garnets, L. D., & Kimmel, D. C. (1993). Introduction: Lesbian and gay male dimensions in the psychological study of human diversity. In L. D. Garnets & D. C. Kimmel (Eds.), *Psychological perspectives on lesbian and gay male experiences* (pp. 1–51). New York: Columbia University Press.

Gonsiorek, J. C. (1995). Gay male identities: Concepts and issues. In A. R. D'Augelli & C. J. Patterson (Eds.), *Lesbian, gay, and bisexual identities over the lifespan: Psychological perspectives* (pp. 24–47). New York: Oxford University Press.

Gonsiorek, J. C., & Rudolph, J. R. (1991). Homosexual identity: Coming out and other developmental events. In J. C. Gonsiorek & J. D. Weinrich (Eds.), *Homosexuality: Research implications for public policy* (pp. 161–175). Newbury Park, CA: Sage.

Greenberg, D. E. (1988). *The construction of homosexuality.* Chicago: University of Chicago Press.

Greene, B. (1994). Mental health concerns of lesbians of color. In L. Comas-Diaz

& B. Greene (Eds.), *Women of color and mental health* (pp. 389–427). New York: Guilford Press.

Greene, B. (1997). (Ed.). *Ethnic and cultural diversity among lesbians and gay men.* Newbury Park, CA: Sage.

Hansen, C. E., & Evans, A. (1985). Bisexuality reconsidered: An idea in pursuit of a definition. *Journal of Homosexuality, 11*(1/2), 1–6.

Hooker, E. (1957). The adjustment of the male homosexual. *Journal of Projective Techniques, 21,* 18–31.

Humphrey, L. (1970). *Tearoom trade: Impersonal sex in public places.* New York: Aldine.

Iasenza, S. (1989). Some challenges of integrating sexual orientations into counselor training and research. *Journal of Counseling and Development, 68,* 73–76.

Kinsey, A. C., Wardell, B. P., Martin, C. E., & Gebhard, P. H. (1948). *Sexual behavior in the human male.* Philadelphia: W. B. Saunders.

Kitzinger, C. (1987). *The social construction of lesbianism.* London: Sage.

Klein, F. (1993). *The bisexual option* (2nd ed.). New York: Harrington Park Press.

Klein, F., Sepekoff, B., & Wolf, T. J. (1985). Sexual orientation: A multi-variable dynamic process. *Journal of Homosexuality, 11*(1/2), 35–49.

Loiacano, D. K. (1989). Gay identity issues among Black Americans: Racism, homophobia, and the need for validation. *Journal of Counseling and Development, 68,* 21–25.

Martin, D. J. (1993). Coping with AIDS and AIDS risk reduction efforts among gay men. *AIDS Education and Prevention, 5,* 104–120.

Martin, J. L., Dean, L., Garcia, M., & Hall, W. (1989). The impact of AIDS on a gay community: Changes in sexual behavior, substance use, and mental health. *American Journal of Community Psychology, 17,* 269–273.

McCarn, S. R. (1991). *Validation of a model of sexual minority (lesbian) identity development.* Unpublished master's thesis, University of Maryland at College Park.

McCarn, S. R., & Fassinger, R. E. (1996). Revisioning sexual minority identity formation: A new model of lesbian identity and its implications for counseling and research. *The Counseling Psychologist, 24,* 508–534.

McDonald, G. J. (1982). Individual differences in the coming out process for gay men: Implications for theoretical models. *Journal of Homosexuality, 8*(1), 47–60.

Morin, S. F. (1977). Heterosexual bias in psychological research on lesbianism and male homosexuality. *American Psychologist, 32,* 629–637.

Moses, A. E. (1978). *Identities management in lesbian women.* New York: Praeger.

Myers, L. J. (1988). *Understanding an Afrocentric worldview: Introduction to an optional psychology.* Dubuque, IA: Kendall/Hunt.

Paul, J. P. (1984). The bisexual identity: An idea without social recognition. *Journal of Homosexuality, 9*(2/3), 45–63.

Ponse, B. (1978). *Identities in the lesbian world: Social constructions of the self.* Westport, CT: Greenwood Press.

Pope, R. L., & Reynolds, A. L. (1991). Including bisexuality: It's more than just a label. In N. J. Evans & V. A. Wall (Eds.), *Beyond tolerance: Gays, lesbians, and bisexuals on campus* (pp. 205–212). Alexandria, VA: American College Personnel Association.

Reynolds, A. L., & Pope, R. L. (1991). The complexities of diversity: Exploring multiple oppressions. *Journal of Counseling and Development, 70,* 174–180.

Rust, P. C. (1992). The politics of sexual identity: Sexual attraction and behavior among lesbian and bisexual women. *Social problems, 39,* 366–386.

Savin-Williams, R. C. (1990). *Gay and lesbian youth: Expressions of identity.* New York: Hemisphere.

Smith, A. (1997). Cultural diversity and the coming-out process: Implications for clinical practice. In B. Greene (Ed.), *Ethnic and cultural diversity among lesbians and gay men* (pp. 279–300). Thousand Oaks, CA: Sage.

Sophie, J. (1985/1986). A critical examination of stage theories of lesbian identity development. *Journal of Homosexuality, 12*(2), 39–51.

Tafoya, T. (1997). Native gay and lesbian issues: The two-spirited. In B. Greene (Ed.), *Ethnic and cultural diversity among lesbians and gay men* (pp. 1–10). Newbury Park, CA: Sage.

Troiden, R. R. (1979). Becoming homosexual: A model of gay identity acquisition. *Psychiatry, 42,* 362–373.

Troiden, R. R. (1989). The formation of homosexual identities. *Journal of Homosexuality, 17*(1/2), 43–73.

Troiden, R. R. (1993). The formation of homosexual identities. In L. D. Garnets & D. C. Kimmel (Eds.), *Psychological perspectives on lesbian and gay male experiences* (pp. 191–217). New York: Columbia University Press.

Troiden, R. R., & Goode, E. (1980). Variables related to the acquisition of a gay identity. *Journal of Homosexuality, 5,* 383–393.

Twining, A. (1983). Bisexual women: Identity in adult development (Doctoral dissertation, Boston University School of Education, 1983). *Dissertation Abstracts International, 44,* 1340A.

Udis-Kessler, A. (1995). Identity/politics: A history of the bisexual movement. In N. Tucker, L. Highleyman, & R. Kaplan (Eds.), *Bisexual politics: Theories, queries, and visions* (pp. 17–30). New York: Harrington Park Press.

Walters, K. L., & Simoni, J. M. (1993). Lesbian and gay male group identity attitudes and self-esteem: Implications for counseling. *Journal of Counseling Psychology, 40,* 94–99.

Weinberg, T. S., Williams, C. J., & Pryor, D. W. (1994). *Dual attraction: Understanding bisexuality.* New York: Oxford University Press.

Zinik, G. (1985). Identity conflict or adaptive flexibility? Bisexuality reconsidered. *Journal of Homosexuality, 11*(1/2), 7–20.

3

"SOMEWHERE IN DES MOINES OR SAN ANTONIO": HISTORICAL PERSPECTIVES ON LESBIAN, GAY, AND BISEXUAL MENTAL HEALTH

ESTHER D. ROTHBLUM

What is gay history? Is it just when we discover that someone from the past had a long-term intimate relationship with someone of the same sex? Or is gay history simply the history of self-identified homosexuals? What do we make of Native American cultures that did not have concepts of homosexuality vs. heterosexuality? ... Unlike other minorities, for whom finding oneself in history is simply a matter of finding out a person's race or religion, gay people have to put together the pieces of a complex puzzle, often using suspicion and loose associations to discover the hidden lineage that is part of our history. (Witt, Thomas, & Marcus, 1995, p. 161)

So many events have influenced the current status of lesbian, gay, and bisexual (LGB) mental health that a whole book could be devoted to this topic alone. In fact, it could be argued that any past legal, political, social, religious, or educational issue related to lesbians, bisexual women, gay men, or bisexual men has affected the status and knowledge of LGB mental health. After describing the history of the language of sexual orientation, this chapter focuses on three historical phenomena that have been important for the current understanding of LGB mental health. The first factor consists of changing social roles—specifically concerning the economy, education, and the military—that allowed some women and men to discover LGB identities in the United States. Second, I briefly review the Harlem Renaissance, Greenwich Village, and the Stonewall uprisings—three phenomena in New York City that profoundly influenced

Adapted from *American Psychologist, 46,* 947–949. Copyright 1991 by the American Psychological Association. Adapted with permission of the author and publisher.

modern-day LGB communities. Third, I review LGB newsletters and organizations that created a national awareness of LGB issues.

The chapter also reviews events and issues specific to LGB mental health and counseling today. These are (a) psychoanalysis and "reorientation" therapy, (b) the sex surveys such as Kinsey's, (c) psychological research concerning LGB issues, and (d) the changing versions of the *Diagnostic and Statistical Manual of Mental Disorders* (DSM) of the American Psychiatric Association.

The purpose of the chapter is to present highlights in LGB history that have influenced LGB-affirmative psychology as it is practiced today. LGB terminology and communities were necessary to the development and practice of a lesbian, gay, and bisexual psychology. In the mental health field itself, research and clinical practice have often had a conflicting past, with research indicating that LGB individuals were similar to heterosexuals in adjustment and mental health while psychotherapists continued to try to "reorient" their LGB clients to become heterosexual. The removal of the diagnosis of "homosexuality" from the DSM and the affirmative stance of the U.S. mental health professions toward LGB issues today are the end result of social and economic changes.

THE HISTORY OF LANGUAGE AND TERMINOLOGY

The Language of Sexual Orientation

What language is used to describe women who had sex with women or men who loved men in earlier centuries and across geographical regions? How is sexual orientation understood when gender itself has had different meanings across time and culture? There have been many books, articles, and posters featuring women and men from the past who were lesbian, gay, or bisexual (or are now believed to have been). How did these people view their own sexuality before the advent of present-day LGB communities? This chapter begins with a historical review of the language that refers to sexual orientation and gender.

Historians generally agree that some form of specialized language is necessary for the development of a group identity. LGB individuals had to view themselves—and be viewed as—different from heterosexuals.

According to Neil Miller (1995), the word *homosexuality* first appeared in print in 1869 in Germany in an anonymous pamphlet urging an end to that country's sodomy law. Regarding early use of the word *gay*, Miller cited Donald Webster Cory's (1960) book *The Homosexual in America*:

> How, when, and where this word originated, I am unable to say. I have
> been told by experts that it came from the French, and that in France

as early as the sixteenth century the homosexual was called gaie; significantly enough, the feminine form was used to describe the male. The word made its way to England and America, and was used in print in some of the more pornographic literature soon after the First World War. Psychoanalysts have informed me that their homosexual patients were calling themselves gay in the nineteen-twenties, and certainly by the nineteen-thirties it was the most common word in use among homosexuals themselves. (pp. 358–359)

In contrast, Emma Donoghue (1993) argued that there has been knowledge of same-sex love for centuries. In her book *Passions Between Women: British Lesbian Culture 1668–1801*, she wrote the following:

The Oxford English Dictionary ... traces "lesbianism" back to 1870, "lesbic" to 1892, and lesbian, as an adjective to 1890 and as a noun to 1925. Similarly, the entries for "Sapphism" start in 1890, with 1902 given as the first date for "Sapphist". These entries give the impression that only after the publications of late nineteenth-century male sexologists such as Havelock Ellis did words for eroticism between women enter the English language.... *Passions Between Women* is urgently committed to dispelling the myth that seventeenth- and eighteenth-century lesbian culture was rarely registered in language and that women who fell in love with women had no words to describe themselves. (pp. 2–3)

Donaghue gives examples of the phrases "lesbian loves," "a lover of her sex," "Sapphic lovers," "woman-lover," and "she loved women in the same manner as men love them" being used in print in the seventeenth and eighteenth centuries (pp. 3–5).

Gert Hekma (1998) found the first use of the word *bisexual* in Dutch in 1877, although it was used in a different context from its current use:

Bisexual referred in this case to a hermaphrodite who started her sexual career as a heterosexual woman in Germany and who continued his career as a heterosexual man in America. In this first case, it is not clear in which sense the adjective was used, but most likely it referred to passing through both sexes: to being a woman with her menses and later being a man with ejaculation, and not to having both sexual object-choices. It was still a time when the attribution of gender could be done on the basis of sexual object-choice: loving a man meant being a woman. (pp. 113–114)

Minton and Mattson (1998) cited the lyrics of a 1940 Broadway musical: "I don't like a deep contralto, or a man whose voice is alto, Zip, I'm a heterosexual" (p. 44). It is interesting that there has been practically no research performed or theories proposed about heterosexuality itself. Although psychological research often compares a sample of LGB individuals to a "control group" of heterosexuals, little is known about heterosexuality. In 1993, Sue Wilkinson and Celia Kitzinger (two lesbian psychologists) edited a volume entirely devoted to heterosexuality among women. They stated in their introduction:

> Heterosexuality has been largely untheorized within both feminism and psychology.... The set of questions we asked in our "Call for Contributions" was a deliberate reversal of those which psychology has traditionally addressed to the topic of lesbianism: What is heterosexuality and why is it so common? Why is it so hard for heterosexuals to change their "sexual orientation"? What is the nature of heterosexual sex? How does heterosexual activity affect the whole of a woman's life, her sense of herself, her relationships with other women, and her political engagements? (p. 1)

Their volume is only the barest introduction to an enormous field, and I encourage researchers and theorists to explore heterosexuality in more depth.

The Language of Gender and Its Relation to Sexual Orientation

Gender is necessary for definitions of sexual orientation. When one conceptualizes gay men as men who love men, or lesbians as women who have sex with women, one has fixed ideas of the terms *men* and *women*. The Western concepts of lesbian, gay, and bisexual assume constancy of gender. It is only in the 1990s that the social sciences are beginning to grapple with ideas of gender as fluid and continuous, but these ideas have a long history in non-European cultures.

Recently, a number of books have appeared on "two-spirit people," a term coined by Native Americans for individuals in their cultures who are gay or lesbian, are transgendered, or have multiple gender identities (see Brown, 1998; Jacobs, Thomas, & Lang, 1997; Roscoe, 1998). Carrie House (1997), of Navajo–Oneida descent, wrote,

> Our oral traditions acknowledge that the he-shes and she-hes (those who hold in balance the male and female, female and male aspects of themselves and the universe) were among the greatest contributors to the well-being and advancement of their communities. They were (and we are) the greatest probers into the ways of the future, and they quickly assimilated the lessons of changing times and people. Recent studies into the lives of she-hes and he-shes have recovered models or near models of this rich, inventive, reverential, and highly productive approach to keeping balance within a society viewed as an extension of nature. (p. 225)

The term *two-spirit* reflects an attempt by Native American communities to redefine their past, in contrast to the way it was depicted by White male anthropologists, and also to distinguish Native American concepts of gender and sexuality from those of the Western gay and lesbian communities. In the late nineteenth century, White male anthropologists "discovered" the *berdache*, a French word for Native American men whose gender roles did not match their anatomical sex. Neil Miller (1995) described the way that berdaches did not fit the categorical Western concepts of sex and gender of the time.

Gloria Wekker (1997) described identity among working-class women of West African origin in Suriname as follows:

> Most Western European languages have only one way to refer to the self—with the personal pronoun "I," "je," "ich," or "ik." This suggests a monolithic, static, unique conception of personhood. In contrast, in Sranan Tongo, the Surinamese creole, there are a wide variety of ways to make statements about the self. In Sranan Tongo it is possible to talk about the self in singular or plural terms, in masculine or feminine forms, and even in third-person constructions, irrespective of one's gender. (p. 331)

Gender intersects with sexuality as Afro-Surinamese women engage in *mati-ism*, or sexual relations with women while also being in relationships with men (Wekker, 1993).

Paula Rust (1996), one of the leading researchers of bisexuality in the United States today, stated the following:

> First of all, in some cultures, sexuality is not perceived to be a source of identity, and a lack of sexual identity in individuals from such cultures is not an indication of psychosexual immaturity or unresolved sexual issues.... Second, even among cultures in which sexuality does serve as a source of identity, the concepts used to understand and organize sexuality often differ from those in European-American culture. (p. 56)

Nevertheless, many people in the United States who identified as lesbian, gay, or bisexual generally followed rigid gender roles until the women's movement of the 1970s provided more alternative gender roles for people in general. Lillian Faderman (1991) and Kennedy and Davis (1993) described the strictly mandated butch versus femme roles, behaviors, and dress codes for women, particularly working-class women who went to gay bars (gay men had the choice of being nelly or butch). There was hostility and suspicion when a woman was "kiki" (neither butch nor femme). Audre Lorde wrote in her autobiography, "I wasn't cute or passive enough to be 'femme' and I wasn't mean or tough enough to be 'butch'" (quoted in Miller, 1995, p. 319). Faderman (1991) stated the following:

> A Columbus, Ohio, woman recalls walking into a lesbian bar in the 1950s and finding that no one would speak to her. After some hours the waitress told her it was because of the way she was dressed—no one could tell what her sexual identity was, butch or femme, and they

were afraid that if she did not know enough to dress right it was because she was a policewoman. (pp. 164–165)

Middle-class and wealthy lesbians tended to avoid a butch or femme appearance and were more likely to "pass" as heterosexual. They often condemned butch and femme roles as increasing society's negative attitudes about lesbians. The organization Daughters of Bilitis urged its middle-class readership to adopt "a mode of behavior and dress acceptable to society" (Faderman, 1991, p. 180). Middle-class lesbians were encouraged to wear feminine, professional clothing and not to appear lesbian. Faderman (1991) pointed out that the same message to blend in reemerged in the late 1980s with the publication of the book *After the Ball* (Kirk, 1989). Consequently, it was poor and working-class lesbians who communicated through their appearance to the dominant culture that lesbians existed, who were portrayed in the media, and who paid for this by frequent police raids in bars and arrests.

In summary, anatomical sex and gender roles (including the appearance of being male or female) intersect with sexual orientation. It is only at the end of the twentieth century that members of LGB communities are beginning to realize the complexities of gender. Not only have bisexual politics emphasized that sexual orientation is fluid but the transgender politics are focusing on gender as fluid. Just as it took language—the terms *gay*, *lesbian*, *bisexual*, and *heterosexual*—to form an awareness of identity in the middle of the twentieth century, so does language allow a continuing expansion of awareness at the end of the millennium. "Transgender" politics have replaced the more binary concept of "transsexualism"; the younger LGB communities often use the word *queer* as a self-descriptor; and cultural and regional variations are affecting language and identity.

HISTORICAL AND ECONOMIC FACTORS

It takes more than language to form a sense of LGB identity. This section reviews some of the societal institutions—urbanization, education, and the military—that allowed some individuals greater freedom of sexual expression and to move away from traditional family roles.

Changing Roles in a Changing Economy

Lillian Faderman (1991) described education as the pathway for women to become lesbians. Education gave women choices other than marriage and motherhood. It also brought women together in all-female colleges and professions. College-educated women were much less likely to marry than those without such education:

> Even worse, some writers eventually came to fear (not without cause) a problem they hardly dared to express: that higher education for females, especially in all-women's colleges, not only "masculinized" women but also made men dispensable to them and rendered women more attractive to one another. (Faderman, 1991, p. 14)

Even today, surveys of lesbians indicate that they are more highly educated than are women represented in the general census data. In the National Lesbian Health Care Survey (Bradford, Ryan, & Rothblum, 1994), 85% of the sample had at least some college education, and more than 30% had an advanced degree. In a more recent survey of nearly 2,400 lesbians (Morris & Rothblum, in press), about three quarters had at least a college degree, and 33% had a graduate or professional degree. Although such "convenience samples" have been criticized for focusing on young, highly educated lesbians who live in urban areas and have access to lesbian newsletters, bars, churches, and so on, it is likely that education continues to be important in allowing women to come out as lesbian or bisexual.

For working-class people who did not have access to higher education, the military served as a vehicle for LGB individuals to come out (Berube, 1990; Faderman, 1991). Faderman (1991) described World War II as a "government-sponsored subculture" (p. 125) where women became aware of their lesbianism:

> Less than a third of a million women served in the military during the war, but many of them were lovers of other women. For those who already identified themselves as lesbians, military service, with its opportunities to meet other women and to engage in work and adventure that were ordinarily denied them, was especially appealing. For many others who had not identified themselves as lesbians before the war, the all female environment of the women's branches of the armed services, offering as it did the novel emotional excitement of working with competent, independent women, made lesbianism an attractive option. The "firm public impression" during the war years that a women's corps was "the ideal breeding ground for lesbians" had considerable basis in fact. (p. 120)

Moreover, World War II created civilian jobs for women that were previously available only to men, and these work settings had predominantly female employees while men were at war. Heterosexuals in the military were exposed to gay men, lesbians, and bisexuals in ways they never would have been in their hometowns. When the war ended, military personnel were shipped back to the large port cities of New York, San Francisco, Boston, and Los Angeles, and many stayed there, creating large LGB communities in these cities (Faderman, 1991).

In contrast to historians who view social institutions (e.g., higher education, the military) as vehicles to becoming LGB, British sociologist Gill Dunne (1997) examined how being out as a lesbian results in more nontraditional jobs and education for women.

> For working-class women who don't have access to higher education, it is hard to imagine having a life that is financially independent of men. Coming out young presents women with an economic problem which cannot be solved by following their peers into dead-end low-paid women's work. Hence the appeal of traditionally male-dominated occupations, like the trades or the military. Having a job in the trades, like being a mechanic, gives women a hell of a lot more financial freedom than working behind a cash register. Women who aren't economically privileged, but who have an early sense of not wanting to be dependent on men, more often try to enter jobs that men have traditionally held. Not because they want to become men, but because they want to earn a living wage. (Dunne, personal communication, January 1998)

John D'Emilio (1992) and Neil Miller (1995) pointed to the role of the changing economy in influencing the birth of the present-day LGB movement. Urbanization and industrialization gave rise to a sense of personal identity and choice outside the structure of the extended family. Individuals could move to cities where they had more anonymity and where they could find a gay subculture. They could choose not to marry, a choice that would have been difficult in agrarian societies. More recently, the National Lesbian Health Care Survey of more than 1,900 lesbians conducted in the mid-1980s (Bradford et al., 1994) asked respondents about geographic moves. Only 10% of the sample were still residing in the town or city in which they had been born. The vast majority resided in large metropolitan areas, with over half living in cities of more than one million residents. There was a general movement away from the Northeast, where 31% of the sample had been born, to the Pacific states. One has only to read the obituaries in the *San Francisco Bay Times* to see how many men moved there from Midwestern or Southern communities. But it is increasingly common to find LGB communities in most towns, no matter how rural or small. Nevertheless, the extended family is still an important issue for LGB individuals who are members of ethnic minority groups (Greene, 1994; Rust, 1996). These authors have reported that members of oppressed groups value the support of their families in a way that members of more privileged groups do not. African American, Latino, Asian American, and Native American communities often value kinship, whereas European American cultures emphasize individuation and separation from families.

New York City: Harlem, Greenwich Village, Stonewall

When LGB individuals were feeling isolated, they could move to or visit urban centers or take solace in the knowledge that such communities existed. New York City became a leading center of LGB communities in the 1920s and 1930s, even while police raids were quite extensive. Miller (1995) stated the following:

> Artistic and bohemian enclaves were among the places where a modern sense of gay and lesbian community first began to emerge. Whether they be New York's Greenwich Village or Jazz Age Harlem or Left Bank Paris, bohemias were self-enclosed geographical and spiritual worlds where unconventionality was prized and new ideas venerated; where women experienced an enhanced degree of freedom; where the power of religion and family to enforce cultural, political, and sexual conformity was limited. (p. 137)

The Harlem Renaissance was important not only in African American history but also in the history of LGB communities. After thousands of African Americans moved from the rural South to the urban North, Harlem became the center for Black music, literature, and politics. Gay parties, balls, and other entertainment flourished in Harlem in the 1920s and 1930s. African American lesbians and gay men were creating a gay subculture that attracted White LGB individuals as well (see Faderman, 1991, and Garber, 1990, for reviews).

The uprisings at the Stonewall Inn Bar at 53 Christopher Street in Greenwich Village in late June and early July 1969 are usually seen as the events that created the modern-day LGB movement. For example, Grube (1990) used 1969, the year of Stonewall, to distinguish men who came out early ("natives") from those who came out more recently ("settlers"). The gay pride marches in most U.S. cities are on or near the date of June 29, to commemorate the time of the Stonewall uprisings.

On that day, the people who were inside the Stonewall Inn Bar in Greenwich Village fought the police who had arrived to raid the bar. Police raids were a normal part of gay life, but this was the first time that the bar patrons fought back. The Stonewall riots continued for several days. Martin Duberman (1993) described the events of that night in his book *Stonewall*. When Duberman interviewed people who had witnessed the Stonewall riots, some remembered a lesbian dressed in men's clothing. Others noticed drag queens locked in a paddy wagon, kicking out with their high heels at the cops.

One of the people who was living in New York City at that time was Ray Rivera. According to Eric Marcus's (1992) oral history, Ray was born in 1951 in the South Bronx. When he was 7, he asked his grandmother to teach him how to sew so he could dress in drag. When he was 10, he tried to kill himself because he thought he was the only faggot in the world. When he was 13, he left home to sell his body on New York City's streets. When he was 18, in the summer, Ray was invited to a birthday party but decided not to go because Judy Garland had just died and he was feeling depressed. So he was home when a friend called Ray and asked him to come along to a bar that Ray had never been to. And that's how Ray Rivera happened to be at the Stonewall Inn Bar at 2:00 a.m. on June 28. Only a small number of "drag queens" were allowed into the Stonewall. Ray, who is Latino, was allowed in because he was dressed as a White woman.

Ray Rivera described that night as follows:

> I don't know if it was the customers or if it was the police, but that night everything just clicked.... When they ushered us out, they very nicely put us out the door. Then we were standing across the street in Sheridan Square Park. But why? Everybody's looking at each other. "Why do we have to keep putting up with this?" Suddenly the nickels, dimes, pennies, and quarters started flying. I threw quarters and pennies and whatnot.... To be there was so beautiful. It was so exciting. I said: "Well, great, now it's my time. I'm out there being a revolutionary for everybody else, and now it's time to do my thing for my own people." ... The police thought that they could come in and say, "Get out," and nothing was going to happen.... This is what we learned to live with at that time. Until that day. (Marcus, 1992, p. 191)

Not all gays in New York participated in or were aware of the Stonewall uprisings. The more conservative gays, in chinos and sweaters, watched cautiously from the sidelines, and some disapproved of the action. The wealthier gay men and lesbians were not at the scene of the Stonewall riots. Some ignored the action when it was reported in the media; others did not hear about it (Duberman, 1993). Nevertheless, Stonewall is considered today the start of the modern LGB movement.

Early Newsletters and Organizations

Not everyone lived in a metropolis. Many people did not know a single other person who was LGB like themselves, but they stayed current with the rising LGB movement through newletters and books.

In Marcus's (1992) oral history, he used the pseudonym "Lisa Ben" for the woman who, in 1945, produced one of the first lesbian newsletters, *Vice Versa*. A secretary in Los Angeles, Lisa typed each issue on her office typewriter, making nine carbon copies. These copies were distributed from friend to friend and had quite a distribution. Lisa said,

> I wrote *Vice Versa* mainly to keep myself company. I called it *Vice Versa* because in those days our kind of life was considered a vice.... There

was never anything in the magazine that was sexy or suggestive. I purposely kept it that way in case I got caught. They couldn't say that *Vice Versa* was dirty or naughty or against the law.... I typed the magazine at work. I had a boss who said, "You won't have a heck of a lot to do here, but I don't want you to knit or read a book. I want you to always look busy." (Marcus, 1992, pp. 8–9)

A more widely known lesbian publication was *The Ladder*, which was published from 1956 to 1972 by the organization Daughters of Bilitis (see Soares, 1998, for a review). *The Ladder* did not use the word *lesbian* until 1967; before that time, it referred to its readers as "variants." To maintain confidentiality, only two copies of *The Ladder*'s mailing list existed, and like *Vice Versa*, *The Ladder* was distributed from friend to friend. One woman interviewed by Soares (1998) said,

After I finished reading it, I would put it in a darkroom bag and put it in the darkroom and I would let other women know where it was or we would pass it on to other women, like we were passing film back and forth because that's the environment we were working in. (p. 29)

The Ladder had an "integrationist" stance, affirming the right of lesbians to assimilate into mainstream culture. This stance later led to conflicts within the organization Daughters of Bilitis, when the emerging lesbian feminist movement had a more separatist approach, and ultimately to the magazine's demise.

The Mattachine Society existed from 1950 to 1953, a strong foundation of the present-day gay rights movement. The founders of this organization, among them Harry Hay and Chuck Rowland, had been involved in communist organizations and had visions of a society that would give gays the same minority-group status as other oppressed groups in the United States. Miller (1995) stated the following:

According to Hay, the name Mattachine derived from a medieval French society of unmarried townsmen who conducted dances and rituals in the countryside during the Feast of Fools at the vernal equinox. The original Mattachines always performed wearing masks; their dance rituals sometimes turned into peasant protests against the aristocracy. Hay chose this name for his new society because he saw the homosexuals of the 1950s as a "masked people, unknown and anonymous, who might become engaged in morale building and helping ourselves and others." (p. 334)

The Mattachine Society began the magazine *One* at a time when it was still illegal to send homosexual material through the U.S. mail.

According to Jay Paul (1998), the first bisexual organization in the United States was the Bisexual Forum in New York City. However, the

Bisexual Center of San Francisco, which spanned the period from 1976 to 1985, had an important role, according to Paul:

> In that span of time, it had a profound impact; it created a sense of a bisexual community, educated the general public and professionals about bisexuality, confronted the gay and lesbian communities about the tendency to render the bisexual invisible, spawned several organizations (including political action groups), and changed the lives of many women and men who had felt marginalized by both the heterosexual and homosexual communities. (p. 130)

Along with newsletters and magazines, alternative bookstores and publishing companies proliferated in the 1970s, giving rise to the large market in LGB books, publishing companies with LGB book series, and "mainstream" bookstores with LGB sections today. In fact, it was precisely the ease with which mainstream publishers and bookstores accepted LGB books that led to the end of many small, alternative, feminist and lesbian presses and women's bookstores. On the other hand, feminist bookstores often survived long after other feminist and lesbian centers ceased to exist, and some continue on today. In her review of lesbian and feminist publishing, Kate Adams (1998) stated the following:

> And to sell and distribute the steadily growing stream of lesbian and feminist books, newspapers, and magazines, a new kind of capitalist enterprise was popping up as well in neighborhoods across the nation: the women's bookstore. In 1973, there were 9 such stores; in 1976, the number had grown to 44; in 1978, 60 bookstores were surviving. Each one served as meeting place, cultural center, and information clearinghouse for its community, and most survived through the 1970s and into the 1980s, long after other kinds of community space—women's centers and buildings, for example—had disappeared. (p. 126)

It is no coincidence, then, that the characters in Alison Bechdel's popular comic strip "Dykes to Watch Out for" are employed in a women's bookstore.

Today, there are hundreds of national, state, and local periodicals about LGB (and transgender) issues. Both university presses and trade publishers routinely publish books about aspects of the LGB experience. Not only LGB but heterosexual people also hear about LGB issues through the printed word as well as radio, television, and films.

THE MENTAL HEALTH FIELD

Psychoanalysis and "Reorientation" Therapy

The practice of psychology was heavily influenced by Freud and subsequent psychoanalytically oriented therapy. Psychotherapists focused on "reorienting" the sexual orientation of LGB individuals to allow them to become heterosexual and engage in "normal sex," that is, heterosexual intercourse.

As in most of his work on mental health, Freud's writings on homosexuality profoundly influenced attitudes and practices of mental health professionals. Most mental health professionals who work with LGB clients are familiar with Freud's quote about homosexuality:

> Homosexuality is assuredly no advantage, but it is nothing to be ashamed of, no vice, degradation; it cannot be classified as an illness; we consider it to be a variation of the sexual function, produced by a certain arrest of sexual development. (Freud, Letter to an American mother, 1935, cited in Drescher, 1998, p. 19)

Drescher (1998) stated the following:

> Although he never dedicated a major work solely to the subject of homosexuality, Freud's contributions on the subject range across a period of almost twenty years (1905, 1908, 1909, 1910, 1911, 1914, 1920, 1923). The contradictions in his voluminous works make Freud's position opaque to the casual, modern reader. Attempts to find "the real Freud" are too often motivated by those who seek his agreement with their own point of view.... Taken out of the historical context in which he wrote, and depending upon the author's selective citations, Freud can be portrayed as either virulently antihomosexual ... or as a closeted friend of gays. (p. 21)

Drescher (1998) described Freud as having an affirmative attitude about homosexuality for the time in which he lived. For example, in the 1930s he signed a statement for the decriminalization of homosexuality in Germany and Austria. Freud also believed that everyone had homosexual as well as heterosexual feelings, which he referred to as *psychological bisexuality*, although he believed that the homosexual part should be sublimated. He also thought that homosexuality was difficult to treat. In his "Psychogenesis of a Case of Homosexuality in a Woman" (1920, cited in Drescher, 1998), he portrayed the woman as a man hater and as suffering from penis envy.

Many of the "reorientation" therapies that existed until the late 1960s were based on psychoanalytic theory. However, their developers differed from Freud in that they did not believe in people's innate bisexuality and instead viewed heterosexual intercourse as the only normal end result of human sexual development (Drescher, 1998). Parental psychopathology was scrutinized, particularly the mother–son relationship.

One of the most poignant accounts of such therapy is Martin Duberman's (1991) book *Cures: A Gay Man's Odyssey*. Duberman was a prize-winning professor of history at Princeton University who had an offer of an endowed chair at Oxford University. Nevertheless, he was given stereotyped diagnoses by therapists including having a weak will, psycho-pathic tendencies, and a tendency to "act out." In 1959 he tried hard to become attracted to a woman but found himself unable to do so; Duberman (1991) described his therapy session:

> Dr. Igen kept the focus steady. He encouraged me to speculate about the source of my "unconscious resistance" to physical love with a woman. Though rarely theoretical, he made reference to a possible "breast complex" and asked me if I had reacted violently to being weaned. When I laughed and said I couldn't remember as far back as yesterday's movie, let alone my experiences in the crib, he replied, with a pained expression, that that too was part of the resistance.... Alarmed at how sulky he looked (would he tell me I was hopeless? would he give up on me?), I offered in quick substitution a lengthy speculation about how unlikely it was that a mother as devoted as mine would have weaned me prematurely and thus provoked my rage. His expression lightened a bit, and he took up the theme of my mother's devotion. "Yes," he said, "devotion embedded in control, de-votion as a mask for seduction. Is it any wonder you have had difficulty ever since in entrusting yourself to a female? You're chronically angry at women and refuse to get it up for them. To enter a vagina is for you to risk being swallowed alive." (pp. 58–59)

Despite societal changes and scientific data indicating that reorien-tation therapy is ineffective (see Haldeman, 1994, for a review of this literature), such therapy continues to be offered today. At a time when U.S. society is more affirmative of LGB cultures and also of changing gen-der roles for heterosexuals, reparative therapists are increasingly coming from a religious rather than scientific perspective (Drescher, 1998). The National Association for Research and Therapy of Homosexuality (NARTH) was founded by reparative therapists. Drescher (1998) stated the following:

> In the current political climate, NARTH's dogmatic views have been marginalized in professional and scientific organizations.... For the present, however, reparative therapists have demonstrated their will-ingness to ally themselves with religious denominations that condemn homosexuality. Because they are unable to find reputable scientific sup-port for their positions, these antihomosexual religious organizations have turned to reparative therapists to treat their flocks and to provide a veneer of modern respectability.... Anti-homosexual politics make strange bedfellows and Freud, the devoutest of atheists ... would find this wedding of psychoanalysis and fundamentalism astonishing." (p. 38)

Given the homophobic history of psychotherapy, it would not be surprising if LGB individuals avoided traditional psychotherapy. Recent research has provided some evidence to the contrary: Lesbians are more likely to seek therapy than heterosexual women (and the same phenomenon may be true for gay men and bisexuals). Kris Morgan (1992) distributed flyers at a women's basketball game inviting spectators to participate in a survey (a creative setting for finding both lesbians and heterosexual women). In this sample, 77.5% of the lesbians and 28.9% of the heterosexual women had been in therapy, an enormous difference. On the Attitudes Toward Seeking Professional Psychological Help Scale, lesbians scored higher than heterosexual women on the subscales Recognition of Personal Need, Tolerance of Stigma, Confidence in the Mental Health Profession, and Counseling as Growth. In a later study, Kris Morgan and Michele Eliason (1992) interviewed 23 lesbians who had been and 17 lesbians who had never been in therapy and found that both groups viewed lesbians to be introspective and saw the lesbian communities as valuing personal growth.

Celia Kitzinger and Rachel Perkins (1993) critiqued the increasing tendency of lesbians to seek therapy in their book *Changing Our Minds*. They argued that psychological terminology (e.g., the "inner child") has replaced political activism in the lesbian communities and that therapy privatizes and individualizes lesbians' lives. At the same time, there are few resources for lesbians with serious, long-term mental health problems, and these authors urge lesbian communities to organize around sharing resources for long-term caregiving.

Charles Silverstein (1991) made sense of this shift from mistrust to advocacy of therapy in his book *Gays, Lesbians, and Their Therapists*. He described three generations of gay therapists. The first, trained and practicing before Stonewall (pre-1969), did not have degrees and practiced as counterculture therapists. They were the only alternative to reorientation therapy at the time. The second generation practiced in the 1970s, at a time when gay liberation led to the first gay counseling centers, staffed by peer counselors. Silverstein recalled this period: "While gays flocked to our services, established professionals, who earned their living by 'curing' gay men and women, saw us as a cabal of reckless incompetents who, when successful, doomed our clients to a life of misery" (p. 5). The third generation, trained in the 1980s, were the first who could be both out as LGB people and admitted to mainstream mental health degree programs.

Sexologists and Sex Surveys

Neil Miller (1995) argued that a crucial factor leading to the formation of present-day LGB identity was medical labeling and terminology at the end of the nineteenth century:

> One crucial factor was biomedical conceptualization of homosexuality in an age that increasingly classified people by their sexual inclinations—the heterosexual and the homosexual; the fetishist, the sadist,

the masochist. This new way of looking at homosexuality tended to stigmatize it, set it apart from the rest of society, and represent it as a medical condition or a symptom of degeneracy. This view, at least early on, insisted that homosexuals possessed characteristics and attributes of the opposite gender. (p. xxiii)

Nineteenth-century sexologists such as Krafft-Ebing and Havelock Ellis published hundreds of case histories of homosexuals. Such research was often conducted among "sexual inverts" (Faderman, 1991) in prisons and psychiatric institutions. Poor and working-class parents were blamed for inappropriate child rearing and a weak genetic pool.

The most influential sexologist of the twentieth century was Alfred Kinsey. After decades as a zoologist, studying and labeling insects, Kinsey applied his scientific skills to interviewing thousands of American men and women about their sexual behaviors. Kinsey managed to portray himself as a family man who just happened to become interested in sex as the result of teaching a course on the subject; in fact, recent revelations have shown that Kinsey himself was bisexual and engaged in sex with his interviewees and members of his research team (Jones, 1997). Furthermore, Kinsey's sampling biases have been critiqued as overrepresenting college students, prisoners, and members of urban gay communities. Nevertheless, Kinsey's reports had a major influence on sexology. They gave rise to the "Kinsey scale," which measured sexual orientation on a continuum and thus included bisexuality; they focused on the prevalence of same-gender behavior even among people who were married or otherwise "conventional"; and they viewed homosexuality and bisexuality as normative. The Kinsey Reports were followed by a number of other "reports" that included data on lesbians, gay men, and bisexuals—by Shere Hite (1976) and Masters and Johnson (1979); one was even called *The Gay Report* (Jay, 1979).

The Role of Psychological Research

It has been only in the past 25 years that psychological researchers have conducted studies of LGB individuals from an affirmative perspective. Before that time, a few studies focused on prisoners or psychotherapy clients who wanted to change their sexual orientation. The focus was often on the pathology of homosexuality.

A landmark study by Evelyn Hooker changed the direction of LGB research. In the 1940s, Hooker was teaching a psychology course through the extension services at the University of California in Los Angeles. Through the friendship and encouragement of a gay male student in her class, she conducted the first study of gay men. In 1953, at the height of McCarthyism, she applied to the new National Institute of Mental Health for a grant to study "normal homosexual men" and compare them with matched heterosexual men. Unlike those described in prior published case studies, these men were not psychiatric patients or prisoners. Each participant was given the Rorschach, the Thematic Apperception Test, and the Make a Picture Story Test; the results were judged by a panel of nationally known psychological experts who did not know the sexual orientation of the participants. At that time, psychologists were convinced that projective test responses would indicate a participant's sexual orientation. When Hooker presented her results—that homosexual men were as well adjusted as heterosexuals—at the American Psychological Association convention in 1956, the ballroom was packed. The study received widespread publicity (see Boxer & Carrier, 1998; Marcus, 1992, for reviews).

Hooker stated the following (in Marcus, 1992):

> But what means the most to me, I think, is . . . excuse me while I cry . . . if I went to a gay gathering of some kind, I was sure to have at least one person come up to me and say, "I wanted to meet you because I wanted to tell you what you saved me from." . . . I know that wherever I go, there are men and women for whom my little bit of work and my caring enough to do it has made an enormous difference in their lives. (p. 25)

Recently, one of Evelyn Hooker's original study participants, Wayne Placek, died and left her a considerable sum of money in his will. He had long since left Los Angeles and was a farmer in Oklahoma, but he always remembered how significant his participation in Hooker's study had been to his life. This money, the Wayne Placek Fund, is now available for LGB research through the American Psychological Foundation.

Hooker's landmark study set the stage for other research that used her method of matching lesbians and gay men with heterosexuals who were demographically similar. In 1969 Hopkins matched 24 lesbians and 24 heterosexual women on age, intelligence, and professional–educational background. She found the lesbian sample to be more independent, resilient, reserved, dominant, "bohemian," self-sufficient, and composed on Cattell's Personality Factor Questionnaire. In another early study using a larger sample (Thompson, McCandless, & Strickland, 1971), lesbians and gay men were matched with heterosexual women and men, respectively, on age and education. Gay men were less defensive and less self-confident than heterosexual men; lesbians were more self-confident than heterosexual women. There were no significant differences between the matched groups on personal adjustment. Given the extremely negative attitudes held by the public and by mental health professionals at this time, it is remarkable that lesbians and gay men were so well adjusted.

Research today does not need to show comparability to heterosexuals to be published in academic journals; there are even academic journals dedicated to LGB issues. It is no longer necessary to demonstrate that LGB individuals are well adjusted. Nevertheless, there have been relatively little research on lesbian and gay mental health issues (compared with the amount of research on lesbian and gay relationships, identity development, coming out, or aging) and practically no research on the mental health of bisexual women and men (see Bieschke, McClanahan, Tozer, Grzegorek, & Park, chapter 13, this volume, for a review).

The Changing *DSM* and the Mental Health Professions

Mental health professionals began to play a significant role when "homosexuality" changed from being a sin to a sickness (Morin & Rothblum, 1991). As described earlier, therapists, especially psychoanalysts, maintained the "normalcy" of heterosexuality in the politically conservative postwar years and interpreted male and female "homosexuality" as deviant. The second edition of the *Diagnostic and Statistical Manual of Mental Disorders* (*DSM–II*; American Psychiatric Association, 1968) included "homosexuality" as a mental illness. This diagnosis was placed in the section on "sociopathy," described as "crimes against society," along with substance abuse and sexual disorders.

By the 1960s the civil rights movement, the women's movement, and the new gay rights movement that followed in the wake of the Stonewall uprisings all served to put pressure on mental health professionals to affirm LGB rights. Much of the LGB advocacy in the mental health professions focused on removing "homosexuality" from the *DSM* list of mental disorders. On December 15, 1973, the American Psychiatric Association removed this diagnosis from its official list of mental disorders (Adam, 1987). However, a residual category of "ego-dystonic homosexuality" was retained to categorize distress experienced by individuals who wished to change their sexual orientation. In 1987, the American Psychological Association urged its members not to use this diagnosis (Fox, 1988) and joined a coalition that eventually succeeded in getting this diagnosis dropped in the *DSM–III–R* (American Psychiatric Association, 1987). These actions helped to counteract the previous association of same-gender sexual orientation with mental illness.

A survey of 2,500 members of the American Psychiatric Association, conducted soon after the removal of "homosexuality" as a diagnostic category from the *DSM* (*Time*, 1978, in Marmor, 1980), found that a majority considered homosexuality pathological and also perceived homosexuals to be less happy and less capable of mature and loving relationships than heterosexuals. More recently, the *APA Task Force Report on Heterosexual Bias in Psychotherapy* (Garnets, Hancock, Cochran, Goodchilds, & Peplau, 1991) surveyed more than 2,500 members of the American Psychological Association and found that psychologists differed in their use of gay-affirmative practice. Biased, inappropriate, or inadequate practice was found in the understanding, assessment, and intervention concerning a wide range of topics such as identity development, lesbian and gay relationships, and parenting.

Changing the *DSM* resulted in more affirmative stances by the mental health professions. In 1975 the American Psychological Association adopted the official policy statement that "homosexuality per se implies no impairment in judgment, stability, reliability, or general social or vocational capabilities" (Conger, 1975, p. 633). Similar resolutions supporting the removal of "homsexuality" from the official list of mental disorders and deploring discrimination based on sexual orientation had been passed before that time by the American Sociological Association, the National Association for Mental Health, the National Association of Social Workers, and the American Psychiatric Association (Adam, 1987). However, the American Psychological Association resolution went further than most earlier resolutions by urging psychologists and all mental health professionals to "take the lead in removing the stigma of mental illness that has long been associated with homosexual orientation" (Conger, 1975, p. 633).

Lesbian and gay activism in the American Psychological Association became organized in 1973 with the formation of the Association of Lesbian and Gay Psychologists, which formed the basis for the current Division 44 (Society for the Psychological Study of Lesbian, Gay, and Bisexual Issues) of the American Psychological Association (see Kimmel & Browning, in press, for a history of APA's Division 44). The Task Force on the Status of Lesbian and Gay Psychologists was formed to address a number of fundamental issues facing lesbian and gay members of the association. This group was succeeded by the Committee on Lesbian, Gay, and Bisexual Concerns, which continues to monitor the association's involvement in the broader agenda of advancing the civil rights of lesbians and gay men.

CONCLUSION

A number of historical events came together to influence modern-day views of LGB mental health. A sense of identity and a language for discussing lesbian, gay, and bisexual issues had to be developed. Through education, the military, and other vehicles for socioeconomic change, some individuals were able to escape traditional pathways to heterosexuality. Large urban areas such as New York City served as a magnet for LGB individuals to allow them to see other people like themselves or to experiment with new gender and sexual orientation roles. Local and national media spread the word about emerging LGB communities.

In the mental health arena, Freud's often contradictory views on homosexuality were translated into a pathology-based psychodynamic model for LGB individuals who sought mental health care. At the same time, sex surveys and psychological research began to demonstrate that there were more LGB people than the general public assumed and that LGB people were as well adjusted as heterosexuals. The *DSM* removed homosexuality from its list of mental disorders, and the mental health professions established divisions that specialized in LGB issues.

The history of lesbians, gay men, and bisexuals is a history of increasing visibility. Following is a quote from Harvey Milk, the openly gay supervisor of San Francisco who was assassinated in 1978 by a homophobic coworker. It sums up the fight for acceptance and equal rights that LGB individuals have been waging over the course of this century and that is far from over despite extraordinary progress. It points out the ways that LGB issues have moved from being pathologized to being accepted, paving the way for the LGB-affirmative psychology that exists today:

> Somewhere in Des Moines or San Antonio, there's a young person who all of a sudden realizes that she or he is gay, knows that if the parents find out they'll be tossed out of the house, the classmates will taunt the child, and the Anita Bryants and John Briggs are doing their bit on TV.
>
> And the child has two options: staying in the closet or suicide. Then one day that child might open a paper that says "Homosexual elected in San Francisco." And now the child has two new options: go to California or stay in San Antonio and fight.
>
> Harvey Milk
> *The Times of Harvey Milk* [Film] 1982

REFERENCES

Adam, B. D. (1987). *The rise of the gay and lesbian movement*. Boston: Twayne.

Adams, K. (1998). Built out of books: Lesbian energy and feminist ideology in alternative publishing. *Journal of Homosexuality, 34* (3/4), 113–141.

American Psychiatric Association. (1968). *Diagnostic and statistical manual of mental disorders* (2nd ed.). Washington, DC: Author.

American Psychiatric Association. (1987). *Diagnostic and statistical manual of mental disorders* (3rd ed., rev.). Washington, DC: Author.

Berube, A. (1990). *Coming out under fire*. New York: Free Press.

Boxer, A. M., & Carrier, J. M. (1998). Evelyn Hooker: A life remembered. *Journal of Homosexuality, 36*(1), 1–17.

Bradford, J., Ryan, C., & Rothblum, E. D. (1994). National Lesbian Health Care Survey: Implications for mental health. *Journal of Consulting and Clinical Psychology, 62,* 228–242.

Brown, L. (1998). *Two-spirit people*. New York: Haworth Press.

Cogan, J., & Erickson, J. (1999). *Lesbians, levis, and lipstick: The meaning of beauty in our lives.* New York: Haworth Press.

Conger, J. (1975). Proceedings of the American Psychological Association, Incorporated, for the year 1974: Minutes of the annual meeting of Council of Representatives. *American Psychologist, 30,* 620–651.

Cory, D. W. (1960). *The homosexual in America.* New York: Castle Books.

D'Emilio, J. (1992). *Making trouble.* New York: Routledge.

Donoghue, E. (1993). *Passions between women: British lesbian culture 1668–1801.* New York: HarperCollins.

Drescher, J. (1998). I'm your handyman: A history of reparative therapies. *Journal of Homosexuality, 36,* 19–42.

Duberman, M. (1991). *Cures: A gay man's odyssey.* New York: Penguin Books.

Duberman, M. (1993). *Stonewall.* New York: Penguin Books.

Dunne, G. A. (1997). *Lesbian lifestyles: Women's work and the politics of sexuality.* Toronto, Ontario, Canada: University of Toronto Press.

Faderman, L. (1981). *Surpassing the love of men.* New York: Morrow.

Faderman, L. (1991). *Odd girls and twilight lovers: A history of lesbian life in twentieth-century America.* New York: Columbia University Press.

Fox, R. E. (1988). Proceedings of the American Psychological Association, Incorporated, for the year 1987: Minutes of the annual meeting of Council of Representatives. *American Psychologist, 43,* 527–528.

Garber, E. (1990). A spectacle in color: The lesbian and gay subculture of Jazz Age Harlem. In M. Duberman, M. Vicinus, & G. Chauncey (Eds.), *Hidden from history: Reclaiming the gay and lesbian past* (pp. 318–331). New York: Penguin Books.

Garnets, L., Hancock, K. A., Cochran, S. D., Goodchilds, J., & Peplau, L. A. (1991). Issues in psychotherapy with lesbians and gay men: A survey of psychologists. *American Psychologist, 46,* 964–972.

Greene, B. (1994). Ethnic-minority lesbians and gay men: Mental health and treatment issues. *Journal of Consulting and Clinical Psychology, 62,* 243–251.

Grube, J. (1990). Natives and settlers: An ethnographic note on early interaction of older homosexual men with younger gay liberationists. *Journal of Homosexuality, 20,* 119–135.

Haldeman, D. C. (1994). The practice and ethics of sexual orientation conversion therapy. *Journal of Consulting and Clinical Psychology, 62,* 221–227.

Hekma, G. (1998). Bisexuality: Historical perspectives. In E. J. Haeberle & R. Gindolf (Eds.), *Bisexualities: The ideology and practice of sexual contact with both men and women* (pp. 113–117). New York: Continuum.

Hite, S. (1976). *The Hite Report: A nationwide survey of female sexuality.* New York: Macmillan.

Hopkins, J. H. (1969). The lesbian personality. *British Journal of Psychiatry, 115,* 1433–1436.

House, C. (1997). Navajo woman warrior: An ancient tradition in a modern world. In S. Jacobs, W. Thomas, & S. Lang (Eds.), *Two-spirit people: Native American gender identity, sexuality, and spirituality* (pp. 223–227). Urbana: University of Illinois Press.

Jacobs, S., Thomas, W., & Lang, S. (1997). *Two-spirit people: Native American gender identity, sexuality, and spirituality.* Urbana: University of Illinois Press.

Jay, K. (1979). *The Gay Report: Lesbians and gay men speak out about sexual experiences and lifestyles.* New York: Summit Books.

Jones, J. H. (1997). *Alfred C. Kinsey: A public/private life.* New York: Norton.

Kennedy, E. L., & Davis, M. D. (1993). *Boots of leather, slippers of gold.* New York: Routledge.

Kimmel, D. C., & Browning, C. (in press). Society for the psychological study of lesbian, gay, and bisexual issues: A division of the American Psychological Association. In D. A. Dewsbury (Ed.), *Unification through division: Histories of divisions of the American Psychological Association.* Washington, DC: American Psychological Association.

Kirk, M. (1989). *After the ball: How America will conquer its hatred and fears of gays in the 90s.* New York: Doubleday.

Kitzinger, C., & Perkins, R. (1993). *Changing our minds: Lesbian feminism and psychology.* New York: New York University Press.

Marcus, E. (1995). *Making history: The struggle for gay and lesbian equal rights 1945– 1990. An oral history.* New York: HarperCollins.

Marmor, J. (1980). Epilogue: Homosexuality and the issue of mental illness. In J. Marmor (Ed.), *Homosexual behavior* (pp. 391–402). New York: Basic Books.

Masters, W., & Johnson, V. (1979). *Homosexuality in perspective.* Boston: Little, Brown.

Miller, N. (1995). *Out of the past: Gay and lesbian history from 1869 to the present.* New York: Vintage Books.

Minton, H. L., & Mattson, S. R. (1998). Deconstructing heterosexuality: Life stories from Gay New York. *Journal of Homosexuality, 36,* 43–61.

Morgan, K. S. (1992). Caucasian lesbians' use of psychotherapy. *Psychology of Women Quarterly, 16,* 127–130.

Morgan, K. S., & Eliason, M. J. (1992). The role of psychotherapy in Caucasian lesbians' lives. *Women and Therapy, 13*(1), 27–52.

Morin, S. F., & Rothblum, E. D. (1991). Removing the stigma: Fifteen years of progress. *American Psychologist, 46,* 947–949.

Morris, J. F., & Rothblum, E. D. (in press). Who fills out a "lesbian" questionnaire? The interrelationship of sexual orientation, years out, disclosure of sexual orientation, sexual experience with women, and participation in the lesbian community. *Psychology of Women Quarterly.*

Paul, J. (1998). San Francisco's Bisexual Center and the emergence of a bisexual movement. In E. J. Haeberle & R. Gindorf (Eds.), *Bisexualities: The ideology* and practice of sexual contact with both men and women (pp. 130–139). New York: Continuum.

Roscoe, W. (1998). *Changing ones: Third and fourth genders in Native North America*. New York: St. Martin's Press.

Rust, P. (1995). *Bisexuality and the challenge to lesbian politics: Sex, loyalty, and revolution*. New York: Columbia University Press.

Rust, P. (1996). Managing multiple identities: Diversity among bisexual women and men. In B. A. Firestein (Ed.), *Bisexuality: The psychology and politics of an invisible minority* (pp. 53–83). Newbury Park, CA: Sage.

Schmeichen, R. (Producer), & Epstein, R. (Producer/Director). (1982). *The Times of Harvey Milk* [Film]. Beverly Hills, CA: Pacific Arts Video.

Silverstein, C. (1991). *Gays, lesbians, and their therapists*. New York: Norton.

Soares, M. (1998). The purloined Ladder: Its place in lesbian history. *Journal of Homosexuality, 34*, 27–49.

Thompson, N. L., McCandless, B. R., & Strickland, B. R. (1971). Personal adjustment of male and female homosexuals and heterosexuals. *Journal of Abnormal Psychology, 78*, 237–240.

Wekker, G. (1993). Mati-ism and Black lesbianism: Two idealtypical expressions of female homosexuality in Black communities of the diaspora. *Journal of Homosexuality, 24*, 145–158.

Wekker, G. (1997). One finger does not drink okra soup: AfroSurinamese women and critical agency. In J. Alexander & C. T. Mohanty (Eds.), *Feminist genealogies, colonial legacies, democratic futures* (pp. 330–332). New York: Routledge.

Wilkinson, S., & Kitzinger, C. (1993). *Heterosexuality: A feminism & psychology reader*. London: Sage.

Witt, L., Thomas, S., & Marcus, E. (1995). *Out in all directions: The almanac of gay and lesbian America*. New York: Warner Books.

4

LESBIAN, GAY, AND BISEXUAL PEOPLE OF COLOR: UNDERSTANDING CULTURAL COMPLEXITY AND MANAGING MULTIPLE OPPRESSIONS

MARY A. FUKUYAMA AND ANGELA D. FERGUSON

The United States of America is composed of many cultural, ethnic, and national groups. Although this country is considered multicultural by many, the dominant culture is primarily the product of Eurocentric philosophies and values; therefore, the psychological literature, research, theoretical paradigms, and practice are imbued with Eurocentric cultural biases (J. H. Katz, 1985; Sue & Sue, 1990). The inclusion of culturally diverse groups has been conspicuously absent in these domains; when included, they are frequently characterized as deficient, deviant, and inferior (Helms, 1989; Herring, 1989; J. H. Katz, 1985). Consequently, the culturally different have experienced discrimination and prejudice not only in the mainstream American society but also in the field of psychology.

In this chapter the focus is on the intersection of cultural variables (ethnicity, race, gender, class), sexual orientation, and the dynamics of oppression. We intend to challenge the status quo of both mainstream society and Eurocentric psychology as we highlight and examine cultural factors that are salient for lesbian, gay, and bisexual (LGB) people of color. We discuss identity theories (concerned with race, sexual orientation, and gender) and how they affect counseling and therapy with these populations, and we make recommendations for positive interventions. We believe that a theme for LGB people of color in the United States is managing social oppressions that take various forms (e.g., racism, heterosexism, homophobia, biphobia). The chapter is organized into the following sections: assumptions and definitions, critique of identity theories, culture-specific perspectives, and implications for counseling.

ASSUMPTIONS AND DEFINITIONS

We have identified three basic assumptions that provide a foundation for this chapter. First, all phenomena have a cultural context. Christensen (1989) defined culture as consisting "of commonalties around which people have developed values, norms, family life-styles, social roles, and behaviors in response to historical, political, economic, and social realities" (p. 275). In the United States, multiple cultures coexist, overlap, and sometimes contradict each other. Studies of acculturation and adaptation indicate that participation in multiple cultures has its unique stressors and implications for mental health. For example, the pressure to assimilate into the dominant culture may result in loss of language, cultural roots, and community ties. For such individuals, the impact is felt in stress, lowered self-esteem, and concurrent social problems such as alcoholism and violence (E. M. J. Smith, 1985). LGB people also feel stress related to "minority status" (DiPlacido, 1998).

Second, we believe that the social structure of American society is based on dominant–subordinate group relations in which the dominant cultural paradigm favors White, heterosexual, male, Christian, and Eurocentric values and marginalizes persons who are different. This structure is at the core of a sociopolitical system that serves to keep the dominant cultural group in economic power and provides these members with privileges not ascribed to those in subordinate roles through various forms of oppression (e.g., sexism, racism). Individuals belonging to or identifying with nondominant cultural groups confront and must cope with one or more forms of oppression on a personal level every day. Oppression itself is a type of "social disease," and it is important not to "blame the victim" for this problem.

Third, the self (identity development, self-esteem, self-concept) is influenced by group memberships. Collective identities (derived from family and ethnic community) may describe more accurately the experiences of people of color than does an individualistic identity. Therefore, psychologists and counselors must examine the dynamics and interactions of multiple cultural identities that are based on group memberships and their accompanying social statuses. Several key definitions follow that clarify further the issues presented in this chapter:

- *Ethnicity*: social groupings based on common ancestry, national origins, foods, music, language, family practices, and political and economic interests. Ethnicity provides an anchor for social identity and historical continuity (McGoldrick, Pearce, & Giordano, 1996).

- *Race*: a determinant of group membership, based largely on geography, national origin, culture, ethnicity, family ties, and economic and political status. Although it was thought to be biologically based, more genetic variability has been found within specified racial groups than between them (King, 1981). Physical characteristics such as skin color have traditionally been used to distinguish group membership, but racial identification is primarily a social construct used to mark social statuses that maintain social divisions and White privilege (Hopps, 1982; Pinderhughes, 1989; Ridley, 1995; Spickard, 1992). In this chapter we prefer to use the phrase "people of color" to describe individuals who belong to visible ethnic or racial minority groups.

- *Racism*: the perpetuation of the myth that Whites are superior to those of other races, which is expressed through social policies and practices that favor Whites; prejudice in combination with institutional and systemic power (J. H. Katz, 1978; Knowles & Prewitt, 1969). We do not include prejudice or bigotry that may exist among various ethnic groups in this definition because it is not a systemic issue.

- *Sexism*: the belief that men are superior to women and that fulfilling specified gender roles is desirable and morally correct. Sexist policies and practices favor traditional masculine values.

Although it is useful to understand the preceding definitions, it is more important to ask how psychologists explore these constructs with clients. How can one measure an individual's racial identity or understand the extent to which people may hold racist or homophobic ideas and attitudes? The issue of identity development is addressed in the next section.

CRITIQUE OF IDENTITY THEORIES

Identity theories have contributed toward an understanding of the relationship between sociocultural factors and the mental health of culturally diverse persons. Various models of identity development have provided a conceptual framework that describes a psychological process by which one moves from nonacceptance to self-acceptance. The relationship of self to one's reference group and to the dominant culture affects this identity development process. Most identity development models are based on a single social identity (e.g., race, gender, or sexual orientation). In this section, we discuss the limitations of single-identity models for understanding LGB individuals' multiple cultural identities. Single-identity theories have overlooked two important dynamics that may exist for LGB people of color: the visibility or invisibility of identity and the saliency of identity. We discuss the negative effects of oppression on members of marginalized groups (Crocker & Major, 1989), and we conclude the section by highlighting some alternative theories applicable to multiple cultural identities.

Identity models have been used to understand an individual's psychological affiliation or connectedness to a particular social identity (Helms, 1990). Several theorists have developed identity models related to race, ethnicity, gender, and sexual orientation (Atkinson, Morten, & Sue, 1989; Banks, 1981; Cass, 1979; Coleman, 1981–1982; Cross, 1991; Downing & Roush, 1985; Helms, 1984, 1986, 1990; McCarn & Fassinger, 1996). Many of the early models of identity explored single social identities and discussed stages or statuses that described the psychological development and experiences of racial identity attitudes (Helms, 1990). Many of these identity models tended to suggest a linear process, although some theorists have discussed the idea that individuals recycle through identity stages in an ongoing process (Parham, 1989).

Identity models also have been developed that describe an individual's perceptions of self related to a particular "ascribed identity" (i.e., that which is attributed to an individual by others; Cross, 1991). These models provide a developmental process for examining the ways in which members of marginalized groups use dominant social groups as reference points for viewing and interpreting themselves and members within their respective reference group. Each stage or ego status represents the extent to which marginalized group members use dominant social groups as reference points. Helms (1990) described this process as the way in which individuals develop their "worldview." She posited that a worldview is a psychological representation of the way in which people view themselves and others relative to their reference group orientation (i.e., group used as reference for self-identity). For example, a young African American woman could identify herself as Black racially but subscribe to White dominant cultural values such as individualism and autonomy.

Many early researchers were interested in understanding the effects of racism and oppression regarding African Americans' racial identity attitudes and reference group orientation. For example, the construct of race represents an individual's "sense of group or collective identity based on one's perception that he or she shares a common racial heritage with a particular racial group" (Helms, 1990, p. 3). The more one perceives a common racial heritage with a particular racial group, the more identification one feels toward that racial group. Identity models provide a conceptual framework for understanding identity attitudes related to reference group orientation, as well as the effects of oppression on both personal and ascribed identity development.

Identity development models also include gender identity and gender role. P. A. Katz's (1979) model described three distinct levels of the way in which boys and girls acquire appropriate gender behavior in terms of sex roles. Other models have examined gender identity relative to female identity. For example, proposed stage models examining female identity have incorporated a feminist developmental perspective (Downing & Roush, 1985; Ossana, Helms, & Leonard, 1992). These models have described the psychological experiences of women's development, particularly in terms of looking at the effects of sexism. However, gender role identity varies within and among cultural groups (Fassinger & Richie, 1997). Many cultures, including the European American culture, value stereotypical gender expectations and ideologies that are associated with patriarchal values (Kimmel & Messner, 1992).

Homophobia (fear of homosexuality) has been used as a means to enforce traditional gender role behavior. For example, boys are coerced into masculine behaviors by threats of being called a "faggot." Girls who act or dress in masculine ways are called "tomboys," although masculinity in girls is not as stigmatizing as femininity in boys. In addition, homophobic comments have been used to dismiss political movements, such as calling feminists "lesbians" as a way to discredit the women's movement (Pharr, 1988).

Until recently, most identity theories and models have been based on single social identities. Theorists have generally discussed and examined a specific social identity as if the group members were homogeneous, monolithic, and lacking multiple identities. Some researchers have attempted to examine multiple layers of identity of culturally diverse individuals in identity formation theories (e.g., Atkinson et al., 1989; Greene, 1986, 1997; Loiacano, 1989; McCarn & Fassinger, 1996; Morales, 1989) and in applications to counseling and psychotherapy (Ferguson, 1995). However, most existing identity theories continue to focus on homogeneous characteristics of group members (Reynolds & Pope, 1991). One of the primary limitations of recognizing only single identities is that individuals who embrace multiple identities are often invisible members within specific social reference groups.

LGB people of color may be coping with feelings of visibility or invisibility in at least two communities in which they live and function: the mainstream LGB community and their respective ethnic communities (Morales, 1989). They are often differentially treated in the White, heterosexual community as well as in their respective heterosexual ethnic communities. Whether visible or not, one's salience of identity, that is, the identity that emerges into one's awareness, often depends on cultural context. An individual's attitudes, feelings, and self-perceptions regarding his or her cultural group memberships are affected by the shifting social, familial, and community contexts the individual moves through on a daily basis. Identities may emerge into awareness as part of group affiliation but also are affected by feelings of difference from the group. For example, an LGB person of color participates in an ethnic community fund-raising dinner. She is invisible as a lesbian, and her identity is affected by homophobic comments. Although her ethnic identity may remain salient and steady in its importance, she may have to work actively at reengaging her links as a lesbian in that context (Deaux, 1993).

Psychological identity theories that do not acknowledge concurrent multiple identities obscure the complexity of integrating multiple social identities and coping with multiple forms of oppression. This manner of exploring identity development dismisses the salience of an individual's existing identities. When these theories are applied to counseling interventions, the erroneous belief that an individual has one prominent, superseding identity is perpetuated. Development of a positive sense of self, particularly when the individual is a member of several marginalized groups, is difficult (Greene, 1994; Myers et al., 1991). When an individual is attempting to integrate multiple identities, it is important to examine multiple layers of oppression (e.g., sexism, racism, homophobia). Members of many visible ethnic groups must face the challenging negative societal and internalized oppressions of racism. Many women also must face the challenges of sexism. Many LGB people of color must face the challenges of homophobia or biphobia (fear of bisexuality). Women who are members of visible ethnic minority groups face the challenges of racism and sexism. LGB women of color face at least two or three challenges: racism, sexism, and homophobia. In addition, bisexual people may feel marginalized within the ethnic lesbian or gay community (Rust, 1996). Forms of racism and homophobia differ when directed at women versus men, just as forms of sexism differ when directed at women of color versus White women. Although individuals' experiences and responses to "isms" differ, A. Smith and Stewart (1983) suggest that the commonality "is the internalization of negative self-image, and a negative image of those most like oneself" (p. 3).

The confluence of factors that may affect the development of one's social identities affects the manner in which an individual integrates those identities. The contexts of family, community, cultural norms and expectations, and oppression can inhibit the expression, salience, and acceptance of one or more identities. Using a single identity framework may be ineffectual and perhaps harmful to the individual. One of the indicators of identity development is the "coming out" process, that is, the recognition of sexual identity in self and gradual disclosure of this identity to others. It has been recommended that the models of identity development that emphasize coming out to family and others as a sign of health do not necessarily apply to all LGB people of color (A. Smith, 1997). Counselors and psychologists must be aware of and knowledgeable about the social identities that individuals embrace. They must also assist individuals in understanding those identities relative to their personal and collective group identity development, group memberships, and personal and collective mental health.

Identity models can be used to facilitate understanding of these dynamics by assisting individuals in exploring the impact of oppressions in their lives related to the ways in which they feel more or less accepting of their respective multiple identities. Psychotherapists must also be aware that the identities of LGB people of color are interrelated and that these clients may experience aspects of their multiple identities in uneven ways. Therapists can assist clients in becoming aware of their respective attitudes, feelings, and beliefs related to their multiple cultural identities.

An alternative identity model developed by Oetting and Beauvais (1990–1991) suggested that individuals may identify with more than one cultural group and that these identities may function independently of each other. The authors suggested that one can have a unicultural, bicultural, or multicultural identification. This model may be useful in exploring multiple cultural identities. For example, Mark might feel positive about being Chinese American, neutral about being male, and negative about being gay. Or Cassandra, who is a biracial African American and Jewish, might be proud to be African American, feel distant from her Jewish identity, and be confused about her bisexuality. The therapist should try to understand the interactions and salience of these identities. Biracial or multiracial people may share experiences with bisexual people in that their identities do not fit into unidimensional categories.

Poston (1990) developed a five-stage biracial identity model that may have relevance to the experiences of bisexual persons. Although this model was not formulated based on sexual identity development, there are parallel processes that may describe the coming out processes for bisexuals. The five stages are personal identity, choice of group categorization, enmeshment–denial, appreciation, and integration. The similarities lie in the forced choice of one ethnic identity (like choosing between being gay or straight) when in fact the individual may identify with more than one ethnic group (or, as a bisexual, be attracted to both genders).

Fox (1996) suggested that bisexual identity development is complex and affected by multiple factors, such as gender, social class, age, ethnicity, sexual and emotional attractions, fantasies, and behaviors. He cited other theorists who have focused on bisexual identity as a process of meeting developmental tasks such as resolving homophobia, developing a support system, or dealing with ongoing emotional adjustments concerning issues of labeling, confusion, and uncertainty.

Walters (1997) proposed an urban, gay, American Indian (GAI) identity development model that incorporates a multilevel context inclusive of self-identity and group identity. She also included levels of acculturation, stages of coming out, and group memberships as dimensions of identity development and integration. This multidimensional model appears similar to McCarn and Fassinger's (1996) model, which includes group membership identity development in addition to individual sexual identity development for lesbians. Developing a sense of group membership with a lesbian and gay community is viewed as a separate but reciprocal process for individual identity development. Group membership identification as being "part of the LGB community" is as important for White LGBs as ethnic community membership is for persons of color. The LGB community provides cultural and social events, support, and political voice, and it substitutes for family for individuals who have been disconnected from their biological families.

These more recent theories that account for multiple cultural identities and cultural complexity have yet to be tested with LGB people of color. We recommend that qualitative research methods be used to elaborate on these experiences. Presently, these models provide a schema for discussing multiple group memberships and identities in interaction with various sources of oppression. We have not addressed other social identities, such as religious identity or the role of parent, but we presume that these roles could be salient and thereby contribute to the complexity of sexual identity development.

CULTURE-SPECIFIC PERSPECTIVES

In this section, we discuss some important factors that relate to selected ethnic groups and influence the identity formation process for people of color. However, we have three major reservations to discuss before embarking on this section. First, there is a paucity of research on LGB people of color (Alquijay, 1997; Ferguson, 1995). Soto (1997) reported that in a 10-year review of gay, lesbian, and bisexual publications, less than 5% of the journal articles focused primarily on the area of race or ethnicity. It is a difficult population to study because LGBs are often hidden within their communities. Second, we run the risk of making overgeneralizations about specific ethnic groups because we cannot fully address "within-group" diversity. Third, the concept of sexual orientation is a Western psychological construct not always found in or stigmatized across other cultures. Evidence of bisexual behaviors in diverse cultures around the world is typically found in anthropological literature (Fox, 1996). Ross, Paulsen, and Stalstrom (1988) cited an early cross-cultural study of same-gender sexual behavior in which 64% of the societies included in the study regarded same-gender sexual behavior as normal or socially acceptable for some or all members of the community. The authors suggested that same-gender sexual behaviors can function positively in several ways within a culture: as recreational, as an educational activity (mentoring), as an emotional preference, and as an indication of social status (dominance vs. submission). These authors posited that sexuality is stigmatized when it violates other cultural rules and values. LGB relationships have been stigmatized in Western civilization because they violate a cultural imperative to procreate (a value derived from historic Judeo-Christian values) and depart from gender role expectations. Note that in some cultures, same-gender sexual behavior is not stigmatized, identity is not based on sexuality, and gay liberation is unknown (Herdt, 1990).

We have decided to highlight four broadly defined ethnic groupings: Native Americans, African Americans, Asian Americans, and Latin Americans. This is not meant to diminish the importance of other cultural groups, but it is beyond the scope of this chapter to include all. The racial and ethnic cultural groups discussed in this section have different values, beliefs, customs, and histories in the United States. They do, however, share many commonalties. Under each cultural group heading, the following dimensions are discussed: demographic and historical perspectives, family and community, gender roles, and religion and spirituality. Case examples are discussed in the final section of the chapter.

Native American Perspectives

Demographic and Historical Perspectives

The indigenous population of the United States consists of more than 500 federally recognized and 200 nonfederally recognized tribes (Walters, 1997). Within this culturally diverse population of more than 2 million people, or about 1% of the total population (U.S. Bureau of the Census, 1998), more than 200 languages are spoken, and over 50% live in urban areas. As a collective experience, the history of Native tribes in America is fraught with traumatic relocation (forced movement to reservations), genocide (war and fatal diseases), and overt assimilation pressures (Indian boarding schools, missionary influences). Native peoples continue to be oppressed in the United States as many struggle with poverty, health problems, and cultural discontinuity. In addition to these systemic factors, LGB Native Americans are faced with homophobic stigmatization.

Family and Community

Extended family relations are central in providing support, and tribal social structures determine family role expectations. Because of past genocide, women may feel pressure to or desire to bear children. The degree to which one identifies as Native American or American Indian is influenced by many factors, such as level of assimilation, tribal membership, and residence (reservation vs. urban areas). LGB Native Americans may feel conflicts in allegiances to two oppressed communities. Walters (1997) suggested that American Indian values of kinship, family, cooperation, and collective identity may directly conflict with Eurocentric gay and lesbian values of individuality and coming out openly (which sets one apart from the group). In early Native American history, some native peoples' sexuality (before Christian missionary influences) was described as including procreation, play, and bisexuality (Brown, 1997). Individuals who displayed cross-gender role preferences were described as "two-spirited," that is, possessing both masculine and feminine qualities (Jacobs, Thomas, & Lang, 1997). In some tribes this was valued, but not so in all cases.

Gender Roles

Gender roles and cross-gender behaviors are frequently associated with sexual orientation issues. Gender role behavior (social constructions of masculinity and femininity) is different from sexual orientation, which involves same-gender erotic and affectional attraction and attachment. The phenomenon of cross-gender role behaviors (i.e., males acting like females, females acting like males) is frequently cited in writings about early Native American sexuality. Some precolonial Native American tribes were tolerant of cross-gender role behaviors and regarded individuals who exhibited them as having special powers (Brown, 1997). In some tribes alternative gender roles were seen positively, whereas in others they were regarded negatively (Crow, Wright, & Brown, 1997). Various distinctions in gender roles have been described, including such terms as "not-women, not-men" (Brown, 1997, p. 5) and "hypermasculine males for warriors, ordinary heterosexual males, and homosexual males" (Tafoya, 1997, p. 1). In traditional tribes, gender roles and sexuality were not limited to dualistic categories. Gender alternatives were not seen as particularly threatening in some tribes. Rather, a difference was regarded as something from which to learn. This more accepting attitude can be traced to Native American spirituality.

Religion and Spirituality

Native American religious orientation has been described as inclusive, with all things being sacred (Tafoya, 1997). Sexuality and gender roles were seen on a continuum represented by a circle rather than limited by linear stages or rigid categories. Human growth and development were seen as ever evolving, in contrast to fitting into reductionistic categories.

However, Western values and Christian proselytizing have subjugated most indigenous peoples of today. Hence, many Native Americans have internalized the homophobic or biphobic attitudes found in the mainstream culture. In some Native American traditions, cross-gender roles and bisexuality were regarded positively; such historical roots may aid Native Americans to claim a positive identity based on these precepts. However, regardless of Native traditions, it is important for Whites not to "exoticize" LGB American Indians, nor to assume that they have acquired a "two-spirit" valuing of their sexuality (Brown, 1997). Walters (1997) recommended that counselors focus on client resilience and positive coping to deal with the double oppressions of racism and heterosexism.

African American Perspectives

Demographic and Historical Perspectives

African Americans make up about 12% of the total population (more than 34 million people) of the United States (U.S. Bureau of the Census, 1998). They are culturally diverse owing, in large part, to the long history of the slave trade in North America, which brought thousands of culturally different African tribes to the United States. People from the Caribbean islands, which were colonized by Europeans for many years, also immigrated to the United States and have contributed to the cultural diversity in African American communities (Greene, 1997). African American gender roles, cultural values and practices, family systems, and sexuality make up a collection of values and customs from African and European cultures.

Family and Community

The African American community historically has valued family and religion as primary sources of emotional support. Although African Americans' cultural origins are diverse, the community shares common forms of oppression, such as racism, sexism, prejudice, and discrimination. For many African Americans, the family and the community provide support and function "as a refuge and buffer against racism in the dominant culture" (Greene, 1994, p. 395).

LGB African Americans face an additional form of oppression, homophobia, from both the White heterosexual community and the African American heterosexual community. B. Smith (1982) asserted that "heterosexual privilege is the only privilege Blacks have. None of us have racial ... privilege, almost none of us have class privilege, maintaining 'straightness' is our last resort" (p. 171). She continued by suggesting that although racism and sexism may be experienced by some within the African American community, African American LGB individuals may also be victimized by heterosexual privilege.

This occurrence raises an interesting point relative to an LGB individual's experience of oppressions and the process of coming out within the African American community. Coming out for African Americans may mean the loss of their connection to heterosexual privilege as well as of their refuge against racism. Therefore, when an African American LGB client is reluctant to come out, the psychotherapist should not immediately interpret this hesitation as being the same as ambivalence or confusion about sexual orientation. It may more accurately represent a time when the African American LGB faces the potential of losing a major support system, with less opportunity to develop another community in which to feel safe and affirmed.

For individuals who come out and who are members of visible racial or ethnic groups, the process may be a more complex experience than for White gays and lesbians (Moore, 1997). Loiacano (1989) conducted structured interviews with six African American lesbians and gay men and stated that "choices about coming out to others, becoming involved in primary relationships, and becoming politically active in the [nonheterosexual] community may be complicated by status as a Black American" (p. 22). His results revealed that African Americans may place less value on coming out to others than their White counterparts, for fear that they may "jeopardize needed support as a racial minority" (p. 24). In other words, racial identity had a higher priority than sexual identity.

Gender Roles

Gender role development varies within the African American community; both the White mainstream society and the African American community generate gender role expectations. Gender roles of African American men and women have been greatly influenced by the legacy of slavery in this country. Many African American communities are commonly viewed as matriarchal; it is said that "African American women play critical roles in keeping Black family ties together and in supporting Black men" (B. Smith, 1982, p. 157). These views contradict Eurocentric ideals of masculine and feminine roles. Fassinger and Richie (1997) suggested that gender roles in patriarchal societies such as the United States embrace a stereotypical gender role ideology in which "women should be gentle and expressive while men should be strong and instrumental; women are best suited to homemaking and child rearing while men are suited to paid work outside the home" (p. 86). Both genders may experience conflict in fulfilling respective traditional masculine and feminine expectations owing to racism and discrimination (Shorter-Gooden & Washington, 1996; Wade, 1996).

Perceptions and knowledge regarding sexuality of African American men and women have also been affected by stereotypes and myths, causing conflict and tension in male–female relationships. Throughout the years, perceptions of beauty based on European standards of features such as skin complexion and hair texture have affected greatly the ways in which African Americans see each other as attractive, romantic partners. Historical efforts to control and exploit African Americans' reproduction (B. Smith, 1982) and the existence of extended family systems (Billingsley, 1968) have influenced the manner in which African American men and women perceive themselves in terms of parental roles, parental responsibilities, gender socialization, and expectations.

Religion and Spirituality

Historically the Black church has played important social and political roles in support of African American families and communities (Richardson, 1991). Both spirituality and religion are key factors in the Black community, and both spirituality and faith have been central to the civil rights movement and other social justice issues. Afrocentric spirituality emphasizes harmony among spiritual, physical, and social aspects of life. This orientation may assist African Americans to integrate their sexuality. Although the African American community publicly opposes homosexuality, there may be tacit tolerance of same-gender liaisons on a private level (Monteiro & Fuqua, 1994). Counselors may want to look for commonalities in multiple oppressions to reinforce strategies to resist negative stereotyping and to increase sources for positive self-esteem.

Asian American Perspectives

Demographic and Historical Perspectives

Asian Americans represent a diverse population of persons of Asian descent, recent immigrants, and refugees from the continent of Asia and the Pacific Rim countries, ranging from India and Pakistan to China, Korea, Japan, the Philippines, Southeast Asia, and the Pacific Islands. Approximately 10 million Asian Americans live in the United States, composing nearly 4% of the total population (U.S. Bureau of the Census, 1998), and more than 50% of Asian Americans are foreign born. With such large numbers of immigrants and refugees, one may assume that acculturation and relocation are major influences on identity development (Espin, 1997).

Pacific Islanders often feel excluded from the umbrella term "Asian American." The experiences of Pacific Islanders are more similar to those of indigenous Native Americans owing to American colonialism and missionary influences in the Pacific Rim. Recent events such as the movement to legalize same-gender marriage in Hawaii have brought more attention to the Pacific Island cultures. In addition, there is a movement to reclaim Hawaii's sovereignty and cultural heritage, which includes a more complex view of bisexuality (Hall & Kauanui, 1994).

Family and Community

The family unit is highly valued, and ancestors and intergenerational connections are emphasized. The family is hierarchical in structure, with roles clearly defined by gender, class, and age. Feelings of obligation (filial duty) and shame dictate and control social behaviors.

Chan (1989, 1997) discussed the reasons that LGB Asian Americans are generally invisible. She suggested that the dimensions of "public self–private self" in East Asian cultures (China, Japan, Korea) dictate the degree of disclosure about intimacy issues. In addition, the self is defined primarily through family and kinship roles, for example, firstborn son. The idea that an individual might come out as a gay man or lesbian is incompatible with the concept of family obligations and duty (Sohng & Icard, 1996).

Attitudes toward same-gender attraction vary among the different Asian groups (Leong, 1996). Traditional East Asian and South Asian cultures restrict heterosexual contact (i.e., dating is not permitted) but allow intimate friendships and bonding to be expressed in same-gender groupings (e.g., gender-segregated schools). In such settings, same-gender sexual behaviors may be tolerated and not taken seriously.

Acculturation into American culture may also influence the degree of openness about LGB identity. It is possible that coming out is an indicator of acculturation toward the values of individuality and openness of expression. However, coming out may place the Asian American in a conflictual situation. A gay Filipino man, who was politically active in his ethnic community, presented such a dilemma:

> To come out in the Filipino community would be double jeopardy. My first concern was that being openly gay would further jeopardize the serious consideration my political viewpoints would be given in the Filipino community. Secondly, to come out in mainstream society would force me to confront the homophobic attitudes of society at large in addition to the racial discrimination that I was already subjected to as an ethnic minority. (Mangaoang, 1994, p. 39)

Gender Roles

Gender roles have powerful influences that are based on traditions and stereotypes. Traditional gender roles for men and women place men in hierarchical positions of power and women as subservient. Men and women must marry and procreate to continue the family name, and these family roles are more important and salient to identity than sexuality.

Negative stereotypes of Asians exist in the White dominant culture (e.g., they may be viewed as asexual males and exotic females). Such distortions continue to be played out in same-gender relationships. For example, within the gay White male community, the term *rice queen* refers to White men who prefer Asian men (who presumably play out female roles). Other Asian American gay and lesbian themes have been explored in film and theater. The film *The Wedding Banquet* is a humorous approach to parental expectations of a Chinese (gay) son to marry. An Indian film *Fire* explores tensions between marital duty and love that develop between two traditional Indian wives who share the same household. Themes of domination were illustrated dramatically in the play M. *Butterfly* by David Henry Hwang (Eng, 1994). The playwright depicted parallels between sexual dominance and political and military dominance by western European powers in Asia.

Religion and Spirituality

A wide variety of religions are represented among Asian Americans, including Hinduism, Islam, Christianity, Buddhism, Confucianism, Taoism, and indigenous forms of spiritualism. Attitudes toward sexuality vary: There are explicit sacred practices (e.g., tantric traditions), and there is repression (e.g., Catholicism). Most religious traditions regulate heterosexual activity as well as prohibit same-gender activity. Sexuality and spirituality are more closely linked in the Hindu traditions, yet most of the symbolic representations are of the union of the masculine and feminine principles. Psychologists and counselors may need to assess levels of acculturation and familial expectations as central themes in working with Asian American clients.

Latin American Perspectives

Demographic and Historical Perspectives

Latin Americans are a culturally diverse mixture of peoples of indigenous, African, Asian, and European roots. This is the fastest growing ethnic group in the United States, with estimated numbers exceeding 30 million and composing 11% of the total population (U.S. Bureau of the Census, 1998). The largest numbers are Mexican Americans, followed by Puerto Ricans, Cuban Americans, and representatives from Caribbean and Central and South American countries.

Family and Community

Latin Americans are family oriented with values of "family unity, welfare and honor" (Garcia-Preto, 1996, p. 151). The family requires loyalty and fulfillment of obligations, and in turn, it provides protection and care as long as one stays within the family system. Deviations in sexuality may be hidden or overlooked for the sake of family continuity. LGB Latinos feel pressure to marry, if only for appearances (*el que diran*, "what they will say"). Extended family includes both blood relations and those acquired through other commitments such as godparents, in-laws, or children informally adopted. Immigration status also affects family, community relations, and pressures to marry.

Gender Roles

An exploration of gender roles in Latin America provides a foundation for understanding variations in sexual expression. Lara-Cantu (1989) developed a sex role inventory that delineated assertive and aggressive dimensions of masculinity and affective and submissive dimensions of femininity. The ideal of *machismo* (manliness, virility) suggests that men are sexually active, and in some cases, men may be sexually active with other men and not be stigmatized. Zamora-Hernandez and Patterson (1996) noted that there was a higher incidence of bisexuality among Latin American men compared with White men in a study of people with the human immunodeficiency virus (HIV). They also found that men may engage in sex with other men without stigma as long as they assume the active role (vs. the passive, or receptive, role). The homosexual label is reserved for a partner who is "female" in the sex act. However, men who are sexually active with other men do not necessarily conform to these narrow roles.

For Latina women, the ideal of *marianismo* suggests that women are submissive, self-sacrificing, and pure. Just as men are expected to be sexually active, women are expected to be "virgins" until marriage and then to devote themselves to child rearing (Vasquez, 1994). For a Latina woman to be interested in sex, interested in another woman, or sexually active outside of marriage would violate gender role expectations (E. Delgado-Romero, personal communication, May 14, 1998). Latin American women are in a process of discovering their voices about sexuality (Alcaron, Castillo, & Moraga, 1993).

Religion and Spirituality

Religion plays an important role in the life of Latin American families, and Catholicism is the predominant religious influence in Latin American countries. Catholicism frequently merges with indigenous religious customs. Some priests have become social activists with regard to human rights issues, but fighting one type of oppression (economic injustice) does not automatically translate into fighting another (heterosexism). In addition, a recent rise in Protestant fundamentalism could increase homophobic attitudes among Latin Americans. Many religions condemn same-gender sexual behavior, although large extended families may be able to absorb deviations from the heterosexual norm. Cultural factors such as preferred language, acculturation, socioeconomic status, religion, educational level, and family and kinship system need to be accounted for in providing psychotherapy for Latin American clients (Carballo-Dieguez, 1989).

IMPLICATIONS FOR COUNSELING

A range of therapeutic issues are raised when working with LGB people of color. In this section we discuss some common themes and make recommendations for practitioners. We again caution the reader about making generalizations but hope that the parameters of this discussion will expand psychologists' abilities to understand the complex dynamics that underlie multiple cultural identities and oppressions. We discuss the impact oppression has on clients' worldviews, the coming out process, and internalized feelings of self-worth. The dynamics of identity saliency and visibility or invisibility are explored. We also make specific recommendations for clinical interventions and discuss selected case examples.

Psychologists are taught to be sensitive to clients' needs and issues but are not taught how to be sensitive to issues of oppression, discrimination, and prejudice. The forces of oppression have shaped the worldviews of clients with multiple identities. As psychologists begin to understand that clients have worldviews that are different from their own, openness to knowing and learning about other cultural groups will increase. Subsequently, psychologists will increase their multicultural counseling competencies (Fassinger & Richie, 1997; Pope & Reynolds, 1997; Sue, Arredondo, & McDavis, 1992; Sue & Sue, 1990).

We recommend that psychologists and counselors examine whether their theoretical orientation allows LGB people of color to feel supported and affirmed in the therapeutic process. Therapists also need to understand clients from a multicultural perspective, which includes exploration of how the individual is affected by various factors such as societal messages, familial messages, group memberships, multiple social identities, oppression, and power. Assessing and understanding the salience of the multiple identities and multiple oppressions of LGB people of color, rather than focusing on only one identity, may assist both the client and the therapist in working through psychological, interpersonal, and emotional issues (Ferguson, 1995).

Coming out is a complex decision-making process for many LGB people of color. There are many places and stages of coming out in one's lifetime; it is a never-ending process. Many LGB people of color have felt diminished and have suffered immeasurably because of oppression. LGB people of color often find refuge in their respective communities and have elected to minimize other aspects of their identities. The decision to disclose sexual orientation—to whom and when—may depend on the intensity of the oppressions. In fact, electing to come out may cause LGB people of color to feel as though they are leaving their place of refuge. Psychologists need to be aware that the decision to come out may bring up feelings of grief and loss. In addition, LGB people of color may have to deal with further oppression in the White gay community. Although LGB people of color may want to affirm their sexual identity, they may not be prepared to leave their cultural environment and enter a hostile social and political climate that may not have sufficient support systems for their psychological well-being. Morales (1989) indicated that LGB people of color balance three identities: "the gay/lesbian community, the ethnic minority community, and the predominantly White mainstream society" (p. 217). For example, by becoming a visible African American LGB, the individual "may run the risk of feeling uprooted as an ethnic person" (Morales, 1989, p. 233).

LGB people of color also may internalize oppression. Feelings of self-hatred and depression and negative attitudes toward the self may be psychological manifestations of internalized oppression. Counselors need to assess the ways in which oppression is experienced from both external and internal sources and how it affects sense of self and perceptions of group memberships. Consider a fictitious case example:

> Maria, a 24-year-old Cuban American, feels positive about herself (i.e., positive personal identity). She is in her first relationship with a woman and sees LGB group membership as irrelevant to her own life circumstances (reference group orientation). Maria's mother has mentioned that she is glad that Maria has light features and is seen as White. Currently, Maria does not feel a commitment to any racial group (ascribed identity). However, Maria's presenting problem is that she feels like an "outsider" with her friends. The counselor may want to explore in what ways Maria is affected by oppressions and how they affect her relationship and group affiliations.

Although each identity may be defined separately, there is an interaction between the person's sense of self and his or her group memberships. Psychologists prepared to assess the impact of multiple oppression can assist clients in coping with these effects, in developing more positive attitudes about their identities, and in learning the skills to resist oppression.

Visibility or invisibility of "minority status" influences identity development and group affiliation. When one is a visible target of oppression, one develops skills for coping and resisting both overt and covert forms of prejudice. LGB people of color may not have the skills or means for counteracting the additional oppression of homophobia or biphobia. The added weight of this oppression may contribute to anxiety, depression, and isolation. When one is an invisible member of an oppressed group, as is more typical of sexual orientation, one is constantly processing decisions about when and if to self-disclose. This constant self-monitoring and vigilance over safety consume a fair amount of psychological energy. In addition, the unguarded homophobic or biphobic comments from loved ones (who otherwise are supportive) can create inner distress. LGB people of color may decide not to take on yet another form of oppression. For some individuals, the additional pressures may seem like too much, whereas others may feel that they have developed "transferable skills" to fight another oppression (e.g., anti-Semitism, sexism, homophobia, biphobia, and racism).

Some people of color resist labeling by sexual orientation. Gay identity and the gay liberation movement have been associated with the White middle class, wherein individuals are able to break from their families and support themselves autonomously (D'Emilio, 1983). People of color may resist joining the gay liberation movement because it is perceived to be joining with the White oppressor and denying one's family ties. In some ways, a gay identity may be a function of acculturation into American society. As was previously discussed, some men of color engage in same-gender sexual behaviors but do not identify themselves as gay (Tsang, 1994; Zamora-Hernandez & Patterson, 1996). We recommend that clients self-select their identity labels and not be pressured to conform to the customary LGB labels.

We recommend also that counselors and psychologists assist LGB clients to find support systems, which may be groups separate from the White gay community. Such separatist groups may be necessary for cultural immersion and safety. For example, LGB people of color may be able to meet on-line through Internet listservs, bulletin boards, and the World Wide Web (Tsang, 1994). Although virtual communication does not eliminate prejudice, it does allow people of color to find each other for support and socializing. In addition, support groups and social networks exist in large metropolitan areas, such as in San Francisco and Washington, DC. We suggest that LGBs also need heterosexual people of color who are "allies" to counteract the effects of homophobia and heterosexism. For example, how can LGB people of color attend a church where the minister continuously condemns "homosexuality" as a sin? LGBs of color may want to find a more progressive church community but may have to deal with integrating into White churches and adapting to cultural differences in styles of worship.

Hoopes (1979) proposed a cultural learning model for adapting to a pluralistic society that suggests that a multicultural approach uses "selective adoption" of cultural behaviors (p. 18). With LGB people of color, there is a blending of subcultures based on race, ethnicity, gender, and sexual orientation. Members of marginalized groups sometimes have the capacity to bridge groups more easily than persons whose identities are embedded in mainstream culture. Although there are benefits of being biculturally skilled, there are also hidden costs, such as experiencing "cultural strain" when there is intense cross-cultural conflict or dissociating parts of one's self in a cultural context where one part is hostile to another.

Consider another fictitious case example:

> Dora is a 33-year-old Dakota who has two children ages 8 and 6. She travels frequently between her tribal home in South Dakota and West Coast urban areas where she has an extended friendship and family network. She has had relationships with both men and women in a "serial monogamous" fashion, and she does not label herself in any particular way regarding her sexual identity. She has formed connections within a lesbian community, and the woman she is currently dating has some concerns about Dora's bisexuality, calling Dora's sexual identity into question. A psychotherapist may want to explore with the client how she negotiates her multiple cultural group connections and identities, as well as explore within the couple relationship the meaning of bisexuality.

CONCLUSION

Whether intentional or not, the LGB liberation movement challenges heterosexual gender norms for everyone. The mainstream culture benefits from broadened expressions of sexuality and gender roles. LGB persons of color are more likely to cross boundaries of gender, class, race, and ethnic origins and thereby break down the "isms" through multiple group memberships and intergroup relationships. Bisexuals in particular model the concept that human sexuality is expressed on a continuum, not in dichotomous boxes. It is important to resist a pathology model for the sexual identity of LGB people of color. Rather, we encourage psychologists to consider the root causes of oppression to be pathological.

Gloria Anzaldua (1987) wrote about living in the borderlands between Texas and Mexico but extended this geographic experience into the psychological realms through her poetry and trilingual prose. We believe the following quote is a fitting conclusion to this chapter:

> I have been straddling that *tejas*–Mexican border, and others, all my life. It's not a comfortable territory to live in, this place of contradictions. Hatred, anger and exploitation are the prominent features of this landscape. However, there have been compensations for this *mestiza*, and certain joys. Living on borders and in margins, keeping intact one's shifting and multiple identity and integrity, is like trying to swim in a new element, an "alien" element. There is an exhilaration in being a participant in the further evolution of humankind, in being "worked" on. (Anzaldua, 1987, p. I)

REFERENCES

Alcaron, N., Castillo, A., & Moraga, C. (Eds.). (1993). *The sexuality of Latinas.* Berkeley, CA: Third Women Press.

Alquijay, M. A. (1997). The relationships among self-esteem, acculturation, and lesbian identity formation in Latina lesbians. In B. Greene (Ed.), *Ethnic and cultural diversity among lesbians and gay men* (pp. 249–265). Newbury Park, CA: Sage.

Anzaldua, G. (1987). *Borderlands/La Frontera: The new mestiza.* San Francisco: Spinsters/Aunt Lute Book Company.

Atkinson, D. R., Morten, G., & Sue, D. W. (Eds.). (1989). *Counseling American minorities: A cross-cultural perspective* (3rd ed.). Dubuque, IA: William C. Brown.

Banks, J. A. (1981). The stages of ethnicity: Implications for curriculum reform. In J. A. Banks (Ed.), *Multi-ethnic education: Theory and practice* (pp. 129–139). Boston: Allyn & Bacon.

Billingsley, A. (1968). *Black families in White America.* Englewood Cliffs, NJ: Prentice-Hall.

Boykin, K. (1996). *One more river to cross: Black and gay in America.* New York: Doubleday.

Brown, L. B. (1997). Women and men, not-men and not-women, lesbians and gays: American Indian gender style alternatives. In L. B. Brown (Ed.), *Two spirit people: American Indian lesbian women and gay men* (pp. 5–20). New York: Harrington Park Press.

Carballo-Dieguez, A. (1989). Hispanic culture, gay male culture, and AIDS: Counseling implications. *Journal of Counseling and Development, 68,* 26–30.

Cass, V. C. (1979). Homosexual identity formation: A theoretical model. *Journal of Homosexuality, 4*(3), 219–235.

Chan, C. S. (1989). Issues of identity development among Asian-American lesbians and gay men. *Journal of Counseling and Development, 68,* 16–20.

Chan, C. S. (1997). Don't ask, don't tell, don't know. In B. Greene (Ed.), *Ethnic and cultural diversity among lesbians and gay men* (pp. 240–248). Newbury Park, CA: Sage.

Christensen, C. P. (1989). Cross-cultural awareness development: A conceptual model. *Counselor Education and Supervision, 28,* 270–289.

Coleman, E. (1981–1982). Developmental stages of the coming out process. *Journal of Homosexuality, 7*(2–3), 31–43.

Crocker, J., & Major, B. (1989). Social stigma and self-esteem: The self-protective properties of stigma. *Psychological Review, 96,* 608–630.

Cross, W. E. (1991). *Shades of Black.* Philadelphia: Temple University Press.

Crow, L., Wright, J. A., & Brown, L. B. (1997). Gender selection in two American Indian tribes. In L. B. Brown (Ed.), *Two spirit people: American Indian lesbian women and gay men* (pp. 21–28). New York: Harrington Park Press.

Deaux, K. (1993). Reconstructing social identity. *Society for Personality and Social Psychology, 19,* 4–12.

D'Emilio, J. (1983). Capitalism and gay identity. In A. Snitow, C. Stansell, & S. Thompson (Eds.), *Power of desire: The politics of sexuality* (pp. 100–113). New York: Monthly Review Press.

DiPlacido, J. (1998). Minority stress among lesbians, gay men, and bisexuals: A consequence of heterosexism, homophobia, and stigmatization. In G. M. Herek (Ed.), *Stigma and sexual orientation: Understanding prejudice against lesbians, gay men, and bisexuals* (pp. 138–159). Newbury Park, CA: Sage.

Downing, N. E., & Roush, K. L. (1985). From passive acceptance to active commitment: A model of feminist identity development for women. *The Counseling Psychologist, 13,* 695–709.

Eng, D. L. (1994). In the shadows of a diva: Committing homosexuality in David Henry Hwang's M. Butterfly. *Amerasia Journal, 20,* 93–116.

Espin, O. M. (1997). Crossing borders and boundaries: The life narratives of immigrant lesbians. In B. Greene (Ed.), *Ethnic and cultural diversity among lesbians and gay men* (pp. 191–215). Newbury Park, CA: Sage.

Fassinger, R. E., & Richie, B. S. (1997). Sex matters: Gender and sexual orientation in training for multicultural counseling competency. In D. B. Pope-Davis & H. L. K. Coleman (Eds.), *Multicultural counseling competencies* (pp. 83–110). Newbury Park, CA: Sage.

Ferguson, A. D. (1995). The relationship between African American lesbians' race, gender, and sexual orientation and self-esteem. *Dissertation Abstracts International, 56*(11) A, 4565.

Fox, R. C. (1996). Bisexuality in perspective: A review of theory and research. In B. A. Firestein (Ed.), *Bisexuality: The psychology and politics of an invisible minority* (pp. 3–50). Newbury Park, CA: Sage.

Garcia-Preto, N. (1996). Latino families: An overview. In M. McGoldrick, J. Giordano, & J. K. Pearce (Eds.), *Ethnicity and family therapy* (2nd ed., pp. 141–154). New York: Guilford Press.

Greene, B. A. (1986). When the therapist is White and the patient is Black: Considerations for psychotherapy in the feminist heterosexual and lesbian communities. *Women and Therapy, 5,* 41–65.

Greene, B. (1994). Lesbian women of color: Triple jeopardy. In L. Comas-Diaz & B. Greene (Eds.), *Women of color: Integrating ethnic and gender identities in psychotherapy* (pp. 389–427). New York: Guilford Press.

Greene, B. (1997). Ethnic minority lesbians and gay men: Mental health and treatment issues. In B. Greene (Ed.), *Ethnic and cultural diversity among lesbians and gay men* (pp. 216–239). Newbury Park, CA: Sage.

Hall, L. K. C., & Kauanui, J. K. (1994). Same-sex sexuality in Pacific literature. *Amerasia Journal, 20,* 75–81.

Helms, J. E. (1984). Toward a theoretical explanation of the effects of race on counseling: A Black and White model. *The Counseling Psychologist, 12,* 153–165.

Helms, J. E. (1986). Expanding racial identity theory to cover counseling process. *Journal of Counseling Psychology, 33,* 62–64.

Helms, J. E. (1989). Eurocentricism strikes in strange ways and in unusual places. *The Counseling Psychologist, 17,* 643–647.

Helms, J. E. (1990). *Black and White racial identity: Theory, research, and practice.* New York: Greenwood Press.

Herdt, G. (1990). Developmental discontinuities and sexual orientation across cultures. In D. P. McWhirter, S. A. Sanders, & J. M. Reinisch (Eds.), *Homosexuality/heterosexuality: Concepts of sexual orientation* (pp. 208–236). New York: Oxford University Press.

Herring, R. D. (1989). The American Native family: Dissolution by coercion. *Journal of Multicultural Counseling and Development, 17,* 4–15.

Hoopes, D. S. (1979). Intercultural communication concepts and the psychology of intercultural experience. In M. D. Pusch (Ed.), *Multicultural education: A cross-cultural training approach* (pp. 10–38). La Grange Park, IL: Intercultural Network.

Hopps, J. (1982). Oppression based on color [Editorial]. *Social Work, 27,* 3–5.

Jacobs, S. E., Thomas, W., & Lang, S. (1997). *Two-spirit people: Native American gender identity, sexuality, and spirituality.* Chicago: University of Illinois Press.

Katz, J. H. (1978). *White awareness: Handbook for anti-racism training.* Norman, OK: University of Oklahoma Press.

Katz, J. H. (1985). The sociopolitical nature of counseling. *The Counseling Psychologist, 13,* 615–624.

Katz, P. A. (1979). The development of female identity. *Sex Roles, 5,* 155–178.

Kimmel, M. S., & Messner, M. A. (1992). *Men's lives.* New York: Macmillan.

King, J. C. (1981). *The biology of race.* Berkeley: University of California Press.

Knowles, L., & Prewitt, K. (1969). *Institutional racism in America.* Englewood Cliffs, NJ: Prentice-Hall.

Lara-Cantu, M. A. (1989). A sex role inventory with scales for "machismo" and "self-sacrificing woman." *Journal of Cross-Cultural Psychology, 20,* 386–398.

Leong, R. (1996). *Asian American sexualities: Dimensions of the gay and lesbian experience.* New York: Routledge.

Loiacano, D. K. (1989). Gay identity issues among Black Americans: Racism, homophobia, and the need for validation. *Journal of Counseling and Development, 68,* 21–25.

Mangaoang, G. (1994). From the 1970s to the 1990s: Perspective of a gay Filipino American activist. *Amerasia Journal, 20,* 33–44.

McCarn, S. R., & Fassinger, R. E. (1996). Revisioning sexual minority identity development formation: A new model of lesbian identity and its implications for counseling and research. *The Counseling Psychologist, 24,* 508–534.

McGoldrick, M., Pearce, J. K., & Giordano, J. (Eds.). (1996). *Ethnicity and family therapy* (2nd ed.). New York: Guilford Press.

Monteiro, K. P., & Fuqua, V. (1994). Black American gay youth: One form of manhood. *High School Journal, 77*(1–2), 20–36.

Moore, L. C. (1997). *Does your mama know? An anthology of Black lesbian coming out stories.* Decatur, GA: Red Bone Press.

Morales, E. S. (1989). Ethnic minority families and minority gays and lesbians. *Journal of Homosexuality, 17,* 217–239.

Myers, L. J., Speight, S. L., Highlen, P. S., Cox, C. I., Reynolds, A. L., Adams, E. M., & Hanley, P. (1991). Identity development and worldview: Toward an optimal conceptualization. *Journal of Counseling and Development, 70,* 54–63.

Oetting, E. R., & Beauvais, F. (1990–1991). Orthogonal cultural identification theory: The cultural identification of minority adolescents. *International Journal of the Addictions, 25,* 655–685.

Ossana, S. M., Helms, J. E., & Leonard, M. M. (1992). Do "womanist" identity attitudes influence college women's self-esteem and perceptions of environmental bias? *Journal of Counseling and Development, 70,* 402–408.

Parham, T. A. (1989). Cycles of psychological nigrescence. *The Counseling Psychologist, 17,* 187–226.

Pharr, S. (1988). *Homophobia: A weapon of sexism.* Berkeley, CA: Chardon.

Pinderhughes, E. (1989). *Understanding race, ethnicity, and power: The key to efficacy in clinical practice.* New York: Free Press.

Pope, R. L., & Reynolds, A. L. (1997). Student affairs core competencies: Integrating multicultural awareness, knowledge, and skills. *Journal of College Student Development, 38,* 266–277.

Poston, W. S. C. (1990). The biracial identity development model. *Journal of Counseling and Development, 69,* 152–155.

Reynolds, A. L., & Pope, R. L. (1991). The complexities of diversity: Exploring multiple oppressions. *Journal of Counseling and Development, 70,* 174–180.

Richardson, B. L. (1991). Utilizing the resources of the African American church: Strategies for counseling professionals. In C. C. Lee & B. L. Richardson (Eds.), *Multicultural issues in counseling: New approaches to diversity* (pp. 65–75). Alexandria, VA: American Counseling Association.

Ridley, C. R. (1995). *Overcoming unintentional racism in counseling and therapy: A practitioner's guide to intentional intervention.* Newbury Park, CA: Sage.

Ross, M. W., Paulsen, J. A., & Stalstrom, O. W. (1988). Homosexuality and mental health: A cross-cultural review. *Journal of Homosexuality, 15*(1–2), 131–152.

Rust, P. C. (1996). Managing multiple identities: Diversity among bisexual women and men. In B. A. Firestein (Ed.), *Bisexuality: The psychology and politics of an invisible minority* (pp. 53–83). Newbury Park, CA: Sage.

Shorter-Gooden, K., & Washington, N. C. (1996). Young, Black, and female: The challenge of weaving an identity. *Journal of Adolescence, 19,* 465–475.

Smith, A. (1997). Cultural diversity and the coming-out process: Implications for clinical practice. In B. Greene (Ed.), *Ethnic and cultural diversity among lesbians and gay men* (pp. 279–300). Newbury Park, CA: Sage.

Smith, A., & Stewart, A. J., (1983). Approaches to studying racism and sexism in Black women's lives. *Journal of Social Issues, 39*, 1–15.

Smith, B. (1982). Racism and women's studies. In G. T. Hull, P. B. Scott, & B. Smith (Eds.), *But some of us are brave* (pp. 157–175). Old Westbury, NY: Feminist Press.

Smith, E. M. J. (1985). Life stress, social support, and mental health issues. *The Counseling Psychologist, 13*, 537–579.

Sohng, S., & Icard, L. D. (1996). A Korean gay man in the United States: Toward a cultural context for social service practice. In J. F. Longres (Ed.), *Men of color: A context for service to homosexually active men* (pp. 115–137). New York: Harrington Park Press.

Soto, T. A. (1997). Ethnic minority gay, lesbian, and bisexual publications: A 10-year review. *Division 44 Newsletter, 13*, 13–14.

Spickard, P. R. (1992). The illogic of American racial categories. In M. P. P. Root (Ed.), *Racially mixed people in America* (pp. 12–23). Thousand Oaks, CA: Sage.

Sue, D. W., Arredondo, P., & McDavis, R. J. (1992). Multicultural counseling competencies and standards: A call to the profession. *Journal of Multicultural Counseling and Development, 20*, 644–688.

Sue, D. W., & Sue, D. (1990). *Counseling the culturally different: Theory and practice* (2nd ed.). New York: Wiley.

Tafoya, T. (1997). Native gay and lesbian issues: The two-spirited. In B. Greene (Ed.), *Ethnic and cultural diversity among lesbians and gay men* (pp. 1–10). Thousand Oaks, CA: Sage.

Tsang, D. C. (1994). Notes on queer n'Asian virtual sex. *Amerasia Journal, 20*, 117–128.

U.S. Bureau of the Census. (1998). Retrieved April 30, 1998 from the World Wide Web: http://www.census.gov.html

Vasquez, M. J. T. (1994). Latinas. In L. Comas-Diaz & B. Greene (Eds.), *Women of color: Integrating ethnic and gender identities in psychotherapy* (pp. 114–138). New York: Guilford Press.

Wade, J. C. (1996). African American men's gender role conflict: The significance of racial identity. *Sex Roles, 34*, 17–33.

Walters, K. L. (1997). Urban lesbian and gay American identity: Implications for mental health service delivery. In L. B. Brown (Ed.), *Two spirit people: American Indian lesbian women and gay men* (pp. 43–65). New York: Harrington Park Press.

Zamora-Hernandez, C. E., & Patterson, D. G. (1996). Homosexually active Latino men: Issues for social work practice. In J. F. Longres (Ed.), *Men of color: A context for service to homosexually active men* (pp. 69–91). New York: Harrington Park Press.

5

APPLYING COUNSELING THEORIES TO LESBIAN, GAY, AND BISEXUAL CLIENTS: PITFALLS AND POSSIBILITIES

RUTH E. FASSINGER

The November 1995 issue of *Consumer Reports* represented a landmark event for anyone interested in public perceptions of psychotherapy. Of the 4,000 readers responding, nine tenths of those who had sought therapy reported significant improvement in their condition, and psychotherapy participants reported as much improvement as those who had received psychotropic medications in addition to therapy. That psychotherapy "works" is finally becoming publicly acknowledged, a fitting, if belated, tribute to a century of development and refinement of clinical practice as well as extensive scholarly exploration of psychotherapy process and outcome.

However, Gordon Paul's famous question remains especially salient to practicing psychotherapists: "What treatment, by whom, is most effective for this individual with that specific problem, under which set of circumstances, and how does it come about?" (Paul, 1969, p. 44). Determining an appropriate, effective approach for a particular client is perhaps the most critical decision in therapeutic practice. The fact that the majority of practicing therapists report that they are functionally eclectic—or at least theoretically pluralistic—in their therapeutic orientation (Arkowitz, 1992; Beutler, 1983; Corey, 1996; Garfield, 1986; Norcross, 1986a; Norcross & Goldfried, 1992) suggests that therapists do, indeed, attempt to use counseling theory selectively and deliberately with their clients.

Given that lesbian, gay, or bisexual (LGB) clients bring a unique set of issues and life circumstances to the therapeutic encounter, it seems useful to explore the applicability of commonly used counseling theories to clinical work with these populations. The purpose of this chapter, therefore, is to offer a brief analysis of widely used psychotherapy frameworks in terms of their usefulness with LGB clients. A detailed explication of each theory is well beyond the scope of this chapter; instead, the theories reviewed here are grouped into four broad classes of therapeutic approaches—humanistic, cognitive–behavioral, psychodynamic, and systems–cultural—and elements of more specific theories (e.g., rational–emotive therapy, person-centered therapy, object relations therapy) are subsumed in those discussions. A thorough working knowledge of a wide variety of counseling theories is assumed on the part of the reader; those with limited exposure to such theories are encouraged to consult the references cited in this chapter for more detailed explanations of basic concepts and terminology.

HUMANISTIC APPROACHES

Overview

Therapies with strong humanistic foundations include person-centered therapy (Raskin & Rogers, 1989; Rogers, 1951, 1957, 1958, 1961), Gestalt therapy (Passons, 1975; Perls, 1973; Polster & Polster, 1973; Yontef & Simkin, 1989), existential therapy (May, 1961; May & Yalom, 1989; Yalom, 1981), and transactional analysis (TA; Berne, 1964). Products of the mid-twentieth century focus on internal subjective experience and existential awareness (Rice & Greenberg, 1992); humanistic approaches share core assumptions regarding self-determination and a positive growth orientation. Self-awareness, freedom of choice, personal responsibility, personal integration and congruence, spontaneity, and inner-directedness are the hallmarks of these approaches. Individual problems are assumed to be caused by an external thwarting of innate tendencies toward self-actualization and self-determination (Rice & Greenberg, 1992). Rogers's (1951, 1957, 1958, 1961) person-centered approach is the historical and conceptual cornerstone of this class of theories, and it is probably safe to say that most counselors and psychotherapists today are trained in the supportive aspects of the therapeutic relationship as postulated by Rogers, even if they do not espouse a purely person-centered therapy approach (Lambert, 1986). Moreover, Rogers's legacy of intensive empirical research into the actual process of counseling has contributed immeasurably to contemporary scholarship on therapy process and outcome (Rice & Greenberg, 1992).

The therapeutic process in the humanistic approaches is phenomenological, client centered, and client supportive. The therapeutic relationship is assumed to be crucial to creating a climate in which one can recognize blocks to growth and freedom, experience aspects of the self previously denied or distorted, accept responsibility for oneself and one's own choices, and develop greater trust in oneself and openness to experience (Rice & Greenberg, 1992). The role of the therapist is to be congruent and authentic in the therapeutic relationship and to communicate respect, accurate empathy, warmth, genuineness, and unconditional acceptance to the client (e.g., Rogers, 1951, 1957). Formal diagnosis is eschewed, and a collaborative understanding of client problems is sought. Although humanistic approaches generally are not focused on specific techniques beyond the importance of the therapeutic relationship, Gestalt and TA approaches use a number of strategies (e.g., script analysis, role-playing, dialoguing with oneself, psychodrama) to help clients confront psychological discrepancies, increase experiencing, and integrate attitudinal and behavioral dichotomies (e.g., Berne, 1964; Perls, 1973; Yontef & Simkin, 1989).

Possibilities

Humanistic approaches are thought to be especially useful for clients experiencing life transitions or developmental crises who would benefit from exploring their own feelings, needs, values, and goals and from freeing themselves from guilt and shame (Corey, 1996). Because the emphasis is on developing one's own internal compass for life's journey rather than attempting to navigate by the expectations and evaluations of others, these approaches seem especially useful for work with LGB clients. Indeed, I believe that a humanistic approach should form the foundation of all work with LGB clients, especially with regard to the central importance of the therapeutic relationship. Conditions of societal, institutional, and individual oppression faced by LGB individuals clearly call for the ameliorative effects of a warm, supportive, and unconditionally respectful relationship. Moreover, the invisibility, secrecy, and shame with which many LGB clients live and work underscore the importance of a genuine, honest encounter with another person, in which congruence, self-acceptance, and personal responsibility for one's choices are both modeled and encouraged.

In terms of specific applications and strategies of humanistic approaches to therapy, the possibilities are seemingly endless. The therapeutic relationship itself serves as a corrective emotional experience for LGB individuals who have been judged negatively and hurt by prejudice and discrimination. Through the unconditional acceptance of the therapist, clients learn self-acceptance and pride; through the congruence and genuineness of the therapist, they learn to integrate their own conflicted feelings and become more open and honest about their lifestyles and identities; and through the active listening and accurate empathy of the therapist, they learn to articulate coherent self-images and clarify their locations in both the LGB and non-LGB communities. Indeed, therapists who work with LGB clients can derive much benefit from returning to Rogers's original (e.g., 1957, 1958) writings on the healing qualities of the therapeutic relationship. Because many professionals are likely to have learned simplistic, skill-oriented versions of Rogers's ideas, much of the richness and complexity may have been lost; reading his thoughts on the power of an accepting relationship in bringing about client change can be an unexpected treat.

In addition to the therapeutic relationship itself, some of the specific techniques of gestalt therapy can be especially useful with LGB populations. Dialogues between polarities and empty-chair strategies can be helpful in clarifying internal conflicts; for example, a client who is struggling with whether she is "really a lesbian" might set up a dialogue between the aspects of herself that are lesbian and the aspects that are not and then explore her thoughts and feelings in the experiencing of those aspects. Role-playing, which also can be in the form of an empty-chair dialogue, can be useful in helping clients to practice self-disclosure to family, friends, coworkers, and others; for example, a client preparing to come out to his homophobic father might set up two chairs in which he alternately sits as he speaks as both himself and his father, thereby actively practicing how he will respond to his father's expected attacks. In group therapy, TA techniques for identifying whether one is acting as a parent, child, or adult in an interpersonal interaction can help clients learn to avoid the games in which they engage to avoid intimacy; this may be especially useful for LGB clients, who often do not have models for healthy intimate relationships with same-sex others.

Pitfalls

Humanistic approaches are not without pitfalls, even in populations for which they appear extremely well suited. The lack of formal diagnostic procedures in these approaches, coupled with the emphasis on acceptance of the client's phenomenological world, may result in a great deal of frustration and wasted time when dealing with clients who exhibit severe pathology or impaired functioning. This is a strong possibility in working with LGB individuals, some of whom have spent long years in secrecy and shame, forming wildly distorted images of the self and failing to develop adequate functional interpersonal skills (e.g., Gonsiorek, 1995). For such clients, the support of the humanistic approaches may not offer enough challenge and confrontation in addressing dysfunctional dynamics and behavior.

Another limitation of the humanistic approaches is that the role of the therapist may seem overly passive to many clients. Especially for LGB clients, who are often hungry for information and direction, the lack of structure and clear direction inherent in the humanistic approaches can make counseling seem pointless. Moreover, there is some indication that clients from particular cultural groups (e.g., Asian Americans) prefer more directive, goal-oriented therapies (e.g., Ponterotto, Casas, Suzuki, & Alexander, 1995; Sue & Sue, 1990). For such clients, the seemingly excessive focus on talking about feelings may appear to be a waste of time, and the therapy process can become stalled by the client's reluctance to engage in such talk.

On the other hand, therapists who wish to use some of the more active therapeutic techniques of the Gestalt approaches must use extreme caution in implementing these strategies. Any technique that focuses on examining and articulating polarities can inadvertently reinforce beliefs that sexual orientation is a dichotomous identity (heterosexual or homosexual) and that healthy functioning requires choosing a category to which one must immutably belong. Not only can this be extremely confusing and damaging to bisexual clients but it runs the risk of rushing any LGB client too quickly through important self-definition processes and can lead to identity foreclosure and premature self-labeling.

Finally, the focus of the humanistic approaches on self-determination and individual autonomy may be at odds with the cultural values of some clients, whose sense of identity may derive from values of collectivism, interdependence, and respect for tradition and authority (Corey, 1996; Ivey, Ivey, & Simek-Morgan, 1997; Sue & Sue, 1990). This conflict presents an intriguing conundrum for the therapist, who must somehow help the LGB client negotiate between the competing demands of adherence to cultural values and traditions (which can be virulently heterosexist and homophobic) and development of self-acceptance, self-appreciation, and responsibility for one's own choices, regardless of how those choices are viewed culturally. Fortunately, the humanistic emphasis on the *client's* views, evaluations, and goals helps to ensure some degree of respect for cultural pluralism and sensitivity in the therapeutic relationship.

Overall, humanistic approaches have much to offer in working with LGB clients. They can aid in the development of clients' self-respect, clarification of values, and fostering of personal congruence, both internally and in relation to others. The potential shortcomings of these approaches in lack of structure and direction can be addressed effectively by the use of more directive approaches, particularly those that are cognitive–

behavioral in emphasis. These approaches are discussed in the following section.

COGNITIVE–BEHAVIORAL APPROACHES

Overview

Therapies that contain strong cognitive and behavioral elements include rational–emotive therapy (Ellis, 1976, 1989; Ellis & Whiteley, 1979; Wessler & Wessler, 1980) and other cognitive therapies (Beck, 1976; Beck & Weishaar, 1989; Freeman & Dattilio, 1992); behavioral, cognitive-behavioral, and social learning approaches (Bandura, 1982; Dobson, 1988; Kazdin, 1994; Meichenbaum, 1977, 1985; Thoreson, 1980; Wilson, 1989; Wolpe, 1990); reality therapy (Glasser, 1980, 1985); Adlerian therapy (Ansbacher & Ansbacher, 1964, Mosak, 1989); and multimodal therapy (Lazarus, 1989). Most of these approaches are rooted in the behavioral movement of the early twentieth century, whose most famous proponents were Watson, Pavlov, and (much later) Skinner (Fishman & Franks, 1992; Hothersall, 1995; Wilson, 1989). The cognitive–behavioral approaches share the assumptions that responses (both cognitive and behavioral) are learned within the context of an ongoing person–environment interaction and that individual problems arise from faulty learnings of one kind or another. Objective evaluation, self-control, self-determination, goal directedness, present centeredness, active engagement, teaching and learning, experimentation, and ongoing assessment are the hallmarks of these approaches (Fishman & Franks, 1992). Although they originally evolved as separate and distinct therapeutic frameworks, cognitive and behavioral approaches have become increasingly integrated over the past several decades. Current adherents of these approaches generally acknowledge the complex interweaving of both cognitive and behavioral elements in individual responses and actions, regardless of where therapeutic attention is focused (Dobson, 1988; Fishman & Franks, 1992; Meichenbaum, 1977).

The process of therapy in cognitive–behavioral approaches follows the reasoned analysis of the scientific method, beginning with thorough assessment and clear setting of goals, followed by experimentation, ongoing evaluation, and establishment of new goals as cognitive and behavioral changes occur (Fishman & Franks, 1992). The role of the therapist is didactic; she or he functions as a teacher–trainer and model who challenges, confronts, and assists the client in identifying difficulties and enacting change. The client is expected to be an active learner and participant in the collaborative therapeutic process. A good working relationship with the therapist is assumed, although the relationship itself is not a focus in the cognitive–behavioral approaches (Dobson, 1988).

Many techniques are used in the various cognitive and behavioral approaches to catalyze change in clients. Contracts often are made, and formal assessments are undertaken (e.g., behavioral analysis, life-history assessment, determination of irrational beliefs); Lazarus's (1989) multimodal assessment framework is especially comprehensive in this regard. Ongoing evaluation by both the therapist and the client is an integral part of treatment, and goals are adjusted accordingly. Techniques such as systematic desensitization, thought stopping, cognitive restructuring, relaxation methods, self-management, stress inoculation, record keeping, and skills rehearsal and training are used liberally. In addition, homework assignments often are given to ensure ongoing commitment and activity on the part of the client (Beck & Weishaar, 1989; Corey, 1996; Dobson, 1988; Ellis, 1989).

Possibilities

Therapies that emphasize cognitive and behavioral change, because of their pragmatic emphasis on unlearning maladaptive response patterns and learning more adaptive responses, are thought to be especially useful for clients whose habituated modes of thinking, feeling, and behaving are causing functional difficulties (Beck & Weishaar, 1989; Corey, 1996; Dobson, 1988). These approaches are used most often in treating specific phobias and anxieties as well as applied widely in institutional settings (e.g., schools, prisons, hospitals) where management of individuals can be maximized through the systematic use of reinforcement techniques. Clients who prefer an active, task-oriented focus in therapy are considered good candidates for cognitive–behavioral approaches (Beck & Weishaar, 1989; Corey, 1996; Dobson, 1988). Moreover, many of the specific techniques are used in group and family counseling, as well as in self-help groups and literature, because they provide self-determined, goal-oriented activity and clear evaluation of results.

Cognitive–behavioral approaches are likely to be quite helpful to LGB clients, who, because of oppression and invisibility, often come to the therapeutic encounter steeped in myths and misinformation about homosexuality. The didactic aspects of cognitive–behavioral approaches allow the therapist to serve as an educator and information resource, and the self-determining aspects of these approaches allow the client to take an active role (e.g., reading, seeking community resources) in learning about being lesbian, gay, or bisexual. Indeed, I believe that the psychoeducational and referral roles of therapists in working with LGB clients are imperative to successful outcomes in fostering healthy LGB development.

In addition, the challenging of dysfunctional patterns of thinking and behaving implicit in these approaches can be useful for LGB clients, who often must overcome a great deal of societally induced, internalized heterosexism and homophobia. Belief systems learned in homophobic families, schools, religious institutions, and the like can be challenged and reevaluated, and more adaptive belief systems can be adopted. For example, a client may be struggling with anxiety over religious teachings that she is sinful and destined for hell; through homework assignments, she can engage in reading and reeducation regarding such teachings, eventually developing less punitive religious beliefs and perhaps even attending a gay-friendly house of worship. Moreover, the emphasis of the cognitive–behavioral approaches on teaching and learning may help to destigmatize personal difficulties and help-seeking behavior. This is especially important for LGB individuals, whose internalized heterosexism and homophobia may have convinced them that they are "sick."

In terms of specific cognitive–behavioral strategies, there are endless possibilities for assisting clients. For example, LGB clients who are extremely panicked about attending LGB community activities or dealing with their families can learn relaxation techniques and other coping strategies. Similarly, LGB clients preparing to come out to families, friends, or colleagues can rehearse their behaviors, strengthening skills that are weak, such as asserting themselves when under attack, in preparation for such events. Cognitive control techniques can be used effectively in helping clients address dysfunctional thinking (e.g., that coming out will completely destroy one's children's lives or that claiming bisexuality implies an underlying lesbian or gay identity that one is avoiding). Stress inoculation training can aid a client in gradually coming out to others in a sequence that becomes increasingly threatening or difficult over time. Finally, the action focus of the cognitive–behavioral approaches makes them especially useful for short-term clinical work, where LGB clients can get immediate assistance with specific developmental tasks.

Pitfalls

Although cognitive–behavioral approaches can be useful in working with LGB clients, the emphasis on goals, tasks, and action may obscure the need for an intimate relationship with the therapist; therapists may become so focused on problem solving that they overlook the value of simply being in a deeply caring relationship with clients. Clients who have internalized a great deal of homophobia and heterosexism are unlikely to be ready to take action quickly, and both client and therapist may become frustrated with lack of progress in the context of the expected focus on forward movement and change. In cases such as these, the lack of attention to feelings may inhibit therapeutic progress.

Moreover, the active challenging of existing modes of thinking and behaving may feel overwhelming to many LGB clients, who already are likely to be feeling under attack by society and who may have experienced physical aggression from others because of their homosexuality (Fassinger, 1991; Herek, 1991, 1998). For such clients, the therapist may appear to be one more critical and insensitive person. In addition, forcefully attacking existing belief systems may be threatening when those belief systems are deeply ingrained and strongly reinforced (e.g., religious beliefs or cultural values). There also is the danger that therapists will impose their own belief systems on clients in an attempt to provide cognitions that are assumed to be more adaptive or healthy (Corey, 1996). This may be an especially egregious error in dealing with clients who are culturally different from oneself; the therapist may misunderstand, ignore, or gloss over core cultural beliefs or values and declare them to be irrational or dysfunctional (Ivey et al., 1997; Sue & Sue, 1990). Fortunately, the emphasis in the cognitive and behavioral approaches on the active participation of the client helps to keep therapy focused on the *client's* problem identification and goals.

Finally, perhaps the most common criticism of the cognitive–behavioral approaches is that they are largely ahistorical, that is, that they ignore clients' past experiences in their families, educational and work institutions, and society at large (Corey, 1996; Fishman & Franks, 1992). Many professionals assume that a thorough understanding of one's past (particularly, experiences in the family), and a recognition of how the past relates to the present, will help to ensure the kind of deep insight that leads to permanent behavioral change. Psychodynamic approaches to therapy, discussed in the following section, may be particularly useful in this regard.

PSYCHODYNAMIC APPROACHES

Overview

Psychodynamic approaches to counseling and therapy subsume a large and diverse assortment of theoretical frameworks including psychoanalysis and psychoanalytic therapy (Arlow, 1989; Freud, 1949; Goldman & Milman, 1978; Jung, 1961; Klein, 1975), ego psychology (Erickson, 1963, 1968, 1982), object relations theory (Fairbairn, 1952; Mahler, 1968; St. Clair, 1986), self psychology (Kohut, 1971, 1977, 1984; Masterson, 1985), and attachment theory (Bowlby, 1969; Winnicott, 1987). A number of these theories might be described more accurately as theories of personality development rather than therapeutic frameworks; clear implications for treatment often are much more difficult to identify in psychoanalytic theories than are explanations of the etiology of pathology (Eagle & Wolitzky, 1992). Nevertheless, all these approaches share, at their core, a focus on intrapsychic processes and the shaping of the present self through early experiences with caregivers and other significant adults. Unconscious motives, intrapsychic conflict, the ego (or self), drives and impulses, defensive mechanisms, and developmental stages are the hallmarks of the various psychodynamic approaches (Eagle & Wolitzky, 1992). Therapeutic success in these approaches is assumed to be manifested in increased insight leading to fairly extensive personality reconstruction (Arlow, 1989; Eagle & Wolitzky, 1992).

Psychoanalytic theory clearly is the "grandfather" of these approaches, and Freud generally is credited with introducing the notion of a "talking cure" for emotional and behavioral problems, thereby laying the foundation for all verbally oriented therapies (Eagle & Wolitzky, 1992; Hothersall, 1995). In comparison with classical psychoanalysis, which evolved out of Freud's drive theory, newer "neo-analytic" or psychodynamic theoretical formulations reflect greater emphasis on the ego, or self; increased attention to differentiating and integrating self and others; greater focus on adaptive functioning; and a more interactive relationship with the therapist. Similarly, the process focus in therapy has shifted from an emphasis on revealing unconscious conflicts to an increasing focus on relationship factors in therapy and their power to correct the destructive effects of early negative experiences (Eagle & Wolitzky, 1992).

The highly intellectual psychodynamic approaches to therapy rely on the desire of the client for deep self-understanding based on a complex analysis of family background and dynamics. Behavioral difficulties are thought to be caused by psychological processes gone awry, for example, unsuccessful resolution of a particular stage of development, thwarting of the formation of healthy attachment bonds, or incorporation of an inappropriate object (e.g., Freud, 1949; Kohut, 1984; Mahler, 1968; Winnicott, 1987). Therapeutic goals thus focus on bringing unconscious motivations and conflicts into conscious awareness, interpreting and understanding their connection to current behavioral problems (including understanding the role of defensive strategies in creating difficulties), and working through those issues to strengthen the self and achieve a more stable personality structure (Eagle & Wolitzky, 1992). The therapist remains somewhat more detached than in other theoretical approaches and focuses on guiding the client through increasing self-awareness by frequent interpretation and explanation; the expectation is that the therapist will become a target of the client's unconscious needs and projections over the course of the clinical work (Arlow, 1989; Eagle & Wolitzsky, 1992).

Techniques used in the various psychodynamic approaches include therapist and client interpretation, free association, dream analysis, hypnosis, analysis of defensive strategies, and analysis of the transferential relationship with the therapist. Formal diagnosis and testing also may be used, and a detailed case history is considered essential. Because of the complexity of the level of insight the client is expected to reach, psychodynamic approaches generally are expected to require more long-term work than other therapies (Corey, 1996; Eagle & Wolitzky, 1992).

Possibilities

Psychodynamic approaches are thought to be particularly useful for highly verbal, fairly well-functioning individuals who want to acquire a deep understanding of their own history and its relation to current behavior (Corey, 1996). These approaches often are sought out by helping professionals and by individuals who have engaged in prior therapy, who wish to extend the insight they already have developed into further self-understanding. The emphasis on the role of early traumatic or inadequate experiences in forming dysfunctional interpersonal patterns clearly is appropriate for individuals who are aware of such events in their lives and wish to explore and understand them. A skilled therapist can aid in interpreting the meanings and impact of those events, and the therapeutic relationship can represent a safe holding environment while one peels away layers of defenses and achieves a clear understanding of past experiences.

It has been my experience that psychodynamic approaches in some form tend to be used more often by therapists in their work with gay men than in work with lesbians; this may be due, in part, to the conscious use of nonsexist or feminist approaches to therapy in many lesbian communities, discussed later in this chapter. For any LGB client, however, the focus of psychodynamic therapies on background and family history may be useful, especially because that kind of analysis can shed light on internal resistance to coming out. A client may feel a particularly precarious bond with one parent, for example, and may be reluctant to come out to that parent for fear (perhaps realistic) of losing the relationship altogether.

An understanding of parent–child dynamics also can aid the LGB client who is experiencing difficulties in achieving intimacy, in seeking or accepting social support, and in understanding habituated and dysfunctional relationship patterns. A client who cannot seem to break out of a pattern of seeking brief, anonymous sexual encounters in favor of desired intimacy might discover that parental attachment patterns have fostered avoidance, and this understanding could lead to focused efforts at overcoming dismissive responses to intimate overtures. Similarly, clients who refuse to explore LGB communities despite an obvious desire to do so might examine the family roots of their "tough it out alone" attitude and thereby overcome internal reluctance to reaching out to others for support.

Many LGB clients form unusually strong attachments to therapists, regardless of the kind of therapeutic relationship deliberately being fostered. This may be the first time the client ever has been open and honest, felt known and understood, or experienced an accepting relationship, and she or he may be working out patterns of intimacy and the expression of heretofore forbidden desires with the safe and supportive therapist. The elements of psychodynamic theories that focus on the analysis of therapeutic relationship dynamics (e.g., transference and countertransference) may be useful in working through the difficulties that these feelings create, for example, helping a client to realize that the warm acceptance she craves from the therapist mirrors what she desires from parents and family.

Finally, some of the specific techniques commonly used in psychodynamic approaches may be useful in analyzing the kinds of experiences LGB individuals often bring to the therapeutic encounter. For example, dreams and fantasies about same-sex encounters can be clear markers of homoerotic tendencies, and thorough discussion and understanding of such dreams and fantasies may help to focus and address clients' confusion about their sexual orientation. Similarly, exploration of images freely associated to particular stimuli (e.g., phrases such as "lesbian mothers" and "gay bars") can function to help clients sort out stereotypes, internal conflicts, and confusion regarding sexual identification and preferences for intimacy.

Pitfalls

Psychodynamic theories occupy the curious position of containing some of the most widely used elements in therapy (e.g., emphasis on client history, centrality of internal conflict, analysis of the therapeutic relationship) yet coming under some of the most intensive criticism. Much of this criticism focuses on the paternalistic aspects of these approaches and their emphasis on intrapsychic processes to the exclusion of contextual and environmental considerations. Indeed, it is difficult to ignore the heterosexist, essentialist underpinnings of these theories; their emphasis on psychopathology; and the use of these theories in mistreating women and gay people, both historically and at present. Moreover, the long-term nature of many of these approaches renders them unrealistic or inaccessible to a large majority of the population. For members of particular cultural groups (including lesbians, gays, and bisexuals), the focus on exposing complex family dynamics, followed by a long process of internal personality reorganization, can be seen as insensitive to the real effects of oppression (racism, sexism, classism, heterosexism, homophobia) on development and functioning.

In addition, many LGB clients may be seeking more immediate solutions to pressing problems: how to deal with erotic feelings about one's roommate, how to come out to one's children, how to deal with a diagnosis of human immunodeficiency virus (HIV) disease, how to handle a dual-career job search, or how to find a gay-friendly place of worship. Although the brief-therapy movement is beginning to spawn some reformulations of psychodynamic treatment, psychodynamic approaches generally are not designed for short-term problem solving, nor are they appropriate for clients clearly needing immediate support and education. Unfortunately, this excludes a large portion of the LGB client population, especially those in the early stages of identity development and coming out and those who are isolated because of geographic location or demographic characteristics.

In short, psychodynamic approaches may be most useful for LGB clients at more advanced stages of identity formation; such individuals have successfully navigated much of the stress of coming out to self and others but may continue to manifest (often subtle) dysfunctional behavioral patterns, or they may wish to develop deeper understandings of themselves. However, for clients who require therapies that help them understand environmental and contextual contributions to their problems, systems–cultural approaches are likely to be preferred; these frameworks are discussed in the following section.

SYSTEMS–CULTURAL APPROACHES

Overview

In addition to the traditional systems theories of therapy and intervention, included here are approaches that deliberately incorporate social and political analysis into therapeutic consideration, because sociopolitical systems are known to exert a profound influence on behavior and functioning (Brown, 1994; Ponterotto et al., 1995; Sue & Sue, 1990). Thus, the systems–cultural approaches discussed here include the familiar, traditional models of family therapy developed in the 1960s and 1970s (Ackerman, 1966; Bowen, 1978; Foley, 1989; Guerin & Chabot, 1992; Haley, 1976; Horne & Passmore, 1991; Madanes, 1981; Minuchin, 1974; Napier & Whitaker, 1978; Satir, 1983), as well as more recently developed frameworks of feminist therapy (Brown, 1994; Enns, 1993, 1997) and multicultural counseling and therapy (Ponterotto et al., 1995; Sue, Ivey, & Pederson, 1996; Sue & Sue, 1990). All share a common focus on the importance of the context in determining behavior, and individuals are seen as part of a mutually interactive system, both influencing and being influenced by all others in the system.

Systems that might become the focus of therapeutic attention range from a small unit such as a couple or family to a very large unit such as a cultural group or a combination of many cultural groups in an enormous social system. The key elements in all of the systems–cultural approaches are assumptions regarding the mutual influence of all parts (e.g., individuals) of a system and the emphasis on historical repetition of systemic patterns that leads to problems for individuals in that system (Foley, 1989). Also critical are the concepts of homeostasis and resistance to change, and the related idea that a void created in a system quickly is filled; thus, there is a focus on establishing and maintaining systemic patterns of power, and there are assumed to be implicit systemic rules and norms that govern behavior (Foley, 1989). Effective systems intervention is expected to require sustained, vigorous, active, dramatic—and sometimes controversial—challenges to the systemic status quo (Guerin & Chabot, 1992).

The intervention process in any systems–cultural approach involves active exploration of the existing system and acquiring an understanding of how it sustains its patterns over time, including an examination of the role that the individual plays in maintaining that system (Foley, 1989). At the couple level, partners might recognize that they have developed a pattern in which one partner consistently ignores her or his own needs in the face of the other's anger or hostility. At the family level, parents might realize that they have allowed one child's chronic behavior difficulties to position that child as the family "problem," overshadowing the needs of the parents and the other siblings. At a cultural level, exploration might focus on helping a woman to understand that her consistent passivity is the result of gender role socialization or aiding a deferent Asian American client in recognizing that her poor work evaluations as a manager are rooted in cultural patterns that are at odds with the more aggressive norms in her workplace.

Because complex systems are presumed to be extremely difficult to change, the role of the therapist is much more active—and proactive—in systems–cultural approaches than in some of the other approaches to therapy and intervention. The therapist serves as a teacher, coach, model, and consultant, actively challenging the assumptions clients hold about the existing system and their location in it, and often functions as an advocate for clients in confronting those systems. The ultimate goal is systemic change, whether familial or societal, and a systems–cultural therapist unabashedly goes about the business of jolting the system as much as possible, using a wide variety of sometimes controversial strategies (Enns, 1997; Foley, 1989). Techniques such as paradoxical instructions, family sculptures, genograms, family trees and family mapping, tracking patterns, structured exercises, anchoring, skills training, political analysis, social or political action, spirituality, drama, music, poetry, movement, and art are used to help clients locate themselves in and subsequently challenge their relevant systems (e.g., Bowen, 1978; Enns, 1997; Haley, 1976; Ivey et al., 1997; Napier & Whitaker, 1978; Satir, 1983).

Possibilities

Asserting that context is critically important in the lives and functioning of LGB people is to state the obvious. It often is noted that LGB people make up one of the few groups in society that it is still acceptable (or even fashionable) to oppress; rampant homophobia and heterosexism create a context for LGB development that is nothing short of lethal (Fassinger, 1991; Herek, 1991, 1998). In such a context, a systems–cultural analysis of individual struggles is imperative for avoiding self-blame or the pathologizing of those who are victimized by existing systems. For example, to recognize that virulent homophobia in one's immediate environment is linked to extreme personal anxiety and fear can help a client channel internal negative affect into externally directed anger and proactive attempts to change the environment (i.e., political activism). Moreover, for LGB people who are members of racial, ethnic, or cultural groups that also are stigmatized, an analysis of the effects of multiple oppressions on individual behavior is critical to healthy development and functioning; such analysis also can help these clients sort out their locations in and commitments to the various cultural (including LGB) communities in which they might take part.

In addition, systems–cultural approaches can be useful in couples, family, and group work with LGB clients. Difficulties in parenting, communication issues, conflict in couples, sibling rivalry and aggression, and other common family problems are best viewed in the context of the expectations, motivations, and resistances inherent in individual family systems, as well as in the larger cultural presses and demands that engulf particular families. For example, in a newly constituted family of two Latina lesbians and their children, the women may struggle with many of the predictable crises of parenting and stepparenting: conflicting loyalties, disciplinary differences, and stepsibling resentment. However, these women must also contend with the pressures of being lesbian parents and with their cultural and gender socialization as Latinas and the discrimination that they are likely to face as a result of their multiple identities as women, lesbians, and Latinas. One need only imagine this hypothetical family as headed by two Black men or an Asian American woman partnered with a European American woman, and the need for some kind of systems–cultural analysis becomes clear.

A feminist political analysis and feminist therapeutic approach also are critically important in working with LGB clients, both females and males. Attitudes about homosexuality and social responses to LGB individuals are so completely linked to assumptions about gender and gender role attitudes (e.g., insisting that lesbians want to be men and believing that all gay men are effeminate) that to ignore those realities does a severe disservice to LGB clients, who daily confront the consequences of those linkages. For example, the particularly vicious homophobia directed against gay men may be rooted in the myth that they want to be (like) women; because women also are victims of widespread societal oppression, gay men may be targeted for increased discrimination through their perceived association with an already-denigrated group (Herek, 1991). An analysis of gender and power, one of the cornerstones of a feminist approach to therapy (Brown, 1994; Enns, 1993, 1997), will serve LGB clients well in helping them to identify and adopt healthy personal attitudes and behavioral responses that are independent of societal proscriptions regarding "appropriate" sex-linked characteristics.

Another cornerstone of feminist therapy that is likely to be effective in work with LGB clients is the emphasis on shared power in the therapeutic relationship (Brown, 1994; Enns, 1997). LGB people, whether male or female, share a common experience of disempowerment, invisibility, and marginalization. Therapeutic relationships in which the therapist holds most of the control simply serve to reinforce the feelings of powerlessness with which LGB individuals struggle daily. Feminist approaches minimize power differences as much as possible, using strategies such as mutually determined goals, open discussions about diagnosis, appropriate self-disclosure by the therapist, mutually determined logistics (e.g., fees, session duration, payment methods), contact outside the therapy hour, and a level of openness and mutuality in the therapeutic relationship that is unparalleled in other approaches (Brown, 1994, Enns, 1997). Certainly for all women, but also for gay and bisexual men, a therapeutic relationship in which one feels powerful can have a significant positive impact on one's feelings of empowerment in the society at large. Feminist approaches to therapy can provide a supportive atmosphere in which all clients can experience themselves moving from the margins to the center of human encounters.

Newly emerging frameworks of multicultural counseling and therapy (Ponterotto et al., 1995; Sue et al. 1996; Sue & Sue, 1990) claim similar strategies for promoting client welfare, particularly for clients in historically oppressed racial or ethnic groups. Political analysis and action, personal empowerment, cultural awareness and sensitivity, and intervention logistics that move beyond the 50-minute office visit are central aspects of multicultural approaches (Ivey et al., 1997). A growing literature on the particular issues faced by LGB people of color (e.g., Greene, 1997) suggests a critical need for attention to ethnic and cultural contexts, and therapeutic approaches that specifically address these issues are imperative for effective work with diverse LGB clients (see Fukuyama & Ferguson, chapter 4, this volume, for a more extensive discussion).

Pitfalls

Injudicious use of systems—cultural approaches can result in problems for both therapists and clients. For some clients, families are not of immediate importance, and excessive focus on the family may obscure more pressing problems. Likewise, premature, excessive, or inappropriate political analysis of societal sexism, racism, heterosexism, and homophobia may be experienced as the therapist "getting up on a soapbox" rather than addressing the real needs of clients, who may be more interested in figuring out how to ask someone out or deciding to come out to their parents during the next holiday dinner. Moreover, levels of development vis-à-vis other identities salient to clients (e.g., racial or ethnic identity, feminist or womanist identity) are likely to be strong determinants of whether clients are developmentally ready to explore the sociopolitical implications of being lesbian, gay, or bisexual as well as the intersection of multiple oppressions they may face.

Another limitation of systems–cultural approaches to therapy is that clients from some cultural groups may be reluctant to talk about family or reticent about exploring interpersonal dynamics, out of a belief that it is dishonorable or rude to do so. Approaches that emphasize disclosure and challenging of family patterns can be insensitive to the elevated and irreproachable position in which family is held in some cultures (Corey, 1996; Ivey et al., 1997; Sue & Sue, 1990). In addition, therapists who attempt to use only systems approaches to intervention may encounter resistance on the part of many clients, who, regardless of cultural background, are likely to present with a variety of clinical issues; some of these may indeed be family and culturally related, but some will be personally and intrapsychically oriented and therefore inappropriate for an exclusively systemic analysis. Fortunately, the cultural sensitivity inherent in several of the systems–cultural approaches may prevent therapists from straying too far from the client's own definition of problems and general frame of reference. In short, systems–cultural approaches to therapy and intervention, if used with care, can add a dimension of contextual analysis that is particularly effective in addressing the oppression faced by LGB clients.

IMPLICATIONS FOR RESEARCH

It should be clear from the foregoing discussion that all therapeutic approaches have something useful to offer in clinical work with LGB clients. Whether the therapeutic focus is on feelings, cognition, behavior, family history, interpersonal relationships, identity, early experiences, socialization, or culture, each approach can provide the therapist with important tools to help the LGB client improve functioning and grow as an individual. Moreover, all of the approaches offer perspectives and techniques that can provide specific guidance for particular issues and problems.

Unfortunately, however, there is little empirical research to date—process or outcome—in which the effectiveness of various conceptual or strategic approaches to therapy with LGB clients has been explored. Much of the literature on counseling and therapy with LGB clients remains issue oriented and anecdotal, and there is little or no empirical support for much of what is becoming common practice in treating these populations. For example, providing LGB clients with reading material is an oft-used strategy for dispelling internalized myths, stereotypes, and homophobia; however, no one has published a study to determine what effect this practice has on the targeted attitudes. Similarly, no researchers to date have investigated the therapeutic efficacy of referral to LGB support groups (another common practice) over and above the effect of individual therapy alone. Linking either of these strategies to a theoretical framework and investigating it in the context of that theory would be an empirical leap that seems almost unthinkable given the current state of the literature.

Indeed, a listing of the kinds of research sorely needed would occupy many pages of this chapter. Suffice it to say that almost nothing is known empirically about the effectiveness of theoretical approaches for LGB clients beyond the general literature on therapy process, outcome, and efficacy. Much of what has been written here is speculation, therefore, and begs for formal investigation: quantitative research, qualitative study, program evaluation. In addition to studies of specific theoretical applications or theory-linked therapeutic techniques, pantheoretical research also is needed, so that the important work of integrating various approaches to therapy with LGB clients can begin. Theoretical convergence in psychotherapy is thought by many to represent the cutting edge of clinical practice and research, and it is predicted that mental health professionals increasingly will describe their primary therapeutic orientation as integrative or eclectic (Arkowitz, 1992; Corey, 1996; Ivey et al., 1997; Norcross, 1986b; Norcross & Goldfried, 1992); therefore, these perspectives are explored briefly in the following section.

THEORETICAL INTEGRATION

Referred to variously as *conceptual integration, functional eclecticism, theoretical assimilation, systematic eclecticism, theoretical convergence, technical eclecticism,* and *psychotherapy integration* (Arkowitz, 1992; Corey, 1996; Garfield, 1986; Lambert, 1986, 1992; Norcross, 1986a, 1986b; Norcross & Goldfried, 1992), theoretical integration is the attempt to "look beyond the confines of single-school approaches in order to see what can be learned from other perspectives. It is characterized by an openness to various ways of integrating diverse theories and techniques" (Arkowitz, 1992, p. 262). The core integrationist assumption is that despite the myriad possibilities of existing theories, no single approach is appropriate for all client issues and problems, and every approach falls short in some area. Theories may be lacking, for example, in explaining client history and dynamics, providing for adequate consideration of the therapeutic relationship, offering specific techniques or strategies to promote client change, or incorporating sociopolitical and cultural variables in explaining client problems.

Although calls for integration and eclecticism have a relatively long history in the psychotherapy literature, it has been only during the last 2 decades that vigorous, sustained attention has been evident (Arkowitz, 1992). There are a number of factors contributing to this upsurge in interest. Probably the most profound change has been the vast improvement in the quality of outcome research, particularly the use of meta-analytic procedures for handling widely disparate data sources (Arkowitz, 1992; Lambert, 1992). Outcome research consistently has revealed that therapy is effective but that there is little difference in efficacy among theoretical orientations, thus dissipating the need for rival claims of universal appropriateness and opening the door for greater rapprochement among the various therapeutic approaches (Arkowitz, 1992; Lambert, 1986, 1992). Other influential factors in the development of integrated models include (a) an increase in the number of different therapies being practiced (current estimates of the number of distinct models range from 250 to 400); (b) more detailed and operational descriptions of therapeutic strategies and techniques; (c) greater attention to short-term treatments; (d) increasing specialization in particular client problems and a concomitant expansion of interaction among professionals with different theoretical orientations working together on common disorders; (e) the development of professional networks related to psychotherapy integration (e.g., journals, societies); and (f) the rise of therapies that deliberately incorporate elements from several theoretical orientations, for example, cognitive–behavioral approaches and mulitmodal therapy (Arkowitz, 1992).

The major impediment to developing useful integrated approaches seems to be disagreement over the level and kind of integration being sought. Arkowitz (1992) presented three distinct categories of therapeutic integration: (a) theoretical integration, in which two or more therapies are conceptually and strategically melded into a new whole that is thought to be better than the individual theories alone; (b) a common factors approach, in which therapeutic change elements shared across different theories are identified; and (c) technical eclecticism, an actuarial approach that focuses on selecting the best treatment for a particular client and problem based on data from similar cases. Whereas the first two approaches are theory driven (one focusing on differences and the other on similarities), the third is empirically derived; moreover, all three rely on different assumptions regarding the appropriate target of integrative efforts as well as what data should be used in support of those efforts. Indeed, Arkowitz (1992) noted that the primary contribution of the literature on therapy integration has been in desegregating the field of psychotherapy; existing approaches to integration are merely frameworks rather than formal theories at present, and much research is needed in operationalizing and testing. the emerging conceptualizations of integrative or eclectic practice.

It should be noted that all of the existing attempts at integration emphasize thoughtful, systematic, coherent articulations of theoretical and technical amalgamation; they are not haphazard, grab-bag approaches that stem from hasty grasps at anything that will work with a particular client at a given moment. Integrative, or eclectic, practice as presented here implies a deliberate, organized effort to combine elements of existing approaches that are internally harmonious as well as compatible with the therapist's own style and values. Radical behaviorism and traditional psychoanalysis, for example, represent points of view that probably are fundamentally irreconcilable, and a therapist who strongly endorses one would be unlikely to find anything useful in the other. However, a flexible, open-minded therapist may well find comfortable partnerships between some cognitive–behavioral and psychodynamic theories; for example, a therapist might use an insight-oriented, interpretive psychodynamic approach to help a lesbian client become aware of distorted attachment patterns she has developed that keep her excessively anxious and self-denying in romantic relationships and then use cognitive restructuring techniques to aid her in overcoming the habituated thinking related to those distortions (e.g., the belief that her only protection from abandonment is to focus on unremitting gratification of her partner's needs).

Similarly, a combination of approaches might be used for a married gay or bisexual male client who wants to disclose and act on his same-sex attractions but fears that such disclosure will shame his family and result in his being ostracized from his community. A warm, empathic, client-centered approach can form a critical foundation for this client in helping him to integrate and value his same-sex needs and desires, and behavioral strategies focused on managing his fear and anxiety, as well as replacing myths about gays and bisexuals with accurate information, can prepare him for the eventuality of coming out. Moreover, for this client, as well as for the lesbian client described previously, feminist and multicultural systems approaches are likely to be necessary in the course of therapy to deconstruct societal and cultural messages about "appropriate" roles and behavior. Couples or family therapy also may be useful for working through the interpersonal difficulties these clients are likely to face.

CONCLUSION

An integrative, or eclectic, approach to psychotherapy offers much promise in addressing the myriad issues that LGB clients bring to the therapy process. Indeed, some level of integration of both theories and techniques is essential in working effectively with LGB clients, whose unique societal location and needs require skilled use of all the therapeutic gifts therapists have to offer.

REFERENCES

Ackerman, N. (1966). *Treating the troubled family*. New York: Basic Books.

Ansbacher, H. L., & Ansbacher, R. R. (Eds.). (1964). *The individual psychology of Alfred Adler*. New York: Harper & Row.

Arkowitz, H. (1992). Integrative theories of therapy. In D. K. Freedheim (Ed.), *History of psychotherapy: A century of change* (pp. 261–303). Washington, DC: American Psychological Association.

Arlow, J. A. (1989). Psychoanalysis. In R. J. Corsini & D. Wedding (Eds.), *Current psychotherapies* (4th ed., pp. 19–64). Itasca, IL: Peacock.

Bandura, A. (1982). Self-efficacy mechanisms in human agency. *American Psychologist, 37*, 122–147.

Beck, A. T. (1976). *Cognitive therapy and emotional disorders*. New York: International Universities Press.

Beck, A. T., & Weishaar, M. E. (1989). Cognitive therapy. In R. J. Corsini & D. Wedding (Eds.), *Current psychotherapies* (4th ed., pp. 285–320). Itasca, IL: Peacock.

Berne, E. (1964). *Games people play*. New York: Grove Press.

Beutler, L. E. (1983). *Eclectic psychotherapy: A systematic approach*. New York: Pergamon Press.

Bowen, M. (1978). *Family therapy in clinical practice*. New York: Jason Aronson.

Bowlby, J. (1969). *Attachment and loss* (Vol. 1). New York: Basic Books.

Brown, L. S. (1994). *Subversive dialogues: Theory in feminist therapy*. New York: Basic Books.

Corey, G. (1996). *Theory and practice of counseling and psychotherapy* (5th ed.). Pacific Grove, CA: Brooks–Cole.

Dobson, K. S. (1988). *Handbook of cognitive–behavior therapies*. New York: Guilford Press.

Eagle, M. N., & Wolitzky, D. L. (1992). Psychoanalytic theories of psychotherapy. In D. K. Freedheim (Ed.), *History of psychotherapy: A century of change* (pp. 109–158). Washington, DC: American Psychological Association.

Ellis, A. (1976). *Humanistic psychotherapy: The rational–emotive approach*. New York: Julian Press.

Ellis, A. (1989). Rational–emotive therapy. In R. J. Corsini & D. Wedding (Eds.), *Current psychotherapies* (4th ed., pp. 197–240). Itasca, IL: Peacock.

Ellis, A., & Whiteley, J. (Eds.). (1979). *Theoretical and empirical foundations of rational–emotive therapy*. Pacific Grove, CA: Brooks/Cole.

Enns, C. Z. (1993). Twenty years of feminist counseling and therapy. *The Counseling Psychologist, 21*, 3–87.

Enns, C. Z. (1997). *Feminist theories and feminist psychotherapies: Origins, themes, and variations*. New York: Harrington Park Press.

Erickson, E. H. (1963). *Childhood and society* (2nd ed.). New York: Norton.

Erickson, E. H. (1968). *Identity: Youth and crisis*. New York: Norton.

Erickson, E. H. (1982). *The life cycle completed*. New York: Norton.

Fairbairn, W. R. D. (1952). *Psychoanalytic studies of the personality*. London: Tavistock Publications and Routledge & Kegan Paul.

Fassinger, R. E. (1991). The hidden minority: Issues and challenges in working with lesbian women and gay men. *The Counseling Psychologist, 19,* 157–176.

Fishman, D. B., & Franks, C. M. (1992). Evolution and differentiation within behavior therapy: A theoretical and epistemological review. In D. K. Freedheim (Ed.), *History of psychotherapy: A century of change* (pp. 159–196). Washington, DC: American Psychological Association.

Foley, V. D. (1989). Family therapy. In R. J. Corsini & D. Wedding (Eds.), *Current psychotherapies* (4th ed., pp. 455–502). Itasca, IL: Peacock.

Freeman, A., & Dattilio, F. M. (1992). *Comprehensive casebook of cognitive therapy.* New York: Plenum Press.

Freud, S. (1949). *An outline of psychoanalysis*. New York: Norton.

Garfield, S. L. (1986). An eclectic psychotherapy. In J. C. Norcross (Ed.), *Handbook of eclectic psychotherapy* (pp. 132–162). New York: Brunner/Mazel.

Glasser, N. (1980). *What are you doing? How people are helped by reality therapy.* New York: Harper & Row.

Glasser, W. (1985). *Control theory: A new explanation of how we control our lives.* New York: Harper & Row.

Goldman, G. D., & Milman, D. S. (1978). *Psychoanalytic psychotherapy*. Reading, MA: Addison-Wesley.

Gonsiorek, J. C. (1995). Gay male identities: Concepts and issues. In A. R. D'Augelli & C. J. Patterson (Eds.), *Lesbian, gay, and bisexual identities over the lifespan: Psychological perspectives* (pp. 24–47). New York: Oxford University Press.

Greene, B. (Ed.). (1997). *Ethnic and cultural diversity among lesbians and gay men.* Thousand Oaks, CA: Sage.

Guerin, P. J., & Chabot, D. R. (1992). Development of family systems theory. In D. K. Freedheim (Ed.), *History of psychotherapy: A century of change* (pp. 225–260). Washington, DC: American Psychological Association.

Haley, J. (1976). *Problem-solving therapy: New strategies for effective family therapy.* San Francisco: Jossey-Bass.

Herek, G. M. (1991). Stigma, prejudice, and violence against lesbians and gay men. In J. C. Gonsiorek & J. D. Weinrich (Eds.), *Homosexuality: Research implications for public policy* (pp. 60–80). Newbury Park, CA: Sage.

Herek, G. M. (Ed.). (1998). *Stigma and sexual orientation: Understanding prejudice against lesbians, gay men, and bisexuals*. Thousand Oaks, CA: Sage.

Horne, A. M., & Passmore, J. L. (1991). *Family counseling and therapy* (2nd ed.). Itasca, IL: Peacock.

Hothersall, D. (1995). *History of psychology* (3rd ed.). New York: McGraw-Hill.

Ivey, A. E., Ivey, M. B., & Simek-Morgan, L. (1997). *Counseling and psychotherapy: A multicultural perspective* (4th ed.). Boston: Allyn & Bacon.

Jung, C. G. (1961). *Memories, dreams, reflections.* New York: Vintage Books.

Kazdin, A. E. (1994). *Behavior modification in applied settings* (5th ed.). Pacific Grove, CA: Brooks/Cole.

Klein, M. (1975). *The psycho-analysis of children.* New York: Dell.

Kohut, H. (1971). *The analysis of the self.* New York: International Universities Press.

Kohut, H. (1977). *The restoration of the self.* New York: International Universities Press.

Kohut, H. (1984). *How does psychoanalysis cure?* Chicago: University of Chicago Press.

Lambert, M. J. (1986). Implications of psychotherapy outcome research for eclectic psychotherapy. In J. C. Norcross (Ed.), *Handbook of eclectic psychotherapy* (pp. 436–462). New York: Brunner/Mazel.

Lambert, M. J. (1992). Psychotherapy outcome research: Implications for integrative and eclectic therapists. In J. C. Norcross & M. R. Goldfried (Eds.), *Handbook of psychotherapy integration* (pp. 94–129). New York: Basic Books.

Lazarus, A. A. (1989). *The practice of multimodal therapy.* Baltimore: Johns Hopkins University Press.

Madanes, C. (1981). *Strategic family therapy.* San Francisco: Jossey-Bass.

Mahler, M. S. (1968). *On human symbiosis or the vicissitudes of individuation.* New York: International Universities Press.

Masterson, J. F. (1985). *The real self: A developmental, self, and object relations approach.* New York: Brunner/Mazel.

May, R. (Ed.). (1961). *Existential psychology.* New York: Random House.

May, R., & Yalom, I. (1989). Existential psychotherapy. In R. J. Corsini & D. Wedding (Eds.), *Current psychotherapies* (4th ed., pp. 363–404). Itasca, IL: Peacock.

Meichenbaum, D. (1977). *Cognitive behavior modification: An integrative approach.* New York: Plenum Press.

Meichenbaum, D. (1985). *Stress inoculation training.* New York: Pergamon Press.

Minuchin, S. (1974). *Families and family therapy.* Cambridge, MA: Harvard University Press.

Mosak, H. H. (1989). Adlerian psychotherapy. In R. J. Corsini & D. Wedding (Eds.), *Current psychotherapies* (4th ed., pp. 65–118). Itasca, IL: Peacock.

Napier, A. Y., & Whitaker, C. A. (1978). *The family crucible.* New York: Harper & Row.

Norcross, J. C. (1986a). Eclectic psychotherapy: An introduction and overview. In J. C. Norcross (Ed.), *Handbook of eclectic psychotherapy* (pp. 3–24). New York: Brunner/Mazel.

Norcross, J. C. (Ed.). (1986b). *Handbook of eclectic psychotherapy*. New York: Brunner/Mazel.

Norcross, J. C., & Goldfried, M. R. (Eds.). (1992). *Handbook of psychotherapy integration*. New York: Basic Books.

Passons, W. R. (1975). *Gestalt approaches in counseling*. New York: Holt, Rinehart & Winston.

Paul, G. L. (1969). Behavior modification research: Design and tactics. In C. M. Franks (Ed.), *Behavior therapy: Appraisal and status* (pp. 29–62). New York: McGraw-Hill.

Perls, F. (1973). *The Gestalt approach and eye witness to therapy*. New York: Bantam Books.

Polster, E., & Polster, M. (1973). *Gestalt therapy integrated*. New York: Brunner/Mazel.

Ponterotto, J. G., Casas, J. M., Suzuki, L. A., & Alexander, C. M. (Eds.). (1995). *Handbook of multicultural counseling*. Thousand Oaks, CA: Sage.

Raskin, N. J., & Rogers, C. R. (1989). Person-centered therapy. In R. J. Corsini & D. Wedding (Eds.), *Current psychotherapies* (4th ed., pp. 155–196). Itasca, IL: Peacock.

Rice, L. N., & Greenberg, L. S. (1992). Humanistic approaches to psychotherapy. In D. K. Freedheim (Ed.), *History of psychotherapy: A century of change* (pp. 197–224). Washington, DC: American Psychological Association.

Rogers, C. R. (1951). *Client-centered therapy*. Boston: Houghton Mifflin.

Rogers, C. R. (1957). The necessary and sufficient conditions of therapeutic personality change. *Journal of Consulting Psychology, 21*, 95–103.

Rogers, C. R. (1958). A process conception of psychotherapy. *American Psychologist, 13*, 142–149.

Rogers, C. R. (1961). *On becoming a person*. Boston: Houghton Mifflin.

Satir, V. (1983). *Conjoint family therapy* (3rd ed.). Palo Alto, CA: Science and Behavior Books.

St. Clair, M. (1986). *Objects relations and self psychology*. Pacific Grove, CA: Brooks/Cole.

Sue, D. W., Ivey, A., & Pederson, P. (1996). *A theory of multicultural counseling and therapy*. Pacific Grove, CA: Brooks/Cole.

Sue, D. W., & Sue, D. (1990). *Counseling the culturally different* (2nd ed.). New York: Wiley.

Thoreson, C. E. (Ed.). (1980). *The behavior therapist*. Pacific Grove, CA: Brooks/Cole.

Wessler, R. A., & Wessler, R. L. (1980). *The principles and practice of rational–emotive therapy*. San Francisco: Jossey-Bass.

Wilson, G. T. (1989). Behavior therapy. In R. J. Corsini & D. Wedding (Eds.), *Current psychotherapies* (4th ed., pp. 241–284). Itasca, IL: Peacock.

Winnicott, L. R. (1987). *The maturational process and the facilitating environment*. New York: International Universities Press.

Wolpe, J. (1990). *The practice of behavior therapy* (4th ed.). Elmsford, NY: Pergamon Press.

Yalom, I. D. (1981). *Existential psychotherapy*. New York: Basic Books.

Yontef, G. M., & Simkin, J. S. (1989). Gestalt therapy. In R. J. Corsini & D. Wedding (Eds.), *Current psychotherapies* (4th ed., pp. 323–362). Itasca, IL: Peacock.

II

COUNSELING AND THERAPY

Theory and research need to be integrated within clinical practice. In addition, counseling and therapy need to inform continuing research and exploration of the therapeutic process. The focus of this part of the book is on the competent, informed, and ethical practice of counseling and psychotherapy with lesbian, gay, and bisexual (LGB) persons based on an integration of current research and theory.

In chapter 6, Susan L. Morrow addresses ethical concerns in therapy with LGB clients. Issues specific to creating an LGB-affirming therapeutic environment and a productive working alliance are outlined and discussed.

In chapter 7, Sari H. Dworkin explores the salient issues that frequently occur in individual therapy with lesbian, gay, and bisexual clients, including the process of self-identifying as LGB, the hardships of dealing simultaneously with homophobia and sexism, and the interaction of socialized gender roles and self-identification.

Kurt A. DeBord and Ruperto M. Perez explore the theory and practice of group counseling with LGB clients in chapter 8. The authors examine and present some of the primary theoretical and practical issues in developing and offering group counseling for LGB persons. The basic tenets of group counseling theory and their application to LGB groups are discussed, along with an exploration and discussion of group format and counselor–therapist considerations.

Chapter 9 is devoted to the influential factors that face older lesbian, gay, and bisexual individuals in therapy. Augustine Barón and David W. Cramer investigate the impact of age on the presenting concerns of LGB individuals and on the counseling process. Case studies feature some of the important areas in counseling, including life transition issues and issues of ageism.

Issues involved in counseling and therapy with adolescents are addressed in chapter 10, authored by Scott L. Hershberger and Anthony R. D'Augelli. A number of important facts and developmental considerations are discussed as they apply to psychotherapy with LGB youth. Given the at-risk nature of LGB adolescents, this chapter is a significant one for professionals involved with this population.

Lesbian, gay, and bisexual family issues are examined in chapter 11, by Connie R. Matthews and Suzanne H. Lease. The authors address the therapeutic situations and opportunities that arise from coming out to one's family, whether it be family of origin or family of choice. The therapist's role in this process also is discussed, along with family counseling and parenting issues for LGB clients.

Finally, in chapter 12, Shelly M. Ossana examines the nature of relationship and couples therapy with LGB clients. The author focuses on issues that emerge in the dating and committed relationships of LGB persons. The effects of gender role socialization as it relates to LGB relationships are examined, and case studies are presented to illustrate and highlight the theory and practice of relationship and couples counseling.

The chapters within this section serve to provide psychologists and counselors with clinical information that is crucial to therapy with lesbian, gay, and bisexual clients. Moreover, the essential strength of this section is in the integration of research and practice, resulting in information that can serve as an invaluable foundation of knowledge and awareness for therapists in their work with lesbian, gay, or bisexual clients.

6

FIRST DO NO HARM: THERAPIST ISSUES IN PSYCHOTHERAPY WITH LESBIAN, GAY, AND BISEXUAL CLIENTS

SUSAN L. MORROW

The silent and passive gay or lesbian who still lives in fear, ignorance, and self-hate is not only the more common outcome of many psychotherapy processes but is a blatant and disturbing result of mistreatment by the therapist. If psychotherapy with gays and lesbians is truly successful, the outcome will be numerous individuals who no longer attempt to conform to a heterosexual world, but who will instead creatively seek the enhancement of their own identities. (McHenry & Johnson, 1993, p. 150)

How would affirmative therapy for lesbian, gay, or bisexual (LGB) clients look if its primary goal, beyond repairing the damage caused by a heterosexist and homophobic society, were the creative enhancement of the identities of LGB people? What would this creative enhancement look like? And what qualities of LGB-affirmative therapists might contribute to creative enhancement of the identities, lives, and communities of LGB individuals?

Laura Brown (1989) wrote of normative creativity as she described a lesbian–gay paradigm for psychology. Because lesbian, gay, and bisexual people fall outside the heterosexual norm, they must of necessity create themselves: their identities, their relationships, and their communities. This somewhat daunting challenge confronts therapists who work with LGB people as well. The task of LGB-affirmative therapists is to view LGB people and issues as central and self-defining as opposed to marginal and defined by a heterosexual norm—not an easy task, even for LGB therapists.

However, before imagining how this goal might be accomplished, it is useful to examine current issues within the profession that affect psychotherapy with LGB people.

PROFESSIONAL STANDARDS AND ETHICS

Medical ethics, encapsulated in the directive by Hippocrates, "Do no harm," underlie the ethics of human service and psychology professions as well. The American Psychological Association's (APA) code of ethics (APA, 1992) addresses this issue by directing psychologists to be competent to treat the populations and problems with which they work. The psychologist should be culturally competent as well, sensitive to the cultures, values, and experiences of oppression of the client (APA, 1991). Therefore, it is imperative that therapists receive formal training, supervision, and ongoing education of both a formal and informal nature, to ensure their competence to work with LGB clients. Because these clients may not come out in the early stages of therapy, referral owing to a therapist's lack of competence or homophobia is often contraindicated; the length of time required to build a trusting relationship and the abandonment and rejection that would be experienced by clients make referral in this situation a poor choice. The burden, then, falls on therapists to be informed and on the programs that prepare them for practice to address biases that may negatively affect the therapeutic relationship as well as the process and outcome of psychotherapy.

In 1986, The Committee on Lesbian and Gay Concerns, the Board of Social and Ethical Responsibility in Psychology, and the Board of Professional Affairs of the American Psychological Association formed the Task Force on Bias in Psychotherapy With Lesbians and Gay Men, to provide an empirical base for developing guidelines for ethical practice. Garnets, Hancock, Cochran, Goodchilds, and Peplau (1991) reported the findings of the task force in terms both of biased, inadequate, or inappropriate practice and of exemplary practice in the following areas: assessment, intervention, identity, relationships, family, and therapist expertise and education. Despite the removal of sexual orientation per se from its lists of mental disorders in 1975 by APA (Garnets et al., 1991), large numbers of therapists still operate with the belief that LGB people are pathological, disordered, or at least deviant. Because of lack of exposure to information and to lesbian and gay people themselves, therapists do not have sufficient knowledge or contact to counter these prejudices. Furthermore, religious biases, societal norms, gender restrictions, and fears surrounding sexuality combine with ignorance to produce homophobia, heterosexism, stigmatization, prejudice, and discrimination against LGB women and men. Therapists are strongly affected by these views, despite the official stance of professional psychological and mental health organizations.

Several factors contribute to the development of homonegative attitudes on the part of therapists. In this chapter, I use the terms *homonegative, homonegativity,* and *homonegativism* (as well as *binegative, binegativity,* and *binegativism*) in place of the more common term *homophobia*. Although *homophobia* has come to encompass a broad range of reactions to LGB people, the root *phobia* implies that discrimination against LGB people is grounded in fear rather than religious and moral chauvinism, misogyny, or any of a host of other negative attitudes. In addition, *homophobia* implies a psychological disorder, thereby failing to hold homonegative individuals and society responsible for the oppression of LGB people (see Kitzinger, 1987, for an in-depth critique of the operational definition of *homophobia*). *Homonegativity* may be defined as negative cognitions and affect about LGB people or orientations (Hudson & Ricketts, 1980).

The implications of homonegativity and heterosexism for psychotherapists are many. The therapist cannot avoid being influenced by societal and professional beliefs and biases concerning LGB people. Because of lack of knowledge about LGB cultures and lifestyles, the therapist may not be aware of unique issues confronting the client, such as identity; the impact of gender stereotyping on early development; specific career-related concerns including job discrimination and harassment; relationship patterns of lesbians and gays; family, parenting, and custody issues; the impact of feminism on lesbian and bisexual women; and different cultural norms for lesbians and gay men (Arizona Psychological Association Executive Council, 1991; Buhrke & Douce, 1991; McHenry & Johnson, 1993). Furthermore, because there is a paucity of information in formal training programs, most therapists are not aware of homonegative and heterosexist bias inherent in many personality theories, therapy approaches, and assessment and diagnostic techniques (Buhrke & Douce, 1991; McHenry & Johnson, 1993; also see Fassinger, chapter 5, this volume). Perhaps most important, therapists may be afraid of or in denial about their own same-sex feelings or feelings toward LGB sexual orientations.

Because of both lack of training and biases, therapists may project their homonegativism onto their clients, thus avoiding certain topics essential to client growth and healing or attributing all of the LGB client's problems to sexual orientation. The therapist may assume that all clients are heterosexual unless proven otherwise or depend on the LGB client to provide education for the therapist. Finally, the therapist may inadvertently discourage the development of a positive LGB identity, bring a client out to others, or make abrupt or inappropriate referrals (Buhrke & Douce, 1991; McHenry & Johnson, 1993). In these cases the client, already suffering from internalized homonegative attitudes and self-hatred, may be further harmed. Even LGB therapists may suffer from internalized homonegativism, lack of awareness of expressions of LGB lifestyles, gender bias, and selective perceptions and cognitive distortions arising from their own life experiences. These issues may in turn negatively affect their work with LGB clients.

Many of these concerns have important implications for therapist education and supervision. Recommendations for training are articulated in depth elsewhere (see Phillips, chapter 14, this volume). The remainder of this chapter identifies background and personal factors that influence therapists who work with LGB clients, discusses therapist orientation to psychotherapy and sociocultural analysis in psychotherapy, and elucidates issues of ethics and boundaries in psychotherapy with LGB clients.

BACKGROUND AND PERSONAL FACTORS INFLUENCING THERAPY

Therapist background and personal factors that may affect the therapeutic relationship include gender, sexual orientation, age and cohort, race or ethnicity, socioeconomic class, and religion, as well as many other variables that arise in a sociocultural context. In addition, the therapist may be affected by attitudes of family members about LGB people; childhood sexual experiences (both traumatic and consensual); type and frequency of exposure to LGB friends, family members, and acquaintances; and a plethora of other life experiences that contribute to the formation of attitudes and values. Herek (1984) identified the sources of homonegative attitudes: experiential, defensive, and symbolic. Sources of *experiential* attitudes include the individual's personal past experiences with LGB people (as well as vicarious experiences through family members and other influential people); *defensive* attitudes arise from individuals' own anxieties or conflicts regarding their sexual orientation; and *symbolic* attitudes are based on ideology and societal norms. A few of these background and personal factors are identified in the following sections, specifically, gender and sexual orientation (as illustrations of Herek's, 1984, experiential sources), defensive sources of homonegativity and binegativity, and religious ideology (symbolic sources).

Gender

Gender appears to be an important variable in attitudes toward LGB people, with women typically found to be less homonegative than men and attitudes toward gay and bisexual men more homonegative than those toward lesbian and bisexual women. For example, women trainees in one investigation were found to be less homonegative than their male counterparts (Gilliland & Crisp, 1995). Therefore, a closer examination of the personal and sociopolitical influences that contribute to higher levels of homonegativity in male therapists (and men in general) may contribute to greater understanding and change. The outcome of a culture that privileges and values men and masculinity is misogyny, the hatred of women and the feminine. Societal stereotypes of LGB people depict lesbians as hypermasculine and gay men as effeminate (Herek, 1993). Bisexual women and men have also been included under these rubrics; however, it is my observation that binegativity has different roots, addressed later in the chapter, that are at play and that bisexual people do not so much transgress gender as they raise the specter of fluidity of sexual identity. Given societal misogyny, the masculine woman is respected whereas the effeminate man is devalued; the man becomes "womanized" in the eyes of others as soon as he comes out, despite his actual gendered characteristics. This phenomenon begins as early as childhood, when the "tomboy" (according to cultural lore, the prelesbian girl) is treated with respect and chosen to be on playground teams, whereas the "sissy" (supposedly the pregay boy) is subject to ridicule and even violence (Morrow, Gore, & Campbell, 1996). It should be noted that nongay boys who are not sufficiently masculine also experience monejgative reactions, often being called "faggot" and taunted for not adhering to gender norms; therefore, antigay oppression affects those who violate gender norms regardless of their sexual orientation.

Herek (1993) and others have noted that heterosexism, which in its extremity takes the form of hate crimes against LGB people, is rooted in gender norms. Therefore, therapists whose gender role orientations are particularly rigid may find themselves uncomfortable and make incorrect assessments of LGB people who do not fit societal gender norms (Hancock, 1995). A lesbian client who wears her usual comfortable garb, without makeup and with a wash-'n'-go haircut, may be inaccurately assessed as depressed because she does not fit the gender stereotype of a heterosexual woman who wants to be attractive to men. Bisexual clients who are part of LGB culture may reflect gender transgressions and be viewed by the therapist as ambivalent about their gender. The therapist may diagnose a flamboyant gay man as narcissistic when the client is simply reflecting and even celebrating his culture. The foregoing descriptors are by no means generalizable to all or even the majority of LGB people; however, these cultural stereotypes about LGB people both within and outside LGB communities are, like many stereotypes, grounded in reality. Therapists' assessments must be grounded in a thorough understanding of the impact of gender on themselves and their clients, as well as informed by a thorough understanding of LGB cultures and diversities, in order to provide ethical service.

Sexual Orientation

The therapist's sexual orientation, whether the same as, similar to, or different from that of the client, has important implications for therapy. When therapists are "insiders" to the population, they may assume similarities between themselves and clients that are unwarranted. As an "outsider," the therapist may overemphasize either similarity or difference. Numerous distortions may occur as a consequence of therapists' unexamined assumptions about clients who are "other." Examples of these assumptions, distortions, and consequences follow, with a focus on both heterosexual and LGB counselors. Many of these issues are a consequence of lack of information on the part of heterosexual therapists about LGB issues, identified by Hancock (1995) as a pivotal concern in relation to LGB clients.

At the start of a therapy relationship, issues of therapist disclosure of sexual orientation may have a critical influence on the course of therapy and the well-being of the client. Hancock (1995) and Isay (1991) both urged even analytically oriented therapists to be aware that nondisclosure conveys important messages to the client. By not disclosing, the therapist collaborates with the larger culture in perpetuating a norm of secrecy and may inadvertently encourage the client to remain in the closet. The therapist must be sufficiently comfortable with her or his own sexual orientation that disclosure is not fraught with ambivalence, and therapists struggling with their own sexual orientation (even unexamined heterosexuality) should not attempt to work with clients who are also in struggle (Gonsiorek, 1989).

A second distortion may occur when heterosexual women therapists, particularly those who have become discouraged in their own lives about establishing egalitarian relationships with men, idealize lesbian lifestyles and relationships. Although it is often the case that lesbian relationships have a baseline of gender equality, power struggles may arise on the basis of race or ethnicity, class, age, or any of a number of other variables. Therapists' idealization of lesbian relationships may influence clients to avoid discussing difficult relationship issues related to inequality and power, particularly if clients feel they must live up to their therapists' fantasies of lesbian relationships. The aware therapist, on the other hand, will be able to name power dynamics as they arise, facilitating open discussion between the partners.

A third distortion may occur when heterosexual therapists assume that the relationship concerns of lesbian, gay, or bisexual couples are overly similar to or, conversely, very different from their own. By minimizing the differences between heterosexual and LGB relationships, the therapist runs the risk of imposing heterosexual standards on clients' relationships. Many "out" lesbian clients report a preference for lesbian, or at least female, therapists (Falco, 1991), and a feminist perspective has been identified as essential in working with this population (Riddle & Sang, 1978). The therapist's awareness of and comfort with alternative value systems such as consensual nonmonogamy, intentional equality, and nontraditional family forms and norms are essential to conducting effective relationship counseling.

Although many trainers, myself included, tend to assume that the audience is heterosexual when training students and therapists about LGB issues, it bears repeating that being a lesbian, gay, or bisexual therapist does not guarantee that one will conduct LGB-affirmative psychotherapy. Internalized heterosexism and homonegativity affect LGB therapists also. The question for LGB therapists is not Am I homophobic or homonegative? but How am I homonegative, and how might that affect my work with heterosexual as well as LGB clients?

Another common assumption is that simply being a good lesbian, gay, or bisexual therapist enables one to work effectively with the full range of LGB people and issues. This is simply not the case. A lesbian therapist who works almost exclusively with women may be out of her element and area of expertise working with a gay or bisexual man. There is no reason to expect a gay man to be less sexist or misogynistic than his heterosexual counterpart. Many lesbian women and gay men hold antibisexual attitudes illustrated by such terms as "fence-sitter" or "only a phase." Bisexual therapists, on the other hand, may become defensive about their orientation because of being marginalized by both heterosexual and lesbian and gay communities.

A particular concern arises related to heterosexual, gay, or lesbian therapists working with bisexual clients. As mentioned earlier, I believe binegativity tends to arise not so much as a result of gender role violations but because bisexual women and men contradict current understandings about the fixedness of sexual orientation. Although constructionist and postmodern analyses indicate that there is much greater fluidity of sexual orientation identity than was believed to be true in the past, the general public, including most therapists, view sexual orientation from the essentialist position in which one's sexual orientation is a stable characteristic of the person (Bohan, 1996; also see Broido, chapter 1, this volume). Indeed, Kinnish (1998) found that sexual orientation appears to be fluid over time for many people, particularly women. However, given the rigidity with which most people view sexual orientation, it is not surprising that bisexual individuals may create discomfort by causing heterosexual, lesbian, and gay people to question the stability of their own orientation. For the heterosexual therapist, unexamined issues around sexual orientation may come into play, in addition to the introduction of potential sexual dynamics between therapist and client that were not considered possible when sexual orientation appeared less ambiguous. For lesbian and gay therapists whose own identities are fixed, additional concerns may be raised. Politically, the idea of sexual orientation fluidity may endanger the stance taken by many gays and lesbians, particularly those from religiously conservative backgrounds, that sexual orientation is unchangeable and therefore legitimate. In addition, many lesbian-identified women came out in a political environment that required them to declare themselves either lesbian or straight, regardless of their actual orientation. Many of these women, who came out during the feminist movement of the 1960s and 1970s after a lifetime of heterosexuality, experienced pressure to "prove" themselves in order to be accepted into the lesbian culture's "feminist fold" (Brown, 1995; Golden, 1987). In addition, bisexuality has been seen by many gays and lesbians as denial or as a phase through which one passes on the way to a "true" identity.

LGB people, like members of other oppressed groups, may be reluctant to acknowledge "dirty laundry" (e.g., partner violence, substance abuse) within their own lives, relationships, and communities. Heterosexual therapists, in their endeavors to be LGB-affirmative, may collude in many of the myths that are perpetuated. Same-sex relationships may be idealized as egalitarian, and therapists may be unwilling to recognize partner abuse in same-sex, particularly lesbian, relationships (Morrow & Hawxhurst, 1989). It is important to recognize that the full range of problems that occur in heterosexual relationships also exist in LGB relationships, including partner abuse, abuse of privilege and power, child abuse and faulty parenting, substance abuse, and sexual acting out. Some problems, such as child sexual abuse, appear to occur rarely in lesbian households and with no greater frequency in gay households as in those in which a heterosexual father is present (APA, 1995). Others, such as substance abuse, may in fact be exacerbated by LGB people's experiences of oppression and by subcultural norms that include socializing in bars (Ratner, 1993). Abuse in relationships may engage different power dynamics from those typically observed in heterosexual battering relationships. Determining issues of safety and appropriate interventions in these cases may be confounded when therapists are unable to depend on gender to cue them as to which member of the relationship may be the batterer. Reluctance on the part of LGB or LGB-affirmative heterosexual therapists to recognize these problems for fear of casting LGB people in a negative light can serve only to undermine the therapy process.

In any area of multicultural counseling, the LGB therapist's stage of identity development will have a strong impact on the therapy. An LGB therapist who experiences fear or shame resulting in a desire to "look straight" is likely to impose those attitudes on clients, however subtly. Therapists who have experienced negative consequences of coming out, such as losing a job or custody of children, may inadvertently transmit their fears to clients, thereby impeding the client's coming out process. Conversely, LGB therapists who are proud of their sexual orientation may express impatience with clients who are struggling to accept their lesbian, gay, or bisexual identity.

LGB-affirmative heterosexual therapists, too, may experience stages of identity development that parallel those of their LGB clients (Gelberg & Chojnacki, 1995). As allies of LGB people, heterosexual therapists may become suspect for being lesbian, gay, or bisexual themselves. Colleagues may disapprove of their advocacy for LGB clients, and affirmative therapists may struggle with whether to be open or "in the closet." Gelberg and Chojnacki described their own stages of development as heterosexual therapists from awareness through ambivalence, empowerment, activism, pride, and integration.

Defensive Sources of Homonegativity and Binegativity

Various forms of homo- and binegativity illustrate Herek's (1993) concept of defensiveness, in which therapists' biases and prejudices are grounded in their anxiety about their own sexual orientation. Professional biases based on personal defenses include attitudes that LGB orientations are inherently pathological, despite official stances taken by professional organizations (Garnets et al., 1991). Biases and prejudices may also occur in the context of gender bias, misogyny, AIDS phobia, antibisexual attitudes, and other forms of oppression and discrimination. One cannot be raised in a society that considers LGB people sick, crazy, sinful, and even evil without being affected by homonegativism. Despite more than 2 decades during which homosexuality has been "declassified" as a mental illness, large numbers of psychologists continue to view same-sex orientation as a form of psychological disorder or developmental arrest. In addition, they often attribute LGB clients' problems to sexual orientation and focus on sexual orientation as a therapeutic issue even when it is irrelevant (Garnets et al., 1991). Subtle forms of bias, such as heterosexual chauvinism in the form of believing that only heterosexual relationships and sexuality can be truly satisfying, may lead to trivializing of LGB relationships, relationship problems, or sexual difficulties. It is crucial that all therapists and therapists-in-training be challenged to confront biases that may affect their effectiveness with LGB clients. In addition, cultural variables other than sexual orientation, such as race or ethnicity, can confound therapist bias (Greene, 1997).

Self-exploration is a key component of becoming an LGB-affirmative counselor. The self-exploration process includes examination of one's own thoughts, feelings, attitudes, beliefs, and values about LGB people and issues, along with gaining an awareness of one's biases and their origins. Therapists should examine their own sexual orientation, what sexual orientation means to them in terms of identity, and how it might relate to the LGB client. At the deepest level, therapists should examine their own same-sex feelings. Finally, when one addresses the discrepancies between one's real and idealized beliefs and feelings, one is able to work through the conflicts that might prevent an empathic stance with LGB clients.

Religious Ideology

Herek (1984) also noted symbolic sources of homonegativity. Because I live and work in a religiously conservative part of the country, I have become particularly aware of the effects of religious fundamentalism on both therapists and clients. It has been my observation that religiously conservative therapists not only can harm LGB clients by attempting or recommending unsubstantiated sexual-orientation conversion therapies (see Haldeman, 1994, for an excellent discussion of the ethics of sexual-orientation conversion therapies) but also can collude in and contribute to shame and guilt perpetuated by religious and cultural ideologies that define LGB people as sinful and unworthy. To adhere to a doctrine that demeans LGB orientations and behaviors while purporting to provide un-biased therapy, or to provide conversion therapy that is based on the presumption that an LGB person is suffering from a disorder, contradicts APA's policy positions and ethical standards (see, e.g., APA, 1997; Conger, 1975; Fox, 1988). Therapists who are unable to maintain a clear distinction between their religious views and therapeutic practice should refer LGB clients to professionals who are LGB affirmative (Standard 1.04, APA, 1992, p. 1600).

Background and personal factors considered within a sociocultural context are influential in providing competent and ethical psychotherapy practice. In addition, the therapist's theoretical orientation to counseling and psychotherapy may have major implications for therapeutic outcomes with LGB clients.

THERAPIST ORIENTATION TO PSYCHOTHERAPY

Painstaking researches [sic] have revealed that classes of human beings exist whose sexual life deviates from the usual one in the most striking manner. One group among these "perverts" has, as it were, expunged the difference between the sexes from its scheme of life. . . . Such persons are called homosexuals or inverts. Often, though not always, they are men and women who otherwise have reached an irreproachably high standard of mental growth and development, intellectually and ethically, and are only afflicted with this one fateful peculiarity. (Freud, 1924, p. 313)

It will be my contention in this chapter that a fixed or exclusive homosexual in our contemporary society is wrong—meaning inefficient, self-defeating, and emotionally disturbed—but that he has an inalienable right, as a human being, to be wrong and should never be persecuted or punished for his errors. Before, however, I establish the right of the homosexual to be wrong, it will be necessary for me to demonstrate, with data stronger than mere opinion, that fixed deviants are mistaken and self-sabotaging in their behavior. (Ellis, 1965, p. 78)

What strange bedfellows are Freud and Ellis in this endeavor to theorize on the subject of homosexuality! Both go on, in their respective writings, to explain that one of the symptoms of the disorder of homosexuality is paranoia. Psychoanalytic theory underlies current perspectives (e.g., Nicolosi, 1991) that view same-sex attraction in men as a result of faulty fathering and attempt to change orientation by providing clients with "appropriate" (nonsexual) bonding experiences with men. Theories about same-sex attraction to women are considerably more complex; however, treatment steps are basically the same. Other efforts to alter sexual orientation include behavioral (including electrical aversion therapy), hormonal, pharmaceutical, and surgical methods (Murphy, 1992). All these approaches lead the informed therapist to ask the question, If same-sex orientation is not a mental disorder, why cure it?

Most therapists are interested not in changing LGB orientations, but in working effectively with clients regardless of sexual orientation. Most therapeutic orientations are not inherently homonegative; however, few address LGB issues in a social context. Historically, therapy has been viewed as apolitical or neutral. However, therapies that do not address the sociopolitical realities of people's lives run the risk of producing a "null" therapeutic environment. The null environment was identified by Freeman (1975) as an academic environment in which neither male nor female students felt supported by faculty but in which women were extraordinarily disadvantaged by this lack of support. Their disadvantage resulted from absence of other supports combined with negative societal messages. LGB clients also are likely to experience less support for their lives and relationships, combined with more negative societal messages, than are heterosexuals. Therefore, it is important that therapists address sociopolitical issues that may not ordinarily be part of their therapeutic repertoire.

The sociopolitical dimensions of LGB client concerns must be addressed regardless of the therapeutic method used by the therapist, because most LGB people live in environments that continually assault their sense of self and create distress that may not be recognized by clients as consequent to living in a homonegative culture. A multicultural feminist sociopolitical analysis can be central to effective work with LGB clients (Brown, 1994; Espín, 1994; Morrow & Hawxhurst, 1998). Such an analysis includes an understanding of the role of gender in the oppression of LGB people, particularly the misogynist underpinnings of homonegativity directed at gay men; how heterosexual privilege and homonegative oppression influence LGB identity and career development; and the ways in which societal prejudices and stereotypes influence self-concept and self-esteem, psychological well-being, and functioning in relationships (Buhrke & Douce, 1991). A multicultural feminist-based analysis also includes an understanding of biculturalism, marginality, and normative difference in LGB people (Brown, 1989), as well as an analysis of privilege and power as they affect clients (Morrow & Hawxhurst, 1998). Heterosexism and other forms of oppression, including the multiple oppressions of LGB people of color, women, and other marginalized groups, are central to a sociopolitical analysis.

Multiple oppressions create an additional burden for LGB people who also experience discrimination based on gender, race or ethnicity, class, age, religion, culture, disability, mental status, appearance, or other variables. Frequently people of color experience "double jeopardy" (or, in the case of women, triple jeopardy) in that they are targets of racism in LGB culture and of homonegativity within their communities of color (see Fukuyama & Ferguson, chapter 4, this volume; Greene, 1997). Bisexual women and men, too, may find that they are unable to be fully themselves in either lesbian–gay or heterosexual culture (Matteson, 1996). Browning, Reynolds, and Dworkin (1991) noted that gay men and lesbians of color are "polycultural and multiply oppressed" (p. 178). Ducharme and Gill (1995) noted that LGB people with disabilities are often considered "doubly disabled" (p. 398).

Clearly, it behooves therapists to be well trained in a broad range of feminist and multicultural perspectives, despite their primary theoretical orientations. A null therapeutic environment may indeed be incompetent practice with populations whose psychological distress stems from oppression. Multicultural competence gains new meaning in work with clients who are members of other marginalized groups in addition to being lesbian, gay, or bisexual, and a sociopolitical analysis may assist clients in unraveling the effects of multiple oppressions. At the heart of competent feminist and multicultural work is therapist self-awareness and self-reflection; in addition, therapist self-knowledge is a key factor in managing ethical issues and boundaries with clients.

THERAPIST, KNOW THYSELF

APA's (1992) "Ethical Principles of Psychologists and Code of Conduct" states the following in Principle D: Respect for People's Rights and Dignity:

> Psychologists are aware of cultural, individual, and role differences, including those due to . . . sexual orientation. . . . [They] try to eliminate the effect on their work of biases based on those factors, and they

do not knowingly participate in or condone unfair discriminatory practices. (pp. 1599–1600)

Included among these biases are therapists' unexamined prejudices in the form of homonegativity and heterosexism (McDermott, Tyndall, & Lichtenberg, 1989); symbolic, transferential, or countertransferential relationships of both client and therapist (Buhrke & Douce, 1991; McHenry & Johnson, 1993); and boundary issues specific to working with LGB clients. In this section, I explore concerns related to therapists' countertransference, or symbolic relationships, with LGB clients and address specific boundary issues related to LGB clients.

Symbolic Relationships

Although client transference is a crucial aspect of the psychotherapy relationship, it is not the subject of this chapter (see Buhrke & Douce, 1991, for an in-depth discussion of client transference). Instead, I focus on common manifestations of therapists' symbolic relationships, or countertransference, as well as cognitive distortions and selective perceptions that evolve from therapists' personal experiences with LGB people. I use Brown's (1994) term *symbolic relationship* instead of the psychoanalytically oriented terms *transference* and *countertransference* to normalize and depathologize the common human experience of revisiting prior significant relationships in present time.

Unresolved symbolic relationships in therapists of all sexual orientations may have negative and often harmful effects on the clients they are trying to help. Among the most damaging can be sexualizing or, conversely, ignoring sexual content in, the client–counselor relationship. Heterosexual people have usually been socialized not to view same-sex attractions as a personal possibility, although "across cultures, bisexual behavior may be more common than either exclusive heterosexuality or homosexuality" (Kauth & Kalichman, 1995, p. 94). If this is the case, it is likely that at least some heterosexually identified therapists may experience same-sex attractions. In a context of societal homonegativity, therapists may refuse to recognize those attractions, thereby allowing unconscious motivations to guide their work. These therapists may bypass important opportunities to assist LGB clients in dealing with their own attractions to the therapist. Worse, the therapist may be rejecting of the client. Depending on their own stages of identity development and relationship needs and experiences, LGB therapists may respond to LGB clients with attractions of their own. In the absence of appropriate supervision with a knowledgeable and competent LGB-affirmative supervisor, the consequences may be costly to client and therapist alike.

In addition to romantic and sexual attractions, a number of factors may influence the symbolic relationships being acted out in the therapy relationship. Heterosexual therapists' personal and professional experiences, particularly if they are limited, may affect their perspectives on working with LGB clients. Earlier relationships with LGB people or with significant others who have strong feelings about LGB people, both positive and negative, may create cognitive distortions, generalizations, and assumptions that may prove countertherapeutic. Because symbolic relationships are always affected by the sociopolitical context in which they evolve, therapists' personal experiences with LGB people always emerge in the context of societal homonegativism. In addition, many heterosexual therapists have had limited contact with people they know to be LGB; sometimes contact occurs only in the therapeutic setting. When therapists' attitudes are formed on the basis of negative societal stereotyping and limited contact with a population who are, by many clinicians' definitions, distressed, further contacts, if not carefully planned, may serve to reinforce existing negative biases.

LGB therapists are subject to many of the same distortions as are heterosexual therapists, particularly if they have not received training and supervision in LGB therapy or have a limited range of contact and experience with LGB people in their own lives. This is particularly true when LGB therapists generalize from their own lesbian, gay, or bisexual experiences to clients who are part of a different context. For example, the lesbian or gay therapist who went through a "bisexual phase" of identity development may assume that the bisexual client's identity is also a phase that the client will "grow out of." A gay or bisexual male therapist may make the "generic gay–bi" assumption, when working with lesbian or bisexual women clients, that cultural values that apply to his own life are equally applicable to his women clients—potentially a huge distortion, particularly with feminist clients. The feminist lesbian or bisexual therapist may oversimplify aspects of gay male culture that she sees as stereotypical or sexist.

LGB-affirmative heterosexual therapists may find themselves in an awkward position when their clients who are victims of heterosexism and homonegativism generalize their experience to heterosexuals in general. All therapists want to be liked by their clients. When a client expresses anger toward the therapist's cultural group, the therapist may feel personally attacked. In addition, the therapist may work to be "politically correct" and therefore avoid taking the risk of offending clients, thereby withholding important feedback from LGB clients (Holahan & Gibson, 1994).

In addition to (and sometimes because of) the effects of symbolic relationships on therapists, boundary issues in the therapeutic relationship often arise. These may be complicated for therapists working with LGB clients, particularly if the therapist is lesbian, gay, or bisexual.

Boundaries

Compilations of actions taken by state and professional boards of psychology over the last 2 decades indicate that by far the greatest number of ethical transgressions are romantic and sexual violations of clients by therapists (Ted Packard, personal communication, July 3, 1997). Lesbian clients with whom I have worked have reported sexually inappropriate advances from heterosexual male therapists who believed that all their clients needed to be "normal" was a positive sexual experience with a man. Heterosexual therapists who have not examined their own sexuality may be more apt to violate sexual boundaries with clients who are uncertain about their sexual orientation. LGB therapists are, unfortunately, not immune from these acts. Because society continues to define LGB people by their sexuality alone—rather than by the full range of affectional, friendship, and cultural aspects of LGB people's lives—LGB therapists can be as vulnerable as their heterosexual counterparts to sexualizing therapeutic relationships, especially if they have not dealt with their own sexuality in the total context of their identity. In addition, the reluctance of therapists to "blow the whistle" on their peers may be amplified in LGB therapeutic communities, where reporting violations may result in uneven treatment for marginalized groups.

A unique type of overlap among LGB therapists and their clients occurs when both therapist and client are active in the same social and political circles. Similar circumstances occur in small communities or when clients seek therapy from members of their own cultural, religious, or racial–ethnic groups. Lyn (1990) found that almost 95% of lesbian and gay therapists had encountered their clients in social contexts. It was particularly common in the early years of feminist therapy for lesbian feminist therapists and their clients to overestimate the extent to which the pair could achieve equality in the therapy relationship. Therapists, therefore, ran the risk of overlooking the ways in which clients felt needy or vulnerable or looked to their therapists for approval in the social or political arena. Often these clients blamed themselves for difficulties in managing the relationship comfortably. Although the goal of a near-egalitarian relationship between therapist and client is well worth striving for, it may be unreachable owing to societal expectations by both therapist and client regarding a hierarchical therapy relationship and the symbolic relationships described previously. Such an assumption belies the power and privilege differential that exists in the therapy relationship and may create expectations on the part of clients that they and their therapists can be friends. This is particularly problematic if both are involved in lesbian feminist community, culture, and politics. The same issues may hold true for gay and bisexual therapists who are politically or socially active in their communities. Therapists are responsible for raising issues of overlap and facilitating a mutual frame for the relationship outside the therapy session.

Therapists in these situations may err in one of two directions. They may set their boundaries so rigidly that clients feel awkward and confused, seeing the therapist as insincere. Conversely, in the interest of being "real" with their clients outside the therapy session, therapists may fail to establish even those boundaries that are appropriate with nonclient community members. Many LGB therapists avoid social, cultural, and political activities to prevent outside contact with their clients. This isolation, in turn, limits therapists' involvement in rich and varied experiences that could inform competent practice. The APA Ethical Principles of Psychologists and Code of Conduct (Standard 1.17) acknowledges that social contact with clients may at times be unavoidable and states that "psychologists must always be sensitive to the potential harmful effects of other contacts on their work" (APA, 1992, p. 1601) as well as on their clients. LGB therapists who find that their community involvement creates overlapping relationships with clients can exercise sensitivity by addressing the potential contacts in advance with their clients, eliciting concerns of the client as well as providing guidelines for appropriate contact in the community setting. Clients should be encouraged to take the lead in greeting their therapists, if they so desire, to prevent embarrassment. The therapist's partner and close friends can be educated not to ask where the therapist has met individuals they are introduced to, to avoid awkward and revealing silences. Reassurances of confidentiality in these situations should be given to the client. In addition, it is helpful if clients understand the therapist's preferred limits in terms of length and depth of conversation in a public setting. Finally, it is often helpful, at the session following the social contact, to process the feelings of both therapist and client and plan for any changes each would like to make for future contacts. For a more extensive treatment of lesbian therapist–client relationships and therapist issues with lesbian clients, see Falco (1991) and Gartrell (1994).

The personal responsibility of therapists working with LGB clients is great. Self-awareness is a critical component of effective and ethical psychotherapy with LGB people. However, therapists tread on shaky ground if they depend on graduate training or personal experiences to provide sufficient education and awareness to conduct LGB-affirmative psychotherapy. The complexities of competent therapy with LGB people demand postgraduation and postlicensure experiences in the form of continuing education, supervision, and consultation. It is only with ongoing commitment to providing truly affirmative therapy for LGB people that therapists will contribute to the creative enhancement of their clients.

CONCLUSION: CREATIVE ENHANCEMENT OF LGB CLIENTS

Recommendations for LGB-affirmative therapy that contributes to the creative enhancement of LGB clients and their identities are grounded in Brown's (1989) conceptualization of a lesbian–gay paradigm for psychology. Morrow (1998) noted that "an LGB paradigm would move LGB issues from the margins to the center" (p. 805). That is, instead of viewing LGB issues from a heterosexual perspective, therapists would immerse themselves sufficiently in the contexts of LGB people's understandings that they could, in essence, begin to ask questions about heterosexuality from the perspective of LGB lives. An example would be to question, on the basis of a deeper understanding of bisexuality, common (and heterosexist) assumptions that people are oriented toward either one gender or the other; one might hypothesize that more individuals than not are to some degree bisexual. To centralize lesbian experience would be to wonder more about what heterosexuality contributes to women's preoccupation with body image. To move gay men from the margins to the center might be to suggest that the physical and emotional distance prescribed between heterosexual men could be depriving them of important intimacy and bonding that are possible only with another man. In short, one would begin to ask questions about heterosexuality generated from norms of LGB cultures and lives— and about lesbian and gay cultures and lives from bisexual women's and men's experiences—instead of vice versa. Bisexuality might become the starting point for derigidifying current notions of sexual orientation. Lesbian women and gay men might begin to claim their right to choose being lesbian or gay instead of needing to defend themselves by claiming that their sexual orientation is inborn. Children might grow up knowing not only that their parents "only wanted what would make them happy" but that their parents would be happy themselves over the choices their children made about love, sex, and relationships. Finally, decentering heterosexual and heterosexist notions of relationship and family could lead to new, healthier ways of being in communion with others as lovers, friends, parents, children, and members of communities.

REFERENCES

American Psychological Association. (1991). *Guidelines for providers of psychological services to ethnic, linguistic, and culturally diverse populations*. Washington, DC: Author.

American Psychological Association. (1992). Ethical principles of psychologists and code of conduct. *American Psychologist, 47*, 1597–1611.

American Psychological Association. (1995). *Lesbian and gay parenting: A resource for psychologists*. Washington, DC: Author.

American Psychological Association. (1997). *Resolution on appropriate therapeutic responses to sexual orientation* [adopted by the American Psychological Association Council of Representatives, August 14]. Washington, DC: Author.

Arizona Psychological Association Executive Council. (1991). *Policy recommendations for psychotherapy with lesbians and gay men*. Phoenix, AZ: Author.

Bohan, J. S. (1996). *Psychology of sexual orientation: Coming to terms*. New York: Routledge.

Brown, L. S. (1989). New voices, new visions: Toward a lesbian/gay paradigm for psychology. *Psychology of Women Quarterly, 13,* 445–458.

Brown, L. S. (1994). *Subversive dialogues: Theory in feminist therapy*. New York: Basic Books.

Brown, L. S. (1995). Lesbian identities: Concepts and issues. In A. R. D'Augelli & C. J. Patterson (Eds.), *Lesbian, gay, and bisexual identities over the lifespan* (pp. 3–23). New York: Oxford University Press.

Browning, C., Reynolds, A. L., & Dworkin, S. H. (1991). Affirmative psychotherapy for lesbian women. *The Counseling Psychologist, 19,* 177–196.

Buhrke, R. A., & Douce, L. A. (1991). Training issues for counseling psychologists in working with lesbian women and gay men. *The Counseling Psychologist, 19,* 216–234.

Conger, J. J. (1975). Proceedings of the American Psychological Association, Incorporated, for the year 1974: Minutes of the annual meeting of the Council of Representatives. *American Psychologist, 30,* 620–651.

Ducharme, S., & Gill, K. M. (1995). Sexuality and disability. In L. Diamant & R. D. McNulty (Eds.), *The psychology of sexual orientation, behavior, and identity* (pp. 398–408). Westport, CT: Greenwood Press.

Ellis, A. (1965). *Homosexuality: Its causes and cure*. New York: Lyle Stuart.

Espín, O. M. (1994). Feminist approaches. In L. Comas-Díaz & B. Greene (Eds.), *Women of color: Integrating ethnic and gender identities in psychotherapy* (pp. 265–286). New York: Guilford Press.

Falco, K. L. (1991). *Psychotherapy with lesbian clients: Theory into practice*. New York: Brunner/Mazel.

Fox, R. E. (1988). Proceedings of the American Psychological Association, Incorporated, for the year 1987: Minutes of the annual meeting of the Council of Representatives. *American Psychologist, 43,* 527–528.

Freeman, J. (1975). How to discriminate against women without really trying. In J. Freeman (Ed.), *Women: A feminist perspective* (pp. 194–208). Palo Alto, CA: Mayfield.

Freud, S. (1924). The sexual life of man. In *A general introduction to psychoanalysis* (Ernest Jones, Trans., pp. 312–328). New York: Washington Square Press.

Garnets, L., Hancock, K. A., Cochran, S. D., Goodchilds, J., & Peplau, L. A. (1991). Issues in psychotherapy with lesbians and gay men: A survey of psychologists. *American Psychologist, 46,* 964–972.

Gartrell, N. K. (1994). Boundaries in lesbian therapist–client relationships. In B.

Greene & G. M. Herek (Eds.), *Lesbian and gay psychology: Theory, research, and clinical applications* (pp. 98–117). Thousand Oaks, CA: Sage.

Gelberg, S., & Chojnacki, J. T. (1995). Developmental transitions of gay/lesbian/bisexual-affirmative, heterosexual career counselors. *Career Development Quarterly, 43,* 267–273.

Gilliland, B., & Crisp, D. (1995, August). *Homophobia: Assessing and changing attitudes of counselors-in-training.* Paper presented at the 103rd Annual Convention of the American Psychological Association, New York.

Golden, C. (1987). Diversity and variability in women's sexual identities. In Boston Lesbian Psychologies Collective (Eds.), *Lesbian psychologies: Explorations and challenges* (pp. 18–34). Urbana: University of Illinois Press.

Gonsiorek, J. (1989). Sexual exploitation by psychotherapists: Some observations on male victims and sexual orientation issues. In G. Schoener, J. Milgram, J. Gonsiorek, E. Luepker, & R. Conroe (Eds.), *Psychotherapists' sexual involvement with clients: Intervention and prevention* (pp. 113–119). Minneapolis, MN: Walk-In Counseling Center.

Greene, B. (Ed.). (1997). *Ethnic and cultural diversity among lesbians and gay men.* Thousand Oaks, CA: Sage.

Haldeman, D. C. (1994). The practice and ethics of sexual orientation conversion therapy. *Journal of Consulting and Clinical Psychology, 62,* 221–227.

Hancock, K. A. (1995). Psychotherapy with lesbians and gay men. In A. R. D'Augelli & C. J. Patterson (Eds.), *Lesbian, gay, and bisexual identities over the lifespan* (pp. 398–432). New York: Oxford University Press.

Herek, G. M. (1984). Beyond homophobia: A social psychological perspective on attitudes toward lesbians and gay men. *Journal of Homosexuality, 10*(1–2), 1–21.

Herek, G. M. (1993). The context of antigay violence: Notes on cultural and psychological heterosexism. In L. D. Garnets & D. C. Kimmel (Eds.), *Psychological perspectives on lesbian and gay male experiences* (pp. 89–107). New York: Columbia University Press.

Holahan, W., & Gibson, S. A. (1994). Heterosexual therapists leading lesbian and gay therapy groups: Therapeutic and political realities. *Journal of Counseling and Development, 72,* 591–594.

Hudson, W. W., & Ricketts, W. A. (1980). A strategy for the measurement of homophobia. *Journal of Homosexuality, 5,* 357–372.

Isay, R. (1991). The homosexual analyst: Clinical considerations. *The psychoanalytic study of the child, 46,* 199–216.

Kauth, M. R., & Kalichman, S. C. (1995). Sexual orientation and development: An interactive approach. In L. Diamant & R. D. McAnulty (Eds.), *The psychology of sexual orientation, behavior, and identity: A handbook* (pp. 81–103). Westport, CT: Greenwood Press.

Kinnish, K. K. (1998). *A multidimensional assessment of stability and flexibility in sexual orientation across the lifespan.* Unpublished master's thesis, University of Utah, Salt Lake City.

Kitzinger, C. (1987). *The social construction of lesbianism*. London: Sage.

Lyn, L. (1990). *Life in the fishbowl: Lesbian and gay therapists' social interactions with their clients*. Unpublished master's thesis, Southern Illinois University, Carbondale.

Matteson, D. R. (1996). Counseling and psychotherapy with bisexual and exploring clients. In B. A. Firestein (Ed.), *Bisexuality: The psychology and politics of an invisible minority* (pp. 185–213). Thousand Oaks, CA: Sage.

McDermott, D., Tyndall, L., & Lichtenberg, J. W. (1989). Factors related to counselor preference among gays and lesbians. *Journal of Counseling and Development, 68,* 31–35.

McHenry, S. S., & Johnson, J. W. (1993). Homophobia in the therapist and gay or lesbian client: Conscious and unconscious collusions in self-hate. *Psychotherapy, 30,* 141–151.

Morrow, S. L. (1998). Toward a new paradigm in counseling-psychology training and education. *The Counseling Psychologist, 26,* 795–806.

Morrow, S. L., Gore, P. A., Jr., & Campbell, B. W. (1996). The application of a sociocognitive framework to the career development of lesbian women and gay men. *Journal of Vocational Behavior, 48,* 136–148.

Morrow, S. L., & Hawxhurst, D. M. (1989). Lesbian partner abuse: Implications for therapists. *Journal of Counseling and Development, 68,* 58–62.

Morrow, S. L., & Hawxhurst, D. M. (1998). Feminist therapy: Integrating political analysis in counseling and psychotherapy. *Women and Therapy, 21*(2), 37–50.

Murphy, T. J. (1992). Redirecting sexual orientation: Techniques and justifications. *The Journal of Sex Research, 29,* 501–523.

Nicolosi, J. (1991). *Reparative therapy of male homosexuality*. Northvale, NJ: Jason Aronson.

Ratner, E. F. (1993). Treatment issues for chemically dependent lesbians and gay men. In L. D. Garnets & D. C. Kimmel (Eds.), *Psychological perspectives on lesbian and gay male experiences* (pp. 567–578). New York: Columbia University Press.

Riddle, D. I., & Sang, B. (1978). Psychotherapy with lesbians. *Journal of Social Issues, 34*(3), 84–100.

7

INDIVIDUAL THERAPY WITH LESBIAN, GAY, AND BISEXUAL CLIENTS

SARI H. DWORKIN

According to the National Gay and Lesbian Task Force Policy Institute (cited in Hancock, 1995), lesbians and gays use the mental health system at higher rates than heterosexuals. In a survey of almost 2,000 lesbians, 73% reported having used the mental health system (National Institute of Mental Health, 1987). No data currently exist for the mental health use of bisexual people, but because bisexual respondents are often grouped with gay and lesbian respondents (Fox, 1996), this finding probably holds true for them as well. At the same time, many LGB people are suspicious of the psychological profession owing to a history of misdiagnosis and the treatment of homosexuality and bisexuality as mental illness (American Psychological Association [APA], 1991; Falco, 1991; Fassinger, 1991). Because LGB clients both use the mental health system in great numbers and are suspicious of it, it is especially important for practitioners to learn how to treat LGB people competently.

Almost every practitioner reports having seen a gay, lesbian, or bisexual client in her or his practice at some point (Hancock, 1995). Counseling with this population requires special knowledge concerning the impact of internalized homophobia or biphobia, the stresses of coming out, and sexual identity development theories. In spite of this, few therapists believe that treating an LGB client is outside their areas of competence (APA, 1991; Clark & Serovich, 1997; Garnets, Hancock, Cochran, Goodchilds, & Peplau, 1991; Hancock, 1995). This is true whether or not the therapist has had any training with the LGB population. The lack of knowledge about bisexuals is even greater than the lack of knowledge about gays and lesbians, because the research about bisexuals is currently being done (Firestein, 1996; Fox, 1996). The literature suggests that few counseling psychology graduate programs offer training for working with nonheterosexual clients. In addition, mental health professionals still publish few articles related to LGB issues in their widely distributed trade journals (APA, 1991; Buhrke & Douce, 1991; Clark & Serovich, 1997; Garnets et al., 1991; Hall, 1997; Phillips, chapter 14, this volume).

This chapter discusses some of the issues relevant to individual therapy with gay, lesbian, and bisexual people. It begins with definitions of key terms and then focuses on assessment concerns, treatment issues, and therapist issues. A discussion of how gender, gender role, disability, ethnicity, culture, class, and locale affect the therapy process is infused into each section.

DEFINITIONS

Following are some key terms used in this chapter to refer to the salient issues in psychotherapy with lesbian, gay, or bisexual clients.

- *Biphobia:* a fear or dislike of people who do not identify or behave as either gay, lesbian, or heterosexual (Hutchins & Kaahumanu, 1991). In the gay and lesbian community, this often manifests as part of heterophobia, or fear or dislike of people who identify as heterosexual or engage in heterosexual activity. In the heterosexual community, it manifests as part of homophobia.
- *Monosexual:* relating sexually to only one gender, as opposed to one who is bisexual and relates to both genders. Homosexual and heterosexual people are monosexual.
- *Gender identity:* a person's sense of being male or female, believed to develop by 3 years of age (Wishik & Pierce, 1995).
- *Sex roles:* culturally and socially defined behaviors for men and women (Wishik & Pierce, 1995).
- *Sexual minorities:* people who are nonheterosexual. In this chapter, the term refers to gays, lesbians, and bisexuals.
- *Polyamory:* referring to people whose relationships are non-

monogamous either sexually or romantically. This term has fewer negative connotations than does *nonmonogamy* in the majority culture of the United States (Halpern & Ashbrook, 1997; Rust, 1996b).

CENTRAL ISSUES OF ASSESSMENT

This section discusses the presenting problem, differential diagnosis, and impact of the presenting problem and differential diagnosis on the therapy process with LGB clients.

Presenting Problem

When a client enters therapy, the first step is to assess what the problem or problems are that will become the focus of treatment. Frequently, when an LGB client enters therapy, whatever problem the client presents is attributed to his or her sexual orientation (APA, 1991; Davison, 1991; Falco, 1991; Greene, 1997; Hancock, 1995). This, often inappropriate, assessment occurs because many therapists still believe that everyone should be heterosexual (Davison, 1991). In contrast, at the other extreme are therapists who completely ignore the sexual identity of the client, treating it as irrelevant (Falco, 1991). Neither position is helpful. The therapist must assess what part of the therapy process sexual identity will play in order to treat the LGB client adequately.

Many factors intersect with sexual identity and must be considered by the therapist. These factors are gender (including gender role socialization), class, race or ethnicity (including the effects of discrimination), locale, and religion (Browning, Reynolds, & Dworkin, 1991; Dworkin, 1996; Dworkin & Gutierrez, 1992; Falco, 1991; Fassinger, 1991; Gonsiorek & Rudolph, 1991; Greene, 1997; Shannon & Woods, 1991; Smith, 1997; Trujillo, 1997). When working with an LGB client who is in a racial, ethnic, or religious minority group, there are additional areas a psychotherapist or counselor should address to assess what will be the focus of treatment (Browning et al., 1991; Dworkin, 1997). These areas include the importance of the family and community links to the client (Dworkin, 1997; Greene, 1997), the importance of religious ties (Dworkin, 1997; Greene, 1997), the level of acculturation and assimilation, the history of discrimination and oppression, the acceptable and unacceptable sexual behaviors within the racial–ethnic or religious community, the view the racial–ethnic or religious community holds about nonheterosexuality (many ethnically and religiously diverse communities view homosexuality as a White phenomenon), and how much racism or anti-Semitism is present in the LGB community (Dworkin, 1997; Greene, 1997; Rust, 1996a).

Once the therapist has determined the impact of these social, environmental, and political factors (the external factors of identity development) on the client's life, he or she can assess the internal dynamics of identity development, particularly family relationships. The family of origin has a major impact on the client's views about self as well as the client's management strategies for self-disclosure of a minority monosexual or bisexual sexual identity. As a result, many LGB clients deal with a shame-based family upbringing, a sense of being defective (Matteson, 1996; Shannon & Woods, 1991). Disclosure always carries the risk of rejection (Falco, 1991; Matteson, 1996), and many clients fear the rejection of their family.

Shannon and Woods (1991) have explained further the importance of family assessment. In counseling gay men, these authors emphasized an exploration of the expression of affection in the family, conflict resolution in the family, the age when the client noticed he was different from other children, and his understanding about this difference. According to Shannon and Woods (1991),

> therapists working with gay male clients need to have a firm foundation of training and experience in conceptualizing and treating addictive disorders including alcoholism and other substance abuse, sexual compulsiveness, and eating disorders. Because of the painful process of coming to terms with one's homosexuality, there is a greater potential for narcissistic injury; this in turn fuels the development of compulsive coping responses. (p. 212)

Even though Shannon and Woods referred specifically to gay men, these areas are also important to explore with lesbian and bisexual clients to determine the breadth of the presenting problem.

The desired outcome of a therapist's assessment of the presenting problem or problems is an appropriate diagnosis. The differential diagnosis of LGB clients, explored in the following section, can be controversial owing to the declassification of homosexuality as a psychiatric illness.

Differential Diagnosis

After the American Psychiatric Association in 1973 and the American Psychological Association in 1975 declassified homosexuality as an illness (Fassinger, 1991; Silverstein, 1991), two reactions became common. On the one hand, many practitioners did not change, continuing to view gay and lesbian clients as sick on the basis of their sexual orientation. These practitioners use psychological and psychiatric diagnosis to maintain the status quo (Fassinger, 1991; Silverstein, 1991) rather than to facilitate client mental health. Silverstein (1991) wrote that "a primary purpose of psychiatric diagnosis, therefore, is an attempt by society to control those people whom it fears" (p. 103). On the other hand, some practitioners stopped diagnosing gay and lesbian clients with psychopathology even when it was clearly indicated (Gonsiorek, 1982; J. Smith, 1988).

It is important to recognize that there are LGB clients who suffer from psychiatric illnesses. Sometimes the mental illness results from the pressures of coming out and dealing with a nonheterosexual identity; at other times, the illness is characterological; and sometimes these two circumstances are combined, and psychological symptoms are exaggerated. Gonsiorek (1982) recommended that a "combination of traditional and gay/lesbian affirmative mental health concepts constitute the necessary and sufficient conditions for competent practice with homosexual populations" (p. 10). This recommendation would apply to bisexual populations as well.

Gonsiorek's (1982) article is particularly useful for practitioners attempting to assess for differential diagnosis:

> In those individuals for whom homosexual thoughts are delusional and have little or no basis in a developed homosexual object-choice, the thoughts will be just that: cerebral, ruminative ideas with little or no component of homosexual desire either in the present or past, as determined by history. (p. 11)

Therefore, a thorough history is essential.

Sometimes, when a psychiatric disorder is evident, the therapist must wait until the client is stabilized before proceeding to explore identity issues. Both Gonsiorek (1982) and Greene (1997) particularly noted the possible presence of borderline personality disorder. The acceptance of an LGB identity is extremely stressful, and an individual may display borderline characteristics that will dissipate once the identity crisis is over. Patients with true borderline personality disorder may look like they are having difficulty adjusting to a sexual minority lifestyle when the real problem is due to characterological defects. According to Gonsiorek (1982), helping such patients to become more cohesive is more important than working on sexual identity issues. The critical issue to assess is whether symptoms are premorbid or are arising because of the identity crisis. For the LGB person, day-to-day living is stressful by virtue of the client's sexual orientation, on top of the stresses that everyone faces in life; therapists need to take this situation seriously (Davison, 1991).

Impact on Therapy

Assessment of the LGB client's problems is no different from the clinical assessment of any client presenting in therapy. The therapist conducts a routine clinical assessment in addition to the following: (a) an examination of internalized homophobia and biphobia (Falco, 1991); (b) an examination of the coming out process, including the costs and benefits of hiding versus revealing (Sophie, 1982); and (c) an examination of erotic fantasies, attractions, and behaviors (Falco, 1991; Matteson, 1996; Shannon & Woods, 1991; Sophie, 1982). If the psychologist uses assessment instruments (e.g., the Minnesota Multiphasic Personality Inventory [MMPI–2] or the Myers–Briggs Type Indicator) along with the clinical interview, he or she must know just what a test may or may not tell about an LGB person. (See Pope, 1992, for an explanation of the research on what major clinical tests can predict about LGB people.)

The clinical assessment helps the therapist and client to develop the treatment plan. For this to be effective, it is important that the therapist truly hear and understand the unique experiences of the client. In discussing therapists' work with lesbians, Browning et al. (1991) stated the following: "Therapists can help empower the lesbian client by acknowledging that she is the expert about her life, by demystifying the process of therapy, by making relevant self-disclosures to facilitate client growth, and by collaboratively negotiating the goals of therapy" (p. 193). The words of these authors are a description of good therapy practices and apply to gay and bisexual clients as well.

In addition to listening to clients' unique experiences, some therapists use structured exercises as part of the assessment or therapy process. Falco (1991) outlined various exercises for helping clients assess the importance of their experience of being part of a sexual minority group. Wishik and Pierce (1995) developed a tool called the Sexual Orientation and Identity Continuum Diagram, which they use in their workshops and therapy practice. This diagram "provides individuals the opportunity to see privately, without embarrassment, where they are in relation to a diverse group of others, encouraging changes in attitudes and behaviors with minimal resistance" (Wishik & Pierce, 1995, p. xii). The continuum consists of three lines that highlight the sexual identity journeys of heterosexuals, gays, lesbians, and bisexuals. The diagram shows the aids and barriers to identifying as an LGB person and allows for sexual identity fluidity. This exercise can be used to help clients assess the impact of a lesbian or gay monosexual or bisexual minority sexual identity on the problems they bring to treatment.

TREATMENT ISSUES

Once the therapist has assessed the presenting concerns of the LGB client, made a diagnosis, and planned therapeutic interventions, the individual therapy begins. There are distinct treatment issues for many LGB clients that result from managing a stigmatized identity. This section covers the following treatment issues: (a) self-identification (including bisexual self-identification); (b) coming out (including the bisexual coming out process); (c) gender, culture, disability, and the coming out process, as well as the impact of these issues on the therapy process; (d) internalized homo-phobia and biphobia; and (e) victimization.

Self-Identification

The process of self-identification as an LGB person is a difficult one. Clients often appear for therapy because of the distress of self-identification of an LGB sexual identity. According to one definition,

> sexual identity is a term for the ways in which a person living in her or his particular cultural and historical context experiences, makes sense of labels, and lives out her or his own combination of sexual orientation, biological sex, and gender. (Wishik & Pierce, 1995, p. 185)

As noted by Reynolds and Hanjorgiris in chapter 2, this volume, there are many models for developing an LGB sexual identity. These models explain how LGB clients acknowledge their orientation to self and others (Caitlin & Futterman, 1997; A. Smith, 1997). The best-known models (Cass, 1979; Coleman, 1982; Troiden, 1989) offer an explanation and de-scription of the critical interaction of internal and external processes of sexual identity development and help people place themselves into a social context (Brown, 1995). Recently, these models have come under attack. Critics have described these models as Eurocentric, based on the experi-ences of White gay men and then generalized to the entire LGB popula-tion; as embodying dichotomous thinking; and as ending with only one outcome (a fixed, integrated gay or lesbian identity across all situations; Brown, 1995; Caitlin & Futterman, 1997; Fassinger, 1991; Gonsiorek & Weinrich, 1991b; Morris, 1997; Wishik & Pierce, 1995). Researchers are discovering that there are many paths to the development of a nonhetero-sexual sexual identity (Falco, 1991; Fassinger, & Miller, 1996; Savin-Williams, personal communication June 3, 1997).

Fassinger and Miller (1996) recently developed an identity develop-ment model that has two separate trajectories. One trajectory looks at the development of the LGB individual's sexual identity, and the other trajec-tory looks at group membership identity development. The results of their research lend support for the different trajectories, although the support is not as strong for members of racial and ethnic minority groups as it is for White LGB people. The authors contended, on the basis of their research, that it is necessary to separate the need to disclose from the development of a cohesive sexual identity.

Other recent models (e.g., Hanley-Hackenbruck, 1989; Morris, 1997) consider the impact of race, ethnicity, gender, culture, and history on sexual identification. However, there is a paucity of research on the complex in-teraction of ethnicity and sexual orientation (Greene, 1997). Greene noted that even practitioners who are LGB-affirmative do not have the tools for effective culturally sensitive therapy.

The consideration of race or ethnicity often is based on the division of people into two categories, Whites versus other races or ethnicities, as though all Whites were the same. Not all Whites feel a part of the dominant Anglo-Saxon Protestant culture (e.g., Greeks and Jews). Therefore, a therapist working with a White LGB person who is coming out should not assume that ethnicity and loyalty to a particular nondominant culture is irrelevant (Dworkin, 1997; Fygetakis, 1997). On the other hand, it is important for therapists to realize that people of color from other countries may not view themselves as part of American minority groups (Greene, 1997). Therapists need to be careful about the assumptions they make on the basis of the color of their client.

Bisexuals experience extreme marginalization from both the heterosexual and the lesbian and gay communities, which can cause additional emotional distress and make self-disclosure more risky (Fox, 1995; Klein, 1993; Matteson, 1996; Rust, 1996a, 1996b). Often this extreme marginalization is due to the fact that the existence of bisexuality as a sexual identity is still controversial (Fox, 1995, 1996; Wishik & Pierce, 1995). Many therapists hold the view that bisexuality is an immature, pathological, transitional stage on the way to a gay or lesbian identity and that it precludes the development of healthy intimacy in relationships (Dworkin, 1996; Fox, 1995, 1996; Klein, 1993; Rust, 1996b; Wishik & Pierce, 1995). Some therapists do not consider bisexuality to be a whole sexual orientation but rather consider bisexual persons as half heterosexual and half homosexual (Rust, 1996b).

People who consider themselves bisexual do so for a number of reasons. Some do so because they feel attracted to both men and women and because they believe they could potentially become involved with either women or men. Others identify themselves as bisexual because they have experienced relationships with both women and men in the past and do not wish to adopt either a lesbian–gay or a heterosexual identity that would effectively deny the reality of part of their sexual feelings or experiences (Rust, 1996b, p. 129).

Reynolds and Hanjorgiris (chapter 2, this volume) note that theories about bisexuality are still in their infancy compared with gay and lesbian sexual development models. However, the emergence of multidimensional theories about sexual identity development has opened the way for consideration of bisexuality (Fox, 1996; Savin-Williams, personal communication, June 3, 1997). Bisexuality, as previously noted in this volume, challenges the dichotomy of homosexual versus heterosexual, challenges gender as a determinant for romantic object choice, and challenges sexual identity as fixed (Firestein, 1996; Fox, 1995, 1996; Matteson, 1996; Rust, 1993, 1996a, 1966b; Weinberg, Williams, & Pryor, 1994).

Once an individual has self-identified as LGB, the next task is determining how and when to come out. The mental health issues associated with this risky process are discussed in the next section.

Coming Out

Shifting one's identity from the socially accepted heterosexual identity to the socially denigrated nonheterosexual LGB identity can cause emotional distress (Caitlin & Futterman, 1997; Gonsiorek, 1995; Hancock, 1995; Morris, 1997; Trujillo, 1997; Wishik & Pierce, 1995). Trujillo (1997) contended that gays and lesbians (as well as bisexuals) expend more energy being gay or lesbian (or bisexual) than heterosexuals expend being heterosexual. Other authors (Fassinger, 1991; Wishik & Pierce, 1995) have agreed, noting that every new setting involves a new decision for an LGB person. Members of sexual minority groups must contend with "triple consciousness" (Trujillo, 1997, p. 271): what society thinks of them, what they think of themselves (Shannon & Woods, 1991), and the dissonance between the two. In a recent study of lesbians, Anderson & Mavis (1996) explored self-efficacy and the coming out process:

> The results suggest that it is not one's actual outness that is significant in lifestyle satisfaction, but rather one's confidence in one's ability to be out that is more important in providing freedom to choose when or if to come out. (p. 50)

Hancock (1995) stated that it is critical for the therapist to assess the ego strength of the client when working on coming out issues. Gender, culture, class, and ethnicity interact with ego strength. The amount of discrimination already faced or anticipated will affect ego strength and how the client manages coming out. Vontress and Epp (1997) explained that minority groups, particularly African Americans, suffer from "historical hostility" (p. 172), which refers to the repressed anger against the dominant culture carried by oppressed groups. This anger may affect not only the coming out process, but the level of suspicion that LGB clients have toward therapists, especially therapists from the dominant culture. Gonsiorek (1995) wrote that psychological adjustment to coming out has some relationship to a client's acceptance or rejection of the illness model of homosexuality as well as to their response to oppression. Discrimination both real and imagined feeds into internalized homophobia.

Some of the mental health problems associated with difficulties in self-identification and in coming out are depression, suicide, somatic concerns, eating disorders, affect disorders, chronic stress, and substance abuse (Caitlin & Futterman, 1997; Smith, 1988). These may be magnified in adolescents who identify as LGB (see Hershberger & D'Augelli, chapter 10, this volume). When assessing adolescents, there is also the risk of misdiagnosis of gender identity disorder because LGB adolescents often display what is considered by society to be gender-inappropriate behaviors (Caitlin & Futterman, 1997).

Serious mental illness can be magnified by the distress of coming out (Caitlin & Futterman, 1997; Gonsiorek, 1995): "The narcissistic injury of disparaged sexuality is not met as a developmental challenge to be surmounted, but rather as another danger that threatens to shatter an already tenuous psychological constitution" (Gonsiorek, 1995, p. 38). The distress may be sharper for men than for women because men seem to experience their shift in identity more abruptly than women do (Gonsiorek, 1995). In addition, men tend to sexualize distress, whereas women are more likely to process emotionally what is happening to them (Browning et al., 1991; Gonsiorek, 1995).

Coming out as bisexual has different challenges from coming out as gay or lesbian. For some bisexuals, sexual identity depends on the gender of the person with whom they are in a relationship. If a bisexual woman is in a relationship with a woman, she may identify as lesbian. If she is in a relationship with a man, she may identify as heterosexual. For other bisexual persons, self-identification may also depend on situational contexts. For example, a bisexual man may identify as gay when he is in a gay bar. Finally, for many bisexuals, identity as bisexual is stable no matter what the context (Dworkin, 1996; Fox, 1995; Matteson, 1996; Weinberg et al., 1994). Bisexuals usually come out later than gays and lesbians, which is thought to result from the lack of support for bisexuals and the belief that sexual orientation is dichotomous (Firestein, 1996; Fox, 1995; Matteson, 1996).

According to Fox's (1995, 1996) survey research on more than 700 bisexually identified women and men, bisexual women usually have heterosexual experiences before they have a homosexual experience. For bisexual men, homosexual attractions and behavior are evident either before or at the same time as heterosexual attraction and behavior. Bisexual women who first identified as lesbian have an added difficulty in coming out because they are often abandoned by their lesbian friends (Matteson, 1996).

Gender, Culture, Disability, and Coming Out

Coming out may cause more emotional distress for people already experiencing prejudice and discrimination, because different denigrated aspects of the client's identity may be more salient at different times. For example, members of racial or ethnic minority groups often feel the need to choose between their minority community and the LGB community for support (Caitlin & Futterman, 1997; Dworkin, 1997; Gonsiorek & Rudolph, 1991; Greene, 1997; A. Smith, 1997). Self-disclosure as a member of a sexual minority group may be more of an issue for clients who experience multiple oppressions.

Most models of sexual identity development incorporate disclosure to others as an important part of identity acceptance. These models assume that a person is either out or not out. If the client is not out, this is viewed as negative (A. Smith, 1997). Hiding one's sexual identity is equated with shame, denial, and self-hatred. A. Smith (1997) noted that this attitude is based on White American culture, in which individuation is seen as important. Trujillo (1997) wrote that it is a White privilege to be able to have sexuality agree with identity. White gays, lesbians, and many bisexuals see disclosure as healthy, but for some people, sexual orientation is private, which does not necessarily indicate a lack of pride or a sense of shame and denial. The emphasis on disclosure completely negates the history of oppression for many members of minority groups and the fear they have of extinction (Dworkin, 1997; A. Smith, 1997). Disclosure in some ethnic groups can disrupt important alliances within the family and the community. A. Smith (1997) stated that "informal norms such as 'Don't ask so they won't tell' may allow families to maintain and accept family members who are gay or lesbian without having to address the issue directly" (p. 286). Often the pressure is not to come out because the ethnic community is more homophobic than the dominant culture (A. Smith, 1997). Therefore, it is important for therapists to recognize what disclosure or nondisclosure means to individual clients and not to base judgments about clients' emotional health or comfort with being LGB on how out they are and how many people they have disclosed their sexual identity to.

In Latino culture, overt disclosure often is not allowed (Greene, 1997). African American LGBs may have an easier time than others because within their culture gender roles are more flexible and families rarely reject their children outright (Greene, 1997). In fact, for some Black families, coming out means being "taken in" (A. Smith, 1997, p. 295). The Black family may reject the idea of a gay or lesbian identity but fully accept the gay or lesbian person as a member of the Black community. The heavy emphasis on marriage in American Indian culture may preclude coming out (Greene, 1997).

There are numerous issues to consider when working with LGB clients of differing ethnicities. Readers are encouraged to refer to Fukuyama and Ferguson, chapter 4, this volume; Greene (1997); Chan (1992, 1995); Morales (1992); Gutierrez and Dworkin (1992); and Rust (1996a) for more information about these issues.

Unfortunately, there is a paucity of information about working with physically disabled LGB clients. For the physically disabled it is often more difficult than for others to disclose sexual minority identity and to obtain information about sexual minority groups (Boden, 1992; Caitlin & Futterman, 1997). Many physically disabled people are dependent on able-bodied significant others for their survival and do not want to alienate their helpers by disclosing an LGB identity or requesting information about LGB identities. Boden (1992) wrote that when working with disabled members of sexual minority groups it is important to understand the social context of disability—the disabled individual's personal experience in an able-bodied world—as well as the experience of being nonheterosexual in a heterosexual world. The shame from a physical defect can generalize to a person's self-organization: "When the feeling of defect is due to a physical difference or disability, shame surrounding the perceived defect—which can be conscious or unconscious—may become a focal point for shame related to other areas of vulnerability" (Boden, 1992, p. 158), such as sexual minority status.

For women there is the stress of living without a man in a society in which a woman is still supposed to depend on a man (Browning et al., 1991; Falco, 1991). When helping a woman determine the costs and benefits of coming out, the therapist must have an understanding of sexism in society (Browning et al., 1991; Murphy, 1992). Sexism proscribes specific roles for women, and lesbians and bisexual women are departing from the traditional feminine role. They also are at higher risk of having sexual abuse in their background. Sometimes a lesbian or bisexual woman is in a female couple in which both partners are experiencing the psychological distresses resulting from a sexual abuse history. In addition, she may be dealing with other sensitive issues such as child custody (Browning et al., 1991). All of the aforementioned issues may affect her acceptance of a sexual minority identity. For women, identity often forms around affectional and even political dimensions (Browning et al., 1991; Faderman, 1991; Fassinger, 1991), whereas for men sexual behavior and fantasy may be the critical dimensions (Gonsiorek, 1995). This may be why women seem to be more fluid and flexible in their sexual identity than men (Dworkin, 1996; Fox, 1995; Golden, 1987; Gonsiorek, 1995; Matteson, 1996; Rust, 1993).

The difficult issues surrounding decisions to come out or not to come out may require more than individual therapy. After a thorough exploration of the coming out issues, the therapist can help the client find and tap into community resources (Falco, 1991; Hancock, 1995; Sophie, 1982). Caitlin and Futterman (1997) provided a checklist to be used with these resources that can help the therapist assess the degree to which they are LGB affirming. Identifying referral sources may prove more challenging to the therapist working with bisexual clients because a readily available bisexual community often does not exist (Dworkin, 1996; Fox, 1995). *The Bisexual Resource Guide* (Ochs, 1995) can help therapists locate the nearest bisexual community. Bibliotherapy can serve as an adjunct to community resources or can substitute for community resources when these resources do not exist. Bibliotherapy (Hancock, 1995; Matteson, 1996; Rust, 1996a,

1996b) can be a powerful tool for helping clients with coming out issues. Fortunately there are many gay- and lesbian-affirmative books, and the scope of bisexual-affirmative literature is rapidly expanding. Community resources and bibliotherapy may help mitigate the damage sustained by many LGB clients from internalized homophobia and biphobia by providing accurate information and a network of healthy LGB people and allies.

Internalized Homophobia and Biphobia

Internalized homophobia or, more broadly, *internalized oppression* "refers to the acceptance and internalization by members of oppressed groups of negative stereotypes and images of their groups, beliefs in their own inferiority, and concomitant beliefs in the superiority of the dominant group" (A. Smith, 1997, p. 289). Internalized homophobia and biphobia develop from the negative messages society puts forth about gays, lesbians, and bisexuals. These messages, especially those about gays and lesbians, are known by childhood (Caitlin & Futterman, 1997).

LGB people are marginalized in American society (Fox, 1995; Hancock, 1995). This marginalization coupled with self-hatred permeates one's entire being. "Negative feelings about one's sexual orientation may be overgeneralized to encompass the entire self. Effects of this may range from a mild tendency toward self-doubt in the face of prejudice to overt self-hatred and self-destructive behavior" (Gonsiorek & Rudolph, 1991, p. 166).

Bisexuals are marginalized in both the gay–lesbian and the heterosexual communities and, therefore, are likely to have internalized negative messages from both communities. Generally, gays and lesbians accuse bisexuals of not accepting their "true" gay or lesbian identity, and heterosexuals are unable to accept the same-gender attractions bisexuals have. Many bisexuals, although certainly not all, stretch traditional norms by experimenting with different types of relationships (Halpern & Ashbrook, 1997; Matteson, 1996; Rust, 1996a). Bisexual people who practice polyamory must fight the "cultural idealization of monogamy" (Rust, 1996b, p. 130), which engenders negative judgments from others as well as from their therapists.

Rust (1996b) is currently involved in ongoing international research about the relational forms of bisexuals. In her analysis of the first 577 questionnaires from the United States, Rust found that bisexual persons were more likely than either heterosexual or homosexual persons to be involved with one or more partners or to desire polyamorous relationships. Many therapists see this as immature or irresponsible and react negatively to bisexual clients who discuss or explore different relational forms. Rust (1996b) stated that "this reaction is conditioned by a sex-negative and monogamy-positive culture and that purely sexual encounters are no more inherently immature or irresponsible than sexual behavior within the context of a relationship" (p. 137). When therapists label these relational forms as immature or irresponsible, they are supporting the internalized biphobia experienced by bisexual clients.

Societal messages are the main reason for internalized homophobia and biphobia. These messages sometimes lead to outright violence against LGB people, and LGB clients may come to therapy after having been the victim of such anti-LGB violence.

Victimization

Anti-LGB violence is more common then most people realize. Herek and others (see Herek & Berrill, 1992) have been researching the prevalence of and psychological effects of these crimes for a number of years. An exploration of all the psychological dynamics involved is beyond the scope of this chapter. It is important for therapists to know that when a person is physically or verbally attacked because of sexual identity or perceived sexual identity, love, sex, and intimacy become paired with feelings of vulnerability (Caitlin & Futterman, 1997; Hancock, 1995; Herek, Gillis, & Cogan, 1997).

All the symptoms commonly associated with posttraumatic stress are likely to follow a physical or verbal attack, in varying degrees of intensity, depending on the circumstances of the attack and the vulnerability of the victim. In a 4-year study of hate crimes against LGB people, Herek et al. (1997) found that stress, depression, and anger lingered for as long as 5 years after the attack. In addition to posttraumatic symptoms, an LGB client can experience anxiety about his or her sexual identification (Bridgewater, 1992). Often there is regression to earlier stages of the coming out process. Bridgewater presented a case study of a gay male survivor of antigay violence and recommended a multifaceted approach including affect regulation and cognitive and behavioral interventions.

Therapists working with LGB clients not only have to be prepared to work on the treatment issues described but also must be ready to respond to the questions that are frequently asked. These questions are explored in the next section.

CLIENT QUESTIONS

Each of the following questions that LGB clients often bring to therapy could constitute a complete chapter by itself. This section briefly explores the following: (a) the question of causality of an LGB orientation, (b) the question "Am I really LGB?" and (c) the question about religion and the acceptance of LGB sexuality.

Question of Causality

Scientists are searching for the "gay gene" (perhaps a search for the bisexual gene will follow) with controversial results (Bailey & Pillard, 1991). Clients often want to know what caused them to become lesbian, gay, or bisexual. (This question seems to be more frequently asked by lesbian or gay clients than by bisexual clients.) The question of causality usually is an indication of internalized homophobia or biphobia, implying "if I knew why, I could change it and become heterosexual." Therefore, it is important to explore with the client what knowing the cause of the LGB orientation would do for him or her (Davison, 1991). A possible response is to share findings from or to refer the client to psychological literature that explores essentialism (where identity is biologically determined) versus constructionism (where identity is constructed out of a historical, cultural context). The reader is encouraged to refer to Broido, chapter 1, this volume, for a more extensive explanation of these two points of view. Another response is to review studies of psychological adjustment and the controversial findings of research into various family dynamics and their effect on sexual orientation. Siegelman (1987) conducted an exhaustive review of empirical data on findings from psychological tests and research on parent–child relationships.

Just as the gay gene has not yet been discovered, the answer to the question about whether homosexuality and bisexuality are fixed or chosen is not known. In their large study of LGB people, Herek et al. (1997) found that most respondents believed they did not choose to be gay, lesbian, or bisexual. However, women and bisexuals were more likely than gay men to believe there was some choice in their sexual identity.

Am I Really Gay, Lesbian, or Bisexual?

Shively and De Cecco (1977) considered sexual identification to have four parts: biological sex, which is noted by chromosomes; gender identity; sex role; and sexual orientation. These may or may not agree; experience often does not match behavior (Gonsiorek & Weinrich, 1991a). To add to the confusion, as previously discussed, there is controversy about whether sexual orientation is fixed or fluid (and best defined by the term *sexual preference*). The therapist should explore with the client (a) sexual behavior, (b) romantic behavior, (c) attractions, (d) fantasies, and (e) thoughts (or fantasies) about future sexual contact with one or the other gender or with both genders (Alquijay, 1997).

It is also important to explore with the client the fact that an LGB identity in this society has come to mean more than sex. The newer layer of meaning, which we name *sexual identity*, concerns socially constructed experiences of identity and of membership in groups (gay men, lesbians, bisexual people) that have developed their own cultures. A third layer of meaning has emerged more recently, called *sexual orientation*. This layer of meaning has to do with what many people, particularly heterosexual and gay men, report as a core knowledge from early childhood about the nature of their sexual inclination and capacities—whether they are homoerotic or heteroerotic. All of these aspects are culturally mediated and individually constructed (Wishik & Pierce, 1995, pp. 182–183).

The question of whether a person is LGB is problematic because behavior does not always reflect identity. The gender of the person with whom the client engages in sexual activity does not always match the sexual identification the client claims. Within the literature on lesbians (Blumstein & Schwartz, 1977; Golden, 1987; Rothblum, 1994), there is the suggestion that some women identify one way publicly (as lesbian) and another way privately (as bisexual). Whereas some researchers have divided lesbian identity into primary versus elective, depending on whether the person's past includes heterosexual behavior (Golden, 1987), most clients are not interested in this classification. The therapist must listen to the unique experience of the client and help him or her to accept the identity that is most comfortable.

Religion

The major organized religions of the United States (Christianity, Judaism, Islam) have not been kind to sexual minorities (O'Neill & Ritter, 1992). Many LGB clients struggle with early religious messages, family religious pronouncements, and, more personally, a deep conflict over whether or not G-d loves them if they are not heterosexual.[1] Some bisexual clients seem to have made peace with their religious beliefs around their same-gender attractions, but if their relationships are polyamorous, they sometimes struggle with religious precepts about adultery. The struggle over whether G-d can love a gay or lesbian person can occur even after a client has rejected religious teachings and accepted his or her sexual identity for years. It is helpful to refer LGB clients who have religious concerns to gay-, lesbian-, and bisexual-affirmative clergy and to books that discuss religious precepts in an LGB-affirmative way. The reader is encouraged to refer to Davidson, chapter 17, this volume, as well as the following resources: *Twice Blessed: On Being Lesbian, Gay and Jewish* (Balka & Rose, 1989), *Coming Out Within: Stages of Spiritual Awakening for Lesbians and Gay Men* (O'Neill & Ritter, 1992), and *Just as I Am: A Practical Guide to Being Out, Proud, and Christian* (Williams, 1992).

The next section explores the need for therapists to examine their

---

[1]In the Jewish religion it is forbidden to name the Supreme Being. Therefore, many Jews use a hyphen between the G and the *d* when writing the English equivalent of the deity's name. I have continued this tradition by writing G-d.

own sexual identity and racial or ethnic identity, some common inappropriate therapist responses, and the biases of the therapist's theoretical orientation. The reader is directed to Morrow, chapter 6, this volume, for an in-depth exploration of therapist issues in working with LGB clients.

THERAPIST ISSUES

Therapist Sexual and Racial–Ethnic Identity

It is essential for therapists to have explored their own sexual identity and to be comfortable with it (Falco, 1991; Hancock, 1995). Therapists who are LGB should not automatically assume that they are competent in working with LGB clients (Hall, 1997). Training for work with nonheterosexual populations should always include an exploration of therapist attitudes and beliefs about sexual identity and sexual orientation. Transference and countertransference are also important areas for exploration. Heterosexual therapists who are insecure in their own sexual identity may experience eroticized countertransference and share too much personal information within the therapy session (Greene, 1997). Brown (1995) cautioned researchers to clarify the sexual identity paradigm they are operating from; this caution is relevant for therapists also: "Adopt a paradigm of multiple, diversely normal streams of sexual identity development with many possible successful outcomes" (p. 14).

Greene (1997) stated that therapists from the dominant culture may be insecure about their racial–ethnic identity as well as their sexual identity. These therapists may be unsure about working with LGB clients from racial or ethnic minority groups. Fearing early termination of clients, they may avoid or minimize sexual issues and foreclose any discussion of sexual identity. On the other hand, Greene warned racial or ethnic minority-group therapists not to overidentify with their racial or ethnic minority-group clients, which can result in ignoring pathology. Therefore, therapists have to be not only sexual identity literate but also culturally literate (Greene, 1997). It is hard, if not impossible, to separate cultural identity from sexual identity, and it is also difficult not to get caught up in personal feelings about the multiple oppressions LGB clients from racial or ethnic minority groups experience. "Therapists err, however, if their feeling sorry for clients or admiring clients (romanticizing clients' struggles) leads them to avoid setting appropriate limits in treatment or calling clients' attention to their own roles in their dilemmas" (Greene, 1997, p. 229).

Therapist Responses

Therapists who have not explored their own sexual identity, ethnic identity, and beliefs about sexual behavior may make inappropriate responses to the presenting concerns of LGB clients. A common therapist misconception that arises from an absence of or inadequate exploration of sexual behavior is that any gay or lesbian experience means the client is gay or lesbian (Baron, 1992; Bi Vocals, 1983; Dworkin, 1996; Fox, 1995). This misconception negates the possibility of a bisexual identity.

Another misconception is that monogamous sexual behavior is necessary for healthy relationships. LGB clients often have relationship patterns that do not fit the traditional monogamous model. Therapists need to examine their assumptions about monogamy and polyamory and make sure that they are not bringing their biases into their work with nonmonogamous couples. An example of therapist bias about sexual behavior is the labeling of extensive sexual activity by gay men as sexual compulsion (Pincu, 1989).

Some concrete examples of inappropriate therapist responses that can result from bypassing the necessary exploration of LGB issues are provided by Falco (1991, pp. 43–45). When a client shares LGB experiences, the therapist might respond, "You're not a lesbian" (or not a gay man, or not a bisexual woman or man). This response negates the experience voiced by the client. Another way the therapist may respond to the client is with a lecture, which is a less subtle homophobic response. The therapist informs the client that homosexuality or bisexuality is unnatural, unhealthy, or a symptom of arrested development. Some therapists make "The Liberal Response," stating that the LGB client is no different from anyone else. Finally, a therapist may make "The Inadequate Response," a total avoidance of the issue of a sexual minority identity. Silverstein (1991) viewed the homophobia of many of these inappropriate responses as psychology's maintenance of middle-class, White culture and its collusion in attempting to wipe out "queer" culture.

Theoretical Orientation

Any theoretical orientation a therapist subscribes to can be useful in working with an LGB client in an affirmative way (see Fassinger, chapter 5, this volume). Even psychoanalysis, which for years set the standard for the "homosexuality as illness" paradigm, is now being explored for useful concepts for gay- and lesbian- (and presumably bisexual-) affirmative treatment (see Glassgold & Iasenza, 1995, *Lesbians and Psychoanalysis*). Falco (1991) speculated on how various psychotherapy schools would respond to working with lesbians in an affirmative way. Some of the theories she speculated about are psychodynamic theory, object relations and developmental theory, existentialism, humanism, systems theory, gestalt theory, and cognitive and behavioral theories. Fassinger (1991; also see chapter 5, this volume) did more than speculate about the use of different theoretical orientations for LGB therapies. She has stated that cognitive therapy can be used to work on irrational thinking and negative self-talk in terms of internalized homophobia and biphobia. Client-centered therapy can help the client express affect and experience nonjudgmental acceptance for sexual minority identity. Gestalt therapy can help the client integrate aspects of conflict and experience vicarious confrontations around sexual identity. Finally, feminist therapy can help the client to explore oppression and sex role socialization.

Gonsiorek (1995), Gonsiorek and Rudolph (1991), and Dworkin (1997) have looked at self psychology and examined how nonheterosexual people (and Jewish women, in Dworkin, 1997) experience narcissistic injury, because only heterosexuality and Christianity are accepted, mirrored, and valued. "Overall, any theoretical approach or intervention should be carefully examined and reexamined throughout implementation for inherent bias and should be applied with sensitivity and professional self-awareness" (Fassinger, 1991, p. 172).

CONCLUSION

Therapists assess, diagnose, and treat clients with the tools provided through many venues, including education, theoretical writings, initial and continued training, professional literature, consultation, and research. Therapy has become more complex owing to the recognition of the many factors that affect mental health. This chapter has explored the interaction of sexual identity with ethnicity, gender, culture, and disability.

Throughout this chapter a few simple but important ideas have been emphasized. The most important one is to hear the client's voice. Therapists are trained to listen and listen closely to clients' stories of their lives and their identities. It is important not to under- or overemphasize a client's LGB identity. The LGB identity may or may not be the critical issue for therapy. Nevertheless, this identity does affect a client's journey through all aspects of his or her life and life systems, as does gender, ethnicity, religion or spirituality, class, ability or disability, and locale (and many other characteristic descriptors). Therapists must help clients to weave all of these seemingly disparate characteristics into an integrated whole that works for their unique lives.

As the APA ethics code prescribes, therapists are enjoined to do good, which means to do good therapy. This cannot be done unless therapists understand the theoretical framework, or therapy paradigm, from which they operate. Fassinger (1991) stated that therapists must also examine these frameworks for any inherent LGB biases. In addition, therapists must critically examine traditional methods of assessment and diagnosis for biases. At the same time, therapists must use these tools when necessary for understanding and appropriately differentiating the underlying emotional distress from characterological issues as well as from the distress of coming out as an LGB person. Therapists must be well versed in the current literature about treatment strategies for LGB people. It is important to remember that it has only been since 1973 that the psychological literature has been lesbian- and gay-affirmative. For bisexual-affirmative therapy, the research is still in its infancy.

There is a great deal of research that needs to be done in the area of individual therapy with LGB clients. As discussed in this chapter (and elsewhere in this volume), new theories of sexual identity development are currently being explored. Multidimensional approaches are making it easier to include bisexuality development as part of identity development research. Process and outcome research, looking at the intersection of client problem, sexual identity, racial or ethnic identity, and other salient aspects of identity and matching that with therapist identity, gender, theoretical orientation, and other characteristics, is still needed. Increasing numbers of therapists operate from a systems perspective, and sexual identity affects many systems, as has been noted in this chapter. Psychologists of today are fortunate to live in an era when the inherent diversity of human beings and human behavior is recognized despite conservative momentum to eradicate any hint of sexual lifestyles other than the nuclear, heterosexual family.

REFERENCES

Alquijay, M. A. (1997). The relationships among self-esteem, acculturation and lesbian identity formation in Latina lesbians. In B. Greene (Ed.), *Ethnic and cultural diversity among lesbians and gay men* (pp. 249–265). Newbury Park, CA: Sage.

American Psychological Association. (1991). *Bias in psychotherapy with lesbians and gay men: Final report of the Task Force on Psychotherapy with Lesbians and Gay Men.* Washington, DC: Author.

Anderson, M. K., & Mavis, B. E. (1996). Sources of coming out self-efficacy for lesbians. *Journal of Homosexuality, 32*(2), 37–52.

Bailey, J. M., & Pillard, R. C. (1991). A genetic study of male sexual orientation. *Archives of General Psychiatry, 48,* 1089–1096.

Balka, C., & Rose, A. (1989). *Twice blessed: On being lesbian, gay and Jewish.* Boston: Beacon Press.

Baron, S. (1992, May). Bisexuality: Having it all. *Lear's,* pp. 55–60, 85.

Bi Vocals. (1983, April 23). Gay-identified bisexuals. *Bi Vocals,* p. 4.

Blumstein, P. W., & Schwartz, P. (1977). Bisexuality: Some social psychological issues. *Journal of Social Issues, 33*(2), 30–45.

Boden, R. (1992). Psychotherapy with physically disabled lesbians. In S. H. Dworkin & F. J. Gutierrez (Eds.), *Counseling gay men and lesbians: Journey to the end of the rainbow* (pp. 157–174). Alexandria, VA: AACD Press.

Bridgewater, D. (1992). A gay male survivor of antigay violence. In S. H. Dworkin & F. J. Gutierrez (Eds.), *Counseling gay men and lesbians: Journey to the end of the rainbow* (pp. 219–230). Alexandria, VA: AACD Press.

Brown, L. (1991). Ethical issues in feminist therapy: Selected topics. *Psychology of Women Quarterly, 15,* 323–336.

Brown, L. S. (1995). Lesbian identities: Concepts and issues. In A. R. D'Augelli & C. J. Patterson (Eds.), *Lesbian, gay, and bisexual identities over the lifespan* (pp. 3–23). New York: Oxford University Press.

Browning, C., Reynolds, A. L., & Dworkin, S. H. (1991). Affirmative psychotherapy for lesbian women. *The Counseling Psychologist, 19,* 177–196.

Buhrke, R. A., & Douce, L. A. (1991). Training issues for counseling psychologists in working with lesbian women and gay men. *The Counseling Psychologist, 19,* 216–234.

Caitlin, R., & Futterman, D. (1997). *Lesbian and gay youth: Care and counseling.* Philadelphia: Hanley & Belfus.

Cass, V. (1979). Homosexual identity formation: A theoretical model. *Journal of Homosexuality, 4,* 219–235.

Chan, C. S. (1992). Cultural considerations in counseling Asian-American lesbians and gay men. In S. H. Dworkin & F. J. Gutierrez (Eds.), *Counseling gay men and lesbians: Journey to the end of the rainbow* (pp. 115–124). Alexandria, VA: AACD Press.

Chan, C. S. (1995). Issues of sexual identity in an ethnic minority: The case of Chinese American lesbians, gay men, and bisexual people. In A. R. D'Augelli & C. J. Patterson (Eds.), *Lesbian, gay, and bisexual identitics over the Lifespan* (pp. 87–101). New York: Oxford University Press.

Clark, W. M., & Serovich, J. M. (1997). Twenty years and still in the dark? Content analyses of articles pertaining to gay, lesbian, and bisexual issues in marriage and family therapy journals. *Journal of Marital and Family Therapy, 23,* 239–253.

Coleman, E. (1982). Developmental stages of the coming out process. In J. C. Gonsiorek (Ed.), *Homosexuality and psychotherapy* (pp. 31–43). New York: Haworth Press.

Davison, G. C. (1991). Constructionism and morality in therapy for homosexuality. In J. C. Gonsiorek & J. D. Weinrich (Eds.), *Homosexuality: Research implications for public policy* (pp. 137–148). Newbury Park, CA: Sage.

de Monteflores, C., & Schultz, S. (1978). Coming out: Similarities and differences for lesbians and gay men. *Journal of Social Issues, 34,* 59–72.

Dworkin, S. H. (1996, August). *Bisexual women, understanding sexual identity: Research in progress.* Paper presented at the 104th Annual Convention of the American Psychological Association, Toronto, Ontario, Canada.

Dworkin, S. H. (1997). Female, lesbian, and Jewish: Complex and invisible. In B.

Greene (Ed.), *Ethnic and cultural diversity among lesbians and gay men* (pp. 63–87). Newbury Park, CA: Sage.

Dworkin, S. H., & Gutierrez, F. J. (1992). *Counseling gay men and lesbians: Journey to the end of the rainbow.* Alexandria, VA: AACD Press.

Faderman, L. (1991). *Odd girls and twilight lovers: A history of lesbian life in twentieth-century America.* New York: Columbia University Press.

Falco, K. L. (1991). *Psychotherapy with lesbian clients: Theory into practice.* New York: Brunner/Mazel.

Fassinger, R. E. (1991). The hidden minority: Issues and challenges in working with lesbian women and gay men. *The Counseling Psychologist, 19,* 157–176.

Fassinger, R. E., & Miller, B. A. (1996). Validation of an inclusive model of sexual minority identity formation on a sample of gay men. *Journal of Homosexuality, 32*(2), 53–78.

Firestein, B. A. (1996). Bisexuality as paradigm shifts: Transforming our disciplines. In B. A. Firestein (Ed.), *Bisexuality: The psychology and politics of an invisible minority* (pp. 263–291). Newbury Park, CA: Sage.

Fox, R. C. (1995). Bisexual identities. In A. R. D'Augelli & C. J. Patterson (Eds.), *Lesbian, gay and bisexual identities over the lifespan* (pp. 48–86). New York: Oxford University Press.

Fox, R. C. (1996). Bisexuality in perspective: A review of theory and research. In B. A. Firestein (Ed.), *Bisexuality: The psychology and politics of an invisible minority* (pp. 3–50). Newbury Park, CA: Sage.

Fygetakis, L. M. (1997). Greek American lesbians: Identity odysseys of honorable good girls. In B. Greene (Ed.), *Ethnic and cultural diversity among lesbians and gay men* (pp. 152–190). Newbury Park, CA: Sage.

Garnets, L., Hancock, K. A., Cochran, S. D., Goodchilds, J., & Peplau, L. A. (1991). Issues in psychotherapy with lesbians and gay men: A survey of psychologists. *American Psychologist, 46,* 964–972.

Glassgold, J. M., & Iasenza, S. (Eds.) (1995). *Lesbians and psychoanalysis: Revolutions in theory and practice.* New York: Free Press.

Golden, C. (1987). Diversity and variability. In Boston Lesbian Psychologies Collective (Eds.), *Lesbian psychologies* (pp. 19–34). Urbana: University of Illinois Press.

Gonsiorek, J. C. (1982). The use of diagnostic concepts in working with gay and lesbian populations. In J. C. Gonsiorek (Ed.), *Homosexuality and psychotherapy: A practitioner's handbook of affirmative models* (pp. 9–20). New York: Haworth Press.

Gonsiorek, J. C. (1995). Gay male identities: Concepts and issues. In A. R. D'Augelli & C. J. Patterson (Eds.), *Lesbian, gay, and bisexual identities over the lifespan* (pp. 24–47). New York: Oxford University Press.

Gonsiorek, J. C., & Rudolph, J. R. (1991). Homosexual identity: Coming out and other developmental events. In J. C. Gonsiorek & J. D. Weinrich (Eds.), *Homosexuality: Research implications and public policy* (pp. 161–176). Newbury Park, CA: Sage.

Gonsiorek, J. C., & Weinrich, J. D. (1991a). The definition and scope of sexual orientation. In J. C. Gonsiorek & J. D. Weinrich (Eds.), *Homosexuality: Research implications for public policy* (pp. 1–12). Newbury Park, CA: Sage.

Gonsiorek, J. C., & Weinrich, J. D. (1991b). Introduction. In J. C. Gonsiorek & J. D. Weinrich (Eds.), *Homosexuality: Research implications for public policy* (pp. xi–xv). Newbury Park, CA: Sage.

Greene, B. (1997). Ethnic minority lesbians and gay men: Mental health and treatment issues. In B. Greene (Ed.), *Ethnic and cultural diversity among lesbians and gay men* (pp. 216–239). Newbury Park, CA: Sage.

Gutierrez, F. J., & Dworkin, S. H. (1992). Gay, lesbian and African American: Managing the integration of identities. In S. H. Dworkin & F. J. Gutierrez (Eds.), *Counseling gay men and lesbians: Journey to the end of the rainbow* (pp. 141–156). Alexandria, VA: AACD Press.

Hall, C. C. I. (1997). Cultural malpractice: The growing obsolescence of psychology with the changing U.S. population. *American Psychologist, 52,* 642–651.

Halpern, E. L., & Ashbrook, P. W. (1997, March). *Responsible polyamory for women (alternative to monogamy).* Structured discussion conducted at the annual convention of the Association for Women in Psychology, Pittsburgh, PA.

Hancock, K. A. (1995). Psychotherapy with lesbians and gay men. In A. R. D'Augelli & C. J. Patterson (Eds.), *Lesbian, gay, and bisexual identities over the lifespan* (pp. 323–336). New York: Oxford University Press.

Hanley-Hackenbruck, P. (1989). Psychotherapy and the "coming out" process. *Journal of Gay and Lesbian Psychotherapy, 1,* 21–39.

Herek, G. M., & Berrill, K. T. (Eds.). (1992). *Hate crimes.* Newbury Park, CA: Sage.

Herek, G. M., Gillis, R. J., & Cogan, J. (1997, May). *Study offers "snapshot" of Sacramento area lesbian, gay and bisexual community.* Available http://psychology.ucdavis.edu/rainbow/default.html

Hutchins, L., & Kaahumanu, L. (Eds.). (1991). *Bi any other name: Bisexual people speak out.* Boston: Alyson.

Klein, F. (1993). *The bisexual option* (2nd ed.). New York: Harrington Park.

Matteson, D. R. (1996). Counseling and psychotherapy with bisexual and exploring clients. In B. A. Firestein (Ed.), *Bisexuality: The psychology and politics of an invisible minority* (pp. 185–213). Newbury Park, CA: Sage.

Morales, E. S. (1992). Counseling Latino gays and Latina lesbians. In S. H. Dworkin & F. J. Gutierrez (Eds.), *Counseling gay men and lesbians: Journey to the end of the rainbow* (pp. 125–139). Alexandria, VA: AACD Press.

Morris, J. F. (1997). Lesbian coming out as a multidimensional process. *Journal of Homosexuality, 33*(2), 1–22.

Murphy, B. C. (1992). Counseling lesbian couples: Sexism, heterosexism, and homophobia. In S. H. Dworkin & F. J. Gutierrez (Eds.), *Counseling gay men and lesbians: Journey to the end of the rainbow* (pp. 63–79). Alexandria, VA: AACD Press.

National Institute of Mental Health. (1987). *National lesbian health care survey* (DHHS Publication Contract No. 86M019832201D). Washington, DC: U.S. Government Printing Office.

Ochs, R. (Ed.). (1995). *The bisexual resource guide*. Available from the Bisexual Resource Center, P.O. Box 639, Cambridge, MA.

O'Neill, C., & Ritter, K. (1992). *Coming out within: Stages of spiritual awakening for lesbians and gay men*. San Francisco: HarperCollins.

Pincu, L. (1989). Sexual compulsivity in gay men: Controversy and treatment. *Journal of Counseling and Development, 68*(1), 63–66.

Pope, M. (1992). Bias in the interpretation of psychological tests. In S. H. Dworkin & F. J. Gutierrez (Eds.), *Counseling gay men and lesbians: Journey to the end of the rainbow* (pp. 277–291). Alexandria, VA: AACD Press.

Rothblum, E. D. (1994). Transforming lesbian sexuality. *Psychology of Women Quarterly, 18,* 627–641.

Rust, P. C. (1993). "Coming out" in an age of social constructionism: Sexual identity formation among lesbian and bisexual women. *Gender & Society, 7*(1), 50–77.

Rust, P. C. (1996a). Managing multiple identities: Diversity among bisexual women and men. In B. A. Firestein (Ed.), *Bisexuality: The psychology and politics of an invisible minority* (pp. 53–83). Newbury Park, CA: Sage.

Rust, P. C. (1996b). Monogamy and polyamory relationship issues for bisexuals. In B. A. Firestein (Ed.), *Bisexuality: The psychology and politics of an invisible minority* (pp. 127–148). Newbury Park, CA: Sage.

Shannon, J. W., & Woods, W. J. (1991). Affirmative psychotherapy for gay men. *The Counseling Psychologist, 19,* 197–215.

Shively, M. G., & De Cecco, J. P. (1977). Components of sexual identity. *Journal of Homosexuality, 3,* 41–48.

Siegelman, M. (1987). Kinsey and others: Empirical input. In L. Diamant (Ed.), *Male and female homosexuality: Psychological approaches* (pp. 33–79). New York: Hemisphere.

Silverstein, C. (1991). Psychological and medical treatments of homosexuality. In J. C. Gonsiorek & J. D. Weinrach (Eds.), *Homosexuality: Research implications for public policy* (pp. 101–114). Newbury Park, CA: Sage.

Smith, A. (1997). Cultural diversity and the coming-out process: Implications for therapy practice. In B. Greene (Ed.), *Ethnic and cultural diversity among lesbians and gay men* (pp. 279–300). Newbury Park, CA: Sage.

Smith, J. (1988). Psychopathology, homosexuality, and homophobia. *Journal of Homosexuality, 15*(1/2), 59–73.

Sophie, J. (1982). Counseling lesbians. *Personnel and Guidance Journal, 60,* 341–345.

Troiden, R. R. (1989). The formation of homosexual identities. *Journal of Homosexuality, 17*(1), 43–73.

Trujillo, C. M. (1997). Sexual identity and the discontents of difference. In B.

Greene (Ed.), *Ethnic and cultural diversity among lesbians and gay men* (pp. 266–278). Newbury Park, CA: Sage.

Vontress, C. E., & Epp, L. R. (1997). Historical hostility in the African American client: Implications for counseling. *Journal of Multicultural Counseling and Development, 25,* 170–184.

Weinberg, M. S., Williams, C. J., & Pryor, D. W. (1994). *Dual attraction: Understanding bisexuality.* New York: Oxford University Press.

Williams, R. (1992). *Just as I am: A practical guide to being out, proud, and Christian.* New York: HarperCollins.

Wishik, H., & Pierce, C. (1995). *Sexual orientation and identity: Heterosexual, lesbian, gay and bisexual journeys.* Laconia, NH: New Dynamics.

8

GROUP COUNSELING THEORY AND PRACTICE WITH LESBIAN, GAY, AND BISEXUAL CLIENTS

KURT A. DeBORD AND RUPERTO M. PEREZ

Group therapy is powerful, dynamic, and effective as an intervention that provides clients with opportunities to address numerous concerns, including relationships, depression, anxiety, family issues, career issues, and other life experiences (Conyne, 1997). Recent empirical work has supported the notion that group work is just as effective as individual therapy (Seligman, 1995). Given this research and the fact that group work is generally more cost-effective than individual counseling, it is a wonder that group therapy is not more consistently considered as a psychotherapeutic option. Because of the advantages it can offer lesbian, gay, or bisexual (LGB) clients, group therapy is emerging as a therapeutic force that must be considered systematically as a potential intervention by those who provide therapy for this population.

Group counseling is unique in the therapeutic benefits it can offer to LGB clients. One such benefit is the opportunity it provides to LGB clients to identify and express feelings about being a "hidden minority" (Fassinger, 1991) and to have those feelings validated by others who share this status. In addition, group therapy affords LGB clients opportunities to openly describe, explore, and understand experiences that no other population is faced with (e.g., coming out, internalized homophobia). Even in therapeutic work with issues that are not specific to LGB individuals, LGB group members can experience safety and emotional validation in an LGB group because of the context shared by its members.

In this chapter we examine the theory, effectiveness, and potentials of group psychotherapy with LGB clients. The chapter is designed to promote LGB group practice and training by adopting Yalom's (1970) set of therapeutic factors and applying them to the existing body of scholarly work on LGB groups. Yalom's theory of group therapy was selected as a conceptual tool because it offers a comprehensive and well-known heuristic for understanding group dynamics as well as the therapeutic effectiveness of groups. Before elaborating on those important areas, the needs for practice, training, research, and further theory development in this area are briefly addressed.

WHY GROUP COUNSELING?

Why is there a need for group work with LGB clients? According to Holahan and Gibson (1994), LGB clients reported that they sought group therapy to help them deal with family and societal rejection. Such rejection is logically a less common motivation among heterosexuals to seek group therapy and an indication that an important difference exists between the therapeutic group needs of LGB and heterosexual clients. Furthermore, LGB clients reported that they sought group therapy to work on self-esteem, family-of-origin issues, and interpersonal skills related to emotional intimacy, which are significant areas for psychotherapeutic group interventions for both LGB and heterosexual clients. However, as mentioned earlier, discussing these issues with group members who share a common identity and similar social contexts can provide numerous opportunities for emotional and cognitive validation in ways that traditional one-on-one therapy cannot.

Primarily because of the pervasive and destructive effects of societal homophobia, the need and demand for therapy by LGB individuals differ from those of non-LGB persons. Herek (1989) and D'Augelli and Rose (1990) have documented the prevalence of homophobia and hate crimes perpetrated against LGBs across the United States. Psychotherapy groups for LGBs are particularly well suited for providing opportunities for obtaining support, safety, and a place of belonging in a societal environment that is hostile to LGBs. Furthermore, groups can provide support and validation in a critical way that individual therapy cannot. That is, LGB groups can empower individual members by allowing them to see the strategies other LGB members have used in coping successfully with a homophobic society. Given this and the fact that Rudolph (1988) reported that more LGB people than heterosexuals seek psychotherapy, a unique need exists for LGB psychotherapy groups and competent psychotherapists to facilitate them (D'Augelli, 1989).

GROUP RESEARCH AND THEORY

Unfortunately, quantitative research in the area of LGB groups is scant and narrowly focused. A thorough literature search uncovered only six quantitative, empirical studies of LGBs (Everaerd et al., 1982; Hedge & Glover, 1990; Mulder et al., 1994; Quadland, 1985; Reece, 1981/1982; Russell & Winkler, 1977). Of these six, only two were published in the past decade, three dealt specifically with sexual dysfunction, and two dealt with issues related to the human immunodeficiency virus (HIV). All six focused solely on men. Generally, as Riva and Smith (1997) concluded in their critique of the current state of group research, "little information is available about the provision of group treatment to gay and lesbian clients." (p. 270). Even less information is available about bisexuals (Wolf, 1987). In terms of recent nonquantitative, nonempirical work, an examination of the past 5 years of the *International Journal of Group Psychotherapy* and the *Journal for Specialists in Group Work* uncovered only one article that focused specifically on groups with lesbian, gay, or bisexual clients (Norsworthy & Horne, 1994). It, too, focused solely on men.

What are common in the scholarly literature on groups are case studies and descriptions of various LGB group experiences (e.g., Westefeld & Winkelpleck, 1983), although many of these are dated. Whereas case studies and other scholarly publications concerning LGB groups can serve to guide the LGB group facilitator through relatively unexplored therapeutic terrain, there is a need, identified by Horne (1994), for research that helps answer questions such as "Does empathy work the same in all groups? With various populations? Is empathy the same for a therapist or counselor leading a group of male sex abusers as it is for an HIV-positive gay men's group?" (p. 139). Until the much-needed research on population-specific group work is conducted, therapists' working hypotheses must be based on the available group research and theory.

Like research, theoretical development in the area of therapy groups has been slow to respond to the significance of LGB diversity. Conyne (1997) made the call for group theories that incorporate the importance and intricacies of multiculturalism, but such a major theoretical shift in the field has yet to occur. In the absence of such a shift, group facilitators are left to determine how to practice ethically and effectively by using the existing theoretical models that are most appropriate to their group dynamics. Under such conditions, it is commonly concluded that "you can't go wrong with those therapeutic conditions" (Conyne, 1997, p. 153). These therapeutic conditions, or therapeutic factors, were first outlined by Yalom (1970) as the necessary ingredients for productive group work. Research on the factors has been substantial, but agreement as to how to measure them (Horne & Rosenthal, 1997) and the consistent inclusion of them in research (Kalodner, Alfred, & Hoyt, 1997) have yet to be achieved. Nonetheless, the widespread acceptance of the importance of the factors to group psychotherapy allows them to be used as theoretical tools with which one can build on the existing body of LGB group work.

As mentioned, in this chapter, we promote LGB group therapy and training by using Yalom's set of therapeutic factors. Although most practitioners are probably already familiar with these factors, we provide definitions of them as well as recommendations about how to consider them in relation to LGB group preparation and process. The body of research on LGB groups may not be extensive, but the authors of published LGB group case studies have been exceptionally astute in articulating their observations regarding the variables that affected the groups about which they wrote (and often facilitated). Their insights into running effective groups (from how to conduct client selection to how to work through termination) are discussed in terms of how they relate to the therapeutic factors. In addition, we include our own insights gained from facilitating LGB groups. The chapter concludes with the identification of important areas for future theory development, research, and practice in the area of LGB group counseling and therapy.

THE THERAPEUTIC FACTORS: APPLICATION TO LGB GROUP THERAPY

Yalom (1995) described 11 therapeutic factors that were derived from his clinical experience as arbitrary constructs. According to Yalom, these constructs are interdependent, critical to the therapeutic process, and relevant to different aspects of client change and growth. For instance, some factors appear most closely related to client behavioral change, whereas others appear more closely related to client learning and insight. In the most recent revision of his landmark book, *The Theory and Practice of Group Psychotherapy*, Yalom articulated how the factors dramatically play themselves out in many psychotherapeutic process-oriented groups. Rather than duplicate his efforts by describing the same dynamics for LGB process groups, we describe here how leaders or facilitators of LGB groups can significantly influence the manifestation of these factors by laying the appropriate groundwork. Rather than separately describing the decisions a group leader must make during the initial developmental stages of a group, those decisions and related variables are each described in relation to their effects on the therapeutic factors. For example, advertisement of the group is discussed in relation to instillation of hope, confidentiality is discussed in terms of group cohesion, and selection of a meeting place is discussed in the section on catharsis. Although nonlinear, this format should provide a pragmatic way for practitioners to conceptualize the formation of an LGB therapy group.

The content and subsequent structure of the chapter are based on the therapeutic factors; the order in which the factors are discussed is based on a developmental sequence. Although the factors are rated differentially important by group members depending on a number of variables (e.g., group type, leader ideology, and member intellectual level), no overarching theoretical model has been proposed to order the factors in any prescribed way. The factors are discussed here in the order in which they emerge in their importance to the life of a typical group (Yalom, 1995). This order provides an easy way to think about group dynamics and the therapeutic factors. However, the chapter's focus on the group groundwork laid by the facilitator challenges readers to consider a group's developmental progression in terms of how early decisions affect later outcomes.

The chapter's organization around the therapeutic factors was based on three considerations. First, differential treatment was given to the factors depending on their theoretical relationship to the groundwork necessary for LGB groups. Thus, some factors (e.g., instillation of hope) are discussed at length, whereas others (e.g., altruism) are only briefly discussed. Second, our placement of topics under the headings of specific therapeutic factors proceeded with regard to conceptual relevance. Although some topics could have been discussed under numerous factors, the most relevant topics to a factor were chosen for their inclusion under that factor. Finally, the 11 therapeutic factors are traditionally considered most germane to process-oriented groups. The focus of this chapter is primarily on LGB process-oriented groups, a term used in this chapter to signify jointly groups that deal primarily with LGB issues and those that are more general in focus. When a therapeutic factor was recognized as particularly relevant to structured or psychoeducational groups, specific mention of that relevance was identified.

Instillation of Hope

Instillation of hope as an agent of therapeutic change typically hinges on members' belief in the group facilitator, the group process, members' abilities to change, and the therapeutic successes of other group members (Yalom, 1995). These elements of hope are essential to group commitment and positive client outcomes (Yalom, 1995) regardless of whether the group is composed of LGB members. However, for LGB clients, instillation of hope can hinge on additional variables. For instance, the mere noticeable existence of an LGB group within a community can create a sense of hope and belonging in potential members before the beginning of the group. D'Augelli's (1989) description of a small community's lack of LGB resources makes clear that what is necessary in many small towns across the United States is an accessible and visible network of LGB support. LGB support and therapy groups can readily fill that gap in many instances. Once the decision has been made to establish an LGB group, hope can be imparted to members and potential members in a number of ways, including advertising, selecting members, placing members in the appropriate group, orienting members, and encouraging member disclosure. With structured groups, hope can also be imparted by designing and announcing a mission statement that clearly communicates hope, as well as by structuring therapeutic group activities around the hopes and dreams of members.

Advertising LGB groups in newspapers and on the radio and television or with flyers posted by local merchants can instill hope in the most closeted of LGB persons. Simply knowing that other LGB people exist who are able to identify as LGB and attend such a group can understandably diminish one's perceived need to continue living in Cass's (1979) stages of denial or identity confusion. Furthermore, if specific attention is given in an advertisement to welcoming bisexuals, less isolation may be experienced by members of this community who sometimes feel marginalized by lesbian and gay organizations. Advertising in various media that will reach numerous racial and ethnic minority groups is also essential in promoting a group that is of service to all members of an LGB community. Finally, building relationships with local business owners who agree to post group flyers allows a powerful message of LGB advocacy to be presented to all who patronize participating establishments (Perez, DeBord, & Brock, in press).

Selection, placement, and orientation of group members in an LGB group are additional points at which hope can be instilled and maintained in the developing LGB group. Most people interested enough in an LGB group to inquire about membership are likely to be good candidates for membership. However, in some environments where homophobia is rampant, it is possible that some people may be interested in gaining access to the group to harass members. To help preserve the safety of the group and the hope that safety provides, it is wise to conduct at least one face-to-face entrance interview with anyone interested in participating in the group. In addition, one major contraindication for LGB group participation is an exaggerated proneness to shame regarding sexual orientation that can be triggered by the slightest indication of rejection from other group members or from the group leader (Hawkins, 1993). As Hawkins noted, clients who are likely to attack other group members because of their own internalized homonegativity will probably benefit from individual psychotherapy before being admitted to an LGB group.

Placing members in the appropriate group is also an important aspect of maintaining and instilling hope. Hawkins (1993) recommended that therapists simultaneously consider a number of client background variables to place clients in the most therapeutically beneficial type of group (i.e., mixed groups with heterosexual and LGB members versus groups with only LGB members). These issues include client reference group, client therapy issues, client stigma-management strategies, and client stage of LGB identity development (Cass, 1979; Troiden, 1988). Although this chapter is exclusively focused on LGB groups, a psychotherapist should not underestimate the power of a mixed group to provide support and empowerment to an LGB member as well as to examine and explore issues of homophobia (Yalom, 1975). An orientation meeting also provides a time when prospective group members can have hope instilled, revived, or strengthened by a facilitator who articulates success stories of past members (with their permission), the goals of the group, and the facilitator's belief in the effectiveness of the group. However, facilitators also have a responsibility to ensure that their clients have a realistic view of what the group is about, because it is possible that some isolated LGB people may have the impression that their first contact with an LGB group will result in an unwavering sense of belongingness.

Self-disclosure is important to the instillation of hope in any group (Yalom, 1995), but it is particularly vital to an LGB group. Assuming that members of an LGB group will be at different stages of LGB identity development and at different levels of functioning and coping, members can benefit greatly by recognizing how others have coped successfully with the hardships and discrimination involved with self-identifying as LGB.

Finally, for structured groups, a number of activities can serve to enhance the hope that group members feel about therapeutic change and about positively expressing their sexual orientation. One such activity involves having group participants write a mission statement for the group that adequately reflects the vision of its members. This statement can be a testament to the pride members feel in their sexual identity and can be relied on as a beacon of hope for new members. Another group activity was proposed by Conlin and Smith (1981/1982); they suggest having one group meeting set aside for members to bring, introduce, and describe the importance to their lives of heterosexual allies (supportive friends or family members) who have played significant roles in their lives, thus decreasing members' sense of social isolation and increasing hope.

Universality

Therapists organizing an LGB group should be aware that universality is consistently one of the more important therapeutic factors affecting group work (Welch, 1996; Yalom, 1995). In describing this factor, Yalom

(1995) noted that it plays itself out as group members openly concede "we're all in the same boat" (p. 6). Although client problems may be complex and diverse, many clients experience relief on realizing that their concerns are not entirely unique to them. The therapeutic force behind this factor for LGB groups and the groundwork decisions related to this factor are presented after the following critical disclaimer is discussed.

This factor necessitates a disclaimer because its therapeutic value is partially woven in paradox. It is multiculturally insensitive to interpret and use universality as a justification for prioritizing member sameness over diversity. DeLucia-Waack (1996) called on group facilitators to acknowledge the fallacious nature of the common assumption that any group can be truly homogeneous. Group counselors and therapists should be willing and able to address the issues related to racial, cultural, gender, age, and socioeconomic diversity within an LGB group early in its development. Avoiding or ignoring how these variables uniquely affect one's personal and LGB identity sends a powerful negative message to group members about the value placed on within-group differences. Furthermore a group facilitator who adopts a culture-sensitive orientation (DeLucia-Waack, 1996) naturally encourages member discussion, confrontation, and clarification of the value placed on both member universality and diversity. In providing examples of exemplary clinical practice with LGB clients, Garnets, Hancock, Cochran, Goodchilds, and Peplau (1991) described ideal practice as that which recognizes the possible synergistic effects of multiple social statuses experienced by ethnic-minority gay men and lesbians (p. 968), particularly the isolating effects of dealing with multiple forms of discrimination and hatred. The paradox involved with this therapeutic factor is that acknowledging and discussing differences between group members often brings into sharp relief the commonalities that they share, including powerful feelings associated with the universal existential issues of isolation and aloneness (Yalom, 1995).

The therapeutic role that universality plays in LGB groups is significant. Although therapists often see LGB group members presenting with the same interpersonal and family-of-origin issues as heterosexual clients (Holahan & Gibson, 1994), LGB group members share the common, non-heterosexual experience of having been societally marginalized because of their sexual–affectional orientation. The positive effects of emotional validation about this experience should not be underestimated. Promoting and recruiting for diversity within a group can magnify this effect by making apparent through member self-disclosures the varied forms LGB phobia, LGB relationships, and LGB lifestyles can take (Perez et al., in press). In other words, if "we're all in the same boat," having a diverse group membership can emphasize how big that boat really is.

Although diversity is important, a few authors have noted the benefits of single-sex LGB groups. For instance, Perez et al. (in press) observed that lesbian and bisexual women may be hesitant to address their reactions to sexism in a mixed LGB group for fear of losing some of the group support and safety they experience in relation to their sexual orientation. It has been observed that members of all-male gay and bisexual groups sometimes become more quickly engaged in self-disclosure than those in mixed groups (Frost, 1996). In explaining this phenomenon, Frost suggested that it may be due to the relief members in an all-male group experience. According to Frost, this relief is experienced because members discover they are not alone in their reactions to stigmatizing societal messages about the incompatibility of possessing healthy masculine traits and being gay or bisexual.

Even though the advantages of a single-sex LGB group are noteworthy, conducting an LGB group that includes both men and women has a few advantages over single-sex groups, including increased opportunities to gain broader perspectives on common LGB issues such as parenting and coping with AIDS (see Frost, 1996, for a more extensive list). A few authors of case studies have recommended having both men and women in an LGB group (Lenihan, 1985; Westefeld & Winkelpleck, 1983). Westefeld and Winkelpleck based their recommendation on the stated preferences of their group members. Lenihan concluded that the potential benefits of a group were greater when it was composed of both men and women, specifically because of the increase in the effects of universality. In particular, she suggested that LGB men and women who openly disclose in a group how they psychologically defend themselves against oppression benefit from knowing that men and women use similar coping strategies. According to Lenihan, group members learn most by having in-group experiences that more readily generalize to the outside world, and single-sex social and work environments are rare.

Generally, the effects of universality in an LGB group help reduce emotional isolation and fears of being unlike anyone else. The facilitator decisions related to universality that must be made during the formation of the group include whether to run a mixed-sex group and how best to intertwine the therapeutic effects of universality and diversity.

Imparting Information

Imparting information through direct instruction has been a part of formal group work since the 1940s (Yalom, 1995). Many groups are designed specifically to convey information and instruction to their members on a number of topics such as stress-management techniques, substance abuse recovery, career decision making, and HIV–AIDS survival. In addition to these types of psychoeducational groups, which are exemplary in their use of this therapeutic factor, process-oriented groups also rely on the imparting of information as a therapeutic change agent.

In our experience, LGB process groups often serve as important stepping-stones for clients who have only recently identified as LGB. It is most often the newly identified who need and want information about their own culture and history to gain an understanding of their own identity. Also, imparting information in a process group can be practical for all members. Finding out about community resources or about how to set up an estate plan that is inclusive of one's partner can be beneficial to nearly all members of an LGB group.

In psychoeducational and structured groups, imparting information often takes the form of didactic instruction provided by the group leader or direct advice provided by group members (Yalom, 1995). This format can provide straightforward information to members about a variety of topics such as health, relationships, and life planning. This format affords group members the opportunity to become informed about topics such as the history of LGB political movements or the impact of LGB contributors to world culture (e.g., in poetry, philosophy, or film). Group leaders of these types of groups must make important decisions in the early life of a group regarding what educational topics will be covered and how the information will be provided. If these decisions are made thoughtfully, this type of group can act as a powerful educational and consciousness-raising agent (much like the role played by heterosexual-affirmative families and schools). In her case study, Masterson (1983) described a lesbian consciousness-raising group whose purpose was, in part, to inform members of how certain defense mechanisms are commonly used by members of minority groups, including aggressor identification and in-group criticism. Lenihan (1985) also acknowledged the importance of informing group members about healthy and unhealthy coping strategies commonly used at different stages of identity development.

In short, imparting information benefits LGB clients in obvious, straightforward ways. Although structured and psychoeducational groups are helpful to clients in providing direct information about special topics, LGB process groups can powerfully benefit members by imparting important information about how other members have successfully progressed through the stages of LGB identity development.

Development of Socializing Techniques

Developing socialization techniques in a group involves learning fundamental social skills. By paying attention to norms and common behaviors in LGB communities, LGB leaders of process groups can consider in advance the possible ways that socialization may occur within a group. In structured groups, a facilitator may decide to plan how to address the socialization of behaviors that are unique to LGB culture.

In process groups, examining social interaction among members is an important therapeutic practice. Facilitating open and genuine communication among members can increase group trust by creating an environment of genuineness and support that lends itself to greater member disclosure and group cohesion. Once healthy group social interaction is established, the group can assist members in the courageous act of self-identifying as LGB for the first time to friends, family members, and co-workers, an important behavior that few LGBs are socialized to do. Too often LGB people must face this task alone, without the support or advice of others. LGB groups can provide these critical therapeutic benefits in a way that few other resources can, especially by providing opportunities for feedback or role-play. Norsworthy and Horne (1994) emphasized that disclosures of coming out stories are typically valuable to other members, particularly those who are considering the consequences of coming out to someone new.

Structured and psychoeducational groups provide a way for LGB members to learn about interpersonal communication skills, managing relationships, and developing a social or support network. In our experience, members of an LGB structured group asserted that they had never been socialized in how to ask others of the same sex out on a date or how to bring up the topic of safer sex. By developing from beginning to end a "dream date" scenario, members helped to socialize each other in these important aspects of LGB behavior.

The development of socialization techniques is clearly a therapeutic factor that can combat the effects of isolation outside the group and sometimes even save lives (e.g., socializing a member about how to discuss safer sex with a prospective partner). Group leaders who consider how to address member socialization before a group starts will be better prepared to meet the unique needs of their LGB clients.

Altruism

Altruism is a factor that overlaps with many of the other factors. Providing information, support, hope, empathic understanding, and encouragement are all aspects of altruistic help giving. As such, altruism can be therapeutic in and of itself for LGB group members. Hawkins (1993) reported that when members intentionally help others to be prouder of their identities as LGB people, they inevitably take some ownership of the pride they are attempting to share. On the other hand, Randall's (1995) examinations of card-sort results from four different process groups indicated that this factor is consistently one of the less important of the therapeutic factors. Given the overlap with other factors, it is not surprising that the significance of altruistic behavior might appear diminished in attempts to assess its value empirically. In any event, the therapeutic aspects of altruism are notable, and for LGB groups, altruistic behavior may be enormously beneficial in giving members a sense of self-worth, value, and purpose.

Imitative Behavior

Imitative behavior benefits group members in that it allows observation of others' problem-solving behaviors and subsequent experimentation with the newly learned strategies. Members can learn problem-solving and communication skills from each other and from group facilitators. Perhaps more important, aspects of LGB pride and beliefs can be modeled and offered to the group. Given the critical role that facilitators play in a group, members often focus their imitative attention on them. Therefore, it is important to consider how the sexual orientation of facilitators has been described in the available literature as important to the success of an LGB group. Deciding how to approach this topic is important for LGB group facilitators early in the life of a group if the potential effects of the decision are to be used therapeutically. This issue is discussed in detail later.

Modeling aspects of LGB pride can be a powerful and facilitative therapeutic force in the life of an LGB group. Group members who have developed a more synthesized LGB identity can model and convey a sense of LGB pride to others in the group who may be in the initial stages of coming out to themselves or others. Masterson (1983) reported that one of the strengths of her consciousness-raising groups was the modeling of alternative attitudinal and emotional states by lesbian members who were considered "more experienced" (p. 29). Conlin and Smith (1981/1982) and Lenihan (1985) also reported that there were therapeutic effects generated in their groups by the modeling of various life and communication styles and by the imitative behavior encouraged by member role-plays.

It is widely recognized that role models provide an important ingredient in effective counseling and that LGB people frequently lack positive role models (Rochlin, 1994). The unique benefit offered by LGB therapists and counselors is that they can serve as positive and strong role models to group members (Conlin & Smith, 1981/1982). In addition, having two LGB cotherapists can emphasize the cultural diversity within an LGB community along a number of dimensions including values, attitudes, and beliefs. It is important for LGB group leaders to consider their own level of comfort in their own LGB identity development. Conlin and Smith (1981/1982) suggested that LGB therapists should be in the latter stages of coming out, having worked through disclosure to friends, family, and colleagues to the extent that this is possible. Depending on the nature of the group, the extent of therapist self-disclosure, and the therapist's visibility in a community, group members might interpret the therapist's hiding or "passing" behavior in the community as a mirror for their own shame. This could interfere with the group leader's perceived trustworthiness and thus the effectiveness of the group.

However, there are no empirical studies that support the notion that LGB groups are better off with LGB facilitators (Chojnacki & Gelberg, 1995). In their review of the literature, Holahan and Gibson (1994) concluded that the lack of LGB facilitators, client needs, and heterosexual facilitator sensitivity sometimes can outweigh the commonly accepted desirability of a client–therapist match on sexual orientation.

Several authors have agreed that a client–therapist match on sexual orientation is not exceptionally important in providing therapeutic benefits to LGB group members (Perez et al., in press; Rochlin, 1994; Schwartz & Harstein, 1986). Lenihan (1985) stated that "the critical factors [in choosing an LGB group facilitator], then, are not sexual orientation, life-style, or gender of the therapist, but professional effectiveness and the quality of the therapeutic relationships established in the group" (p. 736). Schwartz and Harstein (1986) contended that it is a mistake to assume that an LGB sexual orientation qualifies a therapist to facilitate an LGB group. Perez et al. (in press) elaborated on the work of Schwartz and Harstein to outline criteria for a minimum level of "therapeutic effectiveness" for an LGB group facilitator. They identified the following as critical to effective LGB group leadership: (a) knowledge of LGB identity development models, (b) awareness of the unique challenges faced by LGB people of color, (c) familiarity with local LGB resources, (d) understanding of the harmful effects of individual and institutionalized homophobia and heterosexism, and (e) comfort with LGB choices and relationships. Finally, when heterosexual leaders facilitate LGB groups, Holahan and Gibson (1994) have suggested that they self-identify as heterosexual early in the group to avoid undermining group trust. From their experiences with an LGB group, these authors concluded that part of the heterosexual facilitator's earned power to confront members within an LGB group comes from an open, assertive, and nondefensive stance adopted at the beginning of the group.

As a therapeutic factor, imitative behavior can have a powerful impact on LGB group members, especially when group facilitators contemplate and plan for its effects in the early stages of the life of a group. Group leaders can maximize its beneficial impact by spotlighting the behaviors of group members that are consistent with the developmental stage of LGB pride (Cass, 1979).

Corrective Recapitulation of the Primary Family Group

The transference relationships that develop in an LGB group allow for the corrective recapitulation of the primary family group and a great deal of interpersonal learning (see the following section). This therapeutic factor is more pronounced in process groups than in psychoeducational and structured groups because of the interpersonal processing that occurs in the former.

There are a number of transference reactions that members may develop as part of the process group. Lenihan (1985) asserted that transferential patterns or relationships (characterized by unconsciously and automatically relating to other group members as if they were family members, romantic partners, or important others) are common among members in LGB groups. Facilitators can become at least partially aware of the transferential patterns that may develop from group members toward themselves (e.g., idealization) during the initial member-screening interview. Facilitators who attend to this issue will be well equipped to manage their own countertransference reactions as they occur in the group. According to Lenihan, idealizing the facilitator and seeing him or her as lover, psychic, protector, and a nonperson are common transferential patterns in an LGB group. She also pointed out that "because issues of parental love and acceptance are dramatic for homosexuals [sic], the therapist as parent is a common pattern [of transference]" (Lenihan, 1985, p. 734). Taking time to note and record patterns of transference within a group can be helpful in understanding the interpersonal dynamics of individuals in the group as well as the ways in which the group may respond to transferential patterns.

Exploring and articulating how transferential perceptions and relationships have affected in-group interactions can provide group members with opportunities for interpersonal learning and the corrective recapitulation of their primary family group. For many group members, the group becomes a "family of choice" that provides much of the support, encouragement, empathic understanding, and education desired from families of origin. As a result of this transference, group members no longer feel the need to remain closeted and are able to shed many of their "hiding" strategies within the group (Welch, 1996). The opportunity to engage in this corrective emotional experience is unique to LGB interpersonal process groups; it is rarely provided for or attained in individual therapy or other relationships. Facilitators who encourage members to reflect on the recapitulation of family dynamics through transference foster therapeutic insight in a way that few other interventions can do (Conlin & Smith, 1981/1982; Lenihan, 1985; Yalom, 1995).

Interpersonal Learning

The therapeutic factor of interpersonal learning overlaps extensively with recapitulation of the primary family group, group cohesion, and catharsis in that all four factors glean many of their therapeutic benefits from demonstrated trust. With interpersonal learning this trust is manifested in the recognition and modification of interpersonal distortions, often through corrective emotional experiences that include the following: strong emotional expression, group containment and feedback regarding the expression, and client recognition of the maladaptive nature of certain feelings and behaviors (Yalom, 1995). Although this factor is easy to consider in terms of process groups, structured and psychoeducational groups can benefit from this factor by teaching and encouraging the practice of appropriate interpersonal communication and relationship skills. Regardless of the type of group, facilitators should be mindful that preplanning can affect the outcomes concerning this factor. The more that facilitators plan to highlight how group learning can be generalized to nongroup experiences, the more consistently this factor will be used for its therapeutic effects.

In process groups, interpersonal learning helps members to see how the group is a microcosm of larger social systems and, subsequently, how their cognitive and emotional distortions affect their everyday interpersonal interactions. The social microcosm inference may be limited initially by LGB group members' focus on the universality often present in an all-LGB group. According to Lenihan (1985), the intense, often novel feelings of safety springing from universality often promote the loosening of defenses, the development of transference relationships, and an increase in group cohesion, thus allowing for interpersonal learning to occur in a more involved, motivated way.

In short, interpersonal learning is a pivotal process in which group learning is transferred to life outside the group. Facilitators' mindfulness of this factor can increase clients' reflection and understanding of their own interpersonal dynamics and can promote the effectiveness of interrelated therapeutic factors.

Group Cohesion

Group cohesion is perhaps one of the more powerful therapeutic factors in group work. Just as success in individual therapy is mediated by the therapeutic relationship, a successful group experience is mediated by a strong sense of group cohesion, which reflects a feeling of support, encouragement, and acceptance of group members (Yalom, 1995). In process groups, group cohesiveness parallels the working alliance. In psychoeducational and structured groups, group cohesiveness often is evidenced through members' willingness to commit openly to the group's shared goals. Regardless of whether the group is structured or process oriented, a group facilitator's ability to define the group's purpose, attendance agreement, and confidentiality contract is critical to group cohesion during the early stages of a group.

In LGB process groups, explicitly stating the reasons for offering the group serves to enhance trust and promote cohesion (Gambe & Getzel, 1989). In the light of the continued existence of conversion therapy, stating that a group's purpose is to affirm an LGB identity will quite likely relieve fears and encourage a sense of participation and cohesiveness. Lenihan (1985) found that cohesion was aided by articulating the purposes and rules of the group as well as by articulating the commonly held erroneous assumptions that clients had about why the group was offered. This included the common understanding and agreement that the group was not to be used as a social or dating outlet. Holahan and Gibson (1994) also acknowledged the importance of having group discussions about how out-of-group socializing should be managed, but they also recognized how difficult it is to avoid such socializing because LGB communities can be quite small and interconnected, even in cities and large universities.

Yalom (1995) argued that consistent attendance is a reflection of group cohesiveness. Indeed, Frost (1996) reported that some group members identified their contractual agreement to attend a process-oriented group consistently as crucial to their participation. If an LGB group facilitator is to capitalize on cohesion, early attention to attendance rules and norms should be considered a necessity.

Another factor that influences the development of group cohesion is confidentiality. All prospective members should understand and respect the importance of confidentiality (Holahan & Gibson, 1994). A common agreement on confidentiality fosters a sense of safety and trust among members, which are necessary ingredients for group cohesion. Conlin and Smith (1981/1982) argued that the first task of any LGB group is to foster a sense of trust among members, because "gay people frequently grow up lacking trust in themselves and others" (p. 108). They offered a number of suggestions for promoting trust and cohesion, including "reinforcing norms that promote disclosure, support for risk-taking and change, confrontation of homophobia and non-adaptive defenses (e.g., inappropriate humor or sarcasm), and non-sexual intimacy" (p. 108).

In structured and psychoeducational groups, an explicitly stated group purpose, attendance rules, and confidentiality rules are also important to group cohesion, but they may manifest in different ways than in process groups. In our experience, developing a group mission statement and reading it at the beginning of each group meeting were enough to establish a sense of universality and cohesiveness, at least enough to promote self-disclosure and offers of support (Perez et al., in press). Lenihan (1985) found that in making the goals of her structured groups clear and time limited, the development of cohesion was accelerated. Finally, developing goals in structured groups that allow for fun activities such as art therapy, trust walks, and guided fantasy can also contribute to a sense of group cohesion (Conlin & Smith, 1981/1982).

Cohesion is affected by attendance in different ways in structured groups compared with process groups. For example, in a group designed to offer support and information to undergraduate gay and bisexual men, we recognized that a rigid attendance commitment to the group might be experienced as a premature commitment to a gay or bisexual identity (Perez et al., in press). As an alternative, we offered a semistructured, drop-in rap group with an open-door attendance policy that recognized the various developmental needs of group members and still allowed a strong feeling of group cohesion.

In summary, group cohesiveness is a therapeutic factor that promotes intermember trust and makes it more likely that members will take and benefit from more therapeutic risks. Cohesion can be dramatically affected by a group facilitator's early decision making regarding group purpose, group attendance, and confidentiality. Although the decisions regarding these factors may vary with the kind of group being facilitated (i.e., process vs. structured), consideration of their effects is paramount to the successful promotion of group cohesion.

Catharsis

As a therapeutic factor, catharsis was rated as one of the top four in importance among three of four psychotherapy groups described by Randall (1995). However, Yalom (1995) cautioned that these kinds of results are frequently and mistakenly interpreted as indicating that catharsis, by itself, is therapeutic. Analysis of Q-sort data from his therapy groups (Lieberman, Yalom, & Miles, 1973) pointed to the conclusion that catharsis must have been accompanied by the endorsement of two specific items on the Q-sort to be considered therapeutically effective by group members. Those two items were "learning how to express my feelings" and "being able to say what was bothering me" (p. 80). In fact, endorsement of catharsis by itself, as indicated by endorsement of the item "getting things off my chest" (p. 81), without endorsement of one of the other two items, was just as likely to be predictive of negative group outcomes as positive outcomes in Yalom's general psychotherapy groups.

Authors of case studies and one empirical study have focused on the value of this therapeutic factor for LGB groups. Before addressing the pregroup decisions that a facilitator can make regarding maximizing the therapeutic benefits of this factor, we discuss those research results.

Masterson (1983) reported that catharsis acted as a major change agent in her lesbian groups. Gambe and Getzel (1989) reported that "guided group catharsis" (p. 178) was necessary for relieving sadness and grief in their groups of HIV-positive gay men. Furthermore, they felt catharsis was important enough to include it as one of the primary therapeutic objectives for their groups. However, in one of the few methodologically rigorous studies of LGB groups, Mulder et al. (1994) found that among asymptomatic HIV-positive gay men, no outcome differences existed between a waiting-list control group and two 17-session intervention groups on measures of emotional expression and emotional suppression.

Nonetheless, membership in the intervention groups (one cognitive–behavioral and one experiential) reportedly relieved significantly more member distress than membership in the control group.

Although the results appear mixed on the effectiveness of catharsis, the Q-sort studies previously described indicated that group members often find it important. If catharsis is to be promoted in LGB groups, it logically follows that facilitators should attend to the level of safety and confidentiality that group members experience within the group. There are a number of ways to do this. Welch (1996) acknowledged that part of group safety comes from members' knowing that the group meeting place is private. Perez et al. (in press) recommended that the exact meeting time and place be kept private until a brief phone-screening interview could be completed. Perez et al. ensured this with their groups by posting only a contact phone number on all advertisements. Finally, Welch (1996) reported that safety was promoted in his group not only by encouraging confidentiality but also by having members agree on how they would like to be addressed by each other outside the group environment.

Existential Factors

Because of the nature and purpose of process-oriented groups, existential issues are more likely to be present and processed in these than in psychoeducational or other structured groups. Although Yalom (1995) reported that the existential factors have regularly ranked in the top half of factors by most groups he has researched with his Q-sort, the development of existential issues as a therapeutic factor was somewhat of an afterthought. Yalom realized that a number of important sentiments were missing from his Q-sort instrument. Subsequently, he began including items in the Q-sort such as "recognizing that life is at times unfair and unjust" and "learning that I must take ultimate responsibility for the way I live my life no matter how much guidance and support I get from others."

Although these items are clearly related to the oppression that LGB people inevitably deal with, none of the literature on LGB groups has explicitly discussed how to direct the focus of LGB groups to existential issues. Nonetheless, a few facilitators and authors have described group sessions that focused on existential topics, including aging (Conlin & Smith, 1981/1982), independence (Masterson, 1983), isolation (Perez et al., in press), and death of a member (Gambe & Getzel, 1989). To stimulate exploration and discussion of existential issues in groups, group facilitators can explore with group members their ideas regarding life's meaning and purpose, one's being in the world, the role of values and beliefs in developing one's personal philosophy, and the meaning of death.

IMPLICATIONS FOR THEORY, RESEARCH, AND PRACTICE

Theory is needed to direct the research and practice of group counseling, and practice should continue to pose the questions that direct LGB theory and research. To advance the understanding of the benefits of group LGB counseling, theory, research, and practice must be integrated. Accomplishing that task requires consideration of four basic issues, which are described below in terms of their implications for LGB group counseling theory, research, and practice.

First, group theory and therapy involve more than the therapeutic factors. One weakness of group research in general is that previous research has not benefited from an integrated, multidimensional examination or theory of group process (Riva & Smith, 1997). Group theorists need to explore and include multiple developmental, social, and political influences. For LGB groups, it is essential that theories take into account the developmental aspects of LGB identity as well as other influences including race, ethnicity, age, and gender. In addition, it is important for group theories to note the impact of societal oppression, homonegativity, homophobia, biphobia, and heterosexism on group process and outcome.

Second, there are few empirical studies to date in which the nature and effectiveness of group counseling for LGB clients have been examined (Chojnacki & Gelberg, 1995; Perez et al., in press; Riva & Smith, 1997). Most studies are anecdotal and provide descriptions of group interactions and structure. Although they are helpful, these studies do not explain the intricacies of group dynamics. Moreover, replication and generalizability to other LGB group situations are problems. What is needed is to begin empirical examination, both quantitative and qualitative, of LGB group process and the specific ways in which group therapy is effective in addressing the concerns of LGB individuals. Specifically, future researchers need to examine (a) how group counseling is effective for LGB clients; (b) the relationships of different therapeutic factors to significant group issues (e.g., coming out, identity pride); (c) the role of LGB identity development within group process; (d) the impact and influence of racial, ethnic, and gender differences in LGB groups; and (e) the impact and influence of group facilitators on LGB group process and outcome.

One way to spearhead LGB group research is to examine previous group process–outcome research conducted with other populations (e.g., Kivlighan & Angelone, 1992; Kivlighan & Goldfine, 1991; Kivlighan, Jauquet, Hardie, & Francis, 1993; Kivlighan & Lilly, 1997; Kivlighan, Multon, & Brossart, 1996) and to begin to extend these studies to LGB groups. Because previous research has revealed that the therapeutic factors may be differentially significant for a given concern, population (Horne & Rosenthal, 1997; Kaul & Bednar, 1986), or stage of group development (Kivlighan & Mullison, 1988), it is reasonable to hypothesize that the same holds true for LGB therapy groups. Research that investigates the effect of the therapeutic factors on process and outcome for LGB group concerns can be beneficial by providing a deeper understanding of the impact of group counseling on LGB clients.

Third, previous group research in general suffers from several methodological problems and limitations (e.g., sample size, selection bias; Kalodner et al., 1997; Riva & Kalodner, 1997). It would be erroneous to assume that LGB group research is immune to these and other problems. A number of methodological issues exist that are unique to LGB populations (e.g., sample selection, instrumentation bias reflecting possible heterosexist assumptions) and that may complicate LGB group research and LGB research in general. Bieschke et al., in chapter 13, this volume, provide a comprehensive look at the methodological issues specific to LGB research.

Finally, there is a lack of formalized education and training in leading LGB groups. It is critical that group counseling curricula also include LGB developmental theory and that education and training be established and integrated within the group counseling curricula. Practical experience should be provided to afford trainees opportunities to facilitate LGB groups. Internships and postdoctoral training can afford similar experiences as well. In addition, LGB-affirmative supervision is necessary in therapist and counselor training programs. Through such supervision experience, trainees can learn to integrate group theory and LGB issues while exploring their underlying assumptions, biases, and prejudices regarding LGB clients. Psychologists, counselors, and other therapists who are unaware of their beliefs and feelings concerning working with LGB clients or who maintain erroneous assumptions about LGB clients have the potential of hindering, if not damaging, the group or a client's personal growth within the group. These and a variety of other issues must be addressed in supervision sessions or peer consultation with someone who has significant knowledge of LGB theory and issues.

CONCLUSION

Group counseling provides a unique opportunity to meet the mental health needs of lesbian, gay, and bisexual persons and to assist these clients in addressing a variety of life experiences and transitions as well as in coping with the influences of societal oppression and prejudice. Indeed, for a number of LGB individuals, group counseling may initially provide a safe place in which they can talk about their lives and explore concerns and relationships. Although unique challenges face both LGB and non-LGB counselors and psychotherapists who conduct LGB groups, it is incumbent on all potential counselors and therapists to have an awareness of and familiarity with models of LGB developmental theory, the availability of various community resources and events, the influence of personal internal and behavioral biases, and the effects of social and cultural heterosexism, homophobia, and biphobia. In addition, group therapists must also have an awareness of their own strengths and limitations and be confident and comfortable in facilitating group members to examine and explore the various facets of being lesbian, gay, or bisexual.

There are a number of therapeutic benefits for LGB individuals who elect to participate in group counseling. Ultimately, perhaps the most significant therapeutic benefit achieved by group counseling is creating an atmosphere of mutual trust, support, affirmation, and openness to being in genuine relationships with others.

REFERENCES

Cass, V. C. (1979). Homosexual identity formation: A theoretical model. *Journal of Homosexuality, 4*, 219–235.

Chojnacki, J., & Gelberg, S. (1995). The facilitation of a gay/lesbian/bisexual support therapy group by heterosexual counselors. *Journal of Counseling and Development, 73*, 352–354.

Conlin, D., & Smith, J. (1981/1982). Group psychotherapy for gay men. *Journal of Homosexuality, 7*(2–3), 105–112.

Conyne, R. K. (1997). Group work ideas I have made aphoristic (for me). *Journal for Specialists in Group Work, 22*, 149–156.

D'Augelli, A. R. (1989). The development of a helping community for lesbians and gay men: A case study in community psychology. *Journal of Community Psychology, 17*, 18–29.

D'Augelli, A. R., & Rose, M. L. (1990). Homophobia in a university community: Attitudes and experiences of heterosexual freshmen. *Journal of College Student Development, 31*, 484–491.

DeLucia-Waack, J. L. (1996). Multiculturalism is inherent in all group work. *Journal for Specialists in Group Work, 21*, 218–223.

Everaerd, W., Dekker, J., Dronkers, J., van der Rhee, K., Staffeleu, J., & Wiselius, G. (1982). Treatment of homosexual and heterosexual sexual dysfunction in male-only groups of mixed sexual orientation. *Archives of Sexual Behavior, 11*, 1–10.

Fassinger, R. E. (1991). The hidden minority: Issues and challenges in working with lesbian women and gay men. *The Counseling Psychologist, 19*, 157–176.

Frost, J. C. (1996). Working with gay men in psychotherapy groups. In M. P. Andronico (Ed.), *Men in groups* (pp. 163–179). Washington DC: American Psychological Association.

Gambe, R., & Getzel, G. S. (1989). Group work with gay men with AIDS. *Social Casework, 70*, 172–179.

Garnets, L., Hancock, K. A., Cochran, S. D., Goodchilds, J., & Peplau, L. A. (1991). Issues in psychotherapy with lesbians and gay men: A survey of psychologists. *American Psychologist, 46,* 964–972.

Hawkins, D. M. (1993). Group psychotherapy with gay men and lesbians. In H. I. Kaplan & B. J. Sadock (Eds.), *Comprehensive group psychotherapy* (3rd ed., pp. 506–514). Baltimore: Williams & Wilkins.

Hedge, B., & Glover, L. F. (1990). Group intervention with HIV seropositive patients and their partners. *AIDS Care, 2,* 385–396.

Herek, G. M. (1988). Heterosexuals' attitudes toward lesbians and gay men: Correlates and gender differences. *Journal of Sex Research, 25,* 451–477.

Herek, G. M. (1989). Hate crimes against lesbians and gay men. *American Psychologist, 44,* 948–955.

Holahan, W., & Gibson, S. A. (1994). Heterosexual therapists leading lesbian and gay therapy groups: Therapeutic and political realities. *Journal of Counseling and Development, 72,* 591–594.

Horne, A. M. (1994). Developing group work for diverse groups. *Journal for Specialists in Group Work, 19,* 138–139.

Horne, A. M., & Rosenthal, R. (1997). Research in group work: How did we get where we are? *Journal for Specialists in Group Work, 22,* 228–240.

Kalodner, C. R., Alfred, A. R., & Hoyt, W. T. (1997). Group research in applied settings: Examples and recommendations. *Journal for Specialists in Group Work, 22,* 253–265.

Kaul, T., & Bednar, R. (1986). Experimental group research: Results, questions, and suggestions. In S. L. Garfield & A. E. Bergin (Eds.), *Handbook of psychotherapy and behavior change* (3rd ed., pp. 671–714). New York: Wiley.

Kivlighan, D. M., & Angelone, E. O. (1992). Interpersonal problems: Variables influencing participants' perception of group climate. *Journal of Counseling Psychology, 39,* 468–472.

Kivlighan, D. M., & Goldfine, D. C. (1991). Endorsement of therapeutic factors as a function of stage of group development and participant interpersonal attitudes. *Journal of Counseling Psychology, 38,* 150–158.

Kivlighan, D. M., Jauquet, C. A., Hardie, A. W., & Francis, A. M. (1993). Training group members to set session agendas: Effects on in-session behavior and member outcome. *Journal of Counseling Psychology, 40,* 182–187.

Kivlighan, D. M., & Lilly, R. L. (1997). Developmental changes in group climate as they relate to therapeutic gain. *Group Dynamics, 1,* 208–221.

Kivlighan, D. M., & Mullison, D. (1988). Participants' perception of therapeutic factors in group counseling: The role of interpersonal style and stage of group development. *Small Group Behavior, 19,* 452–468.

Kivlighan, D. M., Multon, K. D., & Brossart, D. F. (1996). Helpful impacts in group counseling: Development of a multidimensional rating system. *Journal of Counseling Psychology, 43,* 347–355.

Lenihan, G. O. (1985). The therapeutic gay support group: A call for professional involvement. *Psychotherapy, 22,* 729–739.

Lieberman, M., Yalom, I., & Miles, M. (1973). *Encounter groups: First facts.* New York: Basic Books.

Masterson, J. (1983). Lesbian consciousness-raising discussion groups. *Journal for Specialists in Group Work, 8,* 24–30.

Mulder, C. L., Emmelkamp, P. M. G., Antoni, M. H., Mulder, J. W., Sandfort, T. G. M., & De Vries, M. J. (1994). Cognitive–behavioral and experiential group psychotherapy for HIV-infected homosexual men: A comparative study. *Psychosomatic Medicine, 56,* 423–431.

Norsworthy, K. L., & Horne, A. M. (1994). Issues in group work with HIV-infected gay and bisexual men. *Journal for Specialists in Group Work, 19,* 112–119.

Perez, R. M., DeBord, K. A., & Brock, K. J. (in press). Group counseling for lesbian, gay, and bisexual students. In V. A. Wall & N. J. Evans (Eds.), *Toward acceptance: Sexual orientation and today's college students.* Washington, DC: American College Personnel Association.

Quadland, M. C. (1985). Compulsive sexual behavior: Definition of a problem and an approach to treatment. *Journal of Sex & Marital Therapy, 11,* 121–132.

Randall, D. A. (1995). Curative factor rankings for female incest survivor groups: A summary of three studies. *Journal for Specialists in Group Work, 20,* 232–239.

Reece, R. (1981/1982). Group treatment of sexual dysfunction in gay men. *Journal of Homosexuality, 7*(2–3), 113–129.

Riva, M. T., & Kalodner, C. R. (1997). Group research: Encouraging a collaboration between practitioners and researchers. *Journal for Specialists in Group Work, 22,* 226–227.

Riva, M. T., & Smith, R. D. (1997). Looking into the future of group research: Where do we go from here? *Journal for Specialists in Group Work, 22,* 266–276.

Rochlin, M. (1994). Sexual orientation of the therapist and therapeutic effectiveness with gay clients. In J. Gonsiorek (Ed.), *A guide to psychotherapy with gay and lesbian clients* (pp. 21–29). New York: Harrington Park Press.

Rogers, C., Roback, H., McKee, E., & Calhoun, D. (1976). Group psychotherapy with homosexuals: A review. *International Journal of Group Psychotherapy, 26,* 3–27.

Rudolph, J. (1988). Counselors' attitudes toward homosexuality: A selective review of the literature. *Journal of Counseling and Development, 67,* 165–168.

Russell, A., & Winkler, R. (1977). Evaluation of assertiveness training and homosexual guidance service groups designed to improve homosexual functioning. *Journal of Consulting and Clinical Psychology, 45,* 1–13.

Schwartz, R. D., & Harstein, N. B. (1986). Group psychotherapy with gay men: Theoretical and clinical perspectives. In T. S. Stein & C. J. Cohen (Eds.), *Contemporary perspectives on psychotherapy with lesbians and gay men* (pp. 157–177). New York: Plenum Press.

Seligman, M. E. P. (1995). The effectiveness of psychotherapy: The *Consumer Reports* study. *American Psychologist, 50,* 965–974.

Troiden, R. R. (1988). *Gay and lesbian identity. A sociological analysis.* Dix Hills, NY: General Hall.

Welch, P. J. (1996). In search of a caring community: Group therapy for gay, lesbian, and bisexual college students. *Journal of College Student Psychotherapy, 11,* 27–40.

Westefeld, J. S., & Winkelpleck, J. M. (1983). University counseling service groups for gay students. *Small Group Behavior, 14,* 121–128.

Wolf, T. J. (1987). Group counseling for bisexual men. *Journal for Specialists in Group Work, 12,* 162–165.

Yalom, I. D. (1970). *The theory and practice of group psychotherapy.* New York: Basic Books.

Yalom, I. D. (1975). *The theory and practice of group psychotherapy* (2nd ed.). New York: Basic Books.

Yalom, I. D. (1995). *The theory and practice of group psychotherapy* (4th ed.). New York: Basic Books.

9

POTENTIAL COUNSELING CONCERNS OF AGING LESBIAN, GAY, AND BISEXUAL CLIENTS

AUGUSTINE BARÓN AND DAVID W. CRAMER

The adage "Nobody loves you when you're old and gray" has been modified by lesbian women and gay men to read "Nobody loves you when you're old and *gay*." The similarity in sentiment behind the two sayings reflects the extent to which the travails of aging are the same for both heterosexual and lesbian, gay, and bisexual (LGB) populations. Research conducted thus far has confirmed many similarities. Nonetheless, there are unique challenges in the aging process for lesbians, gays, and bisexuals that clinicians may need to consider. Chief among these are the combined effects of "ableism," ageism, heterosexism, homophobia, racism, and sexism throughout the life spans of individuals. This chapter highlights some of the available research literature regarding aging in LGB people and discusses implications for psychotherapy practice. Among the topics presented

We thank Mary Lou Lumpe, Laura Havlick, and Carolyn Hanna, all of the University of Texas at Austin Counseling and Mental Health Center, for their assistance in preparing the manuscript.

are the importance of generational effects in the study of gay and lesbian aging, the impact of ageism and heterosexism on older LGB individuals, and the importance of social support for successful aging. Actual cases (with pseudonyms) illustrative of the issues being discussed are included to give the reader a sense of how these issues may be presented in a counseling situation. Although this handbook includes bisexuals as part of its focus, our review of the literature on aging, like that of others (e.g., Kimmel & Sang, 1995; Reid, 1995), found few useful references concerning this subgroup. Nonetheless, a section is devoted to speculations about the unique concerns of the bisexual elderly as well. The chapter concludes with suggestions for future research and clinical practice.

THE NOTION OF ACCELERATED AGING

Crucial to an understanding of aging and its effects on individuals are the personal beliefs one has about the beginnings of middle and old age. How people define such markers of the aging process can certainly influence their overall adjustment. Several researchers have investigated when heterosexual and gay or lesbian respondents believe middle and old age start (Atchley, 1977; Bennett & Thompson, 1991; Kelly, 1977, 1980; Minnigerode, 1976; Neugarten, Moore, & Lowe, 1965). In general, both heterosexual and gay or lesbian research participants (mostly White, able-bodied, middle-class men thus far) defined the beginning of middle age as occurring at about 40 years, and old age at about 60 years. Bennett and Thompson (1991) also asked their gay male participants when they thought *other* gay men believed middle and old age began. The results were an average of 39 years for the start of middle age and 54 years for old age.

Such lowered estimates contribute to what is referred to as *accelerated aging*, defined as experiencing oneself as old at an earlier age than one's true chronological age (Friend, 1987). Although "being over the hill" is an issue evidenced by both heterosexual and LGB groups, there is some indication that gay male norms, in particular, can contribute to accentuated feelings and beliefs among some individuals that they are beyond their prime well ahead of their actual age. Thus, the notion of accelerated aging suggests that clinicians should be alert to the possibility that some clients may be prematurely aging themselves through beliefs about being past their prime. From the available evidence, it appears that lesbians are less prone than gay men to connect self-worth to chronological age (Kimmel & Sang, 1995). How present accelerated aging is in the lives of LGB ethnic- or racial-minority subgroups remains unknown.

Case Example

Jerry, in his mid-40s, sought therapy because of depression related to the breakup of a long-term relationship. He and his partner had continued to live together and share a home despite the fact that their sexual relationship had been practically nonexistent for many years. His partner, who had been romantically involved with another man for some time, finally left to take a job in another city. Jerry had not dated in more than 15 years and suddenly felt well beyond his prime and too old to be attractive by his perceptions of gay community standards. The loss of the companionship of his partner was a serious emotional blow. He presented in therapy with overwhelming despair and fear about never being partnered again, with many years of loneliness ahead of him.

Therapy initially focused on Jerry's overwhelming anxiety about how others perceived him. He had been teased intensely as a child and adolescent, and he tended to avoid social situations for fear of being ostracized and humiliated. With support, he was able to venture out more publicly, first in less threatening "straight" settings and eventually to some gay social venues. Jerry also participated in a gay men's therapy group, which further enhanced his self-esteem when group members shared their appreciation of him as a person and their view of him as physically and emotionally attractive. As the group continued, he entertained the idea of seeking a partner again and began to go out on occasional dates.

COHORT EFFECTS: GENERATIONAL FACTORS IN THE STUDY OF AGING

Closely related to accelerated aging in LGB communities is the generational factor (i.e., cohort effects). Because of the continually evolving social consciousness about homosexuality, each generation of lesbians, gays, and bisexuals is influenced by different political and historical forces, which in turn affect identity formation (Gray & Dressel, 1985; Kimmel & Sang, 1995; Reid, 1995; Shannon & Woods, 1991). Thus, a historical, sociopolitical, and contextual understanding is important when individual differences in aging are addressed by the clinician. Kimmel and Sang (1995) noted, for example, that people over the age of 50 today reached their sexual maturity before the full impact of the Stonewall riots of 1969 was felt (see Rothblum, chapter 3, this volume). This same group was in middle adulthood when the AIDS pandemic emerged beginning in the early 1980s and was, therefore, disproportionately devastated.

Lesbians, gays, and bisexuals who are now in their 70s, 80s, and 90s grew up at a time when openness about sexual orientation was much less tolerated than even in the middle of this century. In fact, self-identifying terms such as *gay* and *lesbian* and the concept of coming out did not exist in the early 1900s. Therapists trained after the Stonewall riots may mistakenly interpret older clients' reticence about identifying with "gayness" as a form of homophobia. On the contrary, such clients were socialized during a much different time and place, when the use of such labels was not encouraged. Furthermore, middle-aged gays and lesbians may have difficulty self-identifying with the label "queer," even though it is used with pride by many of today's teenagers and young adults. In fact, the openness of today's gay and lesbian youths stands in sharp contrast to the "closetedness" of past generations.

The important point for therapists is that their ideology, and the labels that go with it, should not blind them to the unique historical circumstances of each older gay or lesbian client. In conducting assessments, clinicians need to consider significant life events within a sociopolitical context to determine how they have contributed to identity formation. A special challenge will be to understand ethnic or cultural dimensions of that history when working with minority-group clients. Seeking consultation from colleagues familiar with various minority-group histories and customs, especially as they relate to sexual orientation, is critical.

Case Example

Sue was in her late 60s and had been in a solid relationship that provided both support and happiness for almost 40 years. However, she and her partner were not "gay"—that is a term with which they did not identify. In describing her relationship, Sue referred to her *spouse*, not *lover*. She preferred to say that she was "married," instead of being "partnered." Her self-identifying label was "homosexual woman," not gay or lesbian. Neither she nor her spouse had ever been active in the gay community, preferring to spend most of their social time in the company of a few other female couples who were of similar age and orientation. Sue had not come out to her family and never discussed the issue of sexual orientation with them.

Sue sought psychotherapy to help her cope with the death of her mother, an event that sparked the uncovering of feelings of guilt, anger, yearnings, and sadness. This multitude of emotions was due not only to the grief of her mother's death but also to Sue's awareness of the emotional distance she had kept with her mother as a way of covering up her sexual orientation. In addition, her mother's death was the catalyst for confronting her own mortality and aging process. Therapy was helpful in normalizing her emotional shifts and addressing her guilt, a feeling based largely on her internalized homophobia—she felt she could have been a "better" daughter if she had been straight.

PSYCHOSOCIAL FACTORS IN THE AGING PROCESS

The available literature on gay, lesbian, and bisexual aging points to a variety of psychosocial variables that must be managed for successful adjustment in later life. This section examines social support, in general, along with specific factors such as early developmental events and their impact on adjustment to old age, the potential crisis created by coming out, and experiences of ageism and homophobia.

Early Developmental Events and Adjustment in Later Life

In a thorough study, Adelman (1991) used discriminant analyses to determine patterns of responses given by 52 mostly White gay men and lesbians with the average age of 65 years. She found that adjustment to aging was related to satisfaction with being gay or lesbian and to same-gender sexual experimentation before self-definition as gay or lesbian. High life satisfaction, low self-criticism, and the presence of few psychosomatic problems were in turn related to these two adjustment factors.

High life satisfaction was also related to five styles of being gay: (a) high salience of homosexuality in the respondent's life, (b) low disclosure about gayness at work, (c) low involvement with other gay people, (d) early age of awareness of one's sexual orientation, and (e) decrease in the importance of one's homosexuality in later years. Some of these findings, such as low involvement with other gay people, contradict those of other studies (Dorfman et al., 1995; Quam & Whitford, 1992), which indicate that social support from other gays and lesbians is a critical factor in adjustment. These contradictions may reflect sampling and cohort differences. Also, although high salience (or relevance) of homosexuality may be a part of a person's identity, this does not necessarily imply that the person will have high disclosure at work about being gay or that there will be high involvement with other gay people. The salience factor, then, is a private, internal characteristic that does not correlate with external behavior in ways that might be assumed.

Of particular note is the finding about early experimentation with same-gender sexual encounters and self-definition of sexual identity. Respondents who reported experimenting first and self-identifying later were found to have high life satisfaction, low self-criticism, and few psychosomatic complaints. The reverse was true for respondents who self-identified as gay or lesbian first and experimented later. Adelman (1991) posited that the sequence of experimentation leading to self-definition provides for withdrawal into a period of internal readjustment, which is useful in dealing with a stigmatizing situation.

Of course, a cohort factor may have been at work here as well, in that previous generations would have lacked the positive role models available today that could contribute to healthy self-identification before experimentation. Nonetheless, Adelman's study underscores the importance of exploring coming out issues and how these have been managed by the individual. The "when, where, how, and to whom" of coming out and the degree of positive self-identification resulting therefrom may provide important prognostic insights into a client's adjustment to the aging process.

As is the case with other constructs and concepts, there are no substantive retrospective analyses of coming out and self-identification among ethnic-minority and other LGB subgroups. One can reasonably assume, however, that the findings would hold for these groups also, because they, too, lacked role models who could have had a positive influence on experimentation and self-labeling.

Case Example

This case, although focused on a client in his late 20s, illustrates how a closeted father in his late 50s negatively influenced the self-identification of his gay son. Tony was a 28-year-old gay man who was overweight, depressed, and highly anxious about the perceived judgments of others regarding his homosexuality. He believed his internalized homophobia resulted in large part from his relationship with his father. Tony suspected his father was gay. He based this on a combination of factors, including finding gay porn videos in the trunk of his father's car, discovering gay magazines hidden in the home, experiencing the extreme discord between his parents, and realizing his father had many opportunities for secretive sexual encounters owing to a frequent out-of-town travel schedule. Tony had confronted his mother with his belief, which she had not denied outright, but he felt unable to talk to his father because their relationship was extremely strained. He saw his father's difficulty with owning up to his sexuality as a direct contributor to his own low self-esteem.

Tony's therapy dealt with the impact of his parent's marital strife on the sense of safety he felt in the world. His father's distance, coupled with his mother's overprotectiveness, prevented him from developing a sense of independence and security. Growing up in a family filled with secrets created distrust of others and a fear of intimacy because he believed that his own needs would be subservient to those of other people. Tony visualized himself becoming a lonely, bitter man as he aged, like his father, thus heightening his suicidal ideation.

Therapy allowed Tony the opportunity to establish a more developed sense of himself. He eventually joined a gay men's therapy group and greatly benefited from the encouragement and challenges provided by group members. A particularly powerful element was his being able to interact with older gay men who displayed greater self-esteem and openness about their sexuality than his father was ever able to do.

Coping With the Crisis of Coming Out

To the extent that people have coped successfully with crises in their lives, the challenges of aging may be better met. One example of a major crisis for lesbians, gays, and bisexuals is coming out to family, friends, and coworkers. Kimmel (1978) noted that once this "coming out crisis is resolved, it may provide a perspective on major life crises and a sense of crisis competence that buffers the person against later crises" (p. 117). Although the argument has much intuitive appeal, available research suggests that LGB-specific crisis coping is not necessarily a major factor in positive adjustment to old age (Lee, 1987). Rather, successful coping with a wide range of "generic" life span developmental challenges appears to be a better predictor. Lee's research further indicated that other factors may better assist people to weather life's challenges, factors that have little to do with one's sexual orientation. These factors include (a) having sufficient financial resources, (b) acquiring advanced education, (c) maintaining good health, and (d) enjoying the emotional support of a partner. To the degree that these four factors are present, regardless of sexual orientation, the ability to cope with crises in later life is significantly enhanced.

These four factors are closely associated with middle-to-upper socioeconomic status (SES). Little is known about coping factors among lower SES LGB groups. Whether or not other factors assist members of lower SES groups to meet the challenges of old age is an open question. Clearly, however, the lack of financial resources affects the availability and quality of daily necessities in later life. Thus, one might expect a more difficult adjustment to old age for lower SES clients, many of whom are women and members of ethnic minority groups, because of their lower life earnings compared with middle- and upper-class White gay and bisexual men.

Within a counseling and psychotherapy setting, therefore, exploration of how successfully the coming out process was managed would be useful, but not to the exclusion of other significant life challenges faced by the client. In addition, a discussion of past, present, and future resources and life conditions will aid in determining a client's coping resilience.

Case Example

Marsha, who was 55, recently found her world turned topsy-turvy after coming out to herself, her husband, her four children, and friends and coworkers. Accepting her lesbianism and publicly coming out resulted in the loss of her 30-year marriage, strained relationships with her children, and the loss of several long-term friendships and many other social supports. Coping with so many losses at one time would tax anyone's coping resources. She found herself depressed, occasionally suicidal, and in constant doubt about her decision to come out. She was also afraid that at her age, she would not be able to adjust to her new "lifestyle." Despite the courage it required of her to come out, she was terrified of being alienated and growing old alone, making it difficult for her to embrace her new possibilities with any kind of excitement or hope.

Through her psychotherapy. Marsha became eager to seek fulfillment of her emotional and sexual desires for another woman, and she quickly found relief and support from community resources focused on LGB parenting, thereby ending much of her isolation. Therapy focused on integrating her whole identity and helping her continue in her role of mother, friend, and coworker while exploring her sexual desires. She often commented on the "oddness" of being a 55-year-old mother who felt like a teenager dating for the first time. Her depression quickly lifted as she grieved the loss of her marriage, some friends, and opportunities missed because of suppressed desires.

Social Support

The adage at the beginning of the chapter about being unloved when old and gay projects the image of lonely and depressed lesbians and gays waiting out their lives. Several studies are available that clearly refute this stereotype. For example, Dorfman et al. (1995) surveyed 108 elderly, mostly White heterosexuals, gay men, and lesbian women, to study the correlates of depression in the participant group. They found all subgroups to be equal in the prevalence of depression (about 15% reached criterion), and all showed relatively high levels of social support available to them. Regression analysis indicated that such support was a critical factor in predicting levels of depression in the samples.

The major difference found was in the *source* of support: Gay men and lesbians derived their support more from friends, whereas heterosexuals garnered it more from family or relatives. Gays and lesbians often refer to this supportive friendship network as a "substitute family" or a "family of choice" (i.e., rather than one determined by biological circumstance). Quam and Whitford (1992) found similar results with a group of lesbian women and gay men in their 50s and 60s. Being active in the gay community was noted as an asset in accepting one's own aging. The support provided by such social connections appears to have a positive benefit in overall adjustment.

Studies of social support have not included significant numbers of culturally diverse participants. Thus, little is known about support networks that exist among ethnic minority gays, lesbians, and bisexuals. Affiliating with a local church provides many minority-group gays and lesbians with some support, but this may come at the expense of keeping one's sexual orientation hidden if the congregation's religious beliefs are homophobic. Also, studies have been conducted mostly in large urban areas where social support networks are well established. A study of social support in smaller cities and rural towns has yet to appear in the literature.

In general, clinicians may find an overrepresentation of depressed elderly clients simply because of the prevalence of this disorder in that age group. The growing interest in gerontology points to increased emphasis on mind–body interactions, which may be exemplified by depression in old age. The complex interplay of medications for various disorders, coupled with the ailments of the aging process, presents clinicians with the challenge of making accurate assessments about underlying factors contributing to dual and triple medical and psychological diagnoses. Research also suggests that clinicians can assist clients in establishing appropriate social supports to improve management of depressive conditions.

Ageism and Heterosexism

Although the effects of ageism may be similar for heterosexuals and LGB people, heterosexism complicates the aging process considerably. For example, one partner of a lesbian couple may be dying in a hospital whose regulations allow only relatives and "legal" partners to be present at bedside. If the partner should die, heterosexual relatives and friends may offer little or no sympathy for a loss they cannot, or do not want to, understand. It is also difficult when lesbians, gays, and bisexuals come out in midlife after having established a family; although coping resources may be greater owing to maturity, they will be taxed that much more during interactions with angry and confused spouses, children, relatives, and friends.

Because health concerns become such a major focus in old age, the sensitivity of health care providers is also a significant issue. Quam and Whitford (1992) noted the fear of one respondent in their study that her lifelong physician might provide her with poor quality care, or even reject her outright as a patient, if he found out she was a lesbian. There are encouraging signs that heterosexism and homophobia among health care professionals are beginning to be addressed through medical education curricula, but much remains to be done (Connolly, 1996; Metz, 1997).

Important Legal Documents

The issues of medical care, death and dying, and coming out in later life underscore the need for careful legal planning for gays, lesbians, and bisexuals. To forestall assaults by family members on the wishes of LGB patients regarding medical treatment and disposition of property, legal devices exist that can minimize risk (Connolly, 1996; Ettelbrick, 1996). Five important documents include a personal will, a medical power of attorney, a general power of attorney, a conservatorship, and a living will (Ettelbrick, 1996). The personal will is indispensable for outlining exactly how an individual wishes to dispose of belongings after death. The medical power of attorney gives the designee the authority to make medical decisions for a patient who is no longer able to do that. A general power of attorney allows a designee to make and implement decisions about a patient's property and related matters when he or she is no longer competent to do so. A conservatorship usually designates a person to carry out business enterprises that an incapacitated individual can no longer perform. The living will (i.e., advance health care directive) is a document in which the patient details what lifesaving and pain-management procedures he or she wishes to undergo or have withheld.

The horror stories of disputes among family members, partners, and incapacitated people, particularly dying AIDS patients, have emphasized the importance of having these various legal documents filed. Although there is no fail-safe way to avoid lawsuits filed by irate relatives and friends, filing these legal papers is a prudent move to protect the dying person's (and the partner's) wishes.

Housing

The present lack of gay- and lesbian-affirmative housing for the elderly is also a serious concern given the impending wave of elderly baby boomers. One study by Waite (1995) noted the hopes of middle-aged lesbian respondents for an "Old Dykes Home" where residents could provide each other support, with the aid of sensitive caregivers. It appears that the community housing support available to heterosexuals is presently lacking for gays, lesbians, and bisexuals. Because gays, lesbians, and bisexuals in their 40s and 50s today are part of the baby boomer generation, it is reasonable to expect that retirement communities of various types geared to these populations will emerge in the twenty-first century, much like gay–lesbian vacation villages have sprung up in the last decade. The challenge with eldercare housing is its labor-intensive cost. Without some type of subsidy, lower SES gays, lesbians, and bisexuals will have difficulty finding suitable housing regardless of how affirmative it may be.

Employment Discrimination

Another outcome of ageism, homophobia, and heterosexism that is receiving increased attention is the "glass ceiling" effect for older gay, lesbian, and bisexual employees (Kimmel & Sang, 1995). Middle-aged workers have questioned the degree to which the combined effects of ageism, heterosexism, racism, and sexism have affected job promotions. Differences in earnings potential between White men and both ethnic minority people and White women have profound implications for retirement. Lower overall salaries for the latter two groups mean lower social security and pension benefits compared with White male workers. The inability to obtain domestic partner retirement benefits compounds this problem further. The legal documents discussed earlier assume grave importance in this context as well, to ensure that beneficiary designations are honored by relatives.

People nearing retirement may present themselves in therapy to review their lives and prepare for leaving the world of work. This can be an occasion for considering how various forms of discrimination have influenced their employment satisfaction and overall achievement (Alexander, 1997). Discrimination based on the interactive effects of ageism and heterosexism may be part of the presenting problem for elderly LGB clients. The clinician's alertness to these effects involves an openness to exploring how social and institutional forces affect the client's emotional state. As the baby boomer "bulge" becomes elderly, clinicians will be called on to advocate increasingly for the psychosocial needs of older LGB clients.

Case Example

Tom was in his early 60s and about 2 years away from retirement. He had a long career as an engineer in a high-technology field. During the last few years on his job, he often felt outdated because he had not been trained much in the latest technology. Although he was closeted at work, he suspected most of his colleagues and his boss knew he was gay. Socially, Tom was quite isolated: He was in a long-term relationship with a man who had several disabilities and functioned primarily in the role of caregiver. His only social outlet was church, where he was also closeted.

Tom indicated his boss had expressed increasing dissatisfaction with his job capabilities and had given him "less demanding" assignments. Tom experienced increasing depression as he worried that his boss wanted to get rid of him. His feelings were intensified by his struggle with being gay and keeping up with the ever-changing engineering field. Therapy assisted Tom in confronting his boss about the reasons for the less demanding assignments. The boss admitted to his own ageist assumptions, believing that Tom wanted to "slow down." Tom was also able to request advanced training, something the boss had also assumed Tom was not interested in owing to impending retirement. The sessions also focused on having Tom begin to expand his circle of friends and supports in anticipation of retiring from his job.

AGING BISEXUALS: DOUBLE JEOPARDY

Woody Allen purportedly asserted that the positive thing about being bisexual is that one doubles the chances of getting a date on a Saturday night. Unfortunately, available evidence suggests that being bisexual usually results in being "double-closeted" (Hansen & Evans, 1985; Lourea,

1985; Zinik, 1985). Many heterosexuals as well as gays and lesbians are uncomfortable with, if not antagonistic toward, bisexuality. Caught in the dichotomy of gay or straight, bisexuals experience discrimination from both groups. Many people believe such a sexual orientation is due to conflicted or confused identity development, retarded psychosexual development, or a defense against one's "true" sexual orientation, presumably homosexual (Hansen & Evans, 1985). In addition to dealing with heterosexism and homophobia, bisexuals as well as gays and lesbians are the targets of erotophobia, defined as society's post-Victorian, negative attitudes regarding sexuality in general. From this viewpoint bisexuals are perceived as inherently promiscuous and nonmonogamous, much like gay men.

Bisexuals are defined in the few studies available as people who eroticize or are sexually aroused by both males and females, engage in or desire sexual activity with both genders, and adopt "bisexual" as their sexual identity label. This definition does not imply that bisexuals are equally attracted to both genders. In fact, data suggest that they are likely to be attracted to one gender over the other, perhaps in a 60:40 or 30:70 balance (Zinik, 1985).

On the basis of Kinsey's studies (Zinik, 1985), estimates of the prevalence of bisexuals in the general population range from 10% to 15%. Of particular note is Kinsey's overlooked finding that significantly higher percentages of his sample exhibited bisexual behavior than exclusively same-gender sexual behavior. Bisexuality, then, is a more prominent phenomenon among both women and men than is generally supposed.

Of particular interest from the standpoint of aging is that a large number of bisexuals discover their homosexual inclinations later in life. Brownfain (1985) found that 20% of bisexual men in his sample experienced their first gay relationship after the age of 40 and 10% had their first experience after 50. Bell, Weinberg, and Hammersmith (1981) found that most bisexuals eroticize the opposite gender first and identify as heterosexual, then discover their homosexual attractions in their late 20s or 30s. On the basis of his study of married bisexual men, Coleman (1985) postulated that for many in his sample, entering into a midlife crisis appeared to be a contributing factor for exploring gayness. Taking stock of their life choices and their hidden, unexpressed desires led many men to acknowledge, and act on, their attractions toward other men.

Because bisexuals often become aware of their orientation at a later age than many gays and lesbians, they are likely to be in a coupled relationship (Lourea, 1985). This scenario suggests six counseling concerns that might arise for couples or individuals. First, the effects of homophobia on each partner must be dealt with, because each will be struggling with various negative attitudes about homosexuality. Second, the issue of whether one has a choice about sexual attractions and feelings may arise. Given the pervasive belief that these feelings are under a person's control, the heterosexual partner may insist that the bisexual partner simply "turn off" the feelings rather than accepting that they are natural and spontaneous. Third, many partners express their insecurities about being able to remain as a couple. Envy as well as jealousy about the bisexual partner's same-gender attractions can lead to feelings of sexual, physical, and emotional inadequacy for the heterosexual partner. Fourth, if the couple desires to stay together, they must address the question of whether to have a monogamous versus an open relationship. Fifth, if the couple has children, the children's future welfare will be a point of significant discussion. Issues of parental rights and shielding children from society's homophobia will be key struggles. Finally, the couple must negotiate the bisexual partner's coming out process, realizing that each step has repercussions for both partners. These six counseling concerns once again highlight the need for social support networks geared to the needs of older bisexual adults.

The preceding points come from a handful of studies focusing predominantly on White, middle-class, able-bodied men in coupled relationships. Studies exploring the demographic diversity of bisexuals have yet to appear in the literature. Clearly, the double assault that bisexuals can experience owing to discrimination against them by both heterosexuals and gays and lesbians underscores their unique marginal position in society, matched only by that of transgendered individuals. Perhaps the soundest conclusion to be drawn about aging bisexuals is that their challenges are largely the same as for gays and lesbians but are further aggravated by the existence of less tolerance and understanding from the society as a whole.

FUTURE RESEARCH

Research on aging in LGB people is in its infancy, and the area is fraught with a variety of methodological problems, not to mention many unanswered questions. Reid (1995) outlined several methodological issues. Sampling in previous research has led to conclusions based largely on White, able-bodied, urban, middle-to-upper-class gay men (Reid, 1995). Most researchers have recruited gays, lesbians, and bisexuals who were members of political and social organizations or were known to other gays and lesbians. Thus, as Harry (1986) noted, knowledge of gays, lesbians, and bisexuals is based largely on people (mostly White men) whose sexual orientation constitutes a significant aspect of their identities because these are the people who volunteer to participate in such studies. Recruitment location usually has been limited to large urban centers such as Los Angeles, New York City, and San Francisco, where sampling is easiest. In addition, gender differences require increased study. As is generally the case concerning research on gays and lesbians, the preponderance of the literature focuses on males. Greater efforts at diversifying samples is crucial to advance knowledge about aging in LGB people. Diversification is needed regarding gender, SES, ethnicity, race, physical abilities, and religion.

Future studies must be designed for sensitivity to cohort effects that might be present. As noted earlier, generational differences are critical for deciphering the special needs of older gay, lesbian, and bisexual subgroups, given the wide age range that older people encompass. For example, gerontologists (e.g., Neugarten, 1985) now speak of at least two groups of older adults: the "young-old" and the "old-old." The young-old are those age 55–60, who may be retired or planning to do so, who may have health problems that are beginning to affect their daily lives, who still have an income, who are active, and who are not dependent on others for assistance. The old-old, age 75 and older, are those who may have significant financial and medical needs owing to a variety of physical ailments and who have suffered multiple losses from the deaths of family members and friends. The old-old cohort will probably continue to pose the most serious challenge to researchers owing to their lesser accessibility for sampling compared with other age groupings.

The variety of research questions yet to be asked is boundless; some of the more salient ones are presented here. As stated at the beginning of the chapter, aging concerns for bisexual men and women have not been explored to any extent. How do their later years compare with those of gays, lesbians, and heterosexuals? Are there recognizable stages or phases of relationship development for LGB couples that are distinct from those of heterosexuals? How do older LGB couples manage differences in career aspirations, sexual openness, and so forth? Conversely, what makes for effective "singlehood" as an LGB person? How valid are models of the coming out process throughout the life span?

What are the psychological and social consequences of the baby boomer generation's reaching old age? As gay men and lesbian women of that generation face the latter part of their lives, how will their heavy losses from AIDS help or hinder their grieving? Similarly, what are the challenges and supports for gays, lesbians, and bisexuals who have lost a long-term relationship, and how do these compare to phases of adjustment for heterosexual widows and widowers? Undergirding all these research questions is the role of cultural and individual differences. The future is indeed rich with research opportunities for addressing significant issues in LGB aging.

IMPLICATIONS FOR CLINICAL PRACTICE

The literature review presented here suggests several noteworthy implications for clinical practice. Cohort effects are crucial for understanding the sociocultural–political and historical context of a client's individual development. The early experiences of an 85-year-old LGB person today can be significantly different from those of a 65-year-old, even though both may be lumped in the category of "senior citizen." For example, a 65-year-old person today may be preparing for retirement, whereas an 85-year-old individual may have been retired already for 20 years or more.

Closely related to cohort effects is the notion of accelerated aging, which may be an issue particularly for middle-aged gay males who may believe that others see them as "over the hill" sooner than is reflected by their actual age. Clinicians should be alert to this premature "mental aging" on the part of some clients.

Regarding sexual identity formation and successful aging, early experimentation with same-gender sexual activity followed by self-identification as gay or lesbian is associated with high life satisfaction, low self-criticism, and few psychosomatic problems, at least among present-day cohorts of gays and lesbians in their 60s and 70s. Evidence also suggests that clinicians would do well to assess how successfully clients have coped with the crisis of coming out, as well as general life challenges, throughout the life span, because success with this challenge may be a good predictor of adjustment to old age. Monetary resources, good health, education, and support from a life partner also appear to make up a critical cluster of coping resources. To the extent that one or more of these factors are missing in a person's life, the task of therapy will be that much more difficult. Indeed, absence of such coping resources argues for an emphasis on providing social services to the client rather than intrapsychic analysis alone. Along these same lines, the social support provided by friends (more than by family members) and community involvement appears to help in the management of depression among older gays and lesbians.

Finally, and perhaps most important, the interactive effects of ageism, heterosexism, and homophobia pose unique challenges for gays, lesbians, and bisexuals. Many of these issues center on the lack of social and institutional support for civil rights regarding such matters as partner benefits; the availability of sensitive and knowledgeable human service caregivers; and affirmative living accommodations for elderly LGB individuals. The role of the therapist with LGB elderly clients, therefore, will increasingly involve advocacy for, and brokering of, social services.

CONCLUSION

Given that gays, lesbians, and bisexuals are part of the aging baby boomer cohort, there will be strength in numbers to effect changes through lobbying and other efforts in the years ahead. In the era of the World Wide Web, the Internet can be used to locate organized activities to assist elderly LGB individuals. One example is the Gay and Lesbian Association of Retiring Persons (http://www.gaylesbianretiring.org) established in 1997 as an alternative and supplement to the American Association of Retired Persons. Another emerging group is Seniors Active in a Gay Environment, whose aim is to support political action as well as research and educational efforts through local and national chapters. As the next millennium approaches, such initiatives will proliferate and intensify, with the exciting promise of significantly advancing the civil rights of all lesbians, gays, and bisexuals.

REFERENCES

Adelman, M. (1991). Stigma, gay lifestyles, and adjustment to aging: A study of later-life gay men and lesbians. *Journal of Homosexuality, 20*(3/4), 7–32.

Alexander, C. J. (1997). *Growth and intimacy for gay men.* New York: Harrington Park Press.

Atchley, R. C. (1977). *The social forces in later life.* Beverly Hills, CA: Sage.

Bell, A. P., Weinberg, M. S., & Hammersmith, S. F. (1981). *Sexual preference: Its development in men and women.* Bloomington: Indiana University Press.

Bennett, K. C., & Thompson, N. L. (1991). Accelerated aging and male homosexuality: Australian evidence in a continuing debate. *Journal of Homosexuality, 20*(3/4), 65–76.

Brownfain, J. J. (1985). A study of the married bisexual male: Paradox and resolution. In F. Klein & T. J. Wolf (Eds.), *Two lives to lead: Bisexuality in men and women* (pp. 173–188). New York: Haworth Press.

Coleman, E. (1985). Integration of male bisexuality and marriage. In F. Klein & T. J. Wolf (Eds.), *Two lives to lead: Bisexuality in men and women* (pp. 189–207). New York: Haworth Press.

Connolly, L. (1996). Long-term care and hospice: The special needs of older gay men and lesbians. In K. J. Peterson (Ed.), *Health care for lesbians and gay men: Confronting homophobia and heterosexism* (pp. 77–91). New York: Harrington Park Press.

Dorfman, R., Walters, K., Burke, P., Hardin, L., Karanik, T., Raphael, J., & Silverstein, E. (1995). Support in the aging process for gays and lesbians. *Journal of Gerontological Social Work, 24*(1/2), 29–44.

Ettelbrick, P. L. (1996). Legal issues in health care for lesbians and gay men. In K. J. Peterson (Ed.), *Health care for lesbians and gay men: Confronting homophobia and heterosexism* (pp. 93–109). New York: Harrington Park Press.

Friend, R. A. (1987). The individual and social psychology of aging: Clinical implications for lesbians and gay men. *Journal of Homosexuality, 14*(1/2), 307–331.

Gray, H., & Dressel, P. (1985). Cohort effects in the study of aging. *The Gerontologist, 25,* 83–87.

Hansen, C. E., & Evans, A. (1985). Bisexuality reconsidered: An idea in pursuit of a definition. In F. Klein & T. J. Wolf (Eds.), *Two lives to lead: Bisexuality in men and women* (pp. 1–6). New York: Haworth Press.

Harry, A. (1986). Sampling gay men. *Journal of Sex Research, 22*(10), 22.

Kelly, J. J. (1977). The aging homosexual: Myth and reality. *The Gerontologist, 17,* 328–332.

Kelly, J. J. (1980). Homosexuality and aging. In J. Marmor (Ed.), *Homosexual behaviour: A modern appraisal* (pp. 230–245). New York: Basic Books.

Kimmel, D. C. (1978). Adult development and aging: A gay perspective. *Journal of Social Issues, 43,* 113–120.

Kimmel, D. C., & Sang, B. E. (1995). Lesbians and gay men in midlife. In A. R. D'Augelli & C. J. Patterson (Eds.), *Lesbian, gay, and bisexual identities over the lifespan* (pp. 190–214). New York: Oxford University Press.

Lee, J. A. (1987). What can homosexual aging studies contribute to theories of aging? *Journal of Homosexuality, 13*(4), 43–71.

Lourea, D. N. (1985). Psycho-social issues related to counseling bisexuals. In F. Klein & T. J. Wolf (Eds.), *Two lives to lead: Bisexuality in men and women* (pp. 51–62). New York: Haworth Press.

Metz, P. (1997). Staff development for working with lesbian and gay elders. In J. K. Quam (Ed.), *Social services for senior gay men and lesbians* (pp. 35–45). New York: Harrington Park Press.

Minnigerode, F. A. (1976). Age-status labeling in homosexual men. *Journal of Homosexuality, 1,* 273–276.

Neugarten, B. L. (1985). Time, age, and the life cycle. In M. Bloom (Ed.), *Life span development* (pp. 113–124). New York: Macmillan.

Neugarten, B. L., Moore, J. W., & Lowe, J. C. (1965). Age norms, age constraints, and adult socialization. *American Journal of Sociology, 70,* 710–717.

Quam, J. K., & Whitford, G. S. (1992). Adaptation and age-related expectations of older gay and lesbian adults. *The Gerontologist, 32,* 367–374.

Reid, J. D. (1995). Development in late life: Older lesbian and gay lives. In A. R. D'Augelli & C. J. Patterson (Eds.), *Lesbian, gay, and bisexual identities over the lifespan* (pp. 215–240). New York: Oxford University Press.

Shannon, J. W., & Woods, W. J. (1991). Affirmative psychotherapy for gay men. *The Counseling Psychologist, 19,* 197–215.

Waite, H. (1995). Lesbians leaping out of the intergenerational contract: Issues of aging in Australia. *Journal of Gay and Lesbian Social Services, 3*(3), 109–127.

Zinik, G. (1985). Identity conflict or adaptive flexibility? Bisexuality reconsidered. In F. Klein & T. J. Wolf (Eds.), *Two lives to lead: Bisexuality in men and women* (pp. 7–9). New York: Haworth Press.

10

ISSUES IN COUNSELING LESBIAN, GAY, AND BISEXUAL ADOLESCENTS

SCOTT L. HERSHBERGER AND ANTHONY R. D'AUGELLI

Lesbian, gay, and bisexual (LGB) adolescents are, in most respects, like other adolescents and thus present to psychologists and counselors with needs and concerns typical of most young people. There are a number of issues, however, that are highly distinctive to LGB young people about which all therapists and counselors working with youths should be knowledgeable. This chapter is concerned with describing these issues with reference to current empirical findings and presenting the implications of the research for counseling LGB youths. A complete description of counseling for LGB youths is beyond the scope of this chapter; the reader is referred to Ryan and Futterman (1998) and M. Schneider (1997) for more detailed information.

THE DEVELOPMENT OF SEXUAL ORIENTATION

Contemporary studies have suggested that most adults who self-identify as lesbian or gay realize their attractions to others of the same sex during early adolescence. The largest of these studies are by D'Augelli and

Hershberger (1993; includes 194 youths), D'Augelli, Pilkington, and Hershberger (1999; includes 260 youths), Herdt and Boxer (1993; includes 202 youths), and Savin-Williams (1990; includes 314 youths). Participants in these projects ranged in age from 14 to 23—far younger than participants whose lives are summarized in the heretofore available information about sexual orientation. For example, lesbian and gay participants described in the Kinsey Institute report *Sexual Preference* (Bell, Weinberg, & Hammersmith, 1981), who were asked to retrospect about their earlier years, averaged from 27 to 37 years of age. The more accurate information obtained in the recent research on the emergence of sexual orientation in adolescence occurs at the same time that LGB youths (and adults) are increasingly visible in society. This greater openness allows researchers the opportunity to study younger samples. It also provides counselors and psychotherapists with a greater challenge because more youths, their parents, and their significant others are seeking assistance at earlier ages. Whereas in earlier generations, LGB people who sought professional assistance did so as adults, today teenagers and college-age young adults more frequently turn to others for support and assistance. Professionals who have contact with youths—teachers; coaches; religious leaders; and all counselors, therapists, and other human service providers—need to be informed about the development of sexual orientation during adolescence, because many youths experience concerns about their same-sex feelings, and more will be forthcoming about these experiences.

A developmental approach to sexual orientation must take into account the individual's developmental status. This means that same-sex eroticism will be experienced, thought about, and expressed not only in different ways at different ages but also in ways that reflect the individual's physical, cognitive, emotional, and social development at a particular point in her or his life. Although no research based on representative samples has explicitly focused on sexual orientation before puberty, the conclusion of the most recent studies is that some personal awareness of same-sex erotic feelings generally predates puberty and that awareness becomes increasingly crystallized at puberty. Sometime thereafter—and there is tremendous individual variability in the timing of this event—the person labels her or his feelings as homoerotic and may self-identify as lesbian, gay, or bisexual. The processes of awareness and self-identification occur simultaneously with the development of more complex cognitive abilities as well as the development of an increasingly independent social life less reliant on family and more focused on peers.

The nature of one's sexual expression—both solitary (fantasy, masturbation) and social (petting, mutual masturbation, oral sex, vaginal sex, and anal sex)—affects the rate at which the solidification of a homoerotic orientation occurs. Interpersonal sexual activity is not a requirement for awareness of orientation, and many youths label themselves as LGB without same-sex sexual behavior. Not engaging in any same-sex sexual activity or any social contact with others who identify as LGB may delay self-labeling, and self-identification as LGB may also be delayed by engagement in opposite-sex sexual activity. Many sexually active LGB youths have a history of opposite-sex sexual behavior, and some heterosexual behavior occurs despite youths' clear self-identification as lesbian or gay. Some of these youths may identify as bisexual; some may be avoiding same-sex sexual experience owing to fear or lack of opportunity; and some are simply experimenting with different sexual partners.

There are many developmental pathways to a same-sex sexual orientation, as there are to a heterosexual or a bisexual orientation. Although the biological processes of puberty accelerate the experience of sexual desire for all adolescents, intense social pressures of adolescence provide powerful barriers to the expression of any nonheterosexual desire. This dynamic makes early adolescence, the teenage years, and early adulthood—the second decade of life, from 10 to 20—a crucial developmental period for LGB people. Conflict may be intense during these years because the expression of homoerotic desire can lead to many problems, and the suppression of the desire can also interfere with adjustment. Because we cannot study youths who will not identify themselves as LGB or acknowledge any same-sex sexual activity, we know little about the many youths whose sexual identity development was thwarted by their fear of the consequences of its expression.

Several milestones in the development of a nonheterosexual sexual orientation have been studied. These milestones reflect the distinctive quality of LGB development, the fact that it involves exiting from pervasive heterosexual expectations and developing a complex, new "self" in the face of widespread cultural stigmatization and discrimination (D'Augelli 1994a, 1994b). Same-sex sexual attraction has been found to occur first before puberty, at about age 10, about the same time that heterosexually identified youths report the beginnings of sexual attractions (McClintock & Herdt, 1996). The self-labeling of same-sex sexual orientation occurs at about age 15. This self-acknowledgment represents the beginning of the process of identity exploration and consolidation, and it is sometimes called "coming out to oneself." Such personal acknowledgment precedes disclosure to someone else, or "coming out." Ordinarily, telling another person for the first time about one's homoerotic orientation is experienced as an extremely difficult act because it involves risk of rejection without the benefits of experience or helping resources. This first disclosure is the first of a lifelong series of coming out processes. The first disclosure to another may follow self-awareness and self-labeling by many years.

There are multiple, overlapping processes involved in the core LGB developmental task of coming out, such as telling family (parents, siblings, grandparents, extended family, and others who are considered to be family members), friends (ranging from casual acquaintances to close friends), and the many important others in one's social network (e.g., neighbors, co-workers, coaches, religious leaders, and teachers). These disclosure processes facilitate an exiting from heterosexual identity and its social expectations. The more people who "know," the more complete is the person's repositioning within an LGB identity. However, this exit from heterosexuality is stressful both for the person, who has been socialized within a heterosexual model, and for her or his social networks, whose expectations have been violated. In essence, the more people who "know," the less control the person has over the consequences of being known to be LGB. This is especially relevant to adolescents whose social worlds can be highly volatile; within most youths' social networks, especially at school and in community settings, such information is rapidly shared. This may partly account for the fact that relatively few LGB youths disclose their sexual orientation to others during junior or senior high school, preferring to defer the disclosure until greater control of its consequences can be arranged.

The disclosure of same-sex or bisexual sexual orientation creates new sets of problems for youths. Coming to terms with one's sexual orientation and its many personal and social dilemmas is considerably different for a 14-year-old and a 25-year-old. The adolescent is still developing in many ways; more important, he or she, under the scrutiny of parents, siblings, and peers, is pressured to conform to heterosexual expectations. Adolescents generally remain in school settings, and the social networks of other youths with whom they have routine social contact are beyond their control. Finally, in contrast to heterosexual adolescents, LGB adolescents have few opportunities to explore their developing identities without risk.

MAJOR STRESSORS IN THE LIVES OF LGB YOUTHS

Current studies have revealed many serious dilemmas faced by LGB adolescents. Some stressors are related to concealment of sexual orientation, and others result from its disclosure. All LGB youths have learned the need to hide, and this long-standing manner of coping exacts its costs in terms of psychological well-being (Martin, 1982). Herdt (1989) identified four characteristics of LGB youths that have consequences for mental health: (a) their invisibility, (b) the assumptions of others—peers and family—that they are defective, (c) the stigmatization that follows the assumption of deviance, and (d) others' assumption that all lesbian and gay individuals are alike. Plummer (1989) added the absence of positive role models and the development of a "negative self" that results from the relentless heterosexism and homophobia of adolescent peer culture. These stressors contribute to the sense of isolation and difference often reported by LGB youths as they come to terms with their sexual orientation. This sense of "otherness" results from isolation from those with similar feelings and from messages that homoerotic desire and identity are legitimate targets for rejection and hate, especially by peers.

During the initial period of recognition and labeling of homoerotic feelings, LGB youths have few resources to aid them in understanding their concerns. Lesbian- and gay-affirming written materials may be inaccessible, or the youth may feel embarrassed to buy them in his or her local community; casual discussions with family and friends are risky; and talking with counseling personnel in schools is hampered by fear of therapists' or counselors' disclosure to others and by fear of judgment. In some urban areas, LGB youths can seek services from community centers, informal groups, and social service agencies devoted to their distinct concerns (Grossman, 1998). In other urban areas, youths can access telephone help and counseling systems anonymously, if they are aware of these systems and can overcome their fears. In many areas, most pointedly in rural areas, however, these resources do not exist, and the sense of isolation and lack of support can be profound. Even when there are helping resources available, few LGB youths overcome hesitancies and seek help. Those who do not remain totally closeted tend to develop a small support system, divulging aspects of their emotional life to well-chosen family members and friends from whom they can predict support and confidentiality. The advent of the Internet and its easy access to resources for LGB and questioning youths will have an enormous impact on the isolation of these youths. Being able to obtain accurate, current information about sexual orientation, to locate local and national resources, and to "chat" with other LGB youths serve to decrease isolation and internalized homophobia and to decrease youths' fear of seeking help from others. Of course, not all youths have access to the Internet, and there are potential risks associated with its use.

Disclosure of Sexual Orientation to Family and Friends

In a recent summary of research on LGB youths' disclosure of their sexual orientation to their families, Savin-Williams (1998) reported considerable variability among studies in the percentages of youths who had told their families—from 25% to 84%, depending on the study. Many problems are exacerbated by the lack of parental, sibling, and extended-family support. The presumption of heterosexuality leaves families unprepared for the expression of homoeroticism, and youths' increased understanding that such a disclosure would not be greeted enthusiastically maximizes secrecy. Whereas most youths from historically disenfranchised groups can rely on family support, LGB youths often cannot. Indeed, given their increasing awareness of social stigmatization, LGB youths often are loath to jeopardize family protection and resources. Youths who reside at home or who are dependent on their families for food and shelter are surely the least likely to risk rejection.

The fears of LGB youths about their families' negative reactions to disclosure of their sexual orientation appear to be justified. Research on parental reactions to disclosure of sexual orientation has revealed considerable upset among parents, many of whom respond very negatively at first (Strommen, 1989). Remafedi (1987a) found that 43% of a sample of gay male adolescents reported strong negative reactions from parents about their sexual orientation. Rotheram-Borus, Hunter, and Rosario (1994) found that coming out to parents and siblings, being discovered as gay by parents or siblings, telling friends or being discovered by friends, and being ridiculed for being gay were the most common gay-related stressors. Using an adult gay male sample, Cramer and Roach (1988) found that 55% of the men's mothers and 42% of their fathers had an initially negative response. Robinson, Walters, and Skeen (1989) sampled parents of lesbian and gay adults through a national support group for parents and found that many reported initial sadness (74%), regret (58%), depression (49%), and fear for their child's well-being (74%). Boxer, Cook, and Herdt (1991) studied parents of LGB youths age 21 and younger. More youths had disclosed to their mothers than fathers. Of the lesbian youths, 63% had disclosed to mothers and 37% to fathers; of the male youths, 54% had disclosed to mothers and 28% to fathers. Parents reported considerable family disruption after the initial disclosure. Herdt and Boxer (1993) found that most youths first disclosed their orientation to friends, with more male than female youths finding this difficult. Nonetheless, youths who have secure relationships with families may experience increased closeness over time after disclosure (Holtzen, Kenny, & Mahalik, 1995).

Victimization of Lesbian, Gay, and Bisexual Youths

LGB youths are subjected to a variety of forms of victimization based on their sexual orientation (D'Augelli & Dark, 1995; D'Augelli, Hershberger, & Pilkington, 1998). Gross, Aurand, and Adessa (1988) found that 50% of a sample of gay men reported victimization in junior high school and 59% in high school; of the lesbians sampled, 12% were victimized in junior high school and 21% in high school. According to a study of New York City LGB youths, 41% had suffered from physical attacks, and nearly half of these attacks were specifically provoked by the youths' sexual orientation (Hunter, 1990). There is also evidence of family victimization of lesbian and gay adolescents (D'Augelli et al., 1998). Lesbian and gay youths are more likely to have been victims of childhood physical or sexual abuse than heterosexual youths. According to national surveys of victimization, between 19% and 41% of lesbian and gay adults have reported family verbal abuse, and between 4% and 7% have reported family physical abuse (Berrill, 1990). Pilkington and D'Augelli (1995) found that more than one third of their LGB youth sample had been verbally attacked by a family member because of sexual orientation and that 10% were physically assaulted by a family member because of sexual orientation. Bradford, Ryan, and Rothblum (1994) reported that 24% of a sample of 1,925 lesbians had been harshly beaten or physically abused while growing up; 21% reported rape or sexual molestation in childhood; and 19% reported childhood incest. Of 1,001 gay and bisexual adult men attending clinics for sexually transmitted diseases, Doll et al. (1992) found that 37% said they had been encouraged or forced to have sexual contact before age 19. Using the same sample, Barthalow et al. (1994) reported a significant association between earlier sexual abuse and current depression, suicidality, risky sexual behavior, and positive serostatus on the human immunodeficiency virus (HIV). Harry (1989) found that gay men were significantly more likely to be physically abused during adolescence than heterosexual men, especially if they had a history of childhood femininity and poor relationships with their fathers. Prevalence estimates of abuse patterns for youths in general survey findings are lower than those reported for LGB youths (Finkelhor & Dziuba-Leatherman, 1994).

In addition to parental conflicts and violence, LGB youths who are open about their sexual orientation face verbal harassment and physical attacks at school and in their local communities. Between 33% and 49% of those responding to community surveys have reported being victimized in school (Berrill, 1990). Remafedi's (1987b) gay male youths' reports were similar, with over half (55%) noting peer verbal abuse and nearly one third (30%) reporting physical assaults. Nearly 40% of the male youths in Remafedi, Farrow, and Deisher's (1991) study said they experienced physical violence. In the study by Bradford et al. (1994), half of the total said they had been verbally attacked, and 6% said they had been physically attacked. Pilkington and D'Augelli (1995) found that 80% of the LGB youths studied reported verbal abuse specifically related to sexual orientation; nearly half reported that such abuse occurred more than twice. Gay male youths experienced significantly more verbal abuse than lesbian youths. Of the total group, 44% had been threatened with physical violence; 23% had personal property damaged; 33% had objects thrown at them; 30% had been chased; and 13% had been spat on. Regarding more serious attacks, 17% had been assaulted (punched, kicked, or beaten), 10% had been assaulted with a weapon, and 22% reported sexual assault. Many reported fear of verbal (22%) or physical (7%) abuse at home; more reported fear of verbal (31%) or physical (26%) abuse at school. Some LGB youths respond to peer harassment at school with truancy or dropping out of school. Remafedi (1987b) found that 39% of his sample of gay and bisexual males were truant on at least 10 occasions and that more than one fourth had left high school before graduating. Using a representative sample of Massachusetts high school LGB-identified and other youths, Garofolo, Wolf, Kessel, Palfrey, and DuRant (1998) found that one third of the LGB youths said they had been threatened with a weapon at school compared 7% of the other youths. In addition, one fourth of the LGB youths said they had missed school within the last month because of fear compared with 5% of the non-LGB youths. In addition to victimization of junior and senior high school–age youths, harassment and violence directed at self-identified lesbian and gay male college and university students have been documented (Comstock, 1991; D'Augelli, 1992).

HIV Issues as Stressors Among LGB Youths

Another area of crucial importance to the mental health of LGB youths is HIV risk and serostatus (Cranston, 1991; Rotheram-Borus, Hunter, & Rosario, 1995). Several studies have shown that gay and bisexual male youths engage in risky sexual behaviors (Kegeles, Hayes, & Coates, 1996). Remafedi (1994) found that 63% of a sample of Minnesota youths had unprotected anal intercourse or used intravenous drugs. Silvestre et al. (1993) studied Pittsburgh gay men who were 22 years old or younger. About 7% were HIV seropositive; of those engaging in receptive anal intercourse, only 12% consistently used condoms, and 39% did not use condoms regularly despite having multiple sexual partners. Stall et al. (1992) studied San Francisco gay men in 1989 and found that the youngest group, who were 18–29 years of age (there were only 20 men under 24 years of age), were at the highest risk. About 10% engaged in unprotected anal sex with multiple partners. Lemp et al. (1994) found that 4% of the 17- to 19-year-olds and 12% of the 20- to 22-year-olds in their San Francisco sample were HIV positive and that one third had engaged in unprotected anal intercourse during the prior 6 months. Unsafe sexual contact was associated with the lack of peer support for safe sex, as well as a history of forced sex. In a study by Rotheram-Borus, Rosario, et al. (1994) of gay male youths in New York, 40% of those engaging in anal sex had not used condoms in the prior 3 months. Dean and Meyer (1995) studied 18- to 24-year-old gay men in New York and found that one third had engaged in unprotected receptive anal intercourse over a 2-year period. HIV risk behavior among young lesbians and female bisexuals has only recently been studied. Cochran and Mays (1996) found that more than one fourth of their sample of 18- to 24-year-old bisexual and lesbian women had heterosexual intercourse in the previous year. Of bisexually identified women, 10% had sex with a gay male partner within the year. Women having sex with a gay man were younger than other women, and many were teenagers.

MENTAL HEALTH PROBLEMS AMONG LGB YOUTHS

High-Risk Behaviors

The accumulated evidence shows that LGB youths are at special risk for a range of health and mental health problems (D'Augelli & Hershberger, 1993; Grossman, 1994; Hetrick & Martin, 1988; Remafedi, 1987a, 1987b; Remafedi, French, Story, Resnick, & Blum, 1998; Rotheram-Borus, Hunter, & Rosario, 1994; Savin-Williams, 1994). There is also evidence of alcohol and drug abuse among LGB youths (Grossman & Kerner, 1998; Rotheram-Borus, Hunter, & Rosario, 1994; Shifrin & Solis, 1992). Mental health problems among young lesbians were first revealed in the national survey data collected in 1987 by the National Lesbian and Gay Health Foundation (Bradford et al., 1994). Mental health problems were common among women age 17–24. Nearly two thirds had received counseling. The most frequently occurring problems taken to counselors were family problems, depression, problems in relationships, and anxiety. A study of gay male university students revealed many personal and emotional problems, especially dealing with parents about their sexual orientation, relationship problems, worry about AIDS, anxiety, and depression (D'Augelli, 1991). In D'Augelli and Hershberger's (1993) report, 63% said they were so worried or nervous in the past year that they could not function, 61% reported feeling nervous and tense at the time of the study, and 73% said they were depressed. In addition, 33% of the youths in the D'Augelli and Hershberger (1993) study reported excessive alcohol use, and 23% reported illegal drug use. Rosario et al. (1996) found that gay and bisexual male youths reported multiple problem behaviors (only 8% reported no conduct problems during the past 6 months). These youths also experienced many stressful life events, with gay-related stressors (those associated with their sexual orientation) correlating significantly with emotional distress and problem behavior. Garofolo et al. (1998) found that LGB youths engaged in more high-risk behaviors, including greater use of alcohol and illegal drugs.

Suicidality

The prevalence of suicide attempts among adolescents is currently estimated to range from 3.5% to 11% (Andrews & Lewinsohn, 1992). Between 10% and 14% of "unsuccessful" attempters eventually die during a subsequent suicide attempt (Diekstra, 1989). Much research has been performed in attempts to isolate the distinguishing characteristics of adolescent suicide attempters and completers (Garland & Zigler, 1993; Lewinsohn, Rohde, & Seeley, 1993). The following risk factors typically have been identified: psychiatric disorders (especially affective disorders, conduct disorder, antisocial personality disorder, substance abuse, and eating disorders), a history of previous suicide attempts, poor coping and problem-solving skills (including low self-efficacy and low social support seeking), hopelessness, stressful life events and chronic physical illness, accessibility to a lethal weapon (especially firearms), a family history of suicide, a recent suicide attempt or completion by a friend or family member, low self-esteem, impulsivity, family violence, peer difficulties, interpersonal conflict with a parent or romantic partner, experiences of intense shame and humiliation (including child abuse and corporal punishment), and lower academic achievement and school problems.

LGB youths have been identified as being at an elevated risk for suicide on the basis of recent studies of LGB youths in a variety of settings. Martin and Hetrick (1988) found that 21% of the 2,000 12- to 21-year-olds interviewed at the New York City Hetrick–Martin Institute—a social service agency for LGB youth—had made a suicide attempt. S. G. Schneider, Farberow, and Kruks (1989) noted that of the 108 men whom they recruited from support groups and university social organizations, 55% reported a history of suicidal ideation, and 20% had made an actual suicide attempt. In two separate nonclinical samples of bisexual and gay male adolescents, Remafedi et al. (1991) found that approximately one third had attempted suicide. Similarly, Hammelman (1993) found that 29% of the lesbian and gay adolescents and young adults whom she recruited from a lesbian–gay support group and other university settings had made a suicide attempt. D'Augelli and Hershberger (1993) discovered that 60% of 194 adolescents had thought of killing themselves and that 42% had made at least one suicide attempt. A recent population-based sample comparing LGB youths and heterosexual youths in Minnesota public schools confirmed the association of sexual orientation with suicide risk (Remafedi et al., 1998). Among the bisexual and gay males, 28% reported a past suicide attempt, compared with 4% of heterosexual males. Among females, the difference was smaller but consistent with the male data: Twenty percent of bisexual and lesbian youths reported a past attempt compared with 14% of heterosexual females. Garofolo et al. (1998) found that 35% of LGB-identified youths acknowledged a suicide attempt within the last year, compared with 10% of non-LGB youths. Waldo, Hesson-McInnis, and D'Augelli (1998) found that 32% of LGB college students attending a rural state university reported a past suicide attempt.

Not all epidemiological studies of adolescent suicide find an elevated rate for LGB youths. Perhaps the strongest evidence against an elevated suicide rate comes from systematically conducted "psychological autopsy" studies, examining the lives of youths who have recently committed suicide. Shaffer (1988) found that only 2.5% of adolescent suicide completers were lesbian or gay, and Rich, Fowler, Young, and Blenkush (1986) identified a rate of 7%. In a more recent study, Shaffer, Fisher, Hicks, Parides, and Gould (1995) found no relationship between sexual orientation and completed suicide. However, statistics from psychological autopsies may be attenuated because of their dependence on interviews with relatives and close friends, who may have been reluctant to identify the suicide completer as homosexual or who may simply have been unaware of the person's sexual orientation. Disagreement concerning the prevalence of suicidal behavior among LGB youths has occasionally been contentious, as reflected in Shaffer's (1993) assertion that lesbian and gay advocates have inflated suicide estimates for political gain. Nonetheless, although many of the studies examining suicidality and sexual orientation are methodologically flawed, it is unlikely that so many studies using a myriad of sampling and analytic strategies would converge on the general conclusion that suicidality is higher among LGB youths if a "true" effect did not exist.

Among the variables that have been linked to an increased risk of suicidality among LGB youths is gender atypicality (Harry, 1983; Saghir & Robins, 1973). Childhood gender atypicality has been linked to a host of negative outcomes including depression, peer rejection, isolation, and ridicule (Coates & Person, 1985; Rosen, Rekers, & Friar, 1977). Traditional masculinity and androgyny have been associated with higher self-esteem and lower rates of substance abuse among girls and boys (Horwitz & White, 1987) as well as better adjustment to stress and reduced fearfulness among male and female college students (Dillon, Wolf, & Katz, 1985; Roos & Cohen, 1987). These associations with androgyny and masculinity probably occur because of the greater independence and assertiveness that typically come from a masculine gender identity. Harry (1983) found that childhood gender role nonconformity was associated with a greater incidence of suicidal ideation and suicide attempts among both heterosexual and homosexual men and women. However, the magnitude of the effect was greater for men than for women, and the prevalence of childhood gender role nonconformity was greater among lesbians and gay men than among heterosexuals. In a more recent study, Remafedi et al. (1991) noted that gay and bisexual male youths with a history of previous suicide attempts were more likely to have a feminine or undifferentiated gender role than were nonattempters. D'Augelli and Hershberger (1993), however, failed to find a similar connection between gender atypicality and suicidality in their sample of LGB adolescents, nor was there any relationship between childhood gender atypicality and current mental health problems in a recent study of LGB youths by D'Augelli et al. (1999).

Alcohol and drug abuse have long been recognized as significant risk factors for suicide attempts and suicide completions in the general population (Motto, 1980; Robins, 1981; Shneidman, Farberow, & Litman, 1970). Furthermore, a number of surveys have found significantly higher frequencies of substance abuse among lesbians and gay men compared with heterosexual adults (Bradford et al., 1994; McKirnan & Peterson, 1989a, 1989b; Saghir & Robins, 1973). Alcohol- and drug-related problems are also prevalent among LGB youths. Fifty-eight percent of Remafedi's (1987a) sample met diagnostic criteria of the *Diagnostic and Statistical Manual of Mental Disorders* (3rd ed.; *DSM–III*; American Psychiatric Association, 1980) for substance abuse disorder. Twenty-five percent of the young female and 37% of the young male participants in D'Augelli and Hershberger's (1993) sample reported problems with excessive alcohol use, whereas 22% and 24%, respectively, reported problems with other drugs. Rosario, Hunter, and Gwadz (1997) reported lifetime prevalence of substance abuse as 41% in lesbian adolescents and 24% in gay male adolescents. Surveys of LGB youths consistently have revealed a connection between substance abuse and suicidality. For example, 85% of the young gay and bisexual male suicide attempters studied by Remafedi et al. (1991), compared with 63% of the nonattempters, reported a history of illicit drug use; nearly 4 times as many suicide attempters than nonattempters (22% vs. 6%) reported having undergone chemical dependency treatment. S. G. Schneider et al. (1989) observed that suicide attempters in their sample of gay male youths were more likely than nonattempters to report a family history of paternal alcoholism.

By no means are LGB suicide attempters a homogeneous group. For example, risk factors differ between single-occasion attempters and multiple-occasion attempters. As noted by Hershberger, Pilkington, and D'Augelli (1996), LGB multiple-occasion attempters are more likely to use violent methods and to self-identify as bisexual; they also express more suicidal ideation. Furthermore, Hershberger et al. (1996) identified three categories, or "types," of LGB suicide attempters. One category includes youths who became aware of their same-sex sexual attractions at younger ages and engaged in same-sex sexual behaviors at younger ages. Perhaps as a necessary consequence of earlier experimentation, these youths also engaged in opposite-sex sexual relations at younger ages. A second category consists of youths who were aware of their same-sex sexual attractions and engaged in sexual behaviors at typical ages but labeled themselves lesbian, gay, or bisexual and subsequently disclosed those identities to others at significantly later ages. These youths were also lower in self-esteem and participated less frequently in lesbian or gay groups. Within the third category are youths who were significantly more open about their sexual orientation and engaged in significantly more same-sex sexual encounters. These youths also lost more friends owing to their sexual orientation, perceived their mothers as more rejecting, and experienced greater victimization of all kinds. Most dramatic was the fact that the incidence of sexual assault was 36% for the first type, 21% for the second type, but 60% for the third type.

IMPLICATIONS OF RESEARCH FOR COUNSELING LGB ADOLESCENTS

The fundamental approach taken by any psychotherapist, counselor, or mental health professional in interacting with LGB youths and youths who are questioning and exploring their sexual identity should be one of acceptance. Unfortunately, this point still needs to be emphasized, because some psychologists and counselors continue to believe that same-sex sexual orientation is dysfunctional and should be changed. Besides the ethical and moral questions concerning whether a same-sex sexual orientation should be changed, it is doubtful that this change can be accomplished even in clients who are most desirous of change (Coleman, 1978; Haldeman, 1994). Despite anecdotal accounts of individuals who have changed their sexual orientation (or at least their sexual behavior), there is no empirical evidence supporting the effectiveness of so-called reparative therapy. In 1997, the American Psychological Association passed a resolution reaffirming the view that LGB people are not in need of treatment as a result of their sexual orientation. This issue may be especially relevant to youths in that their sexual orientation may still be developing. It is of the utmost importance for therapists to avoid making the presumption of heterosexuality for young clients.

Many youths experience same-sex sexual attractions; some engage in same-sex sexual activities; and some self-identify as lesbian, gay, or bisexual. Some heterosexually identified youths engage in same-sex sexual activities and later self-identify as LGB. Counselors who interfere with youths' development because they hold uninformed and biased views about same-sex sexual orientation, and do not allow youths the opportunity to discuss their concerns without fear of judgment or rejection, are engaging in unprofessional practice. A more helpful approach is to view the evolution of adolescents' sexual orientation in the kind of developmental perspective taken in this chapter. Such an approach must take into account the complex relationships between youths' developing attractions, behaviors, and self-identifications and must resist attempts to categorize youths in simplistic terms. In addition, effective counselors need to understand the personal and social contexts in which youths explore their sexual identities, especially contexts in which there may be punitive responses to any expression of same-sex erotic interest. The most important contexts in this regard are the family, the school, and the community, especially youths' peers. On the basis of our review of the literature, we make several general suggestions for professionals working with LGB youths, discussed in the following sections.

Help Youths Explore and Accept Themselves

Self-esteem has been consistently found to be crucial for the healthy development of LGB adolescents. Youths may hold stereotypical views of LGB people and may have internalized, without awareness, many negative messages from families, friends, religious leaders, and the larger culture. These barriers to self-esteem need to be identified and challenged. Youths, for instance, may assume they cannot have long-term relationships, start their own families, or have highly productive and satisfying careers in whatever field they choose. Some may feel that they have a choice to be lesbian, gay, bisexual, or heterosexual. In such cases, it is worth emphasizing that our knowledge of sexual orientation suggests a biological contribution to sexual orientation and that all reputable research concludes that no single cause of any sexual orientation is likely to be discovered. All evidence also suggests that most adolescents know their sexual orientation by the end of their high school years and that many have experienced their attractions for many years. Efforts to deal with possible same-sex sexual orientation by "flight into heterosexuality" should be discouraged. On the other hand, youths will need active assistance in determining how to understand and explore their same-sex orientation in a thoughtful, safe, and healthy way.

Help Youths to Start Dating

It is important to help youths understand the importance of dating in the development of their sexual orientation. In contrast to heterosexual adolescents, LGB youths are unable to engage in same-sex dating unless it is done in secrecy and therefore have little experience with dating when it is age appropriate. More often, their same-sex interests are expressed in sexual behavior that does not occur in the context of romantic relationship development. Among youths in junior high school and high school, sexual activity usually begins as part of the dating ritual. Because same-sex dating is essentially culturally prohibited until adulthood (and even then it is difficult in most settings), sexual activity for LGB youths may occur less often with peers and more often with older partners. Also, LGB youths may engage in heterosexual sexual activity even though they may feel it is inconsistent with their sexual orientation. Counselors should discuss the nature of youths' dating and sexual activities and help youths think about the consequences of their behavior for the development of a healthy sexual identity. This may involve discussing nonjudgmentally the risks involved in sexual expression, especially with older partners. It also involves the risks associated with seeking partners in settings such as bars and clubs, in which an adult-oriented, sexualized atmosphere may pose special risks for LGB youths. Assistance should be given in developing strategies for navigating these situations, but a more important strategy is to encourage youths to seek out social and recreational opportunities for LGB youths overseen by responsible and affirming adults. In such settings, which are available in most communities, a greater emphasis can be placed on social (rather than sexual) ways of relating and on the development of identity without sexual coercion or tension. To accomplish this, psychologists and counselors must be familiar with social and recreational opportunities for LGB youths and must actively assist youths to access these resources.

Help Youths Deal With Family Issues

Counselors can help youths deal with family issues in several ways. Most youths have not disclosed to their families, especially during the earlier phases of their sexual orientation development. Even when "out" to some family members, LGB youths may be closeted to others, creating a complex (and unstable) situation that leaves the person vulnerable. Increasingly, families are showing support for youths who disclose they are LGB; as societal acceptance slowly increases, there is greater visibility, and more accurate information has become available. Yet many youths still experience serious family discord, which may last for years if youths come out at early ages. Because discord can occur with parents, siblings, grandparents, and extended-family members, an assessment of familial response is not a simple task. If youths are already estranged from their families, counselors should be prepared to assist in reuniting them if at all possible, which may involve meetings with members of the family. If this is not possible, counselors can help youths achieve a living status outside the family, perhaps even an independent living status. This is not an easy task, and counselors should be fully aware of social service agencies that are equipped to help in these situations. For youths who are contemplating disclosing their orientation to their families (or anyone else), it is important to discuss the risks involved. The key phrase here is "proceed with caution," a message that is often hard to understand for a young person who wants to express his or her identity in an active way. One can never know how a family will react once faced with the explicit disclosure that a young member is lesbian, gay, or bisexual, because most families make a strong assumption of heterosexuality for all their members. Disclosure to an unsympathetic or hostile family can have many deleterious consequences, most frequently verbal abuse that can last for years if the youth is young and must remain at home. Unless youths are certain of support from family members who matter, they should not be encouraged to disclose.

If youths wish to have family members meet with their therapist, the following questions should be addressed:

1. How much do the family members know?
2. Were they told by the client?

3. If they were not told by the client, how did they find out?
4. Which specific family members know?
5. For each family member who knows, what was her or his reaction?
6. How long have they known?
7. What was the quality of the relationship between client and family before disclosure, and has it changed since?

Intervene for Abused Youths

Counselors should intervene if a youth has been the victim of physical violence or persistent or intense verbal abuse. Verbal abuse including homophobic comments from important adults such as teachers, religious figures, coaches, and therapists or counselors must also be addressed. Intervention can take many forms. If verbal abuse is present within the family, counselors can meet with family members and underscore the importance of stopping the abusive behavior immediately. If extreme verbal abuse or physical violence is present, therapists should seek legal intervention, as they would for any youth in an abusive situation. However, if legal authorities become involved, it is important to understand the implications of this involvement for the youth in terms of others' knowledge of his or her sexual orientation. Similarly, when abuse of any kind occurs within the school setting, counselors should intervene if school authorities fail to address the problem. In general, a crucial role for the therapist of LGB youths is to serve as an advocate for youths who are having problems at home or school.

Be Aware of Developing Mental and Physical Health Problems

LGB youths who are open at school may begin to avoid school if they are victimized in any way. Their academic performance may decline, and they may withdraw from others. Stress may become manifest in LGB youths' escalating use of alcohol and other drugs, including tobacco, but disturbances in eating and other health behaviors may occur as well.

It is crucial to be especially sensitive to indicators of suicidality. Being sensitive includes knowing what the risk factors are for suicidal behavior among adolescents in general and LGB adolescents in particular and knowing whether any of these risk factors are prominent in youths' lives. For example, it would be especially important to be alert to suicidality if a youth is deeply troubled by his or her sexual orientation, has been rejected by peers or has lost friends, or has been rejected or expects rejection from various family members. A youth who has been subjected to persistent, long-term victimization, whether verbal or physical, may be at special risk as well. It is important to remember, however, that most LGB youths are not self-destructive and have developed strong coping mechanisms and social support systems. One should not presume distress simply because an adolescent self-identifies as LGB or discusses same-sex sexual interests or behavior. On the other hand, as youths become increasingly open about themselves with others and have to navigate the many challenges this involves, it is necessary to monitor their coping mechanisms and support systems.

Although LGB youths have a number of special challenges, most of their problems are no different from those of their heterosexual peers. Despite the many complexities in the lives of LGB youths, most have considerable resilience. Being LGB is not the only problem such an adolescent might have, although at times it might overshadow other concerns. In essence, treating LGB youths simultaneously as the same as their peers and different from them is the most appropriate strategy.

CONCLUSION

Many of the issues that trouble LGB youths can be attributed to the difficulty of living in a society that stigmatizes and marginalizes LGB people. To some extent, the hope is that these youths will internalize this disdain, motivating them to cast off their same-sex sexual identities and desires and replace them with the socially sanctioned sexual identities and desires of heterosexuality. Historically, LGB people sought counseling for repair rather than to learn strategies to cope with a hostile environment. Most contemporary counselors and mental health workers now acknowledge that in providing mental health services to LGB people, it is not sexual orientation that needs to be repaired but the hostility expressed against it.

LGB youths not only must deal with the same problems and challenges as other adolescents but also must struggle with problems and challenges that are unique to the experience of being a same-sex-oriented or bisexually oriented young person. The most important problems and challenges are the issues of identity development, dealing with disclosure to families, victimization, HIV risk, and mental health issues. Those who work with LGB youths, whether in counseling or in community settings, must be aware of the special challenges these youths face and must be equipped to address these challenges. Above all, those who work with these youths must be comfortable addressing issues pertinent to LGB youths and be willing to develop interventions to address their special needs.

REFERENCES

American Psychiatric Association. (1980). *Diagnostic and statistical manual of mental disorders* (3rd ed.). Washington, DC: Author.

Andrews, J. A., & Lewinsohn, P. M. (1992). Suicidal attempts among older adolescents: Prevalence and co-occurrence with psychiatric disorders. *Journal of the American Academy of Child and Adolescent Psychiatry, 31,* 655–662.

Bartholow, B. N., Doll, L. S., Joy, D., Douglas, J. M., Bolan, G., Harrison, J. S., Moss, P. M., & McKirnan, D. (1994). Emotional, behavioral, and HIV risks associated with sexual abuse among homosexual and bisexual men. *Child Abuse and Neglect, 18,* 753–767.

Bell, A. P., Weinberg, M. S., & Hammersmith, S. K. (1981). *Sexual preference: Its development in men and women.* Bloomington: Indiana University Press.

Berrill, K. (1990). Anti-gay violence and victimization in the United States: An overview. *Journal of Interpersonal Violence, 5,* 274–294.

Boxer, A. M., Cook, J. A., & Herdt, G. (1991). Double jeopardy: Identity transitions and parent–child relations among gay and lesbian youth. In K. Pillemer & K. McCartney (Eds.), *Parent–child relations throughout life* (pp. 59–92). Hillsdale, NJ: Erlbaum.

Bradford, J., Ryan, C., & Rothblum, E. D. (1994). National Lesbian Health Care Survey: Implications for mental health care. *Journal of Consulting and Clinical Psychology, 62,* 228–242.

Coates, S., & Person, E. S. (1985). Extreme boyhood femininity: Isolated behavior or pervasive disorder. *Journal of the American Academy of Child Psychiatry, 24,* 702–709.

Cochran, S. D., & Mays, V. M. (1996). Prevalence of HIV-related sexual risk behaviors among young 18- to 24-year-old lesbian and bisexual women. *Women's Health, 2*(1–2), 75–89.

Coleman, E. (1978). Toward a new model of treatment of homosexuality: A review. *Journal of Homosexuality, 3,* 180–197.

Comstock, G. D. (1991). *Violence against lesbians and gay men.* New York: Columbia University Press.

Cramer, D. W., & Roach, A. J. (1988). Coming out to Mom and Dad: A study of gay males and their relationships with their parents. *Journal of Homosexuality, 15*(3–4), 79–92.

Cranston, K. (1991). HIV education for gay, lesbian, and bisexual youth: Personal risk, personal power, and the community of conscience. *Journal of Homosexuality, 22*(3/4), 247–259.

D'Augelli, A. R. (1991). Gay men in college: Identity processes and adaptations. *Journal of College Student Development, 32,* 140–146.

D'Augelli, A. R. (1992). Lesbian and gay male undergraduates' experiences of harassment and fear on campus. *Journal of Interpersonal Violence, 7,* 383–395.

D'Augelli, A. R. (1994a). Identity development and sexual orientation: Toward a model of lesbian, gay, and bisexual development. In E. J. Trickett (Ed.), *Human diversity: Perspectives on people in context* (pp. 312–333). San Francisco: Jossey-Bass.

D'Augelli, A. R. (1994b). Lesbian and gay male development: Steps toward an analysis of lesbians' and gay men's lives. In B. Greene & G. M. Herek (Eds.), *Lesbian and gay psychology: Theory, research, and clinical applications* (pp. 118–132). Newbury Park, CA: Sage.

D'Augelli, A. R., & Dark, L. J. (1995). Vulnerable populations: Lesbian, gay, and bisexual youth. In L. D. Eron, J. H. Gentry, & P. Schlegel (Eds.), *Reason to hope: A psychosocial perspective on violence and youth* (pp. 177–196). Washington, DC: American Psychological Association.

D'Augelli, A. R., & Hershberger, S. L. (1993). Lesbian, gay, and bisexual youth in community settings: Personal challenges and mental health problems. *American Journal of Community Psychology, 21,* 1–28.

D'Augelli, A. R., Hershberger, S. L., & Pilkington, N. W. (1998). Lesbian, gay, and bisexual youths and their families: Disclosure of sexual orientation and its consequences. *Journal of Orthopsychiatry, 68,* 361–371.

D'Augelli, A. R., Pilkington, N. W., & Hershberger, S. L. (1999). *Lesbian, gay, and bisexual youths: Relationships among sexual orientation development milestones, gender atypicality, self-acceptance, and adjustment.* Manuscript submitted for publication.

Dean, L., & Meyer, I. (1995). HIV prevalence and sexual behavior in a cohort of New York City gay men (aged 18–24). *Journal of Acquired Immune Deficiency Syndrome and Human Retrovirology, 8,* 208–211.

Diekstra, R. F. (1989). Suicidal behavior in adolescents and young adults: The international picture. *Crisis, 10,* 16–35.

Dillon, K. M., Wolf, E., & Katz, H. (1985). Sex roles, gender, and fear. *Journal of Psychology, 119,* 355–359.

Doll, L. S., Joy, D., Bartholow, B. N., Harrison, J. S., Bolan, G., Douglas, J. M., Saltzman, L. E., Moss, P. M., & Delgado, W. (1992). Self-reported childhood and adolescent sexual abuse among adult homosexual and bisexual men. *Child Abuse and Neglect, 16,* 855–864.

Finkelhor, D., & Dziuba-Leatherman, J. (1994). Victimization of children. *American Psychologist, 49,* 173–183.

Garland, A. F., & Zigler, E. (1993). Adolescent suicide prevention: Current research and social policy implications. *American Psychologist, 48,* 169–182.

Garofolo, R., Wolf, R. C., Kessel, S., Palfrey, J., & DuRant, R. H. (1998). The association between health risk behavior and sexual orientation among a school-based sample of adolescents. *Pediatrics, 101,* 895–902.

Gross, L., Aurand, S., & Adessa, R. (1988). *Violence and discrimination against lesbian and gay people in Philadelphia and the Commonwealth of Pennsylvania.* Unpublished report, Philadelphia Lesbian and Gay Task Force.

Grossman, A. H. (1994). Hiding and coming out: Gay and lesbian youth at risk. In B. Cato, H. Gray, D. Nelson, & P. Varnes (Eds.), *Youth at risk: Targeting in on prevention* (pp. 49–56). Reston, VA: American Association for Leisure and Recreation.

Grossman, A. (1998). The case for a place of their own: Queer youth and urban space. In C. Aitchison & F. Jordan (Eds.), *Gender, space, and identity: Leisure, culture, and commerce* (Publication No. 63, pp. 127–136). Brighton, England: Leisure Studies Association.

Grossman, A. H., & Kerner, M. S. (1998). Support networks of gay male and lesbian youth. *Journal of Gay, Lesbian, and Bisexual Identity, 3,* 27–46.

Haldeman, D. C. (1994). The practice and ethics of sexual orientation conversion therapy. *Journal of Consulting and Clinical Psychology, 62,* 221–227.

Hammelman, T. L. (1993). Gay and lesbian youth: Contributing factors to serious attempts or considerations of suicide. *Journal of Gay and Lesbian Psychotherapy, 2,* 77–89.

Harry, J. (1983). Parasuicide, gender, and gender deviance. *Journal of Health and Social Behavior, 24,* 350–361.

Harry, J. (1989). Parental physical abuse and sexual orientation. *Archives of Sexual Behavior, 18,* 251–261.

Herdt G. (1989). Gay and lesbian youth: Emergent identities and cultural scenes at home and abroad. *Journal of Homosexuality, 17,* 1–42.

Herdt, G. H., & Boxer, A. M. (1993). *Children of horizons: How gay and lesbian teens are leading a new way out of the closet.* Boston: Beacon Press.

Herek, G. M. (1989). Hate crimes against lesbians and gay men: Issues for research and policy. *American Psychologist, 44,* 948–955.

Hershberger, S. L., & D'Augelli, A. R. (1995). The impact of victimization on the mental health and suicidality of lesbian, gay, and bisexual youth. *Developmental Psychology, 31,* 65–74.

Hershberger, S. L., Pilkington, N. W., & D'Augelli, A. R. (1996). Categorization of lesbian, gay, and bisexual suicide attempters. In C. J. Alexander (Ed.), *Gay and lesbian mental health: A sourcebook for practitioners* (pp. 36–60). New York: Haworth Press.

Hershberger, S. L., Pilkington, N. W., & D'Augelli, A. R. (1997). Predictors of suicide attempts among gay, lesbian, and bisexual youth. *Journal of Adolescent Research, 12,* 477–497.

Hetrick, E. S., & Martin, A. D. (1988). *Hetrick–Martin Institute violence report.* New York: The Institute for the Protection of Gay and Lesbian Youth.

Holtzen, D. W., Kenny, M. E., & Mahalik, J. R. (1995). Contributions of parental attachment to gay and lesbian disclosure to parents and dysfunctional cognitive processes. *Journal of Counseling Psychology, 42,* 350–355.

Horwitz, A. V., & White, H. R. (1987). Gender role orientation and styles of pathology among adolescents. *Journal of Health and Social Behavior, 28,* 158–170.

Hunter, J. (1990). Violence against lesbian and gay male youths. *Journal of Interpersonal Violence, 5,* 295–300.

Kegeles, S. M., Hayes, R. B., & Coates, T. J. (1996). The Mpowerment Project: A community level HIV prevention intervention for young gay men. *American Journal of Public Health, 86,* 1129–1136.

Lemp, G. F., Hirozawa, A. M., Givertz, D., Nieri, G. N., Anderson, L., Lindegren, M. L., Janssen, R. S., & Katz, M. (1994). Seroprevalence of HIV and risk behaviors among young homosexual and bisexual men. *Journal of the American Medical Association, 272,* 449–454.

Lewinsohn, P. M., Rohde, P., & Seeley, J. R. (1993). Psychosocial characteristics of adolescents with a history of suicide attempt. *Journal of the American Academy of Child and Adolescent Psychiatry, 32,* 60–68.

Martin, A. D. (1982). Learning to hide: Socialization of the gay adolescent. *Adolescent Psychiatry, 10,* 52–65.

Martin, A. D., & Hetrick, E. S. (1988). The stigmatization of the gay and lesbian adolescent. *Journal of Homosexuality, 15*(1–2), 163–184.

McClintock, M. K., & Herdt, G. (1996). Rethinking puberty: The development of sexual attraction. *Current Directions in Psychological Science, 5,* 178–183.

McKirnan, D. J., & Peterson, P. L. (1989a). Alcohol and drug use among homosexual men and women: Epidemiology and population characteristics. *Addictive Behaviors, 14,* 545–553.

McKirnan, D. J., & Peterson, P. L. (1989b). Psychosocial and cultural factors in alcohol and drug abuse: An analysis of a homosexual community. *Addictive Behaviors, 14,* 555–563.

Motto, J. A. (1980). Suicide risk factors in alcohol abuse. *Suicide and Life-Threatening Behavior, 10,* 230–238.

Pilkington, N., & D'Augelli, A. R. (1995). Victimization of lesbian, gay and bisexual youth in community settings. *Journal of Community Psychology, 23,* 33–56.

Plummer, K. (1989). Lesbian and gay youth in England. *Journal of Homosexuality, 17,* 195–223.

Remafedi, G. (1987a). Adolescent homosexuality: Psychosocial and medical implications. *Pediatrics, 79,* 331–337.

Remafedi, G. (1987b). Male homosexuality: The adolescent's perspective. *Pediatrics, 79,* 326–330.

Remafedi, G. (1994). Predictors of unprotected intercourse among gay and bisexual youth: Knowledge, beliefs, and behavior. *Pediatrics, 94,* 163–168.

Remafedi, G., Farrow, J. A., & Deisher, R. W. (1991). Risk factors for attempted suicide in gay and bisexual youth. *Pediatrics, 87,* 869–875.

Remafedi, G., French, S., Story, M., Resnick, M. D., & Blum, R. (1998). The relationship between suicide risk and sexual orientation: Results of a population-based survey. *American Journal of Public Health, 88,* 57–60.

Rich, C. L., Fowler, R. C., Young, D., & Blenkush, M. (1986). San Diego suicide study: A comparison of gay to straight males. *Suicide and Life-Threatening Behavior, 16,* 448–457.

Robins, E. (1981). *The final months: A study of the lives of 134 persons who committed suicide.* New York: Oxford University Press.

Robinson, B. E., Walters, L. H., & Skeen, P. (1989). Response of parents to learning that their child is homosexual and concern over AIDS: A national survey. *Journal of Homosexuality, 18,* 59–80.

Roos, P. E., & Cohen, L. H. (1987). Sex roles and social support as moderators of life stress adjustment. *Journal of Personality and Social Psychology, 3,* 576–585.

Rosario, M., Hunter, J., & Gwadz, M. (1997). Exploration of substance abuse among lesbian, gay, and bisexual youth: Prevalence and correlates. *Journal of Adolescent Research, 12,* 454–476.

Rosario, M., Meyer-Bahlburg, H. F. L., Hunter, J., Exner, T. M., Gwadz, M., & Keller, A. M. (1996). The psychosexual development of urban lesbian, gay, and bisexual youths. *Journal of Sex Research, 33,* 113–126.

Rosen, A. C., Rekers, G. A., & Friar, L. R. (1977). Theoretical and diagnostic issues in child gender disturbances. *Journal of Sex Research, 13,* 89–103.

Rotheram-Borus, M. J., Hunter, J., & Rosario, M. (1994). Suicidal behavior and gay-related stress among gay and bisexual male adolescents. *Journal of Adolescent Research, 9,* 498–508.

Rotheram-Borus, M. J., Hunter, J., & Rosario, M. (1995). Coming out as lesbian or gay in the era of AIDS. In G. M. Herek & B. Greene (Eds.), *AIDS, identity, and community: The HIV epidemic and lesbians and gay men* (pp. 150–168). Thousand Oaks, CA: Sage.

Rotheram-Borus, M. J., Rosario, M., & Koopman, C. (1991). Minority youths at high risk: Gay males and runaways. In M. E. Colten & S. Gore (Eds.), *Adolescent stress: Causes and consequences* (pp. 181–200). New York: Aldine.

Rotheram-Borus, M. J., Rosario, M., Meyer-Bahlburg, H. F. L., Koopman, C., Dopkins, S. C., & Davies, M. (1994). Sexual and substance use acts of gay and bisexual male adolescents in New York City. *Journal of Sex Research, 31,* 47–57.

Ryan, C., & Futterman, D. (1998). *Lesbian and gay youth: Care and counseling.* New York: Columbia University Press.

Saghir, M., & Robins, E. (1973). *Male and female homosexuality.* Baltimore: Williams & Wilkins.

Savin-Williams, R. C. (1990). *Gay and lesbian youth: Expressions of identity.* Washington, DC: Hemisphere.

Savin-Williams, R. C. (1994). Verbal and physical abuse as stressors in the lives of lesbian, gay male, and bisexual youths: Associations with school problems, running away, substance abuse, prostitution, and suicide. *Journal of Consulting and Clinical Psychology, 62,* 261–269.

Savin-Williams, R. C. (1998). The disclosure to families of same-sex attractions by lesbian, gay, and bisexual youths. *Journal of Research on Adolescence, 8,* 49–68.

Schneider, M. (1991). Developing services for lesbian and gay adolescents. *Canadian Journal of Community Mental Health, 10,* 133–151.

Schneider, M. (Ed.). (1997). *Pride and prejudice: Working with lesbian, gay, and bisexual youth.* Toronto, Ontario, Canada: Central Toronto Youth Services.

Schneider, S. G., Farberow, N. L., & Kruks, G. N. (1989). Suicidal behavior in adolescent and young adult gay men. *Suicidal and Life-Threatening Behavior, 19,* 381–394.

Shaffer, D. (1988). The epidemiology of teen suicide: An examination of risk factors. *Journal of Clinical Psychiatry, 49,* 36–41.

Shaffer, D. (1993, May 3). Political science. *The New Yorker,* 116.

Shaffer, D., Fisher, P., Hicks, R. H., Parides, M., & Gould, M. (1995). Sexual orientation in adolescents who commit suicide. *Suicide and Life Threatening Behavior, 25*(Suppl.), 64–71.

Shifrin, F., & Solis, M. (1992). Chemical dependency in gay and lesbian youth. *Journal of Chemical Dependency Treatment, 5*(1), 67–76.

Shneidman, E. S., Farberow, N. L., & Litman, R. E. (1970). *The psychology of suicide.* New York: Science House.

Silvestre, A. J., Kingsley, L. A., Wehman, P., Dappen, R., Ho, M., & Rinaldo, C. R. (1993). Changes in HIV rates and sexual behavior among homosexual men, 1984 to 1988. *American Journal of Public Health, 83,* 578–580.

Stall, R., Barrett, D., Bye, L., Catania, J., Frutchey, C., Hennessey, J., Lemp, G., & Paul, J. (1992). A comparison of younger and older gay men's HIV risk-taking behaviors: The Communication Technology 1989 Cross-Sectional Survey. *Journal of Acquired Immune Deficiency Syndrome, 5,* 682–687.

Strommen, E. F. (1989). Hidden branches and growing pains: Homosexuality and the family tree. *Journal of Marriage and Family Review, 14,* 9–34.

Waldo, C. R., Hesson-McInnis, M. S., & D'Augelli, A. R. (1988). Antecedents and consequences of victimization of lesbian, gay, and bisexual young people: A structural model comparing rural university and urban samples. *American Journal of Community Psychology, 26,* 307–334.

11

FOCUS ON LESBIAN, GAY, AND BISEXUAL FAMILIES

CONNIE R. MATTHEWS AND SUZANNE H. LEASE

In addressing issues facing lesbian, gay, and bisexual (LGB) families, there are a number of factors for the therapist to consider. This chapter examines the different contexts in which LGB individuals exist within families, including families of origin, traditional nuclear families, and a variety of nonheterosexual family constellations created by choice and necessity. Each set of circumstances presents specific concerns for the LGB individuals, for families, and for therapists. The chapter also addresses some of the additional factors that can come into play when those involved are members of ethnic minority groups that may have different perspectives on family and on sexual orientation from those of the dominant culture. However, before addressing any of these areas, it is important to examine the definition of *family*. A definition of family that is inclusive of LGB members is essential before any therapeutic work can begin.

WHAT IS FAMILY?

In focusing on the LGB families, one of the first issues to confront is the concept of family itself. What do we mean when we refer to family, and where do lesbians, gays, and bisexuals fit into that definition? For many, the very notion of a lesbian, gay, or bisexual family is antithetical to the concept:

> The central heterosexist assumption that everyone is or ought to be heterosexual is nowhere more prevalent than in the area of parent–child relationships. Not only are children usually assumed to be heterosexual in their orientation, but mothers and fathers are also generally expected to exemplify heterosexuality in their attitudes, values, and behaviors. (Patterson, 1995a, p. 255)

Often the idea of lesbians, gays, and bisexuals existing in families, much less heading families, seems unimaginable or impossible (Crawford, 1987; Falk, 1993; Laird, 1993, 1994; Patterson, 1995b; Patterson & Chan, 1996). This attitude is reflected, among other ways, in the absence of attention paid to families of lesbians, gays, and bisexuals in the popular and professional literature as well as in popular film and culture (Casper & Schultz, 1996; Laird, 1996). When lesbians, gays, and bisexuals are considered in relation to families, the association is often one of painful disconnection (Laird, 1996) or of fear, suspicion, or contempt (Ariel & Stearns, 1992; Hargaden & Llewellin, 1996; Strommen, 1990).

Even in this environment of misunderstanding, there has been growing recognition of the varied ways in which lesbians, gays, and bisexuals are maintaining and creating family life in the midst of social stigmatization. Laird (1996), in reviewing both her own research with lesbians and that of several other writers, found that although there may be initial trauma when coming out, lesbians and their families usually have found ways, often complex, to maintain connection. Likewise, Ben-Ari (1995a, 1995b) found that whereas the period preceding parents' learning that a child is gay was often characterized by distance and awkwardness in the parent–child relationship, the postdiscovery relationship sometime was one of greater intimacy and closeness. Dahlheimer and Feigal (1994), Mattison and McWhirter (1995), and Strommen (1990) have offered models that suggest that families move through a coming out process similar to what lesbians, gays, and bisexuals experience in their own identity development and that the initial turmoil may progress to some level of acceptance, or at least acknowledgment, that allows for continued connection. Although none of these writers have denied the struggle that families experience, they do offer hope for finding ways to move beyond or at least carry on in spite of it.

There has also been recent inquiry into the ways that lesbians, gays, and bisexuals create their own "families of choice" (Dahlheimer & Feigal, 1994, p. 66; Laird, 1996, p. 114). Weston (1994) described kinship patterns among lesbians and gays that are often more fluid than in traditional families, incorporating both blood relatives and people consciously chosen on the basis of "symbolic demonstrations of love, shared history, material or emotional assistance, and other signs of enduring solidarity" (p. 527). Patterson (1995b) pointed out that assumptions of biological relatedness in heterosexual families do not always apply to lesbian and gay families, even between parents and children. Dahlheimer and Feigal (1994) discussed ways in which the lesbian and gay community fulfills some of the functions of family in helping to meet the developmental needs of its members. In the midst of, or perhaps because of, the social stigma that often suggests that being lesbian, gay, or bisexual is incompatible with the experience of family, this community and those close to it are finding ways not only to maintain ties with families of origin but also to expand the definition of what constitutes family. The first task, therefore, for therapists wishing to work with LGB families is a self-assessment regarding their own views of family and the assumptions they make about the relationships lesbians, gays, and bisexuals do or do not have to family. At a basic level, this may mean examining one's biases regarding the meaning of family. It is difficult to do effective family therapy when the therapist does not consider the family in question a family. In addition, even the most affirmative therapists may find it necessary to broaden their understanding of family to incorporate the wider systems often included in families of choice.

Conceptualizing this chapter led us in a number of directions as we began to consider the family issues of lesbians, gays, and bisexuals. To begin with, there is the family of origin. Lesbians, gays, and bisexuals face a number of issues relevant to their relationship with their families of origin. Perhaps foremost among these is revealing their sexual orientation. Ben-Ari (1995a, 1995b) described effects on family relationships during the prediscovery, discovery, and postdiscovery periods. Because individuals come out at different stages in their lives (Cass, 1979; Coleman, 1985; Minton & McDonald, 1984), it is important to recognize that the issues related to family may vary depending on when this occurs. For instance, the issues for an adolescent who is still living at home and financially and otherwise dependent on parents may be different from those for a self-sufficient middle-aged adult with relatively little day-to-day contact with the family of origin. Similarly, the families are likely to experience such situations differently as well. The first part of this chapter addresses the concerns likely to arise within the family of origin when a member comes out as lesbian, gay, or bisexual.

Because lesbian, gay, and bisexual individuals may come out at different stages in their lives, it is not uncommon for them to be involved in traditional marital and family relationships when they do. This suggests another set of family issues that can become relevant: coming out to spouse and children. Whether the family decides to separate or to remain intact, this new awareness involves many adjustments, which is another concern to be addressed in focusing on the LGB family.

The last area on which this chapter focuses is the creation of families by lesbians, gays, and bisexuals. Such families might involve lesbian, gay, or bisexual couples who bring children from previous relationships into a new family situation, or it might involve individuals or couples deciding to adopt, become foster parents, or have children through donor insemination. There are many concerns that might present themselves in therapy by people in any of these situations. This section also touches on the possible involvement of extended-family systems that might be considered part of the family of choice.

THE FAMILY OF ORIGIN

Like their heterosexual counterparts, most LGB individuals are born into families or adopted at a very early age and spend at least a portion of their lives connected to those families in one way or another. Furthermore, they are raised with the assumption of heterosexuality that will eventually lead to their marrying someone of the opposite sex and beginning a family of their own. At some point, both the individual and the family must confront the fact that this assumption of heterosexuality is not accurate. This section addresses some of the issues that arise when a family member comes out as gay, lesbian, or bisexual.

There are a number of good resources available to counselors working with the LGB clients coming out to their families (e.g., Borhek, 1993; Fairchild & Hayward, 1979; Silverstein, 1977). Rather than emphasize the coming out process from the LGB individual's perspective, therefore, this chapter addresses the family's process of responding to this new awareness. What is important to keep in mind is that LGB individuals are likely to experience their own continued process of identity development simultaneously with being integrally involved in the family's response to learning about and dealing with this new information. Each process is likely to have an impact on the other. For instance, a less than affirming response on the part of the family of origin may trigger internalized homophobia that the LGB individual has not completely worked through in her or his own coming out process (Laird, 1996). Likewise, as the LGB individual gains confidence in his or her own identity, the family may grow more accepting as well (Iasenza, Colucci, & Rothberg, 1996).

Several writers have addressed the family's coming out process. Mattison and McWhirter (1995) discussed the fact that family members must suddenly reevaluate everything they have heard, learned, said, and accepted about homosexuality in the light of the new revelation that someone they love is homosexual. This brings them face to face with their stereotypes and with myths about LGB people. They are forced to consider those stereotypes in the person of their son, daughter, or other family member. An early reaction may be one of denial, dismissing the newly stated orientation as a phase (Mattison & McWhirter, 1995) or thinking that the child does not know what he or she wants. Alternatively, the announcement could be seen as a rebellion against the parents, especially if there has been a history of tension or poor interactions. Dahlheimer and Feigal (1994) noted that adapting to the family member's disclosure could be considered similar to Kübler-Ross's (1969) stages of dealing with grief. The coming out process for the family is a grief process for the parents, grief for the child they thought they had, for the loss of dreams about a traditional marriage and lifestyle, and possibly for the loss of grandchildren. In the first type of adaptation, which they label *denial and bargaining*, the parents may feel the child's orientation is a bad choice or a sin, or they may believe that the new orientation is something that can and should be cured. If they pursue actions that are based on those beliefs, they are not able to give any support to their child at a time when she or he is most vulnerable and in need of family support and acceptance.

This disavowal of the child's disclosure will stymie any further healthy disclosure or discussion between child and family, and it will prevent the parents from helping the child form a positive identity as an LGB individual. This denial will also prevent parents and other family members from working through negative stereotypical beliefs about lesbians, gays, and bisexuals. An early task for these families is to break their stereotypical beliefs and images, and often they need the help of an outside source to do this. Eliciting these stereotypes may create a great deal of cognitive dissonance for the family as they face the images they have had of the LGB population and then consider their family member in these images. This can be a crucial time for the family, because if family members are not able to get beyond their negative stereotypes, one way for them to restore the homeostasis of the family is to separate themselves from their child, who is no longer seen as an acceptable part of the family.

Dahlheimer and Feigal (1994) noted that in a second type of adaptation to disclosure, grief over the disclosure is expressed as anger toward the newly out member. Family members may be stuck in their angry reaction and may see the child's orientation as a rejection of them and their values, so they respond with hostility. Family responses of refusing to acknowledge the LGB child, disinheritance, or even physical assault are among the experiences of some gays and lesbians who lost their families when they came out to them.

In an adaptation that is characterized by depression, family members may accept their child's orientation but be depressed about what it means both for their child in this society and for themselves. Often a parent's early reaction is fear or guilt that they have done something in their parenting to cause this to happen. This fear or experience of guilt must be directly addressed—as must the homophobic beliefs that underlie it—

before these parents can accept and value their children for who they are. Much of the process with the family members will be eliciting and clarifying the antihomosexual messages the family has learned through general exposure to the societal attitudes toward the LGB population. These attitudes may be intensified by religious beliefs and a church family if the family is active in a denomination that condemns homosexuality as a sin. The family must then struggle with the conflict between the loyalty and love they have for their child and the beliefs of the church, which may be fundamental to their value system.

Part of parents' reaction to a child's news may be based on ignorance about what it means to be lesbian, gay, or bisexual and how it "happened" to their child. Sometimes this ignorance is a true lack of knowledge about an issue (e.g., etiology of a gay orientation, AIDS–related fears and questions), but sometimes it is due to a refusal to be educated about what they and their child are now experiencing. When the latter is the case, it can be useful to explore family members' fears about learning new information and what they believe will occur if they change their views and attitudes. If their views are grounded in their religious beliefs, they will need to be addressed in a respectful manner that incorporates both the importance of the church and the needs of their family member. Laird (1994) discussed the use of narrative as a means of helping lesbian [gay and bisexual] clients learn to retell their stories so that the hatred and self-blame become affirmation. A similar approach can be used with family members who may need to re-create the stories they have of their child or other relatives.

Finally, when the family members have dealt with their denial, anger, and possibly guilt, they may be able to move to a stage of acceptance and hope, in which they see their children with love and pride and accept their diversity as part of their identity. Family members may even become advocates for their children or other lesbians, gays, and bisexuals. Moving to this stage allows families to help their children build their own positive self-identity as gay or lesbian.

Just as the member of the family decides to come out, so does the family. At first the family may feel isolated and cut off from their usual, or "old," community. If they are still caught in their own antigay images, they will find it difficult to tell anyone else about their child out of fear that the people they tell will have the same negative reactions. They may feel isolated from their usual world, as if their world has turned upside down, and yet feel it is impossible to tell anyone about it. Family members may even fear rejection from their own extended families as they begin to consider disclosing their child's orientation, and families may split over the acceptance of the child, especially if the negative family beliefs about homosexuality are deeply rooted in religious beliefs. These issues may be particularly salient in ethnic-minority families or members of other cultural groups that have clear role definitions with respect to family and society

(Liu & Chan, 1996). The therapist working with clients from such cultural backgrounds must be sensitive to the cultural issues while also affirmative of the LGB family member.

Many families find it helpful to become involved with Parents and Friends of Lesbians and Gays (P-FLAG) during this process. P-FLAG serves as both a self-help group and an educational and advocacy organization. With chapters in most major metropolitan areas and many smaller communities, P-FLAG provides a resource for understanding the turmoil that is created when a family member comes out as lesbian, gay, or bisexual and a means for moving beyond it. It also helps break down the shame and isolation that many families experience; many families feel helped by talking with others who have shared their experience. Likewise, many lesbians, gays, and bisexuals are also drawn to P-FLAG as a source of hope that their families can move beyond the initial sense of trauma to a place of acceptance and sometimes affirmation. Ben-Ari (1995b) found that both parents and lesbian and gay children viewed parental participation in support groups as an important contributing factor in their movement toward acknowledging the child's homosexuality. Even when the family is in therapy, it may be important for them to become involved with support groups so that they can make connections with others who share their experience.

It may be especially powerful for the therapist working with the family to remember that it will take some time for the parents to deal with their grief and denial and "catch up" to where their child is. If they did not have any prior knowledge or suspicions about their child's orientation, the disclosure is a shock to them, and they are at the beginning of the process, whereas their child may have already worked through a number of the issues. At the time of disclosure, the LGB family member may expect or want the other family members to be supportive or be disappointed when they are not immediately so. However, the family's reaction can be presented as giving the family members some time to come out themselves and adjust to a new family status as a family with an LGB member; this interpretation may help the newly out person to reframe his or her family's reaction. It also implies that the fact that the family is not immediately supportive does not mean that it will not become so.

Research on coming out within families stresses the long-term nature of the process (e.g., Ben-Ari, 1995a, 1995b; Iasenza et al., 1996; Laird, 1996; Mattison & McWhirter, 1995; Strommen, 1990). Whereas the common assumption is that families are rejecting and lesbians, gays, and bisexuals are turned away when they come out (Laird, 1996), research has revealed that this may be more of a short-term than long-term response. In her study of lesbians, Laird (1996) found that in all cases families found some way to maintain connection, even though that connection may have been complex. Ben-Ari (1995a, 1995b) studied the experiences of lesbians, gay men, and their parents before the parents' learning of the child's sexual orientation, during the discovery period, and after discovery. Both lesbian and gay children and their parents reported distance in the relationship between them before discovery and struggles during the period of discovery; however, 56% of the children reported improvements in the relationships within the family unit, 66% reported improvement in their relationship with their mother, and 44% reported improvement in their relationship with their father after the revelation. Parents reported even more positive responses, with 84% of the mothers and 63% of the fathers indicating that their relationship with their child improved. Note that the parent sample was drawn from parents attending support groups, so it may not be reflective of all parents, but it does offer hope that with some effort coming out within the family does not have to be a tragedy.

Taking a Bowenian approach, Iasenza et al. (1996) stressed the need for assessing multigenerational family dynamics before coming out to the family of origin in an effort to anticipate reactions. They argued that often the response to a child's revelation of sexual orientation is more reflective of ongoing family patterns of interaction than of attitudes toward homosexuality per se and that part of the therapist's role is to help to identify these distinctions. Clarifying these differences allows the overarching family dynamics to be addressed without framing everything in terms of the coming out disclosure. These authors also suggested that true authenticity in family relationships is impossible while sexual orientation remains a secret. Laird (1996) discussed generational concerns from a somewhat different perspective. Arguing that the use of language often varies from generation to generation, she suggested that parents can sometimes accept the fact of their child's sexual orientation but are often unable to verbalize their acceptance owing to the social restraints of earlier periods. She pointed out the need to be sensitive to this possibility and aware of what is occurring within families as well as what is being talked about. Liu and Chan (1996) addressed this issue with respect to ethnic minority families. They suggested that even in cultures with strong strictures against homosexuality and bisexuality, families are often able to maintain connection by focusing on the value placed on family and saying little about sexual orientation.

None of the preceding is meant to suggest that discovery of a child's nonheterosexual orientation does not cause tension within families or to imply that long-term trauma never occurs. What it does suggest is that doom need not be a foregone conclusion. If they are aware of this dynamic, therapists can help provide lesbians, gays, and bisexuals and their families with hope for more positive long-term results even when the short-term situation seems grim. Therapists also need to be aware of generational and cultural differences and to be sensitive to the ways that families may work out their own compromises that allow which families may work out their own compromises that allow connection even when overt affirmation is not evident.

LESBIANS, GAYS, AND BISEXUALS IN TRADITIONAL FAMILIES

Depending on when the LGB individual's own coming out process occurs, he or she may currently be, or have been, in a traditional family relationship before recognizing or acknowledging her or his homosexual or bisexual orientation. This presents a number of issues for the LGB individual and for the family. This section addresses the added complexity that occurs when LGB individuals come out in the context of a traditional heterosexual relationship.

To begin with, although the coming out process always involves moving to an identity as lesbian, gay, or bisexual from an identity that has assumed heterosexuality (i.e., Cass, 1979; Coleman, 1985; Minton & McDonald, 1984), doing so in the context of marriage and family adds layers to the process, not to mention people. For instance, working through the transition from being a member of the dominant group to becoming part of a stigmatized minority group is a painful part of the coming out process for most lesbians, gays, and bisexuals. Even those whose gender, ethnic-minority, religious, or other cultural status may have already given them an understanding of this position often struggle with adding one more stigma. This change can be especially difficult if their status as husband, wife, or parent provided an element of social acceptance. In addition, they must add coming out to spouse and children, if present, to their own internal process and the process of coming out to family of origin. Again, the interaction of these multiple areas can add further complexity. One has to change one's identity from heterosexual to not heterosexual as well as from wife and mother (or husband and father) in the traditional sense to some less socially valued alternative. Bozett (1993) and Patterson and Chan (1996) discussed this transformation process in gay men, reporting that it often involves disengaging from spouse and, perhaps, children and then reengaging in an alternative configuration. This process can involve anger and hostility toward both oneself and one's family, although in the end it can lead to a greater sense of integration.

A number of factors are likely to come into play throughout this process. Often, there is involvement with the legal system, which makes it important for therapists working with LGB families to have some familiarity with relevant legal issues and, especially, to have a well-developed referral system for assessing knowledgeable and affirmative legal professionals (Patterson, 1995a). If there are children, the LGB parent is unlikely to be awarded custody (Falk, 1993; Patterson, 1995a, 1995b, 1996; Patterson & Chan, 1996). Although there is some suggestion that this practice may be changing, it continues to be a serious threat (Hargaden & Llewellin, 1996). Awareness of this possibility may encourage active efforts to conceal one's identity, which may have ramifications for the LGB individual, as well as for those he or she is close to, especially a new partner. Such concealment also increases the vulnerability of any new family arrangements. Crawford (1987) discussed the irony this creates with respect to family boundaries. The LGB family may feel forced to maintain a closed system owing to fear of discovery, yet that very potential suggests boundaries that are constantly threatened with violations over which the family may feel little control. Depending on the ages of children and the nature of the relationship with former spouses, this situation could continue for many years.

Although the focus of this chapter is on therapy with lesbians, gays, and bisexuals, it is important to remember that the spouse and children of the person coming out are clearly also affected. In many cases, they feel confused, betrayed, or deceived. Should this traditional family present for therapy, the therapist striving to be affirmative with the LGB spouse must also be sensitive to the concerns of other family members. Specific concerns that children may have are addressed in the next section. It is also important to remember that should the family decide to separate, they will face many of the same issues faced by other dissolving families in addition to the added concerns created by this situation. As in any work with lesbians, gays, and bisexuals, it is necessary to distinguish between factors that pertain to sexual orientation and those that are separate from it, or at least peripheral to it.

FAMILIES OF CREATION

Although factors surrounding coming out to one's existing family, be it family of origin or current nuclear family, can present stresses that might bring the LGB individual into therapy, they do not present the entire spectrum of family-related issues facing this population. LGB individuals also create and maintain families that are reflective of their nonheterosexual status. This section addresses some of the concerns that can arise within these family constellations, including LGB stepparenting, adoption, and biological parenting through donor insemination. It also addresses some of the ways in which the LGB community is redefining family to include the notion of extended family united by love and commitment rather than blood.

Families Headed by Lesbians, Gays, and Bisexuals

There are a number of ways in which families headed by lesbians, gays, and bisexuals are created (Ariel & Stearns, 1992; Crawford, 1987;

Kirkpatrick, 1996; Laird, 1994; Patterson, 1995a, 1995b; Patterson & Chan, 1996). The largest number of such families are created when one or both members of a couple have children who were born in the context of a heterosexual relationship (Patterson, 1995a; Patterson & Chan, 1996). Lesbians, gays, and bisexuals are also increasingly creating their own families through adoption, foster parenting, and donor insemination. Each of these approaches involves an active decision to parent and has its own set of concerns to be addressed. Although this section includes discussion of bisexual families, there is little literature on the issues encountered by bisexual men and women who choose to parent. The assumption is that when they are involved in same-gender relationships, the issues they face are similar to those experienced by gay and lesbian couples. Nevertheless, that is a largely untested assumption. Rust (1996) discussed the tendency to define bisexual individuals according to the relationship they are in at the time, hence rendering the bisexual orientation largely invisible. It is quite possible and probably likely that this is occurring in the literature on bisexual families. Clearly this is an area for additional research and theory building.

Lesbian, Gay, and Bisexual Stepfamilies

In LGB families in which children from previous relationships are brought to the current relationships, stepfamilies are formed. These families often get caught between not being recognized as families and being treated just like any other family, without consideration of their unique status (Crawford, 1987). LGB stepfamilies experience some problems that are similar to those in heterosexual stepfamilies (jealousy, new house rules and roles, stepparent–stepchild conflict), but they also experience problems that are unknown in heterosexual blended families (Baptiste, 1987). These special issues can include problems brought on by being members of a stigmatized group in which the relationships are disapproved of by the majority of society, lack of formal or legal recognition of lesbian and gay families, nonheterosexual lifestyles being seen as incompatible with child rearing, fear of losing custody, and the perceived need for secrecy.

Lesbians, gays, and bisexuals are themselves socially stigmatized, and this stigma extends to the families they create. They can often experience this stigma from both directions: They may find themselves misunderstood and excluded from the LGB community owing to their parental–family status as well as from the heterosexual community owing to sexual orientation (Crawford, 1987). The additional stress of coping with society's disapproval can add to the difficulties of combining a family and may hinder the blending process. Therapists working with LGB families need to be aware of how these pressures can play themselves out in the couple and family relationship. It is also vital that therapists be familiar with resources and support services in the community. Many communities are beginning to establish formal and informal networks and services specifically geared to aiding LGB families (Patterson, 1995a). Therapists must be prepared to help families make these connections.

Because there is no legal or formal recognition of lesbian or gay marriages and families, there are few guidelines for resolving separation or custody issues. This can make roles that are already unclear for the nonbiological or nonadoptive parent even more difficult to define, especially if the true nature of the relationship is not revealed. Furthermore, the lack of legal status for the family as a whole and especially for the nonbiological or nonadoptive parent may place increased emphasis on the emotional vulnerabilities (Crawford, 1987). The possible role complications experienced by the nonbiological or nonadoptive parent are elaborated on in the next section. Therapists must be attuned to these issues and be able to recognize them. Because the LGB stepfamily may not be seen as a legitimate family form, family issues may be seen as the result of the LGB identity or as individual issues rather than as family issues. Although individuals in families may continue to work through their own concerns regarding sexual orientation (coming out is an ongoing and often long-term process), it is not helpful or appropriate to attribute all problems within a family to issues about sexual orientation. Failure on the part of the therapist to recognize the family as a family and family issues as family issues only adds to the destructive forces of society at large.

Often the stigma associated with LGB families goes beyond absence of recognition and lack of protection to active disdain and discrimination. A nonheterosexual lifestyle may be seen as incompatible with child rearing owing to fears that LGB individuals are unfit parents and that children raised by them will be psychologically maladjusted, suffer extreme social stigmatization, or assume a homosexual orientation themselves (Ariel & Stearns, 1992; Hargaden & Llewellin, 1996; Patterson, 1995a, 1996). These attitudes continue despite a growing body of research that indicates that these concerns about both parents and children are unfounded. (For more extensive literature reviews on this work, see Bozett, 1993; Falk, 1993; Kirkpatrick, 1996; Patterson, 1995a, 1995b, 1996; Patterson & Chan, 1996.) Given the level of misperception and, often, hostility toward LGB parents, there may be little support for the difficulties the blended family may face. Again, the therapist should be familiar with resources in the community where such support may be available. It is also important for the therapist to assess her or his own attitudes and biases and not contribute to the negative response. Therapists should avoid the seemingly benign stance of neither condemning nor affirming nonheterosexual orientations. This so-called neutral approach often reflects the view that although LGB parents may not do harm to children, the children are still better off residing with heterosexual parents given the choice.

Given the inclination of representatives of the legal system to act in accordance with prevalent fears and misconceptions, gay parents live in fear of losing custodial rights over children if their orientation is known. Even those already without primary custody might fear loss of, or limits to, visitation rights. The response is often to conceal their orientation, sometimes at great personal cost to themselves and their relationship with their partner. It is vital that the therapist recognize the very real basis for these fears. LGB parents are at great risk for being denied custody of their children (Falk, 1993; Patterson, 1995a; Patterson & Chan, 1996). Thus, problems that result from living in the midst of this fear must be taken seriously and not be dismissed as overreactions. The therapist should also have some familiarity with the legal status of LGB families in her or his community and state, as well as with attorneys who are knowledgeable and affirmative. The National Gay and Lesbian Task Force has a web page (http://www.ngltf.org) that provides a good starting point for an overview of state laws as well as assistance with reaching LGB-affirmative lawyers and lawmakers.

Because of the need or perceived need for secrecy, the usual problems of parenthood are increased; the secrecy itself can be a stressor that contributes to relationship difficulties and limits the support that can be sought. Many common informal support systems, such as the ones that include friends, neighbors, and colleagues at work, cannot be accessed if the true nature of the relationship cannot be revealed (Crawford, 1987; Kirkpatrick, 1996). This can be especially pertinent for nonbiological parents, who may not even be able to acknowledge their stepparent status. In addition, joys and celebrations cannot be shared. Problems can arise, too, in relationships between the family and the respective families of origin. Different expectations are often placed on family members who are single (even single parents) than on those who have their own families (Laird, 1996). This can apply especially to things like holidays, felt obligations to the family of origin, and whether a partner is included in family occasions. This issue may be more salient for some ethnic minorities for whom obligation to family of origin is especially valued (Liu & Chan, 1996).

In some instances, the couple's relationship must be kept secret even from the children in the household (Patterson & Chan, 1996). This may limit the support that partners can get even from each other, both in terms of the family and with respect to the function of the home as a refuge from the prejudice of the outside world. Similarly, it can limit the openness with which issues within the family can be addressed. The therapist may need to help family members negotiate boundaries with respect to secrecy and openness, especially if individual family members are at different places in their own development or feel different needs. Therapists who are themselves lesbian, gay, or bisexual may need to assess their own needs and values in this area so that they can adequately hear the variety of perspectives that clients may present. These concerns may be relevant to all LGB families, whether or not they are stepfamilies.

Choosing to Have Children

Although many LGB families are formed when partners bring children into the relationship from previous heterosexual relationships, increasingly, couples and individuals are deciding to have children (Kirkpatrick, 1996; Patterson, 1994, 1995b, 1996). There are a variety of options available for doing this, including adoption, foster parenting, and donor insemination. In the first two instances, the parent or parents and child are not biologically related; in the latter situation, one parent is biologically related to the child. There are several possible arrangements within the different options as well, although in most instances one person becomes the parent of record, which can create difficulties with regard to role definition for a couple. Furthermore, depending on the regulations in different states and communities, it may be necessary for individuals or couples who have been somewhat open about their sexual orientation to become secretive, especially with respect to adoption or foster care (Crawford, 1987). Lesbians, gays, and bisexuals are also developing their own creative ways of choosing to parent. For instance, a lesbian and a gay man or a lesbian couple and a gay male couple may agree to joint biological or custodial parenting arrangement (Ariel & Stearns, 1992; Hargaden & Llewellin, 1996). Therapists working with LGB families must be open to the variety of configurations that individuals and couples may choose and must be knowledgeable, or able to become knowledgeable, about the issues pertinent to each. Ariel and Stearns (1992), Hargaden and Llewellin (1996), and Kirkpatrick (1996) have offered overviews of some of the issues involved when lesbians, gays, and bisexuals choose to create their own families. Again, therapists must be familiar with the resources available to assist individuals and couples as they pursue these options (Patterson, 1995a). In many circumstances, it is necessary to have contacts with professionals who are able to provide legal assistance.

Although all couples or individuals considering having children often go through a decision-making process to determine whether they should parent, there are some unique issues for LGB couples who are considering having children. Crawford (1987) stressed the need for lesbians to have a safe space to work through these decisions; confronted with a social system that often condemns them, lesbian couples must be able to work through their questions and concerns about parenting without having to justify their right *to be* parents. The same applies to gay and bisexual individuals and couples. Some of the issues they may need to work through may be related to their own internalized homophobia, which makes them question their own fitness for parenting. In addition, even couples who are confident in their right to parent and their fitness as parents may question the wisdom of bringing children into a situation where they, too, will be subject to social stigmatization. Therapy must be a safe space to discuss these issues if it is to be effective. Hargaden and Llewellin (1996) suggested that therapists make a point of expressing an affirmation of the *right* of nonheterosexual families to have children, to make it clear that they do not have to justify their choice owing to their sexual orientation. At the same time, it is appropriate for all potential parents to explore their desires and motives for parenting. Therapists must not back away from this step simply because they are scared of appearing to require justification from the client.

Deciding to have children may further complicate an LGB couple's relationship with their families of origin (Crawford, 1987; Patterson, 1995a, 1995b). Even when the family was somewhat accepting (or at least tolerant) of their sexual orientation and perhaps even of the couple relationship, reactions may be different when the prospect of children is considered because of the myths about molestation and psychological difficulties that children may experience (Ariel & Stearns, 1992). This response may be in sharp contrast to the joy and excitement that is often expressed when heterosexual couples announce impending parenthood. If the LGB partners have heterosexual siblings for whom this was the case, a different reaction may be especially painful.

Once the choice to parent is made, there are still a number of factors to be considered. Many of these are related to the roles that both parents will play and how those roles may differ if only one member of the couple is publicly acknowledged as a parent (Ariel & Stearns, 1992; Crawford, 1987; Kirkpatrick, 1996; Patterson, 1995b, 1996). Without social or legal recognition and lacking established models, nonheterosexual families must come up with their own approaches to parenting. Some of the areas to be addressed include financial arrangements, wage working versus home and family care, dealing with outside entities, and negotiating levels of openness with children's peers and their families. These issues may be particularly delicate for the noncustodial parent, who may feel especially vulnerable without any formal recognition of his or her role, perhaps even within the family. The position of the nonbiological or nonadoptive parent can be especially precarious in the case of ending the relationship. Retaining custody or even continued contact with the child or children may be difficult when the partner's coparenting status was never formally recognized. Negotiating role expectations and protection for all involved in the case of a separation may be an important part of therapy, one that is hard for couples to address at a point in their relationship when they are feeling strong and connected. Therapists may need to be persistent in encouraging couples to consider these issues. More creative parenting arrangements may require even more attention to these details to be sure that all parties involved understand and agree ahead of time on the arrangements and expectations (Ariel & Stearns, 1992).

Choosing to have children also entails choices of whether to come out to a variety of people who will be involved in the child's life. These include members of the medical community, child care workers, school officials, and the children's peers and their parents. Decisions need to be made concerning how open to be as a family and as a gay parent when dealing with these organizations. Coming out issues that were thought to be long resolved may reemerge in a different context when the decision to parent is made (Ariel & Stearns, 1992). This reemergence of difficult or painful issues may confuse individuals and lead them to doubt their decision to have children. Realizing that this process is a natural developmental outgrowth of having to consider how one will deal with these societal institutions may provide clients with some perspective and allay fears or doubts about their competence to raise children.

LGB families who choose parenting face many of the same issues that stepfamilies and blended families face. The perceived need for secrecy and the invisibility of the nonbiological, nonadoptive, or nonfoster parent can present similar problems in families of choice as in stepfamilies. Furthermore, in many locales the inability of lesbians, gays, and bisexuals to adopt as a couple can be problematic. In addition, being unable to reach out to support systems can be especially isolating for individuals or couples who are first-time parents. Even when families feel able to be open, they often feel caught between two worlds. Although they may receive assistance as parents from the heterosexual community, they often lack acceptance owing to sexual orientation. On the other hand, the LGB community may be accepting with respect to sexual orientation but dismissive of the parenting role. Again, the need for the therapist to recognize and support the dual realities and to be able to help clients connect with others who can do likewise seems evident.

Some have argued that there is a lack of established models and traditions of parenting for LGB families (Ariel & Stearns, 1992; Crawford, 1987); however, others have suggested that there are opportunities to create new models (Laird, 1994, 1996; Weston, 1994). Laird (1994) suggested that models can come from different sources, including heterosexuals as well as lesbians, gays, and bisexuals. She stressed the importance of developing rituals and traditions that speak to the lives of the families created, stating the need to find ways to celebrate achievements and successes, heal from losses, and connect with others when society as a whole does not recognize those milestones. Weston (1994) found that the lack of established rituals meant that new ways needed to be discovered, which took time, but that being able to stay connected over time and be a part of emerging rituals and traditions was one of the things that helped to define kinship.

Children's Concerns

Studies have indicated that children of lesbian and gay parents do not experience significantly greater long-term problems in terms of psychological adjustment, relationships with parents, or social stigmatization than children of heterosexual parents (most often compared to children of divorced parents; see Bozett, 1993; Falk, 1993; Kirkpatrick, 1996; Patterson, 1995a, 1995b, 1996; Patterson & Chan, 1996, for more extensive reviews). Nonetheless, there are short-term issues and life disruptions that can occur at the time of the parent's disclosure and at certain developmental points in the children's lives. Knowledge of these issues allows them to be addressed and resolved at an early stage so they do not present more complicated issues later.

Crawford (1987) noted that just as LGB parents face being perceived as different and inappropriate as parents, their children may also feel that they are different from their peers. This may be especially difficult for children who were the products of heterosexual marriages and are now living with LGB stepparents. Suddenly, they may worry about being seen as different by the world when they had not previously felt different from their peers (Hargaden & Llewellin, 1996). Talking with the children openly about this life transition may help them to verbalize their anxiety and possible anger at what they perceive is a dramatic change in their lives. Children's feelings of anger or distress over the composition of their new family should be attended to and validated but addressed in a way that allows them to learn to cope with the situation and recognize the oppression in the larger society as it now affects them.

Because of custody concerns, some lesbian and gay parents who are living with their same-sex partners are afraid to be open about that relationship. Even if they disclose the nature of the relationship to their children, they often caution their children about the need for secrecy. This need to live a secretive life can create a burdensome fear of discovery for the children (Baptiste, 1987; Crawford, 1987), who might withdraw from peers and other social interactions because they fear they will accidentally reveal the information. Even if the parents are openly out and the children have no need for secrecy, the children may have little peer support because their peers have been exposed to the prejudices about homosexuality that are still prevalent in this society (Sears, 1993–1994). When faced with other children's comments, they may not have any strategies for dealing with those children. Children who are experiencing these concerns can be assisted by therapists in learning coping skills to deal with the anger or sense of isolation. Therapists can help children understand the comments their classmates make by putting those comments in the context of what society believes about LGB relationships and the fact that many people mimic what society believes even if they do not understand it. Helping children, as well as their parents, see the larger sociological perspective can assist them in reframing the comments and making them less personal in nature.

Older children and adolescents must make their own decisions about coming out concerning their parents, and they run the risk of being singled out by their peer groups. They may not want to bring peers or dates home with them, or they may deny the partner's existence or importance in the family if they do. This attitude may be extremely difficult for the coparenting partner to endure, and therapists may provide some assistance in framing the adolescent's actions as a process the child is going through rather than a direct rejection of the partner. Similarly, the therapist can help the children and parents negotiate agreements regarding when, to whom, and under what circumstances they will each be open about the nature of the family relationships. Adolescents may also be struggling with their own identity, including their sexuality, and they may not be happy about a parent who seems to have changed all the rules midstream. If the child is older at the time the parent comes out, he or she might conclude that homosexuality and the new partner are the causes of the divorce, which can lead to resentment, anger, and acting out around the partner as a way of expressing pain and confusion about the loss of the previously intact family.

Families of Choice

Although Dahlheimer and Feigal (1994) proposed different types of adaptation families go through when a family member comes out, they have stated that some families do not reach a stage of acceptance; therefore, they stressed the importance of lesbians, gays, and bisexuals finding their families elsewhere in the community. They have suggested that these families of choice are able to fulfill the functions that families of origin normally serve. First, families are usually seen as sources of protection for their members, yet the family of origin may not be willing or able to serve this function for its LGB member. Families of choice may fulfill this role through providing community as well as working through advocacy groups and lobbying for legislation on important issues such as partner benefits and hate crime bills.

Second, families are also sources of socialization, yet the most supportive families of origin may not have the knowledge needed to help their members learn the skills for living in a society in which their sexual orientation is considered by many to be unacceptable. Families of choice in the LGB community can teach individuals how to relate to both the majority and minority cultures (i.e., to be bicultural), how to decide when and to whom disclosures should be made, how to make those disclosures,

and how to address gender role issues in partnerships in which both partners have been socialized to assume the same role. The family of choice
also provides places for meeting, organizing, and connecting with others
in the community.

A third function of families is to provide a sense of self-esteem to
their members. Many LGB individuals have taken in years of antigay messages from society before they come out, and these messages have perme-
ated the core of their self-concept. The LGB community serving as a sur-
rogate family can provide role models, coping skills, and positive messages
to offset the power of these negative stereotypes.

A fourth family function is to provide members with a sense of identity and belongingness. The LGB community can help break down the
isolation that many lesbians, gays, and bisexuals experience as they begin
to discover and claim their orientation. Connecting with the community
can help turn what seemed like an unusual or deviant identity into an
accepted, valued component of the self. Finally, Dahlheimer and Feigal
(1994) noted that families teach survival skills for meeting the challenges
of daily interactions. However, the family of origin may not be able to
teach its LGB member the skills needed for living in a culture where homophobia is present because they have not had to face those experiences
and learn the skills for themselves. The LGB community and smaller support groups within the community can take on this function by establishing
information networks and forums that address issues ignored by the nongay
community.

An important role of therapists working with LGB clients is to facilitate connections with the larger LGB community for clients so that
these necessary family functions can occur. Clients who are newly out may
have little or no idea about how to find support networks among the LGB
population or how to learn the self-protective survival skills they may need
to negotiate both their minority and the majority cultures. It is also important for therapists to recognize the variety of ways in which lesbians,
gays, and bisexuals create family and to be open to incorporating all manner of family in therapy as appropriate (Weston, 1994). For instance, ex-
partners often remain in close connection and may be considered family
even though the partner relationship has dissolved. Likewise, members of
the larger community may share parenting responsibilities and may need
to be included in matters pertaining to children. Therapists who are affirmative of nonheterosexual relationships but limited in how they conceptualize family may miss important opportunities for support (or areas of
turmoil) when working with LGB families. Laird (1996) stressed the importance of looking for strengths and capabilities for resilience. Sources of
strength may be found outside of what is traditionally considered immediate family.

ETHNIC-MINORITY GAYS, LESBIANS, AND BISEXUALS

Lesbians, gays, and bisexuals who are members of racial or ethnic minority groups face many of the same concerns of majority-group lesbians, gays, and bisexuals, as well as challenges specific to their ethnic-minority membership. Morales (1990) noted that ethnic lesbians and gay men live in three separate communities: the gay and lesbian community, the ethnic-minority community, and the larger society. These three communities all fulfill basic needs for the individual, but no community fulfills all needs, and the needs are not easily integrated. Many ethnic-minority communities are not accepting of LGB individuals, and the LGB community has learned the racial prejudices of the larger society (Chan, 1989; Greene, 1994; Loia-cano, 1989; Morales, 1990). In addition, the larger society has stereotypes and prejudices about both groups. This need to live in three separate worlds can leave ethnic LGB individuals feeling fragmented. They must expend constant effort to live in all of their worlds, each of which fails to fulfill significant needs (Morales, 1990). This multiple minority membership can lead to increased feelings of isolation, depression, and confusion about identity, both as a lesbian, gay male, or bisexual and as a member of an ethnic minority group.

Isolation can be increased by distance from a family who otherwise might be providing support. Minority parents provide support and protect their children from societal racial discrimination whenever possible and teach them skills for surviving in both the majority and minority cultures. But for many ethnic-minority communities, the social norms and values about homosexuality foster homophobic attitudes. Consequently, many ethnic lesbians, gays, and bisexuals face rejection rather than support from their ethnic communities. Some ethnic lesbians, gays, and bisexuals may restrict their coming out because they fear losing or negatively affecting the support they receive from their families and the members of ethnic communities who do not discuss or accept their orientation. This rejection is especially intense because the nuclear and extended family and community are important for many ethnic minorities.

As a visible minority group, the ethnic community provides a sense of identity, strength, and protection that members may not receive from any other source but is automatically provided to members of the dominant majority culture. Coming out to the ethnic community risks rejection or ostracism from the community, which otherwise provides validation. The weight of that threat is great, and many ethnic lesbians, gays, and bisexuals are reluctant to sacrifice that family and community support. Decisions of ethnic lesbians, gay males, or bisexuals about coming out need to be made with the importance of and consequences to family in mind. Therapists working with these individuals must help them to assess their own situation (Ibrahim, 1991), with attention to a sense of racial identity (Atkinson,

Morten, & Sue, 1993), sexual orientation, gender, and physical ability; they should discuss with their clients the possible reactions of family and community members as well as how to cope with negative responses.

The multiple minority-group memberships experienced by ethnic lesbians, gays, and bisexuals and the balancing of those separate identities create anxiety for this population. Giving preference to one identity component over the other is seen as a personal betrayal of the nonpreferred identity. Learning to integrate the identities or make choices about when to live one more fully than another allows the ethnic-minority LGB individual to develop effective coping strategies and successfully manage internal conflicts. Therapists can assist in this process by norming the conflicts among identities, weighing the pros and cons of emphasizing one identity over another, and discussing situations in which it may be more appropriate to emphasize one identity over another. Therapists also can facilitate contact with other ethnic-minority lesbians, gays, and bisexuals who are managing these conflicts and who can serve as role models and provide support.

FUTURE RESEARCH

Despite a growing body of work on LGB families, some areas require more attention. Much of the research to date has been driven by the need and desire to respond to the historical (and continuing) prejudice in the legal system against LGB families (Falk, 1993; Patterson, 1995a, 1995b, 1996; Patterson & Chan, 1996). Although this work has been and continues to be important, it is more reactive than proactive; because LGB families have been seriously harmed by social reactions, it is appropriate that the first line of research has been directed toward stopping the harm. There is now a need to be more proactive, however, and to learn more about how LGB families can foster resilience in the midst of an oppressive social system as well as how therapists can help strengthen such families. Like much of the work in this field, the preponderance of research to date has been conducted with White, well-educated, middle-class families (Patterson, 1995a, 1995b, 1996; Patterson & Chan, 1996). There is clearly a need for more work with a greater diversity of families. Because families have traditionally serve the vital role of support system for members of ethnic minority groups, it is critical to learn more about how to help ethnic-minority LGB clients maintain that connection while also fully integrating their sexual orientation. There is also a need to look more closely at issues specific to bisexual clients. We found almost nothing that directly addressed family issues pertaining to this population. It makes sense to intuit that bisexual families would experience many of the issues common to lesbian and gay families, especially when the current family configuration involves a same-sex couple. This is why we have included them in this chapter. We recognize that this is an assumption that may not hold up to empirical investigation; there is a need for research regarding the particular issues that bisexual families face. If the notion of family must be expanded to include nontraditional families, researchers also must recognize the diversity of experience within those families and make a commitment to developing an understanding of those differences as well as of common issues they share by virtue of being outside the traditional view of family.

There is also a need for research that contributes to theory building. Traditional family theories tend to be built on a presumption of heterosexuality (Demo & Allen, 1996). To the extent that alternatives are even addressed, they are seen as problematic or reflective of failures in family processes. It is time to develop new definitions of family that incorporate the variety of experiences that gays, lesbians, and bisexuals have in families into existing theories in ways that show the strengths and resiliencies of these families while acknowledging the reality of the stresses that can accompany social stigmatization and oppression.

CONCLUSION

Clearly the most important first step in working with LGB families is to recognize not only the legitimacy of such families but also the variety of ways in which family might be conceptualized. It is equally important to be aware of the different ways that sexual orientation intersects with family issues. This awareness is as vital for therapists who work primarily with individuals as it is for those who specialize in work with families, because the family, in its varied forms, can have a substantial impact on the individual's developing identity as an LGB person. Furthermore, it is not enough for therapists to be supportive in their own right; they must also be able to connect both the LGB individual and the family with other avenues of support in the community. This means learning what is available in the community and developing referral procedures. Because the legal system frequently comes into play, especially for families headed by lesbians, gays, and bisexuals, some knowledge of this system, particularly the names of affirmative professionals, is necessary as well. It is also important for the therapist to be sensitive to religious, cultural, and generational issues that might affect both the family's response to issues related to sexual orientation and the nonheterosexual member's response to the family. Finally, it is important to distinguish between family issues that are also sexual orientation issues and family issues that are separate from or peripheral to sexual orientation issues.

REFERENCES

Ariel, J., & Stearns, S. M. (1992). Challenges facing gay and lesbian families. In S. H. Dworkin & F. J. Gutiérrez (Eds.), *Counseling gay men and lesbians: Journey to the end of the rainbow* (pp. 95–112). Alexandria, VA: American Association for Counseling and Development.

Atkinson, D. R., Morten, G., & Sue, D. W. (1993). *Counseling American minorities* (4th ed.). Dubuque, IA: Brown & Benchmark.

Baptiste, D. A., Jr. (1987). Psychotherapy with gay/lesbian couples and their children in "stepfamilies": A challenge for marriage and family therapists. *Journal of Homosexuality, 14*, 223–238.

Ben-Ari, A. (1995a). Coming out: A dialectic of intimacy and privacy. *Families in Society: The Journal of Contemporary Human Services, 76*, 306–314.

Ben-Ari, A. (1995b). The discovery that an offspring is gay: Parents', gay men's, and lesbians' perspectives. *Journal of Homosexuality, 30*, 89–112.

Borhek, M. V. (1993). *Coming out to parents: A two-way survival guide for lesbians and gay men and their parents.* Cleveland, OH: Pilgrim Press.

Bozett, F. W. (1993). Gay fathers: A review of the literature. In L. D. Garnets & D. C. Kimmel (Eds.), *Psychological perspectives on lesbian and gay male experiences* (pp. 437–457). New York: Columbia University Press.

Casper, V., & Schultz, S. (1996). Lesbian and gay parents encounter educators: Initiating conversations. In R. C. Savin-Williams & K. M. Cohen (Eds.), *The lives of lesbians, gays, and bisexuals: Children to adults* (pp. 305–330). Fort Worth, TX: Harcourt Brace.

Cass, V. C. (1979). Homosexual identity formation: A theoretical model. *Journal of Homosexuality, 4*, 219–235.

Chan, C. S. (1989). Issues of identity development among Asian-American lesbians and gay men. *Journal of Counseling and Development, 68*, 16–20.

Coleman, E. (1985). Developmental stages of the coming out process. In J. C. Gonsiorek (Ed.), *A guide to psychotherapy with gay and lesbian clients.* New York: Harrington Park Press.

Crawford, S. (1987). Lesbian families: Psychosocial stress and the family-building process. In Boston Lesbian Psychologies Collective (Eds.), *Lesbian psychologies* (pp. 195–214). Urbana: University of Illinois Press.

Dahlheimer, D., & Feigal, J. (1994). Community as family: The multiple-family contexts of gay and lesbian clients. In C. H. Huber (Ed.), *Transitioning from individual to family counseling* (pp. 63–74). Alexandria, VA: American Counseling Association.

Demo, D. H., & Allen, K. R. (1996). Diversity within lesbian and gay families: Challenges and implications for family theory and research. *Journal of Social and Personal Relationships, 13*, 415–434.

Fairchild, B., & Hayward, N. (1979). *Now that you know: What every parent should know about homosexuality.* New York: Harvester/Harcourt Brace Jovanovich.

Falk, P. J. (1993). Lesbian mothers: Psychosocial assumptions in family law. In

L. D. Garnets & D. C. Kimmel (Eds.), *Psychological perspectives on lesbian and gay male experiences* (pp. 420–436). New York: Columbia University Press.

Greene, B. (1994). Ethnic-minority lesbians and gay men: Mental health and treatment issues. *Journal of Consulting and Clinical Psychology, 62,* 243–251.

Hargaden, H., & Llewellin, S. (1996). Lesbian and gay parenting issues. In D. Davies & C. Neal (Eds.), *Pink therapy: A guide for counselors and therapists working with LGB clients* (pp. 116–130). Philadelphia: Open University Press.

Iasenza, S., Colucci, P. L., & Rothberg, B. (1996). Coming out and the mother–daughter bond: Two case examples. In J. Laird & R. J. Green (Eds.), *Lesbians and gays in couples and families* (pp. 123–136). San Francisco: Jossey-Bass.

Ibrahim, F. (1991). Contribution of cultural worldview to generic counseling and development. *Journal of Counseling and Development, 70,* 13–19.

Kirkpatrick, M. (1996). Lesbians as parents. In R. P. Cabaj & T. S. Stein (Eds.), *Textbook of homosexuality and mental health* (pp. 353–370). Washington, DC: American Psychiatric Press.

Kübler-Ross, E. (1969). *On death and dying.* New York: Macmillan.

Laird, J. (1993). Lesbian and gay families. In F. Walsh (Ed.), *Normal family processes* (2nd ed., pp. 282–328). New York: Guilford Press.

Laird, J. (1994). Lesbian families: A cultural perspective. In M. P. Mirkin (Ed.), *Women in context: Toward a feminist reconstruction of psychotherapy* (pp. 118–148). New York: Guilford Press.

Laird, J. (1996). Invisible ties: Lesbians and their families of origin. In J. Laird & R. J. Green (Eds.), *Lesbians and gays in couples and families* (pp. 89–122). San Francisco: Jossey-Bass.

Liu, P., & Chan, C. S. (1996). Lesbian, gay, and bisexual Asian Americans and their families. In J. Laird & R. J. Green (Eds.), *Lesbians and gays in couples and families: A handbook for therapists* (pp. 137–152). San Francisco: Jossey-Bass.

Loiacano, D. K. (1989). Gay identity issues among Black Americans: Racism, homophobia, and the need for validation. *Journal of Counseling and Development, 68,* 21–25.

Mattison, A. M., & McWhirter, D. P. (1995). Lesbians, gay men, and their families: Some therapeutic issues. *Psychiatric Clinics of North America, 18,* 123–137.

Minton, H. L., & McDonald, G. J. (1984). *Homosexual identity formation as a developmental process, 9,* 91–104.

Morales, E. S. (1990). Ethnic minority families and minority gays and lesbians. In F. W. Bozett & M. B. Sussman (Eds.), *Homosexuality and family relations* (pp. 217–239). New York: Harrington Park Press.

Patterson, C. J. (1994). Children of the lesbian baby boom: Behavioral adjustment, self-concepts, and sex role identity. In B. Greene & G. M. Herek (Eds.), *Psychological perspectives on lesbian and gay psychology: Theory, research, and clinical applications* (pp. 156–175). Newbury Park, CA: Sage.

Patterson, C. J. (1995a). Lesbian and gay parenthood. In M. H. Bornstein (Ed.),

Handbook of parenting: Vol. 4. Status and social conditions of parenting (pp. 255–274). Mahwah, NJ: Erlbaum.

Patterson, C. J. (1995b). Lesbian mothers, gay fathers, and their children. In A. R. D'Augelli & C. J. Patterson (Eds.), *Lesbian, gay, and bisexual perspectives over the lifespan: Psychological perspectives* (pp. 262–290). New York: Oxford University Press.

Patterson, C. J. (1996). Lesbian and gay parents and their children. In R. C. Savin-Williams & K. M. Cohen (Eds.), *The lives of lesbians, gays, and bisexuals: Children to adults* (pp. 274–304). Fort Worth, TX: Harcourt Brace.

Patterson, C. J., & Chan, R. W. (1996). Gay fathers and their children. In R. P. Cabaj & T. S. Stein (Eds.), *Textbook of homosexuality and mental health* (pp. 371–393). Washington, DC: American Psychiatric Press.

Rust, P. C. (1996). Monogamy and polyamory: Relationship issues for bisexuals. In B. A. Firestein (Ed.), *Bisexuality: The psychology and politics of an invisible minority* (pp. 127–148). Newbury Park, CA: Sage.

Sears, J. T. (1993–1994). Challenges for educators: Lesbian, gay, and bisexual families. *High School Journal, 77*(1–2), 138–156.

Silverstein, C. (1977). *A family matter: A parent's guide to homosexuality*. New York: McGraw-Hill.

Strommen, E. F. (1990). Hidden branches and growing pains: Homosexuality and the family tree. In F. W. Bozett & M. B. Sussman (Eds.), *Homosexuality and family relations* (pp. 9–34). New York: Harrington Park Press.

Weston, K. (1994). Building gay families. In G. Handel & G. G. Whitchurch (Eds.), *The psychosocial interior of the family* (4th ed., pp. 525–533). New York: Aldine de Gruyter.

12

RELATIONSHIP AND COUPLES COUNSELING

SHELLY M. OSSANA

All couples desire companionship, intimacy, and love. Same-sex couples and heterosexual couples deal with similar issues, including balancing autonomy and intimacy, handling money decisions, dealing with in-laws, and balancing relationship and career responsibilities. However, there are several important differences between heterosexual couples and same-sex couples. Gender role socialization has a unique influence in relationships between two people of the same gender. In addition, the dominant culture is rejecting of same-sex relationships. As a result, the various overt and covert manifestations of homophobia and heterosexism figure prominently in the lives and relationships of gay men and lesbians. Nonetheless, in spite of numerous obstacles, lesbian women and gay men appear to have relationships that are as satisfying as those of their heterosexual counterparts (Kurdek, 1988, 1995b; Peplau & Cochran, 1990).

This chapter explores various dimensions of same-sex relationships, including commonalities with heterosexual relationships as well as unique

Candace Galen and Laurie B. Mintz provided invaluable assistance throughout the preparation of this chapter. I would also like to thank Mandy Manderino for helpful comments on a draft.

considerations. The impact of gender role socialization, which has been theorized to play a major role in the relationships of gay men and lesbians, is discussed. Additional issues unique to same-sex couples, such as the impact of homophobia and heterosexism, the lack of rituals and role models, and the roles of secrecy and the coming out process, are addressed with particular attention to how these issues affect the types of problems gay and lesbian couples bring to therapy. Therapist skills and attitudes necessary for effective work with gay and lesbian couples are reviewed.

Several caveats are in order. First, there is little empirical work on gay and lesbian couples. A recent content analysis of articles published in the marriage and family therapy literature from 1975 to 1995 revealed that only .006% of the articles focused on lesbian, gay, or bisexual (LGB) issues (Clark & Serovich, 1997). In considering the present review of salient empirical studies in the current literature, the reader should be mindful that this body of work is in its infancy, permitting only speculative conclusions. There is an even greater scarcity of theoretical and empirical work on multicultural issues in same-sex relationships. In a recent survey of journal articles on LGB issues, it was concluded that only 4.5% of these focused primarily on race or ethnicity (Soto, 1997). A similar paucity of information hampers any discussion of unique relationship issues for bisexuals. Owing to both the lack of information and space constraints, multicultural and bisexual issues are not covered here in depth. Nevertheless, these two issues are important topics that warrant further theoretical work and empirical investigation. Finally, it must be noted that to date the vast majority of research on lesbians and gay men has been conducted with White, middle-class participants. Therefore, caution should be exercised in generalizing from the empirical studies reviewed in this chapter to diverse populations.

COMMONALITIES BETWEEN SAME-SEX AND HETEROSEXUAL COUPLES

Same-sex couples and heterosexual couples are faced with a variety of common issues, including those concerning children, sex, money, communication, family of origin, conflict resolution, and balancing work with personal commitments. Few, if any, differences have been reported in relationship satisfaction between same-sex and heterosexual couples (Peplau & Cochran, 1990). In fact, the quality of lesbian and gay male relationships generally has been reported to be comparable to (and for lesbian relationships, sometimes better than) that of heterosexual relationships (R. Green, Bettinger, & Zachs, 1996; Kurdek, 1988, 1995b). The correlates of relationship quality are similar for all couples: appraisals that the relationship includes many rewards and few costs; personality characteristics such as high expressiveness; partners' placing higher value on security, permanence, shared activities, and togetherness; less belief that disagreement is destructive; higher mutual trust; better problem-solving and conflict-resolution skills; more frequent shared or egalitarian decision making; and greater satisfaction with perceived social support (Kurdek, 1995b; Peplau, 1991).

In addition, McWhirter and Mattison (1984) proposed that same-sex relationships and heterosexual relationships follow a similar developmental progression. Their model, based on work with gay male couples, suggests the relationship typically begins with intense feelings of romantic love and idealization of the partner's qualities. As individual needs then emerge, conflict-resolution strategies must be developed. Although each member of the couple may become more autonomous over time, mutual trust and commitment deepen as the relationship matures.

ISSUES UNIQUE TO SAME-SEX COUPLES

Several issues have a unique impact on the relationships of same-sex couples. These include gender role socialization, homophobia, heterosexism, the lack of role models and rituals, and the coming out process.

Socialization Squared?

Much of the literature on same-sex couples emphasizes the impact of gender role socialization on the dynamics and difficulties of these relationships. This literature is predicated on the assumption that gender role socialization affects children who grow up to be gay, lesbian, or bisexual in the same manner that it affects children who grow up to be heterosexual. On the basis of this assumption, various authors (e.g., Brown, 1995; Krestan & Bepko, 1980; Rubin, 1983) have suggested that same-sex relationships are characterized by a "doubling" of the qualities traditionally associated with each gender role. Although this proposition makes intuitive sense, it has been based largely on clinical observations rather than empirical investigations. Furthermore, the assumption that a duplication of qualities related to one or the other gender role is inherently problematic in same-sex relationships seems to reflect both sexist and heterosexist biases.

R. Green et al. (1996) suggested that as both children and adults, lesbians and gay men are less conforming to their respective gender roles than their heterosexual counterparts. If the formation of sexual orientation has its roots in childhood, gay men and lesbians may differ from their heterosexual peers from an early age, and the gender role socialization process may affect them in unique ways. Research in this area is in its infancy, and further prospective and retrospective studies are needed to clarify the impact of gender role socialization on same-sex relationships.

Gender Role Socialization and Relationship Dynamics

American culture socializes men and women to conform to gender-based roles. Women are traditionally socialized to prize intimacy and commitment to relationships, to place others' needs before their own, to be exceptionally sensitive and nurturant, and to conceal competitive or aggressive reactions (Roth, 1985). Men, in contrast, are socialized to value independence, assertiveness, emotional stoicism, leadership, and achievement (Levant, 1995).

Gender role socialization affects all men and women in our culture, to a greater or lesser degree. However, the impact of this process on gay men and lesbians, and on various dimensions of their adult relationships, may not be as straightforward, or as negative, as previously theorized. Considerable research has shown that lesbians and gay men are substantially less conforming to their respective gender roles in childhood (R. Green et al., 1996). A meta-analysis of 41 retrospective studies (Bailey & Zucker, 1995) revealed that lesbians recalled markedly more cross-gender behavior as children than did their heterosexual counterparts. For example, lesbians recalled more interest in boys' competitive sports and boys' play materials and being more likely to be perceived by their peers as tomboys. This study revealed an analogous profile for adult gay men, who recalled more behavior traditionally associated with the female gender role during childhood (e.g., participating in more solitary and artistic activities, having less interest in rough play and competitive sports).

Two prospective studies (R. Green, 1987; Zuger, 1984) in which individuals were followed from early childhood to early adulthood revealed compelling evidence to suggest that "feminine" boys (e.g., those who demonstrated a behavioral and attitudinal preference for activities typically associated with the female gender role) were significantly more likely than "nonfeminine" boys to become gay or bisexual men. No prospective studies of "tomboys" have been conducted to determine whether girls who demonstrate greater interest in activities associated with the male gender role are more likely to become lesbian adults. However, Bailey and Zucker's (1995) meta-analysis showed that lesbians were more likely to have been tomboyish children than were heterosexual women. These findings suggest that many gay men and lesbians were less conforming to their respective gender roles in childhood, although the relationship between childhood gender role and adult sexual orientation was less robust for lesbian women than for gay men.

Kurdek (1987) found that the self-concepts of gay men incorporated more expressiveness (e.g., tenderness, compassion, warmth) than those of heterosexual men but equivalent amounts of instrumentality (e.g., assertiveness, leadership). Kurdek (1987) also reported that the self-concepts of lesbians included more instrumentality than those of heterosexual women but comparable amounts of expressiveness. Various studies (see Pillard, 1991, for a review) have corroborated these findings, suggesting that gay and lesbian adults are more androgynous, and hence less conforming to traditional gender roles, than their heterosexual counterparts.

Gender Role Socialization and Gay Male Relationships

Despite evidence that gay men are relatively less conforming to the male gender role, gay male couples are viewed as more likely than heterosexual couples to struggle with relationship problems stemming from an overdevelopment of skills and values associated with traditional masculinity (e.g., George & Behrendt, 1988; Johnson & Keren, 1996). For example, Hawkins (1992) suggested that male socialization for achievement, competitiveness, sex, and aggression is related to problems commonly presented by gay couples in therapy, including conflicts over finances or jobs, anger and violence, jealousy, and sexual difficulties. He deduced that male socialization leads to deficits in interpersonal skills, hence compounding communication problems for gay men. Other authors (Elise, 1986; Krestan & Bepko, 1980; Rubin, 1983) have similarly suggested that as a result of gender role socialization, gay men have difficulties with dependency, intimacy, and expressiveness and that they frequently use emotional disengagement as a way of coping with relationship pressures. At present, there is little evidence to support this popular view.

Evidence indicating that many gay men were less conforming to their gender role as children suggests that socialization may affect them and their adult relationships in unique ways. If many gay men were more "feminine" as children, it seems likely that they experienced ridicule, rejection, and disapproval for these behaviors. Our society is much less tolerant of cross-gender behavior for boys than for girls (Martin, 1990). In addition, "masculine" characteristics are more esteemed by the dominant culture and are viewed as intrinsic to maleness. Complicating this picture is the societal message that being male and being gay are antithetical to each other. As a result, boys who demonstrate feminine behaviors not only may experience intense pressure to repress these traits but also may internalize the message that they are lacking fundamental qualities of maleness. These sexist and homophobic messages about masculinity and gayness are likely to affect all boys whose same-sex attractions make them feel different from their peers and disapproved of by society at large.

How might male socialization affect boys who express feminine traits as children? In a model that has been applied to heterosexual couples, Hendrix (1988) proposed that traits or characteristics that are disapproved of or ridiculed by society, parents, or peers may become denied or repressed. These societal injunctions not only limit an individual's self-acceptance and ability to be "whole" but also influence the types of traits that attract individuals to others. One manifestation of this process for gay men might be attraction to very masculine men and repression or rejection of feminine characteristics in others and the self. A similar process may apply to gay men who did not display particularly feminine characteristics as children but nonetheless internalized the message that such characteristics are bad, especially because they are associated with deficits in maleness by the dominant culture.

Gay and bisexual youths age 17–23 interviewed by Savin-Williams (1996) about their early recollections revealed that although most youths were strongly attracted to the masculinity of boys and men, some felt more comfortable in the presence of girls and women. These youths felt judged as "weird" by other boys, lacked the desire to interact with their male peers, and found emotional sustenance and acceptance in the company of girls. At the same time, they typically experienced an intense erotic attraction to male bodies from a very early age.

These findings suggest that for some gay men, the feminine "part" of themselves may have been expressed and accepted more in relationships with women, whereas sexual feelings and behaviors may have been more prominent in relationships with other men. Ironically, the very traits that some gay men have learned to devalue and suppress in themselves, particularly in relationships with other men, provide some of the essential ingredients for successful intimacy.

Several clinical implications arise from these speculations. First, gay men may need help in recovering and valuing childhood traits that were previously associated with pain, rejection, humiliation, and judgment. As part of this process, each member of the couple may need assistance in developing ways of showing encouragement and acceptance of these traits in his partner. Second, a discussion of the effects of socialization, particularly those concerning the meanings of masculinity, is important in facilitating understanding of nonconscious processes that underlie relationship attitudes and functioning.

Clearly, if an overabundance of "masculine" characteristics appears to exist in gay male relationships, the reasons for this may be much more complex than "socialization squared." Research is needed to clarify the various ways gender role socialization might affect gay male relationships. In clinical settings, the relevance of these issues must be interpreted in the context of the relationship norms of gay culture and the values and priorities of each gay couple.

Gender Role Socialization and Lesbian Relationships

In lesbian relationships, the gender role socialization process has been theorized to create problems opposite to those posited for gay male relationships. Many authors (Burch, 1982, 1986; Krestan & Bepko 1980; Roth,

1985) have suggested that the major effect of female socialization on lesbian couples is one of "fusion," or enmeshment. Fusion can be described as a relational process in which the boundaries between the individual partners are blurred and a premium is placed on togetherness and emotional closeness. This process is thought to be exaggerated by the effects of societal oppression, which creates a "two against the world" posture (Krestan & Bepko, 1980). Again, the literature on fusion is largely theoretical and based on clinical observations. Systematic research is needed not only to clarify the impact of fusion on relational functioning but also to determine whether it exists to a greater degree among lesbians than heterosexuals or gay men. Whereas an awareness of this relational process may have conceptual value, clinicians should be mindful that empirical evidence is sparse at present.

More recently, several authors (R. Green et al., 1996; Slater & Mencher, 1991) have provided evidence that many of the relational features characterized as fusion (e.g., exceptional emotional closeness and togetherness) are related to the high levels of relationship satisfaction reported by lesbian couples. This kind of intense intimacy may encourage personal growth and risk taking by creating deeper trust and safety (Mencher, 1990). In addition, lesbian couples may use fusion to strengthen their identity in a culture that largely negates their existence.

Slater and Mencher (1991) proposed that fusion is primarily a desirable relationship feature that creates difficulties only when it is present at extremely high or extremely low levels. They suggested that extremely high levels of fusion may result in stagnation of both individual development and growth of the relationship, whereas extremely low levels of fusion may result in persistent feelings of disconnection that increase the risk of separation, especially in the face of external stresses. These observations suggest that it is important for therapists (and researchers) to clearly discern healthy intimacy from potentially problematic relationship patterns such as enmeshment and emotional disengagement. Like all couples, lesbian couples are likely to struggle with issues of how to balance intimacy and autonomy needs. However, when assessing the meaning of these relational issues for lesbian couples, it is most important to use a lesbian rather than heterosexual normative framework.

Gender Role Socialization and Sexuality

Convincing evidence for conformity to certain aspects of gender role socialization may be most apparent in the sexual behavior of gay men and lesbians. Considerable research has shown that gay male couples are markedly less monogamous than heterosexual or lesbian couples. Studies conducted before the acquired immunodeficiency syndrome (AIDS) epidemic reported monogamy rates for gay men ranging from zero (McWhirter &

Mattison, 1984) to 18% (Blumstein & Schwartz, 1983). More recent studies have revealed a rise in monogamy rates for gay men from 48% (Parker, 1995) to 63% (Demian, 1994). Although the reported rates of monogamy have significantly increased over time in apparent response to the AIDS epidemic, gay couples still report rates of nonmonogamy that are significantly higher than those for lesbian or heterosexual couples (R. Green et al., 1996).

However, several authors (Blumstein & Schwartz, 1983; McWhirter & Mattison, 1984) have suggested that gay men have traditionally viewed sexual activity outside the primary relationship as recreational. Blumstein and Schwartz (1983) found that although the majority of gay male partners were nonmonogamous, few ever had a meaningful affair. This study also found that gay men had high expectations for fidelity in their relationships, which was defined in terms of emotional commitment rather than sexual exclusivity. These results indicate that for gay men, sex outside the relationship may not be emotionally involving or have the same meaning (e.g., lack of commitment, disloyalty, betrayal) as such behavior typically has for heterosexual or lesbian couples (R. Green et al., 1996). Many gay male couples that view sex in this manner may prefer consensual nonmonogamous relationships. Various researchers have found comparable relationship quality for sexually monogamous and nonmonogamous gay male couples (Blasband & Peplau, 1985; Blumstein & Schwartz, 1983; Kurdek, 1988). These results further support the importance of interpreting relational structures and their merits and difficulties within a same-sex rather than a heterosexual norm.

In contrast to gay men, lesbians place a high value on romantic love and monogamy (Downey & Friedman, 1995). Lesbians and heterosexual women are less interested in casual sex and place less importance on a partner's physical attractiveness than gay and heterosexual men (Bailey, Gaulin, Agyei, & Glaude, 1994). Various studies have shown that approximately 75% of lesbians express a preference for a monogamous relationship (Blumstein & Schwartz, 1983; Schneider, 1986). Behaviorally, the majority of coupled lesbians describe themselves as monogamous (Blumstein & Schwartz, 1983; Schreurs, 1993).

In general, emotional intimacy is an important aspect of sexual desire and expression for women (Downey & Friedman, 1995). Women also prefer longer periods of sexual arousal than men (Masters, Johnson, and Kolodny, 1994). With regard to frequency of sexual experiences, Blumstein and Schwartz (1983) found that lesbian couples have sex less often than either gay male or heterosexual couples, regardless of relationship duration. However, various studies have indicated that lesbians report equal or greater sexual satisfaction compared with heterosexual women (Blumstein & Schwartz, 1983; Nichols, 1990; Schreurs, 1993).

In summary, with regard to sexual behavior, gay men and lesbians appear to demonstrate attitudes and behavior that are consistent with their respective gender roles. One implication is that lesbians may place primary value on emotional relatedness when choosing a partner, which may subsequently lead to problems with boundary maintenance and sexual desire. Gay men, on the other hand, may emphasize sexual attractiveness when choosing a partner, which may subsequently contribute to problems with emotional intimacy.

Impact of Cultural Oppression

Homophobia and heterosexism are profound influences in the lives of same-sex couples. All gay men and lesbians grow up in a dominant culture that views homosexuality as basically wrong (Cabaj, 1988). Societal homophobia takes various forms, including outright hostility and violence, prejudice and discrimination, and lack of legal sanctioning and protection for same-sex partners and their families. Homophobia and heterosexism also take more insidious forms, such as the lack of attention to happy and satisfied same-sex couples in the media and the treatment of coupled gay men or lesbians as though they were single and without the responsibilities and commitments of their heterosexual counterparts (Brown, 1995). When internalized by gay men and lesbians, homophobia may take various forms, including self-hatred, self-judgment, guilt, and pessimism about the viability of long-term same-sex relationships (Brown, 1995; Downey & Friedman, 1995).

The effects of external homophobia are numerous. Some, including fear of violence; fear of discrimination; and fear of judgment or rejection by coworkers, family members, and friends, can limit the couple's ability to feel safe and be open. These fears create ongoing stress surrounding coming out and its associated risks. Legislated homophobia in the form of an absence of legal protection and recognition leaves same-sex couples at risk for loss of child custody and exclusion from important medical decisions concerning the partner. Similarly, the lack of rituals and the right to marry legally excludes same-sex couples from the social validation and legal benefits of marriage that are automatically afforded to heterosexual couples.

Homophobia and heterosexism force same-sex couples to face ongoing dilemmas about how much and with whom to risk coming out. Often, the decision is between coming out, with its risk of rejection, discrimination, and marginalization, and keeping one's sexual orientation a secret and facing isolation, lack of support, and the duress of leading a "double life." The discontinuity between "passing as just friends" in certain settings and experiencing the freedom to be a couple in others creates a tremendous strain on same-sex couples. In effect, because of societal oppression and fear of reprisal, many same-sex couples feel forced into behavior that is invalidating of their relationship.

The coming out process, so vital to validation, social support, self-acceptance, and personal integrity, also necessitates that gay men and lesbians face potential estrangement from their coworkers, families, friends, and religious establishments as well as disruption of their future plans. These issues can create tension and conflict for the couple when partners disagree about how much to be "out" or are at different stages of self-acceptance and expression (Roth, 1985). The various stresses created by cultural oppression are among the reasons same-sex couples seek counseling. Regardless of the specific reasons presented, all same-sex relationships occur in a context of oppression and must be approached with these societal influences in mind.

REASONS FOR SEEKING THERAPY

The reasons that same-sex couples seek therapy are often similar to those of heterosexual couples: difficulties communicating, conflicts about money, sexual issues, and balancing career and family responsibilities. Unique concerns that same-sex couples may bring to counseling include issues related to homophobia and the coming out process, conflicts arising from differences between the partners in the development of their identity as gay or lesbian, difficulties related to the lack of role models and socially sanctioned rituals, and issues related to the effects of gender role socialization on relationship roles and communication patterns.

Homophobia and the Coming Out Process

Decisions about coming out are an integral part of the fabric of gay and lesbian relationships. These decisions are frequently extremely stressful, particularly when there is disagreement between the partners about how much to be out and to whom. Many gay men and lesbians have reality-based fears about disclosing their sexual orientation. As a survival strategy, same-sex couples may develop creative ways of buffering themselves from the damaging effects of secrecy (Laird, 1993), although its impact is frequently subtle and far-reaching. Couples are forced to be hypervigilant against language and behavior that are revealing or overtly affectionate and to adapt their level of expressed intimacy to each situation (Laird, 1994). As a result, couples experience a variety of invalidating responses, from being treated as "single" by coworkers to being excluded from their partner's family functions. In addition, couples feel forced to act in ways that are incongruous with their true selves and that can erode self-acceptance and establish patterns of caution and inhibition that impede intimacy in a variety of relationships.

Berger (1990) found that the extent to which individuals were "out" to significant others (e.g., parents, siblings, best friends, employers) was related to their relationship satisfaction. Being out to distant others had no effect on relationship satisfaction. In addition, Kurdek (1988) found that high social support was related to psychological adjustment for gays and lesbians in cohabitating relationships. The stress of staying closeted can magnify other relationship difficulties and take energy away from addressing those issues (Patterson & Schwartz, 1994). Because coming out issues are central for same-sex couples, it is important for therapists to assess thoroughly the history and current status of each partner's sexual identity development and level of self-disclosure.

Therapists can assist couples with coming out issues in various ways including (a) promoting dialogue about the meanings the partners give to their own and the other's decisions regarding how much to be out, (b) encouraging discussion about the risks and benefits of being out versus closeted in specific settings and with particular people, (c) helping each partner deal with the losses associated with either choice, (d) promoting understanding and respect for different timetables in the coming out process, (e) providing reading material, (f) helping partners prepare and develop coping responses for dealing with others' reactions if they do choose to come out, (g) educating couples about the evolving nature of the coming out process and normalizing the feelings likely to be experienced along the way, and (h) helping couples access resources and support within the gay and lesbian communities. Therapists should be mindful that coming out issues are complex and that it is important not to present a value bias in this regard but to help couples stay aligned as they discuss and negotiate this emotionally laden and frequently difficult process.

Differences in Identity Development

Each partner in a same-sex couple has had different experiences in the development of their sexual identity. Lesbians typically discover their sexual identity at a later point in life than gay men, who are frequently aware of, and act on, their same-sex attractions during adolescence (Garnets & Kimmel, 1991). Within a lesbian couple, one partner may have identified herself as lesbian relatively early and had little heterosexual experience, whereas her partner may have been heterosexually married with children and had few, if any, previous relationships with other women (Brown, 1995). These variations also occur for gay men, although they seem to be more common for lesbians. A variety of issues may arise in couples in which one partner has identified him- or herself as gay or lesbian for a long time and the other is newer to same-sex relationships. In these relationships, the more "experienced" member of the couple may worry about whether the partner's sexual orientation is transient or whether the partner will eventually want to pursue other dating relationships. The less experienced member of the couple may feel insecure and threatened by the partner's level of "outness" and involvement in the gay and lesbian community.

Another important consideration for therapists is the milieu in which each partner came out (Brown, 1995), which requires an assessment of the following: the general societal attitude (e.g., before vs. after the gay and lesbian liberation movement); the community atmosphere (conservative vs. liberal, rural vs. urban); family reactions, including any cultural or religious beliefs about homosexuality; and peer reactions. Differences in these life experiences and their manifestations may become a source of stress and conflict for couples and can influence the extent to which negative messages about being gay or lesbian are internalized. The therapist should be alert for the subtle and nonconscious ways internalized homophobia may affect relationship functioning (Brown, 1995). Therapists can help couples depersonalize these issues by helping them understand the influence of culture and society and by promoting a dialogue between partners about the individual meanings of their differences.

Exclusion From Socially Sanctioned Rituals

Rituals are important for marking and resolving major life events and for connecting couples to their families and the larger community (Laird, 1994). Rituals also send a message of cultural validation, which can provide a sense of legitimacy and essential external support during times of relationship difficulty (Slater & Mencher, 1991). The lack of legal and social validation for same-sex couples often enables invalidating responses from others, such as excluding partners from family and job functions and treating the relationship as nonexistent. The stress associated with dealing with these overt and covert reactions may motivate couples to seek therapy.

Therapy can provide same-sex couples with an arena for discussing and creating meaningful rituals. In addition, simply by providing an affirmative environment, therapy provides a ritual that legitimizes and validates the many strengths and resources of same-sex couples. In fact, many same-sex couples do not need intensive therapy, but rather "a witnessing and validation of their coming together, a function that no rabbi, minister, judge, nor priest has done for them" (Falco, 1990, p. 117).

Lack of Role Models

In the absence of social and legal validation and readily available role models, gay men and lesbians often create their own relationship norms. Various studies (Blumstein & Schwartz, 1983; Peplau, 1991) have shown that same-sex couples place high value on role flexibility and equality in their relationships. Equality is especially important to lesbian couples (Kurdek, 1995a). Although this flexibility may be liberating, the emphasis that same-sex couples place on equality can lead to conflict regarding unavoidable inequities such as discrepancies in education level or income (Murphy, 1992). These conflicts can be compounded if couples are closeted, because the partners may have little exposure to models of how inequities are resolved within the context of a gay or lesbian relationship. Therapists can play a part by providing gay and lesbian couples with access to such role models through readings or community resources. Therapy also provides an arena for gay and lesbian couples to discuss the meanings of inequities in their relationships and to develop realistic and mutually satisfying expectations regarding relationship roles and equality.

The Impact of Gender Role Socialization

Most couples are faced with the challenge of negotiating differences between the partners in their needs for emotional closeness and autonomy (Roth, 1985). Relational styles favoring intimacy or autonomy are influenced by patterns learned in the family of origin, socialization, personality styles, individual differences in psychological functioning, current stressors, and idiosyncratic couple dynamics. Therapists should assess all such factors, because their salience varies among couples. Although the effects of gender role socialization are discussed in more detail here because of their special influence on the functioning of same-sex couples, it is important not to overemphasize their meaning to the neglect of other salient factors.

For some same-sex couples, particular relationship difficulties may arise from gender role socialization. For lesbians, these difficulties may take the form of an overemphasis on empathy and relational harmony that inhibits autonomy and direct expression of individual wants and needs (Patterson & Schwartz, 1994). Some lesbian couples may need help viewing differences as valuable, rather than threatening, and developing associated skills (e.g., assertiveness). In effect, partners in lesbian couples may need help developing and valuing aspects of themselves that are traditionally associated with the male gender role. These include capacities to be more assertive, to enjoy more fully the purely physical aspects of sex, to express anger, and to prioritize personal needs. In some cases, one or both partners already possess these qualities but may be reluctant to express them. This reluctance may have several causes, such as the societal message that these characteristics are "unbecoming" in women and the lack of "permission" for either partner to display qualities that are traditionally ascribed to the man in heterosexual relationships.

The converse may be true for some gay men. Johnson and Keren (1996) observed that male couples in therapy demonstrated "less investment in discussion of relational process and emotional responsivity than lesbian couples; easier access to anger than sadness, vulnerability, or dependence; and more urgency about problem resolution and termination" (p. 236). These results suggest that some gay male couples may benefit from developing certain skills and attributes traditionally associated with the female gender role, including the ability to express a range of emotions, an emphasis on cooperation rather than competition, greater comfort with vulnerability and interdependence, more emphasis on emotional relatedness than physical attractiveness, and greater enjoyment of the emotional aspects of sex. Just as lesbians may have learned to inhibit or hide certain "masculine" qualities, gay men may be reluctant to express particular "feminine" qualities. Each partner may be waiting for the other to take on the complementary role in this regard. Therapy can help gay men and lesbians develop and value parts of themselves that have been "disowned" or devalued as a result of socialization or homophobia and can provide a safe haven for experimenting with new behaviors.

Children and Parenting Issues

Increasingly, gay and lesbian couples are also parents (G. D. Green & Bozett, 1991). These couples face many of the same parenting issues as their heterosexual counterparts. However, same-sex families are uniquely configured and face numerous stressors such as homophobia and lack of adequate legal protection. Lesbian and gay parents create families in a variety of ways. One or both partners may bring children to the relationship from a previous, usually heterosexual, relationship; the couple may adopt with legal rights to the child belonging to only one partner; or one of the partners in a lesbian couple may give birth to a biological child (Brown, 1995).

Same-sex parents face a variety of unique issues that intensify and complicate what is already one of life's biggest challenges. Custody issues are often prominent for couples in which one partner was previously heterosexually married. The legal and emotional risks of coming out become even more profound when children are involved (Patterson & Schwartz, 1994). In most same-sex families, one partner is the "biological" parent and the other is the "nonbiological" parent, which gives rise to a variety of legal and emotional issues. When same-sex couples decide to become parents, the complexity and difficulty of the issues involved are likely to bring up feelings of grief and anger about the effects of homophobia and heterosexism on one of the most fundamental of life's choices. Therapists can help same-sex couples with these issues by (a) communicating an awareness that many gay men and lesbians are, or will be, parents; (b) helping partners communicate clearly about their feelings and values regarding parenting; (c) promoting dialogue about ways each partner can feel equally important and valued as a parent; (d) suggesting legal resources and procedures that provide some protection for gay and lesbian families; and

(e) helping partners stay aligned as a couple as they negotiate these complex and difficult issues.

Substance Abuse

Research has suggested that lesbians and gay men are more likely to have problems with drugs or alcohol than their heterosexual counterparts (Cabaj, 1992). Substance abuse problems may be abating in response to the AIDS epidemic and increasing opportunities for socializing in places other than bars. Nonetheless, it is critical for therapists to assess the role of alcohol and drugs on same-sex couples' social and interpersonal functioning.

Sexual Abuse

Because lesbian couples are composed of two women, they are more likely than heterosexual couples to include an adult survivor of assault or childhood sexual abuse (Brown, 1995). As a result, the impact of childhood trauma on adult relationship functioning may be a more salient factor for lesbian couples. Although the incidence is likely to be lower, it is also important to assess for past sexual abuse in gay male couples. Lew (1988) observed that American culture allows little room for men to be considered victims and that early sexual experiences for men are often viewed as a demonstration of masculinity. As a result, inappropriate or abusive sexual experiences may not be labeled as such by gay men or may be associated with tremendous shame or confusion about how these experiences affected their sexual identity development. A thorough sexual history is important for understanding and appropriately treating sexual issues brought to counseling by same-sex couples.

AIDS

AIDS has had a dramatic impact on all aspects of gay men's intimate relationships. In a matter of years, the kind of sexual activity that had previously seemed "liberating" became potentially life threatening (Nichols, 1989). As a result, the incidence of casual and anonymous sex among gay men has declined, and more gay men are choosing sexually monogamous relationships (Berger, 1990; Seigel & Glassman, 1989). Gay men whose dating relationships were primarily focused on sexual activity may be new to the fundamentals of courtship and emotional intimacy (Nichols, 1989). Living in the age of AIDS intensifies a variety of relationship issues for gay men. For example, fears of infecting or being infected with the human immunodeficiency virus (HIV) may create sexual problems regardless of agreements about monogamy or nonmonogamy (Patterson &

Schwartz, 1994). In addition, Paradis (1991) has argued that the unresolved grief resulting from the loss of friends or former partners to AIDS may interfere with the ability of many gay men to be intimate. The stigma associated with AIDS may trigger additional feelings of internalized homophobia and may compound already difficult coming out issues. Therapists working with gay male couples must be alert to the variety of complex and profound influences the AIDS epidemic has on individual and relationship functioning.

Sexual Issues Specific to Gay Men

Many gay men report difficulty maintaining sexual interest and arousal in long-term and sexually monogamous relationships (Brown, 1995). Gay culture has traditionally valued sexual attractiveness and freedom, although, as noted previously, these patterns appear to be changing owing to the impact of the AIDS epidemic. As a result, gay male couples may not have developed emotional skills necessary for long-term intimacy (Brown, 1995) and may lack knowledge about the developmental changes typically experienced by gay male couples in long-lasting relationships. Such couples can benefit from psychoeducation regarding the developmental stages through which gay male relationships typically pass (McWhirter & Mattison, 1984) and techniques designed to eroticize intimacy in long-term relationships (Shernoff, 1999). Gay couples may also need assistance discussing and clarifying the meaning of commitment. Couples who choose to be sexually monogamous can benefit from additional support and validation from the therapist if they experience their choice as unsupported by the larger gay community. Other couples may need the therapist's assistance discussing and negotiating the details of nonmonogamy agreements. In any case, when working with same-sex couples, therapists should be careful to leave their assumptions about what constitutes "normal" sexual behavior at the office door.

Sexual Issues Specific to Lesbians

A variety of studies have shown that gay men and heterosexuals have more sex than do lesbians (Blumstein & Schwartz, 1983; Nichols, 1990; Schreurs, 1993). However, these studies have operationalized "more" in terms of frequency and have not considered the amount of time spent in each sexual interaction. Perhaps lesbians have fewer sexual contacts but spend significantly more time in each encounter. Some lesbian couples may place less importance on sexuality relative to other aspects of the relationship, such as emotional intimacy and shared values (Blumstein & Schwartz, 1983). These differences in the sexual behavior of gay men and lesbians may also have a biochemical component given that men, on average, produce much greater quantities of the hormone (testosterone) that fuels sex drive than do women (Love, 1999). In any case, most lesbians report that sexuality is a satisfying part of their life (Schreurs, 1993).

When lesbians present sexual difficulties as an issue in therapy, several unique factors should be assessed in addition to those considered for all couples (e.g., history of sexual abuse, communication problems). Infrequent sexual contact may be a nonconscious strategy for obtaining some degree of separateness in couples for whom there is too much emotional intimacy and togetherness (Hall, 1984). Stated more positively, in some lesbian couples, intimacy needs may be saturated by emotional closeness and activity sharing, leaving less motivation for sexual forms of connection. These couples may benefit from a description of the concept of fusion and its manifestations in lesbian relationships. Therapists can help lesbian couples see the benefits of separate activities and assist each partner in finding a comfortable balance between intimacy and autonomy.

Sexual difficulties can also be a product of socialization and internalized homophobia. Women in our culture are taught that they are not supposed to be interested in or initiate sex (Roth, 1985). Compounding these negative messages are the societal proscriptions against sexual involvement with another woman. Therapeutic interventions should be focused on surfacing nonconscious beliefs and attitudes, providing conceptual descriptions of the impact of socialization and homophobia, and skill development (e.g., assertiveness and risk taking).

Multicultural Issues

Issues of race and ethnicity can profoundly influence the intimate relationships of gay men and lesbians. However, little has been written about the impact of multicultural issues on same-sex relationships. Owing to a dearth of information and the complexity of the issues involved, this topic cannot be thoroughly explored in this chapter (see Greene, 1997, for a discussion of unique issues for ethnic-minority lesbians and gay men). Nonetheless, therapists must be mindful of the possible importance of multicultural issues. The following speculative considerations highlight some key points in exploring multicultural issues with same-sex couples.

First, ethnicity may have a profound effect on the importance and meaning of family to each partner. Various authors (Boyd-Franklin, 1990; Greene, 1997; Smith, 1997) have noted the importance of the family as the primary social unit in many ethnic groups. This cultural value may create difficulties for same-sex couples when partners differ in the importance they place on family connections. Such difficulties are magnified when cultural or religious views about homosexuality are particularly negative. Several authors (Liu & Chan, 1996; Morales, 1992) have suggested that disapproval of homosexuality is more intense in certain ethnic-minority groups than in the dominant White culture. For ethnic-minority clients, culturally specific disapproval may result in intense internal conflict between their identity as gay or lesbian and their ethnic identity, complicating already difficult coming out issues. This kind of internal struggle can translate into relationship conflicts about the importance each partner places on his or her primary relationship versus the importance of ties to his or her family and ethnic community (Johnson & Keren, 1996). Coming out to family members is sometimes viewed by partners as a barometer of their importance to each other. Therapists should help couples explore the deeper issues involved in coming out decisions, so that differences between the partners are better understood and the influences of ethnicity are disentangled from the meaning and value each partner attaches to the relationship.

Ethnicity also has a profound influence on gender role expectations (Greene, 1997). Given the potential importance of gender role socialization in same-sex relationships, therapists should carefully explore cultural expectations regarding gender role behavior, the extent to which these have been internalized, and the meanings each partner gives to departing from these culturally based norms.

Finally, the gay and lesbian community to which a couple belongs may have particular attitudes (positive or negative) toward various configurations of mixed-race couples. These attitudes can profoundly influence the degree to which the couple feels accepted within the community. In addition, trust issues may arise if one partner believes that the other's motivation for being in the relationship is related to extrinsic factors (e.g., status or acceptance in the gay or lesbian community) rather than intrinsic factors.

All same-sex couples in which one or both partners belong to a racial or ethnic minority group face issues related to being a "dual minority." These couples face possible difficulties related to the complex interplay of ethnicity and sexual orientation, including reconciling cultural differences within the relationship and recognizing and dealing with multilayered forms of oppression.

In summary, the influence of multicultural issues on same-sex couples is complex and poorly understood. To explore multicultural issues effectively with same-sex couples, therapists should assess the extent to which each partner identifies with his or her racial or ethnic group and carefully examine culturally based values and beliefs about sexuality and homosexuality, gender roles, and the importance of family. Most important, therapists should explicitly acknowledge the importance of multicultural issues and provide a safe forum in which the couple can explore their influence on relationship issues.

Relationship Issues of Bisexuals

There is scant information available concerning unique relationship issues of bisexuals. The complexities of this topic are beyond the scope of this chapter; however, therapists should be mindful of several key issues when counseling mixed-orientation couples.

Issues of commitment and monogamy can take on added significance in relationships in which one partner is bisexual (Rust, 1996). The gay or lesbian partner may experience ongoing insecurities about the possibility of losing his or her mate to someone who possesses a quality he or she cannot possibly provide (i.e., the opposite gender). The bisexual partner's self-identification can also be interpreted by the gay or lesbian partner to mean that he or she is not fully committed to the relationship. Therapists should help couples discuss commitment issues and the implications, if any, of each partner's sexual orientation identity for commitment to the relationship. Rust found that bisexuals were also more likely than lesbians and gay men to prefer a nonmonogamous relationship. Thus, therapists may need to help mixed-orientation couples negotiate the specifics of a relationship style (nonmonogamy or monogamy) that works for both partners, bearing in mind that the bisexual partner and the gay or lesbian partner may have differing preferences in this regard.

Mixed-orientation couples may also experience a lack of acceptance from the gay or lesbian community. Such couples can feel misunderstood and disapproved of by both gay and straight friends. Paul (1996) suggested that therapists should help clients examine and challenge biphobic assumptions, whether they originate in the dominant culture or in the gay or lesbian subculture. Given the lack of support often experienced by mixed-orientation couples, it is especially important for the therapist to communicate an attitude of acceptance and validation for each partner's sexual orientation and the couple's choices about monogamy or nonmonogamy. Therapists should be able to suggest community resources that are available for individual bisexuals and mixed-orientation couples.

CASE EXAMPLES

The following cases illustrate many of the issues unique to gay (Case Example 1) and lesbian (Case Example 2) couples that have been explored in this chapter. Specifically, these cases highlight the following issues: the impact of gender role socialization, differences between partners in their coming out experiences, family-of-origin influences, the impact of childhood sexual abuse, multicultural issues, sexual issues, and differences between partners in their sexual orientation identity development.

Case Example 1

Paul and Mike were both in their mid-20s and had been in a committed relationship for 1 year when they sought treatment. They reported conflicts about sex and "arguing all the time" as their primary presenting problems. Paul was Mike's first same-sex partner. Mike had recently come out to his family and close friends and had received primarily accepting responses. Paul had come out at age 15 to his parents, and they both had responded with hostility and rejection. Before meeting Mike, he had been in several relationships including one that he characterized as abusive. Mike reported that he was always the initiator of sex and felt rejected by Paul's seeming lack of interest. Because this was his first same-sex relationship, Mike felt insecure about his competence as a lover and also experienced intense sexual desire driven partly by the "newness" of this relationship. Mike also worried that perhaps he was not as exciting to Paul as his previous partners had been. These feelings caused Mike to feel extremely threatened by Paul's interactions with other gay men. A repeating pattern developed in which they would attend social functions involving other gay men, both would have several beers, and a fight would ensue in which Mike would become increasingly angry and Paul would withdraw.

Further exploration of Paul's sexual history revealed that his first sexual experiences at age 13 were with a man in his late 20s. He reported feeling "curious" at first but increasingly trapped and violated as these experiences continued. As therapy progressed, Paul shared more about these traumatic experiences and began to recognize their many ramifications in his adult relationships. Mike developed a much deeper understanding of Paul's strong reactions to feeling pressured sexually and was able to take these reactions less personally.

An exploration of family of origin and social influences revealed that Mike had felt rejected for ways that he was "sensitive" and experienced a lot of pressure to participate in athletics and display emotional self-sufficiency. These influences manifested themselves in his relationship with Paul as a tendency to funnel all feelings into anger or sexuality and a reluctance to show neediness or vulnerability. Paul felt as though he was not "good enough" in his family, and these feelings were intensified by his parents' hostile reaction when he came out to them. Paul dealt with his insecurities by withdrawing, a pattern modeled by his father. As these previously nonconscious beliefs and corresponding coping styles surfaced in therapy, Mike and Paul developed more compassion for each other and greater understanding of the triggers of their conflicts. With Paul's encouragement and support, Mike was able to show more of his "sensitive" side and express his desire to be taken care of at times. As Mike "backed off," Paul was able to be more expressive and take more initiative in both emotional and sexual intimacy. Both reported that their new understanding of family-of-origin issues, socialization, differences in their coming out experiences, and the role of alcohol in their relationship difficulties was central to breaking these patterns and deepening their relationship.

Case Example 2

Liz and Janet had been living together in a committed relationship for 3 years at the time they sought treatment. Liz, a White lawyer in her early 40s, had been previously married to a man and had only recently begun thinking of herself as lesbian. Janet, an African American nurse in her late 30s, had self-identified as lesbian from age 18 and had been involved in several long-term same-sex relationships. Liz and Janet reported family problems and coming out issues as their primary presenting problems.

Liz described her parents as "racist and homophobic" and had not told them explicitly about her relationship with Janet for fear they would "disown" her. Since her divorce, Liz's relationship with her parents had been steadily improving, and she was fearful of jeopardizing this newfound harmony. Janet had come out to her parents in her early 20s, and they had become very accepting of her sexual orientation over time. Janet was close to all members of her family, especially her mother, and she and Liz spent a considerable amount of time with them individually and as a couple. Liz reported that she "liked" Janet's family but experienced their frequent requests for Janet's time and emotional support as demanding and intrusive at times. Liz and Janet found themselves fighting about these family issues with increasing frequency.

As therapy progressed, Liz revealed that she was feeling increasingly uncomfortable with the amount of time they were spending with Janet's family. She felt as though Janet placed primary importance on her relationship with her family and treated her and their relationship as "peripheral." She had previously been reluctant to say anything about this because she felt "grateful" that Janet's family was so accepting of their relationship. She also worried that her concerns would be viewed as racist because Janet had described this type of closeness as typical of many African American families. Janet revealed that she felt hurt and offended that Liz had not explicitly told her parents about their relationship. Although Janet and Liz had been together for 3 years, Liz's parents had yet to meet Janet, and Liz attended family functions by herself. Janet had a deepening resentment about this exclusion and also feared that this meant that Liz was not fully committed to their relationship. On some level, both Liz and Janet perceived the other as choosing her family of origin over their relationship.

In therapy, Janet and Liz began to discuss openly the meanings that they had attached to the other's decisions about family relationships, hidden fears, and the role of cultural differences in their relationship. Janet developed a greater understanding of why Liz became so angry and upset when she "dropped everything" to be with her family. Liz recognized the fear and rejection underneath Janet's angry withdrawal when she spent holidays alone with her family. Both realized the many ways that family pressures and expectations had become divisive in their relationship and began talking about ways of strengthening their boundaries as a couple and affirming their importance to each other. Therapy provided Liz and Janet with a forum for developing strategies to prioritize their relationship while also addressing needs and concerns regarding their respective families. Most important, through this process, Liz and Janet became realigned as a couple and were able to take gradual steps toward resolution of these issues.

Therapist Attitudes and Skills

Like all effective therapists, those working with same-sex couples should possess fundamental attributes including empathy, respect, good assessment skills, and an understanding of relationship dynamics and family-of-origin influences. In addition, effective therapy with gay and lesbian couples requires an exploration of the broader cultural forces that profoundly influence their relationships. Same-sex relationships are influenced not only by the norms and values of the larger society but also by those of the gay or lesbian subculture to which the partners belong. An awareness of these influences enables the couple to make more conscious decisions about which cultural values they want to embrace and which they want to discard (Markowitz, 1997). This awareness also helps the couple to externalize appropriately, rather than internalize, problems stemming from negative societal injunctions. In addition, appropriate externalization promotes mutuality in the resolution of relationship difficulties.

Brown (1995) contended that therapists should also possess knowledge about the unique challenges and normative issues faced by well-functioning same-sex couples. She suggested several ways of obtaining this information, including social and professional contacts with a variety of same-sex couples, familiarity with the professional and popular literature about gay and lesbian individuals and couples, and awareness of the norms of the gay and lesbian communities in which the practitioner works.

Gay, lesbian, or bisexual therapists must make individual decisions about the appropriateness and therapeutic value of disclosing their sexual orientation to clients. One survey (Modrcin & Wyers, 1990) indicated that the sexual orientation of the therapist was not an important consideration for most gay and lesbian respondents in their choice of a professional. Nonetheless, when gay and lesbian therapists are out to their clients, they can serve as important role models, and this disclosure may help clients feel more deeply understood and accepted. In some cases, the therapist may be the only person with whom the couple feels comfortable asking questions about what is "normal" in gay and lesbian cultures and with whom ways of dealing with coming out issues or creating rituals can be discussed. The power of providing this kind of "parental" role model to gay and lesbian clients, whose biological parents rarely belong to the same sexual orientation minority group, cannot be underestimated. However, in some circumstances, coming out to clients may detract from the couples' experiences and create hesitancy to share negative reactions about gay and lesbian norms (Paul, 1996). Being "out" to clients can also create complications when the therapist and his or her clients belong to the same gay or lesbian community (see Smith, 1990, for a discussion of this issue). Decisions about disclosure should be based on the individual practitioner's comfort level and what is most therapeutic for each couple.

More important than the therapist's sexual orientation is his or her attitude, which should be gay and lesbian affirmative. Therapists who go beyond an attitude of passive acceptance to one of active validation and affirmation provide an invaluable service to their clients.

CONCLUSION

Although similar to their heterosexual counterparts in several ways, same-sex couples face unique difficulties that are frequently related to the oppressive context in which their relationships occur. These difficulties include the stress surrounding the risks of coming out and the insidious effects of being denied social and legal validation. Same-sex couples may also face unique difficulties related to gender role socialization, although empirical evidence in support of this view is scant, except as it pertains to sexuality. Problems related to gender role socialization may include an overemphasis on relational harmony and empathy for lesbian couples. For gay men, concerns related to gender role socialization may take the form of difficulties with emotional intimacy and vulnerability. Further research is needed to illuminate the impact of gender role socialization on same-sex relationships.

Therapists working with same-sex couples must maintain a keen awareness of the influences of the larger culture on relationship difficulties. When couples understand these influences, they can more appropriately externalize particular relationship difficulties and attain mutuality in the resolution process. Therapists are most effective in helping couples realize these rewards when therapy is provided within a context of acceptance and validation for same-sex couples and empathy guided by an understanding of the unique challenges they face.

REFERENCES

Bailey, J. M. (1996). Gender identity. In R. C. Savin-Williams & K. M. Cohen (Eds.), *The lives of lesbians, gays, and bisexuals: Children to adults* (pp. 71–93). Orlando, FL: Harcourt Brace.

Bailey, J. M., Gaulin, S., Agyei, Y., & Glaude, B. A. (1994). Effects of gender and sexual orientation on evolutionarily relevant aspects of human mating psychology. *Journal of Personality and Social Psychology, 66,* 1081–1093.

Bailey, J. M., & Zucker, K. J. (1995). Childhood sex-typed behavior and sexual orientation: A conceptual analysis and quantitative review. *Developmental Psychology, 31,* 43–55.

Berger, R. M. (1990). Passing: The impact on the quality of same-sex couple relationships. *Social Work, 35,* 328–332.

Blasband, D., & Peplau, L. A. (1985). Sexual exclusivity versus openness in gay couples. *Archives of Sexual Behavior, 14,* 395–412.

Blumstein, P., & Schwartz, P. (1983). *American couples: Money, work, and sex.* New York: Morrow.

Boyd-Franklin, N. (1990). *Black families in therapy: A multisystems approach.* New York: Guilford Press.

Brown, L. (1995). Therapy with same-sex couples: An introduction. In N. S. Jacobson & A. S. Gurman (Eds.), *Clinical handbook of couple therapy* (pp. 274–291). New York: Guilford Press.

Burch, B. (1982). Psychological merger in lesbian couples: A joint ego psychological and systems approach. *Family Therapy, 9,* 201–208.

Burch, B. (1986). Psychotherapy and the dynamics of merger in lesbian couples. In T. S. Stein & C. J. Cohen (Eds.), *Contemporary perspectives on psychotherapy with lesbians and gay men* (pp. 57–71). New York: Plenum Press.

Cabaj, R. P. (1988). Gay and lesbian couples: Lessons on human intimacy. *Psychiatric Annals, 18*(1), 21–25.

Cabaj, R. P. (1992). Substance abuse among gays and lesbians. In J. H. Lowinson, P. Ruiz, & R. B. Millman (Eds.), *Substance abuse: A comprehensive textbook* (pp. 852–860). Baltimore: Williams & Wilkins.

Clark, W. M., & Serovich, J. M. (1997). Twenty years and still in the dark? Content analysis of articles pertaining to gay, lesbian, and bisexual issues in marriage and family therapy journals. *Journal of Marital and Family Therapy, 23,* 239–253.

Demian, A. S. B. (1994). Relationship characteristics of American gay and lesbian couples: Findings from a national survey. In L. A. Kurdek (Ed.), *Social services for gay and lesbian couples* (pp. 101–117). Binghamton, NY: Harrington Park Press.

Downey, J. I., & Friedman, R. C. (1995). Internalized homophobia in lesbian relationships. *Journal of the American Academy of Psychoanalysis, 23,* 435–447.

Elise, D. (1986). Lesbian couples: The implication of sex differences in separation–individuation. *Psychotherapy, 23,* 305–310.

Falco, K. L. (1990). *Psychotherapy with lesbian clients: Theory into practice*. New York: Brunner/Mazel.

Garnets, L., & Kimmel, D. (1991). Lesbian and gay male dimensions in the psychological study of human diversity. In J. Goodchilds (Ed.), *Psychological perspectives on human diversity in America* (pp. 143–192). Washington, DC: American Psychological Association.

George, K. D., & Behrendt, A. E. (1988). Therapy for male couples experiencing relationship problems and sexual problems. In E. Coleman (Ed.), *Psychotherapy with homosexual men and women: Integrated identity approaches for clinical practice* (pp. 77–88). New York: Haworth Press.

Green, G. D., & Bozett, F. W. (1991). Lesbian mothers and gay fathers. In J. C. Gonsiorek & J. D. Weinrich (Eds.), *Homosexuality: Research implications for public policy* (pp. 197–214). Newbury Park, CA: Sage.

Green, R. (1987). *The "sissy boy syndrome" and the development of homosexuality*. New Haven, CT: Yale University Press.

Green, R., Bettinger, M., & Zachs, E. (1996). Are lesbian couples fused and gay male couples disengaged? In J. Laird & R. Green (Eds.), *Lesbians and gays in couples and families* (pp. 185–230). San Francisco: Jossey-Bass.

Greene, B. (1997). Ethnic minority lesbians and gay men: Mental health and treatment issues. In B. Greene (Ed.), *Ethnic and cultural diversity among lesbians and gay men* (pp. 216–239). Newbury Park, CA: Sage.

Hall, M. (1984). Lesbians, limerence, and long-term relationships. In J. Loulan (Ed.), *Lesbian sex* (pp. 141–150). New York: Spinsters.

Hawkins, R. L. (1992). Therapy with the male couple. In S. H. Dworkin & F. J. Gutierrez (Eds.), *Counseling gay men and lesbians: Journey to the end of the rainbow* (pp. 81–94). Alexandria, VA: American Counseling Association.

Hendrix, H. (1988). *Getting the love you want: A guide for couples*. New York: Holt.

Johnson, T. W., & Keren, M. S. (1996). Creating and maintaining boundaries in male couples. In J. Laird & R. Green (Eds.), *Lesbians and gays in couples and families* (pp. 231–250). San Francisco: Jossey-Bass.

Krestan, J. A., & Bepko, C. S. (1980). The problem of fusion in the lesbian relationship. *Family Process, 19,* 277–289.

Kurdek, L. A. (1987). Sex-role self-schema and psychological adjustment in coupled homosexual and heterosexual men and women. *Sex Roles, 17,* 549–562.

Kurdek, L. A. (1988). Relationship quality of gay and lesbian cohabiting couples. *Journal of Homosexuality, 15,* 93–118.

Kurdek, L. A. (1995a). Developmental changes in relationship quality in gay and lesbian cohabiting couples. *Developmental Psychology, 31,* 86–94.

Kurdek, L. A. (1995b). Lesbian and gay couples. In R. D'Augelli & C. J. Patterson (Eds.), *Lesbian, gay, and bisexual identities over the lifespan: Psychological perspectives* (pp. 243–261). New York: Oxford University Press.

Laird, J. (1993). Women's secrets—Women's silences. In E. Imber-Black (Ed.), *Secrets in families and family therapy* (pp. 243–267). New York: Norton.

Laird, J. (1994). Lesbian families: A cultural perspective. In M. P. Mirkin (Ed.), *Women in context: Toward a feminist reconstruction of psychotherapy* (pp. 118–148). New York: Guilford Press.

Levant, R. F. (1995). Toward the reconstruction of masculinity. In R. F. Levant & W. S. Pollack (Eds.), *A new psychology of men* (pp. 229–251). New York: HarperCollins.

Lew, M. (1988). *Victims no longer.* New York: Harper & Row.

Liu, P., & Chan, C. S. (1996). Lesbian, gay, and bisexual Asian Americans and their families. In J. Laird & R. Green (Eds.), *Lesbians and gays in couples and families* (pp. 137–152). San Francisco: Jossey-Bass.

Love, P. (1999, March/April). What is this thing called love? *Family Therapy Networker,* pp. 34–44.

Markowitz, L. (1997, September/October). The cultural context of intimacy. *Family Therapy Networker,* pp. 51–58.

Martin, C. L. (1990). Attitudes and expectations about children with nontraditional and traditional gender roles. *Sex Roles, 22,* 151–165.

Masters, W. H., Johnson, V. E., & Kolodny, R. C. (1994). *Heterosexuality.* New York: HarperCollins.

McWhirter, D., & Mattison, A. (1984). *The male couple.* Englewood Cliffs, NJ: Prentice-Hall.

Mencher, J. (1990). *Intimacy in lesbian relationships: A critical re-examination of fusion* (Work in Progress No. 42). Wellesley, MA: Wellesley College, Stone Center for Women's Development.

Modrcin, M. J., & Wyers, N. L. (1990). Lesbian and gay couples: Where they turn when they need help. *Journal of Gay and Lesbian Psychotherapy, 1*(3), pp. 89–104.

Morales, E. (1992). Latino gays and Latina lesbians. In S. H. Dworkin & F. J. Gutierrez (Eds.), *Counseling gay men and lesbians: Journey to the end of the rainbow* (pp. 125–139). Alexandria, VA: American Counseling Association.

Murphy, B. C. (1992). Counseling lesbian couples: Sexism, heterosexism, and homophobia. In S. H. Dworkin & F. J. Gutierrez (Eds.), *Counseling gay men and lesbians: Journey to the end of the rainbow* (pp. 46–51). Alexandria, VA: American Counseling Association.

Nichols, M. (1989). Sex therapy with lesbians, gay men, and bisexuals. In S. R. Lieblum & R. C. Rosen (Eds.), *Principles and practice of sex therapy* (pp. 269–297). New York: Guilford Press.

Nichols, M. (1990). Lesbian relationships: Implications for the study of sexuality and gender. In D. P. McWhirter, S. A. Sanders, & J. M. Reinisch (Eds.), *Homosexuality/heterosexuality: Concepts of sexual orientation* (pp. 350–364). New York: Oxford University Press.

Paradis, B. A. (1991). Seeking intimacy and integration: Gay men in the era of AIDS. *Smith College Studies in Social Work, 61,* 260–274.

Parker, D. A. (1995). *The cruising project report.* Unpublished manuscript, San Francisco State University, Center for Education and Research in Sexuality.

Patterson, D. G., & Schwartz, P. (1994). The social construction of conflict in intimate same-sex couples. In D. D. Cahn (Ed.), *Conflict in personal relationships* (pp. 3–26). Hillsdale, NJ: Erlbaum.

Paul, J. P. (1996). Bisexuality: Exploring/exploding the boundaries. In R. C. Savin-Williams & K. M. Cohen (Eds.), *The lives of lesbians, gays, and bisexuals: Children to adults* (pp. 436–461). Orlando, FL: Harcourt Brace.

Peplau, L. A. (1991). Lesbian and gay relationships. In J. C. Gonsiorek & J. D. Weinrich (Eds.), *Homosexuality: Research implications for public policy* (pp. 177–196). Newbury Park, CA: Sage.

Peplau, L. A., & Cochran, S. D. (1990). A relational perspective on homosexuality. In D. P. McWhirter, S. A. Sanders, & J. M. Reinisch (Eds.), *Homosexuality/heterosexuality: Concepts of sexual orientation* (pp. 321–349). New York: Oxford University Press.

Pillard, R. C. (1991). Masculinity and femininity in homosexuality: "Inversion" revisited. In J. C. Gonsiorek & J. D. Weinrich (Eds.), *Homosexuality: Research implications for public policy* (pp. 32–43). Newbury Park, CA: Sage.

Roth, S. (1985). Psychotherapy with lesbian couples: Individual issues, female socialization, and the social context. In M. McGoldrick, C. M. Anderson, & F. Walsh (Eds.), *Women in families: A framework for family therapy* (pp. 286–307). New York: Norton.

Rubin, L. B. (1983). *Intimate strangers: Men and women together.* New York: HarperCollins.

Rust, P. (1996). Monogamy and polyamory: Relationship issues for bisexuals. In B. A. Firestein (Ed.), *Bisexuality: The psychology and politics of an invisible minority* (pp. 127–148). Newbury Park, CA: Sage.

Savin-Williams, R. C. (1996). Dating and romantic relationships among gay, lesbian, and bisexual youths. In R. C. Savin-Williams & K. M. Cohen (Eds.), *The lives of lesbians, gays, and bisexuals: Children to adults* (pp. 166–180). Orlando, FL: Harcourt Brace.

Schneider, M. S. (1986). The relationship of cohabiting lesbian and heterosexual couples: A comparison. *Psychology of Women Quarterly, 10,* 234–239.

Schreurs, K. M. G. (1993). Sexuality in lesbian couples: The importance of gender. *Annual Review of Sex Research, 4,* 49–66.

Seigel, K., & Glassman, M. (1989). Individual and aggregate level change in sexual behavior among gay men at risk for AIDS. *Archives of Sexual Behavior, 18,* 335–348.

Shernoff, M. (1999, March/April). Monogamy and gay men. *Family Therapy Networker,* pp. 63–71.

Slater, S., & Mencher, J. (1991). The lesbian family life cycle: A contextual approach. *American Journal of Orthopsychiatry, 61,* 372–382.

Smith, A. (1990). Working within the lesbian community: The dilemma of overlapping relationships. In H. Lerman & N. Porter (Eds.), *Feminist ethics in psychotherapy* (pp. 92–105). New York: Springer.

Smith, A. (1997). Cultural diversity and the coming out process: Implications for clinical practice. In B. Greene (Ed.), *Ethnic and cultural diversity among lesbians and gay men* (pp. 279–300). Newbury Park, CA: Sage.

Soto, T. A. (1997). Ethnic minority gay, lesbian, and bisexual publications: A ten year review. *Division 44 Newsletter, 13*(5), 13–14.

Zuger, B. (1984). Early effeminate behavior in boys: Outcome and significance for homosexuality. *Journal of Nervous and Mental Disease, 172,* 90–97.

III

RELEVANT ISSUES FOR THERAPY, THEORY, AND RESEARCH

To ignore the topics in the following chapters would be a disservice to lesbian, gay, and bisexual (LGB) individuals. The first two parts of the book have provided clear images of LGB lives from historical, conceptual, empirical, and therapeutic perspectives. However, mental health practitioners and researchers must go beyond consideration of these perspectives to affirm LGB lives. To take seriously the challenge of LGB affirmation requires examination of the factors that influence the daily lives of LGB persons, as well as those that affect therapy with them. After examining those factors, it is necessary to act. If one is committed to intervening therapeutically in the lives of LGB people, one must be willing to change the environments for learning, teaching, and providing services, as well as for experiencing and nurturing one's body, sense of agency, and spirituality. The chapters in this section describe numerous significant ways in which changes can be made.

In chapter 13, Kathleen J. Bieschke and colleagues thoroughly review and critique the significant findings from four major research areas that have focused on the therapeutic treatment of LGB clients. Although the chapter highlights counseling and therapy, it is well suited for placement in this section because it bears primarily on the ways in which research efforts can change and have changed to become more informative and LGB affirmative. The authors' position at the beginning of the section allows the chapter to act as an excellent segue from an exclusive focus on counseling and therapy to one on LGB affirmation, broadly defined. One of the standout features of this chapter is its critique of research on LGB-negative therapy (i.e., conversion therapy). The authors also hone their critiquing skills on research concerning counselor attitudes toward LGB clients, LGB client preferences for counselors, and counseling outcomes. Finally, the authors provide insightful recommendations for changes in research and practice on the basis of the studies reviewed.

Chapter 14, authored by Julia C. Phillips, directly challenges directors of graduate training programs to educate students about the importance of LGB-affirmative methods in conducting research and providing mental health services. This chapter's practical approach is one of its greatest strengths. It provides sharp "how-to" advice about changing the institutional, classroom, laboratory, and practicum settings so that each is more sensitive to LGB populations. Faculty and students alike should read this chapter and jointly set their training standards to meet this chapter's clarion call.

In chapter 15, Barry A. Schreier and Donald L. Werden describe the importance of intervening in community and university settings to foster more consistent practice of LGB-affirmative attitudes and policies. These authors first outline the empirically demonstrated efficacy of psychoeducational programming and then articulate the practical need for more of it. By taking this approach, they clearly establish a sound basis for their arguments regarding the necessity of programming as an alternative to traditional means of psychotherapeutic intervention. Their adopted model of "nurturance" in creating programs dictates that heterosexual and LGB people alike will benefit from participation in program activities. Like the previous chapter, this one is exceptional in its offerings of suggestions and ideas, including numerous ideas for developing, advertising, and assessing programs.

Chapter 16, by James M. Croteau and colleagues, explores one of the few areas of LGB psychology in which a considerable body of systematic, empirical research has been published. The authors summarize the scholarly work in vocational psychology in a tabular format that is enormously informative and creative. They thoroughly review and critique the research and theory in vocational psychology that relate to timely and important topics such as discrimination in the workplace and perceptions of occupational choice by LGB people. In the spirit of the scientist–practitioner model, this chapter concludes with clearly explicated agendas for research and practice based on what is known from the scholarly work reviewed.

In sharp contrast with the area of LGB vocational psychology, the empirical research on LGB spirituality is nearly nonexistent. However, spiritual concerns are of monumental importance to many LGB clients. In chapter 17, Mary Gage Davidson takes a sensitive look at numerous religious perspectives on LGB lives as well as at the theoretical and practice-oriented literature that informs mental health care providers about LGB spirituality. Her attention to the diversity of spiritual expressions by LGB people is enlightening and challenges counselors to be similarly appreciative of these many possible expressions. The chapter relates the coming out process to one conception of spiritual growth that is likely to facilitate counselor empathy and understanding for clients who see the two processes as emotionally and conceptually related. The chapter ends with challenges and recommendations for researchers, theoreticians, and directors of graduate training programs.

In keeping with the focus on issues critical to the daily lives of LGB people, chapter 18, the final chapter in this section, deals with the significant behaviors that LGB people engage in that can have dramatic effects on their physical and emotional health. Michael R. Kauth, Marcia J. Hartwig, and Seth C. Kalichman provide illuminating statistics and other information about the health care and health risk conduct of many LGB people, covering such topics as health care use, involvement in exercise, sexual behavior, and substance use. With an emphasis on wellness, this chapter challenges mental health care providers (and researchers) to conceptualize clients from a holistic perspective, one that is inclusive of physical health. In this chapter, as well as the previous ones, therapeutic intervention with LGB clients takes on new dimensions, which these authors are adept at highlighting.

The chapters in this section implore practitioners, researchers, and theoreticians to think about counseling and therapy with LGB clients in multifaceted ways. Mental health professionals will have a difficult time completing this section without being moved to consider in new ways how therapy is affected by a wide range of influences, from training environments to religious doctrines. Unfortunately, the influences of race and culture on LGB psychology have barely been touched by sound, systematic research; the same is true of research and theory on bisexuality. The authors of these chapters have regularly noted these gaps in LGB psychology and have called for a change in how LGB populations are examined. This call and numerous others await the adventurous reader of the following pages.

13

PROGRAMMATIC RESEARCH ON THE TREATMENT OF LESBIAN, GAY, AND BISEXUAL CLIENTS: THE PAST, THE PRESENT, AND THE COURSE FOR THE FUTURE

KATHLEEN J. BIESCHKE, MARY McCLANAHAN, ERINN TOZER, JENNIFER L. GRZEGOREK, AND JEESEON PARK

Almost all early discussions of lesbian, gay, or bisexual (LGB) persons assumed that such orientations indicated profound psychopathology. Caprio (1954), for example, considered same-sex orientations to be indicative of deep-seated and unresolved neuroses. Bergler (1956) believed that gay men and lesbians suffered from a neurotic disease stemming from their striving for defeat, humiliation, and rejection. Socarides (1968) spared no hyperbole when he wrote that being lesbian or gay:

> is a masquerade of life in which certain psychic energies are neutralized and held in a somewhat quiescent state. However, the unconscious manifestations of hate, destructiveness, incest, and fear are always threatening to break through. Instead of union, cooperation, solace, stimulation, enrichment, healthy challenge, and fulfillment, there are only destruction, mutual defeat, exploitation of the partner and the

self, oral-sadistic incorporation, aggressive onslaughts, attempts to alleviate anxiety and a pseudo-solution to the aggressive and libidinal urges which dominate and torment the individual. (p. 32)

Each of these early discussions of sexual orientation, it should be noted, was theoretical in nature. Scant attention was given to the fact that almost all of the few early empirical studies conducted involved participants from hospitals, prisons, or outpatient clinics (Moses & Hawkins, 1982). There was little, if any, attempt to study LGB individuals who were well adjusted and satisfied with their orientation.

Three studies in particular signaled a shift from this assumption of psychopathology. Kinsey and his colleagues studied male sexuality (Kinsey, Pomeroy, & Martin, 1948) and then female sexuality (Kinsey, Pomeroy, Martin, & Gebhard, 1953). Kinsey and his colleagues found that for both men and women, sexuality encompassed a continuum with far more people experiencing same-sex attraction, fantasy, and activity than had previously been believed. The two Kinsey studies provided the earliest empirical data to contradict the assumptions that sexuality was a dichotomous phenomenon (heterosexual or homosexual) and that few people experienced same-sex attractions. A few years later, in 1957, Evelyn Hooker compared the Rorschach and Thematic Apperception Test response profiles of 35 heterosexual men and 35 gay men. Neither group was a clinical sample. She used a double-blind technique, so that test interpreters did not know to which group any given profile belonged. Hooker found no differences in the two groups' levels of psychological adjustment. This landmark study was the first to refute the prevailing assumption that same-sex orientations were, by their very nature, pathological. These three studies represented a profound departure from the theoretical, biased writings that had previously held sway.

Although these studies heralded considerable change, it would be misleading to state that the field of psychology has been uniformly and consistently progressive in its study and treatment of LGB persons. As Phillips (chapter 14, this volume) discusses, there is still wide latitude in the types and quality of training that mental health professionals receive regarding ethical and effective therapy with LGB clients. This is due in part to the dearth of reliable data. Theoretical work in this area abounds, but there are few empirical studies. From a scientist–practitioner model, it is imperative that this imbalance be corrected. Moreover, the research must be unbiased and informed if it is to counteract the homophobia and prejudice that have dictated much of the existing inquiry into LGB lives.

The purpose of this chapter is to evaluate the existing state of research on the treatment of LGB clients. We begin with a review of the empirical studies investigating the effectiveness of conversion therapy. Conversion therapy has been practiced for over a century; its endurance—and the renewed popularity it now enjoys—probably represents the epitome of un-affirmative treatment. We provide both an ethical and a methodological critique of this body of literature. We also provide a critique of the literature that has assessed mental health professionals' attitudes toward LGB clients and draw some conclusions about how these attitudes have changed over time. We then attempt to assess how these attitudes have influenced use of psychotherapy and counseling by LGB clients and discuss the factors that have influenced the effectiveness of treatment of LGB persons. To conclude the chapter, we provide a set of methodological guidelines to consider when examining treatment effectiveness with LGB clients and a research agenda aimed at purposefully facilitating research in this area. We believe that these domains encompass the most critical areas of both theory and practice in the treatment of LGB clients. In addition to reviewing the past (and sometimes present) sins of psychology, we wish to address current attitudes and interventions. Finally, we believe that it is important to provide guidelines for more proactive, affirmative research, in the hope that future reviewers of this topic will have more promising findings to report.

We wish to emphasize at the outset that much of the existing research has addressed the experience of middle-class, White men with relatively high levels of formal education. It is imperative that readers approach this chapter with this fact in mind; it is equally imperative that future research be proactive in rectifying this bias.

CONVERSION THERAPY

Most of the early treatment of LGB clients was founded on a belief that same-sex attraction was pathological; therefore, the desired outcome of such treatment was conversion to heterosexuality. The conceptual underpinnings of conversion therapy are heavily rooted in the psychodynamic belief that same-sex attraction represents a deviation from normal sexual and gender development. In addition, as Moses and Hawkins (1982) pointed out, the Judaic and Christian beliefs that homoerotic behavior is an abomination contributed to the early psychiatric view of LGB individuals. Murphy (1992) noted that conversion therapy (also known as re-orientation therapy) first appeared in the 1800s when a man was instructed to ride a bicycle to exhaustion to eradicate his attraction to other men. Other common techniques designed for men included rest, visits to prostitutes, marriage, use of alcohol and other drugs, isolation with a woman for 2 weeks, inhalation of repulsive substances, deprivation of fluids accompanied by a diuretic, electroshock, injection or ingestion of chemicals to induce convulsions, lobotomies, and castration.

Inherent in conversion therapy research is a sexist bias; this research has focused almost exclusively on men. For example, when the technique of isolating an individual with a woman for 2 weeks is used, it is assumed that the individual placed in isolation is a man. Like others in society, proponents of conversion therapy seem to be more threatened by gay men than lesbian women.

Although its techniques have changed during the past century, conversion therapy continues to be practiced today. Current interventions are likely to include covert sensitization or other cognitive–behavioral techniques in an attempt to suppress an individual's attraction to others of the same sex. Some psychologists, such as Socarides, still believe that same-sex attractions are pathological, despite the removal of homosexuality as a disorder from the American Psychiatric Association's *Diagnostic and Statistical Manual of Mental Disorders (DSM)* in 1973. Socarides (1997) noted, "Homosexuality is a psychological and psychiatric disorder, there is no question about it. . . . It is a purple menace that is threatening the proper design of gender distinction in society" (p. 2).

Other proponents of conversion therapy focus less on the question of psychopathology and instead advocate the role of self-determination and autonomy in acquiescing to a client's request to be reoriented to heterosexuality. Cautela and Kearney (1986) noted, "From both an ethical and a practical point of view it is our contention that the decision of whether or not to change an individual's sexual orientation must be made by the client rather than by society at large or subgroups of that culture" (p. 119). More than a decade later, Yarhouse (1998) advocated that clients—if given full information regarding conversion therapy—have the right to pursue reorientation and that psychologists have the right to practice such techniques. Specifically, Yarhouse posited that

> psychologists presume that people are autonomous, self-determining agents, particularly with respect to their ability to make decisions concerning their work in therapy. Although some clients may pursue treatment for same-sex attraction and/or behavior due to internalized feelings of societal rejection, others may choose to pursue change and may appeal to normative religious or cultural values they hold concerning the purpose and design of human sexuality and sexual behavior (Yarhouse, 1998, p. 250)

Ethics of Conversion Therapy

The ethics of practicing conversion therapy have been hotly debated. Certainly, there are numerous ethical considerations that contraindicate conversion therapy. Several of the ethical guidelines set forth by the American Psychological Association (APA) clearly indicate that the assumptions and practices of conversion therapy are unethical. For example, the APA code of ethics stipulates that psychologists practice with integrity; psychologists "strive to be aware of their own belief systems, values, needs, and limitations and the effect of these on their work" (APA, 1992, Principle B, p. 1599). Yet inherent in conversion therapy is the premise that same-sex orientations are pathological, an arrest in normal development, or (less stigmatizing but still homophobic and harmful in nature) not as well accommodated in society as a heterosexual orientation. Clinicians who offer or even consider conversion therapy for their clients are ignoring the sociopolitical context that perpetuates both external and internal homophobia. Their values and belief systems are imparted to clients in a detrimental way (see Haldeman, 1994, and Tozer & McClanahan, in press, for an exhaustive discussion of these prohibitions). Moreover, in August of 1997 APA passed a resolution regarding the ethics of conversion therapy. Specifically, APA stated that it "supports the dissemination of accurate information about sexual orientation, and mental health, and appropriate interventions in order to counteract bias that is based in ignorance or unfounded beliefs about sexual orientation" (APA, 1997, p. 2). APA did not explicitly ban conversion therapy because such therapy has not been demonstrated to cause harm.

The preponderance of the available literature on conversion therapy is theoretical in nature. The following review critiques the few empirical studies designed to assess the effectiveness of conversion therapy and demonstrates why such therapy is inappropriate.

Methodological Critique

Proponents of conversion therapy state that there are effective means of changing one's sexual orientation (e.g., Bieber et al., 1962; Masters & Johnson, 1979; Mintz, 1966; Nicolosi, 1993). Closer scrutiny of the methods used in the research supporting conversion therapy, however, reveals numerous flaws that render such a claim highly disputable. First, sampling problems are numerous. For example, a study by Bieber et al. (1962) is often cited as a landmark success in the reorientation literature. He claimed a 27% success rate, in itself a relatively low percentage. His sample of 106 gay and bisexual men, however, included 27 men who were diagnosed with schizophrenia. Moreover, the inclusion of bisexuals also made this a skewed sample, because bisexuals certainly are better able to access and act on preexisting opposite-sex attractions. When bisexuals were factored out of the results, the conversion rate dropped to 14%. Masters and Johnson's (1979) conversion study, which included 54 men and 13 women, had a similar sampling problem. Of this sample, only 18% could be considered exclusively or almost exclusively gay or lesbian. In addition to the inclusion of bisexuals, some studies had very small samples. Conrad and Wincze's (1976) study, for example, had only 4 participants (one of whom was a pedophile). Furthermore, high dropout rates aggravated the problems related to small sample size (e.g., Mintz, 1966).

In many studies of the effectiveness of conversion treatment, outcome measures were problematic. As Masters and Johnson (1979) noted, "the therapist is the least acceptable authority to define levels of successful treatment in his or her own clinical program" (p. 380). Many researchers of conversion therapy used therapist report as the sole means of measuring change (e.g., Bieber et al., 1962; Mintz, 1966). This method is inherently biased owing to the demand effects of the study. It stands to reason that if one volunteers for reorientation therapy, one would strive to believe and report that change did occur. In contrast, Conrad and Wincze (1976) used more exhaustive outcome measures, including measures of physiological arousal, behavioral change, and client self-report. It is interesting that although self-report measures tended to support a claim of successful reorientation, little physiological or behavioral change ensued. As Conrad and Wincze (1976) stated, "if this tendency is common to subjects undergoing this type of treatment, and there is reason to believe it may be, it alone could be responsible for the contradiction between favorable reports and the absence of corroborative data" (p. 165).

In all of the preceding studies, behavioral change (whether reported by the client or by the therapist) was the criterion for successful conversion to heterosexuality. It is misleading to assert, however, that a change of behavior denotes an actual reorientation or conversion. Even some proponents of conversion therapy admit that it is not possible to change someone's sexual orientation; rather, they believe that clients are regaining control over behaviors previously thought to be beyond their control (McConaughy, Armstrong, & Blaszczynski, 1981).

Finally, note that in Mintz's (1966) study, none of her 10 participants actually requested reorientation or conversion therapy. These men had presented for assistance with anxiety and vocational difficulties. Although Mintz stated that she would not try to "cure" these individuals, she reported her data in terms of conversion outcomes, thereby revealing her assumption that treatment effectiveness was predicated on reorientation to heterosexuality. Likewise, only 64 of 106 participants studied by Bieber et al. (1962) wanted to be converted to heterosexuality. In both studies, the measure of successful treatment, whether implicitly or explicitly stated, was deemed to be a heterosexual orientation. Such practices raise serious ethical issues regarding the pursuit of a researcher's agenda at the expense of the participants.

Summary

There are numerous methodological flaws—including biased sampling, questionable outcome measures, and a failure to distinguish between behavioral change and actual reorientation—that make claims of successful reorientation suspect. These flawed studies constitute the bulk of treatment-effectiveness studies conducted before the 1970s, and they are still cited to support the viability of conversion therapy. Despite the methodological and ethical problems of conversion therapy, it is still in practice today. We contend that such practice is unethical and inappropriate treatment for LGB clients. Mental health professionals must be knowledgeable regarding the flaws of conversion therapy if they are to provide the most affirmative and effective treatment possible.

Effective treatment is also predicated on a thorough and honest appraisal of one's attitudes and beliefs regarding sexual orientation. The following section provides a historical and current overview of mental health professionals' attitudes toward sexual orientation.

ATTITUDES TOWARD LGB CLIENTS

In the early 1970s, awareness of treatment issues related to LGB clients began to occur. This was prompted by the gay liberation movement and the emergence of sex research as a scientific discipline (Silverstein, 1996), as well as by changes in professional viewpoints. Certainly, research findings pertaining to mental health professionals' attitudes toward LGB clients are greatly affected by societal and professional change. First, we briefly review the empirical research on the attitudes of therapists toward LGB clients before the mid-1980s. After providing a summary of that research, we examine whether such attitudes are still prevalent today. A methodological critique of these studies is provided, as well as suggestions for future research.

Early Empirical Studies

It is not surprising that several early survey studies had mixed findings concerning mental health professionals' attitudes and beliefs related to LGB clients, including the etiology of sexual orientation, treatment strategies, and diagnosis. In general, mental health professionals seemed to agree that same-sex attraction is not a mental disorder (Davison & Wilson, 1973; Fort, Steiner, & Conrad, 1971; Graham, Rawlings, Halpern, & Hermes, 1984). In addition, according to Fort et al., the majority (97%) of counselors reported that they would work with LGB clients toward goals other than change of sexual orientation. Regarding treatment strategies, early studies revealed that the majority of counselors reported that they would help LGB clients to become more at ease with their sexual orientation. In general, counselors also reported that they believed that LGB clients could lead a happy life without changing their sexual orientation. There were some exceptions to these general conclusions. Fort et al. reported that the majority of counselors perceived same-sex attraction as a "personality disorder" or a "sexual deviation" (p. 347). Davison and Wilson (1973) presented evidence that some counselors were willing to work toward the goal of changing LGB clients' sexual orientation.

Several studies indicated that counselors held stereotypical beliefs about LGB individuals similar to beliefs that were prevalent in society. Davison and Wilson (1973) found that counselors rated LGB clients as being less good, more tense, less dominant, and less feminine or masculine than heterosexual clients. Garfinkle and Morin (1978) revealed that counselors rated heterosexuals as being more psychologically healthy than gay or lesbian clients. They also reported that heterosexuals were considered more psychologically healthy because heterosexual men and women exhibited a lesser degree of female-valued sex role stereotypes than did gay or lesbian clients. On the basis of the results, the authors concluded that gay men might be perceived negatively because these men violate sex role expectations and are perceived to exhibit female qualities, which have been traditionally considered less healthy than male qualities.

Several researchers have reported sex differences in mental health professionals' attitudes toward LGB clients. Thompson and Fishburn (1977) revealed that female counseling trainees were more informed about and more comfortable with their attitudes toward same-sex attraction than were male trainees. Moreover, female counseling trainees showed greater consistency than their male counterparts between their opinions about etiology and their attitudes toward same-sex attraction. In addition, male therapists were consistently more negative in their judgment regarding the perceived lack of psychological health among gay and lesbian clients than were female therapists. Similarly, Garfinkle and Morin (1978) reported that male therapists rated gay and lesbian clients as less resilient than did female therapists.

Therefore, although the majority of mental health professionals in the 1970s reported holding affirmative, nonpejorative attitudes toward LGB clients, there was a significant proportion that believed that such an orientation was indicative of psychopathology. Some even believed that such clients should be "reoriented" toward heterosexuality. Gay men were perceived more negatively than lesbians, and female mental health providers were perceived to be more affirmative and less negative about the psychological health of their LGB clients.

Recent Empirical Studies

The study of counselor attitudes has become more complex, providing evidence that negative attitudes toward LGB clients persist. Glenn and Russell (1986) reported that counselors rated LGB clients as being weaker, more powerless, less delicate, and less active than heterosexual clients. One group also examined how stereotypes and biases held by counselors affect counseling interactions. Using an illusory correlation paradigm, Casas, Brady, and Ponterotto (1983) examined the impact of counselors' stereotyping on their information processing regarding clients identified by sex and sexual orientation. The results showed that counselors make more errors when they process information related to gay and lesbian clients. The number of inaccuracies associated with information processing further increased when information was incongruent with commonly held stereotypes related to LGB individuals. For example, participants were more likely to recall that a heterosexual man was monogamous even though, on the stimulus cards presented to participants, monogamy was more often associated with gay men.

Further efforts have been made to examine how stereotypes and bias affect counseling interactions. In 1986, a task force of the APA's Committee on Lesbian and Gay Concerns conducted a survey of 6,580 psychologists to examine the range of bias that may occur in psychotherapy when working with lesbians and gay men (Garnets, Hancock, Cochran, Goodchilds, & Peplau, 1991). Of the 2,544 psychologists who returned the survey, 1,481 respondents reported that they knew of psychotherapy experiences with gay and lesbian clients. These respondents were asked to provide critical incidents of psychotherapy experiences of lesbians and gay men and the source of the information. Seventeen themes reflecting biased, inadequate, or inappropriate practice were identified. These practices reflected a wide range of obvious and subtle forms of bias manifested in counseling interactions (e.g., automatically attributing a client's problems to his or her sexual orientation, encouraging the client to change his or her sexual orientation). Fourteen themes illustrating exemplary practice were also identified, and the authors concluded that psychologists can and do provide appropriate and sensitive services to lesbian and gay clients.

Two groups examined how therapists' homophobia affects their reactions toward videotaped clients in analogue sessions (Gelso, Fassinger, Gomez, & Latts, 1995; Hayes & Gelso, 1993). In both studies, therapists' reactions on three dimensions were measuerd: a cognitive dimension, as measured by recall errors; an affective dimension, as measured by state anxiety; and a behavioral dimension, as measured by approach and avoidance behavior. In Hayes and Gelso's study, therapist discomfort level did not differ according to client sexual orientation. However, male therapists' homophobia did predict their behavioral avoidance (e.g., responses that discourage, inhibit, or divert further exploration such as disapproval, silence, or ignoring) with gay men. In a subsequent study, Gelso et al. reported that both male and female therapists made more recall errors when interacting with lesbian clients than they did when interacting with heterosexual female clients. These results also showed that there was a significant relationship between homophobia and a behavioral measure of approach and avoidance responses. It is important to note that in both of these studies it was reported that counselors exhibited much lower levels of homophobia on a paper-and-pencil instrument than did the general public. The authors posited that social desirability might help explain such findings.

Other studies have demonstrated the existence of heterosexism toward LGB clients. For example, Rudolph (1989) indicated that counselors had divergent attitudes toward different aspects of same-sex attractions. Specifically, Rudolph reported that counselors exhibited affirmative attitudes in noneroticized contexts, which are "distant" from actual experiences and conceptual in nature (e.g., contexts of morality, psychopathology, and civil liberties); conversely, counselors were more likely to exhibit negative attitudes toward eroticized interactions (e.g., being attractive, or attracted to, a person of the same sex). In an analogue study using audiotaped clients, Glenn and Russell (1986) examined heterosexual bias in counseling. They showed that counselors had a tendency to use the term *boyfriend* when identifying the partner of a female client with unidentified sexual orientation.

An emerging body of literature has stressed the importance of affirmative attitudes when working with LGB clients (Atkinson & Hackett, 1988; Betz, 1991; Brown, 1992; Browning, Reynolds, & Dworkin, 1991; Fassinger, 1991; A. S. Hall & Franklin, 1992; Tozer & McClanahan, in press). In these nonempirical writings, the authors have argued that a failure to recognize and validate LGB clients' experiences may lead to damaging outcomes in therapy. In only one study has there been an attempt to identify the factors that are predictive of career counselors' affirmative attitudes and behaviors when working with LGB clients. Bieschke and Matthews (1996) reported that a nonheterosexist organizational climate and the degree to which counselors defined diverse populations as cultural minority groups influenced the extent to which career counselors engaged in more affirmative behaviors.

Methodological Critique

Some of the inconsistencies in the preceding findings reflect one of the methodological problems found in such studies. The survey methods used in most studies (Davison & Wilson, 1973, Fort et al., 1971; Graham et al., 1984), and the homophobia scale used in many studies (Bieschke & Matthews, 1996; Gelso et al., 1995; Hayes & Gelso, 1993) may not accurately reflect mental health professionals' attitudes. Given the political sensitivity of the issue and increased emphasis on multicultural awareness among practitioners, one could argue that participants in these studies provided "appropriate" answers, which may or may not have coincided with their actual attitudes.

Another major problem in the literature is a lack of sensitivity toward subgroups of nonheterosexuals. Many researchers have inappropriately generalized their results to bisexual clients even though bisexual clients were not included in their sample. To date, there is no published research that focuses exclusively on therapists' attitudes and behaviors toward bisexual individuals. In most studies, attitudes toward both gay men and lesbian women are discussed under the generic term *homosexuals*. Moreover, in only one study (Bieschke & Matthews, 1996) was information gathered on the sexual orientation of the counselors. Given that LGB mental health providers are also products of their society, further investigation of the role of LGB therapists' heterosexist biases or internalized homophobia would be beneficial. It seems, however, that a comprehensive investigation of the effect of therapist sexual orientation on therapeutic outcomes would be difficult to achieve given the lack of an instrument to measure heterosexist bias or internalized homophobia (e.g., Gelso et al., 1995; Hayes & Gelso, 1993). Note that most studies have focused exclusively on White therapists' attitudes and behaviors toward gay and lesbian clients.

Clearly, therapists' attitudes and values are formed through a myriad of sources, some of which seem to be mutually exclusive. For example, the messages counselors receive from society at large and from their training programs may be incompatible with each other and, in turn, may leave counselors confused and indecisive about their attitudes. When working with gay or lesbian clients, even well-meaning mental health providers with much experience and knowledge related to gay and lesbian clients may be susceptible to the more subtle forms of heterosexual bias prevalent in society (Brown, 1996; Rudolph, 1989).

Summary

In general, the body of research suggests that mental health providers do not perceive same-sex attraction as psychopathology and that they would be supportive of LGB clients who are coming to terms with their sexual identity. In addition, three studies revealed that mental health providers exhibited much lower levels of homophobia than the general public (Bieschke & Matthews, 1996; Gelso et al., 1995; Hayes & Gelso, 1993). When therapist attitudes were assessed using methods that were less obvious than a questionnaire or a survey, however, therapists seemed to be vulnerable to acting on the basis of stereotypes persistently held by the general public (Garnets et al., 1991; Gelso et al., 1995; Hayes & Gelso, 1993). Furthermore, behaviors were manifested in analogue sessions (e.g., inaccurate information processing, cognitive errors, avoidance behaviors) that were inconsistent with the affirmative treatment strategies endorsed by counselors in surveys.

LGB CLIENTS' USE OF COUNSELING AND PERCEPTIONS OF HELPFULNESS

Given the continuing controversy over conversion therapy as well as recent research that demonstrates that therapists continue to bring heterosexual biases to their work with clients, one might expect the use of therapy to be quite low among LGB individuals. Furthermore, one might expect that LGB clients would not perceive therapy to be particularly helpful. To the contrary, as the following section illustrates, usage rates among lesbian and gay clients have been found to be quite high, as have perceptions of helpfulness. In fact, Garnets et al. (1991) found that nearly all of the psychotherapists in their sample reported having seen at least one lesbian or gay client during their career. It is impossible to speculate about usage rates and perceptions of helpfulness among bisexual clients, because there have been no studies examining this population.

Use of Counseling

There is a considerable amount of research evidence to suggest that gay men and lesbian women use counseling at a high rate. Most recently, Liddle (1996) compared a group of heterosexual clients with a subgroup composed of a national sample of gay men and lesbians. Gay men and lesbian participants reported seeing significantly more therapists than did heterosexual participants (a mean of 4.32 vs. 3.08). Furthermore the same gay or lesbian clients reported an average of 82 sessions with each therapist, in comparison with 29 sessions for heterosexual participants. These results confirmed previous results indicating that both gay men (Bell & Weinberg, 1978; Mapou, Ayres, & Cole, 1983) and lesbians (Bell & Weinberg, 1978; Bradford, Ryan, & Rothblum, 1994; Morgan, 1992) used therapy at a higher rate than did heterosexuals.

The study by Bradford et al. (1994) is notable for both its size and the diversity of its sample. These authors used a large (N = 1,925) national sample and found that White and Latina lesbians used counseling (74% and 70%, respectively) at a slightly higher rate than African American lesbians (61%). Bradford et al. also found that women with advanced degrees saw mental health providers at a higher rate than those with less than a high school degree (80% compared with 67%), which corresponds with Morgan's (1992) finding that those who were highly educated had more positive views toward psychotherapy.

Caution must be exercised when generalizing these results, however. The samples used in most of these studies were composed primarily of highly educated, middle-class, White individuals. The sample used by Bradford et al. (1994) was the exception. As stated, none of these results are generalizable to bisexual individuals because no data have been collected on the therapy usage rates for this group.

Perceptions of Helpfulness

Even a cautious interpretation of the reported usage rates leads one to believe that psychotherapy has a different meaning for gay men and lesbians than for heterosexual people. Liddle (1997b) summarized the reasons proposed in the literature (e.g., Morgan & Eliason, 1992) to explain why gay men and lesbians use psychotherapy at a higher rate. She stated that in addition to having many of the same life issues as heterosexual people, gay men and lesbians also have to cope with additional issues such as oppression and isolation, stigma management, sexual identity development, and internalized homophobia. Furthermore, she reported that gay men and lesbians might lack support from nonprofessional sources typically available to heterosexual people.

Liddle (1999) explored changes over time in gay and lesbian clients' perceptions of the helpfulness of therapists who were heterosexual or whose sexual orientation was unknown. She found that the correlation between perception of helpfulness and the year that the counseling took place was significantly stronger for gay and lesbian clients than for a sample of heterosexual clients. Liddle noted that the positive upswing of perceptions of helpfulness occurred around the late 1980s, approximately 15 years after professional organizations passed resolutions supporting the removal of homosexuality from the *DSM*. She stated that it may have taken 15 years for the new research and writing to influence practicing therapists and training programs significantly.

Examining the role psychotherapy plays in the lives of lesbians has generated a considerable amount of research interest. Lucas (1992) assessed lesbians' preferences for a variety of health care services. Psychological counseling was ranked relatively highly, and 42% of the participants indicated that it was a priority health care service. Through content analysis, Trippett (1993) identified the following four changes lesbian women would like to see in the mental health system: (a) changes in treatment modalities (including less use of medication), (b) practical changes (including making counseling accessible to everyone), (c) provider attitudinal changes (including more awareness of attitudes and beliefs about lesbians), and (d) changes in the type of therapist typically encountered (including the desire for more women therapists and, specifically, more lesbian therapists).

Two qualitative studies have been done to examine the quality of mental health care lesbians received (J. M. Hall, 1994; Morgan & Eliason, 1992). As one might imagine, these studies go far beyond the somewhat simplistic finding that lesbians have found therapy helpful, as evidenced by prevalence of usage and ratings of helpfulness. J. M. Hall's ethnographic study focused on a racially diverse group of 35 San Francisco lesbians in long-term alcohol recovery, and Morgan and Eliason interviewed 40 White lesbians regarding the role of therapy in the lives of lesbians. Both groups found that lesbians perceived therapy to be useful and identified the ability to discuss issues within a supportive environment as particularly important.

On the other hand, relatively little is known about the counseling experiences of gay men. We were able to locate only one study that examined their experiences. Mapou et al. (1983) surveyed 96 White gay men who were members of one of several gay organizations in a Southern city. More than half of the respondents had some counseling experience. Of those responding, the majority reported being satisfied with their experience, although a significant percentage (approximately half) did not report an opinion.

Like many of the studies discussed in this chapter, the results of the preceding studies were somewhat limited in their generalizability. With few exceptions (e.g., J. M. Hall, 1994), these studies used samples of White, educated gay men and lesbian women. Although the generalizability of the results presented in the qualitative study is also somewhat limited, such studies are to be commended for increasing the understanding regarding the role of psychotherapy within the lives of lesbians. Again, no studies have been done to examine bisexual individuals' perceptions of counseling.

Summary

Gay men and lesbians use therapy at a high rate, and little is known about the usage of therapy by clients who identify as bisexual. In general, lesbian and gay clients report feeling satisfied with the help they have received from mental health providers. Considerably more is known about the counseling experiences of lesbian women than of gay men; this is one of the few areas of research in which the focus has been more on lesbians than on gay men. Some of these studies have demonstrated that lesbians and gay men use therapy at a higher rate than do heterosexual clients; these studies further support the need for therapists to seek specific training to work with this population.

FACTORS THAT INFLUENCE THERAPIST PREFERENCE AND THERAPY OUTCOMES

The previous section has illustrated that therapy has a particular meaning for LGB clients and that most of those who have used it have found it to be quite helpful. The empirical literature has begun to identify the factors that influence helpfulness. Specifically, the literature has focused on LGB individuals' preferences for mental health providers and how these may affect outcomes. The two areas in which empirical studies have been conducted include (a) the factors that affect therapist preference and (b) how therapist variables affect perceived treatment outcomes. We turn now to a discussion of these two areas of research.

Therapist Preference Studies

Several studies have examined whether LGB individuals are more likely to select counselors whose sexual orientation matches their own. These studies have indicated that therapist sexual orientation does appear to influence therapist selection, although not unilaterally. Brooks (1981) found that 70% of her lesbian participants said they would prefer to see a lesbian counselor, whereas the rest of the participants said they either had no preference (20%) or would prefer a heterosexual counselor (10%). Likewise, in their analogue study, Atkinson, Brady, and Casas (1981) found that gay and lesbian participants rated homosexual counselors significantly more favorably than heterosexual counselors or counselors whose sexual orientation was not mentioned. Similarly, Liddle (1997b) reported that gay men were more likely to choose gay or bisexual male therapists and lesbians were more likely to choose lesbian or bisexual female therapists. In this study, lesbians were much more likely to choose a therapist of the same sexual orientation than were gay men. Thus, the preference for a similar sexual orientation, although present in both sexes, was more pronounced in lesbians. Furthermore, two studies (Kaufman et al., 1997; McDermott, Tyndall, & Lichtenberg, 1989) revealed that whereas lesbians and gay men preferred counselors of the same sexual orientation, this preference was much more pronounced for those who had sex-related concerns than for those whose concerns were not sex related.

Only one researcher (Moran, 1992) found that LGB individuals did not rate counselors with the same sexual orientation more favorably than heterosexual counselors. In this study an analogue method was used in which lesbians and gay men were asked to watch a 15-minute video recording of a contrived counseling session and then rate the counselor on attractiveness and expertness. Findings revealed no differences on these ratings when participants were told the counselor was of the same versus of a different sexual orientation. However, participants were asked to rate counselors' attractiveness and expertness instead of indicating preferences for a certain type of counselor. Moreover, Moran suggested that this finding might have reflected the fact that the videotaped "sessions" centered on issues of depression and existential concerns rather than sexual orientation issues. He further concluded that the results of the study offer support for the notion that sexual orientation of the counselor might be more salient for clients who have sexual orientation concerns than for those who do not.

Two studies explicitly examined whether LGB individuals preferred counselors of the same sex. Kaufman et al. (1997) found that although a significant number of LGB individuals preferred counselors of the same sex, lesbians rated sex of the counselor as significantly more important than did gay men or bisexuals. Similarly, Liddle (1997b) found that all respondents were more likely to choose a therapist of the same sex but that this preference was more marked for lesbians and bisexual women than for gay and bisexual men.

Other factors that have been examined with regard to counselor preference include counselor attitudes (Atkinson et al., 1981), counselor experience (Moran, 1992), and level of clients' openness (i.e., "outness") about their sexual orientation (Kaufman et al., 1997). A study by Atkinson et al. (1981) focused on whether counselors' attitude similarity regarding gay advocacy affected gay males' ratings of perceived counselor attractiveness and credibility. Participants gave higher ratings to counselors who had attitudes similar to their own. In his study of counselor experience, Moran (1992) found that counselors labeled as more experienced (whether they were labeled as heterosexual or lesbian) were rated more favorably by lesbians but not by gay men. Finally, Kaufman et al. (1997) hypothesized that LGB clients would be more likely to choose a counselor of the same sexual orientation if the clients were more open about their own sexual orientation. This hypothesis was not supported by their data; level of client openness about their sexual orientation was unrelated to their likelihood of choosing a therapist of the same orientation.

Factors That Affect Client Perception of Therapy Outcome

Studies of perceived therapeutic outcomes have indicated that sex and sexual orientation tend to be important factors. Liljestrand, Gerling, and Saliba (1978) found that LGB individuals indicated significantly more favorable outcomes when their therapists were of the same sex and sexual orientation. Brooks (1981) asked a large sample of lesbians who had been in therapy to report their counselors' sex and sexual orientation and to rate their counselors according to how helpful they had been. She found that overall, 77% of participants perceived that their therapy experience was of at least some benefit. All therapists, whether heterosexual male, heterosexual female, gay male, or lesbian, were more likely to be perceived as either *fairly helpful* or *very helpful* than *not helpful* or *destructive*. However, lesbian and female heterosexual therapists were significantly more likely to be rated as helpful than were male heterosexual therapists. There were no significant differences in perceived helpfulness among the other groups of therapists (e.g., between heterosexual females and gay males or between gay males and lesbians). Brooks noted also that about three fourths of her lesbian participants who rated therapy as being destructive had a heterosexual male therapist, although she noted that a relatively small number of individuals (10%) rated therapy as being destructive.

A similar study conducted by Liddle (1996) included a sample of gay men in the analyses and yielded results that were consistent with Brooks's (1981) findings. That is, heterosexual male therapists were seen as being the least helpful. Liddle (1996) found that heterosexual female therapists and LGB therapists were seen as being equally helpful. She suggested that these findings might be owing to the fact that heterosexual men are consistently found to have more negative attitudes toward LGB individuals than are women. However, the finding that heterosexual female therapists were seen as being as helpful as LGB therapists led Liddle (1996) to conclude that heterosexual therapists can be effective when working with lesbian or gay male clients.

Liddle (1996) also asked participants to rate the perceived effectiveness of their therapists on 13 items derived from a study of exemplary and inadequate practices with LGB individuals by Garnets et al. (1991). Results indicated that therapists who used those practices that psychologists characterized as exemplary (e.g., "Your therapist was not afraid to deal with your sexual orientation when it was relevant") were 6–12 times more likely to be rated as being fairly or very helpful by LGB individuals. By contrast, therapists engaged in practices characterized as being inadequate (e.g., "Your therapist indicated that he or she believed that a gay or lesbian identity is bad, sick, or inferior") were as much as 4 times more likely to be rated as unhelpful. LGB clients whose therapists engaged in these inadequate practices were as much as 5 times more likely than others to terminate therapy after just one session. Moreover, in another study, Liddle (1997b) found that 63% of gay men and lesbian participants prescreened their therapists for gay-affirmative attitudes (e.g., consulted with those in the gay community or asked the therapist about his or her experience with lesbians or gay males). Prescreened counselors were significantly more likely to be rated as helpful than those who were not prescreened. Results from these studies indicate that there are behaviors and attitudes of therapists, regardless of sex or sexual orientation, that facilitate a therapeutic relationship that is perceived as being more helpful.

Methodological Critique

Although the shift away from exclusively examining therapists' and trainees' perceptions of LGB individuals' therapy preferences and outcomes is both admirable and necessary, this body of research is nonetheless plagued with some of the same methodological problems as is other LGB research. One of the most common problems with these and other studies with LGB individuals concerns sampling. Researchers have been unsuccessful for the most part at obtaining samples of LGB individuals who are racially, ethnically, and geographically diverse. Most of the participants in these studies are White, highly educated, and from middle socioeconomic backgrounds. Of these studies, only one by Liddle (1996) involved a geographically diverse sample, with participants from 29 states and 3 Canadian provinces.

In addition, many of these studies either did not include a subset of bisexual participants (Liddle, 1997b; McDermott et al., 1989; Moran, 1992) or simply grouped bisexual men and women with lesbians and gay men (Liddle, 1996). Only Kaufman et al. (1997) systematically attempted to measure attitudes of bisexual men and women. It is apparent that much more research with bisexual men and women is needed.

Like other studies cited in this chapter, two of the studies cited in this section involved an analogue approach to determine counselor preference (Atkinson et al., 1981; Moran, 1992). Most other studies used survey methods to elicit LGB individuals' therapist preferences. Researchers often simply asked participants to state preferences for a variety of therapist variables without asking whether the participants had ever been in therapy or how they chose a particular therapist (Kaufman et al., 1997; McDermott et al., 1989). Considering the relatively high rate of therapy use by gay men and lesbians (Mapou et al., 1983; Morgan, 1992), this seems an important variable to consider when measuring therapist preferences. It is difficult to extrapolate from current studies whether the participants answered with regard to previous therapy experiences or simply in a hypothetical sense. There may be substantial differences between the attitudes of participants who have been in therapy and those who have not. Moreover, although counselor preference and outcome studies are less prone to the problem of attaining socially desirable answers than are studies of therapists' and trainees' perceptions, analogue and hypothetical survey data may not reflect actual behavior of LGB individuals. One researcher (Liddle, 1996, 1997b) attempted to address these issues by measuring preferences and outcomes of LGB individuals who had been in therapy at least once. In addition, in an early study Liljestrand et al. (1978) used an interview method with matched therapist–client pairs to measure therapy outcomes. Clearly, however, studies that have explicitly examined current or former LGB clients' attitudes toward therapy are currently in the minority.

Summary

A tentative conclusion from the preceding studies of counselor preference and outcome is that LGB individuals have a slight tendency to prefer therapists who are of the same sex and sexual orientation. In addition, these data indicate that female counselors, whether heterosexual, lesbian, or bisexual, tend to be perceived as being more helpful than heterosexual male counselors. There is some evidence that this perception is more pronounced among lesbians than among gay men or bisexuals. Also, Liddle (1996) provided initial evidence that there are certain practices that counselors engage in that may be either facilitative or harmful for LGB clients.

RECOMMENDATIONS

Methodological Recommendations and Research Agenda

The methodological concerns that plague the research studies in this chapter are not inconsistent with those that have been expressed about other research areas focused on LGB individuals (e.g., Bieschke, Eberz, & Wilson, in press; Buhrke, Ben-Ezra, Hurley, & Ruprecht, 1992; Croteau, 1996; Lonborg & Phillips, 1996). These authors have expressed concerns similar to ours about this body of literature, including the lack of programmatic, theory-driven research; sampling problems; the relative lack of attention to bisexual individuals and, to a lesser extent, lesbians; and the measurement of independent and dependent variables. We have developed a research agenda that both builds on previous research and addresses our methodological criticisms.

As noted previously, with few exceptions most of the research studies examining the treatment of LGB individuals have been independent of each other; that is, they did not build on existing theory or knowledge. Programmatic research that focuses on further replication and expansion of current findings and theory is necessary. Our confidence in the results pertaining to countertransference with LGB clients (Gelso et al., 1995; Hayes & Gelso, 1993) and factors influencing help seeking (Liddle, 1996, 1997b, 1999) is strengthened because there have been multiple studies in these areas, each of which contributes to a more complex view of these phenomena. Liddle (1997a) discussed the importance of thinking programmatically about one's research, particularly when attempting to collect data from a relatively elusive population. She noted that by being planful and creative, she was able to conduct four studies from two waves of data collections by using matched subsets of participant and comparison samples.

Perhaps most important, however, is that researchers carefully consider the purpose of their program of research. Currently there is not an organizational or theoretical framework that ties the work focused on LGB treatment effectiveness together. With the exception of the studies pertaining to conversion therapy, however, a spirit of affirmation for LGB individuals does seem to be evident. We believe that theory development is called for, specifically with regard to affirmative therapy with LGB clients. Tozer and McClanahan (in press) defined *affirmative therapy* as "therapy that celebrates and advocates the authenticity and integrity of LGB persons and their relationships." Further elaboration of this concept, including the incorporation of the existing research and theoretical work (e.g., Browning et al., 1991; Dworkin, chapter 7, this volume), could lead to the development of a theoretical framework to guide researchers interested in developing efficacious treatment methods for use with this population. We advocate the development of a comprehensive theoretical framework, one that incorporates issues such as organizational climate (e.g., Bieschke & Matthews, 1996), theoretical orientation (e.g., Fassinger, chapter 5, this volume), and gender and sex role expectations (e.g., Liddle, 1996).

The development of this framework might be best accomplished with the use of diverse methods, including both quantitative and qualitative research designs. As mentioned previously, if quantitative methods are used, research questions can be limited by the lack of a large sample size. Qualitative methods are not typically hampered by concerns for sample size and are often particularly useful when engaging in theory building. Finally, qualitative methods can help researchers tap into smaller segments of the larger population, including participants who are diverse in terms of ethnicity, race, socioeconomic status, education, and LGB identity status. The research in this area to date has focused primarily on participants who are White and highly educated. Both quantitative and qualitative research designs must strive for diverse samples if researchers are to develop a theoretical framework that is applicable to all members of this population.

Representative sampling is just one of the problems researchers must successfully resolve. A related and perhaps more pressing issue is defining just who is a member of the LGB population. One concern we had about the research in this area was the lack of attention to bisexual individuals. Bisexuals were either excluded or grouped together with gay men or lesbians. We were unable to locate any study in which bisexuals were the sole focus of the investigation. Transgendered individuals, who are increasingly being considered members of the LGB community, were not addressed in any study. Concern about the failure of researchers and scholars to be inclusive is not limited to the studies in this chapter (Croteau & Bieschke, 1996; Croteau et al., 1998; Morrow, 1998). The underlying question is, of course, whether clients who are bisexual or transgendered represent different populations or segments of a larger population. Careful consideration of the purpose of a research investigation will help researchers to make deliberate choices about whether these individuals should be included, focused on exclusively, or excluded altogether.

Another definitional issue that researchers in this area must address pertains to the measurement of both independent and dependent variables. The difficulties researchers have faced when attempting to measure homophobia is a good example. Homophobic attitudes have been theorized to influence outcome of treatment. Yet counselors have been found to have lower levels of homophobia than the general population (Bieschke & Matthews, 1996; Gelso et al., 1995; Hayes & Gelso, 1993), perhaps because mental health professionals are aware that they "should" be affirmative. Although homophobic attitudes have not been associated with behaviors toward LGB clients, there is some indication that heterosexist attitudes may influence counselor behaviors (e.g., Gelso et al., 1995). Given that there is not at present a valid and reliable measure of heterosexist attitudes, researchers must either develop such a measure or think creatively about how to solve this problem. For example, a measure of social desirability might be administered along with a measure of homophobia, to assess the extent to which counselors are portraying themselves as they believe they "should."

A related issue is the development of measures that assess therapeutic outcomes. To date, effective treatment has been primarily defined in terms of LGB clients' perceptions of helpfulness. Such a definition seems limited, yet the question of what outcomes are most salient is debatable. Here again the existence of a theoretical framework would be useful; researchers could draw on this model to guide them in their selection of outcomes and in the development of measures. Regardless of the outcomes identified, researchers must be sure to attend to the psychometric properties of the measurement of these variables.

Although our research agenda has focused primarily on affirmative psychotherapy, it would be incomplete if we did not address the need for more research focused on conversion therapy. As stated previously, we believe that providing such treatment is unethical, even for research purposes. Yet investigating the effects of such therapy is important, particularly for political reasons, because enough compelling evidence does not exist to ban such treatment. Perhaps retrospective studies focused on those who have participated in conversion therapy in the past would provide researchers and practitioners in this area with sufficient information about the effects of such treatment.

Practice Recommendations

Although the research in this area is sparse and limited by the lack of an organizational or theoretical framework, there are conclusions that can be drawn from this body of work that have implications for how mental health professionals can work most effectively with LGB clients. These implications focus on two issues. First, what type of therapy is most effective when working with these clients? Second, how might individual therapists practice within their own theoretical orientation to increase their effectiveness with LGB individuals?

No studies have examined whether a particular theoretical orientation is more effective when working with LGB clients. In fact, as we have discussed in this chapter, most research in this area has focused on what factors contribute to effective treatment. Fassinger (chapter 5, this volume) provided an excellent discussion of how therapists might work effectively with LGB clients using a variety of theoretical orientations. Fassinger's chapter, however, rests on the premise that a therapist operates from an affirmative worldview. That is, the therapist "celebrates and advocates the authenticity and integrity of lesbian, gay, and bisexual persons and their relationships" (Tozer & McClanahan, in press). As we have discussed, a considerable body of work has been published in an attempt to demonstrate that conversion, or reorientation, therapy is effective. We believe that the evidence often used to support the use of conversion therapy is seriously methodologically flawed. We recommend that such therapy not be considered as an option when working with LGB clients, not only for this reason but because such treatment does not have as one of its core assumptions affirmation of clients' sexual orientation.

Although LGB individuals represent a relatively small percentage of the population, they use therapy at a greater rate than heterosexual clients (e.g., Liddle, 1996). Therefore, it is not unlikely that every mental health practitioner will eventually encounter an LGB client. Furthermore, therapy seems to play a unique role, particularly for lesbian clients (e.g., Morgan & Eliason, 1992). Given that LGB clients represent a hidden minority (i.e., their sexual orientation is not an obvious part of their identity as race or sex often is), it is entirely probable that therapists encounter LGB clients without knowing it. There is considerable evidence that counselors are at the very least heterosexist. We believe that all mental health professionals must develop their awareness of their homophobic and heterosexist beliefs and how these beliefs influence their behaviors with clients (see chapters 6, by Morrow, and 14, by Phillips, this volume, for suggestions on how to address this issue).

Research evidence suggests that LGB clients prefer a therapist who is of the same sexual orientation and sex and that female therapists tend to be perceived as more helpful than heterosexual male therapists. This perception is more pronounced among lesbian and bisexual women. Nevertheless, both male and female heterosexual therapists can be effective with LGB clients, particularly if they engage in affirmative practices (see Garnets et al., 1991). These findings suggest that therapists must be aware of the possibility that being of a different sexual orientation or sex may influence client perceptions of the effectiveness of therapy. At the very least, practitioners must be aware of other mental health professionals and services in the community for instances when referral is appropriate.

CONCLUSION

Our review of the literature suggests that although members of the mental health profession historically have viewed an LGB sexual orientation as pathological, such attitudes are not prevalent today. In fact, mental health professionals have been found to have lower levels of homophobia than members of the general population. There is, however, some evidence to suggest that heterosexist attitudes negatively influence counselor behaviors. Even so, LGB clients use counseling at a greater rate than do heterosexual clients. Clients who identify as LGB have a slight preference for therapists who are of the same sexual orientation. Regardless of sexual orientation, however, female therapists are perceived to be more helpful than heterosexual male counselors.

There is a need for more research focused on the effectiveness of treatment of LGB clients. In addition to the research agenda we presented, a valuable resource for researchers in this area is an article by Herek, Kimmel, Amaro, and Melton (1991), who have provided researchers with questions aimed at assisting in the design of research studies free from heterosexist bias. Programmatic research pertaining to treatment effectiveness is particularly needed, and scholars must develop an organizational or theoretical framework focused on affirmative therapy to guide further research. The development of such a framework would guide decisions regarding samples, methodology, and outcome measures.

We believe that research should focus primarily on the effects of affirmative therapy, although the existence of conversion therapy cannot be ignored. Although we do not believe the use of such therapy is defensible, either ethically or methodologically, we believe that investigating both the long- and short-term effects of such therapy is important.

The limited research presented here has implications for practice. First, there is no evidence to support the use of conversion therapy. Second, heterosexist beliefs and attitudes have the potential to influence how therapists behave with clients; practitioners should strive to become aware of their heterosexism and be cognizant of how it might influence their behavior with clients. Practitioners should also be mindful that LGB clients have a slight preference for counselors who are of the same sex, sexual orientation, or both. Certainly, practice should guide future research. Without an exchange of information between researchers and practitioners, the goal of developing effective and affirmative therapy for clients who identify as gay, lesbian, or bisexual cannot be achieved.

REFERENCES

American Psychological Association. (1992). Ethical principles for psychologists and code of conduct. *American Psychologist, 47,* 1679–1693.

American Psychological Association. (1997). *Resolution on appropriate therapeutic responses to sexual orientation.* Washington, DC: American Psychological Association.

Atkinson, D. R., Brady, S., & Casas, J. M. (1981). Sexual preference similarity, attitude similarity, and perceived counselor credibility and attractiveness. *Journal of Counseling Psychology, 28,* 504–509.

Atkinson, D. R., & Hackett, C. (1988). *Counseling non-ethnic American minorities.* Springfield, IL: Charles C Thomas.

Bell, A. P., & Weinberg, M. S. (1978). *Homosexualities: A study of diversity among men and women.* New York: Simon & Schuster.

Bergler, E. (1956). *Homosexuality: Disease or way of life?* New York: Collier Books.

Betz, N. E. (1991). Implications for counseling psychology training programs: Reactions to the special issue. *The Counseling Psychologist, 19,* 248–252.

Bieber, I., Dain, H., Dince, P., Drellich, M., Grand, H., Gundlach, R., Kremer, M., Rifkin, A., Wilbur, C., & Bieber, T. (Society of Medical Psychoanalysts). (1962). *Homosexuality: A psychoanalytic study.* New York: Basic Books.

Bieschke, K. J., Eberz, A. B., & Wilson, D. (in press). Empirical investigations of the gay, lesbian, and bisexual college student: Are they worth the effort? In N. Evans & V. Wall (Eds.), *Toward acceptance: Sexual orientation and today's college campus.* Washington, DC: American College Personnel Association.

Bieschke, K. J., & Matthews, C. (1996). Career counselor attitudes and behaviors toward gay, lesbian, and bisexual clients. *Journal of Vocational Behavior, 48,* 243–255.

Bradford, J., Ryan, C., & Rothblum, E. D. (1994). National lesbian health care survey: Implications for mental health care. *Journal of Consulting and Clinical Psychology, 62,* 228–242.

Brooks, V. R. (1981). Sex and sexual orientation as variables in therapists' biases and therapy outcomes. *Clinical Social Work Journal, 9,* 198–210.

Brown, L. S. (1992). While waiting for the revolution: The case for a lesbian feminist psychotherapy. *Feminism: Psychology, 2*(2), 239–253.

Brown, L. S. (1996). Ethical concerns with sexual minority clients. In R. P. Cabaj & T. S. Stein (Eds.), *Textbook of homosexuality and mental health* (pp. 897–916). Washington, DC: American Psychiatric Press.

Browning, C., Reynolds, A. L., & Dworkin, S. H. (1991). Affirmative psychotherapy for lesbian women. *The Counseling Psychologist, 19,* 177–194.

Buhrke, R. A., Ben-Ezra, L. A., Hurley, M. E., & Ruprecht, L. J. (1992). Content analysis and methodological critique of articles concerning lesbian and gay male issues in counseling journals. *Journal of Counseling Psychology, 39,* 91–99.

Caprio, F. (1954). *Female homosexuality: A psychodynamic study of lesbianism.* New York: Citadel Press.

Casas, J. M., Brady, S., & Ponterotto, J. G. (1983). Sexual preference biases in counseling: An information processing approach. *Journal of Counseling Psychology, 30,* 139–145.

Cautela, J., & Kearney, A. (1986). *The covert conditioning handbook.* New York: Springer.

Conrad, S. R., & Wincze, J. P. (1976). Orgasmic reconditioning: A controlled study of its effects upon the sexual arousal and behavior of adult male homosexuals. *Behavior Therapy, 7,* 155–166.

Croteau, J. M. (1996). Research on the work experiences of lesbian, gay, and bisexual people: An integrative review of methodology and findings. *Journal of Vocational Behavior, 48,* 195–208.

Croteau, J. M., & Bieschke, K. J. (1996). Beyond pioneering: An introduction to the special issue on the vocational issues of lesbian women and gay men. *Journal of Vocational Behavior, 48,* 119–124.

Croteau, J. M., Bieschke, K. J., Phillips, J. C., Lark, J. S., Fischer, A. R., & Eberz, A. B. (1998). Toward a more inclusive and diverse multigenerational community of lesbian, gay, and bisexual affirmative counseling psychologists. *The Counseling Psychologist, 26,* 809–816.

Davison, G., & Wilson, G. T. (1973). Attitudes of behavior therapists toward homosexuality. *Behavior Therapy, 4,* 686–696.

Fassinger, R. E. (1991). The hidden minority: Issues and challenges in working with lesbian women and gay men. *The Counseling Psychologist, 2,* 157–176.

Fort, J., Steiner, C. M., & Conrad, F. (1971). Attitudes of mental health professionals toward homosexuality and its treatment. *Psychological Reports, 29,* 347–350.

Garfinkle, E. M., & Morin, S. F. (1978). Psychologists' attitudes toward homosexual psychotherapy clients. *Journal of Social Issues, 34,* 101–112.

Garnets, L., Hancock, K. A., Cochran, S. D., Goodchilds, J., & Peplau, L. A. (1991). Issues in psychotherapy with lesbians and gay men: A survey of psychologists. *American Psychologist, 46,* 964–972.

Gelso, C. J., Fassinger, R., Gomez, M. J., & Latts, M. G. (1995). Countertransference reactions to lesbian clients: The role of homophobia, counselor gender, and countertransference management. *Journal of Counseling Psychology, 42,* 356–364.

Glenn, A. A., & Russell, R. K. (1986). Heterosexual bias among counselor trainees. *Counselor Education and Supervision, 26,* 222–229.

Graham, D. L. R., Rawlings, E. I., Halpern, H. S., & Hermes, J. (1984). Therapists' need for training in counseling lesbians and gay men. *Professional Psychology: Research and Practice, 15,* 482–496.

Haldeman, D. C. (1994). The practices and ethics of sexual orientation conversion therapy. *Journal of Consulting and Clinical Psychology, 62,* 221–227.

Hall, A. S., & Franklin, H. R. (1992). Affirming gay men's mental health: Counseling with a new attitude. *Journal of Mental Health Counseling, 14,* 362–374.

Hall, J. M. (1994). Lesbians recovering from alcohol problems: An ethnographic study of health care experiences. *Nursing Research, 43,* 238–244.

Hayes, J. A., & Gelso, C. J. (1993). Male counselors' discomfort with gay and HIV-infected clients. *Journal of Counseling Psychology, 40,* 86–93.

Herek, G. M., Kimmel, D. C., Amaro, H., & Melton, G. B. (1991). Avoiding heterosexist bias in psychological research. *American Psychologist, 46,* 957–963.

Hooker, E. (1957). The adjustment of the male overt homosexual. *Journal of Projective Techniques, 21,* 17–31.

Kaufman, J. S., Carlozzi, A. F., Boswell, D. L., Barnes, L. L. B., Wheeler-Scruggs, K., & Levy, P. A. (1997). Factors influencing therapist selection among gays, lesbians, and bisexuals. *Counselling Psychology Quarterly, 10,* 287–297.

Kinsey, A. C., Pomeroy, W. B., & Martin, C. E. (1948). *Sexual behavior in the human male.* Philadelphia: W. B. Saunders.

Kinsey, A. C., Pomeroy, W. B., Martin, C. E., & Gebhard, P. (1953). *Sexual behavior in the human female.* Philadelphia: W. B. Saunders.

Liddle, B. J. (1996). Therapist sexual orientation, gender, and counseling practices as they relate to ratings of helpfulness by gay and lesbian clients. *Journal of Counseling Psychology, 43,* 394–401.

Liddle, B. J. (1997a). Doing research on therapy with gay and lesbian clients. *Division 44 Newsletter, 13*(2), 14–15.

Liddle, B. J. (1997b). Gay and lesbian clients' selection of therapists and utilization of therapy. *Psychotherapy, 34,* 11–18.

Liddle, B. J. (1999). Recent improvement in mental health services to lesbian and gay clients. *Journal of Homosexuality, 33,* 123–132.

Liljestrand, P., Gerling, E., & Saliba, P. A. (1978). The effects of social sex-role stereotypes and sexual orientation on psychotherapeutic outcomes. *Journal of Homosexuality, 3,* 361–372.

Lonborg, S. D., & Phillips, J. M. (1996). Investigating the career development of gay, lesbian, and bisexual people: Methodological considerations and recommendations. *Journal of Vocational Behavior, 48,* 176–194.

Lucas, V. A. (1992). An investigation of the health care preferences of the lesbian population. *Health Care for Women International, 13,* 221–228.

Mapou, R. L., Ayres, J., & Cole, S. P. (1983). An analysis of problem areas and counseling experiences of gay white males. *American Journal of Community Psychology, 11,* 323–336.

Masters, W. H., & Johnson, V. E. (1979). *Homosexuality in perspective.* Boston: Little, Brown.

McConaughy, N., Armstrong, M. S., & Blaszczynski, A. (1981). Controlled comparison of aversive therapy and covert sensitization in compulsive homosexuality. *Behavior Research and Therapy, 19,* 425–434.

McDermott, D., Tyndall, L., & Lichtenberg, J. W. (1989). Factors related to counselor preference among gays and lesbians. *Journal of Counseling and Development, 68,* 31–35.

Mintz, E. (1966). Overt male homosexuals in combined group and individual treatment. *Journal of Consulting Psychology, 30,* 193–198.

Modrcin, M. J., & Wyers, N. L. (1990). Lesbian and gay couples: Where they turn when help is needed. *Journal of Gay and Lesbian Psychotherapy, 1*(3), 89–104.

Moran, M. R. (1992). Effects of sexual orientation similarity and counselor experience level on gay men's and lesbians' perceptions of counselors. *Journal of Counseling Psychology, 39*, 247–251.

Morgan, K. S. (1992). Caucasian lesbians' use of psychotherapy. *Psychology of Women Quarterly, 16*, 127–130.

Morgan, K. S., & Eliason, M. J. (1992). The role of psychotherapy in Caucasian lesbians' lives. *Women & Therapy, 13*, 27–52.

Morrow, S. L. (1998). Toward a new paradigm in counseling psychology training and education. *The Counseling Psychologist, 26*, 797–808.

Moses, A. E., & Hawkins, R. O. (1982). *Counseling lesbian women and gay men.* Columbus, OH: Mosby.

Murphy, T. F. (1992). Redirecting sexual orientation: Techniques and justifications. *Journal of Sex Research, 29*, 501–523.

Nicolosi, J. (1993). Let's be straight: A cure is possible. *Insight on the News, 9*, 22–24.

Rudolph, J. (1989). Impact of contemporary idealogy and AIDS on the counseling of gay clients. *Counseling and Values, 33*, 96–108.

Silverstein, C. (1996). History of treatment. In R. P. Cabaj & T. S. Stein (Eds.), *Textbook of homosexuality and mental health* (pp. 3–31). Washington, DC: American Psychiatric Press.

Socarides, C. (1968). *The overt homosexual.* New York: Grune & Stratton.

Socarides, C. (1997, November). *"Healing" homosexuality.* [On-line] Retrieved November 14, 1997 from the World Wide Web: http://www.religioustolerance. org/hom_exod.html

Thompson, G. H., & Fishburn, W. R. (1977). Attitudes toward homosexuality among graduate counseling students. *Counselor Education and Supervision, 17*, 121–130.

Tozer, E. E., & McClanahan, M. K. (in press). Treating the purple menace: Ethical considerations of conversion therapy and affirmative alternatives. *The Counseling Psychologist.*

Trippett, S. E. (1993). Lesbians' mental health concerns. *Health Care for Women International, 15*, 317–323.

Yarhouse, M. A. (1998). When clients seek treatment for same-sex attraction: Ethical issues in the "light to choose" debate. *Psychotherapy, 35*(2), 248–259.

14

TRAINING ISSUES AND CONSIDERATIONS

JULIA C. PHILLIPS

The main purpose of this chapter is to provide information on the theory and practice of lesbian-, gay-, and bisexual-affirmative training in graduate programs in psychology. Drawing from research results and suggestions in the literature, I outline practical strategies in both the science and practice of psychology that program administrators, faculty, and supervisors can incorporate in their work with graduate students. The need for training in lesbian, gay, and bisexual (LGB) issues is most clearly indicated by empirical research in this area on heterosexist biases in therapy. However, this need is also supported by an examination of the ethical obligations of psychologists and the inadequacy of traditional generalist training to produce psychologists who can work effectively with special populations.

The need for psychology graduate programs to include LGB-related training is documented in studies in which it has been found that students and mental health practitioners believe that their programs have not trained them adequately to work with LGB clients or perceive heterosexism in their education. Mental health practitioners, including psychologists and psychologists-in-training, have reported feeling less competent and less well prepared to work effectively with lesbian and gay clients (Allison, Crawford, Echemendia, Robinson, & Knepp, 1994; Graham, Rawlings, Halpern, & Hermes 1984; Phillips & Fisher, 1998; Thompson & Fishburn, 1977) and even less well prepared to work with bisexual clients (Phillips & Fisher, 1998). Students have reported that lesbian and gay issues are integrated into only a small number of classes (Buhrke, 1989a; Phillips & Fisher, 1998; Pilkington & Cantor, 1996) and that even fewer classes integrate bisexual issues (Phillips & Fisher, 1998). Students have reported that they know more about lesbian and gay issues than do supervisors or faculty (Buhrke, 1989a) and that when LGB issues are discussed in class, the students initiate discussion (Phillips & Fisher, 1998). An alarming number of heterosexist and stereotypical comments made by instructors, seen in textbooks, and heard from supervisors in practicums and internships have been documented; some of these vividly illustrate that students continue to have interactions with psychologists who believe, teach, and practice on the basis of outdated and empirically unsupported notions that homosexuality and bisexuality are inherently pathological (Pilkington & Cantor, 1996). Students also perceive heterosexism in their experiences with research in their programs, including both a lack of support and overt discouragement from faculty from pursuing LGB research interests (Buhrke, 1989a; Pilkington & Cantor, 1996). When seeking a mentor, students who were both LGB and members of ethnic-minority groups also reported difficulty in balancing their needs for an LGB mentor and an ethnic-minority mentor who validated both aspects of their identities or who shared research interests in both areas (Lark & Croteau, 1998). Finally, only about half the students reported being encouraged to explore heterosexist biases in course work and during practicums (Phillips & Fisher, 1998), and the modal number of LGB clients seen during practicums was zero (Allison et al., 1994; Buhrke, 1989a; Phillips & Fisher, 1998).

Given the inadequacies in training, it is not surprising that research has also documented the existence of heterosexist biases in therapy (e.g., Casas, Brady, & Ponterotto, 1983; Garfinkle & Morin, 1978; Garnets, Hancock, Cochran, Goodchilds, & Peplau, 1991; Glenn & Russell, 1986; Thompson & Fishburn, 1977). The presence of such biases also supports the need for graduate programs to provide better LGB-related training. Examples of heterosexist biases range from pathologizing or denigrating clients because of their sexual orientation to having inadequate knowledge bases about LGB issues, lifestyles, and resources. Other examples include differential assessment and treatment of LGB clients and overlooking the impact on them of oppression and discrimination. Gay and lesbian clients reported dissatisfaction with therapy because of perceived heterosexism in their psychotherapists (Bell & Weinberg, 1978; Saghir & Robins, 1973), and Moss (1995) reported that bisexual clients perceived more heterosexist bias in their psychotherapists than did gay or lesbian clients. To date, no studies have addressed the effectiveness of psychotherapists in working with clients with multiple minority statuses or the degree to which racism interacts with heterosexism in counseling. However, Garnets et al. (1991) did suggest that the recognition of multiple oppression and racism when working with lesbian and gay clients was an example of exemplary practice with those clients.

In addition to empirical research that clearly documents the need for LGB-related training, the Ethical Principles of Psychologists and Code of Conduct (American Psychological Association [APA], 1992) supports the need for programs to provide specialized training in LGB issues. For example, the ethics code recognizes the need for psychologists to have specific training in working with special populations, including those related to sexual orientation, in order to provide competent services in their roles as researchers, teachers, therapists, and supervisors. Two other APA resolutions also suggest the need for LGB-related training. First, the resolution *Discrimination Against Homosexuals* encourages psychologists to work proactively to remove the stigma of mental illness associated with homosexuality (Conger, 1975). Second, the recently adopted *Resolution on Appropriate Therapeutic Responses to Sexual Orientation* also suggests that APA supports "the dissemination of accurate information about sexual orientation, and mental health, and appropriate interventions as a means of counteracting unfounded heterosexist biases" (DeLeon, 1998, p. 934).

Finally, the need for specialized training in LGB issues is supported by similar arguments suggesting that specialized training is necessary for psychologists to work competently with other diverse populations, including women (see Enns, 1993, for review) and culturally, linguistically, and ethnically diverse populations (e.g., APA, 1993; Atkinson, Morten, & Sue, 1989; LaFromboise, Foster, & James, 1996). Generalist training does not ensure the cross-cultural competence of psychologists, because such training historically has been provided from a predominately White male worldview (LaFromboise et al., 1996). Similarly, generalist training does not ensure that psychologists will be able to work competently with LGB clients or to produce scientifically valid research on LGB issues because it has historically been provided from a heterosexual worldview (Phillips & Fisher, 1998). If psychology graduate programs do not provide specialized training in LGB issues, practitioners will be more likely to do harm to LGB clients (McHenry & Johnson, 1993; Morin & Charles, 1983) and scientists will be more likely to produce heterosexually biased or invalid studies (Herek, Kimmel, Amaro, & Melton, 1991).

In summary, the reasons for considering how to improve graduate training in LGB issues are compelling. Research clearly has demonstrated a need for such training. Empirical studies of graduate training have revealed inadequacies in LGB-related training, as well as an alarming number of instances of heterosexism and homophobia. It is not surprising, then, that the existence of heterosexist bias in therapy is also well documented.

In its ethics code and other resolutions, APA also clearly supports the need for graduate programs to provide LGB-related training. Finally, increased attention to specialized training in LGB issues is necessary because training from a heterosexist worldview is not likely to produce psychologists who are competent to work with LGB issues in the science and practice of psychology.

IMPROVING TRAINING IN LGB ISSUES

The remainder of this chapter is devoted to strategies and suggestions for fostering the growth of LGB-affirmative scientist–practitioners in graduate training. Key components of LGB-affirmative training include providing students with an LGB-affirmative training environment, conveying accurate information about sexual orientation and LGB people, raising awareness of the effects of oppression and heterosexism on self and other, offering opportunities to learn and practice LGB-affirmative counseling skills with LGB-affirmative supervision, and providing research training that is LGB affirmative (Bieschke, Eberz, Bard, & Croteau, 1998; Buhrke & Douce, 1991; Green, 1996; Murphy, 1992; Stein & Burg, 1996). Although many of these components are interconnected, each is discussed in a separate section for organizational purposes.

LGB-Affirmative Training Environments

Ideally, training environments should be characterized by the absence of homophobia and heterosexism and the presence of LGB-affirmative attitudes and behaviors. In such an environment, faculty would view LGB people as a valued part of a diverse population. Faculty would be equally comfortable with LGB people and heterosexual people. They would admire their unique strengths as an oppressed group and would work actively to combat heterosexism and advocate for equal rights for LGB people. Finally, LGB people, issues, and events would be naturally integrated into the daily training environment for students. Unfortunately, such training environments are rare. This section focuses on ways that faculty can create and maintain LGB-affirmative training environments both organizationally and individually.

Organizational Strategies

At the macro level, faculty in positions of power can provide leadership and advocacy in the broader organizations that compose students' training environments. Bieschke et al. (1998) suggested assessing the university environment for both overt (e.g., university policies) and subtle (e.g., discrimination against LGB scholarship by tenure committees) indicators of the climate for LGB people. In addition to assessing the environment, leaders can advocate for change in these areas when necessary. For example, leaders can advocate for the inclusion of sexual orientation in the university nondiscrimination policy and for domestic partnership benefits for LGB faculty, staff, and students. Furthermore, department chairs and program directors can emphasize that LGB scholarship by students and faculty will be valued and rewarded on the same level as other types of scholarship in terms of teaching, research, and service. For example, department chairs can encourage and reward faculty members for service to the university in a role such as faculty advisor to the university's LGB student group. Finally, training directors can also assess training environments at various practicum and internship sites with regard to LGB issues. They can then offer knowledge and guidance to LGB students who are trying to find the best fit to meet their training needs. When appropriate, training directors can also offer constructive feedback to supervisors at practicum and internship sites.

Within the program, faculty in positions of power should provide strong and active leadership in creating an LGB-affirmative environment. Leaders' advocacy efforts and role modeling are powerful influences on the behaviors and attitudes of the rest of the faculty. Betz (1991) suggested that an absence of LGB-affirmative leadership will at best create a null environment in which there are no forces to counteract the societal heterosexism that negatively influences students and faculty and will at worst create an environment of fear and prejudice. All faculty, but especially faculty in positions of power, should ensure that the atmosphere is safe for faculty, staff, and students to be openly identified as gay, lesbian, or bisexual by modeling and rewarding behaviors that increase safety. Some guidelines suggested by Buhrke and Douce (1991) for creating a safe environment include objecting to antigay jokes and stereotypes; understanding the dynamics of oppression, supporting LGB faculty and students in facing oppression, and recognizing their strengths for doing so; viewing LGB issues as part of diversity and recognizing the interrelatedness of all oppressions; initiating discussions of LGB issues instead of always relying on LGB-identified persons to do so; asking LGB people how out they wish to be before disclosing their sexual orientation to others, especially in letters of recommendation, but also in casual interactions; inviting openly identified LGB professionals to present on both LGB issues and other topics; and recruiting faculty and students who are openly identified as LGB. An additional suggestion for creating an LGB-affirmative training environment is to include LGB issues in program materials. For example, LGB-related activities and scholarship by faculty and students can be highlighted in brochures describing the program to the public. Finally, flyers of conferences related to sexual orientation can be displayed along with those of other conferences.

Individual Strategies

In the absence of strong leadership regarding LGB issues or in situations involving overt homophobia, faculty and students should not underestimate their power to influence others. Each time anyone raises LGB issues, whether in class, in a paper, or in a practicum, other students and faculty members will be educated, and their awareness will be raised. In a null environment, LGB students, especially those who are early in their own coming out process, have a greater need for support from their advisors and mentors (Lark & Croteau, 1998). Especially if local support is less than optimal, faculty can help students find additional support at the regional and national levels. Excellent opportunities for networking and support are available within APA (e.g., Division 44, Division 17's Section for LGB Awareness, and APA Graduate Students' Committee on LGB Concerns). Faculty can facilitate referral of students to these groups by having their brochures and applications readily available. Many of these groups also operate listservs that can enhance feelings of belonging and support.

At the individual level, faculty can enhance the training environment for LGB people through informal acts that create cohesion and positive relationships. For example, individuals can be inclusive of LGB people's romantic partners when organizing social gatherings and show interest in LGB people's romantic relationships in the same way that they show interest in heterosexual people's relationships. Actively supporting LGB people in their grief at the loss of a romantic partner or relationship can also provide a welcome buffer to the isolation that can occur in a heterosexist society for LGB people. Asking LGB people if they are willing to tell you about their experiences as a lesbian woman, gay man, or bisexual person is a way to demonstrate interest in their lives and a desire for understanding the unique experiences of LGB individuals. Finally, Bieschke et al. (1998) noted that faculty advisors and mentors can actively support students by recognizing and responding to the significant anxiety that students may have concerning the development and integration of their personal and professional identities.

Finally, faculty and clinical supervisors should take inventory of their own knowledge base and biases regarding LGB issues to enhance their own contributions to the training environment (Bruss, Brack, Brack, Glickauf-Hughes, & O'Leary, 1997; Long, 1996; Russell & Greenhouse, 1997; Stein & Burg, 1996). Many resources are available for faculty who need an update on LGB issues including the *Journal of Homosexuality* and the *Journal of Gay and Lesbian Psychotherapy*. In addition, several counseling journals have devoted entire issues or special sections to gay and lesbian issues, albeit with only cursory attention to bisexual issues in most (e.g., *The Counseling Psychologist* [Heppner, 1998; Stone, 1991], *Journal of Counseling and Development* [Dworkin & Gutierrez, 1989], and *Journal of Vocational Behavior* [Croteau & Bieschke, 1996]). Furthermore, numerous books have provided information on the unique issues involved in counseling LGB people (e.g., Cabaj & Stein, 1996; D'Augelli & Patterson, 1995; Firestein, 1996). In addition to heterosexist biases that have already been recognized, biases in the area of gay and lesbian issues that were previously unexamined have now begun to be recognized and challenged. For example, although racism and stereotyping have historically led to a neglect of ethnic-minority issues within the LGB literature, scholarship on multiple identities is growing (e.g., Greene, 1997). In addition, psychologists have recently begun to study bisexuality as a legitimate sexual orientation, to provide data about the lives of bisexual people, and to identify unique issues in counseling bisexual men and women (Firestein, 1996; Fox, 1996; Matteson, 1996). In addition to learning more about these topics, educators may need to reflect on the effects of racism in their attention to LGB issues and to examine their biases with respect to bisexual people.

In summary, training environments can be assessed for heterosexist biases, and strategies can be implemented to make them more LGB-affirmative. Faculty in positions of power can encourage and enact organizational changes in their programs, departments, and university communities at large. Individual faculty members and supervisors also have the power to create LGB-affirmative training environments in their daily interactions with students and through the process of learning about LGB issues themselves. In addition to learning in a training environment that is LGB-affirmative, students also need to be exposed to accurate information about the lives of LGB people.

Knowledge About LGB Issues

Students must gain accurate information about lesbian women, gay men, and bisexual men and women not only for its own sake but also because it will help them to dispel myths and stereotypes about LGB people, thus increasing the likelihood that they form LGB-affirmative attitudes. Teaching students about LGB issues can best be accomplished by integrating, as appropriate, LGB issues into individual courses in the curriculum (Buhrke, 1989b; Burhke & Douce, 1991; Murphy, 1992; Norton, 1982; Stein & Burg, 1996). Ideally, programs would also offer a separate course devoted to LGB issues. The following sections contain specific suggestions for integrating LGB issues into various therapy-related courses, ethics courses, and testing and assessment courses, as well as a discussion of separate courses on LGB issues. Regarding courses that are not mentioned here, faculty should ask themselves, "Given my knowledge of the theory and research in this particular area, how has heterosexism been evident, and how are issues different for LGB people?" Faculty can also quickly and easily run a computerized search on PsycINFO (or any similar search engine) combining the topic areas of the course and LGB issues to find recent information. Key terms to use with PsycINFO include *male homosexuality, lesbianism, bisexuality,* and *attitudes toward homosexuality.*

Therapy

Information on the presence of heterosexism in various approaches to psychotherapy can be highlighted in the introduction to counseling theories course, and in advanced courses and seminars, professors can provide more in-depth coverage of the ways that particular theories have been criticized as heterosexist (Buhrke & Douce, 1991). Discussing the ways that current theorists have modified traditional theories to eliminate heterosexism is also warranted. Theories that explicitly incorporate how oppression affects mental health should also be presented (e.g., feminist therapy [Worrell & Remer, 1992], multicultural relational therapy [McClure & Teyber, 1996]).

In group therapy courses, faculty can integrate LGB issues in a number of ways. First, discussions about how a particular group will or will not meet an LGB client's needs depending on his or her stage of identity development can be incorporated into sections on inclusion and exclusion criteria for composing groups (Burhke & Douce, 1991). Second, LGB groups can be discussed in the section on theme groups (Burhke & Douce, 1991). Discussing LGB theme groups offers a prime opportunity for students to learn the complexities of group dynamics, specifically how the dynamics can be differentially affected depending on whether group leaders are themselves lesbian, gay, or bisexual. Faculty can also assign articles about heterosexual students' facilitating LGB theme groups to stimulate discussion (Chojnacki & Gelberg, 1995; Holahan & Gibson, 1994).

Concerning couple, marital, and family therapy courses, Green (1996) noted that faculty must teach students first about well-functioning LGB people in couples and families, because many students have not learned such information from their daily lives or past education. Helping students recognize the impact of oppression and discrimination on same-sex couples and families will help them to avoid overpathologizing clients. Faculty can mention special issues facing LGB couples and families, including those related to multiple minority statuses (see Laird & Green, 1996; Matthews & Lease, chapter 11, this volume; Ossana, chapter 12, this volume). Faculty can also teach students methods of helping couples explore and cope effectively with the issues related to monogamy and polyamory that may be present for some bisexual clients, as well as for lesbian, gay, and heterosexual clients (Matteson, 1996; Rust, 1996b).

LGB issues can be integrated in a number of ways into career-counseling courses. Faculty can highlight the heterosexism inherent in some career development theories (see, e.g., Buhrke & Douce's, 1991, discussion of Harren's, 1979, theory of career decision making). Faculty can begin discussions on special issues that LGB clients may encounter in career development, including fighting inaccurate stereotypes about which occupations are and are not appropriate for LGB people, weighing the benefits and risks of coming out in the workplace, dealing with workplace discrimination, and coping with dual career issues in the absence of societal recognition of their partnership status (Croteau et al., chapter 16, this volume; Morgan & Brown, 1991; Orzek, 1992). Instructors can also draw on recently published theoretical and empirical articles to educate students concerning career counseling and career-development issues for LGB people (e.g., Bieschke & Matthews, 1996; Croteau, 1996).

LGB issues can easily be integrated into seminars focused on counseling special populations, such as seminars on multicultural counseling, gender issues in counseling, and counseling persons with disabilities. Because these courses typically focus on the dynamics of oppression, individuals' identity development as members of a minority group, and unique characteristics of particular cultures, students will gain a framework from which to consider LGB individuals as an oppressed group with special issues for counseling (Buhrke, 1989b; Buhrke & Douce, 1991). Focusing on people with multiple minority statuses highlights the fact that minority communities also struggle with their own prejudices. For example, racism exists in the LGB community as does heterosexism in ethnic-minority communities. For clients with multiple identities, the task of developing a positive identity as a member of multiple groups may be both more challenging and more rewarding (see Rust, 1996a, for a discussion of bisexual people managing multiple identities; also see Fukuyama & Ferguson, chapter 4, this volume).

Ethics

In ethics and professional development courses, instructors should include sexual orientation as a facet of diversity that is covered by the Ethical Principles of Psychologists and Code of Conduct (APA, 1992). Instructors can provide students with copies of LGB-related policies and resolutions that have been adopted by APA, including the original statement, *Discrimination Against Homosexuals* (Conger, 1975), and the recently adopted *Resolution on Appropriate Therapeutic Responses to Sexual Orientation* (DeLeon, 1998). LGB-related policy statements, which include resolutions titled *Child Custody and Placement* (Conger, 1977), *Employment Rights of Gay Teachers* (Abeles, 1981), and *LGB Youths in the Schools* (DeLeon, 1993), are easily accessible on APA's web site (http://www.apa.org/pi/statement.html). Ethics instructors can also include LGB issues in discussions related to managing conflicts between religious values and professional ethics, particularly when working with students who are overtly hostile or homophobic. Beginning counselors often struggle with religious values that conflict with professional ethics in a variety of areas, including the roles of women and men, premarital sex, abortion, divorce, and sexual orientation (see Davidson, chapter 17, this volume).

Testing and Assessment

Norton (1982) pointed out that attention should be given in testing and assessment courses to the validity of various tests for lesbian women, gay men, and bisexual men and women. Little research exists on heterosexist biases in different tests or test items. Students can hypothesize about how heterosexism may influence test results and can generate strategies for the use, possible modification, and interpretation of tests with LGB clients. Furthermore, because understanding the LGB client's stage of identity development is crucial when conceptualizing clients or determining diagnoses, clinical strategies for assessing a client's stage of identity development can also be presented in class. Finally, instructors can help students understand how societal prejudice and internalized homophobia can lead to symptoms of mental illness, including depression and anxiety (Garnets et al., 1991).

Separate Courses

A separate course or seminar is an ideal setting for providing students with in-depth knowledge about LGB issues as well as opportunities for additional experiential activities designed to foster LGB-affirmative attitudes. Specific descriptions of course objectives and special topics to be included in such a course can be found in the literature (Gilliland & Crisp, 1995; Stein & Burg, 1996). Faculty who are interested in developing such a course should consult with others who have already done so. A listing of programs with courses integrating LGB issues, including courses devoted solely to LGB issues, is available from APA's Public Interest Directorate on their web site (www.apa.org/pi/lgbc/lgbsurvey/table3.html). Note that on its own, a separate course cannot be considered to be an adequate substitute for integrating LGB issues throughout a program's curriculum.

In summary, there are a variety of ways to integrate knowledge about LGB issues into the typical courses taught in graduate school. Doing so not only will make students more knowledgeable about LGB issues but also will help them to combat myths and stereotypes about LGB people. Although accurate information is essential, programs also need to raise students' awareness of LGB issues in more personal and experiential ways, so that students become aware of the impact of heterosexism on themselves and their clients. This awareness should also help students become more comfortable in interacting with LGB people.

Raising Awareness of LGB Issues

Raising students' awareness of the impact of heterosexism and homophobia on themselves and others is a key component of effective training in LGB issues. Brown (1996) suggested that all counselors assume the presence of heterosexist and homophobic biases in themselves and make concomitant efforts to seek and rid themselves of those biases. The specific goals of raising awareness are presented here, along with examples of experiential exercises and assignments designed to meet those goals.

An initial goal of awareness-raising activities is to help students to identify previously unrecognized instances of heterosexism. Exploring the concept of heterosexual privilege is one method for doing so. Heterosexual privileges are societal rights and privileges enjoyed by heterosexual people but not by LGB people. Students can be given examples of heterosexual privileges, such as the right to a legally and religiously sanctioned marriage, the exposure as children to schoolbooks that showed positive portrayals of people of one's sexual orientation, the ability to show affection for a romantic partner in public without fear of reprisals, and the ability to obtain and keep housing without being discriminated against because of one's sexual orientation. Students can then be asked to brainstorm about other ways that heterosexual privilege exists in the common experiences of daily living. In addition, the experiences of bisexual people should be highlighted, including the fact that bisexual people in same-sex relationships don't have heterosexual privilege, whereas those in opposite-sex relationships have some but not all of the privileges.

Another goal of enhancing awareness is to increase students' understanding of how heterosexism affects the psychological, intellectual, vocational, spiritual, and financial lives of LGB people. Guided imagery can be used to meet this goal as well as to raise students' awareness of how heterosexual privilege pervades the daily lives of all people. For example, an instructor might ask students to imagine themselves with a current, past, or future romantic partner while the instructor describes daily life activities in a world in which the vast majority of people are lesbian or gay and only a small minority of people are heterosexual. Students who do this exercise with reference to an opposite-sex partner typically describe feelings of isolation, fear, embarrassment, and anger, thus increasing their understanding of LGB people's experiences in society today.

A third goal is to provide students with opportunities to examine how heterosexism has shaped their own attitudes, values, beliefs, feelings, and behaviors. This goal is a particularly important first step for students who are especially homophobic. Students can be asked to reflect on the different messages they received during childhood, adolescence, and adulthood about LGB people, including messages that were overt (e.g., it was an insult to be called "gay" or "queer" in adolescence) and messages that were subtle (e.g., children's books with no stories about children with LGB parents implied that all parents were heterosexual). Students should consider various sources of messages such as family, peer groups, television, movies, books, magazines, religious institutions, schools, news reports, textbooks, government, and laws. Journal writing is another beneficial way for students to explore their attitudes and feelings but in a more private manner. Murphy (1992) suggested that students explore in their journals issues related to how they feel about their own sexual orientation, how they feel about the sexual orientation of clients, the impact of heterosexism on their lives, and the impact of LGB issues on therapy and the therapeutic relationship. When reading students' journals, instructors should ensure confidentiality, respect where the student is in his or her development, reward exploration and growth, and gently confront heterosexism when it is evident. Given the sensitive nature of these issues, instructors should offer students the option of requesting that instructors not read particular journal entries, without a penalty to their grade.

A final goal for enhancing awareness involves exposing students to positive experiences with LGB people. Having personal contact with LGB people is especially important for students who have had limited contact with LGB people or who are especially homophobic. Personal contact will increase comfort with LGB people, dispel myths and stereotypes about them, offset the negative reactions that society has conditioned students to feel, and improve psychotherapists' self-efficacy in working with LGB clients (Flores, O'Brien, & McDermott, 1995). Encouraging students to do the things they will suggest to their clients who are in the coming out process is warranted. For example, reading LGB novels and newspapers and watching LGB-related films are nonthreatening ways to start. Attending local and regional events, such as LGB-related festivals, pride marches, musical programs, and informational presentations, is also useful. Students can also attend meetings of the LGB student group on campus. In the event that little is available locally, students should be encouraged to attend LGB-related programs and activities when they go to regional and national conferences. Finally, Green (1996) suggested assigning students the task of conducting a personal interview with an LGB person and has provided a thorough structured questionnaire for students to use in their interviews.

Clinical Practice

Once students have received accurate information about the lives of LGB people and have engaged in awareness-raising activities in an LGB-affirmative training environment, the next step is to gain clinical skills in working with LGB clients and to deepen their understanding of LGB issues in clinical contexts. Prepracticums, practicums, and predoctoral internships all present unique opportunities for students to do this. This section discusses teaching LGB-affirmative therapy techniques in a group setting for students early in their development, providing an LGB-affirmative training environment in advanced clinical settings, and attending to LGB-related issues in clinical supervision using a developmental model. It should be noted that supervising psychologists and training directors should tailor their training to meet the individual needs of each student. Depending on the opportunities for training on LGB issues available to a student in the past and his or her ability and willingness to take advantage of those opportunities, psychologists may have to provide basic education and awareness raising in addition to facilitating students' development as clinicians.

Teaching Clinical Skills In a Group Setting

Students with little experience are especially appreciative if they are given examples of what LGB-affirmative therapists tend to do and say and what they tend not to do and say. An article by Garnets et al. (1991) can be used to give students those examples. A creative way to use this study in an interactive fashion is to do a "read-around" exercise (Morgan, personal communication, September 1993). An instructor can copy the article and cut out the examples of negative bias in therapy and the examples of affirmative therapy. In a group setting, the biased examples are given to students, and each is asked to read one example aloud, in turn, until all examples are read. The affirmative examples are then read aloud in a similar manner. Discussion can follow, after which students practice affirmative therapy skills by role-playing.

Role-playing in a group setting is an excellent way for students to learn and practice clinical skills, including LGB-affirmative therapeutic techniques (Long, 1996). Instructors can demonstrate LGB-affirmative therapy by playing the role of the psychologist while LGB-identified guests play the roles of clients and the students observe. A discussion can follow that highlights the instructors' LGB-affirmative techniques, as well as identifies instances in which the client might have perceived heterosexism in the psychologist. Students can then play the role of the psychologist and receive feedback from the professor, their classmates, and the guests. Role-playing and receiving constructive feedback may be particularly valuable for students who are struggling with homophobia. Care should be taken to bring in guests who are knowledgeable about issues related to being LGB and how being LGB does or does not affect other issues. Issues to be role-played can include general mental health concerns (e.g., depression, anxiety), normal developmental issues (e.g., career development, grief and loss, parenting), and specific concerns related to being an LGB person (e.g., coming out to parents, dealing with harassment and discrimination).

LGB-Affirmative Training Environments in Advanced Clinical Settings

Psychologists at students' practicum and internship sites can be powerful role models of LGB affirmation by creating LGB-affirmative organizational environments. Bieschke and Matthews (1996) reported that a nonheterosexist organizational climate was predictive of both career counselors' LGB-affirmative behaviors with LGB clients and culturally affirmative behaviors with all clients. In addition to implementing suggestions mentioned previously for creating an affirming environment overall, supervisors at these sites can implement strategies to create nonheterosexist organizational climates (Bieschke & Matthews, 1996; Eldridge & Barnett, 1991). For example, supervisors can put LGB-inclusive categories and language on their forms, publicly display LGB-affirmative signs or symbols such as the upside-down pink triangle or the rainbow flag, and have in the waiting room copies of an LGB magazine such as *The Advocate*. Furthermore, psychologists can have LGB therapy books on their shelves and pamphlets about LGB issues available for students. A thorough list of community resources and referrals should also be available (Murphy, 1992).

Finally, the organizational environment of advanced clinical settings should offer students regular opportunities for learning about LGB issues. LGB issues can be integrated into training seminars in the same way that they are integrated into courses. Seminars on LGB issues should be provided on a regular basis, as well. It can also be highly beneficial for students to have access to tapes of a counselor modeling LGB-affirmative therapy with an LGB client. Finally, advanced clinical settings should offer opportunities for practicum students and interns to work with a psychologist providing cotherapy to LGB clients, couples counseling to same-sex or bisexual couples, group therapy with an LGB theme group, or outreach programming for an LGB organization.

Issues in Clinical Supervision

Bruss et al. (1997) advocated applying a developmental model of supervision to students working with LGB clients by matching supervisory interventions to supervisees' developmental level. Beginning counselors will need more structure in exploring LGB-related issues in supervision. For example, beginning counselors should be challenged by supervisors to think about what assumptions they make, how the language they use will communicate those assumptions to clients, and what the effect will be on clients (Buhrke & Douce, 1991; Long, 1996). Supervisors can encourage students to avoid making assumptions about a client's sexual orientation and to use gender-neutral terms such as *romantic partner* instead of *girlfriend* or *boyfriend*. Students should also be encouraged to consider that persons with either same-gender partners or opposite-gender partners may be bisexual. Furthermore, beginning supervisees will most likely need reassurance that having stereotypes and biases is common for new counselors and that they will be judged positively for acknowledging, exploring, and working on changing those biases.

In contrast, supervision during advanced practicums and internships is an excellent time for students to explore more fully their own thoughts, feelings, experiences, and biases related to LGB issues because they are generally more confident and comfortable with their skills at this time (Bruss et al., 1997). Hancock (1995) and Morrow (chapter 6, this volume) provide excellent summaries of countertransference issues that psychologists may face while working with lesbian and gay clients. For example, heterosexual psychologists may struggle with feelings of discomfort related to erotic transference from a same-sex client, and lesbian or gay psychologists may overidentify with the client. Issues related to countertransference with bisexual clients may also be present for both heterosexual and gay or lesbian supervisees. Supervisees may unconsciously reward a bisexual client for behaviors that mirror their own sexual attractions (i.e., heterosexual counselors may focus more on the client's opposite-sex feelings and behaviors, and lesbian or gay supervisees may focus more on the client's same-sex feelings and behaviors). Finally, Russell and Greenhouse (1997) discussed another example of transference–countertransference issues resulting from internalized homophobia and nondisclosure of sexual orientation. In that case, a parallel process existed between the client–counselor dyad and the supervisee–supervisor dyad. Openly discussing these issues resulted in growth for all three.

In summary, students need to incorporate their knowledge about LGB issues in their therapy while they are developing their identities as therapists. Instructors can use strategies that provide concrete examples of LGB-affirmative therapy skills to beginning counselors in group settings. Supervisors can match their interventions to the developmental level of their supervisees by providing more structure and reassurance to their beginning supervisees and more in-depth exploration of LGB issues to their more advanced supervisees. Finally, psychologists at advanced clinical sites can role-model LGB affirmation by taking measures to make their organizational environments more LGB-affirmative. The final area that graduate programs must address to make their training environments more LGB-affirmative is research.

Research Training

Whereas most of the past literature on creating LGB-affirmative training environments has focused on the practice of psychology, recently comprehensive attention has been given to creating an LGB-affirmative research training environment (Bieschke et al., 1998). Bieschke et al. suggested that in the absence of an LGB-affirmative environment in the university, department, or program, it is difficult to create an LGB-affirmative research training environment. However, those challenges must not deter faculty from implementing strategies for an LGB-affirmative research training environment one at a time. An LGB-affirmative research training environment is characterized by the presence of faculty doing research on LGB issues, LGB-affirmative advising and mentoring by faculty, and integration of LGB issues into courses on research methods and statistics.

Faculty can serve as powerful role models for students—in building students' self-efficacy in doing LGB-related research and in mediating their anxiety about being involved in LGB-related research—if they themselves are also researching LGB issues (Bieschke et al., 1998). In their role as advisor, faculty must be sure that the messages they send to students about doing LGB-related research are balanced. Research has suggested that students perceive both overt and subtle discouragement from faculty about doing LGB-related research (Buhrke, 1989a; Pilkington & Cantor, 1996). When discussing the ramifications of doing LGB-related research, therefore, faculty should discuss the potential discrimination students may face in some academic environments as well as a number of positive factors. Besides providing encouragement and support, faculty can provide information about scholars who have been successful, satisfied, supported, and rewarded in LGB-related research (Bieschke et al., 1998). As advisors, faculty members can also be aware of the personal issues that students have in developing their research interests in LGB issues. Both LGB and heterosexual students may be concerned with the correct or incorrect assumptions that others will likely make about their sexual orientation if they choose to do LGB-related research (Bieschke et al., 1998; Lark & Croteau, 1998). For LGB students in various stages of identity development and for heterosexual students in various stages of development related to being an LGB ally, these may be powerful concerns. Finally, faculty should help students network within national organizations to increase their exposure to other psychologists interested in LGB-related research.

Several authors have made suggestions for integrating LGB issues and avoiding heterosexist bias in research that professors can present in research methodology courses (Bieschke et al., 1998; Buhrke & Douce, 1991; Herek et al., 1991). Discussions of LGB-related research offer an excellent opportunity for students to think critically about all phases of research, including operationalization of variables, sampling, data collection procedures, and data analysis. For example, discussions can focus on ways to meet the challenge of obtaining a random sample of LGB people given their relative invisibility and potential reluctance to self-identify. Different methods for assessing the sexual orientation of participants may be identified, because sexual behavior, sexual identity, and sexual orientation do not always match. Students should be challenged to consider how a research design may be weakened by the researcher's failure to recognize that samples are generally made up of both heterosexual and LGB participants and that the research question under study may be affected by sexual orientation. Finally, in statistics courses, faculty can use examples in class and on tests that are inclusive of diverse sexual orientations.

CONCLUSION

Because of the clear need for improved training in LGB issues in graduate programs in psychology, I have discussed issues relevant to such training and provided practical strategies and suggestions that program administrators, faculty, and supervisors can incorporate in their work with graduate students. Effective training in LGB issues involves providing an LGB-affirmative training environment to students, educating students about the lives of LGB people, enhancing students' awareness of the impact of heterosexism on themselves and others, teaching them developmentally appropriate clinical skills for working with LGB clients, and offering LGB-affirmative research training. It is recommended that program administrators, individual faculty, and clinical supervisors review the suggestions made in this chapter with regard to their own programs, teaching, and training activities. In addition, open discussions with colleagues can lead to group decisions about what changes need to be made. Although large-scale change may be warranted in many cases, making changes on a large scale often begins with small, individual acts. The key to large-scale change is continual evaluation and forward movement, especially by those who are in positions of power. When large-scale change is not warranted, additional changes can further enhance an environment that already has elements of LGB affirmation present.

Researchers should continue to monitor the effectiveness of graduate programs in the provision of training in LGB issues. Previous studies have indicated that the quality of training varies widely across programs. It is also likely that the quality of training varies within programs, depending on which aspect is being evaluated (e.g., overall environment, infusion of LGB issues into the curriculum, teaching of clinical practice, research). Methods for gathering data on the effectiveness of programs that are less likely to be affected by sampling biases should be used to obtain a truer picture of the state of training in LGB issues. Future theory and research can be undertaken to identify the relationships between particular elements of training and particular aspects of students' professional development.

Mediating factors owing to individual differences in these relationships can also be discussed theoretically and examined empirically.

Although research has indicated that training in LGB issues has been less than optimal and that societal backlash against LGB issues has been strong, the future of LGB training in graduate programs in psychology is promising. The first generation of LGB-affirmative scholars has pioneered the way for the second and third generations to continue to augment the knowledge base of LGB issues and to influence positively the attitudes of colleagues, students, and society at large (Croteau et al., 1998). As each reader of this chapter implements suggestions for improving LGB-related training of graduate students, current and future generations of psychologists will be positively affected and, in turn, will positively affect others.

REFERENCES

Abeles, N. (1981). Proceedings of the American Psychological Association, Incorporated, for the year 1980: Minutes of the annual meetings of the Council of Representatives. *American Psychologist, 36,* 552–586.

Allison, K. W., Crawford, I., Echemendia, R., Robinson, L., & Knepp, D. (1994). Human diversity and professional competence: Training in clinical and counseling psychology revisited. *American Psychologist, 49,* 792–796.

American Psychological Association. (1992). Ethical principles of psychologists and code of conduct. *American Psychologist, 47,* 1597–1611.

American Psychological Association. (1993). Guidelines for providers of psychological services to ethnic, linguistic, and culturally diverse populations. *American Psychologist, 48,* 45–48.

Atkinson, D. R., Morten, G., & Sue, D. W. (1989). *Counseling American minorities: A cross-cultural perspective.* Dubuque, IA: William C. Brown.

Bell, A. P., & Weinberg, M. S. (1978). *Homosexualities: A study of diversity among men and women.* New York: Simon & Schuster.

Betz, N. E. (1991). Implications for counseling psychology training programs: Reactions to the special issue. *The Counseling Psychologist, 19,* 248–252.

Bieschke, K. J., Eberz, A. B., Bard, C. C., & Croteau, J. M. (1998). Using social cognitive career theory to create affirmative lesbian, gay, and bisexual research training environments. *The Counseling Psychologist, 26,* 735–753.

Bieschke, K. J., & Matthews, C. (1996). Career counselor attitudes and behaviors toward gay, lesbian, and bisexual clients. *Journal of Vocational Behavior, 48,* 243–255.

Brown, L. S. (1996). Ethical concerns with minority patients. In R. P. Cabaj & T. S. Stein (Eds.), *Textbook of homosexuality and mental health* (pp. 897–916). Washington, DC: American Psychiatric Press.

Bruss, L. V., Brack, C. J., Brack, G., Glickauf-Hughes, C., & O'Leary, M. (1997).

A developmental model for supervising therapists treating gay, lesbian, and bisexual clients. *The Clinical Supervisor, 15,* 61–73.

Buhrke, R. A. (1989a). Female student perspectives on training in lesbian and gay issues. *The Counseling Psychologist, 17,* 629–636.

Buhrke, R. A. (1989b). Incorporating lesbian and gay issues into counselor training: A resource guide. *Journal of Counseling and Development, 68,* 77–80.

Buhrke, R. A., & Douce, L. A. (1991). Training issues for counseling psychologists working with lesbians and gay men. *The Counseling Psychologist, 19,* 248–252.

Cabaj, R. P., & Stein, T. S. (Eds.). (1996). *Textbook of homosexuality and mental health.* Washington, DC: American Psychiatric Press.

Casas, J. M., Brady, S., & Ponterotto, J. G. (1983). Sexual preference biases in counseling: An information processing approach. *Journal of Counseling Psychology, 30,* 139–145.

Chojnacki, J. T., & Gelberg, S. (1995). The facilitation of a gay/lesbian/bisexual support-therapy group by heterosexual counselors. *Journal of Counseling & Development, 73,* 352–354.

Conger, J. J. (1975). Proceedings of the American Psychological Association, Incorporated, for the year 1974: Minutes of the annual meetings of the Council of Representatives. *American Psychologist, 30,* 620–651.

Conger, J. J. (1977). Proceedings of the American Psychological Association, Incorporated, for the year 1976: Minutes of the annual meetings of the Council of Representatives. *American Psychologist, 32,* 408–438.

Croteau, J. M. (1996). Research on the work experiences of lesbian, gay, and bisexual people: An integrative review of methodology and findings. *Journal of Vocational Behavior, 48,* 195–209.

Croteau, J. M., & Bieschke, K. J. (1996). Special issue on the vocational issues of lesbian women and gay men [Special issue]. *Journal of Vocational Behavior, 48*(2).

Croteau, J. M., Bieschke, K. J., Phillips, J. C., Lark, J. S., Fischer, A. R., & Eberz, A. B. (1998). Toward a more inclusive and diverse multi-generational community of LGB affirmative counseling psychologists. *The Counseling Psychologist, 26,* 809–816.

D'Augelli, A. R., & Patterson, C. J. (Eds.). (1995). *Lesbian, gay, and bisexual identities over the lifespan: Psychological perspectives.* New York: Oxford University Press.

DeLeon, P. H. (1993). Proceedings of the American Psychological Association, Incorporated, for the year 1992: Minutes of the annual meetings of the Council of Representatives. *American Psychologist, 48,* 745–788.

DeLeon, P. H. (1998). Proceedings of the American Psychological Association, Incorporated, for the year 1992: Minutes of the annual meetings of the Council of Representatives. *American Psychologist, 53,* 882–939.

Dworkin, S. H., & Gutierrez, C. J. (1989). Gay, lesbian, and bisexual issues in counseling [Special issue]. *Journal of Counseling and Development, 68*(1).

Eldridge, N. S., & Barnett, D. C. (1991). Counseling gay and lesbian students. In

N. J. Evans & V.A. Wall (Eds.), *Beyond tolerance: Gays, lesbians, and bisexuals on campus* (pp. 147–178). Alexandria, VA: American College Personnel Association.

Enns, C. Z. (1993). Twenty years of feminist counseling and therapy: From naming biases to implementing multifaceted practice. *The Counseling Psychologist, 21,* 3–87.

Firestein, B. A. (Ed.). (1996). *Bisexuality: The psychology and politics of an invisible minority.* Newbury Park, CA: Sage.

Flores, L. Y., O'Brien, K. M., & McDermott, D. (1995). *Counseling psychology trainees' perceived efficacy in counseling lesbian and gay clients.* Paper presented at the 103rd annual meeting of the American Psychological Association, New York.

Fox, R. C. (1996). Bisexuality in perspective: A review of theory and research. In B. A. Firestein (Ed.), *Bisexuality: The psychology and politics of an invisible minority* (pp. 3–50). Newbury Park, CA: Sage.

Garfinkle, E. M., & Morin, S. F. (1978). Psychologists' attitudes toward homosexual psychotherapy clients. *Journal of Social Issues, 34,* 101–112.

Garnets, L., Hancock, K. A., Cochran, S. D., Goodchilds, J., & Peplau, L. A. (1991). Issues in psychotherapy with lesbians and gay men: A survey of psychologists. *American Psychologist, 46,* 964–974.

Gilliland, B., & Crisp, D. (1995, August). *Homophobia: Assessing and changing attitudes of counselors-in-training.* Paper presented at the 103rd Annual Convention of the American Psychological Association, New York.

Glenn, A. A., & Russell, R. K. (1986). Heterosexual bias among counselor trainees. *Counselor Education and Supervision, 25,* 222–229.

Graham, D. L. R., Rawlings, E. I., Halpern, H. S., & Hermes, J. (1984). Therapists' need for training in counseling lesbians and gay men. *Professional Psychology: Research and Practice, 15,* 482–496.

Green, R.-J. (1996). Why ask, why tell? Teaching and learning about lesbians and gays in family therapy. *Family Process, 35,* 389–400.

Greene, B. (Ed.). (1997). *Ethnic and cultural diversity among lesbians and gay men.* Newbury Park, CA: Sage.

Hancock, K. (1995). Psychotherapy with lesbians and gay men. In A. R. D'Augelli & C. J. Patterson (Eds.), *Lesbian, gay, and bisexual identities over the lifespan: Psychological perspectives* (pp. 398–432). New York: Oxford University Press.

Harren, V. A. (1979). A model of career decision making for college students. *Journal of Vocational Behavior, 14,* 119–133.

Heppner, P. P. (1998). Lesbian, gay, and bisexual affirmative training [Special issue]. *The Counseling Psychologist, 26*(5).

Herek, G. M., Kimmel, D. C., Amaro, H., & Melton, G. B. (1991). Avoiding heterosexist bias in psychological research. *American Psychologist, 46,* 957–963.

Holahan, W., & Gibson, S. A. (1994). Heterosexual therapists leading lesbian and gay therapy groups: Therapeutic and political realities. *Journal of Counseling & Development, 72,* 591–594.

LaFromboise, T. D., Foster, S., & James, A. (1996). Ethics in multicultural counseling. In P. B. Pedersen, J. G. Draguns, W. J. Lonner, & J. E. Trimble (Eds.), *Counseling across cultures* (4th ed., pp. 47–72). Thousand Oaks, CA: Sage.

Laird, J., & Green, R.-J. (Eds.). (1996). *Lesbians and gays in couples and families: A handbook for therapists.* San Francisco: Jossey-Bass.

Lark, J. S., & Croteau, J. M. (1998). Lesbian, gay and bisexual doctoral students' mentoring relationships with faculty in counseling psychology: A qualitative study. *The Counseling Psychologist, 26,* 754–776.

Long, J. K. (1996). Working with lesbians, gays, and bisexuals: Addressing heterosexism in supervision. *Family Process, 35,* 377–388.

Matteson, D. R. (1996). Counseling and psychotherapy with bisexual and exploring clients. In B. A. Firestein (Ed.), *Bisexuality: The psychology and politics of an invisible minority* (pp. 185–213). Newbury Park, CA: Sage.

McClure, F. H., & Teyber, E. (Eds.). (1996). *Child and adolescent therapy: A multicultural relational approach.* San Diego, CA: Harcourt Brace Jovanovich.

McHenry, S. S., & Johnson, J. W. (1993). Homophobia in the therapist and gay or lesbian client: Conscious and unconscious collusions in self-hate. *Psychotherapy, 30,* 141–151.

Morgan, K. S., & Brown, L. S. (1991). Lesbian career development, work behavior, and vocational counseling. *The Counseling Psychologist, 19,* 273–291.

Morin, S. F., & Charles, K. A. (1983). Heterosexual issues in psychotherapy? In J. Murray and P. R. Abramson (Eds.), *Bias in psychotherapy* (pp. 309–338). New York: Praeger.

Moss, J. F. (1995, August). *Gay, lesbian, and bisexual clients' perceptions of bias in psychotherapy.* Paper presented at the 103rd Annual Convention of the American Psychological Association, New York.

Murphy, B. C. (1992). Educating mental health professionals about gay and lesbian issues. *Journal of Homosexuality, 22,* 229–246.

Norton, J. L. (1982). Integrating gay issues into counselor education. *Counselor Education and Supervision, 21,* 208–212.

Orzek, A. M. (1992). Career counseling for the gay and lesbian community. In S. H. Dworkin & F. J. Gutierrez (Eds.), *Counseling gay men and lesbians: Journey to the end of the rainbow* (pp. 23–33). Alexandria, VA: American Association for Counseling and Development.

Phillips, J. C., & Fisher, A. R. (1998). Graduate students' training experiences with gay, lesbian, and bisexual issues. *The Counseling Psychologist, 26,* 712–734.

Pilkington, N. W., & Cantor, J. M. (1996). Perceptions of heterosexual bias in professional psychology programs: A survey of graduate students. *Professional Psychology: Research and Practice, 27,* 604–612.

Russell, G. M., & Greenhouse, E. M. (1997). Homophobia in the supervisory relationship: An invisible intruder. *Psychoanalytic Review, 84,* 27–42.

Rust, P. (1996a). Managing multiple identities: Diversity among bisexual women and men. In B. A. Firestein (Ed.), *Bisexuality: The psychology and politics of an invisible minority* (pp. 53–83). Newbury Park, CA: Sage.

Rust, P. (1996b). Monogamy and polyamory: Relationship issues for bisexuals. In B. A. Firestein (Ed.), *Bisexuality: The psychology and politics of an invisible minority* (pp. 127–148). Newbury Park, CA: Sage.

Saghir, M., & Robins, E. (1973). *Male and female homosexuality: A comprehensive investigation.* Baltimore: Williams & Wilkins.

Stein, T. S., & Burg, B. K. (1996). Teaching in mental health training programs about homosexuality, lesbians, gay men, and bisexuals. In R. P. Cabaj & T. S. Stein (Eds.), *Textbook of homosexuality and mental health* (pp. 621–631). Washington, DC: American Psychiatric Press.

Stone, G. L. (1991). Counseling lesbian women and gay men [Special issue]. *The Counseling Psychologist, 19*(2).

Thompson, G. H., & Fishburn, W. R. (1977). Attitudes toward homosexuality among graduate counseling students. *Counselor Education and Supervision, 17,* 121–130.

Worrell, J., & Remer, P. (1992). *Feminist perspectives in therapy: An empowerment model for women.* Chichester, England: Wiley.

15

PSYCHOEDUCATIONAL PROGRAMMING: CREATING A CONTEXT OF MENTAL HEALTH FOR PEOPLE WHO ARE LESBIAN, GAY, OR BISEXUAL

BARRY A. SCHREIER AND DONALD L. WERDEN

The effects of attitudes and practices that tend to omit, exclude, over-look, or misrepresent lesbian, gay, and bisexual (LGB) people are evidenced in the presenting problems of many LGB clients (Albee, 1995; Uribe & Harbeck, 1991). These problems include (a) feeling disconnected from a sense of identity and community, (b) depression stemming from self-hate or feelings of failure for being someone who is less than societally ideal, and (c) high levels of fear or emotional flatness resulting from having to hide and change one's natural sense of self (Browning, Reynolds, & Dworkin, 1991; Shannon & Woods, 1991).

Service delivery options typically available to mental health providers include individual, group, and couples counseling approaches (see chapters 7, 8, and 12, this volume, respectively). As is indicated in many of the preceding chapters, working with LGB clients can be developmentally enriching for both client and therapist (Silverstein, 1991). Despite the benefits to be gained from traditional forms of service delivery, some LGB clients may continue to feel marginalized in these contexts and shy away from mental health services because they find them as stifling as the dominant culture in which they live (Greene, 1994; Liddle, 1996). To compensate for these problems, alternative forms of service delivery need to be designed to reach individuals who are not currently using counseling services and would like to do so. Furthermore, the extant alternative interventions should be improved in terms of their usefulness, advocacy, and effectiveness (Mazumdar, 1992).

This chapter consists of a discussion of psychoeducational programming (herein referred to as *programming*), which we consider an integral component in the effective delivery of mental health services (Drum & Figler, 1973; Ivey & Authier, 1978). The following issues regarding the use of programming to deliver broadly defined mental health services are included: (a) efficacy of psychoeducational and preventive programming, (b) theoretical bases for effective programming, (c) creative programming ideas, (d) programming marketing tools, and (e) measuring programming efficacy.

DEFINITION OF TERMS

The terms *outreach*, *prevention*, and *programming* are often used interchangeably and, in general, suggest mental health services that are provided "outside" the confines of the mental health center (Croteau & Tinsley, 1984). The term *outreach* is often used in social work and community psychology to denote community interventions by indigenous outreach workers for the purpose of altering environmental conditions. These interventions are designed to decrease mental health problems (Garnets & D'Augelli, 1994) and maladaptive behaviors (Booth & Koester, 1996; Kelly, Murphy, Sikkema, & Kalichman, 1993; Singer & Marxuach-Rodriquez, 1996). In university counseling centers, outreach is likely to be defined as "any organized program, workshop, media effort, class, or systematic attempt to provide psychological education [that also] includes systematic attempts to modify the campus environment" (Stone & Archer, 1990, p. 557). In this chapter, *outreach* is defined as any purposeful intervention, conducted outside the office setting, that attempts to impart information to modify a specific psychological environment.

The term *prevention* refers to efforts designed to promote health and counteract risk factors proactively (Coie et al., 1993; Price, Cowen, Lorion, & Ramos-McKay, 1988). The intention of prevention programs is to build adaptive strengths in the healthy or at-risk consumer before a problem has manifested (Albee & Gullotta, 1997).

The term *programming* has been defined as service delivery that provides cognitively oriented information and experiences that lead to improvement in an individual's mental health or to the acquisition of psychological knowledge or skill (Watkins, 1985). Programs can be designed to address flexibly the person–environment interaction and to promote intrapsychic solutions to problems. According to Cowen (1984) and Drum (1984), well-designed programs are (a) targeted toward specific participants and needs; (b) designed to assist participants in achieving a consistent, congruent, and positive sense of self; (c) time limited (Watkins, 1985); (d) facilitated by designated individuals; and (e) evaluated for effectiveness (Schreier, 1995).

A synthesis of the previous definitions is germane to create a suitable framework for discussion that encompasses the breadth and depth of programming. Programming is defined, therefore, as any proactive, remedial, or early-intervention outreach effort that is cognitively oriented and time limited and is designed to enhance intrapsychic change, modify the interpersonal–social context, and create systemwide enhancement of the mental health of a targeted population.

EFFICACY OF PSYCHOEDUCATIONAL AND PREVENTIVE PROGRAMMING

Efficacy research on programming designed to address issues faced by LGB individuals is scarce. Garnets and D'Augelli (1994) issued a strong call to community psychologists to "confront their silence about working with lesbians and gay men" (p. 464). Rotheram-Borus and Fernandez (1995) drew attention to the fact that "community-level interventions that attempt to increase society's acceptance of homosexuality and of homosexual young people are desperately needed" (p. 32). A review of psychological abstracts between 1990 and 1998 revealed that more than 80% of articles concerning programming with LGB populations addressed only the needs of gay men who are positive for the human immunodeficiency virus (HIV) and the societal perceptions of gay men who are HIV positive. Whereas this literature highlights the effectiveness of efforts to reduce the incidence of HIV and the acquired immunodeficiency syndrome (AIDS) in the LGB community (House & Walker, 1993; Icard, Schilling, El-Bassel, & Young, 1992; Kegeles, Hays, & Coates, 1996), specific design or implementation models of outreach programming not addressing HIV/AIDS are underrepresented in the literature. As such, this review of the efficacy of programming emphasizes the literature on HIV/AIDS programming and programming in general.

During the past 2 decades, prevention programming has been shown to be effective in increasing knowledge about HIV/AIDS and decreasing involvement in risky behaviors in specific populations (Brand, Lakey, &

Berman, 1995; House & Walker, 1993; Marx, Franks, Kahn, Haynes Stansted, & Werdegar, 1997). The use of peer educators and of cognitive–behavioral interventions has been effective in maintaining behavioral change over time (Kegeles et al., 1996; Kelly, St. Lawrence, & Hood, 1989; Stevens, 1994; St. Lawrence, Brasfield, & Jefferson, 1995). The success of many HIV/AIDS interventions has encouraged the continued refinement of HIV/AIDS programming and has inspired more research (Kelly et al., 1993; O'Keefe, Nesselhof-Kendall, & Baum, 1990).

The effectiveness of non-HIV/AIDS programming has also been consistently supported, as demonstrated by the results of meta-analyses (Durlak & Wells, 1997; Lipsey & Wilson, 1993). A meta-analysis is a method for combining the results of a number of related studies to determine the overall effectiveness of interventions. Treatment effects from each study, reported as mean scores, are combined, averaged, and standardized into standard deviation units to produce a grand mean treatment effect score. Durlak and Wells (1997) conducted a meta-analytic review of 177 primary prevention programs for children and adolescents and determined that treatment participants performed between 59% and 82% better than control group participants.

In a meta-analytic review of 302 psychological, behavioral, and educational interventions, Lipsey and Wilson (1993) calculated a grand mean treatment effect of 0.50 (SD = 0.29), suggesting that treatment interventions were 67% more effective in producing positive change than were control group activities. Lipsey and Wilson refined their review by dropping 146 studies to avoid the introduction of potential bias from methodological flaws. They then found a grand mean treatment effect of 0.47 (SD = 0.28). Grand mean scores for analyses focusing on psychoeducational treatments and primary preventions ranged from 0.30 to 1.51, supporting the contention that programming and prevention efforts are effective service delivery alternatives. Although these studies did not review interventions and programs for LGB people, the positive results reported can be extrapolated to encourage more research and the development of programming to address LGB needs and concerns. The following theoretical underpinnings of program development can stimulate thinking along these lines.

THEORETICAL BASES FOR EFFECTIVE PSYCHOEDUCATIONAL PROGRAMMING

The foundation of effective programming lies in grounding programming in strong theoretical bases. The following section covers three areas of programming theory. This overview discusses how to target programming, how to increase the level of attitude and belief change, and how to include emotionality in programming.

Program Development

It is important to direct programming toward the modification of intolerant environments and of the attitudes and beliefs that perpetuate the intolerance (Schreier, 1995). However, focusing programming on a context of intolerance raises this question: For whom should programming be developed? Ideally, programming is most effective when it assists both victims and perpetrators, regardless of the participants' sexual–affectional identities. Psychotherapeutic healing and growth is as much the result of contextual change as of individual change (McNamara & Rickard, 1989).

Programs addressing intolerance can offer a number of opportunities to change negative attitudes and beliefs. Furthermore, effective programs challenge individuals to explore how such beliefs limit their own personal growth and self-awareness. For instance, LBG individuals who are anxious about their identities (see Reynolds and Hanjorgiris, chapter 2, this volume, and Rothblum, chapter 3, this volume) could readily benefit from self-empowerment and self-nurturance programming (Brand et al., 1995; Garnets & D'Augelli, 1994).

Whereas it is important to develop programming to meet the needs of specific participants, such programming should not alienate participants for whom the programming is not specifically designed. Developing programming to meet a broad range of demands can be difficult. The core conditions of counseling (Ivey, Ivey, & Simek-Downing, 1987; Rogers, 1951) must be met: Program participants must feel respected, heard, and nurtured to derive benefits from the program. Didactic interventions and participatory experiences contribute to the effectiveness of such a program (Drum, 1984).

It is incumbent on programmers to develop programming that is inclusive of the needs of LGB communities and that accounts for the diversity within these communities. Programmers should look beyond developing programming based solely on sexual orientation, because LGB people vary in race, sex, age, and other characteristics. These demographic factors influence the experiences of LGB people within LGB communities and thus affect programming considerations. Croteau, Nero, and Prosser (1993) stressed the importance of considering the social and cultural group contexts of program participants before the development and implementation of programming. People who are gay and African American commonly face degrees of intolerance that people who are gay and White do not (Croteau et al., 1993). Race and ethnicity can influence how an individual values his or her LGB identity. For instance, gay men who are African American and gay men who are White are both gay, but they may view their experiences of being gay differently on the basis of racial identity. This difference may be exacerbated by the fact that gay male communities are viewed as predominantly White (Icard et al., 1992). The negative impact of White privilege (McIntosh, 1998) and sexual racism (Greene, 1994) are obvious even within a gay context. The dynamic interplay between racial or ethnic identity and LGB identity can also be difficult because of the conflicts between values that are predominant in different cultural groups. This is especially true for values concerning procreation, continuation of family lines, religiosity, maintaining ties to ethnic background, degree of acculturation and assimilation, and history of ethnic-group oppression (Greene, 1994; Russell & Quirolgico, 1997). In addition, people who are bisexual experience being part of the nonheterosexual communities differently from those who are gay or lesbian (Morales, 1990; Supple, 1984). Bisexuals are often rejected from the gay and lesbian communities, as they are from the heterosexual communities, because of biphobia (Schreier, 1997).

When designing effective programming, awareness of participants' needs and characteristics is imperative for creating the best fit between the goals of the program and participants' needs. Programs that are designed to improve the lives of LGB people must include people who perpetuate intolerance and those who suffer from it. Therefore, programmers must be familiar with a wide variety of personal characteristics that are typical of the audiences they will be addressing. Initially, it might appear difficult to develop programming to bridge the differences between LGB participants and homophobic–biphobic participants. A model of nurturance provides an effective approach for dealing with the needs of such a diverse population of potential participants (Schreier, 1995).

Model of Nurturance

Nurturance is defined as a state of being that allows, accepts, and encourages someone or something (Whitehead & Nokes, 1990). Tolerance merely allows; it lacks the dimensions of acceptance and encouragement (Stevenson, 1989). The constructs of tolerance and nurturance often reflect the attitudes that programmers have toward program participants. These constructs also guide program developers as they set the focus of a specific program (Schreier, 1995).

Programs based on a tolerance model usually are constructed for audiences that contain members who do not affirm LGB people. Schreier (1995) suggested that a tolerance model (a) induces shame and awareness of the negative consequences of intolerance, (b) provides limits and rules about what behaviors are and are not acceptable, (c) operates on the assumption that individuals are resistant to new ideas, and (d) assumes that having to deal with LGB people is a necessary evil. Most programmers tend to model tolerant behaviors. Tolerance was the priority of D'Augelli and Rose (1990) when they called for interventions to erase homophobic–biphobic activity on college campuses by communicating the negative consequences of discrimination. Iasenza and Troutt (1990) suggested that programs should encourage potential perpetrators of intolerance to examine and articulate the prejudices, stereotypes, cultural similarities and differences, homophobic–biphobic attitudes, and heterosexist beliefs that affect their lives. This type of programming is not to be discouraged because it serves an important purpose in encouraging participants not to become perpetrators of acts of intolerance. However, it is important to recognize that the effects of tolerance-based programming may be limited because it focuses on only one part of the population affected by these attitudes and beliefs. A programming model based on nurturance may be more productive because it is simultaneously directed toward LGB people and heterosexuals (Schreier, 1995).

Programmers address the broader population by providing participants with alternative attitudes that allow them to view LGB people positively. For example, programmers can explain ways in which LGB people can be empowered. Programmers also can introduce ways in which LGB people and heterosexuals can facilitate empowerment in others (Cranston, 1991). Although such efforts are typically focused on ideal goals, they can have, at the very least, the important effect of raising awareness. Whereas heterosexuals gain knowledge and may become LGB advocates, LGB people benefit by stimulating their own empowerment through self-advocacy. Programming must create opportunities for LGB people to feel empowered, to recognize their vital role in the community, and to feel supported (Body, 1986).

Programmers should attempt to foster the excitement and the interest of participants to meet the multiple goals of raising awareness, facilitating attitudinal change, and fostering environmental change. A nurturance model recognizes that participants are curious, experimental, and often open to new ideas presented in genuine and nonadversarial ways. Multiple characteristics of LGB people can be included and affirmed. For instance, programming should be developed that explores the experiences of having multiple identities (e.g., an LGB identity and a racial-minority identity). Such a program can be inclusive of all racial–ethnic groups and sexual–affectional orientations. It is the dynamic of nurturance that makes the difference, and nurturance can be used to bridge any number of defining characteristics.

Finally, programmers may feel pressed to develop special programming exclusively for LGB people because they are typically excluded by society. Special programming would not be necessary if programmers would incorporate nurturing references to LGBs into all programming. Following is a list of some of the elements involved in using a nurturance model in program development:

- *Nonheterosexist language.* Use affirming, nonheterosexist language for discussing everyday examples, such as: "Dating is a concern whether we are talking about men dating women,

men dating men, or women dating women." "This example is about Bill and Mark, who have been together for 10 years."

- *Statements of inclusion.* Include statements in advertising materials that all people are welcome. Make the statements inclusive of race, creed, color, sexual–affectional identity, gender, age, social class, religious or spiritual affiliation, physical ability, veteran status, familial status, ancestry, and so on.

- *Bibliographies.* When providing lists for further reading, include titles focused on LGB people. Make these publications as openly available as other publications (Geller, 1991).

- *Confrontation of defamatory humor.* Actively question the use of any defamatory humor that occurs during programs.

- *Reporting.* Report all homophobic–biphobic and gay-bashing activities that you see, hear, or reasonably suspect to local authorities who are responsible for tracking and responding to hate crimes.

- *Information.* Use programming opportunities to provide information on activities, support groups, and social events for LGB people and their allies. Provide referral information for individuals who are dealing with coming out issues or with homophobic–biphobic attitudes and heterosexist beliefs.

- *Displays of pride.* Purchase a button that affirms LGB pride and wear it during the program, or display other outward signs of affirmation.

- *Movies.* If movies or videos are used, use ones that are about LGB people.

- *Resource lists.* Have resource lists available that include LGB-affirmative counseling services, advocacy agencies, community organizations, reading materials, social and political organizations, civil rights groups, and local business establishments.

- *Laws, by-laws, and ordinances.* Learn about city, state, federal, and institutional ordinances and laws concerning the civil rights of LGB people. Have copies of these readily available for participants.

- *Addressing personal attitudes and beliefs.* Address your own homophobic–biphobic attitudes and heterosexist beliefs. Read about LGB lives. Attend workshops and seminars sponsored by a university or by local communities. Attend local LGB university or community events. Obtain personal counseling concerning any of these issues if you feel they impair your ability to promote a message of nurturance.

Each recommendation can assist programmers in creating a positive atmosphere where LGB people are consistently valued, thereby fostering for them a therapeutic context. The goal, of course, is to create programming that builds a bridge between divergent participants. Programmers must maintain beliefs that communicate and model nurturance to all participants. The beliefs and attitudes of participants, however, must be directly considered when developing effective programming. Schreier (1995) and Drum (1984) suggested that designing programs to provide opportunities for participants to access their emotions is one means of facilitating the growth experience. For this reason, programmers are encouraged to provide opportunities for participants to examine the full range of their emotions about LGBs.

Accessing Emotionality

Programming is often geared toward presenting information or engaging participants at a cognitive level (i.e., accessing beliefs and attitudes; Drum, 1984; Watkins, 1985). However, emotions affect the attitude change process by influencing what information is attended to, encoded, and retrieved (Eagley & Chaiken, 1993). Homophobic–biphobic attitudes and heterosexist beliefs are most effectively changed when there is exposure to and interaction with LGB people (Burkholder & Dineen, 1996). When LGB people share information about themselves and their experiences, heterosexuals have opportunities to gain firsthand experiences with LGB people and potentially to dispel their negative stereotypes (Garnets & D'Augelli, 1994).

Fear and anxiety are emotions that are closely linked with homophobic–biphobic beliefs and heterosexist attitudes, because heterosexual self-concepts can be challenged by the presence of LGB people (Kruks, 1991; Lewes, 1992; Meisenhelder, 1994; Slater, 1993; Stein, 1996). The relative importance of attitudes and beliefs is noteworthy because they are intrinsic to the self-concept; assuage the psychological needs for consistency, predictability, and security; and defend against chaos, threat, and dysfunction (Simoni, 1996). A sense of harmony is highly valued by most individuals. As a result, beliefs and attitudes are fairly resistant to change (Quackenbush, 1989).

Programming designed to change beliefs or to provide safety for exploring sexual–affectional identity requires interventions that go beyond the dissemination of information, exercises that are cognitively based, or exposure to LGB people. The emotional component of attitudes and beliefs can be directly addressed to inspire lasting changes. The appeal for emotional transformation can take varied forms such as (a) eliciting feelings of self-dissatisfaction concerning a given attitude or belief (Rokeach, 1984), (b) appealing to the commonality of emotional experiences and of natural curiosity (Schreier, 1995), (c) presenting information that suggests that more positive emotional experiences result from adopting new attitudes or beliefs (Abelson, 1986), and (d) demonstrating the emotional dysfunctionality of targeted attitudes or beliefs (Ajzen & Fishbein, 1980).

We suggest that programmers direct their efforts toward meeting the needs of specific participants, use an inclusive model of nurturance, consider participants' social and cultural group contexts, and address the emotional experiences that participants associate with their beliefs and attitudes. The challenge is to develop the programming that includes these factors and delivers service to LGB people.

CREATIVE PSYCHOEDUCATIONAL PROGRAMMING IDEAS

With several theories delineated for developing effective programming to assist LGB people, it is important to provide examples that address the challenge of putting theory into practice. Readers are encouraged to use the following exercises as a starting point for creating their own programming ideas.

Exercise 1: Walk a Mile in My Shoes

People who have never experienced the coming out process often misunderstand it (Muchmore & Hanson, 1991). The coming out process may be denigrated by some who feel they do not want to come out because their sexual–affectional identity is no one else's business or it is only one part of their life (Rotheram-Borus & Fernandez, 1995). The process can be especially difficult for LGB people of color because of the possibility of experiencing racism within the LGB community (Garnets & D'Augelli, 1994; Greene, 1994; Icard et al., 1992). Research indicates that individuals are more congruent in their self-concepts if they come out to important others and are supported in the process (Muchmore & Hanson, 1991). However, coming out can result in the loss of significant relationships (Berzon, 1992; Fairchild, 1992) and the deterioration of critical aspects of everyday life such as mental and physical health (Browning et al., 1991; Shannon & Woods, 1991), social affiliations (Fassinger, 1991; Rotheram-Borus & Fernandez, 1995), career position (McNaught, 1992), and financial standing (Link & Coleman, 1992). Therefore, it may be important to focus on the emotionality underlying the process of coming out. In addition, the emotional experiences of loss associated with coming out include loss of heterosexual privilege, change in family status, rejection by friends and family, loss of safety, and absence of positive role models (Muchmore & Hanson, 1991; Rotheram-Borus & Fernandez, 1995).

Most individuals in society, whether LGB or heterosexual, have experienced loss in one form or another. Consideration of the coming out process provides a chance to demonstrate that not everyone experiences overwhelming loss during the process and that, in fact, many individuals have positive coming out experiences. This approach allows for a model of nurturance to be introduced that demonstrates the benefits of coming out and the importance of being an ally to those coming out. The following single-session exercise offers participants a chance to connect with each other over the common emotional experience of loss.

This exercise can be used as a starting point for discussion within community-based support groups (i.e., Parents, Families, and Friends of Lesbians and Gays). When presenting this exercise, one can discuss the universality of loss and the types of loss LGB people might experience when coming out. It is vital to process this exercise emotionally and intellectually with participants so that they have an empathic understanding of the effects of homophobic–biphobic attitudes and heterosexist beliefs. The exercise takes about 1 hour.

Preparing Stage

Ask all participants to tear white sheets of paper into 16 equal-sized pieces. Ask them to divide these pieces into four piles categorized as "people," "roles" (e.g., parent, son, daughter, student), "possessions," and "activities."

Personalizing Stage

Ask participants to write down the following on the separate pieces of paper: the names of four people they care about, four life roles, four possessions, and four activities that are special and central to their current lives.

Experiencing Stage

Explain that loss can come in many forms and that the first form of loss is predictable loss. Explain that as one is coming out, one can often guess how, when, and where losses will occur. Ask participants to look at their piles and pick one piece of paper from each pile that names something or someone they could do without. Instruct them to crumple the four pieces of paper and to throw them to the floor.

Explain that another form of loss is loss that is somewhat predictable, in that one knows loss is going to occur, but is unpredictable concerning which areas of life the loss will affect. With the piles still separate, ask participants now to turn their papers over so they cannot see what is written on them. Tell them to pick one paper from each group and to crumple it and throw it to the floor without looking at it. Ask participants not to turn the remaining pieces over.

Explain that loss also can be completely unpredictable and that even though one feels protected from loss, one can quite easily become vulnerable. Explain that when people feel that they have sustained all the loss they can, there comes more loss. Some get lucky and have little or no loss; others are unfortunate and lose everything. Finally, explain that people act on their homophobic–biphobic attitudes and heterosexist beliefs in a manner that is unaware of the devastation it creates. Move among participants and take their remaining papers according to the types of loss being discussed. From some take all, from some take a few, and from some take nothing. Return to any individual who has not lost anything, and take everything. When taking papers from participants, crumple them and throw them onto the floor.

Processing Stage

Process participants' reactions to help them understand how their emotional experiences may match the emotional experience of coming out. Open the discussion for questions before ending the exercise.

This exercise exposes individuals to the possibility of loss that can be associated with coming out. It provides didactic material and experiential examples of loss to facilitate the connection with emotionality that is necessary to create attitude change (Eagley & Chaiken, 1993).

Exercise 2: We Are Not Alone

LGB people struggle with many diverse issues as they arrive at an understanding and affirmation of their sexual–affectional identity. Issues encountered by LGB people of color compound those struggles as they reconcile multiple identities (Garnets & D'Augelli, 1994). Heterosexuals may experience conflict and confusion when they try to understand and relate to the process of coming out or when people they know come out to them. A breakthrough point occurs in the acceptance of LGB sexual–affectional orientation when people are able to reattribute their homophobic–biphobic attitudes and heterosexist beliefs that they had previously introjected (Lima, Lo Presto, & Sherman, 1993). This process fosters the ability to place these attitudes and beliefs into the larger social context rather than having them maintained as an injurious part of the self-concept (Moss, 1992).

The following exercise is modeled after programming by Weiss and Orysh (1994) and Howard-Hamilton, Ferguson, Rolle, and Alexander (1997). This program is based on an all-day retreat model that encourages follow-up support and therapy group options. Under the model of nurturance, facilitators need to decide beforehand how heterosexuals can be included.

Icebreaker

Give all participants a list of personal qualities. Group members mingle with each other and discover who is described by the qualities. For instance, qualities can include "Is taller than father," and "Is out to parents." Participants keep track of who possesses what qualities. After all blanks are completed, participants discuss collectively the information about each other they found interesting or unique.

Life Story Drawings

Invite participants individually to come to a board and draw pictures that depict their life stories from the time they first had feelings, ideas, or perceptions that they were lesbian, gay, or bisexual. After all participants have drawn their stories, break up into small groups to discuss participants' stories and their current feelings about how their sexual–affectional identities resulted from the experiences they related in the drawings. Subsequently, engage participants in a discussion about their beliefs and attitudes about themselves, their sexual–affectional identities, their emotionality, and the connections among these factors.

Self-Perception Cookies

Provide participants with two large gingerbread cookies (or drawings of same) and assorted pieces of fabric, colored markers, yarn, glue, and tape. Ask participants to dress up each cookie. The first is to be dressed as participants see themselves. The second is to be dressed as participants think society-at-large sees them. Break into small groups to discuss the disparities and similarities that participants see between their two figures and between others' two figures. Discuss the fact that their figures represent how participants want to be and how they think they should be to be congruent with societal beliefs and attitudes.

Lavender Bingo

Give participants a bingo sheet that has 20 items related to LGB culture. Call out information that is related to items on the bingo cards, and ask participants to mark the items off accordingly. Participants have to know facts about the items to mark them. In this way, participants are able to validate what they know about LGB culture or to learn new things. For instance, for the item "Barney Frank," the facilitator might say, "The first openly gay U.S. congressperson to be elected." When someone obtains bingo, the winning participant must call off and explain each item marked.

Quilting Identity and Roles

Give participants a drawing of a quilt made up of blank panels and several threads that run the length of the quilt. Instruct participants to fill in the panels so that each panel represents an aspect of their lives. Mention that some aspects of their lives are more than just parts and instead run the length of their lives. Direct participants to fill in the threads with aspects of their lives that represent more than a panel. Break into small groups to discuss how participants filled in their quilts. Encourage participants to discuss where on their quilts they have portrayed their sexual–affectional identities. Encourage participants to discuss the various quilt designs as well as the placement and depictions of sexual–affectional identity.

Are You or Aren't You?

Give participants a face-down card that reads either "gay," "lesbian," "bisexual," or "heterosexual." Participants interact in dyads by discussing imaginary weekend activities they participated in, assuming the identities indicated on the cards. The primary rule of this activity is that participants cannot share the sex or the name of any significant other with whom they shared their weekend. Participants mingle and have one-to-one conversations with others in 2-minute rounds. In each round, participants note the names of each person with whom they talk, the sexual–affectional identity they thought each person had, and the reasons for their decisions. After several rounds, assemble the group and record this information on the board. Lead a discussion about how stereotypes and faulty beliefs influence interpersonal interactions.

Final Discussion and Wrap-Up

In addressing participants' newfound understandings about LGB people, the final discussion can focus on several issues including (a) what participants discovered about their own beliefs and attitudes, (b) how their beliefs and attitudes affect others, (c) what changes they perceive in their beliefs and attitudes as a result of the experience, (d) how their beliefs and attitudes influence how out they are and to whom they are out, (e) how they respond to others who have come out to them, and (f) what changes participants will make in their lives as a result of the program.

At this point, participants can be invited to join follow-up support or therapy groups for further exploration of sexual–affectional identity issues. Participants can be encouraged to organize a follow-up retreat or to organize as a group to plan other activities (e.g., social or political activities).

These retreat exercises are designed to assist participants in understanding and affirming LGB sexual–affectional identity. They can be used individually or collectively. Each exercise challenges misconceptions, misinformation, and maladaptive attitudes and beliefs through thoughtful discussion and meaningful experience.

MARKETING PSYCHOEDUCATIONAL PROGRAMMING

Although a theoretical understanding of programming is critical to program effectiveness, a program is worthless if no one attends (Schreier & Bialk, 1997; Williams, 1998). The effort to provide creative, innovative, and effective programs is regularly challenged by the necessity of getting participants to attend (Trice, Desio, & Haire, 1989; Wittmann, 1988). A solution to this common problem involves adding basic marketing strategies to programmers' expertise (Gilchrist & Stringer, 1992). Some of the elements that contribute to effective marketing follow, including suggestions for advertising and establishing contacts to disseminate information in major community areas.

Mental Health Agencies and Managed Care Providers

Contact the people responsible for distribution of promotional materials within several mental health agencies. Provide a day of free sample programming for these agencies and follow up by distributing weekly program announcements to agency staff members. Meet with managed care providers in an attempt to become a service provider and to inform them of the economic viability of programming (Kagan, Kagan, & Watson, 1995). These actions stimulate community awareness and encourage mental health agencies to advertise available programming. Such efforts also generate invitations to do in-house programming. Finally, these actions provide a connection with mental health agencies and managed care systems that can result in referrals.

Other Health Professionals

Send flyers to other professionals that describe programs and related information (i.e., referral information and costs). Contact those who can engage in joint programming efforts. If fees are charged, offer discounts to clients who are referred by other professionals. Also, encourage in-house referrals from colleagues. These actions can help coordinate programming activities of various professionals by fostering multiprofessional coalitions. These actions also multiply marketing resources and provide programming information directly to referral sources.

Lesbian, Gay, and Bisexual Referral Sources

List program information with LGB networks (e.g., event calendars, community newspapers, bulletin boards in local establishments, signs at major events). Distribute programming announcements to LGB social, political, civil, and religious organizations. Get listed in LGB publications as a service provider with specialization in working with these communities. These actions create greater community awareness of program offerings by accessing existing LGB networks and by targeting specific programs to identifiable groups (e.g., a program on body image offered to a lesbian athletics group or a program on race relations targeted to an LGB civil rights group; Paul & Crego, 1979).

Media

List workshops in all community weekly or daily publications (e.g., free calendars of ongoing events), and work with the organizers of these publications to run feature stories on program offerings. List programs on LGB electronic billboards. Distribute announcements of future programming to attendees at each program. Make use of existing, free, and highly accessed advertising venues such as the Internet, printed media, and word-of-mouth promotion.

EVALUATING PSYCHOEDUCATIONAL PROGRAMMING

Measures of programming efficacy should achieve two primary goals (Cowen, 1984; Drum, 1984; Posavac & Carey, 1992). The first is validating the extent to which intended outcomes were obtained. The second is identifying what elements of the program contributed to the achievement of intended outcomes. For instance, an evaluation instrument could assess whether homophobic–biphobic attitudes and heterosexist beliefs changed and what aspects of the program contributed to those changes. These factors can be assessed at the individual and system levels (Johnson, 1997).

On an individual level, variables that can be measured to determine successful outcomes include (a) programmer style, (b) fit between goals and methods used to achieve the goals, (c) clarity about the objectives stated and used, and (d) degree of fit between participants' perceived needs and the goals and objectives of the program (Antonowicz & Ross, 1994). Feedback derived from individual participant needs is necessary for an understanding of the impact of the intervention and of the future refinement of the program (Drum, 1984). Multiple measures should be taken to assess information such as (a) opportunities for participants to interact, (b) degree to which specific questions were addressed, (c) acquisition of new information, and (d) level of respect felt by the participants as a function of the program's content and the programmer's leadership style.

On a systemic level, Johnson (1997) recommended that programmers assess the program's impact on the greater system (i.e., impact of programming on policies, procedures, and incidents of homophobia and biphobia). The efficacy of programming in reducing homophobic–biphobic attitudes and heterosexist beliefs in the workplace can be measured by evaluating changes in workplace policy regarding inclusiveness of LGB people. It also can be measured by tracking reductions in homophobic-based incidents in the workplace.

Self-report measures can be highly effective in measuring pre- and postprogramming attitudes and beliefs and the overall satisfaction with the program (Lennon, Maloney, Miller, Wright, & Chambliss, 1997). The usefulness of self-report measures is clear when time, labor, and financial resources are limited. Self-report measures for assessing levels of homophobic–biphobic attitudes and heterosexist beliefs include the Modified Attitudes Toward Homosexuality Scale (J. H. Price, 1982), the Affective Reactions to Homosexuality Scale (Innala & Ernulf, 1987), and the Homophobic Behavior of Students Scale (Van de Ven, Bornholt, & Bailey, 1996). See Schwanberg (1993) for a listing and critique of each measure. It is recommended that pre- and posttest measures be taken in a nonequivalent control group matched on characteristics (i.e., sex, age, class) with program participants (Heppner, Kivlighan, & Wampold, 1992; Petitpas & Chapagne, 1988).

Finally, cost-effectiveness must be considered (Cronin, 1991). A cost–benefit ratio can be constructed by looking at (a) the costs of alternative approaches, (b) the benefits of such approaches, (c) the contrast between time spent and the number of participants reached, and (d) the growth in business as a result of services delivered (Pisapia, 1994).

CONCLUSION

Mental health professionals have many options at their disposal when deciding how best to provide mental health services to LGB or heterosexual people. Service provision can range from traditional counseling services to alternative forms of service provision, such as those delivered through programming.

Readers are encouraged to develop programs that are sensitive to the societal and cultural diversity inherent in their participants. Programming must focus on individuals who are the targets of homophobic–biphobic attitudes and heterosexist beliefs as well as those who internalize and externalize these attitudes and beliefs. Programming is most beneficial when it focuses on creating a nurturing environment (Schreier, 1995) and when it examines the full cognitive and emotional range of beliefs and attitudes about LGB people (Eagley & Chaiken, 1993).

Some mental health practitioners may decide not to use LGB programming because of the limited amount of research that has been conducted in this area. However, the effectiveness of programming is supported in the literature. Given the growing demand for mental health professionals to deliver more service with fewer resources, creative programming can effectively meet this demand. However, without further outcome research to validate empirically the efficacy of LGB programming, mental health practitioners may continue to shy away from effective modes of nontraditional service delivery. Clearly, there is a need for additional research on the use of programming in the mental health arena, its methods, and its efficacy (Garnets & D'Augelli, 1994).

There is one final consideration programmers must ponder regarding LGB issues. Given the potential volatility of these issues, programmers have to consider carefully the program's content. The programmer can become tokenized, either by a specific program audience or within the general community (Dillon, 1986). Individuals who are tokenized often are discounted, objectified, and seen as less able than individuals who are not tokenized (MacCorquodale & Jensen, 1993). The tokenized individual becomes "the gay–lesbian–bisexual spokesperson" when requests for programming occur, even when the person is not in that category. The potential volatility of LGB programming may lead others to shy away from programming, especially when a spokesperson has already been identified.

The American social environment is more nurturing toward LGB people now than it has ever been. This cultural shift is due, in part, to a general liberalization of beliefs and attitudes and to the dissipation of myths about the lives of LGB individuals. The breakdown of myths and misconceptions has occurred mostly because of the greater visibility of LGBs. However, many of these individuals continue to experience fear and intimidation from an intolerant society. Society continues to exert tight control on the comfort people have in being themselves and in sharing themselves with others. Programming, when effectively developed and sufficiently marketed, can lead to improvement in individuals' mental health. In doing this, the process of generating a more inclusive social context for LGB people can continue.

REFERENCES

Abelson, R. P. (1986). Beliefs are like possessions. *Journal for the Theory of Social Behaviour, 16,* 223–250.

Ajzen, I., & Fishbein, M. (1980). *Understanding attitudes and predicting social behavior.* Englewood Cliffs, NJ: Prentice-Hall.

Albee, G. (1995). Counselling and primary prevention. *Counselling Psychology Quarterly, 8,* 205–211.

Albee, G. W., & Gullotta, T. P. (1997). Primary prevention's evolution. In G. W. Albee & T. P. Gullotta (Eds.), *Primary prevention works* (pp. 3–22). Newbury Park, CA: Sage.

Antonowicz, D. H., & Ross, R. R. (1994). Essential components of successful rehabilitation programs for offenders. *International Journal of Offender Therapy and Comparative Criminology, 38,* 97–104.

Berzon, B. (1992). Telling the family you're gay. In B. Berzon (Ed.), *Positively gay: New approaches to gay and lesbian life* (pp. 67–78). Berkeley, CA: Celestial Arts.

Body, G. (1986). *The healthy community.* Workshop presented at the Northeast Lesbian and Gay Student Union Conference, Brown University, Providence, RI.

Booth, R. E., & Koester, S. K. (1996). Issues and approaches to evaluating HIV outreach interventions. *Journal of Drug Issues, 26,* 525–539.

Brand, E. F., Lakey, B., & Berman, S. (1995). A preventive, psychoeducational approach to increase perceived social support. *American Journal of Community Psychology, 23,* 117–135.

Browning, C., Reynolds, A. L., & Dworkin, S. H. (1991). Affirmative psychotherapy for lesbian women. *The Counseling Psychologist, 19,* 177–196.

Burkholder, G. J., & Dineen, A. (1996). Using panel presentations to increase awareness of experiences of gay, lesbian, and bisexual people. *Journal of College Student Development, 37,* 469–470.

Coie, J. D., Watt, N. F., West, S. G., Hawkins, J. D., Asarnow, J. R., Markman, H. J., Ramey, S. L., Shure, M. B., & Long B. (1993). The science of prevention: A conceptual framework and some direction for a national research program. *American Psychologist, 48,* 1013–1022.

Cowen, E. L. (1984). A general structural model for primary prevention program development in mental health. *The Personnel and Guidance Journal 62,* 485–490.

Cranston, K. (1991). HIV education for gays, lesbians, and bisexual youth: Personal risk, personal power, and the community of conscience. *Journal of Homosexuality, 22,* 247–259.

Cronin, C. (1991). Counseling center outreach: A guide to simple, inexpensive programming. *International Journal for the Advancement of Counselling, 14,* 253–261.

Croteau, J. M., Nero, C. I., & Prosser, D. J. (1993). Social and cultural sensitivity to group-specific HIV and AIDS programming. *Journal of Counseling and Development, 71,* 290–296.

Croteau, J. M., & Tinsley, D. J. (1984). Training paraprofessionals in programming: An experimental course incorporating developmental theory. *Journal of College Student Personnel, 25,* 553–554.

D'Augelli, A. R., & Rose, M. L. (1990). Homophobia in a university community: Attitudes and experiences of heterosexual freshmen. *Journal of College Student Development, 31,* 484–491.

Dillon, C. (1986). Preparing college health professionals to deliver gay-affirmative services. *Journal of American College Health, 35,* 546–552.

Drum, D. J. (1984). Implementing theme-focused prevention: A challenge for the 1980's. *The Personnel and Guidance Journal, 62,* 509–514.

Drum, D. J., & Figler, H. E. (1973). *Outreach in counseling*. Cranston, RI: Carroll Press.

Durlak, J. A., & Wells, A. W. (1997). Primary prevention mental health programs for children and adolescents: A meta-analytic review. *American Journal of Community Psychology, 25,* 115–152.

Eagley, A.H., & Chaiken, S. (1993). *The psychology of attitudes*. Orlando, FL: Harcourt Brace Jovanovich.

Fairchild, B. (1992). For parents of lesbians and gays. In B. Berzon (Ed.), *Positively gay: New approaches to gay and lesbian life* (pp. 67–90). Berkeley, CA: Celestial Arts.

Fassinger, R. E. (1991). The hidden minority: Issues and challenges in working with lesbian women and gay men. *The Counseling Psychologist, 19,* 157–176.

Garnets, L. D., & D'Augelli, A. R. (1994). Empowering lesbian and gay communities: A call for collaboration with community psychology. *American Journal of Community Psychology, 22,* 447–470.

Geller, W. W. (1991). Lesbian and gay topics: Awakening a campus. *Journal of College Student Development, 32,* 91–92.

Gilchrist, L. A., & Stringer, M. (1992). Marketing counseling: Guidelines for training and practice. *Counselor Education and Supervision, 31,* 155–161.

Greene, B. (1994). Ethnic-minority lesbians and gay men: Mental health and treatment issues. *Journal of Consulting and Clinical Psychology, 62,* 243–251.

Heppner, P. P., Kivlighan, D. M., & Wampold, B. E. (1992). *Research design in counseling*. Pacific Grove, CA: Brooks/Cole.

House, R. M., & Walker, C. M. (1993). Preventing AIDS via education. *Journal of Counseling and Development, 71,* 282–289.

Howard-Hamilton, M. F., Ferguson, A. D., Rolle, K., & Alexander, T. (1997). Border crossings: A black cultural retreat. *Journal of College Student Development, 38,* 307–308.

Iasenza, S., & Troutt, B. V. (1990). A training program to punish prejudicial attitudes in student leaders. *Journal of College Student Development, 31,* 83–84.

Icard, L. D., Schilling, R. F., El-Bassel, N., & Young, D. (1992). Preventing AIDS among Black gay men and Black gay and heterosexual male intravenous drug users. *Social Work, 37,* 440–445.

Innala, S. M., & Ernulf, K. E. (1987). The relationship between affective and cognitive components of homophobic reaction: Three cross-national replications. *Archives of Sexual Behavior* (16)6, 501–509.

Ivey, A. E., & Authier, J. (1978). *Microcounseling: Innovations in interviewing, counseling, psychotherapy, and psychoeducation*. Springfield, IL: Charles C Thomas.

Ivey, A. E., Ivey, M. B., & Simek-Downing, L. (1987). *Counseling and psychotherapy: Integrating skills, theory, and practice*. Englewood Cliffs, NJ: Prentice-Hall.

Johnson, E. P. (1997). *Manual: A practical guide for workplace educators*. (ERIC Document Reproduction Service No. ED 410 386)

Kagan, N. I., Kagan, H., & Watson, M. G. (1995). Stress reduction in the workplace: The effectiveness of psychoeducational programs. *Journal of Counseling Psychology, 42*, 71–78.

Kegeles, S. M., Hays, R. B., & Coates, T. J. (1996). The Mpowerment Project: A community-level HIV prevention intervention for young gay men. *American Journal of Public Health, 86*, 1129–1136.

Kelly, J. A., Murphy, D. A., Sikkema, K. J., & Kalichman, S. C. (1993). Psychological interventions to prevent HIV infection are urgently needed: New priorities for behavioral research in the second decade of AIDS. *American Psychologist, 48*, 1023–1034.

Kelly, J. A., St. Lawrence, J. S., & Hood, H. V. (1989). Behavioral intervention to reduce AIDS risk activities. *Journal of Consulting and Clinical Psychology, 57*, 60–67.

Kruks, G. (1991). Gay and lesbian homeless street youth: Special issues and concerns. *Journal of Adolescent Health, 12*, 515–518.

Lennon, L., Maloney, C., Miller, J., Wright, C., & Chambliss, C. (1997). *The challenges of evaluating formal parental programming.* (ERIC Document Reproduction Service No. ED 410 514)

Lewes, K. (1992). Homophobia and the heterosexual fear of AIDS. *American Imago, 49*, 343–356.

Liddle, B. J. (1996). Therapist sexual orientation, gender, and counseling practices as they relate to ratings of helpfulness by gay and lesbian clients. *Journal of Counseling Psychology, 43*, 394–401.

Lima, G., Lo Presto, C. T., & Sherman, M. F. (1993). The relationship between homophobia and self-esteem in gay males with AIDS. *Psychotherapy, 25*, 69–76.

Link, D., & Coleman, T. F. (1992). Job security in the workplace: Legal protections for lesbians and gay men. In B. Berzon (Ed.), *Positively gay: New approaches to gay and lesbian life* (pp. 171–182). Berkeley, CA: Celestial Arts.

Lipsey, M. W., & Wilson, D. B. (1993). The efficacy of psychological, educational, and behavioral treatment: Confirmation from meta-analysis. *American Psychologist, 48*, 1181–1209.

MacCorquodale, P., & Jensen, G. (1993). Women in the law: Partners or tokens? *Gender and Society, 7*, 582–593.

Marx, R., Franks, P. E., Kahn, J. G., Haynes Stansted, K. C., & Werdegar, D. (1997, Spring). HIV education and prevention in California: Problems and progress. *AIDS & Public Policy Journal, 12*, 31–45.

Mazumdar, S. (1992). HIV programming can be counterproductive: An analysis of approaches to programming. *Journal of Environmental Psychology, 12*, 65–91.

McIntosh, P. (1998). White privilege: Unpacking the invisible knapsack. In M. McGoldrick (Ed.), *Re-visioning family therapy: Race, culture, and gender in clinical practice* (pp. 147–152). New York: Guilford Press.

McNamara, K., & Rickard, K. M. (1989). Feminist identity development: Implications for feminist therapy with women. *Journal of Counseling and Development*, 68, 184–188.

McNaught, B. (1992). Take back the day: Opening the corporate closet. In B. Berzon (Ed.), *Positively gay: New approaches to gay and lesbian life* (pp. 195–201). Berkeley, CA: Celestial Arts.

Meisenhelder, J. B. (1994). Contributing factors to fear of HIV contagion in registered nurses. *Journal of Nursing Scholarship*, 26, 65–69.

Morales, E. (1990). Ethnic minority families and minority gays and lesbians. *Marriage and Family Review*, 14, 217–239.

Moss, D. (1992). Introductory thoughts: Hating in the first person plural: The example of homophobia. *American Imago*, 49, 277–291.

Muchmore, W., & Hanson, W. (1991). *Coming out right: A handbook for the gay male*. Boston: Alyson.

O'Keefe, M. K., Nesselhof-Kendall, S., & Baum, A. (1990). Behavior and prevention of AIDS: Bases of research and intervention. *Personality and Social Psychology Bulletin*, 16, 166–180.

Paul, S. C., & Crego, C. A. (1979). Marketing counseling center programs in a student consumer society. *Journal of College Student Personnel*, 20, 135–139.

Petitpas, A., & Chapagne, D. E. (1988). Developmental programming for intercollegiate athletes. *Journal of College Student Development*, 29, 454–460.

Pisapia, J. (1994). *How to conduct a cost-effectiveness analysis*. (ERIC Document Reproduction Service No. ED 411 354)

Posavac, E. J., & Carey, R. G. (1992). *Program evaluation: Methods and case studies*. Englewood Cliffs, NJ: Prentice-Hall.

Price, J. H. (1982). High school students' attitudes towards homosexuality. *Journal of School Health*, 52, 469–474.

Price, R. H., Cowen, E. L., Lorion, R. P., & Ramos-McKay, J. (Eds.). (1988). *14 ounces of prevention: A casebook for practitioners*. Washington, DC: American Psychological Association.

Quackenbush, R. L. (1989). Comparison and contrast between belief system and cognitive theory. *Journal of Psychology*, 123, 315–328.

Rogers, C. R. (1951). *Client centered therapy*. Boston: Houghton Mifflin.

Rokeach, M. (1984). A belief system theory of stability and change. In S. J. Ball Rokeach, M. Rokeach, & J. W. Grube (Eds.), *The great American values test: Influencing behavior and belief through television* (pp. 17–38). New York: Free Press.

Rotheram-Borus, M. J., & Fernandez, M. I. (1995). Sexual orientation and developmental challenges experienced by gay and lesbian youths. *Suicide and Life-Threatening Behavior*, 25, 26–34.

Russell, P. C., & Quirolgico, R. (1997, March). *Lesbians, gays, and bisexuals of color*. Paper presented at the meeting of the American College Personnel Association, Chicago.

Schreier, B. A. (1995). Moving beyond tolerance: A new paradigm for programming about homophobia/biphobia and heterosexism. *Journal of College Student Development, 36,* 19–26.

Schreier, B. A. (1997). Talking 'bout my generation: Responding to bisexual and transgendered student identities. *Commission VII: Counseling and Psychological Services, 24*(2), 4–5.

Schreier, B. A., & Bialk, S. E. (1997). Marketing an educational programming workshop series: An effective model and plan. *Journal of College Student Development, 38,* 89–90.

Schwanberg, S. L. (1993). Attitudes towards gay men and lesbian women instrumentation issues. *Journal of Homosexuality, 26,* 99–136.

Shannon, J. W., & Woods, W. J. (1991). Affirmative psychotherapy for gay men. *The Counseling Psychologist, 19,* 197–215.

Silverstein, C. (1991) Psychotherapy and psychotherapists: A history. In C. Silverstein (Ed.), *Gays, lesbians, and their therapists* (pp. 1–14). New York: Norton.

Simoni, J. M. (1996). Pathways to prejudice: Predicting students' heterosexist attitudes with demographics, self-esteem, and contact with lesbians and gay men. *Journal of College Student Development, 37,* 68–78.

Singer, M., & Marxuach-Rodriquez, L. (1996, Summer). Applying anthropology to the prevention of AIDS: The Latino Gay Men's Health Project. *Human Organization, 55,* 141–148.

Slater, B. R. (1993). Violence against lesbian and gay male college students. *Journal of College Student Psychotherapy, 8,* 177–202.

Stein, T. B. (1996). Homosexuality and homophobia in men. *Psychiatric Annals, 26,* 37–40.

Stevens, P. E. (1994). HIV prevention education for lesbians and bisexual women: A cultural analysis of a community intervention. *Social Science & Medicine, 39,* 1565–1578.

Stevenson, M. R. (1989). Promoting tolerance for homosexuality: An evaluation of intervention strategies. *Journal of Sex Research, 25,* 500–511.

St. Lawrence, J. S., Brasfield, T. L., & Jefferson, K. W. (1995). Cognitive–behavioral intervention to reduce African American adolescents' risk for HIV infection. *Journal of Consulting and Clinical Psychology, 63,* 221–237.

Stone, G. L., & Archer, J. (1990). College and university counseling centers in the 1990's: Challenges and limits. *The Counseling Psychologist, 18,* 539–607.

Supple, F. (1984). In defense of a multidimensional approach to sexual identity. *Journal of Homosexuality, 10,* 7–14.

Trice, A. D., Desio, D, & Haire, J. R. (1989). Personalizing career development outreach for college students. *College Student Journal, 23,* 251–254.

Uribe, V., & Harbeck, K. M. (1991). Addressing the needs of lesbian, gay, and bisexual youth: The origins of PROJECT 10 and school-based intervention. *Journal of Homosexuality, 22,* 9–28.

Van de Ven, P., Bornholt, L., & Bailey, M. (1996). Measuring cognitive, affective, and behavioral components of homophobic reaction. *Archives of Sexual Behavior, 25,* 155–179.

Watkins, C. E. (1985). Psychoeducational training in counseling psychology programs: Some thoughts on a training curriculum. *The Counseling Psychologist, 13,* 295–302.

Weiss, C. R., & Orysh, L. K. (1994). Group counseling for eating disorders: A two-phase treatment program. *Journal of College Student Development, 35,* 487–488.

Whitehead, M. M., & Nokes, K. M. (1990). An examination of demographic variables, nurturance, and empathy among homosexual and heterosexual Big Brother/Big Sister volunteers. *Journal of Homosexuality, 19,* 89–101.

Williams, L. B. (1998). Belly up 3 feet from the shore. *About Campus, 3,* 27–28.

Wittmann, P. P. (1988). Marketing counseling: What counseling can learn from other health care professionals. *Counselor Education and Supervision, 27,* 308–314.

16

LESBIAN, GAY, AND BISEXUAL VOCATIONAL PSYCHOLOGY: REVIEWING FOUNDATIONS AND PLANNING CONSTRUCTION

JAMES M. CROTEAU, MARY Z. ANDERSON, TERESA M. DISTEFANO, AND SHEILA KAMPA-KOKESCH

The past 25 years have seen a shift in the psychological study of lesbian, gay and bisexual (LGB) issues from a framework of pathology to a framework of affirmation (Croteau & Bieschke, 1996; Garnets & Kimmel, 1990; Morin & Rothblum, 1991). The psychosocial issues of LGB people have become a focus of study in this new affirmative framework (Garnets & Kimmel, 1990). Of these psychosocial issues, the "unique work-related concerns, behaviors, and needs" (Croteau & Bieschke, 1996, p. 119) of LGB people began to receive attention in the literature in the 1980s. Since 1993, the amount of literature on LGB career and work issues has more than doubled. This increase has been influenced by major contributions in two of the leading career and vocational psychology journals. In 1993 and 1995, the *Career Development Quarterly* (*CDQ*) published special sections on this topic, and in 1996 the *Journal of Vocational Behavior* published an entire issue on this topic. These contributions have moved the study of LGB issues into the mainstream of vocational and career psychology and are cited throughout the chapter. Indeed, a new era of scholarship seems to be emerging that is characterized by stronger theoretical and empirical work that rests on the foundations of the existing "pioneering" work (Croteau & Bieschke, 1996).

This chapter is intended to help move LGB vocational psychology "beyond pioneering" (Croteau and Bieschke, 1996, p. 119) by encouraging career scholars to build on the foundational literature to construct a knowledge base grounded in research and theory. The chapter is also designed to help practitioners ground their career-counseling work in that emerging knowledge base. We hoped to maximize understanding of the current foundations of LGB vocational psychology and to suggest possible blueprints for constructing future research, theory, and practice that build on those foundations. Whereas we emphasize some details of existing scholarship to assist those who want to join in efforts to build the literature, the information in the chapter should also help practitioners ground their practice in the current literature. The chapter is organized into four main sections: definitions and parameters used to structure the chapter, a chart of existing literature, discussion of the existing foundational literature, and recommendations for building the LGB vocational psychology literature.

PERTINENT DEFINITIONS AND PARAMETERS

Lesbian, gay, and bisexual career or vocational psychology is the overarching phrase that defines the content and parameters of this chapter. *Lesbian, gay,* and *bisexual* are terms used to refer to people who define themselves as having a same-sex sexual orientation. Individual articles in the LGB vocational psychology literature often focus on only one or two of the distinct subgroups within this umbrella phrase. For example, many focus exclusively on lesbian women, and others focus on lesbian women and gay men. Bisexual people are typically only nominally included. Because these different foci combined with likely differences in the career psychology of each group make the integration task of this chapter difficult, we use the following strategy: When drawing conclusions or summarizing content, we use language inclusive of a subgroup if one source that supports the conclusion has included that subgroup. Furthermore, if any one subgroup has been included to a much greater or lesser extent in any content area, we note that explicitly in the text.

We use the terms *career* and *vocational* interchangeably to encompass the full spectrum of career development in LGB individuals, including exploration of career-related interests, abilities, and attitudes; career choice and decision making; and career implementation, adjustment, and maintenance. We use the term *psychology* to refer to content that explicitly focuses on social, emotional, or intellectual aspects of work and career within the individual. For instance, articles focused on workplace policies are not included for review unless they are focused on the effects of policies on individual LGB workers. In addition to the parameters described by the phrase *lesbian, gay, and bisexual career and vocational psychology*, we have set two other parameters. We excluded the few sources that were written before 1980 owing to how dramatically different we believe the social context of LGB lives was before that time, and we excluded unpublished sources because they may not have been peer reviewed and may be relatively unaccessible. Most books on LGB career issues have a popular or nonpsychological focus; however, we do make references to the content of a few books that fit chapter parameters.

CHARTING OF RELEVANT LITERATURE

Table 1 contains an overview of the published scholarly journal articles on LGB vocational psychology found in our search of the literature from 1980 to 1996. The first column identifies article citations. Columns 2 through 6 contain the most frequently discussed content areas in the literature. We arrived at those content areas by applying a systematic process similar to that used in developing codes or categories in qualitative analysis. The column for a particular content area is checked if the article emphasized that content area. Column 7 indicates the particular segment of the population addressed in each article. Column 8 indicates which aspects of career development are emphasized. The type (practice, theory, or research) and focus of each article are indicated in the final two columns.

CURRENT PERSPECTIVES AND DEVELOPMENTS

Discussion of the current foundational literature is organized into five subsections, each focusing on a major content area in the literature. A sixth subsection summarizes four additional content areas that are discussed to a notable but less frequent extent.

LGB Identity Development

Sexual identity development theory is probably the most frequently discussed conceptual framework in the general LGB psychology literature. Thirteen sources focused on this framework in examining the career lives of this population (see Table 1). Bisexual identity development was seldom

TABLE 1
Content and Focus of Journal Articles in LGB Vocational Psychology 1980–1996

Reference	LGB identity development	Discrimination and climate	Managing sexual identity	Societal messages and interests	Practitioner interventions	Lesbian, gay, or bisexual	Exploration, choice, and implentation	Type of article	Stated focus
Belz, 1993					✓	G	CI	P	Case study analysis
Bieschke & Matthews, 1996					✓	LGB	N/A	R	A study of career counselor behaviors that are LGB client affirming
Boatwright et al., 1996	✓		✓			L	EC	R	A study of lesbian identity development and effects on career trajectory
Chojnacki & Gelberg, 1994	✓	✓			✓	LGB	CI	T	Suggested person–environment career counseling be applied with LGB clients
Chung, 1995		✓		✓		LGB	C	T	Suggested person–environment framework be applied to LGB career decision making
Chung & Harmon, 1994				✓		G	C	R	A study of "the career interests and aspirations of gay men" (p. 224)
Croteau, 1996		✓	✓			LGB	I	R	Review "of nine published studies on the workplace experiences of LGB people" (p. 195)
Croteau & Bieschke, 1996						LGB	N/A		Overview of existing literature; advocates a move "beyond pioneering" (p. 119)
Croteau & Hedstrom, 1993		✓	✓		✓	LG	CI	P	Case study analysis
Croteau & Lark, 1995		✓	✓			LGB	I	R	A study of work experiences of LGB student affairs professionals
Croteau & Thiel, 1993	✓				✓	LGB	CI	P	Examined need to integrate sexual orientation into career counseling through case examples

Reference				Population	Focus	Type	Description
Croteau & von Destinon, 1994	✓	✓		LGB	I	R	A study of discrimination during job search for LGB student affairs professionals
Driscoll et al., 1996	✓	✓		L	I	R	A study of disclosure, climate, and occupational adjustment of lesbian women
Dunkle, 1996	✓			LG	EC	T	Lesbian–gay identity development and Super's career-development model
Elliot, 1993			✓	LGB	ECI	P	Suggestions for effective counseling of lesbian and gay "cultural minority" (p. 210)
Etringer et al., 1990	✓			LG	C	R	A study of how sexual orientation may affect the decision-making process
Fassinger, 1995	✓	✓		L	CI	T	Discussed identity development and "vocational psychology of lesbians" (p. 148)
Fassinger, 1996	✓	✓		L	CI	T	Explored the applicability of women's career development models to lesbians
Griffin, 1992	✓	✓		LG	I	R	A study of work experiences of K–12 educators and their empowerment
Hall, 1986	✓	✓		L	I	R	A study of the work experiences of lesbians in corporate settings
Hetherington, 1991	✓			LG	ECI	P	Suggestions for career practitioners working with LGB college students
Hetherington & Orzek, 1989	✓		✓	L	C	P	Suggestions for career counselors working with lesbian women
Hetherington et al., 1989			✓	G	ECI	P	Suggestions for career counseling with gay men

Table continues

TABLE 1 (Continued)

Reference	LGB identity development	Discrimination and climate	Managing sexual identity	Societal messages and interests	Practitioner interventions	Lesbian, gay, or bisexual	Exploration, choice, and implentation	Type of article	Stated focus
Levine & Leonard, 1984		✓	✓			L	I	R	A study of the work experiences of lesbian women
Lonborg & Phillips, 1996						LGB	EC		Suggested improved methodology and content in LGB career research
Milburn, 1993					✓	G	CI	P	Presented a case study for analysis by Belz and Croteau & Hedstrom
Mobley & Slaney, 1996	✓			✓		LG	CI	T	Examined the applicability of Holland's theory to LGB career development
Morgan & Brown, 1991	✓	✓	✓	✓	✓	L	CI	T	Examined the applicability of women's career models to lesbians
Morrow et al., 1996	✓	✓		✓		LG	CI	T	Applied sociocognitive career theory to lesbian and gay people
Olson, 1987		✓	✓			LG	I	R	A study of work experiences of lesbian and gay teachers
Orzek, 1992	✓					LGB	C	P	Examined unique issues for LGB career decision making using case studies
Pope, 1995					✓	LGB	N/A		Reviewed literature that made suggestions for career counseling
Prince, 1995	✓			✓		G	EC	P	Applied development concepts about gay men to the area of career
Sailer et al., 1994					✓	LGB	N/A	P	Suggestions for developing an affirming career center

Author			Population	Type	Article	Description
Schachar & Gilbert, 1983	✓	✓	L	I	R	A study of interrole and intrarole conflicts of lesbian workers
Schmitz, 1988		✓	LG	C	P	"Identifies resources available to assist gay and lesbian career planning and job search" (p. 51)
Schneider, 1986	✓	✓	L	I	R	A study of workplace climate and disclosure among lesbian women
Van Den Bergh, 1994	✓	✓	L	I	P	Overview of LGB issues for EAP professionals
Woods & Harbeck, 1992	✓	✓	L	I	R	A study of work experiences of lesbian physical educators

Note. LGB = lesbian, gay, and bisexual; L = lesbian women; G = gay men; B = bisexual people; E = career exploration; C = career choice; I = career implementation; R = research; T= theory; P = practice; a blank cell indicates the article was a review or other type of article; K = kindergarten; EAP = Employee Assistance Program.

explored in the general psychology literature and almost never explored in vocational psychology literature; therefore, our summary refers only to lesbian and gay people.

Lesbian and gay sexual identity development can be defined as the process of changing one's current dominant heterosexual cultural beliefs, values, attitudes, behaviors, and identification to those of a minority lesbian or gay culture and identification (Prince, 1995). Furthermore, it is the process by which a person overcomes or manages internalized and externalized homophobia and heterosexism, resulting in the development of a positive sense of self as lesbian or gay. This process is further described in several other chapters of this volume (see Broido, chapter 1, this volume, and Reynolds and Hanjorgiris, chapter 2, this volume) and is not described here.

Several theory-based articles have appeared, describing sexual identity development in the context of formal career theories (Dunkle, 1996; Mobley & Slaney, 1996; Morrow, Gore, & Campbell, 1996); other writers have focused on identity development in the context of understanding issues unique to women or men (Fassinger, 1995, 1996; Morgan & Brown, 1991; Prince, 1995). Chojnacki and Gelberg (1994) suggested using sexual identity development to assess the "person" in a person–environment conception of lesbian and gay career issues. Several authors have published useful case illustrations involving the application of identity development concepts (Chojnacki & Gelberg, 1994; Croteau & Thiel, 1993; Orzek, 1992).

We highlight three general ideas found in the literature on practice and theory. First, individuals can be at any stage of identity development when they deal with any vocational issue across the spectrum of career development. Identity development can affect career development in a wide variety of permutations. Second, the career development of lesbian and gay persons can be stalled, delayed, or misdirected as a result of the amount of psychic energy required to integrate a positive lesbian or gay identity into the total self-concept. Last, sexual identity theory can help career practitioners avoid the mistake of assuming that all lesbian and gay clients are monolithic by helping them understand the various ways that sexual orientation can affect career developmentally.

In the only empirical study of sexual identity and career development, Boatwright, Gilbert, Forrest, and Ketzenberger (1996) interviewed 10 self-identified lesbian women who described their sexual identity development to be a "personally demanding" process that tended to "delay, disrupt, and in some cases seriously derail" their vocational lives (p. 210). As a consequence, most women felt their career development was behind that of their heterosexual counterparts at some point in their lives. These findings support several of the ideas in the practice and theory literature concerning the interaction of sexual identity and career development.

The general LGB psychology literature on sexual identity development has focused on models that involve coming to a clear definition of self as lesbian or gay and incorporating that identity into one's life in visible ways. Identity development theorists are just beginning to recognize that coming to a clear and open identification with being lesbian or gay may not be the only route to dealing successfully with same-sex attractions for people in all cultures and social contexts. More information about these and other limitations of traditional identity development models may be found in earlier chapters of this volume (see Broido, chapter 1, and Reynolds & Hanjorgiris, chapter 2). These more complex and inclusive ideas about identity development have been only briefly considered in the career literature (e.g., Fassinger, 1995, 1996; Morgan & Brown, 1991; Prince, 1995).

Discrimination and Climate in the Workplace

Issues concerning discrimination toward LGB workers were discussed in 11 LGB vocational psychology theory and practice articles (see Table 1). Workplace discrimination is one of the most frequent factors subjected to empirical research. In the research studies identified, lesbians were studied in all 11, gay men in 4, and bisexual people in 2. Therefore, summaries and conclusions are applicable with greatest certainty to lesbian women and with least certainty to bisexual people.

Discrimination against LGB workers is pervasive. Croteau (1996) noted that from 25% to 66% of the respondents in three of the studies he reviewed reported experiencing discrimination and that these figures were in agreement with other data summarized by previous authors (Croteau & Lark, 1995; Croteau & von Destinon, 1994; Levine 1979; Levine & Leonard, 1984). In two studies, 44% to 60% of workers reported anticipating future discrimination (Croteau & Lark, 1995; Levine & Leonard, 1984). LGB respondents who answered open-ended questions in qualitative studies also frequently depicted work lives marked by discrimination and fear of discrimination (Griffin, 1992; Hall, 1986; Woods & Harbeck, 1992).

Levine and Leonard (1984) suggested a distinction between informal and formal discrimination that seems to fit the descriptions of discrimination given by participants in a variety of studies (Croteau, 1996). Formal discrimination involves adverse decisions in the conditions of employment based on the worker's sexual orientation (e.g., in hiring, wages, retention and promotion, work evaluations, and policies that limit benefits for domestic partners). Informal discrimination involves hostility or adversity in the work environment or climate (e.g.,"verbal harassment and property violence"; "loss of credibility, acceptance, or respect by co-workers and supervisors"; Croteau, 1996, p. 199). Some authors highlighted the importance of the latter type of discrimination. Driscoll, Kelley, and Fassinger

(1996), for instance, noted that a hostile environment detracts from the emotional and relational benefits of work.

Managing Sexual Identity at Work

The decisions and actions of LGB people concerning the concealment or disclosure of their sexual orientation at work were seen as central tasks in 4 theory or practice articles and in 11 empirical studies (see Table 1). Like the articles about discrimination, these articles focused most often on lesbian women and least often on bisexual people. Once again, summaries and conclusions are applicable with greatest certainty to lesbian women and with least certainty to bisexual people. Croteau (1996) summarized the findings that had the strongest support in 9 studies published before 1995. He concluded, in part, that there is great variability in the degree of disclosure by LGB workers as evidenced by large variation in levels of disclosure within and across studies. More recent findings also indicated similar variation (Boatwright et al., 1996; Driscoll et al., 1996).

Research concerning variables associated with levels of disclosure is sparse. Comparison and integration across studies can be made for only a few variables. Higher levels of disclosure at work have been related to greater frequency of discrimination (Croteau & Lark, 1995; Croteau & von Destinon, 1994; Levine & Leonard, 1984). Disclosure, however, was also found to have either a positive relationship or no relationship to job satisfaction (Croteau & Lark, 1995; Croteau & von Destinon, 1994; Driscoll et al., 1996). From these data, some authors hypothesized that more open individuals benefit from their openness perhaps owing to increased feelings of integrity or the reward of role modeling for other LGB workers (Croteau, 1996; Croteau & Lark, 1995; Croteau & von Destinon, 1994; Driscoll et al., 1996; Fassinger, 1996). These benefits may mitigate the negative effects of greater discrimination, leaving more open workers at least as satisfied with their jobs as less open workers.

In quantitative studies, sexual identity management has been conceptualized as degree of disclosure, measured largely through self-report of how many people at work are thought to know one's minority sexual orientation. Qualitative research offers a more complex picture and challenges the adequacy of conceptualizing sexual identity management as degree of disclosure. Croteau (1996) reviewed six qualitative studies and concluded that a model constructed by Griffin (1992) seemed to fit well with participants' descriptions of identity management across the studies. Griffin proposed four categories of identity management strategies along a continuum from totally closeted to publicly out. Closest to the totally closeted end of the continuum are "passing" strategies involving leading others to believe that one is heterosexual. Next are "covering" strategies involving actions that prevent others at work from knowing one is lesbian or gay without pretending heterosexuality. The third strategy on the continuum is being "implicitly out," which involves actions that are honest about one's life but not actually labeling oneself as gay or lesbian. "Explicitly out" strategies involve directly disclosing one's gay or lesbian identity at work.

According to Griffin (1992), use of strategies is governed largely by the tension between fear of discovery and the need for self-integrity. Fear of discovery, which could lead to negative job consequences, motivates workers to pass or cover in an attempt to protect themselves from such consequences. Concealment may have such protective effects because less discrimination has been reported in several studies by those who are less out (Croteau & Lark, 1995; Croteau & von Destinon, 1994; Levine & Leonard, 1984). Worker reports in qualitative studies also have supported Griffin's notion that fear of discrimination and harassment motivates participants to conceal their identities. Workers reported constant vigilance to protect themselves from being "found out" (e.g., Griffin, 1992; Hall, 1986; Woods & Harbeck, 1992). On the other hand, Griffin posited that self-integrity provides motivation for being implicitly or explicitly out.

Although there is research support for the notion that tension between fear and integrity contributes to the individual variation in identity management strategies, several authors have suggested that other factors may also determine which strategies are used. For instance, two studies (Driscoll et al., 1996; Schneider, 1986) indicated that environmental (e.g., general sociability of the work environment or hostile work climate) and personal (e.g., having previous experiences with work losses caused by disclosure of sexual identity or having longer duration of romantic relationship) factors may influence identity management.

Societal Messages and Occupational Interests, Choices, and Perceptions

Eight theory and practice articles and one empirical article have focused on possible influences of family and societal messages about gender and sexual orientation on the vocational interests, abilities, and perceptions of lesbian and gay people (see Table 1). Bisexual people are considered nominally in only one theoretical article (Chung, 1995). Therefore, this discussion refers only to lesbian women and gay men.

The literature has centered around two specific hypotheses about societal messages and career issues. First, several authors in the area of vocational psychology hypothesized that gender role socialization influences the development of vocational interests in gay and lesbian people in a manner distinct from that of heterosexual people (Chung, 1995, Chung & Harmon, 1994; Fassinger, 1995, 1996; Hetherington & Orzek, 1989; Morgan & Brown, 1991; Morrow et al., 1996). These authors often have cited existing gender-related research suggesting that familial and societal messages discouraging gender nontraditional behavior and interests are communicated early in life and that lesbian and gay people are more likely to be gender nontraditional than are heterosexual people. These ideas were extended to the vocational area, and lesbian and gay people were hypothesized to have gender nontraditional occupational interests frequently and to lack support for exploring and developing those interests. It was hypothesized, therefore, that lesbian and gay people may experience restricted occupational choice, increased career indecision, and decreased career satisfaction. In contrast, a few authors offered speculation that the career development of lesbian women is advantaged because lesbian women are more likely to reject pressure to pursue gender traditional interests and occupations (Fassinger, 1995, 1996; Morgan & Brown, 1991). Empirical investigation of the relationship between gender-related interests and career variables is limited to a single study of gay men. Chung and Harmon (1994) found that gay men were more likely than heterosexual men to endorse gender atypical interest patterns and to aspire to gender nontraditional occupations, although sex-role orientation did not mediate the relationship between sexual orientation and interests as expected.

The second general hypothesis in this area is that lesbian and gay people internalize societal vocational stereotypes about LGB people and develop perceived occupational opportunity structures defining which occupations are accessible to them (Fassinger, 1995, 1996; Morrow et al., 1996; Prince, 1995). The salience and nature of the effect of this perceived opportunity structure have been described as interacting with variation in identity management and identity development (Fassinger, 1995, 1996; Hetherington & Orzek, 1989; Morgan & Brown, 1991). There are no studies directly investigating the influence of perceived opportunity structure on lesbian and gay people (Chung, 1995). However, three studies provided tentative support for the notion that prejudicial stereotypes may restrict perceived opportunity structure for careers involving work with children (Griffin, 1992; Schneider, 1986; Woods & Harbeck, 1992).

Career Practitioners and Their Interventions

Numerous theory and practice articles concerning the effective provision of career counseling have been published, whereas only two research studies have addressed this content area (see Table 1). In one review of career intervention literature, Pope (1995) examined about half of the literature cited previously in addition to unpublished sources and reported the nine broad practice suggestions found most frequently in the literature. We focused on the articles that gave the most specific ideas for providing LGB-sensitive career services (Belz, 1993; Chojnacki & Gelberg, 1994; Croteau & Hedstrom, 1993; Croteau & Thiel, 1993; Elliot, 1993; Morgan & Brown, 1991; Sailer, Korschgen, & Lokken, 1994). According to these authors, counselors need to create a context that invites LGB people to feel free to seek services, disclose their sexual identity, and explore LGB-unique career concerns. Suggestions for establishing such a context included displaying LGB-affirmative artwork, pamphlets, and books; providing inclusive written language in all paperwork and forms; conducting outreach with LGB organizations; and hiring openly LGB staff. Furthermore, it is important that practitioners use language that is inclusive of same-sex relationships and does not assume heterosexuality. Career practitioners should also be familiar with available LGB-specific career resources and referrals. Two recent books have given the most comprehensive, up-to-date listing of a wide variety of such resources (Friskopp & Silverstein, 1995; Gelberg & Chojnacki, 1996). In addition, several authors have suggested that career counselors apply the general concepts of effective multicultural counseling (Croteau & Hedstrom, 1993; Elliot, 1993; Morgan & Brown, 1991). These recommendations are consistent with calls for affirmative approaches to counseling in non-career-focused LGB counseling and therapy literature (see Rothblum, chapter 3, and Dworkin, chapter 7, this volume).

Pope (1995) noted that the career intervention literature is "anecdotal and based on clinical observation" (p. 192). Indeed, only two empirical articles were found concerning career practitioners and their interventions (Bieschke & Matthews, 1996; Griffin, 1992). In a national study of career counselors, Bieschke and Matthews (1996) identified three factors related to self-reported affirmative counselor behaviors: (a) working in an organizational climate perceived by counselors as nonheterosexist; (b) counselors' identifying as lesbian, gay, or bisexual; and (c) counselors' defining a broad range of populations as cultural minority groups. These findings have provided initial support for the practice-based recommendations that counselors focus particular attention on the counseling environment and operate from a multicultural framework. The other study in this content area was the participatory qualitative research project that produced the model of sexual identity management described previously (Griffin, 1992). In addition to providing information about their work lives, the participating lesbian and gay teachers took part in a series of individual and group experiences. They found these experiences to be affirming, supportive, and empowering, suggesting group career interventions can be helpful to LGB people in their work lives.

Other Areas Less Fully Discussed in the Literature

In the process of identifying the five major content areas discussed previously, we identified four content areas that were discussed briefly across a few published sources but seemed particularly compelling areas for future scholarship. The first of these areas concerns dual-career and multiple-role issues, discussed primarily in terms of lesbian women. Issues discussed are similar to those in the women's career development literature on this topic (Fassinger, 1995, 1996; Morgan & Brown, 1991; Morrow et al., 1996). Issues specific to lesbians are also discussed, including greater equality in lesbian versus heterosexual relationships related to dual-career and family-maintenance issues, dealing with differences between partners in sexual identity management, and external pressures associated with wage inequities and employment benefits not being extended to partners and family. There are also two interesting research findings related to lesbians and their multiple roles: Longer duration of lesbian relationships was related to greater workplace disclosure and less work-related stress (Driscoll et al., 1996), and the most frequent interrole conflict experienced was that between worker and lover (Schachar & Gilbert, 1983).

The second content area covered briefly in a few theory and practice articles concerned how involvement in LGB communities affects career lives (Fassinger, 1995, 1996; Hetherington, 1991; Schmitz, 1988). Involvement in LGB communities was seen as having the potential for creating conflict (e.g., by increasing the risk of sexual orientation being revealed at work). However, benefits of involvement such as job-related networking and support for job-related stress were also articulated by the 10 lesbian women interviewed by Boatwright et al. (1996).

The third content area discussed briefly in a few theory and practice articles is the need for LGB role models during career exploration and choice, particularly because of the effects of invisibility, leading to the lack of opportunity for LGB young people to learn from their LGB elders in most social contexts (Fassinger, 1995; Hetherington, 1991; Hetherington, Hillerbrand, & Etringer, 1989; Hetherington & Orzek, 1989). Reports from qualitative studies have indicated that some LGB people desire role models, yet some LGB people may be ambivalent about being role models owing to the risks of being out (Griffin, 1992; Olson, 1987; Woods & Harbeck, 1992). Interpretations of some quantitative research (Croteau & Lark, 1995; Croteau & von Destinon, 1994; Driscoll et al., 1996) have suggested that being an openly LGB role model may have positive effects.

The final content area concerns the lack of diversity other than sexual orientation in the LGB vocational psychology literature. Participants in general LGB psychology research have to a large extent been White, formally well educated, employed in professional-type occupations, lesbian or gay identified, and at least somewhat open and connected to LGB communities. The LGB vocational psychology literature has the same limitations. Thus, current LGB vocational psychology represents only a select group of LGB people. Although this lack of inclusion has been criticized in the literature, there has been almost no inclusion of LGB people of color or other diverse LGB people.

BUILDING LGB VOCATIONAL PSYCHOLOGY PRACTICE, THEORY, AND RESEARCH

Previous sections of this chapter contribute to the construction of a knowledge base by presenting a broad map of existing literature and summarizing the most frequently discussed content. In the final section, we first explore the extent to which existing literature informs career practice and make direct suggestions to practitioners based on that literature. Then we make recommendations for research methods and scholarship that will extend LGB vocational psychology and more firmly ground it in theory and research.

Informing Competent LGB Vocational Psychology Practice

We use the foundational LGB vocational psychology literature to develop preliminary ideas about what constitutes good practice. Borrowing the structure used by Fassinger and Richie (1997), we use the concept of multicultural competence and its three elements (knowledge, attitudes, and skills) to organize the next two subsections on how the LGB vocational psychology literature informs career practice.

Competence in Knowledge

Four of the five most discussed content areas in the literature described previously focus on the knowledge element of competence with this population; that is, on understanding the career and work lives of LGB clients. The first content area, sexual identity development, has been examined largely from a practice and theory perspective. This literature is unanimous in admonishing career practitioners to recognize that sexual identity development influences career development for LGB clients. Career counselors who consider sexual identity development as a context within which career development occurs will recognize the myriad of ways that being LGB interacts with career development. They will avoid unwarranted assumptions about how being LGB interacts with career concerns that may not apply to specific individuals. One example of an unwarranted assumption is that all LGB clients will be aware of and ready to explore the interaction between sexual identity development and career; this may not be true for clients early in their sexual identity development. More informed career counselors will frame discussion of the influence of sexual identity on career concerns in a manner suited to individual readiness. The full range of interaction between sexual identity and career development is illustrated by case examples provided in the LGB vocational psychology literature (e.g., Belz, 1993; Chojnacki & Gelberg, 1994, 1996; Croteau & Hedstrom, 1993; Croteau & Thiel, 1993; Milburn, 1993; Orzek, 1992).

Concerning the second and third content areas discussed previously, researchers have found that workplace discrimination and hostility are pervasive for LGB workers and that sexual identity management is a central task in the face of actual or feared discrimination and hostility. Furthermore, there is great variation in how open individuals will be concerning sexual orientation, and the variation in openness is influenced by a complex set of personal and work-related variables. Griffin (1992) offered a promising conceptual framework for career practitioners in understanding and discussing various strategies for managing sexual identity in the face of actual or potential discrimination. Career counselors can use Griffin's model to assist clients in exploring the full range of sexual identity management strategies from passing to being explicitly out. Existing research indicates that concerns about past, present, and anticipated discrimination is a key factor in identity management decisions. Griffin's model points to the dynamic tension between fear of discrimination and personal integrity in making decisions about identity management in the workplace. In addition to helping clients explore this dynamic tension, career counselors need to assist clients in considering several less discussed and studied factors that may influence identity management. Examples of such factors include the degree to which a work environment is sociable, whether the client is partnered, the influence of each partner's sexual identity management strategies on the other, the longevity of the partner relationship, and the presence of children. Although the literature is weak in this area, we believe it is essential to facilitate integration of other social and cultural identities that interact with career into discussions of sexual identity management. For example, decision making about sexual identity management for African American clients will undoubtedly be influenced by the experience of racism in the workplace, the cultural context for definitions of sexual identity, and the possibility of feeling marginalized within the safety of their "home" African American community.

The last and least frequently examined area in which career practitioners must be knowledgeable concerns societal messages about gender and sexual orientation and the effects of these messages on the career interests, choices, and perceptions of LGB clients. The major thesis of this largely theoretical literature is that gender-based societal messages may affect LGB clients differently from heterosexual people owing to the hypothesized greater salience and frequency of gender nontraditionality among this population. Furthermore, images of appropriate and acceptable occupations for LGB people may create issues related to perceived opportunity structure similar to the opportunity structure issues of women and people of color. It is critical for career counselors to assess and increase client awareness of how societal messages about gender and sexual orientation have influenced the development of career interests and choices.

Competence in Attitudes and Skills

The content area labeled "career practitioners and their interventions" was the only content area that addressed the final two competency areas. The attitudinal component of competence involves the counselors' awareness of their own overt and subtle homophobic and heterosexist biases and their efforts to manage and overcome such attitudes. Much of the vocational psychology practice literature admonishes practitioners to deal with their homophobia or heterosexism but says little beyond that admonishment. Practitioners are referred to the more general counseling literature reviewed in other chapters in this book for recommendations concerning development of LGB-affirmative attitudes.

The skill element refers to the appropriateness and effectiveness of counselors' behaviors and interventions with LGB people. As reviewed previously, the practice-oriented literature offers suggestions concerning effective skills. We have two additional broad suggestions. First, because many LGB-unique career concerns are a result of societal oppression, it seems critical that practitioners rely on career-counseling approaches that place sufficient emphasis on understanding environmental influences on career development. The emphasis on environmental factors in sociocognitive career theory and women's career development models makes application of these and similar conceptual frameworks especially helpful (e.g., Fassinger, 1996; Morgan & Brown, 1991; Morrow et al., 1996). Second, we recommend that career counselors move beyond the traditional exclusive emphasis on intrapersonal approaches to individual counseling and testing to embrace interventions and advocacy activities that more directly address external oppression. Examples of oppression-sensitive interventions include assisting clients to develop skills for assessing and building affirmation in workplace environments and assisting clients to develop and maintain career-related networks within the LGB community. Findings from Griffin's (1992) research also suggest that small-group activities may be particularly effective for empowering clients to confront and cope with career-related oppression. Examples of advocacy activities include working to create an LGB-affirmative counseling environment, pressing for inclusion and affirmation with employers, developing and maintaining strong relationships with LGB communities, and securing LGB-specific career information resources.

Advancing Research and Theory Development in LGB Vocational Psychology

In the preceding discussion, we examined LGB vocational psychology from the perspective of how it informs competent career practice. In this section, we give four recommendations for future scholarship that will improve and expand research methodology and theory building.

Future Practice-Oriented Scholarship Should Rely on Research and Theory

When the literature on the career issues of this population first emerged in the late 1980s and early 1990s, many authors focused on educating career counselors concerning the basic issues in the career lives of this population (e.g., Elliot, 1993; Hetherington et al., 1989; Hetherington & Orzek, 1989; Van Den Bergh, 1994). These authors were pioneering in providing needed guidance often without the benefit of much research or theory base. In the past few years, original research, research integrations, and theory applications have begun to establish a research and theory base on which to offer guidance to career practitioners. Gelberg and Chojnacki's (1996) book is probably the most comprehensive practitioner-oriented publication; however, it does not include some of the recent more rigorous theory and research efforts. Future writing geared toward practitioners should include the growing theory and research now being generated and enunciate how (or whether) LGB practice recommendations are based in theory, research, or both.

Broad Descriptive Research Is Still Needed in Most Areas

Most content areas in LGB vocational psychology are in the early stages of development of a research and theory base. Research and theory building have barely begun in three of the five identified major content areas: (a) effect of LGB identity development on career development; (b) relationship of societal messages about gender and sexual orientation with career interests, choices, and perceptions of LGB people; and (c) attitudes and interventions of career practitioners. Other issues that have received even less attention include how the career lives of LGB people are affected by multiple life roles and dual-career relationships, LGB communities, career role models and mentors, and diverse social group identities other than sexual orientation. The lack of a descriptive base concerning bisexual people and LGB people of color is particularly striking. A descriptive base is needed in all of these areas. Scholarly writing based on practical experience in these areas might help begin to establish this descriptive foundation. Quantitative and qualitative research that is exploratory and broadly focused will be key to establishing a descriptive base.

Qualitative designs eliciting LGB persons' own descriptions of their career-related experiences are useful for generating initial information. For instance, Boatwright et al. (1996) generated open-ended questions concerning the intersections of lesbian identity development and career development, conducted interviews employing these questions with 10 lesbian women, and analyzed the data to describe the topic areas covered by their questions. The qualitative research that helps form the descriptive base for understanding the more developed content areas of discrimination and identity management can also serve as useful design examples for establishing a descriptive base in other areas (e.g., Griffin, 1992; Woods & Harbeck, 1992).

Researchers can also generate quantitative descriptive questions for inclusion in survey-style research designs. Several researchers have used this design to help provide a descriptive base concerning discrimination and sexual identity management (Croteau & Lark, 1995; Croteau & von Destinon, 1994; Levine & Leonard, 1984). These research designs yield information that is as useful as the questions generated by the researcher. Researchers, therefore, need to tap carefully whatever information is in the literature and be systematic in their own thinking to develop such questions.

Hypothesis-Testing and Theory-Building Research Is Now Possible

The authors that reviewed research methods in LGB vocational psychology emphasized the need for theory-based and hypothesis-testing research (Croteau, 1996; Lonborg & Phillips, 1996). Discrimination or hostile climate and sexual identity management in the workplace are content areas that have some descriptive base and thus can most easily lead to hypothesis-testing and theory-building inquiries. In addition, broad and exploratory descriptive work on discrimination and sexual identity management is still needed, particularly concerning segments of LGB workers who have been studied little or not at all, including bisexual people, people of color, and people in nonprofessional and lower paid occupations.

Existing research suggests the importance of studies that examine hypothesized relationships among discrimination, hostile climate, sexual identity management, and job satisfaction, along with other internal and external variables as discussed in our summary of the sexual identity management content area. One recent study can serve as an example of such a design for future researchers. Driscoll and her colleagues (1996) developed a model to explain the relationships among disclosure, workplace climate on LGB issues, stress, coping, and job satisfaction and then tested that model through the path analysis of data from 123 lesbian women in a variety of occupations. Research studies that identify a priori research or theory-based hypotheses concerning the complex relationships among relevant variables will further establish the knowledge base about discrimination and work climate in the career lives of LGB people.

Theory building can also occur through research efforts that are cumulative and involve movement toward defining important variables within a theoretical framework. Griffin (1992), for example, took qualitative data from individual and group interviews with a small group of lesbian and gay educators and analyzed the data to develop the model of sexual identity management discussed previously. Some of the present authors and their colleagues have begun the process of operationalizing Griffin's conceptual definition of sexual identity management (Anderson, Chung, Croteau, & Distefano, 1998) by generating items on the basis of qualitative descriptions of identity management given by workers in six studies (Friskopp & Silverstein, 1995; Griffin, 1992; Hall, 1986; Olson, 1987; Woods, 1994; Woods & Harbeck, 1992). Efforts such as these that build on previous descriptive research to construct and operationalize conceptual models can be used as models for research in other areas.

Even in content areas with less descriptive bases, the research could move toward more hypothesis testing and theory-based inquiry by applying theoretically derived and researched concepts from areas outside LBG vocational psychology. Recently, a number of authors have made explicit suggestions for LGB vocational psychology research from a variety of theoretical perspectives: (a) broad career theories including Super's theory (Dunkle, 1996), Holland's theory (Mobley & Slaney, 1996), and sociocognitive theory (Morrow et al., 1996); (b) women's career theories including those of Farmer (1985), Astin (1984), and Gottfredson (1981; Chung, 1995; Chung & Harmon, 1994; Fassinger, 1995, 1996; Lonborg & Phillips, 1996; Morgan & Brown, 1991); and (c) theories from general LGB psychology (Croteau, 1996; Lonborg & Phillips, 1996), including concepts such as internalized homophobia (Shidlo, 1994) and the interaction of ethnic–cultural identity with LGB identity (Greene, 1997).

Future Research Efforts Should Improve on and Broaden Research Designs

Lonborg and Phillips (1996) discussed methodological considerations and recommendations for research across all areas of LGB vocational psychology. Croteau (1996) critiqued the current methods and made suggestions for future research within the more narrow area of LGB workplace experiences. These authors discussed comprehensively what needs to be done to improve methodology and expand the variety of research designs in LGB vocational psychology. The following discussion provides an overview of their ideas and presents some additions and illustrations.

In terms of quantitative research, both of the aforementioned methodological reviews (Croteau, 1996; Lonborg & Phillips, 1996) focused on diversifying samples. Lonborg and Phillips discussed difficulties with, and strategies for, probability sampling of the LGB population. When probability sampling is not possible, both articles recommended diversifying convenience samples. A major factor in future successful research will be the use of creative and cost-efficient ways to involve diverse LGB people in research, particularly segments of the population frequently that are neglected (e.g., people of color, bisexual people, people in nonprofessional jobs). Both reviews contain many good suggestions for doing so.

In addition to sampling issues, Croteau (1996) pointed to problems with defining and measuring variables in quantitative research on workplace experiences (e.g., single-item measurement and measurement by unique sets of questions with no indications of validity or reliability). The definition and measurement of discrimination are cited as an example of this problem in many studies. Two efforts at better measurement of this variable illustrate the direction needed to be taken in research. Driscoll et al. (1996) adapted a measure of gender-related inequities in campus environments to measure hostile climate toward lesbians in the workplace. The present authors are developing a measure of discrimination and hostile climate based on descriptions of discrimination in existing research (Anderson et al., 1998).

Croteau (1996) and Lonborg and Phillips (1996) also pressed for increasing the variety of research designs in quantitative research. Most quantitative research has been correlational survey research with less sophisticated data analysis techniques. Lonborg and Phillips suggested and illustrated the use of "quasi-experimental designs, factor analytic studies, path analysis, and structural equation modeling" (p. 189). They suggested and discussed the use of longitudinal methods. Croteau emphasized field, analogue, and interventional research of all types and gave examples.

Both methodological reviews also discussed improving qualitative methodology in the study of LGB vocational psychology. Lonborg and Phillips (1996) discussed the use of three basic data collection designs: structured interviews, focus groups, and critical incident techniques. Croteau (1996) emphasized the usefulness of qualitative designs to study LGB workers who have currently been ignored and suggested data collection methods other than interviews or written responses (e.g., field observation, participant journaling of work experiences). Lonborg and Phillips described qualitative methods as good techniques for generating information for description "when little is known about a particular population" (p. 187). Croteau agreed and added that open-ended inquiries "allow the concepts and models to emerge from the unique experiences and perspectives of the socially marginalized group" (p. 228).

CONCLUSION

Carol, a veteran elementary school teacher, recently fell in love with another woman for the first time in her life. She comes to career counseling concerned about how her relationship and newly emerging lesbian identity will affect her career. She is particularly worried about how open she can afford be at the school where she works. Frank, a college senior who has identified as gay since his freshman year, wants to participate in campus-based recruitment services. He wants to interview with the on-campus recruiters who are LGB affirmative. Frank is also Latino and wants employers with whom he interviews to be nonracist and affirmative of his Latino culture. He asks for the advice of a career practitioner. Chris, a bisexual man, has worked in an accounting firm for 15 years and has been denied promotion several times. Although he has tried to keep his work and personal life separate, he wonders if his boss suspects he is bisexual and has denied him promotions for this reason. He does not know where to turn for help. Mary, a 16-year-old, has suspected she is a lesbian but has never told anyone. She, like many of her peers, has not thought much about her career but is exploring career-related interests in the context of everyday activities. Because she does not want to reveal her lesbian identity, she has confined her activities to those that are gender traditional. Where will she be in 2 years, when high school graduation creates the necessity of initial career and educational choices?

These examples provide a glimpse into the career struggles unique to LGB people, especially in the context of homophobia and heterosexism in the world of work. The LGB vocational psychology literature has begun to point to many of the issues faced by Carol, Frank, Chris, Mary, and so many other LGB people. LGB people develop their career identities in the context of, and in complex interaction with, their sexual identities. LGB people struggle to cope with career and workplace discrimination. In the face of such discrimination, LGB people often face decisions about workplace sexual identity management that involve painful choices requiring sacrifice of either personal integrity or personal safety. LGB people face obstacles to developing interests and making career choices that are personally congruent as opposed to being based on heterosexist societal messages about careers. Furthermore, LGB people also struggle to integrate their socially stigmatized partner relationships, alternative family structures, and racial and ethnic cultural identities with their career lives in ways the literature has barely begun to address.

The current LGB vocational psychology literature has laid the foundation for understanding these unique and significant career issues. In this chapter, we first reviewed and organized the current LGB vocational psychology literature so that researchers, theorists, and practitioners could more easily build on current foundations in their future work. Then we suggested future directions for practitioners, researchers, and theorists. Career practitioners must use the current foundations of LGB vocational psychology in their work with the Franks and Carols who come for career assistance, and the current literature does provide some direction. To make substantive progress in improving the career lives of LGB people, however, we believe that the primary challenge is the construction of a broader, more inclusive, and more rigorous knowledge base for LGB vocational psychology. Let construction begin!

REFERENCES

Anderson, M. Z., Chung, Y. B., Croteau, J. M., & Distefano, T. M. (1998). *Keys to understanding workplace dynamics: Improved variable definitions and measurement*. Manuscript in preparation.

Astin, H. S. (1984). The meaning of work in women's lives: A sociopsychological model of career choice and work behavior. *The Counseling Psychologist, 12*, 117–126.

Belz, J. R. (1993). Sexual orientation as a factor in career development. *Career Development Quarterly, 41*, 197–200.

Bieschke, K. J., & Matthews, C. (1996). Career counselor attitudes and behaviors towards gay, lesbian, bisexual clients. *Journal of Vocational Behavior, 48*, 243–255.

Boatwright, K. J., Gilbert, M. S., Forrest, L., & Ketzenberger, K. L. (1996). Impact of identity development upon career trajectory: Listening to the voices of lesbians. *Journal of Vocational Behavior, 48*, 210–228.

Chojnacki, J. T., & Gelberg, S. (1994). Toward a conceptualization of career counseling with gay/lesbian/bisexual persons. *Journal of Career Development, 21*(1), 3–10.

Chojnacki, J. T., & Gelberg, S. (1996). *Career and life planning with gay, lesbian, and bisexual persons*. Alexandria, VA: American Counseling Association.

Chung, Y. B. (1995). Career decision making of lesbian, gay, and bisexual individuals. *Career Development Quarterly, 44*, 178–190.

Chung, Y. B., & Harmon, L. W. (1994). The career interests and aspirations of gay men: How sex-role orientation is related. *Journal of Vocational Behavior, 45*, 223–239.

Croteau, J. M. (1996). Research on the work experiences of lesbian, gay and bisexual people: An integrative review of methodology and findings. *Journal of Vocational Behavior, 48*, 195–209.

Croteau, J. M., & Bieschke, K. J. (1996). Beyond pioneering: An introduction to the special issue on the vocational issues of lesbian women and gay men. *Journal of Vocational Behavior, 48*, 119–124.

Croteau, J. M., & Hedstrom, S. M. (1993). Integrating commonality and difference: The key to career counseling with lesbian women and gay men. *Career Development Quarterly, 41*, 201–209.

Croteau, J. M., & Lark, J. S. (1995). On being lesbian, gay or bisexual in student affairs: A national survey of experiences on the job. *NASPA Journal, 32*, 189–197.

Croteau, J. M., & Thiel, M. J. (1993). Integrating sexual orientation in career counseling: Acting to end a form of the personal-career dichotomy. *Career Development Quarterly, 42*, 174–179.

Croteau, J. M., & von Destinon, M. (1994). A national survey of job search experiences of lesbian, gay and bisexual student affairs professionals. *Journal of College Student Development, 35*, 40–45.

Driscoll, J. M., Kelley, F. A., & Fassinger, R. E. (1996). Lesbian identity and self-disclosure in the workplace: Relation to occupational stress and satisfaction. *Journal of Vocational Behavior, 48,* 229–242.

Dunkle, J. H. (1996). Toward an integration of gay and lesbian identity development and Super's life-span approach. *Journal of Vocational Behavior, 48,* 149–159.

Elliot, J. E. (1993). Career development with lesbian and gay clients. *Career Development Quarterly, 41,* 210–226.

Etringer, B. D., Hillerbrand, E., & Hetherington, C. (1990). The influence of sexual orientation on career decision making: A research note. *Journal of Homosexuality, 19,* 103–111.

Farmer, H. S. (1985). Model of career and achievement motivation for women and men. *Journal of Counseling Psychology, 32,* 363–390.

Fassinger, R. E. (1995). From invisibility to integration: Lesbian identity in the workplace. *Career Development Quarterly, 44,* 149–167.

Fassinger, R. E. (1996). Notes from the margins: Integrating lesbian experience into the vocational psychology of women. *Journal of Vocational Behavior, 48,* 160–175.

Fassinger, R. E., & Richie, B. S. (1997). Sex matters: Gender and sexual orientation in training for multicultural counseling competency. In D. B. Pope-Davis & H. L. K. Coleman (Eds.), *Multicultural counseling competencies: Assessment, education and training, and supervision* (pp. 83–110). Newbury Park, CA: Sage.

Friskopp, A., & Silverstein, S. (1995). *Straight jobs, gay lives: Gay and lesbian professionals, the Harvard Business School, and the American workplace.* New York: Scribner.

Garnets, L., & Kimmel, D. (1990). Lesbian and gay male dimensions in the psychological study of human diversity. In J. D. Goodchilds (Ed.), *Psychological perspectives on human diversity in America. Master lecturers' psychology series* (pp. 137–192). Washington, DC: American Psychological Association.

Gelberg, S., & Chojnacki, J. T. (1996). *Career and life planning with gay, lesbian, & bisexual persons.* Alexandria, VA: American Counseling Association.

Gottfredson, L. S. (1981). Circumscription and compromise: A developmental theory of occupational aspirations. *Journal of Counseling Psychology, 28,* 545–579.

Greene, B. (Ed.). (1997). *Ethnic and cultural diversity among lesbians and gay men: Vol. 3. Psychological perspectives on lesbian and gay issues.* Newbury Park, CA: Sage.

Griffin, P. (1992). From hiding out to coming out: Empowering lesbian and gay educators. In K. M. Harbeck (Ed.), *Coming out of the classroom closet* (pp. 167–196). Binghamton, NY: Harrington Park Press.

Hall, M. (1986). The lesbian corporate experience. *Journal of Homosexuality, 12,* 59–75.

Hetherington, C. (1991). Life planning and career counseling with gay and lesbian students. In N. Evans & V. Wall (Eds.), *Beyond tolerance: Gays, lesbians and bisexuals on campus* (pp. 131–146). Alexandria, VA: American College Personnel Association.

Hetherington, C., Hillerbrand, E., & Etringer, B. (1989). Career counseling with gay men: Issues and recommendations for research. *Journal of Counseling & Development, 67,* 452–454.

Hetherington, C., & Orzek, A. (1989). Career counseling and life planning with lesbian women. Special Issue: Gay, lesbian and bisexual issues in counseling. *Journal of Counseling & Development, 68,* 52–57.

Levine, M. P. (1979). Employment discrimination against gay men. *International Review of Modern Sociology, 9,* 151–163.

Levine, M. P., & Leonard, R. (1984). Discrimination against lesbians in the work force. *Signs: Journal of Women in Culture and Society, 9,* 700–710.

Lonborg, S. D., & Phillips, J. M. (1996). Investigating the career development of gays, lesbians, and bisexuals: Methodological considerations and recommendations. *Journal of Vocational Behavior, 48,* 176–194.

Milburn, L. (1993). Career issues of a gay man: Case of Allan. *Career Development Quarterly, 41,* 195–196.

Mobley, M., & Slaney, R. B. (1996). Holland's theory: Its relevance for lesbian and gay career clients. *Journal of Vocational Behavior, 48,* 125–135.

Morgan, K. S., & Brown, L. S. (1991). Lesbian career development, work behavior and vocational counseling. *The Counseling Psychologist, 19,* 273–291.

Morin, S., & Rothblum, E. (1991). Removing the stigma: Fifteen years of progress. *American Psychologist, 46,* 947–949.

Morrow, S. L., Gore, P. A., Jr., & Campbell, B. W. (1996). The application of a sociocognitive framework to the career development of lesbians and gay men. *Journal of Vocational Behavior, 48,* 136–148.

Olson, M. R. (1987). A study of gay and lesbian teachers. *Journal of Homosexuality, 13,* 73–81.

Orzek, A. M. (1992). Career counseling for the gay and lesbian community. In S. H. Dworkin & F. J. Gutierrez (Eds.), *Counseling gay men and lesbians: Journey to the end of the rainbow* (pp. 23–34). Alexandria, VA: American Association for Counseling and Development.

Pope, M. (1995). Career interventions for gay and lesbian clients: A synopsis of practice, knowledge and research needs. *Career Development Quarterly, 44,* 191–203.

Prince, J. P. (1995). Influences upon the career development of gay men. *Career Development Quarterly, 44,* 168–177.

Sailer, D. D., Korschgen, A. J., & Lokken, J. M. (1994). Responding to the career needs of gays, lesbians, and bisexuals. *Journal of Career Planning and Employment, 54,* 39–42.

Schachar, S. A., & Gilbert, L. A. (1983). Working lesbians: Role conflicts and coping strategies. *Psychology of Women Quarterly, 7,* 244–256.

Schmitz, T. J. (1988). Career counseling implications with the gay and lesbian population. *Journal of Employment Counseling, 25,* 51–56.

Schneider, B. E. (1986). Coming out at work: Bridging the private/public gap. *Work and Occupations, 13,* 463–487.

Shidlo, A. (1994). Internalized homophobia: Conceptual and empirical issues in measurement. In B. Green & G. M. Herek (Eds.), *Lesbian and gay psychologies: Theory, research and clinical application: Vol. 1: Psychological perspective on lesbian and gay issues* (pp. 176–205). Newbury Park, CA: Sage.

Van Den Bergh, N. (1994). From invisibility to voice: Providing EAP assistance to lesbians at the workplace. *Employee Assistance Quarterly, 9*(3/4), 161–177.

Woods, S. E. (1994). *The corporate closet.* New York: Free Press.

Woods, S. E., & Harbeck, K. M. (1992). Living in two worlds: The identity management strategies used by lesbian physical educators. In K. M. Harbeck (Ed.), *Coming out of the classroom closet* (pp. 141–166). Binghamton, NY: Harrington Park Press.

17

RELIGION AND SPIRITUALITY

MARY GAGE DAVIDSON

Institutionalized religion has been a vehicle for intolerance and op-pression of gay, lesbian, and bisexual men and women since the early Mid-dle Ages (Boswell, 1980). Historically, monotheistic religions—among them Islam, Judaism, and Christianity—have denied acceptance to openly lesbian, gay, and bisexual (LGB) individuals and couples. Within each of these three traditions today, different sects, movements, and denominations vary in their degree of tolerance, but full inclusion and celebration of openly gay, lesbian, and bisexual men and women remain the exception to the rule.

Many experts have articulated a belief that because of the oppression of heterosexist society, gay, bisexual, and lesbian persons are more in need of, and more open to, spiritual nourishment than others (Fortunato, 1982; Garanzini, 1989; O'Neill & Ritter, 1992; Struzzo, 1989). Gorman (1991), for example, speaks of the 1980s as a time when "spirituality has finally come out of the closet" for gay men, accompanying "an awakening of interest in things of the spirit broadly defined" (p. 47). Thus, spirituality has become an "emic category" (Gorman, 1991, p. 45), and its expression a recognized part of gay, bisexual, and lesbian life in the U.S. (Gorman,

409

1991; Highleyman, 1995). What does this mean for those in psychology who work with gay, lesbian, and bisexual persons? In short, it means that for psychologists, familiarity with and openness to religion and spirituality become a necessity.

To more fully understand many gay, lesbian, and bisexual men and women, and to intervene most successfully in eliminating homophobia, biphobia, and its sequelae, psychologists must be aware of the homo- and biphobia historically and currently imposed by traditional religion. As psychologists, we must be able to recognize and be comfortable discussing spiritual and religious issues. Further, we must begin to understand spirituality not simply as an issue or concern, but as a lived dimension and transformative worldview in the lives of some gay, lesbian, and bisexual persons. Only then can we help clients transform conflicts into psychological and spiritual growth (Browning, Reynolds, & Dworkin, 1991; Haldeman, 1996; Nelson, 1982; Ritter & O'Neill, 1989).

The first purpose of this chapter is to provide a brief overview of selected religious positions toward gay, lesbian, and bisexual persons, with an emphasis on Christianity. The second is to describe the ways in which spirituality and religion have been embraced by gay, lesbian, and bisexual men and women and to introduce readers to the religious and spiritual issues involved in their psychotherapy. The spiritual coming-out process will be presented as a prototype for considering spirituality as a dimension of the whole person as well as a rough framework and itinerary for psychotherapy. Finally, some recommendations will be presented for further research, theory development, and training to increase our understanding of religion and spirituality as they relate to LGB persons.

DEFINITIONS AND DISCLAIMERS

The purpose of this chapter, as articulated above, is descriptive, exploratory, and propositional. Thus, it is different from others in this volume. Because very little empirical research exists as a basis for conclusions and generalizations, the intent is to provide more critical analysis than proven hypothesis, and more conjecture than conclusion. Spirituality and religion, as topics, are difficult both to define and quantify. Thus, several definitions and disclaimers are necessary for this chapter. *Spirituality* refers to that "vast realm of human potential dealing with ultimate purposes, with higher entities, with God, with love, with compassion, with purpose" (Tart, 1992, p. 4). In contrast, *religion* refers to an integrated system of beliefs in a superhuman power (Morris, 1970), as well as to the social institutions that house, organize, nourish, and direct the expression of belief among its followers. Religion, although neither necessary nor sufficient for the presence of spirituality, does not exclude the possibility of its presence. In this chapter, the term *spirituality* will be used to indicate a whole dimension and realm of consciousness related to human growth, and to "impl[y] . . . the *experiences* that people have about the meaning of life, God, [and] ways to live" (Tart, 1992, p. 4).

In articulating the need for psychologists to include religious issues and a spiritual dimension in their work, I do not intend to suggest that spirituality is necessary or healthy for every gay, lesbian, and bisexual man and woman. For some persons, religious and spiritual practices are neither relevant nor important. The focus of this chapter is on the majority of persons for whom spirituality and religion are concerns. This chapter will also address the diversity in gay, lesbian, and bisexual males and females, as well as the distinctiveness of the three groups. I do not believe that religious and spiritual expression and development will be identical either within or among gay, lesbian, and bisexual male and female communities. Rather than categorizing and making distinctions, my intention is to ex-plicate a variety of spiritual expressions and processes as a beginning step in understanding this important topic.

Similarly, whenever mention is made in this chapter of spiritual com-monalities that many members of a racial, ethnic, or cultural group may share, my attempt is not to categorize all members of a given group, nor to gloss over important and significant group- and individual differences that exist. Substantive distinctions exist, especially in Native American cultures, among different indigenous groups and among individuals within each group. Categorical generalizations would be both inaccurate and dis-respectful of diversity.

Another disclaimer relates to the lack of literature exclusively dedi-cated to the religious or spiritual concerns of bisexual men and women. Although some writers and researchers do describe spiritual traditions and expressions of gay men and lesbians, only a few resources refer to or specify bisexual spirituality. Bisexuality has generally been neglected as a research topic, because its place as a viable identity has been denied by both gays and lesbians, and heterosexual persons (Queen, 1996). In this chapter, I include bisexual men and women in the discussion either when the liter-ature actually cites this group, or when it describes conditions that indis-criminately reject gays, lesbians, and bisexual persons. For example, dis-cussions in the literature that reflect strict gender roles maintained through heterosexist intolerance would be relevant to both gays and lesbians, as well as to bisexual persons. My discussion will reflect the paucity of avail-able information. However, in no way do I intend to denigrate the concerns of bisexual men and women.

Finally, I do not wish to imply that psychologists cannot be effective without recognizing a spiritual dimension in their own lives or without being well-versed in a variety of religious traditions. I am suggesting, how-ever, that without an awareness of, and openness to, spiritual concerns, psychologists limit the scope and depth of their work with gay, lesbian, and bisexual clients.

THREE MONOTHEISTIC RELIGIONS AND INTOLERANCE: A BRIEF REVIEW

Western institutionalized religion and its heritage have had a profound influence on gay, lesbian, and bisexual persons living in the United States. Essential sacred texts shared by both Christians and Jews contain ideas that exclude gays, lesbians, and bisexual persons. Both Torah and the Old Testament contain the Pentateuch, the Five Books of Moses, from which passages (e.g. Genesis 1:27 and Leviticus 18:22) have been quoted by orthodox Jews and traditional Christians to condemn same-sex affectional orientation (Alpert, 1997; Helminiak, 1994). In this chapter, the term *Judeo-Christian* is used to refer to those values and beliefs that are drawn from common sacred texts, shared by some Jews and Christians, and used to prohibit or render invisible gay, lesbian, and bisexual relationships. Although the Judeo-Christian tradition has hegemony in United States culture and is emphasized in this chapter, a brief consideration of Islam is included first, because Islam is the world's fastest growing religion and the West's closest geographic and conceptual neighbor (Blumenfeld & Raymond, 1988). This section is intended to provide an understanding of the background against which gay, lesbian, and bisexual persons struggle when seeking to define religious and spiritual dimensions in their lives.

Although the Koran does not condemn same-sex affectional orientation per se, Islamic doctrine views sexual acts between two males as a type of adultery. Heterosexual marriage is the expected norm, and sex outside of marriage is a sin—theoretically punishable by death but requiring impossibly strenuous requirements for evidential proof (Dynes & Donaldson, 1992). Fundamentalists within the Shiite sect, however, condemn sex acts between males and impose harsh and violent penalties on the receptive partner in anal intercourse (Blumenfeld & Raymond, 1988).

Within Judaism, traditional opinion dictates an historical prohibition of sexual acts between same-sex partners as sin (Umansky, 1997). Thus, "heterosexual marriage is the only route to religious and personal fulfillment" (Kahn, 1989, p. 47). This is due, in part, to the fact that for some, the union between male and female is viewed as a fundamental basis for Jewish family life (Kimelman, 1994). Inroads toward tolerance and acceptance have been made within more progressive Reform and Reconstructionist movements in the last several decades. For example, lesbian rabbi Rebecca Alpert (1997) has sought to reinterpret and transform Jewish sacred texts from a uniquely lesbian Jewish perspective. However, for Orthodox Jews, sexual acts by same-sex partners remains a violation of nature (Blumenfeld & Raymond, 1988; Cooper, 1989; Dynes & Donaldson, 1992).

The Roman Catholic Church offers perhaps the most clearly articulated, although much debated, sexual ethic: Sex is only moral and good within heterosexual, monogamous marriage where the theoretical potential for procreation exists (Nugent & Gramick, 1989). In 1986, Cardinal Ratzinger, in a letter to the Bishops of the Catholic Church on the pastoral care of homosexual persons, stated that "[a]lthough the particular inclination of the homosexual person is not a sin, it is a more or less strong tendency ordered toward an intrinsic moral evil; and thus the inclination itself must be seen as an objective disorder" (Ratzinger, 1994, p. 40). This position obviously does not validate the goodness and worth of gay, lesbian, or bisexual men and women. However, more and more gay and lesbian Catholics are choosing to affirm both their sexual and their Catholic identity as the Church continues to wrestle with the issue of same-sex affectional orientation (Nugent, 1992; Sullivan, 1997).

Within Protestant denominations, stances on same-sex affectional orientation range from the rejecting, punishing position of Biblical fundamentalists to qualified acceptance of many mainstream denominations. Qualified acceptance often means adopting a position of hating the sin (sexual acts between same-sex partners) but loving the sinner (LGB persons). This position puts gays, lesbians, and bisexual men and women in a cruel double bind: Affirmation by the church community is available only through celibacy or (false) heterosexual marriage (Nelson, 1982). The few denominations that offer full acceptance include the Friends (Quakers) and Unitarian Universalists. These denominations, as well as certain congregations in other denominations, welcome the diversity offered by gay, lesbian, and bisexual men and women (Blumenfeld & Raymond, 1988; Nugent & Gramick, 1989; Siker, 1994).

The Church of Jesus Christ of the Latter Day Saints (LDS), or the Mormon church, deserves special consideration because of its unique position in Christian theology and because of its rapid growth. Projections on the basis of birthrates and new conversion rates place Mormonism among the major world faiths by the year 2080 (Stark, 1994). Traditional Mormon doctrine promotes a uniquely heterosexist and patriarchal family-centered theology in which both premarital and extramarital sex are completely unacceptable (Heaton, Goodman, & Holman, 1994). Childbearing itself has great theological significance for Mormons, who have historically exceeded the national average family size (Heaton, 1986). Thus, the LDS church's position toward same-sex affectional orientation is predictably condemnatory; the Church views any same-sex attraction as a (perverted) choice that must be suppressed or reoriented into heterosexual marriage. Persons who "indulge" in what is viewed as unnatural behavior face excommunication (Schow, 1997).

Time has been on the side of gays and lesbians, however. Activists have used scientific evidence of biological influences on sexual orientation (LeVay, 1995; Money, 1987) to weaken the prejudices of many churches and synagogues. In addition, "conversion" therapy, often supported by Christian fundamentalists and aimed at changing clients' sexual orientation, has failed to "cure homosexuality" (Haldeman, 1996), and this has added "evidence" to biological hypotheses. The use of a monosexual argument that persons are biologically predisposed to be attracted to only one gender, whether it be the same or the other sex, however, does not assist bisexual males and females in their struggle against religious intolerance. As Driver (1982) has indicated, in some ways bisexuality is "the [Christian] church's deepest sexual fear" (p. 18). If the sexual loves and attractions of persons are not clear and exclusive, then "[t]his is as much as to say that all sexual love is good, and that its form does not matter" (p. 18). This position undermines a basic (though anachronistic and damaging) emphasis in the New Testament, particularly the Pauline letters, which claims celibacy as the human ideal. Sex within marriage, a compromise for those not capable of abstinence, has procreation as its only purpose. Although liberal Protestant theology has rejected this position by supporting sexuality within marriage as a means of fostering intimacy as well as procreation (Nugent & Gramick, 1989), a fundamental erotophobia continues to feed homo- and biphobia and remains strong in the (Christian) culture.

In contrast, Islamic tradition does not include the view of human nature as "fallen," nor is celibacy valued as an avenue for spiritual devotion. In fact, celibacy is discouraged, because sexuality is understood to be a gift from Allah (Blumenfeld & Raymond, 1988). Thus, in this culture, the erotophobia of the Christian tradition is absent; however, the individual's role in heterosexual marriage and family is viewed as a primary and compelling obligation to God and to society. It is on these grounds, and because of a prohibition against avoiding excess, that sexual acts outside of heterosexual marriage are disfavored (Blumenfeld & Raymond, 1988; Schild, 1992).

In summary, the three monotheistic religions discussed above—Islam, Judaism, and Christianity—each paint a backdrop of intolerance against which LGB persons have had to define their religious and spiritual beliefs. Despite some moderation of position, the institutions of both Christianity and Judaism have not supported gay men, lesbians, or bisexual persons either "professionally, liturgically/pastorally, or doctrinally" (Clark, Brown, & Hochstein, 1990, p. 265). Instead these institutions have been the "arbiter[s] of homophobic judgement, fostering rejection and alienation not only within gay/lesbian individuals and gay/lesbian relationships, but also between gays/lesbians and both their families of origin and their native cultural ethos" (p. 268). In the remainder of this chapter, I focus primarily on Christianity because of its salience in the United States, as reflected in the literature.

THE RELIGIOUS AND SPIRITUAL EXPRESSIONS
OF LGB PERSONS

Given the historical oppression of traditional religion, it is surprising that gay men and lesbians consistently participate in institutional forms of Judaism and Christianity. Gay men represent a disproportionately large percentage of Catholic clergy (Curb & Manahan, 1985; DeStefano, 1986). They also have formed official and unofficial support groups in every Christian denomination, fought vigorously for ordination of gay and lesbian clergy, and established their own denomination (Universalist Fellowship of Metropolitan Community Church) as well as a loose federation of synagogues [World Congress of Gay and Lesbian Jewish Organization] (Clark et al., 1990).

For gay, lesbian, and bisexual people who wish to remain within traditional religious institutions, one strategy has been to separate God and spirit from the history of those social institutions of organized religion that reject homosexuality. For example, Episcopalian priest and civil rights activist Malcolm Boyd (1994) has asserted that "God never planned anything in terms of making gays suffer. God created. It isn't God who's ever persecuted gay people" (p. 244). Although religious beliefs may incorporate oppression and may be used to justify prejudice, they are not the cause of intolerance (Boswell, 1980).

A body of excellent scholarship generated by Christian apologists (e.g. Boswell, 1980; Countryman, 1988; Helminiak, 1994; Nelson, 1982; Scroggs, 1983) shows that attempts to "proof-text" or use specific Biblical passages to condemn sexual acts between same-sex partners (typically male) are based on inadequate interpretations and inaccurate translations. Others, including feminist and gay liberation theologians, such as Rosemary Ruether, Carter Heyward, J. Michael Clark, and R. Cleaver, assert unique theological opportunities inherent in the marginal and oppressed position of gays, bisexual men and women, and lesbians. Rather than eternally trying to justify bi- and same-sex affectional orientation in existent traditions, this position articulates a new theology of liberation. As Clark (1991) has stated, "Gay people must make a commitment to be a force to be reckoned with in theology by claiming and assuming our right to theologize and to speak prophetically" (p. 28).

In response to hostility and rejection, some gays, lesbians, and bisexual people have turned from traditional religion as well as from a belief in God. Many have found alternatives to monotheistic religions in paganism, Greek and Eastern mythology, witchcraft and magic, and Native American traditions (Browning et al., 1991; Dynes & Donaldson, 1992; Highleyman, 1995; Ritter & O'Neill, 1989). Buddhism and its practices have been a welcome alternative to many, because it "contains no trace of homophobia" (Dynes & Donaldson, 1992, p. xiii). Others have joined the New Age movement to find alternative spiritual communities (Dynes & Donaldson, 1992; Highleyman, 1995).

The gay, lesbian, and bisexual community offers many related definitions of spirituality. For example, according to the informants of anthropologist E. Michael Gorman (1991), spirituality may be described as: "a connection with one's inner self connected to a larger consciousness"; "being the truth that I know, and not hiding"; or "a movement toward wholeness, to live values around authenticity." Spirituality may also refer to "our experience of the spirit and our place in the universe," "or an experience of God" (p. 45). Eric Law (1997), a Chinese gay Episcopal priest, views spirituality as "the ability to make connections: connections with myself, especially parts of myself that I dislike and deny; connection with others, not just those who are like me but also those who are different and even my enemies; and connection with God through Jesus Christ" (p. 345). N. Wilson (1995) relates coming out to telling the truth—a defining aspect of gay, lesbian, and bisexual male and female spirituality. She envisions spirituality as "claim[ing] purpose and meaning for gay and lesbian people on the planet" (p. 41). Finally, for Rainone (1987), feminist spiritual practice is aimed at developing "a sense of compassion for oneself as well as for others" (p. 350).

LGB persons have found and created myriad models and definitions, both within and outside of traditional religions, for spiritual expression. As Boyd (1987) has stated, "We gay people, in our diversity, will never follow simply one path in spirituality" (p. 83).

BENEFITS AND FUNCTIONS OF RELIGION AND SPIRITUALITY FOR LGB PERSONS

As is clear from the above definitions, religion and spirituality provide new ways of viewing and relating to the world for many gay, lesbian, and bisexual men and women. O'Neill and Ritter (1992) posit three basic functions of a spiritual dimension in an LGB person's life: affirming one's basic goodness, developing a sense of community, and providing a way of connecting with a God or creator. These functions will be elaborated on below and include multicultural examples provided in the first section, Affirmation of Basic Goodness.

Affirmation of Basic Goodness

Bi- and homophilic religion and spirituality affirm the basic goodness of gay, lesbian, and bisexual men and women. Within a church or synagogue that celebrates diversity, gay, lesbian, and bisexual members "contribute to the wholeness, the multidimensionality of creation" (Wilson, 1995, p. 41). A "creation-centered spirituality" (Struzzo, 1989) in which all creation is celebrated replaces the redemption or fall model with its emphasis on being born into sin. For example, Gorman (1991) has spoken of the *kerygma* ("good news") that gay is good.

This affirmation of basic goodness leads to a recognition of the unique contributions of gay, lesbian, and bisexual men and women. From a position on the margins of society the hypocrisy of traditional orthodoxy becomes apparent and can be articulated (Clark, 1991; Cleaver, 1995; Shallenberger, 1994). Gays, lesbians, and bisexuals give voice to the need for liberation of all who are oppressed and marginalized (Clark, 1991; Cleaver, 1995; Heyward, 1984; Miller, 1997). These liberation theologists offer a radical critique of blind conformity to rigid gender roles, the "erotization of dominance and dependency" in heterosexual relationships (N. Wilson, 1995, p. 44), and male heterosexual preoccupation with competition and dominance (Hay, 1994).

Gay, lesbian, and bisexual males and females, by standing in opposition to traditional Judeo-Christian condemnation of sexuality outside of procreation, insist that our bodies and sexuality are good (Heyward, 1984). They offer an alternative to the destructive dualism where spirit and body are placed in opposition, the earth is ravaged, and the physical realm is denigrated, or equated with lust and sin. As Starhawk (1995) writes, "we as bisexuals can, out of our unique experiences, define a new morality based on the honoring of our inner, body-rooted authority and the integrity of the earth-body of which we are each a part" (p. 328). Bisexual male and female spirituality can thus involve a reclamation of the earth as erotic, and of pleasure as sacred (Starhawk, 1995). This "erotic inclusiveness" offers a basis for "multicultural awareness and openness to a variety of viewpoints" (Bennett, 1992, p. 226). Similarly, Clark (1993), an ethicist and theologian, asserts the need for a gay ecotheology to protect and nurture the earth and its nonhuman inhabitants.

Spirituality, according to some polytheistic traditions such as those among Native populations in America, also provides unique and positive roles of gay, lesbian, and bisexual persons. Both the shaman, who is concerned with ecstatic experiences and contact with the other world, and the two-spirited person, a cultural mediator and restorer of balance (Hall, 1994; Hay, 1994), are associated with fluid gender roles. Likewise, African and Afro-Haitian religious traditions, such as *vodun* and *Yoruba*, offer a different "theology of gender" (Farajaje-Jones, 1995, p. 124). Among the latter, some manifestations of the divine (*orisha*) are bigendered, and the body and sexuality are perceived as a gift (Farajaje-Jones, 1995). These examples have been embraced by some writers as models for gay, lesbian, and bisexual male and female gifts of creativity, mediation, and transcendent ability (Farajaje-Jones, 1995; Hay, 1994; Roscoe, 1994; Steinbrecher, 1994).

Greek and Roman myths also confirm gay and lesbian presence in history and culture, describing certain special abilities and relationships that are often missing in Judeo-Christian culture (Downing, 1997; Roscoe, 1995). As Roscoe (1995) points out, myths can lead to a discovery of archetypal images that shape the psyche of gay men. These archetypes offer corrective viewpoints for the many religious and psychological theories that describe same-sex affectional orientation as heterosexual development gone awry. Finally, myths, by tapping into the unconscious parts of the mind, offer to gay, lesbian, and bisexual men and women the possibility of spiritual and psychological transformation. Roscoe (1995) encourages not "blind imitation" of these myths and traditions, but the use of them by LGB persons to facilitate a deeper self-understanding that promotes the discovery of more—and more thoughtful—options for action. He states that "[m]yths are to be imagined, not imitated. Used in this way, they can lead to ethical choices attuned to the complex world we live in" (p. 19).

This first function of a spiritual dimension—an affirmation of basic goodness of LGB persons—thus encourages the recognition of LGB persons' unique contributions and positive roles in community. The articulation of these role models not only encourages gay, lesbian, and bisexual men and women but offers an extremely important and corrective contribution to society in general.

Connecting to Community and to a God

A second basic function of spirituality and religion involves the presence of a supportive community (O'Neill & Ritter, 1992). Rituals such as coming-out celebrations, commitment ceremonies, anniversaries, and celebrations of other important times affirm and support their participants (Rainone, 1987). Community fosters the sharing of life images with others (O'Neill & Ritter, 1992) and a sense of belonging that is vitally important for LGB persons who are too often rejected by their biological families, their work environment, and their culture. Especially within the scope of the AIDS crisis, gay, lesbian, and bisexual persons have often filled the role of caring for others. Helping the dying has also often been a part of participating in a spiritual community (Boyd, 1994; Gorman, 1991; Ramer, 1994).

According to O'Neill and Ritter (1992), the third and final function of spirituality is to provide "a pathway to the creator" (p. 39). A connection with the divine and the transcendent can provide hope (Gorman, 1991) and moral guidance, particularly when the AIDS crisis raises agonizing questions about the meaning and purpose of life and death (Helminiak, 1995). Gay, lesbian, and bisexual men and women have continued the fight for official, ordained roles in churches and synagogues, thereby claiming professional access to God. In this section, three functions of spirituality and religion have been described. Clearly, the affirmation of goodness, a sense of community, and a connection with God or a creator can assume great significance in the daily lives of LGB persons and can promote healthy self-esteem and a sense of belonging.

THE SPIRITUAL COMING OUT PROCESS:
AN ITINERARY FOR THERAPY

As Haldeman (1996) has stated, "the spiritual components of identity development . . . have scarcely been mentioned in the mental health literature" (p. 882). However, several writers describe a process that is variously termed "a spiritual quest" (Helminiak, 1995, p. 307), "coming out within" (O'Neill & Ritter, 1992, p. 1), "coming out inside" (Thompson, 1987, p. 241), "choosing exile and beginning the journey out" (Miller, 1997, p. 235), and "embracing the exile" (Fortunato, 1982). This process articulates the progression of spiritual development in an individual.

In the literature, different models use the language and metaphors of the particular tradition to which they belong, whether they be Christian (Fortunato, 1982; Miller, 1997), Eastern mystical (Harvey, 1994), dynamic psychological (Isay, 1994; Walker, 1994), Tibetan Buddhist (Hopkins, 1997), or mythic (Roscoe, 1995). The spiritual coming-out process, in each of these descriptions, begins with oppression and consequent loss familiar to the gay community and ultimately leads to spiritual deepening (Clark et al., 1990; Fortunato, 1982; Garanzini, 1989; Miller, 1997; Struzzo, 1989).

Fortunato (1982), O'Neill and Ritter (1992), and Struzzo (1989) have articulated a paradigm of spiritual development that fits broadly within the Western, Judeo-Christian *Weltanschauung* ("world view"). This model is outlined below because it is useful for those LGB persons seeking to remain within the Judeo-Christian tradition. However, it may not be relevant to persons seeking non-Western paths and traditions.

In this paradigm of spiritual development, gay, lesbian or bisexual men and women, after first attempting to deny the reality of deprivations resulting from oppression, may then come to a fuller understanding of the losses they have experienced and mourn them. These losses can then be integrated into one's identity, reformulated, and transformed as the individual is released from expectations of the life images that do not fit

(O'Neill & Ritter, 1992). Many of these life images are derived from a Western myth that promises power and success to those who fit in and conform (Fortunato, 1982). The transformation of loss into spiritual awakening can involve experiencing oneness with others, God, or both (O'Neill & Ritter, 1992); "having direct contact in the soul, the core of being, with the Source" (Harvey, 1994, p. 52); or embracing the "awesome and liberating reality that *all* creation is redeemed" (Fortunato, 1982, p. 43).

O'Neill and Ritter (1992) present five themes that delineate a spiritual development that stems from a concern with fitting in with heterosexual society. While these themes are phrased in secular language, they still retain implicit ties to a Christian moral worldview. They include a progression "from rigidity to openness . . . from external authority toward personal integrity . . . from disconnectedness toward inter-relatedness . . . from self-centeredness toward generativity," and "from a literal interpretation of pain and loss as personal, toward a symbolic understanding of loss as universal" (pp. 209–211). Thus, the goals of transformation, put in secular language, include authenticity, openness, and growing compassion for other marginalized people (O'Neill & Ritter, 1992). Such self-transcendence is seen as particularly important for gays, lesbians, and bisexual men and women because adaptation to dominant culture so often involves an unhealthy rejection of one's identity (Clark et al., 1990; Fortunato, 1982; Struzzo, 1989).

Other authors have sought to describe models of spiritual development without implicit or explicit ties to the Western Judeo-Christian world view. For example, on the basis of what he terms a *nontheistic, fully psychological approach*, Helminiak has stated, "If all spirituality is grounded in what is inherent in humanity as such, if the core of spirituality is basic human integrity, the option to affirm *oneself* rather than societal and religious expectations is pivotal to all spiritual development" (Helminiak, 1987, as cited in Helminiak, 1995, p. 307).

The tasks of spiritual development are not far removed from gay, lesbian, and bisexual male and female affirmative psychotherapy (Haldeman, 1996; Rainone, 1987). Rainone, for example, has compared feminist spiritual development with psychotherapy, and finds five similarities among the two. First, both deal with self-renewal and affirm and strengthen self-identity. Second, both help the individual to become more consciously aware of feelings. Third, both offer a perspective that allows choices to be made about whether and how to express these feelings. Fourth, both help individuals confront what is harmful in their lives on both conscious and unconscious levels. Finally, both facilitate making greater peace with one's self and others.

Haldeman (1996) has described spiritual and psychological identity as two parallel and overlapping processes. Spiritual development heals the wounded spirit, and psychological identity development mitigates the impact of sociocultural damage. Both allow individuals to express and release pain and then move on and both "facilitate . . . the repair and growth of the whole person" (Haldeman, 1996, p. 884). Thus, the difficulty in separating psychological therapeutic processes from spiritual development becomes evident. Acceptance and celebration of one's sexual orientation, one's life, and one's self can be mediated through both psychological and spiritual or religious processes. Optimally, the two may overlap as psychologist and client participate in an awareness of the spiritual dimensions of personal growth.

SPECIFIC ISSUES IN PSYCHOTHERAPY

LGB-affirming psychotherapy can be described as a process that helps the client move through the coming-out process by incorporating both sexual identity and spiritual development (Fortunato, 1982; Garanzini, 1989; Haldeman, 1996; Struzzo, 1989). Although the relation between coming out as lesbian, gay, or bisexual and spiritual development has not been clearly delineated, Wagner, Serafini, Rabkin, Remien, and Williams (1994) indicate that for gay men, the process of integrating one's religion and sexual orientation leads to a shorter delay in the coming-out process.

To provide conditions for psychotherapy where such an integration of religion, spirituality, and sexual orientation can occur and where therapy is sensitive to religious and spiritual dimensions in LGB persons' lives, therapists need to create an environment that fosters a "basic openness and understanding of the dimensions of spirituality, a general vocabulary for such experience, and an appreciation for the particular functions of spirituality in the patient's life" (Haldeman, 1996, p. 883–884). Within this environment, many different combinations of theoretical orientation and spiritual tradition are possible and productive.

Five issues relevant to a therapeutic process that is sensitive to LGB clients' religious and spiritual concerns are discussed below. These include an awareness of the interplay of client gender, sexual orientation, and ethnicity with religion or spirituality; the relation between family of origin and traditional religious values and their impact on the client; the inherent difficulty that occurs when bi- and homophobic religions function as a client's major source of support; the spiritual impact of AIDS; and finally, the therapists' own prejudices and intolerance toward religion and spirituality.

Awareness of Ethnicity, Gender, and Sexual Orientation

The consideration of the synergistic interplay between a client's ethnicity, gender, and sexual orientation, and his or her spiritual concerns, can be a complex task for the therapist. Quantitative research in this area is minimal and often nonconclusive. However, religious affiliation, often linked to cultural heritage and ethnicity, has been found to be related to attitudes toward same-sex affectional orientation (Jensen, Gambles, & Olsen, 1988; Lottes & Kuriloff, 1992). Certain racial and ethnic groups may feel forced to choose between their culturally or racially mediated religion and the gay, lesbian, and bisexual male and female community, often feeling excluded by both (Folayan, 1992; Gutierrez, 1992; Law, 1997). As Gock (1992) indicates, "the process of integrating one's multiple identities requires some additional and independent tasks not experienced by . . . those in the mainstream lesbian and gay community" (p. 249).

The issue of integrating multiple identities is complicated further by the hegemony of religious or spiritual beliefs within certain cultures. For example, as Folayan (1992) has stated, "The most solid community-based institution within the African-American community is the church. Whatever the denomination . . . , they consistently condemn gay men and lesbians for their sexual orientation and condone by their tacit approval the rampant homophobia directed towards Black gay men and lesbians" (p. 238). She goes on to poignantly describe the "sense of exile, of being cast out from the larger community around [herself and other African-American gays and lesbians]" (Folayan, 1992, p. 238).

For many male and female Latin Americans, the cultural power of institutionalized religion, specifically Catholicism, looms large. Catholicism's emphasis on conservative and traditional family values strongly influences the Latin American culture and supports the rejection of gays, lesbians, and bisexual persons (Carballo-Dieguez, 1989). Thus, to come out as gay, lesbian, or bisexual in this culture may mean a triple loss of family, community, and church. Therapists must be mindful of the multiplicity of losses, exponential in their ability to produce psychic pain, as they work with LGB persons from ethnic and racial backgrounds where homophobic institutionalized religion is a bonding and influential force within the culture.

For some ethnic groups, such as Native Americans, even the discrete categorization of sexual orientation and gender is problematic and alien to their worldview (Tafoya, 1992; A. Wilson, 1996). In addition, the Western notion of self-actualization through individuated identity does not fit their strong community ethic. An important point to keep in mind is that for some cultures, all aspects of identity (sexual orientation, spiritual development, race, gender) can be interconnected and fluid. As an indigenous American woman states, "We (two spirits) become self-actualized when we become what we've always been, empowered by our location in our communities" (A. Wilson, 1996, p. 310). Classifying sexual identity and spiritual development into stages, or separating them from community, may neither fit nor be helpful.

A similar linguistic and philosophical problem relates to applying

Western terminology to Muslims. The Western concept of same-sex orientation stemming from personality and identity has typically resulted in a condemnation of the "homosexual" person. In contrast, according to Islamic law, only specific same-sex acts are condemned, not persons. In Islamic culture, sexual acts are determined not by a person's individual identity, but by the social role pattern and circumstances in which a person finds him or herself (Schild, 1992). Thus, concepts like "heterosexuality" and "homosexuality" lose meaning in this non-Western culture, and applying these categories to persons from this cultural background can result in misunderstanding.

Because cultural, gender, and age differences in identity development exist for gays, lesbians, and bisexual men and women (Fox, 1996), it is probable that similar distinctions inform the process of spiritual development. For example, in a qualitative study on values and the identities of lesbian and gay religious leaders, Fischer (1989) found gender differences in stories reflecting spiritual and identity development. Women emphasized the meaning of relationship, as well as a sense of the importance of nature and human community in the revelation of the self, whereas men identified the self as the central figure and saw coming out as the pivotal moment in the story. While the women's stories described a flow of experiences, the men's narrative took the form of a journey. If spiritual coming-out processes are related to socially constructed gender roles as well as sexual orientation, it is incumbent on therapists to be aware of gender issues as well as sexual orientation in clients working on spiritual concerns.

It is clear from the above discussion that a therapist faces many complex and interrelated therapeutic concerns when working with LGB clients from different cultures as they seek to integrate spiritual or religious concerns in their lives. To summarize, therapists would benefit from being sensitive to gender, sexual orientation, and cultural differences that exist in spiritual development, as well as to inherent difficulties that arise when Western categories and definitions of both gender and sexual orientation are applied to non-Western individuals.

Impact of Family of Origin

A second therapeutic issue relates to the impact of the client's family of origin on his or her religious and spiritual concerns. Research by Newman and Muzzonigro (1993) has indicated that race has no effect on an adolescent male's coming-out process, but that the presence of traditional family values (adherence to religion, and emphasis on marriage and procreation) does. Adolescents from traditional families perceived increased disapproval and rejection because they were gay, which ultimately heightened their sense of being "different." Other studies have also found a positive correlation between intolerance and traditional beliefs (Jensen et al.,

1988; Lottes & Kuriloff, 1992). Thus, therapists must be aware of the impact of oppressive religion and prejudice not only on clients' spiritual development but also as mediated through their family of origin. Families often use religious arguments as grounds for abuse and rejection of gay, lesbian, and bisexual children. Therapy can help clients not only to deal with the pain and loss associated with a rejecting family but also to examine religious and moral assumptions held by the client's family of origin. On examination, some of these assumptions may no longer be relevant to the client, or part of their "life image" (O'Neill & Ritter, 1992, p. 5).

Client Involvement in Bi- or Homophobic Religious Communities

A third therapeutic issue arises when the therapist recognizes that the client is involved in a bi- or homophobic religious community that may be the client's major source of social support. The therapist's task becomes to assist clients to fully explore the conflict between their love for their families and religion and the hurtful, potentially damaging elements of these. Through this process, clients may increase their awareness of this conflict and the dilemma it presents to make more conscious choices about how to proceed. A knee-jerk abandonment of either family relationships or valued religion can result in extreme isolation in the same way that leading a double life to maintain ties inevitably results in alienation from self and valued others. Because families of origin and treasured religions are each part and parcel of the client's identity, the transformation or rejection of their destructive parts is a slow and painful process. When clients are ready, therapists can help them distinguish between spirituality and the oppressive aspects of traditional religion, or assist them in becoming aware of alternatives to organized religion (Shannon & Woods, 1991).

The Impact of AIDS

A fourth issue for psychotherapists relates to the challenges presented by AIDS. Two aspects of the AIDS crisis are particularly relevant to therapists working in a religiously and spiritually sensitive way with LGB clients. One involves the spread of the disease and the strain of living with the human immunodeficiency virus, which has provoked a spiritual crisis about the meaning and purpose of life (Fortunato, 1987; Helminiak, 1995); a second relates to how traditional religion has exacerbated the suffering of those with AIDS by increasing bi- and homophobia. This latter concern will be explored first.

Although one study found that fear of AIDS is not related to religiosity, "subjects who attended church on a monthly basis were more AIDS-phobic than those who attended church weekly, rarely, or never" (Kunkel

& Temple, 1992, p. 1038). Religiosity was found to be related to homophobia, however. Members of the Church of Latter-day Saints and those who attended church weekly were found to be more homophobic than participants who selected the response category "other" for religion and those who never attended church, respectively (Kunkel & Temple, 1992).

One particularly toxic myth relating the disease to sexual orientation is that AIDS is the "scourge of God" (Dunphy, 1987; Fortunato, 1987). Some LGB clients who have grown up with the image of a vengeful God, or those who come from families where such beliefs predominate may struggle privately with the belief that persons with AIDS are being punished by God. Sensitive inquiry by therapists about these emotionally charged beliefs, with the goal of bringing them into the therapeutic space for discussion, can be extremely important in decreasing clients' fear and isolation.

Another virulent and related form of biphobia has portrayed bisexual persons, particularly males and African Americans (Farajaje-Jones, 1995), as the bridge over which AIDS has traveled from the gay male to the heterosexual population. Stokes, Taywaditep, Vanable, and McKirnan (1996), citing 1994 Centers for Disease Control statistics, have stated that a larger role has been played by males who inject drugs and that only 15% of women infected through heterosexual contact were infected by bisexual males. However, research indicates that many bisexual men do not disclose to female partners that they have had sexual activity with other men. Rila (1996) concluded that although women who have sex with African American and Latino men may be at greater risk of HIV infection due to a "hidden bisexual male population" (p. 175), all women are at risk in this regard. A further important conclusion extrapolated from this research relates to a need to balance the helpfulness of tracing etiology of infection with an overriding concern for safer sex for everyone, regardless of sexual orientation.

Although this issue has not been investigated directly, it is probable that institutionalized religion, particularly important in both Latino and African American culture, may be one factor promoting the homophobia that can lead to failure to disclose same-sex activities in this bisexual male population. Therapists must help their clients work through both the internalized homophobia as well as the perceived homophobia from others that makes honest disclosure of past sexual history difficult (Stokes et al., 1996). These researchers recommend that therapists be prepared to ask specific questions about sexual activity with male and female partners rather than relying on clients' self-identification as "bisexual."

A second aspect of the AIDS crisis relates to the direct and indirect suffering that often precipitates a spiritual journey. Clients may reevaluate and reconcile with the religion of their upbringing, find a new spiritual practice, or be coerced into conversion, which entails a repudiation of their whole gay, lesbian, or bisexual life when faced with AIDS (Helminiak, 1995). Here, the therapeutic task includes supporting the client's examination of religious and spiritual beliefs to see if they can be embraced with integrity and if they support or sabotage spiritual growth toward personal wholeness. AIDS and its sequelae, rather than leading to despair, can serve as a "challenge to all of us to become as awake and enlightened as possible" (Harvey, 1994, p. 57) and can point out to gay, lesbian, and bisexual persons their unique calling in life.

Therapist Self-Awareness

A final issue for psychotherapy that is sensitive to the religious and spiritual concerns of LGB clients involves therapist self-awareness. Therapists who are not aware of their own moral and religious assumptions and who have not already tried to work through any bi- and homophobic feelings will have a difficult time promoting their clients' spiritual explorations. Clearing out vestiges of bi- and homophobia is an ongoing process for professionals and clients, but it is incumbent on therapists to be constantly vigilant about our own prejudices and intolerance. In addition, therapists' biases against organized religion or New Age spirituality must be addressed and critically examined before working with clients for whom religion and spirituality are sustaining. It is important to know and to be able to refer clients both to traditional and nontraditional spiritual and religious resources in one's own community and to validate clients' needs for such a spiritual community (Browning et al., 1991).

RECOMMENDATIONS FOR RESEARCH, THEORY,
AND TRAINING

As mentioned in the introduction to this chapter, research and theory to date have failed to address the spiritual development and needs of bisexual male and female clients. It is probable that distinctions will be found between the spiritual experiences, needs, and concerns of bisexual men and women and those of gays and lesbians.

The sparse research literature relevant to gay and lesbian spirituality is limited in its scope. Treating religion primarily as a categorical variable or demographic description, these quantitative approaches to the topic fail to consider spirituality as a dimension and vehicle for human growth. Qualitative research that is capable of treating spirituality phenomenologically, especially that which addresses the process of spiritual coming out and its relation to sexual, gender, and racial identity, is needed. Analogously, psychologists also lack any comprehensive theory that reflects a view of persons as physical, sexual, emotional, and spiritual wholes. Such a theory incorporating a fuller phenomenology of a more holistic personhood could guide research on the relations among sexual identity or orientation, spiritual identity, and gender roles. At present, different theories exist for these various dimensions of personhood, but no overarching and inclusive theory brings them together in a useful gestalt.

The theoretical debate between social constructivist and essentialist views on sexual identity also has ramifications for spiritual and religions concerns. Although this debate is far from settled, essentialist views on inherent characteristics and an inborn uniqueness associated with being gay have fostered gay and lesbian pride that is mitigated against political and religious intolerance (Starhawk, 1995) and pointed to a special spiritual sensibility among gay and lesbian persons (Bronski, 1987; Hay, 1987, 1994; Isay, 1994; Walker, 1994).

However, as mentioned above, the essentialist position does not fit the experience of many bisexual men and women. Bisexual male and female supporters of the constructivist position suggest that the use of immutable or inherent characteristics in developing a spirituality based on connections between modern gays or lesbians, Native American shamans, or Greek or Roman divinities reflects oppressive identity politics (Bennett, 1992; Highleyman, 1995). In pursuing a nondichotomous, erotically and multiculturally inclusive spirituality, bisexual men and women resist being pinned down by sexual identity or socially derived and created categories (Highleyman, 1995; Starhawk, 1995). However, the energy generated by this debate has vitalized theory, research, and practice and should be encouraged, because "both modern spirituality and modern sexual identities are in flux" (Hutchins & Kaahumanu, 1991, p. 92).

Finally, psychology training programs need to include course work and supervision on religious concerns and the spiritual dimension of life, because the majority of Americans (72%) report that religion is the most important influence on their lives (Bergin & Jensen, 1990). Thus, psychologists-in-training should become familiar with, open to, and capable of discussing spiritual or religious concerns with clients and research subjects, whether clients are gay, straight, or bisexual.

CONCLUSION

In this chapter, I have provided a brief overview of selected religious positions toward LGB persons as a backdrop for a description of how and why LGB persons have embraced spiritual and religious concerns. In addition, I have presented a prototype for psychotherapy that is inclusive of a spiritual and religious life dimension and the spiritual coming-out process. I have also raised several issues to be considered by therapists working with

LGB clients. Finally, I enumerated the limitations of current research and theory.

The paucity of useful research and theory about spiritual development for gays, lesbians, and bisexual men and women is related to the discipline of psychology's historic reticence regarding spirituality and religion. Responding to the philosophy of positivistic science and to attempts to remain within one's area of expertise, psychologists have attempted to take a value- and morally neutral stance in psychotherapy, often leaving religious and spiritual concerns to ministers, priests, rabbis, pastoral counselors, and spiritual advisors (Jones, 1994). However, the zeitgeist is changing with the rise of postmodernist and postpositivist science, which teaches that all data are laden with theory and that all science is value based. Commonalities are now recognized among the profession of psychology and religion. Voices within the profession are encouraging practitioners as well as academics to develop a working relationship with spiritual and religious concerns (Bergin, 1991; Jones, 1994). The unique significance of, and issues related to, spirituality of gay, lesbian, and bisexual men and women have been outlined in this chapter, as well as a growing awareness that such concerns and processes are intimately related to "psychological" growth. By including religions and spiritual issues in therapy, research, and practice and by viewing spirituality as a dimension of the whole person (and as a dimension of the profession), psychologists stand to broaden and deepen the scope and helpfulness of our work with all clients. Just as sexual orientation cannot be reduced to a specific type of sexual act, neither can spirituality be equated with a demographic variable. Thus, psychologists' incorporation of religious and spiritual concerns is particularly appropriate here, because bisexual, gay, and lesbian persons as well as their allies have done much to provide an appreciation for inclusiveness and diversity in psychology and to move it beyond narrowly defined, positivistic science.

REFERENCES

Alpert, R. (1997). *Like bread on the Seder plate: Jewish lesbians and the transformation of tradition*. New York: Columbia University Press.

Bennett, K. (1992). Feminist bisexuality: A both/and option for an either/or world. In E. R. Weise (Ed.), *Closer to home: Bisexuality and feminism* (pp. 205–232). Seattle, WA: Seal Press.

Bergin, A. E. (1991). Values and religious issues in psychotherapy and mental health. *American Psychologist, 46*, 394–403.

Bergin, A. E., & Jensen, J. (1990). Religiosity of psychotherapists: A national survey. *Psychotherapy, 27*, 3–7.

Blumenfeld, W. J., & Raymond, K. (1988). *Looking at gay and lesbian life*. New York: Philosophical Library.

Boswell, J. (1980). *Christianity, social tolerance, and homosexuality*. Chicago: The University of Chicago Press.

Boyd, M. (1987). Telling a lie for Christ? In M. Thompson (Ed.), *Gay spirit: Myth and meaning* (pp. 78–87). New York: St. Martin's Press.

Boyd, M. (1994). Survival with grace. In M. Thompson, (Ed.), *Gay soul: Finding the heart of gay spirit and nature* (pp. 229–246). San Francisco: Harper & Row.

Bronski, M. (1987). Reform or revolution? The challenge of creating a gay sensibility. In M. Thompson (Ed.), *Gay spirit: Myth and meaning* (pp. 10–15). New York: St. Martin's Press.

Browning, C., Reynolds, A. L., & Dworkin, S. H. (1991). Affirmative psychotherapy for lesbian women. *The Counseling Psychologist, 19*, 177–196

Carballo-Dieguez, A. (1989). Hispanic culture, gay male culture, and AIDS: Counseling implications. *Journal of Counseling and Development, 68*, 26–30.

Clark, J. M. (1991). Prophesy, subjectivity, and theodicy in gay theology: Developing a constructive methodology. In M. L. Stemmeler & J. M. Clark (Eds.), *Constructing gay theology* (pp. 27–44). Las Colinas, TX: Monument Press.

Clark, J. M. (1993). *Beyond our ghettos: Gay theology in ecological perspective*. Cleveland, OH: Pilgrim Press.

Clark, J. M., Brown, J. C., & Hochstein, L. M. (1990). Institutional religion and gay/lesbian oppression. In F. W. Bozett & M. B. Sussman (Eds.), *Homosexuality and family relations* (pp. 265–284). New York: Haworth Press.

Cleaver, R. (1995). *Know my name: A gay liberation theology*. Louisville, KY: Westminster John Knox Press.

Cooper, A. (1989). No longer invisible: Gay and lesbian jews build a movement. In R. Hasbany (Ed.) *Homosexuality and religion* (pp. 83–94). New York: Haworth Press.

Countryman, L. W. (1988). *Dirt, greed and sex: Sexual ethics in the New Testament and their implications for today*. Philadelphia: Fortress Press.

Curb, R., & Manahan, N. (Eds.). (1985). *Lesbian nuns*. Tallahassee, FL: Naiad.

DeStefano, G. (1986). Gay under the collar: The hypocrisy of the Catholic Church. *The Advocate, 439*, 43–48.

Downing, C. (1997). Lesbian mythology. In G. D. Comstock & S. E. Henking (Eds.), *Que(e)rying religion: A critical anthology* (pp. 415–440). New York: Continuum.

Driver, T. F. (1982). The contemporary and Christian contexts. In E. Batchelor, Jr. (Ed.), *Homosexuality and ethics* (pp. 14–21). New York: Pilgrim Press.

Dunphy, R. (1987). Helping persons with AIDS find meaning and hope. *Health Progress, 67*(4), 58–63.

Dynes, W. R., & Donaldson, S. (1992). *Studies in homosexuality: Vol. XII. Homosexuality and religion and philosophy*. New York: Garland.

Farajaje-Jones, E. (1995). Fluid desire: Race, HIV/AIDS, and bisexual politics. In N. Tucker (Ed.), *Bisexual politics: Theories, queries, and visions* (pp. 119–130). New York: Haworth Press.

Fischer, C. B. (1989). A bonding of choice: Values and identity among lesbian and gay religious leaders. In R. Hasbany (Ed.), *Homosexuality and religion* (pp. 145–174). New York: Haworth Press.

Folayan, A. (1992). African-American issues: The soul of it. In B. Berzon (Ed.), *Positively gay: New approaches to gay and lesbian life* (pp. 235–239). Berkeley, CA: Celestial Arts.

Fortunato, J. E. (1982). *Embracing the exile: Healing journeys of gay Christians*. New York: Seabury Press.

Fortunato, J. E. (1987). *AIDS: The spiritual dilemma*. San Francisco: Harper & Row.

Fox, R. C. (1996). Bisexuality in perspective: A review of theory and research. In B.A. Firestein (Ed.), *Bisexuality: The psychology and politics of an invisible minority* (pp. 3–50). Newbury Park, CA: Sage.

Garanzini, M. J. (1989). Psychodynamic theory and pastoral theology: An integrated model. In R. Hasbany (Ed.), *Homosexuality and religion* (pp. 175–194). New York: Haworth.

Gock, T. (1992). Asian–Pacific Islander issues: Identity integration and pride. In B. Berzon (Ed.), *Positively gay: New approaches to gay and lesbian life* (pp. 247–252). Berkeley, CA: Celestial Arts.

Gorman, E. M. (1991). A special window: An anthropological perspective on spirituality in contemporary United States gay male culture. In M. L. Stemmeler & J. M. Clark (Eds.), *Constructing gay theology* (pp. 45–61). Las Colinas, TX: Monument Press.

Gutierrez, E. (1992). Latino issues: Gay and lesbian latinos claiming *La Raza*. In B. Berzon, (Ed.), *Positively gay: New approaches to gay and lesbian life* (pp. 240–246). Berkeley, CA: Celestial Arts.

Haldeman, D. C. (1996). Spirituality and religion in the lives of lesbians and gay men. In R. P. Cabaj & T. S. Stein (Eds.), *Textbook of homosexuality and mental health* (pp. 881–896). Washington, DC: American Psychiatric Press.

Hall, C. (1994). Great spirit. In M. Thompson, (Ed.), *Gay soul: finding the heart of gay spirit and nature* (pp. 117–132). San Francisco: Harper & Row.

Harvey, A. (1994). Rebirth through the wound. In M. Thompson, (Ed.), *Gay soul: Finding the heart of gay spirit and nature* (pp. 47–64). San Francisco: Harper & Row.

Hasbany, J. (Ed.) (1989). *Homosexuality and religion*. New York: Haworth Press.

Hay, H. (1987). A separate people whose time has come. In M. Thompson (Ed.), *Gay spirit: Myth and meaning* (pp. 279–291). New York: St. Martin's Press.

Hay, H. (1994). Reinventing ourselves. In M. Thompson, (Ed.), *Gay soul: Finding the heart of gay spirit and nature* (pp. 79–98). San Francisco: Harper & Row.

Heaton, T. (1986). How does religion influence fertility? The case of the Mormons. *Journal for the Scientific Study of Religion, 25*, 248–58.

Heaton, T., Goodman, K., & Holman, T. (1994). In search of a peculiar people: Are Mormon families really different? In M. Corwall, T. Heaton, & L. Young, (Eds.), *Contemporary Mormonism: Social science perspectives* (pp. 87–117). Urbana: University of Illinois Press.

Helminiak, D. A. (1994). *What the bible really says about homosexuality*. San Francisco: Alamo Square Press.

Helminiak, D. A. (1995). Nonreligious lesbians and gays facing AIDS: A fully psychological approach to spirituality. *Pastoral Psychology, 43*, 301–318.

Heyward, C. (1984). *Our passion for justice: Images of power, sexuality, and liberation*. Cleveland, OH: Pilgrim Press.

Highleyman, L. A. (1995). Identity and ideas: Strategies for bisexuals. In N. Tucker (Ed.), *Bisexual politics: Theories, queries, and visions* (pp. 73–92). New York: Haworth Press.

Hopkins, J. (1997). The compatibility of reason and orgasm in Tibetan Buddhism: Reflections on sexual violence and homophobia. In G. D. Comstock & S. E. Henking (Eds.), *Que(e)rying religion: A critical anthology* (pp. 372–383). New York: Continuum.

Hutchins, L., & Kaahumanu, L. (Eds.). (1991). *Bi any other name: Bisexual people speak out*. Boston: Alyson Publications.

Isay, R. A. (1994). Rising to love. In M. Thompson, (Ed.), *Gay soul: Finding the heart of gay spirit and nature* (pp. 33–46). San Francisco: Harper & Row.

Jensen, L. D., Gambles, D., & Olsen, J. (1988). Attitudes toward homosexuality: A cross-cultural analysis of predictors. *International Journal of Social Psychiatry, 34*, 47–57.

Jones, S. L. (1994). A constructive relationship for religion with the science and profession of psychology: Perhaps the boldest model yet. *American Psychologist, 49*, 184–199.

Kahn, Y. H. (1989). Judaism and homosexuality: The traditionalist/progressive debate. In R. Hasbany (Ed.), *Homosexuality and religion* (pp. 47–82). New York: Haworth Press.

Kimelman, R. (1994). Homosexuality and family-centered Judaism. *Tikkun, 9*, 53–57.

Kunkel, L. E., & Temple, L. L. (1992). Attitudes towards AIDS and Homosexuals: Gender, marital status, and religion. *Journal of Applied Social Psychology, 22*, 1030–1040.

Law, E. (1997). A spirituality of creative marginality. In G. D. Comstock & S. E. Henking (Eds.), *Que(e)rying religion: A critical anthology* (pp. 343–346). New York: Continuum.

LeVay, S. (1995). Sexual orientation and its development. In R. M. Baird & M. K. Baird (Eds.), *Homosexuality: Debating the issues* (pp. 62–70). Amherst, NY: Prometheus Books.

Lottes, I. L., & Kuriloff, P. J. (1992). The effects of gender, race, religion, and political orientation on the sex role attitudes of college freshmen. *Adolescence, 27*, pp. 675–688.

McNeill, J. J. (1988). *The church and the homosexual*. Boston: Beacon Press.

Miller, R. (1997). On my journey now. In G. D. Comstock & S. E. Henking (Eds.), *Que(e)rying religion: A critical anthology* (pp. 232–235). New York: Continuum.

Money, J. (1987). Sin, sickness, or status? Homosexual gender identity and psychoneuroendocrinology. *American Psychologist, 42*, 384–99.

Morris, W. (Ed.). (1970). *The American Heritage dictionary of the English language* (6th ed.). New York: American Heritage.

Nelson, J. B. (1982). Religious and moral issues working with homosexual clients. *Journal of Homosexuality, 7*(2 & 3), 163–175.

Newman, B. S., & Muzzonigro, P. G. (1993). The effects of traditional family values on the coming-out process of gay male adolescents. *Adolescence, 28*, 213–234.

Nugent, R. (1992). Catholicism: On the compatibility of sexuality and faith. In B. Berzon (Ed.), *Positively gay: New approaches to gay and lesbian life* (pp. 156–167). Berkeley, CA: Celestial Arts.

Nugent, R., & Gramick, J. (1989). Homosexuality: Protestant, Catholic and Jewish issues; A fishbone tale. In R. Hasbany (Ed.), *Homosexuality and religion* (pp. 7–46). New York: Haworth.

O'Neill, C., & Ritter, K. (1992). *Coming out within: Stages of spiritual awakening for lesbians and gay men*. San Francisco: Harper & Row.

Queen, C. (1996). Bisexuality, sexual diversity, and the sex-positive perspective. In B. A. Firestein (Ed.), *Bisexuality: The psychology and politics of an invisible minority* (pp.103–124). Newbury Park, CA: Sage.

Rainone, F. L. (1987). Beyond community: Politics and spirituality. In Boston Lesbian Psychologies Collective (Eds.), *Lesbian psychologies* (pp. 344–353). Urbana: University of Illinois Press.

Ramer, A. (1994). Tribal wisdom. In M. Thompson, (Ed.), *Gay soul: Finding the heart of gay spirit and nature* (pp. 65–78). San Francisco: Harper San Francisco.

Ratzinger, J. (1994). Letter to the bishops of the Catholic church on the pastoral care of homosexual persons. In J. S. Siker (Ed.), *Homosexuality and the church: Both sides of the debate* (pp. 39–48). Louisville, KY: Westminster John Knox Press.

Rila, M. (1996). Bisexual women and the AIDS crisis. In B. A. Firestein (Ed.), *Bisexuality: The psychology and politics of an invisible minority* (pp. 169–184). Newbury Park, CA: Sage.

Ritter, K. Y., & O'Neill, C. W. (1989). Moving through loss: The spiritual journey of gay men and lesbian women. *Journal of Counseling and Development, 68*, 9–15.

Roscoe, W. (1994). The geography of gender. In M. Thompson, (Ed.), *Gay soul: Finding the heart of gay spirit and nature* (pp. 99–116). San Francisco: Harper & Row.

Roscoe, W. (1995). *Queer spirits: A gay men's myth book*. Boston: Beacon Press.

Schild, M. (1992). Islam. In A. Schmitt & J. Sofer (Eds.), *Sexuality and eroticism among males in Moslem societies* (pp. 179–187). New York: Harrington Park.

Schow, W. (1997). Homosexuality, Mormon doctrine, and Christianity: A father's perspecctive. In G. D. Comstock & S. E. Henking (Eds.), *Que(e)rying religion: A critical anthology* (pp. 255–264). New York: Continuum.

Scroggs, R. (1983). *Homosexuality in the new testament: Contextual background for contemporary debate*. Philadelphia: Fortress Press.

Shallenberger, D. (1994). Gifts of gay and lesbian ministry. *Pastoral Psychology, 43,* 105–113.

Shannon, J. W., & Woods, W. J. (1991). Affirmative psychotherapy for gay men. *The Counseling Psychologist, 19,* 197–215.

Siker, J. S. (Ed.). (1994). *Homosexuality in the church: Both sides of the debate.* Louisville, KY: Westminster John Knox Press.

Starhawk. (1995). The sacredness of pleasure. In N. Tucker (Ed.), *Bisexual politics: Theories, queries, and visions* (pp. 325–329). New York: Haworth Press.

Stark, R. (1994). Modernization and Mormon growth: The secularization thesis revisited. In M. Corwall, T. Heaton, & L. Young, (Eds.), *Contemporary Mormonism: Social science perspectives* (pp. 13–23). Urbana: University of Illinois Press.

Steinbrecher, E. (1994). Sex with god. In M. Thompson, (Ed.), *Gay soul: Finding the heart of gay spirit and nature* (pp. 197–210). San Francisco: Harper & Row.

Stokes, J. P., Taywaditep, K., Vanable, P., & McKirnan, D. J. (1996). Bisexual men, sexual behavior, and HIV/AIDS. In B. A. Firestein (Ed.), *Bisexuality: The psychology and politics of an invisible minority* (pp. 149–168). Newbury Park, CA: Sage.

Struzzo, J. A. (1989). Pastoral counseling and homosexuality. In R. Hasbany (Ed.), *Homosexuality and religion* (pp. 195–221). New York: Haworth Press.

Sullivan, A. (1997). Alone again, naturally: The Catholic church and the homosexual. In G. D. Comstock & S. E. Henking (Eds.), *Que(e)rying religion: A critical anthology* (pp. 238–250). New York: Continuum.

Tafoya, T. (1992). Native gay and lesbian issues: The two-spirited. In B. Berzon (Ed.), *Positively gay: New approaches to gay and lesbian life* (pp. 253–260). Berkeley, CA: Celestial Arts.

Tart, C. T. (Ed.). (1992) *Transpersonal psychologies: Perspectives on the mind from seven great spiritual traditions*. San Francisco: Harper & Row.

Thompson, M. (1987). *Gay spirit: Myth and meaning*. New York: St. Martin's Press.

Umansky, E. M. (1997). Jewish attitudes toward homosexuality: A review of contemporary sources. In G. D. Comstock & S. E. Henking (Eds.), *Que(e)rying religion: A critical anthology* (pp. 181–187.) New York: Continuum.

Wagner, C., Serafini, J., Rabkin, J., Remien, R., & Williams, J. (1994). Integration of one's religion and homosexuality: A weapon against internalized homophobia? *Journal of Homosexuality, 26,* 91–110.

Walker, M. (1994). Coming out inside. In M. Thompson, (Ed.), *Gay soul: Finding the heart of gay spirit and nature* (pp. 247–263). San Francisco: Harper & Row.

Wilson, A. (1996). How we find ourselves: Identity development and two-spirit people. *Harvard Educational Review, 66,* 303–317.

Wilson, N. (1995). *Our tribe: Queer folks, God, Jesus, and the Bible*. San Francisco: Harper & Row.

18

HEALTH BEHAVIOR RELEVANT TO PSYCHOTHERAPY WITH LESBIAN, GAY, AND BISEXUAL CLIENTS

MICHAEL R. KAUTH, MARCIA J. HARTWIG, AND
SETH C. KALICHMAN

LIMITS AND DEFINITIONS

The limits of a chapter on health behavior affecting lesbians, gays, and bisexuals (LGBs) is that although an extensive literature exists regarding health risks, disease and disorder have gripped the attention of most health researchers, whereas wellness has been virtually ignored. In this chapter, we provide a brief overview of the research on health risk behavior relevant to LGBs as well as the sparse literature on optimizing health and wellness.

Health can be conceptualized as an integration of optimal emotional, cognitive, and physical functioning. For our purpose, however, *health* will be defined as optimizing physical functioning and freedom from disease, and *health behavior* is any action or belief that affects physical functioning, for better or worse. Although psychotherapists are usually concerned only with emotional health, physical health and the effect of risk behaviors are interactive elements of global functioning and should not be ignored. Emotional health is discussed in several chapters of this text and will not be repeated here. Our goal is to provide clinicians with a basic working knowledge of physical health behaviors affecting LGBs.

THE MEDICALIZATION OF SEXUALITY AND ACCESS TO AND UTILIZATION OF HEALTH CARE

For many people, including some psychotherapists, same-sex erotic behavior seems more related to illness than health. The link between same-sex feelings and disease dates back to at least the late nineteenth century. At that time, medicine and the emerging field of psychiatry transformed the "problem" of same-sex feelings and behavior from vice to sickness and offered various noxious treatments and "cures" (Foucault, 1978/1990; Greenberg, 1988; Halperin, 1990). Throughout the past century, several medical and psychiatric writers have claimed that same-sex activity leads to nervous exhaustion, chronic fatigue, wasting, uncontrolled masturbation, and insanity. They have treated the malady in various ways—with emetics, surgical and chemical castration, forced opposite-sex erotic activity and marriage, psychotherapy, electroconvulsive shock, brain surgery, and institutionalization (Bullough, 1976; Murphy, 1992). Not until 1973 did a vocal group of psychotherapists and gay activists convince the psychiatric governing body, the American Psychiatric Association, that the diagnosis of homosexuality was driven by social prejudice rather than by science and thereby force the removal of the disorder from the diagnostic manual (Bayer, 1981). Of course, eliminating a diagnosis did not eradicate prejudice and misconceptions among mental health professionals and the public. A few years later, the AIDS epidemic reinforced the perceived link between male same-sex behavior and disease. Protests from gay activists and a few health care professionals, as well as changing demographics of those infected with HIV, have weakened but not eliminated the belief that same-sex erotic behavior itself is unhealthy.

Health care professionals who hold negative views of LGBs or of same-sex erotic behavior may incorrectly assess health risk, misattribute symptom cause, and provide inadequate medical care. Many health care providers assume that all patients are heterosexual and fail to ask about their patient's sexual identity (Douglas, Kalman, & Kalman, 1985). Providers who are uncomfortable with a patient's same-sex erotic activity may broadcast various verbal and nonverbal messages that signal their disapproval and lack of support for identity disclosure (Douglas et al., 1985; Prichard et al., 1988). Such messages and the general clinical milieu may communicate less sympathy and more blame toward gay and bisexual patients for their illness (Kelly, St. Lawrence, Smith, Hood, & Cook, 1987a; 1987b). An unsupportive clinical environment inhibits men and women from disclosing their sexual orientation to a health care provider out of fear of disapproval or rejection (Savin-Williams, 1994), and such fears are not unfounded. For some LGBs, disclosure has led to a physician's refusal to provide care, although reliable estimates of treatment refusal are difficult to determine (Deevey, 1990; Harvey, Carr, & Bernheine, 1989; Kass, Faden, Fox, & Dudley, 1992).

For many of these reasons, lesbians in particular often neglect regular medical care (American Medical Association [AMA], 1996; Stevens, 1992). Many lesbians, and women in general, view the traditional medical establishment as patriarchal, patronizing, and focused only on women's reproductive health. Lesbians who avoid traditional health care report doing so because of the absence of low-cost, natural, or alternative medical care; failure to provide holistic care; lack of preventive approaches; rarity of women-managed clinics; and poor rapport and communication by physicians (Trippet & Bain, 1992). For example, one female respondent complained in a survey about a male physician's attitude toward her disclosure of same-sex erotic behavior, claiming that "(h)e got up, left the room and had a nurse finish the questioning" once she had told him that she was a lesbian (Smith, Johnson & Guenther, 1985). Lesbians from ethnic minority groups and those from lower socioeconomic standings have even greater difficulty accessing health care and establishing a therapeutic relationship with a physician than White middle-class lesbians (Stevens, 1994; Taylor & Repetti, 1997). In another survey, a lesbian of color stated that "I can't get the same quality of care as somebody who is white. I can't get the same quality of care as somebody who is straight. Compound that with the fact that I don't have any money. I don't have any insurance. . . . It is almost the kind of fear that I can't even talk about" (Stevens, 1994). For the disadvantaged, health care can be too costly or unavailable. Whereas married heterosexual women benefit from their husband's health insurance, many single women and lesbians have no such coverage and lack their own health insurance.

Little is known about how gay and bisexual men access health care, although some men fear discrimination and rejection by a provider (Kass et al., 1992). Likewise, ethnic minority and economically disadvantaged gay and bisexual men have fewer health care resources available to them (cf. Taylor & Repetti, 1997). Yet, HIV-seropositive gay men as a group have been successful in resisting passive compliance with the dictatorial medical establishment and have demanded to be treated as partners in their health care. As a complement to traditional medicine, many HIV-infected gay men have participated in underground treatment networks and pursued nontraditional health care alternatives, such as new unapproved medications, megavitamins, acupuncture, and biofeedback (Shilts, 1987; Suarez & Reese, 1997).

Although health care access and an open relationship with a provider are essential, equally important for healthy behavior among LGBs is self-acceptance and comfort with same-sex erotic activities and sexual identity. Positive self-regard lowers health costs related to problem drinking, sexual risk taking, and emotional disorders (McDonald, 1982; Paul, Weinrich, Gonsiorek, & Hotvedt, 1982). Furthermore, openness about sexual orientation is associated with fewer physical illnesses in gay men (Cole, Kemeny, Taylor, & Visscher, 1996; Weinberg & Williams, 1974). Although no evidence has yet been reported, a similar relationship between openness about sexuality and health is likely to exist for bisexuals and lesbians. Being closeted about sexual identity in all or several aspects of life is correlated with somatic symptoms.

Still, comfort with sexuality is only one factor in health-promoting behavior. Health attitudes specific to LGBs overlay strong cultural health beliefs grounded in ethnicity, race, gender, education, socioeconomic status (SES), age and developmental phase, and religious beliefs and must also be taken into account. For instance, SES is strongly linked to higher prevalence and incidence of most chronic and infectious disorders and higher rates of mortality across populations and across all developmental phases (Adler, Boyce, Chesney, Folkman, & Syme, 1993; Williams & Collins, 1995). Across every level of SES, African Americans, for example, have more health problems than Whites (Williams & Collins, 1995). Early negative childhood experiences in the family and with peers can also set the stage for poor adult health behavior (Taylor & Repetti, 1997). Lack of social integration among adults impairs immune functioning and contributes to various health problems (House, Landis, & Umberson, 1988; Kiecolt-Glaser, Malarkey, Cacioppo, & Glaser, 1994), whereas being in an intimate relationship has several positive health benefits (Kiecolt-Glaser et al., 1994). In summary, the health behavior of LGBs is dependent to a large extent on a host of interrelated demographic and social factors, as well as the unique influences of sexuality.

With this level of complexity in the determination of physical health, theoretical models that generally rely on single or few factors related to information processing and health attribution, without regard to demographic and social variables, have little predictive value. In subsequent sections we will note the application of certain theoretical models to LGB health issues and speculate upon health risk and wellness outcomes in areas where actual data is scarce.

HEALTH RISK BEHAVIORS

Lesbians and Bisexual Women

The physical health profile for women who partner exclusively with women is generally positive. There are almost no identified medical problems specific to lesbians. Woman-to-woman sexual contact is not associated with increased risk of gynecological problems over heterosexual women (Johnson, Guenther, Laube, & Keettel, 1981), and lesbians have a lower risk of cervical cancer than heterosexual women, who are more likely to be exposed to sexually transmitted diseases (Mitchell, Drake, & Medley, 1986). Yet, the herpes simplex II virus and human papillomavirus are transmitted via genital–genital and oral–genital contact, putting women who partner exclusively with women at low but potential risk. In addition, while the incidence of breast cancer among lesbians and bisexual women is unknown (Rankow, 1995), the risk of breast cancer increases among women who have delayed childbirth, do not breast-feed, never become pregnant, or who have consumed large amounts of alcohol—conditions that characterize lesbians more often than heterosexual women (Bradford & Ryan, 1988; Johnson, Smith, & Guenther, 1987; Skinner, 1994). The incidence of ovarian cancer among lesbians is also uncertain but thought to be low (The Cancer and Steroid Hormone Study of the Centers for Disease Control and the National Institute of Child Health and Human Development, 1987). Still, oral contraceptives are thought to provide a slightly protective effect against ovarian cancer, and women who partner exclusively with women are less likely to use oral contraceptives.

Effective health maintenance requires regular screening and prevention activities, such as regular gynecological exams and routine evaluation for hypertension, coronary artery disease, anemia, hypercholesterolemia, and colon and other cancers (Rankow, 1995). As noted earlier, many lesbians and bisexual women avoid routine medical checkups, which carries serious health consequences (Stevens, 1992; Trippett & Bain, 1992). Lesbians, for example, average 12 to 22 months longer between Papanicolaou smears than heterosexual women (Biddle, 1993; Robertson & Schacter, 1981). As one woman explained, "If you are a lesbian, you have to deal with health care providers' assumptions and their homophobia. So you . . . stay away. If you have a chronic health problem, the combination is like a one–two punch and you are down for the count" (Stevens, 1994). If the lesbian or bisexual woman is a person of color, poor, without insurance, with little formal education, or living in a rural environment, health care options are limited, even if good health is valued and desired.

Non-HIV Sexually Transmitted Diseases (STDs)

Women who partner exclusively with women and whose partner also does not have male sex partners are at low risk for most bacterial and viral STDs (Degen & Waitkevicz, 1982; Johnson et al., 1987; White & Levinson, 1993). However, women who have any male partners are at risk of STDs, which are epidemic among men and bisexual women. An estimated 75% to 90% of lesbians report having had sex with a man during their lifetime, most often in their early sexually active years (Rankow, 1995). One survey of 1,086 women noted that 53% of lesbians and 90% of bisexual women recently had sex with a male partner (Einhorn & Polgar, 1994). Women who have sex with men who themselves have male partners are at further risk of HIV infection.

If infected, several STDs can be transmitted by woman-to-woman sexual contact, including *Chlamydia trachomatis*, venereal warts caused by human papillomavirus (HPV), and *Trichomonas vaginalis* (Johnson et al., 1987). In addition, bacterial vaginosis and genital HPV increase the risk of cervical cancer and occur with notable frequency among lesbians who have had male partners. Thus, although the risks for disease transmission between women appear low, considerable risk exists if a woman has male partners.

HIV Infection and AIDS

Research has not demonstrated conclusive risks for HIV transmission through woman-to-woman sexual contact, primarily because many lesbian and bisexual women also have male partners. In a large-scale study of 960,000 women who donated blood at blood centers in the United States in 1990, 106 HIV-infected women were identified, and none reported having sex exclusively with women (Petersen et al., 1992). All had male sex partners or had injected drugs. Still, concerns about woman-to-woman HIV transmission are fueled by case studies of infected lesbians who report their only having female sex partners. Rich, Buck, Tuomala, and Kazanjian (1993), for example, described a 24-year-old HIV-infected woman who had been in a monogamous sexual relationship with a 38-year-old woman who had a history of injection drug use and who died from complications of AIDS. The younger woman denied injecting drugs and denied having any male partners. Still, the risk of woman-to-woman transmission of HIV to date appears low.

Bisexual women, however, bear significant risk of HIV infection (Kennedy, Scarlett, Duerr, & Chu, 1995). Bevier, Chiasson, Heffernan, and Castro (1995) reported that bisexual women attending an STD clinic in New York City were more likely to have injected drugs, used crack cocaine, and traded sex for drugs or money than were heterosexual women. Seventeen percent of bisexual women were HIV-infected compared with 11% of heterosexual women. Finally, among 850 women who patronized bars that catered mostly to gay and bisexual men, 39% of bisexual women had sex with a man who they knew or suspected was also having sex with men (Norman, Perry, Stevenson, Kelly, & Roffman, 1996). Twenty percent of bisexual women reported having male partners with injection-drug use histories.

Effective HIV risk-reduction strategies for both men and women usually take a cognitive–behavioral approach that includes accurate information, personalization of risk, identification of risky situations, management of behavior-change barriers, instruction in condom use and needle cleaning, and training in assertive communication skills (Kalichman, 1995). Most successful HIV risk-reduction interventions developed from social cognitive theory, which emphasizes increased knowledge, personalization of risk, skills training, modeling, corrective feedback, and problem solving. However, any HIV intervention must be culturally sensitive to the targeted population. Assertive sexual communication, for example, carries significant risk for some women. Poor women and those living in ethnic communities that value traditional gender roles may be punished for being assertive in sexual situations. In these cases, safer sex and behavior must be placed in the context of health and reproductive concerns to reduce the possibility of suspicious and angry reactions from male sexual partners.

Body Image and Diet

One study suggests that lesbians are far less concerned about their physical attractiveness than heterosexual women and are more satisfied with their bodies. Consequently, they are less vulnerable to eating disorders (Siever, 1994). Only 4% of lesbians reported clinical symptoms of an eating disorder compared with 14% of heterosexual women. However, this study has yet to be replicated, and the author cautioned that participants' responses may reflect political values more than actual attitudes and behavior.

Alcohol and Substance Abuse

One of the most biased and poorly researched areas of LGB health behavior has been alcohol use. Popular clinical lore holds that one third of lesbians and gay men are problem drinkers, although early studies that described problem drinking in the gay community (e.g., Fifield, 1975, and Zehner & Lewis, 1983) calculated estimates of alcohol use from *bar samples* (see Bux, 1996). Other early studies (Saghir & Robins, 1973) poorly defined problem drinking and used dissimilar comparison groups. In a recent literature review, Bux concluded that lesbians and gay men were not at significantly higher risk of heavy drinking and that early claims about non-acceptance of a lesbian or gay identity, gender role conflict, or the "gay lifestyle" leading to alcohol problems were unsupported. None of the studies reviewed by Bux described drinking among bisexuals, and few determined consumption rates by ethnicity. Of course, ethnic and racial background, as well as SES, can play a significant role in attitudes about alcohol consumption. Despite numerous studies on alcohol use, these are areas that have yet to be fully explored among LGBs.

One study of 3,400 lesbians and gay men, recruited through newspaper advertisements and social organizations in Chicago, noted that lesbians were less likely than heterosexual women to abstain from alcohol (McKirnan & Peterson, 1989). The proportion of heavy drinkers (over 60 drinks per month) among lesbians was comparable to the general population (15% vs. 14%; Clark & Midanik, 1982). A separate study of 1,067 lesbians and gay men from metropolitan Lexington and Louisville, KY, reported heavy drinking—five or more days in the past month and five or more drinks on a single occasion—among only 8% of lesbians (Skinner & Otis, 1992) compared with 3% of heterosexual women (National Institute on Drug Abuse, 1991).

Still, for some lesbians and bisexual women, drinking is a problem. Perhaps more for gay and bisexual men than lesbians or bisexual women, bars have typically been a place to meet other people with same-sex interests. Being in a bar increases the likelihood of alcohol consumption and abuse through reduction of anxiety and inhibitions (Isrealstam & Lambert, 1984). For women who are not comfortable with their sexuality, alcohol and other disinhibiting substances may lessen guilt and shame associated with same-sex attraction and behavior (Mayer, 1983). The downside, of course, is that intoxication reduces self-control and impairs judgment, which may lead to sexual or physical lapses in safety.

Gay and Bisexual Men

Generally, gay and bisexual men have no greater physical health problems than heterosexual men, with a few exceptions (AMA, 1996). There is evidence to suggest that among gay men, being "closeted" and uncomfortable with a gay identity contributes to increased somatic symptoms. In the early 1970s, Weinberg and Williams (1974) found that closeted gay and bisexual men were more likely to report frequent psychosomatic symptoms than those who were "out." More recently, a study of 222 gay and bisexual men who were not infected with HIV reported that the incidence of skin cancers and moderately serious infectious diseases such as bronchitis and sinusitis increased in direct proportion to concealment of sexual identity (Cole et al., 1996). Although the degree of openness about sexual identity was rated across family, friends, and social and occupational environments, demographics, health-relevant behavioral patterns, mood, repressive coping style, and social desirability responses were not able to account for health differences between the two groups. While speculative at this point, this data suggest that gay and bisexual men who are self-accepting and "out" in most environments have fewer health problems than those who are secretive.

Other health problems are more common among gay and bisexual men than heterosexual men. For instance, men who have sex with men are more likely to experience medical problems related to having a greater number of sexual contacts and participation in specific sexual behaviors.

Gay and bisexual men tend to be sexually active at a younger age than heterosexual men and report more lifetime sexual partners (Rotheram-Borus & Gwadz, 1993). Furthermore, men who have sex with men are more likely to engage in anal intercourse and to have oral–anal and digital–anal contact than heterosexual men (Friedman & Downey, 1994). As a result, gay and bisexual men more commonly experience (a) STDs; (b) intestinal diseases such as amebiasis, hepatitis, and cytomegalovirus (CMV) infections; (c) complications of traumatic anal intercourse such as fecal incontinence, hemorrhoids, or anal fissures; and (d) immune-related disorders caused by HIV (Owen, 1985). The more common of these health problems—STDs and HIV—are discussed in more detail below. Most of these problems have severe health consequences if unidentified or untreated. Therefore, regular self-exams, medical checkups, and open communication with a knowledgeable provider are essential components of good health care.

Non-HIV STDs

As they are within the general population, STDs are epidemic among gay and bisexual men (Friedman & Downey, 1994). Men who have sex with men are particularly susceptible to contracting bacterial infections such as gonorrhea, syphilis, urethritis, and a variety of oral and gastrointestinal infections through oral and anal intercourse (Eng & Butler, 1997). While bacterial infections are generally curable when diagnosed and treated early, emerging antibiotic-resistant strains of gonorrhea have created a new threat of ever more severe infections.

Viral infections constitute an even greater health threat than bacterial infections, principally because viral infections are usually incurable. Gay and bisexual men who contract (HPV) infection, the source of genital warts and dysplasia, are also at increased risk for anal and penile cancer, with the majority of such cancers being associated with HPV (Eng & Butler, 1997). Herpes simplex viruses (HSV) are extremely prevalent—some studies identify as many as 95% of the gay men sampled indicating exposure to HSV (Drew, Buhles, & Erlich, 1992). Worse, several life-threatening viruses are prevalent among gay and bisexual men, particularly all forms of hepatitis—especially hepatitis B—and HIV (AMA, 1996). Viral STDs share a close link to HIV–AIDS, which is especially alarming for gay and bisexual men. Not only do STDs and HIV have a common route of transmission, but STDs increase the risk of HIV-transmission risk through local sites of infection. Coinfection with several STDs also accelerates the immune-suppressing effects of HIV and speeds progression of the disease.

HIV Infection and AIDS

The AIDS epidemic has added an entirely new dimension to the health of gay and bisexual men. In the United States, for example, HIV first appeared among men who had sex with men and then spread between partners via anal intercourse without a condom. While men who have sex with men have a high HIV seroprevalence rate, gay and bisexual men are only at high risk for HIV infection when they engage in receptive anal intercourse without a condom—the single highest risk behavior for transmitting HIV (Kingsley et al., 1987). Across an array of samples and research methodologies, most studies find that about one third of men have recently engaged in unprotected anal intercourse (Kalichman, Kelly, Morgan, & Rompa, 1997; Kelly et al., 1991; Lemp et al., 1994; Ostrow, DiFranceisco, Chmiel, Wagstaff, & Wesch, 1995). Even more alarming, unprotected anal intercourse is relatively common among younger (under 30) gay men and non-gay-identified men who have sex with men.

Currently, 47% of AIDS cases among men are attributable to unprotected sex with men—a 10% decline from just 7 years ago—and less than half of new HIV infections among men are due only to unprotected sex with men (Centers for Disease Control, 1991; Centers for Disease Control and Prevention, 1997). Substantial evidence suggests that HIV transmission has reached a plateau among men who have sex with men in major urban centers such as New York City (Dean & Meyer, 1995; Fordyce et al., 1995). Since 1985, HIV-transmission rates among gay and bisexual men have declined, and the number of AIDS cases due to male–male contact has dropped since 1991. However, some gay and bisexual men experience occasional lapses into unprotected anal intercourse, and other men are unable or unwilling to stop having anal sex without a condom (Kelly et al., 1991). Safer sex lapses have been attributed to fatalism among gay men living in cities devastated by AIDS and a complacency that comes with a seemingly endless epidemic (Kalichman et al., 1997). In addition, a resurgence of HIV infections, or a second wave, may be occurring among gay and bisexual men who are tired of safer sex precautions or who feel immune to infection.

Although the risks of unprotected anal intercourse for HIV transmission are clear, risks for oral sex remain ambiguous. Oral–genital HIV transmission is biologically plausible when oral mucosa are exposed to infected semen or vaginal fluids (Baba et al., 1996). Early epidemiological studies failed to establish a link between oral sex and HIV infection (Lyman, Winkelstein, Ascher, & Levy, 1986; Winkelstein, Samuel, & Padian, 1987), and laboratory research found only small amounts of the HIV in saliva (Levy, 1992) and identified enzymes in saliva that inactivate the virus (Fultz, 1986). Later studies of male–female couples who engaged only in oral sex without condoms and where one partner was HIV infected also failed to substantiate risks for HIV infection posed by oral sex (DeVincenzi, 1994). Other cohort studies have reported similar findings (e.g., Ostrow et al., 1995), suggesting that risk of HIV infection from oral sex is minimal. Still, early safer sex messages admonished gay and bisexual men to *avoid* oral sex entirely, or to use condoms. Oral–genital sex is far more common among men who have sex with men than anal intercourse, making public health messages about the *theoretical* risks of oral sex seem anxiety provoking. Without clear epidemiological evidence of HIV risk during oral sex, public health messages that discourage oral sex will be ignored. Still, many HIV educators and clinicians are uncomfortable with any uncertainty about the link between oral sex and HIV transmission and recommend protected oral sex for added safety.

Recent years have witnessed an explosion of new drugs to manage HIV disease. Current use of protease inhibitors, or, medications designed to obstruct the maturation of live HIV, as part of a drug "cocktail" containing two antiretrovirals such as AZT or 3TC appear to produce dramatic health benefits for many people infected with HIV. However, the triple therapy is costly, the regime is complicated, and any treatment noncompliance risks the development of resistance to these and similar drugs. In addition, one third of HIV patients are unable to tolerate one or more of these medications, making triple pharmacotherapy impractical for a significant number of people. Concurrently, many HIV-infected gay and bisexual men have turned to complementary and alternative medicines (CAMs) to manage symptoms and enhance well-being (Suarez & Reese, 1997). CAMs include, for example, diet and nutrition changes, mind–body control, manual healing, and herbal medicines. Although the direct health benefits of CAMs are unknown, gay and bisexual men who use such strategies seem to perceive more control over their HIV symptoms, enhance coping, and reduce stress that can negatively affect immune functioning (Dorian & Garfinkel, 1987).

As noted earlier, effective HIV sexual-risk-reduction efforts usually include cognitive–behavioral interventions (Kalichman, 1995). Risk reduction interventions have been most successful among White, educated, gay men than among gay and bisexual men of color and lower SES, populations that are generally difficult to reach. However, while intervention efforts have reduced the overall rate of HIV infection among gay and bisexual men, many men continue to engage in unprotected sex with men. In spite of thousands of AIDS-related deaths and years of HIV-education and risk-reduction efforts, about one third of gay and bisexual men have recently engaged in unprotected anal sex (Kalichman et al., 1997; Ostrow et al., 1995), and a significant proportion of gay and bisexual men who practice safer sex occasionally lapse (Kelly et al., 1991). Much still needs to be done to reach all men who have sex with men and assist them in maintenance of safer sex efforts.

Body Image and Diet

Siever (1994) found that gay men and heterosexual women were more dissatisfied with their physical appearance than lesbians or heterosexual men. Perhaps as a consequence, 17% of gay men reported symptoms of an eating disorder compared with 3% of heterosexual men. Both gay men and heterosexual women believe that physical appearance is very important to their male partners—a finding that was substantiated by men in the sample. However, further research is needed to corroborate these findings.

Alcohol and Substance Abuse

Although gay and bisexual men rarely abstain from alcohol, they are not at higher risk of problem drinking (Bux, 1996). Contrary to early studies, a recent literature review found few drinking-related problems among gay men and a general trend toward decreases in alcohol consumption. Bux attributed these findings to a greater emphasis in recent years on health-related behavior among the gay community. Furthermore, alcohol consumption is similar for gay and heterosexual men. Two large-scale studies described 13% to 15% of gay men as heavy drinkers (McKirnan & Peterson, 1989; Skinner & Otis, 1992), and a third study of 624 gay men in New York City found that 9% to 12% of men met the *Diagnostic and Statistical Manual of Mental Disorders—III* (DSM-III; American Psychiatric Association, 1987) criteria for abuse or dependence (Martin, Dean, Garcia, & Hall, 1989). These figures are comparable to proportions of heavy drinking in the general population (14%; Clark & Midanik, 1982) and no different than figures for heterosexual men (National Institute on Drug Abuse, 1991). None of the studies reviewed by Bux reported on drinking among lower SES or ethnic gay men and bisexuals.

All the same, drinking is a problem for some gay and bisexual men, and bars have commonly been the place where men with same-sex interests go to meet other men. Of course, being in a bar increases the likelihood of alcohol use and abuse (Isrealstam & Lambert, 1984). Furthermore, alcohol and substances are used by some men to lessen guilt and shame associated with same-sex feelings and sexual behavior or to facilitate and enhance the performance of certain sexual acts such as anal intercourse (Mayer, 1983). Disinhibition from drinking or drug use, therefore, is especially risky for gay and bisexual men. Several studies have noted that recreational drug use is associated with having more than one sexual partner and engaging in high HIV sexual-risk behavior (Ostrow et al., 1990; Siegel, Mesagno, Chen, & Christ, 1989). The relationship between substance use and unsafe sexual practices is complicated, however, by factors such as anxiety reduction and thrill seeking (Leigh & Stall, 1993; Siegel et al., 1989).

The prevalence and frequency of recreational drug use among HIV seronegative lesbians and gay men are less well-known than data about drinking. A few studies have noted that lesbians and gay men use a variety of substances more often than heterosexuals (Bradford, Ryan & Rothblum, 1994; McKirnan & Peterson, 1989; Stall & Wiley, 1988). However, Stall and Wiley pointed out that differences between gay and heterosexual men are the result of very frequent substance use among gay men younger than 35. Prevalence rates do not suggest that gay men are at greater risk of drug dependence or "addiction" than heterosexual men.

WELLNESS

Psychosocial researchers have devoted little attention to health promotion and wellness. Most studies of LGBs have focused on disease and dysfunction. We have already noted that discomfort with same-sex feelings and being closeted is associated with an increased number of somatic complaints among gay men (Cole et al., 1996). On the other hand, a few studies have found that self-acceptance of same-sex erotic feelings and "coming out" is related to positive self-regard, the absence of depression, fewer alcohol-related problems, a lower risk of unsafe sexual activity, and successful aging (Quam & Whitford, 1992; Sadava & Thompson, 1986; Siever, 1994). Before extrapolating from these data, we must point out that self-acceptance is not easy and may be especially difficult for ethnic LGBs for whom sexual identity is in conflict with ethnic identity (Chan, 1993; Icard, 1986). African Americans, Asian Americans, and Hispanics, for example, tend to view same-sex erotic behavior as somehow conflicting with family and ethnic-community involvement, and many ethnic LGBs feel pressured to choose between their ethnic community and the gay/lesbian community (Icard, 1986). Acceptance of multiple identities requires a great deal of effort.

Because acceptance and disclosure of sexual identity among LGBs is linked to fewer health risks, it is possible to speculate that positive self-regard facilitates health-promoting behaviors. LGBs who feel good about themselves may be more likely to eat a balanced diet, exercise regularly, drink moderately, avoid tobacco, practice safer sex, have medical checkups, manage stress, participate in the gay and general community, and pursue life-enhancing activities. Indeed, several of these suppositions are supported (Cole et al., 1996; Quam & Whitford, 1992; Sadava & Thompson, 1996; Siever, 1994).

First, a growing trend toward exercise has been observed among LGBs. Membership in health clubs and the number of local gay sports teams have risen dramatically. Amateur competition in the Gay Games expanded from a few thousand athletes during the first games in 1982 to more than 15,000 athletes in 1994 for the fourth games in New York City ("Score Card #2,"

1994). Yet, fascination with physical fitness by LGBs is probably fueled by more than the desire to avoid illness. For instance, interest in sports and physical fitness may have achieved acceptability and social status by the "coming out" of gay and lesbian athletes—Greg Louganis, Martina Navratilova, Bob Paris, Muffin Spencer-Devlin, Bruce Hayes, and Rudy Galindo. In addition to the health benefits of exercise, participation in local gay sports groups expands social networks and resources and facilitates community involvement. Furthermore, for some gay and bisexual men, looking like the "picture of health" defends against the perception of emasculation and vulnerability to HIV infection. A pumped and buffed body not only challenges the notion of impotence associated with disease but presents an image of virile masculinity (Pronger, 1991).

Second, the growing interest in CAMs among gay men and lesbians suggests more than a lack of confidence in traditional medicine. The popularity of nonmedical approaches to health, healing touch, massage, relaxation techniques, acupuncture, aromatherapy, vitamins, dietary supplements, and naturally occurring mood stabilizers and immune boosters points toward a desire by LGBs for *optimal* physical health and well-being. Many alternative health approaches gained popularity at women's health fairs and through gay men's frustrations with traditional Western medical treatment of AIDS but have now found growing acceptance in popular culture. As marginalized members of American culture, LGBs may be less committed to and less satisfied with traditional health approaches and more likely to experiment with new methods. Although the efficacy of alternative medicines is an empirical question that has yet to be answered, the use of these approaches contributes to stress reduction, a sense of worth, empowerment, and an internal locus of control, all of which have their own positive health benefits (Suarez & Reese, 1997). In this context, use of CAMs can be viewed as an attempt to take control of one's life and to decide how well to live.

The pursuit of life-enhancing activities and wellness is likely to promote a sense of happiness or well-being (Diener & Diener, 1996). To what degree LGBs find happiness or whether LGBs are happier than heterosexuals is, again, an empirical question ripe for research. At any rate, clinicians can facilitate the process of well-being for LGB clients by meeting and moving beyond the immediate tasks of symptom alleviation and management. Clinicians must acknowledge the synergy of physical and mental health and take a holistic approach to patient care. Holistic psychotherapy focuses not only on managing emotional distress but on fulfilling dynamic life tasks of spirituality, self-regulation, work, friendship, and love (Witmer & Sweeney, 1992). Witmer and Sweeney's model of wellness asserts that purposefulness can be found through spirituality, control and fitness achieved through moderation, self-efficacy developed through work, community and belongingness discovered through friendships, and companionship fostered through intimate loving relationships. Achievement of well-being through the exploration of life tasks is strikingly similar to Frankl's (1959/1984) hypothesis that meaningfulness is found by losing oneself in the larger pursuit of work, nature and art, and loving relationships. No matter what global wellness model is used, psychotherapists can assist LGB clients in moving beyond minimally adaptive functioning to the richer achievement of wholeness and happiness.

METHODOLOGICAL LIMITATIONS

Several common methodological problems limit the generalizability of studies discussed in this chapter. First, most studies of LGBs use small convenience samples that overrepresent those who are comfortable with a gay identity, including those connected to the (White) gay community, and those who are politically active, engaging in risky behavior, or motivated to participate in a study about people with same-sex erotic interests (Berrill, 1992). Yet, finding a diverse group of men and women with same-sex erotic interests outside of traditional gay-identified environments presents immense difficulties to researchers. Second, most studies that were cited in this chapter described predominantly White, well-educated, urban, gay men who differ considerably from ethnically and socially diverse men and women. In addition, bisexuals are rarely treated as a separate group. For convenience, many researchers pooled gay and bisexual men, although gay and bisexual men may not be similar at all. Fourth, studies often lacked matched comparison groups of heterosexuals that would enhance the meaning of results. Finally, as mentioned before, most research about LGB has been limited to disease and dysfunction rather than adaptive functioning and wellness.

Future research should improve on noted methodological shortcomings and also examine health promotion, quality of life, and coping with the chronic stress of living in a heterosexist culture. Cross-cultural studies of people with same-sex erotic feelings would further aid in understanding how Western culture affects health behavior among LGBs.

CONCLUSION

This chapter is intended to provide psychotherapists with basic knowledge about physical health risks and wellness behaviors relevant to LGBs. While LGBs share much of the same physical health concerns as heterosexuals, LGBs have few unique health risks. Most of the health risks that exist are generally associated with disease transmission through unprotected sexual contact with male partners. Additional information about

LGB health behavior can be found in Kauth and Prejean (1997) and VanScoy (1997). Much past research has focused on health risks. Consequently, little is known about health promotion and wellness relevant to LGBs. However, extrapolation from available data and recent observations suggest that many LGBs are actively engaged in various wellness strategies. Clinicians are encouraged to use a holistic model of wellness with LGB clients.

REFERENCES

Adler, N. E., Boyce, W. T., Chesney, M. A., Folkman, S., & Syme, S. L. (1993). Socioeconomic inequalities in health: No easy solution. *Journal of the American Medical Association, 269,* 3140–3145.

American Medical Association, Council on Scientific Affairs. (1996). Health care needs of gay men and lesbians in the United States. *Journal of the American Medical Association, 275,* 1354–1359.

American Psychiatric Association. (1987). *Diagnostic and statistical manual of mental disorders.* (3rd ed., rev.). Washington, DC: Author.

Baba, T. W., Trichel, A. M., An, L., Liska, V., Martin, L., Murphey-Corb, M., & Ruprecht, R. M. (1996). Infection and AIDS in adult macaques after nontraumatic oral exposure of cell-free SIV. *Science, 272,* 1486–1489.

Bayer, R. (1981). Homosexuality and American psychiatry: The politics of diagnosis. Princeton, NJ: Princeton University Press.

Berrill, K. T. (1992). Antigay violence and victimization in the United States: An overview. In G. M. Herek and K. T. Berrill (Eds.), *Hate crimes: Confronting violence against lesbians and gay men* (pp. 19–45). Newbury Park, CA: Sage.

Bevier, P., Chiasson, M., Heffernan, R., & Castro, K. (1995). Women at a sexually transmitted disease clinic who report same-sex contact: Their HIV seroprevalence and risk behaviors. *American Journal of Public Health, 85,* 1366–1371.

Biddle, B. S. (1993). *Health status indicators for Washington area lesbians and bisexual women: A report on the Lesbian Health Clinic's first year.* Washington, DC: Whitman Walker Clinic, Inc.

Bradford, J., & Ryan, C. (1988). *The national lesbian health care survey.* Washington, DC: National Lesbian and Gay Health Foundation.

Bradford, J., Ryan, C., & Rothblum, E. D. (1994). National lesbian health care survey: Implications for mental health care. *Journal of consulting and clinical psychology, 62*(2), 228–242.

Bullough, V. L. (1976). *Sex, society, & history.* New York: Science History Publications.

Bux, D. A. (1996). The epidemiology of problem drinking in gay men and lesbians: A critical review. *Clinical Psychology Review, 16*(4), 277–298.

The Cancer and Steroid Hormone Study of the Centers for Disease Control and the National Institute of Child Health and Human Development. (1987). The reduction in risk of ovarian cancer associated with oral contraceptive use. *England Journal of New Medicine, 316,* 650–655.

Centers for Disease Control. (1991). *HIV/AIDS surveillance report,* 1–22. Atlanta, GA: Author.

Centers for Disease Control and Prevention. (1997). *HIV/AIDS surveillance report,* 9, 1–39. Atlanta, GA: Author.

Chan, C. S. (1993). Issues of identity development among Asian American lesbians and gay men. In L. D. Garnets & D. C. Kimmel (Eds.), *Psychological perspectives on lesbian and gay male experiences* (pp. 376–388). New York: Columbia University Press.

Clark, W. B., & Midanik, L. (1982). Alcohol use and alcohol problems among U.S. adults: Results of the 1979 national survey. In *Alcohol and health: Alcohol consumption and related problems* (Alcohol and Health Monograph No. 1, DHHS Publication Number 81-600185, pp. 3–52). Washington, DC: U.S. Government Printing Office.

Cole, S. W., Kemeny, M. E., Taylor, S. E., & Visscher, B. R. (1996). Elevated physical health risk among gay men who conceal their homosexual identity. *Health Psychology, 15,* 243–251.

Dean, L., & Meyer, I. (1995). HIV prevalence and sexual behavior in a cohort of New York City gay men (aged 18–24). *Journal of Acquired Immune Deficiency Syndromes and Human Retrovirology, 8,* 208–211.

Deevey, S. (1990). Older lesbian women: An invisible minority. *Journal of Gerontological Nursing, 16,* 35–39.

Degen, K., & Waitkevicz, H. J. (1982, May). Lesbian health issues. *British Journal of Sexual Medicine, 2,* 40–47.

DeVincenzi, I. (1994). A longitudinal study of human immunodeficiency virus transmission by heterosexual partners. *New England Journal of Medicine, 331,* 341–346.

Diener, E., & Diener, C. (1996). Most people are happy. *Psychological Science, 7,* 181–185.

Dorian, B., & Garfinkel, P. E. (1987). Stress, immunity and illness: A review. *Psychological Medicine, 17*(2), 393–407.

Douglas, C. J., Kalman, C. M., & Kalman, T. P. (1985). Homophobia among physicians and nurses: An empirical study. *Hospital & Community Psychiatry, 36,* 1309–1311.

Drew, W. L., Buhles, W., & Erlich, K. S. (1992). Management of herpes virus infections (CMV, HSV, VZV). In M. A. Sande and P. A. Volberding (Eds.), *The medical management of AIDS* (3rd ed., pp. 359–382). Philadelphia: W. B. Saunders.

Einhorn, L., & Polgar, M. (1994). HIV-risk behavior among lesbians and bisexual women. *AIDS Education and Prevention, 6,* 514–523.

Eng, T. R., & Butler, W. T. (1997). *The hidden epidemic: Confronting sexually transmitted diseases.* Washington, DC: National Academy of Medicine.

Fifield, L. H. (1975). *On my way to nowhere: Alienated, isolated, and drunk.* Los Angeles: Gay Community Services Center.

Fordyce, E. J., Williams, R. D., Surick, I. W., Shum, R., Quintyne, R., & Thomas, P. (1995). Trends in the AIDS epidemic among men who reported sex with men in New York City: 1981–1993. *AIDS Education and Prevention, 7,* 3–13.

Foucault, M. (1990). *The history of sexuality, Volume I: An introduction* (Robert Hurley, Trans.). New York: Vintage Books. (Original work published 1978)

Frankl, V. E. (1984). *Man's search for meaning. Revised and updated.* New York: Washington Square Press. (Original work published 1959)

Friedman, R. C., & Downey, J. I. (1994). Homosexuality. *New England Journal of Medicine, 331,* 923–930.

Fultz, P. N. (1986). Components of saliva inactivate human immunodeficiency virus. *Lancet, ii,* 345–349.

Greenberg, D. F. (1988). *The construction of homosexuality.* Chicago: University of Chicago Press.

Halperin, D. M. (1990). One hundred years of homosexuality and other essays on Greek love. New York: Routledge.

Harvey, S. M., Carr, C., & Bernheine, S. (1989). Lesbian mothers: Health care experiences. *Journal of Nurse-Midwifery, 34,* 115–119.

House, J. S., Landis, K. R., & Umberson, D. (1988). Social relationships and health. *Science, 241,* 540–545.

Icard, L. (1986). Black gay men and conflicting social identities: Sexual orientation versus racial identity. In J. Gripton and M. Valentich (Eds.), Special issue of the *Journal of Social Work & Human Sexuality: Social Work Practice in Sexual Problems, 4,* 83–93.

Isrealstam, S., & Lambert, S. (1984). Gay bars. *Journal of Drug Issues, 14,* 637–653.

Johnson, S. R., Guenther, S. M., Laube, D. W., & Keettel, W. C. (1981). Factors influencing lesbian gynecological care: A preliminary study. *American Journal of Obstetrics and Gynecology, 140,* 20–28.

Johnson, S. R., Smith, S. M., & Guenther, S. M. (1987). Comparison of gynecologic health care problems between lesbians and bisexual women. *Journal of Reproductive Medicine, 32,* 805–811.

Kalichman, S. C. (1995). *Understanding AIDS: A guide for mental health professionals.* Washington, DC: American Psychological Association.

Kalichman, S. C., Kelly, J. A., Morgan, M., & Rompa, D. (1997). Fatalism, future outlook, current life satisfaction, and risk for human immunodeficiency virus (HIV) infection among gay and bisexual men. *Journal of Consulting and Clinical Psychology, 65,* 542–546.

Kass, N. E., Faden, R. R., Fox, R., & Dudley, J. (1992). Homosexual and bisexual mens' perceptions of discrimination in health services. *American Journal of Public Health, 82,* 1277–1279.

Kauth, M. R., & Prejean, J. (1997). Health behavior in gay men. In D. S. Gochman (Ed.), *Handbook of Health Behavior Research: Volume III* (pp. 141–162). New York: Plenum Press.

Kelly, J. A., Kalichman, S. C., Kauth, M. R., Kilgore, H. G., Hood, H. V., Campos, P. E., Rao, S. M., Brasfield, T. L., & St. Lawrence, J. S. (1991). Situational factors associated with AIDS risk behavior lapses and coping strategies used by gay men who successfully avoid lapses. *American Journal of Public Health, 81,* 1335–1338.

Kelly, J. A., St. Lawrence, J. S., Smith, S., Jr., Hood, H. V., & Cook, D. J. (1987a). Medical students' attitudes toward AIDS and homosexual patients. *Journal of Medical Education, 62,* 549–556.

Kelly, J. A., St. Lawrence, J. S., Smith, S., Jr., Hood, H. V., & Cook, D. J. (1987b). Stigmatization of AIDS patients by physicians. *American Journal of Public Health, 77,* 789–791.

Kennedy, M., Scarlett, M., Duerr, A., & Chu, S. (1995). Assessing HIV risk among women who have sex with women: Scientific and communication issues. *Journal of the Medical Women's Association, 50,* 103–107.

Kiecolt-Glaser, J. K., Malarkey, W. B., Cacioppo, J. T., & Glaser, R. (1994). Stressful personal relationships: Immune and endocrine function. In R. Glaser and J. Kiecolt-Glaser (Eds.), *Handbook of human stress and immunity* (pp. 321–339). San Diego, CA: Academic Press.

Kingsley, L. A., Detels, R., Kaslow, R., Polk, B. F., Rinaldo, C. R., & Chmiel, J. (1987). Risk factors for seroconversion to human immunodeficiency virus among male homosexuals. *Lancet, 1*(8529), 345–349.

Leigh, B. C., & Stall, R. (1993). Substance use and risky sexual behavior for exposure to HIV: Issues in methodology, interpretation, and prevention. *American Psychologist, 48,* 1035–1045.

Lemp, G. F., Hirozawa, A. M., Givertz, D., Nieri, G. N., Anderson, L., Lindegren, M. L., Janssen, R. S., & Katz, M. (1994). Seroprevalence of HIV and risk behaviors among young homosexual and bisexual men. *Journal of the American Medical Association, 272,* 449–454.

Levy, J. A. (1992). Viral and immunologic factors in HIV infection. In M. A. Sande & P. A. Volberding (Eds.), *The medical management of AIDS* (3rd ed.) (pages 18–32). Philadelphia: W. B. Saunders.

Lyman, D., Winkelstein, W., Ascher, M., & Levy, J. A. (1986). Minimal risk of transmission of AIDS-associated retrovirus infection by oral–genital contact. *Journal of the American Medical Association, 255,* 1703.

Martin, J. L., Dean, L., Garcia, M., & Hall, W. (1989). The impact of AIDS on a gay community: Changes in sexual behavior, substance use, and mental health. *American Journal of Community Psychology, 17,* 269–293.

Mayer, K. H. (1983). Medical consequences of the inhalation of volatile nitrites. In D. G. Ostrow, T. A. Sandholzer, and Y. M. Felman (Eds.), *Sexually transmitted diseases in homosexual men: Diagnosis, treatment and research.* (pp. 237–242). New York: Plenum Press.

McDonald, G. J. (1982). Individual differences in the coming-out process for gay men. *Journal of Homosexuality, 8,* 47–60.

McKirnan, D. J., & Peterson, P. L. (1989). Alcohol and drug use among homosexual men and women: Epidemiology and population characteristics. *Addictive Behaviors, 14,* 545–553.

Mitchell, H., Drake, M., & Medley, G. (1986). Prospective evaluation of risk of cervical cancer after cytological evidence of human papillomavirus infection. *Lancet, 2,* 573–575.

Murphy, T. F. (1992). Redirecting sexual orientation: Techniques and justifications. *The Journal of Sex Research, 29,* 501–523.

National Institute on Drug Abuse. (1991). *National household survey on drug abuse: Population estimates 1991* (DHHS Publication No. ADM 92–1887). Washington, DC: U.S. Government Printing Office.

Norman, A. D., Perry, M., Stevenson, L. Y., Kelly, J. A., & Roffman, R. (1996). Lesbian and bisexual women in small cities—At risk for HIV? *Public Health Reports, 111,* 347–352.

Ostrow, D., DiFranceisco, W., Chmeil, J., Wagstaff, D., & Wesch J. (1995). A case–control study of human immunodeficiency virus type-1 seroconversion and risk-related behaviors in the Chicago MACS/CCS cohort, 1984–1992. *American Journal of Epidemiology, 142,* 1–10.

Ostrow, D. G., VanRaden, M. J., Fox, R., Kingsley, L. A., Dudley, J., Kaslow, R. A., & the Multicenter AIDS Cohort Study (MACS). (1990). Recreational drug use and sexual behavior change in a cohort of homosexual men. *AIDS, 4,* 759–765.

Owen, W. F. (1985). Medical problems of the homosexual adolescent. *Journal of Adolescent Health Care, 6,* 278–285.

Paul, W., Weinrich, J. D., Gonsiorek, J., & Hotvedt, M. (1982). *Homosexuality: Social, psychological, and biological issues.* Beverly Hills, CA: Sage.

Petersen, L. R., Doll, L., White, C., Chu, S., and the HIV Blood Donor Study Group. (1992). No evidence for female-to-female HIV transmission among 960,000 female blood donors. *Journal of Acquired Immune Deficiency Syndromes, 5,* 853–855.

Prichard, J. G., Dial, L. K., Holloway, R. L., Mosley, M., Bale, R. M., & Kaplowitz, H. J. (1988). Attitudes of family-medicine residents toward homosexuality. *The Journal of Family Practice, 27,* 637–639.

Pronger, B. (1991). *The arena of masculinity: Sports, homosexuality, and the meaning of sex.* New York: St. Martin's Press.

Quam, J. K., & Whitford, G. S. (1992). Adaptation of age-related expectations of older gay and lesbian adults. *The Gerontologist, 32,* 367–374.

Rankow, E. J. (1995). Lesbian health issues for the primary care provider. *Journal of Family Practice, 40,* 486–493.

Rich, J. D., Buck, A., Tuomala, R., & Kazanjian, P. (1993). Transmission of human immunodeficiency virus infection presumed to have occurred via female homosexual contact. *Clinical Infectious Diseases, 17,* 1003–1005.

Robertson, P., & Schacter, J. (1981). Failure to identify venereal disease in a lesbian population. *Sexually Transmitted Diseases, 8,* 75–76.

Rotheram-Borus, M. J., & Gwadz, M. (1993). Sexuality among youths at high risk. *Child and Adolescent Psychiatric Clinics of North America, 2*, 415–431.

Sadava, S. W., & Thompson, M. M. (1986). Loneliness, social drinking, and vulnerability to alcohol problems. *Canadian Journal of Behavioral Science, 18,* 133–139.

Saghir, M. T., & Robins, E. (1973). *Male and female homosexuality: A comprehensive investigation.* Baltimore: Williams & Wilkins.

Savin-Williams, R. C. (1994). Verbal and physical abuse as stressors in the lives of lesbian, gay male, and bisexual youths: Associations with school problems, running away, substance abuse, prostitution, and suicide. *Journal of Consulting and Clinical Psychology, 62*, 261–269.

"Score card #2." (1994). *OUT, 13,* 103.

Shilts, R. (1987). *And the band played on: Politics, people, and the AIDS epidemic.* New York: St. Martin's Press.

Siegel, K., Mesagno, F. P., Chen, J. Y., & Christ, G. (1989). Factors distinguishing homosexual males practicing risky and safer sex. *Social Science Medicine, 28,* 561–569.

Siever, M. D. (1994). Sexual orientation and gender as factors in socioculturally acquired vulnerability to body dissatisfaction and eating disorders. *Journal of Consulting and Clinical Psychology, 62,* 252–260.

Skinner, W. F., (1994). The prevalence and demographic predictors of illicit and licit drug use among lesbians and gay men. *American Journal of Public Health, 84,* 1307–1310.

Skinner, W., & Otis, M. D. (1992). Drug use among lesbian and gay people: Findings, research design, insights, and policy issues from the Trilogy Project. In J. Kelly (Ed.), *The research symposium on alcohol and other drug problem prevention among lesbians and gay men.* Sacramento, CA: EMT Group.

Smith, E. M., Johnson, S. R., & Guenther, S. M. (1985). Health care attitudes and experiences during gynecologic care among lesbians and bisexuals. *American Journal of Public Health, 75,* 1085–1087.

Stall, R., & Wiley, J. (1988). A comparison of alcohol and drug use patterns of homosexual and heterosexual men: The San Francisco Men's Health Study. *Drug and Alcohol Dependence, 22,* 63–73.

Stevens, P. E. (1992). Lesbian health care research: A review of the literature from 1970 to 1990. Special Issue: Lesbian health: What are the issues? *Health Care for Women International, 13,* 91–120.

Stevens, P. E. (1994). Protective strategies of lesbian clients in health care environments. *Research in Nursing & Health, 15,* 217–229.

Suarez, T. S., & Reese, F. L. (1997). Alternative medicine use, perceived control, coping, and adjustment in African American and Caucasian males living with HIV and AIDS. *International Journal of Rehabilitation and Health, 3,* 107–118.

Taylor, S. E., & Repetti, R. L. (1997). Health psychology: What is an unhealthy environment and how does it get under the skin? *Annual Review of Psychology, 48,* 411–447.

Trippet, S. E., & Bain, J. (1992). Reasons American lesbians fail to seek traditional health care. Special issue: Lesbian health: What are the issues? *Health Care for Women International, 13*, 145–153.

VanScoy, H. C. (1997). Lesbian health issues. In D. S. Gochman (Ed.), *Handbook of health behavior research: Volume III* (pp. 141–162). New York: Plenum Press.

Weinberg, M. S., & Williams, C. J. (1974). *Male homosexuals: Their problems and adaptations*. New York: Penguin Books.

White, J., & Levinson, W. (1993). Primary care of lesbian patients. *Journal of General Internal Medicine, 8*, 41–47.

Williams, D. R., & Collins, C. (1995). U.S. socioeconomic and racial differences in health: Patterns and explanations. *Annual Review of Sociology, 21*, 349–389.

Winkelstein, W., Samuel, M., & Padian, N. S. (1987). The San Francisco Men's Health Study III: Reduction in human immunodeficiency virus transmission among homosexual/bisexual men, 1982–1986. *American Journal of Public Health, 77*, 685–689.

Witmer, J. M., & Sweeney, T. J. (1992). A holistic model for wellness and prevention over the life span. *Journal of Counseling & Development, 71*, 140–148.

Zehner, M. A., & Lewis, J. (1983). Homosexuality and alcoholism: Social and developmental perspectives. *Journal of Social Work and Human Sexuality, 2*, 75–89.

AUTHOR INDEX

References in italics refer to listings in the reference section.

Bednar, R., 201, *204*
Behrendt, A. E., 279, *299*
Bell, A. P., 43, 44, 49, *51*, 218, *222*,
    226, 242, 320, *332*, 338, *354*
Belz, J. R., 386, 394, 397, *405*
Ben-Ari, A., 250, 251, 255, *271*
Ben-Ezra, L. A., 36, *52*, 327, *332*
Bennett, K., 417, 427, *428*
Bennett, K. C., 208, *222*
Bepko, C. S., 277, 279–281, *299*
Berger, M. B., 42, *51*
Berger, R. M., 284, 289, *298*
Bergin, A. E., 427, 428, *428*
Bergler, E., 309, *332*
Berrill, K. T., 170, *179, 242*, 450
Berman, S., 362, *377*
Berne, E., 108, 109, *127*
Bernheine, S., *452*
Berube, A., 63, 76
Berzon, B., 368, *377*
Bettinger, M., 276, *299*
Betz, N. E., 318, *332, 341, 354*
Beutler, L. E., 108, *127*
Bevier, P., *450*
Bialk, S. E., 373, *381*
Biddle, B. S., *450*
Bieber, I., 313, 314, *332*
Bieber, T., *332*
Bieschke, K. J., 8, 318, 319, 327–329,
    332, 333, 340, 342, 343, 345,
    350, 352, *354, 355*, 383, 384,
    386, 395, *405*
Billingsley, A., 93, *101*
Bi Vocals, 174, *177*
Blasband, D., 282, *298*
Blaszczynski, A., 314, *334*
Blenkush, M., 234, *245*
Blum, R., 233, *245*
Blumenfeld, W. J., 412–414, *428*
Blumstein, P. W., 43, 44, *51*, 172, *177*,
    282, 286, 290, *298*
Boatwright, K. J., 386, 390, 392, 396,
    400, *405*
Boden, R., 168, *177*
Body, G., 365, *377*
Bohan, J. S., 6, 7, 8, 143, *154*
Bolan, G., *242, 243*
Boll, L. S., *242*
Booth, R. E., 360, *377*
Borhek, M. V., 252, *271*
Bornholt, L., 375, *381*
Bornstein, K., 24, *30*

Boswell, D. L., *334*
Boswell, J., 409, 415, *429*
Bowen, M., 119, 120, *127*
Bowlby, J., 115, *127*
Boxer, A. M., 73, 76, 226, 230, *242, 244*
Boyce, W. T., *450*
Boyd, M., 416, 418, *429*
Boyd-Franklin, N., 291, *298*
Boykin, K., *101*
Bozett, F. W., 257, 260, 265, *271, 288,
    299*
Brack, C. J., 342, *354*
Brack, G., 342, *354*
Bradford, J., 3, 8, 63, 64, 76, 231, 233,
    236, *242*, 320, *332, 450*
Brady, S., 36, 37, *51*, 317, 323, *332*, 338,
    355
Brand, E. F., 361, 363, *377*
Brannock, J. C., 40, *52*
Brasfield, T. L., 362, *381, 453*
Bridgewater, D., 170, *177*
Brock, K. J., 188, *205*
Brod, H., 16, *30*
Bronski, M., 427, *429*
Brooks, V. R., 323–325, *332*
Brossart, D. F., 201, *204*
Brown, J. C., 414, 415, 419, 420, *429*
Brown, L., 60, *76, 177*, 277, 283, 285,
    286, 288–290, 296, *298*
Brown, L. B., 90, 91, *101*
Brown, L. S., 26, *30*, 37, 38, 46, 49, *51*,
    52, 119, 121, 122, *127*, 137,
    144, 147–149, 153, *154*, 163,
    173, *177*, 318, 319, *332*, 345,
    347, *354, 357*, 388, 390, 391,
    393–396, *399*, 402, *407*
Brownfain, J. J., 218, *222*
Browning, C., 50, *52*, 75, 78, 148, *154*,
    159, 162, 166, 168, *177*, 318,
    328, *332*, 359, 368, *377*, 410,
    416, 426, *429*
Bruss, L. V., 342, 350, 351, *354*
Buck, A., *454*
Buhles, W., *451*
Buhrke, R. A., 36, 49, *52*, 139, 148, 149,
    154, 158, *177*, 327, *332*, 338,
    340, 341, 343, 345, 350, 352,
    355
Bullough, V. L., *450*
Burch, B., 280, *298*
Burg, B. K., 340, 342, 343, 346, *358*
Burke, P., *222*

Burkholder, G. J., 367, *377*
Busse, W. J., 36, 37, *51*
Butler, J., 16, 22, *30*
Butler, W. T., *451*
Bux, D. A., *450*
Bye, L., *247*

Cabaj, R. P., 4, 8, 283, 289, 298, 343, *355*
Cacioppo, J. T., *453*
Caitlin, R., 163, 165–170, *177*
Calhoun, D., *205*
Campbell, B. W., 141, 156, 390, *407*
Campos, P. E., *453*
The Cancer and Steroid Hormone Study of the Centers for Disease Control and the National Institute of Child Health and Human Development, *450–451*
Cantor, J. M., 338, 352, *357*
Caprio, F., 309, *332*
Carballo-Dieguez, A., 97, *101*, 422, *429*
Carey, R. G., 374, *380*
Carlozzi, A. F., *334*
Carr, C., *452*
Carrier, J. M., 73, *76*
Casas, J. M., 5, 8, 111, *130*, 317, 323, *332*, 338, *355*
Casper, V., 250, *271*
Cass, V. C., 27, 30, 31, 36, 37–39, *52*, 84, *101*, 163, *177*, 188, 189, 195, 203, 251, 257, *271*
Castillo, A., 96, *101*
Castro, K., *450*
Catania, J., *247*
Cautela, J., 312, *333*
Centers for Disease Control, *451*
Centers for Disease Control and Prevention, *451*
Chabot, D. R., 119, 120, *128*
Chaiken, S., 367, 370, 375, *378*
Chambliss, C., 375, *379*
Chan, C. S., 22, 23, 31, 46, 52, 48, *52*, 94, *101*, 167, *177*, 255, 256, 261, 268, *271, 272*, 291, 300, *451*
Chan, R. W., 250, 257, 259–261, 265, 269, *273*
Chang Hall, L. K., 23, *31*
Chapagne, D. E., 375, *380*
Chapman, B. E., 37, 40, *52*

Charles, K. A., 339, *357*
Chen, J. Y., *455*
Chesney, M. A., *450*
Chiasson, M., *450*
Chmiel, J., 453, *454*
Chojnacki, J. T., 145, 155, 195, 201, 203, 344, *355*, 386, 390, 394, 395, 397, 400, 405, *406*
Christ, G., *455*
Christensen, C. P., 82, *101*
Chu, S., 453, *454*
Chung, Y. B., 45, *52*, 386, 393, 394, 402, *405*
Clark, J. M., 414, 415, 417, 419, 420, *429*
Clark, W. B., *451*
Clark, W. M., 158, *177*, 276, *298*
Clausen, J., 14, 17, 21, 22, 25, 28–30, *31*
Cleaver, R., 417, *429*
Coates, S., 235, *242*
Coates, T. J., 232, 244, 361, *379*
Cochran, S. D., 3, 8, 74, *77*, 138, *154*, 158, *178*, 190, 204, 232, *242*, 275, 276, *301*, 317, 333, 338, *356*
Cogan, J., *77*, 170, *179*
Cohen, L. H., 235, *246*
Coie, J. D., 360, *377*
Cole, S. P., 320, *334*
Cole, S. W., *451*
Coleman, E., 36, *52*, 84, *101*, 163, *177*, 218, 222, 237, *242*, 251, 257, *271*
Coleman, T. F., 368, *379*
Collins, C., *456*
Colucci, P. L., 252, *272*
Committee on Lesbian and Gay Concerns, 15, *31*
Comstock, G. D., 232, *242*
Conger, J. J., 75, *77*, 146, *154*, 339, 345, *355*
Conlin, D., 189, 194, 196, 198, 200, *203*
Connolly, L., 215, *222*
Conrad, F., 315, *333*
Conrad, S. R., 313, 314, *333*
Conyne, R. K., 183, 185, 186, *203*
Cook, D. J., *453*
Cook, J. A., 230, *242*
Cooper, A., 413, *429*
Corey, G., 108, 109, 111, 113, 115, 117, 123, 124, *127*
Cory, D. W., *77*

Countryman, L. W., 415, *429*
Cowen, E. L., 360, 361, 374, *377, 380*
Cox, C. I., *104*
Cox, S., 44, *52*
Cramer, D. W., 230, *242*
Cranston, K., 232, *242*, 365, *377*
Crawford, I., 337–338, *354*
Crawford, S., 250, 258–265, *271*
Crego, C. A., 374, *380*
Crisp, D., 141, *155*, 346, *356*
Crocker, J., 84, *101*
Cronin, C., *377*
Cross, W. E., 40, *52*, 84, *101*
Croteau, J. M., 7, 8, 327, 328, 333, 338, 340, 342, 343, 345, 352, 354, *354*, 355, 357, 360, 363, *377*, 383, 384, 386, 387, 390–397, 401–403, *405*
Crow, L., 90, *101*
Curb, R., 415, *429*

Dahlheimer, D., 250, 251, 253, 266, 267, *271*
Dain, H., *332*
Dank, B. M., 36, *52*
Dankmeijer, P., 27, *31*
Dappen, R., 232, *247*
Dark, L. J., 230, *243*
Dattilio, F. M., 112, *128*
D'Augelli, A. R., 4, 8, 184, 185, 188, 203, 225–227, 230–236, *242–245, 247*, 343, *355*, 360, 361, 363, 364, 367, 368, 370, 376, *377, 378*
Davies, M., *246*
Davis, M. D., 61, *78*
Davison, G. C., 159, 161, 171, *178*, 315, 316, 318, *333*
Dean, L., 42, *54*, 232, *243*, 451, *453*
Deaux, K., 86, *102*
DeBord, K. A., 188, *205*
De Cecco, J. P., 17, 24, 27, *31*, 44, *52*, 171, *180*
Deevey, S., *451*
Degen, K., *451*
Deisher, R. W., 231, *245*
Dekker, J., *203*
DeLeon, P. H., 339, 345, *355*
Delgado, W., *243*
Delgado-Romero, E., *96*
DeLucia-Waack, J. L., 190, *203*

Demian, A. S. B., 282, *298*
D'Emilio, J., 64, *77*, 99, *102*
Demo, D. H., 270, *271*
de Monteflores, C., 36, 37, 46, *52, 178*
Desio, D., 373, *381*
DeStefano, G., 415, *429*
Detels, R., *453*
DeVincenzi, I., *451*
De Vries, M. J., *205*
Dial, L. K., *454*
Diekstra, R. F., 233, *243*
Diener, C., *451*
Diener, E., *451*
DiFranceisco, W., *454*
Dillon, C., 376, *377*
Dillon, K. M., 235, *243*
Dince, P., *332*
Dineen, A., 367, *377*
DiPlacido, J., 82, *102*
Distefano, T. M., 402, *405*
Dobkin, A., 22, *31*
Dobson, K. S., 112, 113, *127*
Doll, L. S., *243*, *454*
Donaldson, S., 412, 413, 416, *429*
Donoghue, E., 59, *77*
Dopkins, S. C., *246*
Dorfman, R., 211, 214, *222*
Dorian, B., *451*
Douce, L. A., 139, 148, 149, *154*, 158, *177*, 340, 341, 343, 345, 350, 352, *355*
Douglas, C. J., *451*
Douglas, J. M., 242, *243*
Downey, J. I., 42, *53*, 282, 283, *298*, *452*
Downing, C., 418, *429*
Downing, N. E., 84, 85, *102*
Drake, M., *454*
Drellich, M., *332*
Drescher, J., 69, 70, *77*
Dressel, P., 209, *222*
Drew, W. L., *451*
Driscoll, J. M., 387, 391–393, 396, 401, 403, *406*
Driver, T. F., 414, *429*
Dronkers, J., *203*
Drum, D. J., 360, 361, 363, 367, 374, *377, 378*
DuBay, W. H., 17, 19, 25, 28, *31*
Duberman, M., 65, 66, 69, *77*
Ducharme, S., 148, *154*
Dudley, J., 452, *454*
Duerr, A., *453*

460   AUTHOR INDEX

Green, R. J., 276–278, 281, 282, 299, 340, 344, 348, *356, 357*

Greenberg, D. E., 17, 22, *32*, 41, *53, 452*

Greenberg, L. S., 108, 109, *130*

Greene, B. A., 46, *53, 54*, 64, *77*, 85, 86, 91, *102*, 122, *128*, 145, 148, *155*, 159, 161, 163, 164, 167, 173, 174, *179*, 268, 272, 291, 292, 299, 343, 356, 360, 364, 368, *378*, 402, 406

Greenhouse, E. M., 342, 351, *357*

Griffin, P., 387, 391–396, 398, 399, 401, 402, *406*

Griggs, C., 24, *32*

Gross, L., 230, *243*

Grossman, A. H., 229, 233, *243, 244*

Grube, J., 65, *77*

Guenther, S. M., *452, 455*

Guerin, P. J., 119, 120, *128*

Gullotta, T. P., 360, *376*

Gundlach, R., *332*

Gutierrez, C. J., 343, *355*

Gutierrez, E., 422, *430*

Gutierrez, F. J., 4, 8, 159, 167, 178, *179*

Gwadz, M., 236, 246, *455*

Hackett, C., 318, *332*

Haire, J. R., 373, *381*

Haldeman, D. C., 70, *77*, 146, *155*, 237, *244*, 313, *333*, 410, 414, 420, *430*

Haley, J., 119, 120, *128*

Hall, A. S., 318, *333*

Hall, C. C. I., 158, 173, *179*, 417, *430*

Hall, J. M., 321, *333*

Hall, L. K. C., 94, *102*

Hall, M., 291, 299, 387, 391, 393, 402, *406*

Hall, W., 42, *54, 453*

Halperin, D. M., *452*

Halpern, E. L., 159, 169, *179*

Halpern, H. S., 315, *333, 356*

Hammelman, T. L., 234, *244*

Hammersmith, S. F., 218, *222*

Hammersmith, S. K., 226, *242*

Hancock, K. A., 3, 8, 74, *77*, 138, 141, 142, *154, 155*, 157–159, 165, 168–170, 173, 178, *179*, 190, *204*, 317, *333*, 338, 351, *356*

Hanley, P., *104*

Hanley-Hackenbruck, P., 163, *179*

Hansen, C. E., 44, *54*, 217, 218, *222*

Hanson, W., 368, *380*

Harbeck, K. M., 359, *381*, 389, 391, 393, 394, 396, 401, 402, *408*

Hardie, A. W., 201, *204*

Hardin, L., *222*

Hargaden, H., 250, 258, 260, 262, 263, *272*

Harmon, L. W., 386, 393, 394, 402, *405*

Harren, V. A., 345, *356*

Harrison, J. S., *242, 243*

Harry, A., 219, *223*

Harry, J., 231, 235, *244*

Harstein, N. B., 195, *205*

Hart, J., 22, 27, *32*

Harvey, A., 419, 420, 426, *430*

Harvey, S. M., *452*

Hasbany, J., *430*

Hawkins, D. M., 188, 189, 193, *204*

Hawkins, J. D., *377*

Hawkins, R. L., 279, *299*

Hawkins, R. O., 310, 311, *335*

Hawxhurst, D. M., 144, 147, 148, *156*

Hay, H., 417, 418, 427, *430*

Hayes, J. A., 317, 319, 327, 329, *333*

Hayes, R. B., 232, *244*

Haynes Stansted, K. C., 362, *379*

Hays, R. B., 361, *379*

Hayward, N., 252, *271*

Heaton, T., 413, *430*

Hedge, B., 185, *204*

Hedstrom, S. M., 386, 394, 395, 397, *405*

Heffernan, R., *450*

Hekma, G., 59, *77*

Helminiak, D. A., 412, 415, 419, 424, 426, *431*

Helms, J. E., 81, 84, 85, *102–104*

Hendrix, H., 279, *299*

Hennessey, J., *247*

Herdt, G. H., 89, *103*, 226, 227, 228, 230, *242, 244, 245*

Herek, G. M., 115, 121, *128*, 140, 141, 145, 146, *155*, 170, 171, *179*, 184, *204, 244*, 331, *334, 339*, 352, *356*

Hermes, J., 315, *333*, 338, *356*

Herring, R. D., 81, *103*

Hershberger, S. L., 226, 230, 233–236, *243, 244*

Hesson-McInnis, M. S., 234, *247*

Lonborg, S. D., 327, *334*, 388, 401–403, *407*
Long, B., *377*
Long, J. K., 342, 349, 350, *357*
Lopez, S. R., 4, 8
Lo Presto, C. T., 370, *379*
Lorber, J., 16, 22, *32*
Lorion, R. P., 360, *380*
Lottes, I. L., *431*
Lourea, D. N., 217, 218, *223*
Love, P., 291, *300*
Lowe, J. C., 208, *223*
Lucas, V. A., 321, *334*
Lyman, D., *453*
Lyn, L., 151, *156*

MacCorquodale, P., 376, *379*
Madanes, C., 119, *129*
Mahalik, J. R., 230, *244*
Mahler, M. S., 115, 116, *129*
Major, B., 84, *101*
Malarkey, W. B., *453*
Mallon, D., 42, *51*
Maloney, C., 375, *379*
Manahan, N., 415, *429*
Mangaoang, G., 94, *103*
Mapou, R. L., 320, 322, 326, *334*
Marcus, E., 57, 65, 66, 73, 78, *79*
Markman, H. J., *377*
Markowitz, L., 296, *300*
Marmor, J., 74, *78*
Martin, A. D., 228, 233, 234, *244, 245*
Martin, C., 19, *32*
Martin, C. E., 43, *54*, 310, *334*
Martin, C. L., 279, *300*
Martin, D. J., 42, *54*
Martin, J. L., 42, *54, 453*
Martin, L., *450*
Marx, R., 362, *379*
Marxuach-Rodriquez, L., 360, *381*
Masters, W. H., 72, *78*, 282, *300*
Masterson, J. F., 115, *129*, 192, 194, 199, 200, *205*
Masters W. H., 313, 314, *334*
Matteson, D. R., 148, *156*, 160, 162, 164–166, 168, 169, *179*, 343, 344, *357*
Matthews, C., 318, 319, 328, 329, 332, 345, 350, *354*, 386, 395, *405*
Mattison, A. M., 250, 252, 253, 255, *272*, 277, 282, 290, *300*

Mattson, S. R., 59, *78*
Mavis, B. E., 165, *176*
May, R., 108, *129*
Mayer, K. H., *453*
Mays, V. M., 232, *242*
Mazumdar, S., 360, *379*
McCandless, B. R., 73, *79*
McCarn, S. R., 37, 40, 41, 46, 47, *54*, 84, 85, 88, *103*
McClanahan, M. K., 313, 318, 328, 330, *335*
McClintock, M. K., 227, *245*
McClure, F. H., 344, *357*
McConaughy, N., 314, *334*
McDavis, R. J., 97, *105*
McDermott, D., 149, *156*, 323, 326, *334*, 348, *356*
McDonald, G. J., 41, 48, *54*, 251, 257, *272, 453*
McGoldrick, M., 83, *103*
McHenry, S. S., 137, 139, 149, *156*, 339, *357*
McIntosh, M., 18, 20, *32*
McIntosh, P., 364, *379*
McKee, E., *205*
McKirnan, D. J., 236, *242, 245*, 425, *433, 454*
McNally, E. B., 41, *53*
McNamara, K., 363, *379*
McNaught, B., 368, *380*
McNeill, J. J., *431*
McWhirter, D. P., 250, 252, 253, 255, *272*, 277, 281, 282, 290, *300*
Medley, G., *454*
Meichenbaum, D., 112, *129*
Meisenhelder, J. B., 367, *380*
Melton, G. B., 331, *334*, 339, *356*
Mencher, J., 281, 286, *300, 301*
Mesagno, F. P., *455*
Messner, M. A., 85, *103*
Metz, P., 215, *223*
Meyer, I., 232, *243, 451*
Meyer-Bahlburg, H. F. L., *246*
Midanik, L., *451*
Milburn, L., 388, 397, *407*
Miles, M., 199, *205*
Miller, B. A., 37, 41, 42, 47, *53*, 163, *178*
Miller, J., 375, *379*
Miller, N., 58, 61, 64, 65, 67, 71, *78*
Miller, R., 417, 419, *431*
Milman, D. S., 115, *128*

SUBJECT INDEX

Gender identity, 158
Gender roles
among African Americans, 92–93
among Asian American, 94–95
among Latin Americans, 96
among Native Americans, 90
Gender role socialization, 277–283
and gay male relationships, 279–280
and lesbian relationships, 280–281
and relationship dynamics, 278–279,
287–288
and sexuality, 281–283
and vocational interests, 393–394
General power of attorney, 216
Generational factor (in aging), 209–210
Gestalt therapy, 108
Gonorrhea, 113
Gonsiorek, J. C., 161
Gorman, E. Michael, 416
Graduate training. *See* Training
Group counseling, 183–203
altruism as factor in, 193–194
catharsis as therapeutic factor in, 199–
200
cohesion of group in, 197–199
development of socialization techniques in, 192–193
existential factors in, 200
future research, areas for, 201–202
imitative behavior as benefit of, 194–
195
imparting information in, 191–192
instillation of hope in, 187–189
interpersonal learning as benefit of,
196–197
need for, with LGB clients, 184–185
with single-sex groups, 190–191
theoretical underpinnings of, 185–186
transference relationships in, 195–196
universality as factor in, 189–191
Group memberships, 82–83
Guilt, in family of LGB individuals, 253–
254

Harlem Renaissance, 65
Hawaii, 94
Hayes, Bruce, 448
Health behavior(s), 435–450
of bisexuals, 437–447
and definition of health, 435–436
of gay men, 437, 442–447

of lesbians, 437, 439–442
and prejudice in medical profession,
436–437
risk behaviors, 438–447
and wellness, 447–449
Hekma, Gert, 59
Helms, J. E., 84
Herpes simple viruses (HSV), 443
Heterosexism, 283
and ageism, 215–217
and identity development, 35
internalized, 113–114
as term, 7
in therapist, 139
and training, 338
Heterosexual (as term), 15, 17
Heterosexuality, as possible identity, 14–
15
Heyward, Carter, 415
Hinduism, 95
Historical aspects of LGB mental health,
57–76
early newsletters/organizations, 66–68
economic factors, 63–64
educational factors, 62–63
New York City, role of, 65–66
and "reorientation" therapy, 68–71
research, role of psychological, 72–75
and sexology as field, 71–72
specialized language, use of, 58–62
istory of Sexuality (Michel Foucault), 18,
20–21
HIV. *See* Human immunodeficiency virus
Homonegativity (in therapist), 139–140,
145–146
Homophobia, 85, 139
and coming out process, 284–285
and identity development, 35, 50–51
internalized, 113–114
in LGB clients, 169–170
societal, 283
as term, 7
Homosexual (as term), 6, 15, 17, 18
The Homosexual in America (Donald
Webster Cory), 58–59
Homosexuality
APA position on, 3
diagnosis of, 160–161
in *DSM*, 74–75
same-gender desire vs., 15–16
as term, 18
Hooker, Evelyn, 72–73, 310

Lesbian(s)
  and gender role socialization, 280–281
  health behaviors of, 437, 439–442
  idealization of relationships between,
    by women therapists, 142
  identity development in, 38–40
  newsletters/organizations for, 66–68
  quality of mental health care received
    by, 321–322
  relationships between, 280–282, 287,
    290–291
  as term, 15
  use of therapy by, 70–71
LGB identity (as term), 6
Liddle, B. J., 321, 325
Living will, 216
Louganis, Greg, 448

M. *Butterfly* (David Henry Hwang), 95
Machismo, 96
Make a Picture Story Test, 73
Managed care providers, 373
Marginalization, 169
Marianismo, 96
Massachusetts, 232
Masters, W. H., 313, 314
Mattachine Society, 67
McCarn, S. R., 40–42, 47
McIntosh, Mary, 20
Media, 374
Medical power of attorney, 216
Mental health agencies, 373
Milk, Harvey, 76
Miller, Neil, 58–59, 61, 64, 65, 71–72
Minnesota, 232
Modeling, and group therapy, 194–195
Monogamous relationships, 281–282, 290
Monosexual (as term), 158
Monotheistic religions, 409, 412–415
Moran, M. R., 323–324
Morgan, Kris, 71
Multicultural competence, 397–399
Multicultural therapy, 119
Multimodal therapy, 112

NARTH (National Association for Re-
    search and Therapy of Homosex-
    uality), 70
National Association for Mental Health,
    75

National Association for Research and
    Therapy of Homosexuality
    (NARTH), 70
National Association of Social Workers,
    75
National Gay and Lesbian Task Force,
    261
National Gay and Lesbian Task Force
    Policy Institute, 157
National Institute of Mental Health, 72
National Lesbian Health Care Survey,
    63, 64, 233
Native Americans, 36, 60–61, 64, 89–91,
    411, 417, 422
Navratilova, Martina, 448
Newsletters, first LGB, 66–68
New York City, 65–66, 230, 232
Null environment, 50, 147
Nurturance, 364–367

Object relations theory, 115
Oetting, E. R., 87
Older LGB individuals. *See* Aging
Old Testament, 412
Oral sex, 444–445
Organizations, first LGB, 66–68
Orientation
  affectional, 6
  sexual, 6
Outcome, therapy, 324–327
Outreach, 360

Pacific Islanders, 93–94
Parents and Friends of Lesbians and Gays
    (P-FLAG), 255
Parents and parenting, 250, 262–264,
    288–289
Paris, Bob, 448
Passions Between Women (Emma Dona-
    ghue), 59
Paul, Gordon, 107
Perkins, Rachel, 71
Personality Factor Questionnaire, 73
Person-centered therapy, 108
P-FLAG (Parents and Friends of Lesbians
    and Gays), 255
Physical abuse, 231, 240
Pittsburgh, 232
Placek, Wayne, 73

Plato, 15–16
Polyamory, 158–159
Ponse, B., 39
Poston, W. S. C., 87
Posttraumatic stress, 170
Powers of attorney, 216
Presentation, client, 159–160
Prevention, 360
Professional standards, 138–140, 152
Programmatic research, 309–311, 327–329
Programming, psychoeducational. *See* Psychoeducational programming
Protestant fundamentalism, 96, 414
Protestantism, 413
Psychoanalysis, 68–69, 115, 116
Psychoanalytic therapy, 115
Psychodynamic therapeutic approaches, 115–119
    benefits of, 117–118
    pitfalls of, 118–119
Psychoeducational programming, 359–376
    cost-effectiveness of, 375
    and definition of programming, 360–361
    and demographic factors, 363–364
    development of, 363–364
    efficacy of, 361–362
    emotional component of attitudes/beliefs, 367–368
    evaluation of, 374–375
    exercise examples, 368–372
    marketing of, 373–374
    nurturance as component of, 364–367
    terminology related to, 360–361
    theoretical bases for effective, 362–368
Psychological autopsies, 234–235
Psychopathia Sexualis
        (R. von Krafft-Ebing), 18–19
PsycINFO, 344

Q-sort, 200
Qualitative research, 328, 400–401
Quantitative research, 328, 401, 421–422
Questions, client, 170–173

Race/racial identity, 5, 83
    of African Americans, 84–85

and family, 268–269
and LGB relationships, 291–292
and self-identification, 164
Racism, 83
Rational–emotive therapy, 112
Reality therapy, 112
Referral sources, LGB, 373–374
Relationship counseling. *See* Couples counseling
Religion and spirituality, 409–428
    among African Americans, 93
    among Asian American, 95
    among Latin Americans, 96–97
    among Native Americans, 90–91
    benefits of, 416–419
    client questions about, 172–173
    and cognitive–behavioral therapeutic approach, 114
    and coming out process, 419–421
    definitions of, 410–411
    future research, areas for, 426–427
    and intolerance of monotheistic religions, 412–415
    of LGB persons, 415–419
    and therapeutic process, 421–426
    of therapist, 146
"Reorientation" therapy, 68–71. *See also* Conversion therapy
Research on LGB counseling/therapy, 4
Research training, 351–353
Rich, Adrienne, 21
Risk behaviors, 361–362
    among gay/bisexual men, 442–447
    among lesbian/bisexual women, 438–442
    among LGB youths, 233
Rituals, socially-sanctioned, 286
Rivera, Ray, 65–66
Rogers, Carl, 108–110
Role models, 286–287, 396
Role-playing (as training technique), 349–350
Roman Catholicism, 96, 413, 422
Rorschach Test, 73, 310
Ruether, Rosemary, 415
Rust, Paula, 61, 169–170

Same-sex sexual attraction, development of, 226–227
San Francisco, 232

Self-esteem
  and family, 267
  of LGB adolescents, 238
Self-identification (of LGB clients), 163–165
Self-identity, development of. *See* Identity development
Self psychology, 115
Sexism, 83, 311–312
Sexology, 72
Sex roles, 158
Sexual abuse, 289
Sexual identity, 22–24, 171. *See also* Identity development
Sexually transmitted diseases (STDs), 439–440, 443. *See also* Acquired immunodeficiency syndrome
Sexual minorities, 158
Sexual orientation
  bisexual, 44
  development of, 225–228
  disclosure of. *See* Coming out
  emergence of, as concept, 18
  fixed vs. fluid nature of, 170–171
  and gender, 46
  language of, 58–60
  and suicide, 235
  as term, 6
  of therapist, 142–145, 195, 323–324, 330
Sexual Orientation and Identity Continuum Diagram, 162
Sexual preference, 171
Sexual Preference, 226
Shamans, 417
Shannon, J. W., 160
Silverstein, Charles, 71
Skills, 399
Smith, A., 46–47
Smith, B., 91–92
Socarides, C., 309–310, 312
Social constructionism, 14, 16–17, 22–29
  applications of, 26–27
  assumptions of, 25–26
  current perspectives on, 22–24
  definition of, 16–17
  and essentialism, 28–29
  and future research/theory development, 24–25
  and role of therapist, 29
Socialization, gender role. *See* Gender role socialization

Socialization techniques, development of, 192–193
Social structure, American, 82
Social support, and aging, 214–215
Socioeconomic status, 213, 438
Spencer-Devlin, Muffin, 448
Spirituality. *See* Religion and spirituality
Standards, professional, 138–140, 152
STDs. *See* Sexually transmitted diseases
Stepfamilies, LGB, 259–262
Stonewall riots, 65–66, 210
Stress, posttraumatic, 170
Substance abuse, 235–236, 289, 441–442, 446–447
"Substitute" family, 214
Suicidality, 233–236, 240–241
Symbolic relationships (in therapy), 149–150
Symposium (Plato), 15–16
Systems–cultural therapeutic approaches, 119–123
  benefits of, 120–122
  pitfalls of, 122–123

TA (transactional analysis), 108
Terminology, LGB, 5–7, 15, 58–62
Thematic Apperception Test, 73, 310
Therapeutic approaches, 107–126
  with adolescents, 237–241
  cognitive–behavioral, 112–115
  humanistic, 108–112
  psychodynamic, 115–119
  research implications of, 123–124
  systems–cultural, 119–123
  theoretical integration of, 124–126
  and training, 344–345
Therapist(s), 137–153
  and aging issues, 210
  attitudes of, toward LGB clients, 315–319
  background/personal factors of, 140–146
  and boundaries, 151–152
  gender of, 140–141
  homonegativity/binegativity in, 145–146
  in humanistic therapeutic approaches, 111
  and individual therapy, 173–175
  preference of LGB clients for, 323–324

and professional standards/ethics, 138–
140
psychotherapeutic orientation of, 146–
148
religious ideology of, 146
self-awareness of, 148–152, 426
sexual identity of, 173–174
sexual orientation of, 142–145, 195,
323–324, 330
and social constructionism and role of,
29
and symbolic relationships with clients,
149–150
theoretical orientation of, 174–175
training of. *See* Training
Therapy
approaches to. *See* Therapeutic approaches
couples. *See* Couples counseling
group. *See* Group counseling
and identity development, 49–51
individual. *See* Individual therapy
with LGB people of color, 97–100
role of spirituality in, 421–426
therapist orientation to, 146–148
The Times of Harvey Milk (film), 76
Torah, 412
Training, 337–354
and clinical practice, 348–351
environments for LGB-affirmative,
340–343
in graduate programs, 337–338
and increased awareness of LGB issues,
347–348
and knowledge about LGB issues, 343–
347
need for LGB-related, 337–339
research, 351–353
Transactional analysis (TA), 108
Transference, 149, 195–196
Treatment, in individual therapy, 162–
170
Trichomonas vaginalis, 440
"Two-spirit people," 60

Use of therapy by LGB individuals, 320–
321
group therapy, 184
lesbians, 70–71
and perceptions of helpfulness, 321–
322

rates for, 3, 157
reasons for, 28

Verbal abuse, 231, 240
Vice Versa, 66
Victimization
as issue in individual therapy, 170
of LGB youths, 230–232
Violence, anti-LGB, 170, 231–232, 240
Viral infections, 443
Vocational psychology, 383–404
advancing research/theory development
in LGB, 399–403
career counseling, 394–395
current research on, 385, 390–396
definition of LGB, 384
and discrimination issues, 391–392
and dual-career issues, 395–396
and family/societal messages, 393–394
and involvement in LGB communities,
396
and management of sexual identity in
work environment, 392–393
and multicultural competence, 397–
399
and need for LGB role models, 396
published articles on (table), 385–389
and sexual identity development, 385,
390–391
terminology related to, 384–385

"Walk a Mile in My Shoes" (exercise),
368–370
Walters, K. L., 88
Wayne Placek Fund, 73
"We Are Not Alone" (exercise), 370–
372
The Wedding Banquet (film), 95
Wellness, 447–449
Wilkinson, Sue, 59–60
Wills, personal, 215–216
Woods, W. J., 160
Workplace, discrimination in, 216–217,
391–392, 398, 401
World War II, 63

Yalom, I. D., 186, 187, 189–190
Yarhouse, M. A., 312
Youth, LGB. *See* Adolescents, LGB

ABOUT THE EDITORS

Ruperto M. Perez is a counseling psychologist in the Counseling and Testing Center at The University of Georgia, where he serves as counseling services coordinator. He is also adjunct assistant professor and Diversity Research Team member in the counseling psychology program, Department of Counseling and Human Development Services at The University of Georgia. He received his MA in counseling psychology from Boston College and his PhD in counseling psychology from the University of Missouri–Columbia. His clinical and research interests include counseling lesbian, gay, and bisexual individuals, counseling persons of color, and training and supervision. He has presented a number of professional programs on counseling issues with lesbian, gay, and bisexual clients. In addition, he is actively involved in Division 17 of the American Psychological Association as a member of the Section for Lesbian, Gay, and Bisexual Awareness, as Vice President for Diversity and Public Interest, and as post-chair of the Section on Ethnic and Racial Diversity.

Kurt A. DeBord earned his PhD in counseling psychology from the University of Missouri–Columbia after receiving a BS in psychology from Ball State University. He is currently an assistant professor of psychology at Lincoln University in Jefferson City, Missouri. He has published research in the areas of rape prevention, gender roles, drug and alcohol involvement, and lesbian, gay, and bisexual concerns. He is currently involved in research on the relationship between racism and biphobia as well as research on teaching interventions.

Kathleen J. Bieschke is an associate professor of counseling psychology at the Pennsylvania State University, where she also serves as director of training. She received a BS in psychology and an MS in clinical psychology from Illinois State University and a PhD in counseling psychology from Michigan State University. Her research focuses on issues pertaining to lesbian, gay, and bisexual people. In addition, she has studied the research training of doctoral students and has written about the creation of training environments that are affirming of lesbian, gay, and bisexual clients.